# The
# Governing
## of
# Men

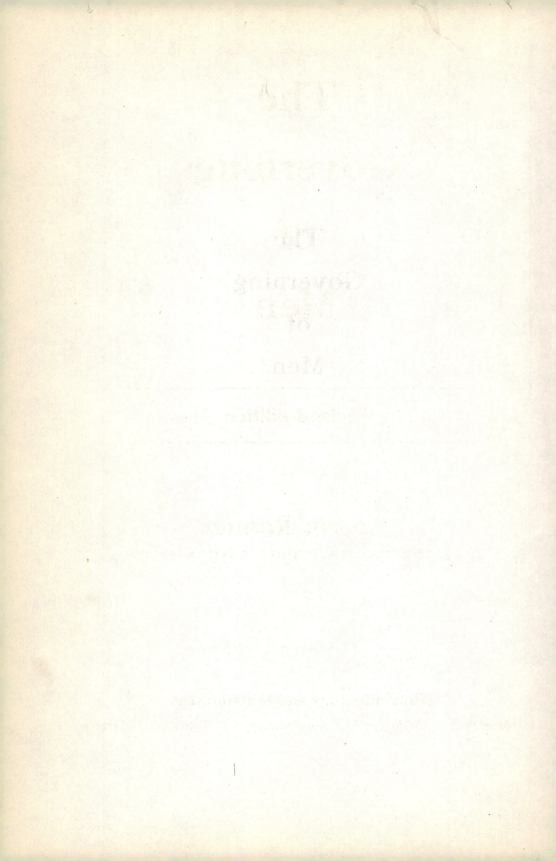

# The
# Governing
# of
# Men

---

**revised edition**

---

## *Austin Ranney*
THE UNIVERSITY OF WISCONSIN

**Holt, Rinehart and Winston, Inc.**

New York    Chicago    San Francisco    Toronto    London

*To Betsey, with love*

# Preface

"Ye shall know the truth; and the truth shall make ye free." These wingéd words nobly express the faith long held by most human beings of whatever creed that knowledge and understanding of the physical and social world in which he lives is man's principal tool for building the good life in the good society.

Politics and government are among man's oldest and most universal activities and institutions. Many of the greatest minds in history have pondered their nature and possibilities and have enriched us with their reflections. In our own time the study of politics and government has acquired a new and terrible urgency; for, through control of thermonuclear energy and access to outer space, man now possesses the technical means either to destroy himself or to build a new life of undreamed richness. Whatever choices he makes will emerge from political conflict and be implemented by governmental action.

Most American colleges and universities and an ever-growing number in other nations presently give the study of politics and government prominent places in their curriculums, partly as vocational training for public service, partly as general training for citizenship, but mainly as a necessary part of a liberal education intended to make men free by increasing their understanding of the physical and social world around them. In most American schools the study of these matters is primarily the province of departments variously called "political science" or "government" or "politics." Each perennially faces the pedagogical problem of introducing students to this vast, complex, and challenging subject. Two approaches are most commonly used. The first, most frequently employed in the United States, is the detailed study of American government. The second, which may be called the "principles-of-political-science" approach, seeks to describe the traits universal to the governing processes of all human societies and the nature and consequences of the major variations in these processes among different societies.

For a number of years I have taught an introductory undergraduate course using the second approach. My experiences have sensitized me to certain problems arising from its use, and the present book represents my judgment about how to deal with them.

One problem is that of giving students some sense of the relevance of politics and government to their own personal lives. Many of my students begin with the belief that politics is a rather dirty game played by *other* people and that government is something remote from the really important personal concerns of life. My failures in the classroom have taught me that merely exhorting students to regard government as important has little impact on their perceptions of what is important to *them*. In this book, accordingly, I have taken as my points of departure certain situations that all students have experienced and recognize as basic to their lives, and have tried to show, step by step, how these situations affect and are affected by what happens in such apparently remote places as United Nations headquarters, Washington, London, Paris, Moscow, Peking—and the students' state capitols and city halls. I have drawn most of my illustrations from current political conflicts in an effort to emphasize the concrete activities and interrelations of real human beings underlying such necessary but highly abstract terms as *nationalism, democracy, federalism, civil rights,* and the like.

Another problem is that of making students aware of the intellectual processes underlying the facts and conclusions presented by political science. If a teacher seeks to "give students the facts," he certainly must set forth the facts he considers significant and the explanations of them he considers valid and meaningful. If he also wishes to "teach students to think," he must tell them something about the processes by which he and his colleagues have gathered the facts and drawn conclusions about them. I believe that the first objective should have the main priority in an introductory course and textbook in political science, and that such courses and books should devote most of their space to describing what political scientists have learned and avoid trying to make research scholars out of beginning students. But I also believe that the second objective should receive some attention as well, and that such a course and book should say something about the nature and problems of political science (as in Chapter 24) and about the particular analytical framework within which the facts of politics and government are described and explained (as in Chapters 1 and 2).

In all of these respects the second edition of this book is identical with the first. Yet the march of world political events has been so rapid—and the advance of political science's ability to interpret and explain them has been so marked—that while the book's framework remains the same, much of its content has been altered to fit the late 1960's.

Like the author of any textbook, I am indebted to many colleagues and friends. I realize that much of whatever merit—but none of whatever errors —it may have is due to their help, and I am grateful for the opportunity traditionally provided by the preface to make public my thanks to those to whom I am most deeply in debt. In addition to general thanks to the authors of the many works cited in the text for the insights and information they have provided, I wish to make the following particular acknowledgments of help directly received and valued: to Elizabeth M. Ranney, who read the entire manuscript and commented on it with an architect's understanding of order and a wife's sympathy and encouragement; to my good friends and generous colleagues, Vice-Chancellor Jack W. Peltason of the University of California, Irvine, and Professor Charles B. Hagan of the University of Illinois, each of whom not only read and improved a number of chapters but in the process greatly contributed to my education; to the following colleagues who cheerfully read and perceptively criticized particular chapters: Professors William Albig, Valentine Jobst III, Benjamin B. Johnston, Charles M. Kneier, Phillip Monypenny, and Clyde F. Snider, all of the University of Illinois; Charles S. Hyneman of Indiana University; Evron M. Kirkpatrick of the American Political Science Association; Joseph G. LaPalombara of Yale University; Warren E. Miller of the Inter-University Consortium for Political Research and the University of Michigan; James N. Murray of the University of Iowa; Dean Richard L. Park of the University of Pittsburgh; Professors Charles W. Anderson, Donald S. Carlisle, Bernard C. Cohen, Leon D. Epstein, David Fellman, Fred R. von der Mehden, and M. Crawford Young, all of the University of Wisconsin; and the late and mourned Sigmund Neumann of Wesleyan University. Finally, my thanks go to Mrs. Helen T. Cropp, who expertly and uncomplainingly typed most of the manuscript of the first edition; and to Joseph A. Ranney III, who rendered great help in the assembly of the manuscript for this edition.

A.R.

*Madison, Wisconsin*
*September 1965*

# Contents

PREFACE   *v*


**part one**
## General Themes and Principal Variations               **1**

  1.  Politics in Human Life                               *3*
  2.  The Governing of Nations                           *20*
  3.  The Functions of Modern Governments                *41*
  4.  Forms of Government                                 *59*
  5.  Models of Democracy and Dictatorship               *79*


**part two**
## The Constitutional Position of the Individual        **103**

  6.  The Anatomy and Physiology of Constitutions       *105*
  7.  Citizens, Aliens, and Immigrants                  *126*
  8.  The Rights of Man: principles and problems        *149*
  9.  The Rights of Man: challenges and responses       *173*


**part three**
## Political Agencies and Processes                     **203**

10.  Public Opinion: nature and determinants             *205*
11.  Public Opinion: communication and measurement       *232*
12.  Theory and Practice of Political Representation      *257*
13.  Choosing Representatives: Suffrage, Nominations, and
     Elections                                        *282*
14.  Voting Behavior                                     *309*
15.  Political Parties and Party Systems                  *331*
16.  Pressure Groups and Pressure Politics               *365*

[ ix ]

## part four
### Governmental Agencies and Processes 391

17. The Legislative Process 393
18. The Executive Process 427
19. The Administrative Process 457
20. Law and the Judicial Process 484
21. Local Government and Federalism 516

## part five
### International Relations 545

22. International Politics 547
23. The Quest for Peace in the Thermonuclear Age 577

## part six
### The Current State of Political Science 611

24. Inside Political Science 613

SELECTED BIBLIOGRAPHY 634

INDEX 663

# part one

## General Themes
## and
## Principal Variations

# 1

## Politics in Human Life

**M**AN is an inquisitive animal. He not only lives his life, but he is also curious about it. None of us are so swamped by the demands of day-to-day living that we never pause and ask, "How did we get here?" "Why are we here?" "What's it all about, anyway?"

Man is also, in Aristotle's famous phrase, a "political animal." When we reflect upon the course of our lives and try to understand what has happened to us and why, we realize that our stories must be told largely in terms of our relations with other people—our parents, teachers, sweethearts, friends, enemies, bosses, subordinates, and so on. Aristotle insisted that one who does not live together with his fellow creatures in society must be either below mankind and therefore a beast, or above mankind and therefore a god.

Man the inquisitive animal has always been curious about the political and governmental environment in which man the political animal lives. Who among us has never asked such questions as "Why do I have to go into the army?" "What right has the government to tax away so much of my income?" "Who is going to win the election?" "Is there going to be a war?"

Most of us are better at asking such questions than we are at answering them. For one thing, getting answers is harder and more uncomfortable than asking questions: not only does it take more time and energy; the man who gives answers usually exposes himself to a kind of criticism and even ridicule that seldom disturbs the man who only asks questions. Then, too, most of us have to earn a living and simply cannot devote much time or energy to finding more and better explanations of how and why our politico-governmental system behaves as it does. In short, the demands of our daily lives do not keep us from asking questions, but they do prevent most of us from seeking answers in any but the most casual, sporadic, and after-hours manner.

However, a few persons, generally called "political scientists," *do* make a full-time job of investigating the nature of politics and government. The purpose of this book is to describe something of what political scientists have learned about these matters. The purpose of this introductory chapter is to explain what politics is "about"—that is, what kinds of human behavior are "political" and therefore relevant to our concerns in this book.

## What Is "Politics"?

### *In Everyday Conversation*

We all know *something* about "politics." The word and its derivatives pop up again and again in everyday thinking, conversation, and reading. When a football player tells us that "X was elected captain because of politics, not merit," or when a university president charges that "politicians are interfering with higher education," or when a newspaper columnist writes that "farm subsidies are economically senseless but it is politically impossible for Congress to abolish them," most of us will feel that we know what such statements mean. Indeed, most of us are likely to nod sagely and perhaps add a sigh for the imperfections of human nature.

These and similar commonly heard statements give some clues to what "politics" means to most of us. For one thing, "politics" has something to do with "allocating values"—with deciding who gets the lion's share and who the mouse's. For another, it operates not only in "the government" but in private groups as well—e.g., in a football team as well as in Congress. And for still another, it often connotes selfish squabbling for private gain rather than statesmanlike cooperation for the common good.

Most political scientists incorporate the first two elements in their conceptions of politics, but reject the third. They observe that even people who dislike "politicians" and admire "statesmen" can never agree on just which public figures should be given which label. To some, for example, Franklin Roosevelt was a great "statesman," while to others he was a "politician of the cheapest sort." Similar disagreements have existed about almost every other prominent leader from Thomas Jefferson and Abraham Lincoln to Winston Churchill and Charles de Gaulle.

Basically, such disagreements arise from the fact that "statesman" is a laudatory term while "politician" is a term of opprobrium. Thus most persons who use them regularly are really only telling us that they like certain public figures and dislike others. This observation has led one commentator to define a statesman as "a dead politician," and another to declare that "a statesman is a politician held upright by pressures from *all* sides." It has also inclined most political scientists to give the terms "politics" and "politician" the more neutral and descriptive meanings we shall use in this book.

## Politics as Policy Making

In its broadest sense "politics" includes the decision-making and -enforcing processes in any organization which makes and enforces rules for its members; and several political scientists have studied these processes in such organizations as labor unions, business corporations, medical associations, and the like.[1] But most political scientists have concentrated on the processes of governments rather than on private organizations,[2] and it seems desirable to have the same focus in an introduction to the discipline.

As the word will be used in this book, accordingly, *politics is the process of making governmental policies*. Let us see just what is involved in this definition.

### The Meaning of "Governmental Policies"

When governmental officials are called upon to take some course of action (or inaction) in a particular field, they are always faced with a number of alternatives which *might* be pursued—that is, which are technically possible. They cannot, however, simultaneously undertake *all* these courses of action, if for no other reason than that some are bound to be inconsistent with others, and if all were pursued simultaneously some actions would cancel out others. In such a situation, public officials always select from the available alternatives the few which they intend to actually put into effect. The courses of action thus chosen are, for the moment, governmental *policies*; and the *process* by which the policy makers choose which alternatives they will and will not use is, according to our definition, *politics*.

A good illustration for this point can be taken from the area of foreign policy. Those who make the foreign policy of the United States have, for some years, been called upon to do something about the attempts of the Soviet Union and its communist allies to control an ever-increasing portion of the world's peoples. Our policy makers have the physical power available to undertake one or more of many different lines of action in

---

[1] Cf. Harold D. Lasswell and Abraham Kaplan, *Power and Society* (New Haven, Conn.: Yale University Press, 1950); and David Easton, *The Political System* (New York: Alfred A. Knopf, Inc., 1953).

[2] We shall consider the distinctions between governments and private organizations in Chapter 2.

response to communist aggression. They could, for example, start a preventive war now; they could inform the communists that we will fight if there is any further aggression; they could raise the living standards of the uncommitted peoples to try to prevent the latter from voluntarily embracing communism; they could abandon all resistance and simply surrender; and so on. Policy makers cannot, however, do all these things at once; some (e.g., preventive war and complete surrender) are bound to cancel out others. So they have rejected certain of these possible courses of action and adopted others. These adopted lines of action, taken together, have become the American *policy* toward communist aggression.

### Some Aspects of Politics

In order better to understand the process by which American foreign policy—or governmental policy in any other field—is made, one must know something about the following matters.

*Formal Policy-Making Procedures.*   According to the formal rules of procedure as laid down by the Constitution, acts of Congress, and other documents, which public officials are in charge of determining our foreign policy? What formal procedures, such as laws, executive proclamations, and formal instructions to ambassadors, do these officials employ?

*Informal Policy-Making Procedures.*   Of the many public officials who participate in making our foreign policy, whose suggestions are most often accepted and whose are most often rejected? In other words, who appears to have the most *influence*? Are they the same people in whom the formal organization charts vest principal legal powers? If not, why? What accounts for the variations in influence among the President, the secretary of state, congressmen, state department employees, presidential advisers, and so on? (In Chapter 6 we shall have more to say about the differences between "formal" and "informal" policy-making procedures.)

*Selection of Public Officials.*   How do particular people come to occupy these offices at particular times? By what formal and informal procedures are such officials nominated and elected or appointed? What are the effects of personnel-selecting procedures on the policy-making process?

*Relation of Public Officials to Persons outside the Formal Government.*   What persons other than public officials are actively interested in our foreign policy? How do they show their interest? Which of them attempt to influence the formulation of particular policies? What methods of influence do they use? Which of them have the greater influence? Why?

*Relation of "Policy Makers" to "Administrators."*   Do State Department employees, ambassadors, generals, admirals, and other officials formally charged with carrying out our foreign policy actually put it into effect as the policy makers intend? If not, how do they modify it? What influence have policy makers over administrators, and vice-versa?

## Some Characteristics of Politics in
## All Nations

Most of this book is devoted to a description of principal political and governmental "systems"—patterns of governmental policy making and policy execution—in the modern world. In the course of that description we shall repeatedly encounter two basic facts about the governing of men. First, certain general themes are characteristic of politics and government in all modern nations. In other words, there are certain respects in which these phenomena are essentially alike wherever we look. Second, there are a number of significant variations in these phenomena from nation to nation—variations that help to produce important differences in the lives and fortunes of the nations and peoples concerned.

An understanding of both the general themes and the principal variations is necessary for the student of political science. Accordingly, Chapters 1 through 3 are devoted to the consideration of the former, and Chapters 4 and 5 to an introduction to the latter.

### Politics Is Conflict

The first characteristic of politics in all modern nations is the fact that it involves conflict—that is, some form of struggle among human beings

Politics Is Conflict: Birmingham, Alabama, April, 1963. (Wide World Photos, Inc.)

who are trying to realize different goals and opposing interests. Political conflict is not an unfortunate and temporary aberration from the norm of perfect cooperation and harmony. It stems from the very character of human life itself.

### Conflict in Human Life

One universal and basic trait of human life, as we noted at the outset of this chapter, is the fact that people live together, not in isolation from one another. To be a human being is to interact with, to affect and be affected by, other human beings every day of one's life. To interact with one's fellows is, to some extent at least, to conflict with them. Let us see why.

Although all human beings are alike in certain respects, no human being is exactly like any other in every respect. One of the most significant respects in which human beings differ from one another is the fact that each has a somewhat different set of values from those held by his fellows. Now a "value," as social scientists usually employ the term, is an object of desire—something some person wants, whether it be passing grades, a Cadillac, social prestige, peace of mind, or a brave new world. Social scientists agree that not only do different persons want different things, but every person in some way *acts* to realize certain of his values. Wherever human beings come into contact with each other, their values are to some extent in conflict. To the extent that some values are satisfied, other values will necessarily go unsatisfied. For example, if taxes are increased to pay for a veterans' bonus, taxpayers will be unhappy; if the Republican party captures the presidency, Democrats will be unhappy; if farm prices are high and industrial prices low, farmers will be happy and industrialists and workers unhappy; and so on.

Accordingly, each of us finds that to some extent he is in competition with his fellows. As he lives his daily life and tries to date the prettiest girls, make the basketball team, get good grades, earn money, win the approval of his parents, bosses, and peers, and achieve his goals he finds his compatriots also want these satisfactions and that not everyone can or does have equal success in achieving them. Each of us strives in all sorts of ways —working and resting, studying and practicing, even lying and cheating—to achieve his particular goals while competing with those of his fellows who are trying to achieve conflicting goals. Conflict should be thought of as an essential and inescapable consequence of the fact that we live together rather than in isolation from each other.

### Political Conflict in Society

Wherever human beings live together in a society, most of them feel that certain values can be fully satisfied only by authoritative rules binding upon the *whole* society and everyone in it. For example, many Americans who believe that racial segregation in public schools is a great injustice to Negro children would not be satisfied merely with getting permission for a few to attend unsegregated schools while all the others continue to study under Jim Crow laws. They demand that *all* Negro children be permitted to attend unsegregated schools and will settle for nothing less. For another example, most persons who advocate preventive war with Soviet Russia are not likely to be satisfied by obtaining permission to shoot at the Soviet ambassador with their squirrel rifles. They are likely to demand that the armed forces of the entire nation launch an all-out war on Russia.

Most persons regard governmental action as the most promising way of getting authoritative rules binding upon the whole society. Conflict over what such rules shall be is, according to our definition, *political* conflict. Of course, not all conflicts among individuals and groups in any society are fought out by political means. Many occur largely or entirely outside the structure of politics and government. It is also true, however, that no society is entirely without internal political conflict; and, as we shall observe repeatedly in the course of this book, in modern nations most value-conflicts about which men feel strongly sooner or later become, for good or ill, political in nature.

Just as interpersonal conflict is an inescapable aspect of human life, political conflict is an inescapable aspect of human society.

### Political Conflict is Group Conflict

Political scientists are coming more and more to agree on a second general characteristic of politics: that contestants in political conflict are *groups* of human beings, not isolated individuals acting without reference to or support from other individuals. The contest between Johnson and Goldwater for the American presidency in the 1964 election, for example, was far from being a contest between those two individuals alone. Each of them was supported and influenced by political parties, labor unions, farmer organizations, business associations, ethnic groups, and numerous other bodies. To describe such an election solely in terms of what Johnson and Goldwater did would be to present only a partial picture of the situation and could be highly misleading. The conflict between Roy Wilkins of the NAACP and Governor George Wallace of Alabama over racial segregation in southern public schools directly involves the Supreme Court, Congress, the President, the National Association for the Advancement of Colored People (NAACP), White Citizens' Councils, northern whites and Negroes, southern whites and Negroes, and a host of other groups.

The defendant in a murder trial may appear at first glance to be an individual with no group support or interest behind him. Certainly the standard title of such a trial—*The People of the State of Illinois v. John Doe*—seems to suggest that the contest is taking place between Mr. Doe on the one hand and everybody else in Illinois on the other. If this is

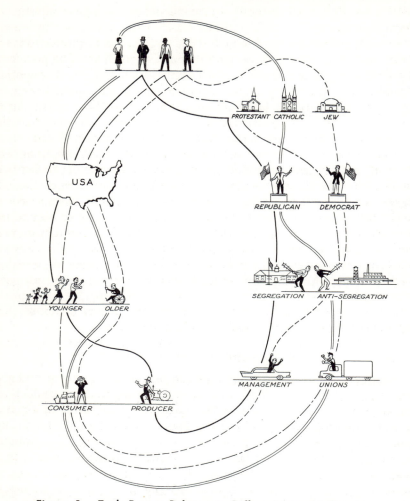

*Figure 1.* Each Person Belongs to Different Interest Groups. As One Issue Succeeds Another, the Lineup of Allies and Antagonists Changes.

indeed the situation, it seems a highly unequal contest, and one wonders how Mr. Doe can have the slightest chance of winning. The fact is, however, that he has considerable support from others. For example, many people in the community believe that every person accused of crime should be given a fair trial, and they have written into the state Constitution such protections for Doe as the guarantee of counsel paid for by the state if he cannot afford to hire one himself, the power to subpoena witnesses on his behalf, and the right to unseat jurors prejudiced against him. Mr. Doe, like every other individual engaged in politico-governmental conflict, is not alone.

Politics, then, may most usefully be thought of as the conflict among groups over the formulation of governmental policy. Let us now consider the different kinds of groups and determine which are the most prominent in politics.

### Varieties of Human Groups

CATEGORIC GROUPS. A categoric group is any aggregate of individuals sharing one or more common characteristics, such as persons under twenty-one years of age, persons earning more than $5,000 a year, residents of Illinois, tool-and-die makers, blondes, outfielders, and so on. The individuals in any particular categoric group may or may not be conscious of their common characteristic, regard it as important, and direct their behavior accordingly. Few brown-eyed people, for example, feel strong bonds of kinship with other brown-eyed people or are acutely aware of a wide gulf between their interests and the interests of blue-eyed people; they are not likely, therefore, to unite with other brown-eyed persons to advance the cause of brown-eyedness against the blue-eyed peril. Most Negroes, on the other hand, can hardly help being aware of their differences from white people, and they form organizations like the NAACP to improve their social status. In other words, any particular categoric group may or may not be socially or politically significant.

INTEREST GROUPS. The American political scientist David B. Truman defines an interest group as "any group that, on the basis of one or more shared attitudes, makes certain claims upon other groups in the society for the establishment, maintenance, or enhancement of forms of behavior that are implied by the shared attitudes."[3] In this sense, an interest group is a categoric group whose members are to some extent conscious of their common characteristics, regard themselves as having a common value or "interest" arising from these characteristics, and to some extent direct their behavior to advance their common interest. Doctors of medicine, for example, share the common characteristic of having received a certain kind of training and the M.D. degree from a medical school. They are also conscious that their training and skills differ from the training and skills of chiropractors, herbalists, and faith healers. Most medical doctors, therefore, join a professional association (the American Medical Association) which, among other things, works to withhold from persons who do not have the M.D. degree such privileges as legally calling themselves "M.D.'s" or "physicians" or "surgeons," performing operations, and prescribing certain

---

[3] David B. Truman, *The Governmental Process* (New York: Alfred A. Knopf, Inc., 1951), p. 33.

drugs. These attitudes and behaviors make doctors, in our terminology, an interest group.

"ORGANIZED" AND "UNORGANIZED" INTEREST GROUPS.   Some interest groups pursue their goals with little or no conscious and planned cooperative activity, but make their weight felt mainly by spontaneous parallel action. When the price of meat rises above a certain level, many housewives may individually and without mutual consultation decide to boycott the butchers and feed their families macaroni and cheese until meat prices come down. Although they now become a full-fledged interest group, and their parallel activity will have a powerful impact on the price of meat, they constitute, in our terminology, an *unorganized* interest group.

On the other hand, members of certain other interest groups regularly try to achieve their common goals by direct association, conscious planning, and "organization." Medical doctors, for example, do not try to retain their preferred position over chiropractors merely by individual and uncoordinated protests, and letters-to-the-editor. They *organize*—that is, they meet together, form a professional association with bylaws, dues, and officers, decide what must be done, and assign the various jobs to different members of the association. If they do these organizing jobs well, their members and officers act together cooperatively much as the organs of the body interact with each other—hence the origin of the term "organ-ized" to describe such a group.

POLITICAL INTEREST GROUPS.   Any interest group, organized or unorganized, which to some extent pursues its goals by political action—that is, by seeking to obtain governmental policies which will help achieve its goals and/or hinder opposing groups from achieving theirs—is a political interest group. Some political commentators use the term "pressure group" to denote such associations, but the term has doubtful utility because of its bad moral connotation and because the word "pressure" usually refers to certain kinds of tactics employed by some, but not all, politically oriented groups. In this book, therefore, we shall employ the more neutral and descriptive term "political interest group" except when we have occasion to refer to groups using "pressure" tactics described in Chapter 16.

### Characteristics of Group Conflict in Politics

Group conflict in politics in every human society displays, to a greater or lesser degree in particular societies, these main characteristics.[4]

MULTIPLICITY.   Every kind of distinction among human beings—whether based on race, religion, age, occupation, educational level, or whatever—

---

[4] See the somewhat different list of characteristics in E. E. Schattschneider, *Party Government* (New York: Holt, Rinehart and Winston, Inc., 1942), pp. 18–34.

gives rise to categoric groups, and some of these categoric groups become political interest groups. The more complex the society the more distinctions there are among its members, and the more likely it is to contain large numbers of political interest groups. A highly complex society like that of the United States probably contains more categoric groups than can ever be counted. The surest proof of this statement is the incredible variety of bases on which organized interest groups are formed in America. The following list is a small sample of the national associations listed in the *World Almanac*, but it illustrates how many extraordinary and diversified interests Americans feel are worth organizing to advance.[5]

American League to Abolish Capital Punishment
Alcoholics Anonymous
Anti-Defamation League of B'nai B'rith
American Automobile Association
Association of Professional Ball Players of America
Big Brothers of America
Blizzard Men and Ladies of 1888
Chinchilla Breeders of America
Circus Fans Association of America
International City Managers' Association
American Civil Liberties Union
National Collegiate Athletic Association
Ducks Unlimited
American Feline Society
Future Farmers of America
Federation of the Handicapped
Hay Fever Prevention Society
International Concatenated Order of Hoo Hoo
National Horseshoe Pitchers Association of America
Izaak Walton League of America
Association for the Promotion of the Study of Latin
Magicians Guild of America
Planned Parenthood Federation of America
Poetry Society of America
Rodeo Cowboys Association
Save-the-Redwoods League
Soaring Society of America
National Speleological Society
National Temperance League
American Wedding Society
Woodmen of the World

Another method for determining the multiplicity of interest groups in

---

[5] The names are taken from the *World Almanac*, 1965 (New York: New York *World-Telegram and The Sun*, 1965, pp. 546–560.

the United States is to list the number of units stemming from a few of the more obvious group-formation bases.

Number of families (households): 57,200,000
Religious denominations: 254; local congregations: 300,056
Business firms: 4,800,000
Farms: 3,700,000
National and international unions: 181
Local unions: 77,000
Units of government
    Nation: 1
    States: 50
    Counties: 3,043
    Municipalities: 17,997
    Townships and towns: 17,144
    School districts: 34,678
    Special districts: 18,323
    TOTAL: 91,236

If politics is a contest among political interest groups, then the United States—like any complex modern nation—has an almost infinite number of active and potential contestants.

OPPOSITION. Every political interest group has opposition—that is, some group or combination of groups seeking conflicting goals. To reword the same point, no proposal for governmental policy ever enlists *all* the members of the society in its support. The closest a nation comes to such a policy is usually the win-the-war policy adopted during times of armed conflict. Even then, an opposition of pacifists, who oppose all war-prosecuting measures, and of traitors, who seek to bring about an enemy victory, still exists. Every political interest group, accordingly, encounters some opposition in its efforts to induce the government to adopt policies favorable to its interests.

There are many variations in the kind of opposition particular groups face in particular situations. Opposing groups may be organized or unorganized, large or small, powerful or weak, and so on. The degree of hostility between opposing groups ranges all the way from the mild disagreement of groups favoring and opposing free barber service for congressmen to the bitter and uncompromising conflict that results in civil war.

As we have already noted, not all group conflict is fought out by political means, but many of the most serious and divisive types of social competition in modern nations are to a considerable degree conducted in the political arena. Such political competition may include (1) competition among cities, states, and regions for industry, teachers, labor, population, and water; (2) competition between labor and management over wages, hours, working conditions, and union status; (3) competition among ethnic groups for status, power, and prestige; (4) competition among religious

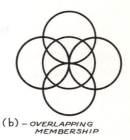

Figure 2. The Overlapping Membership of Political Groups.

groups for membership and status; (5) competition among various income-level groups over governmental taxes and expenditures, and for various kinds of special privilege; and (6) competition among businessmen, farmers, and workers for favored positions in the economy.[6]

Other examples will no doubt suggest themselves to the reader.

OVERLAPPING MEMBERSHIP.  Political interest groups in any complex modern society do not have mutually exclusive memberships—that is, they do not contain people who are members of a particular group but no other. Represented graphically, political interest groups in such a society relate to each other as shown in part b of Figure 2.

As Figure 2 suggests, each group shares a number of its members with other groups, although no two groups claim identical membership.

This phenomenon of overlapping membership stems from a society which has many distinctions among its members and therefore many bases for group formation; hence each individual belongs to a great many different groups, and no two individuals belong to exactly the same groups. The reader can check the validity of this generalization by comparing his group memberships with those of his close friends and associates. He is likely to find, for example, that friend X is a college student, Protestant, of Scottish descent, and a fraternity man; friend Y is a college student, Protestant, of German descent, and an independent; while friend Z is a college student, Catholic, of Italian descent, and a fraternity man.

IMPERFECT MOBILIZATION.  Since membership in political interest groups overlaps, no group can mobilize the all-out support of all its members. The degree of mobilization it can muster is likely to vary considerably from issue to issue in at least the following two respects. First, the *number* of mem-

---

[6] Cf. Austin Ranney and Willmoore Kendall, *Democracy and the American Party System* (New York: Harcourt, Brace & World, Inc., 1956), pp. 465–466.

bers who support a group to *any* degree fluctuates. Recent studies of voting behavior, for example, have shown that all the major voting groups studied —older and younger people, Protestants and Catholics, rich people and poor people, Negroes and whites, and so on—are internally divided in their voting preferences. Table 1 shows how some of them were split in the 1960 American presidential election.

### Table 1. Preferences of Certain Voting Groups in the 1960 Presidential Election

| VOTING GROUP | VOTED FOR KENNEDY | VOTED FOR NIXON | VOTED FOR OTHER | DID NOT VOTE |
|---|---|---|---|---|
| Men | 43% | 39% | * | 18% |
| Women | 35 | 40 | * | 25 |
| Protestants | 28 | 49 | * | 23 |
| Catholics | 72 | 15 | * | 13 |
| White | 39 | 42 | * | 19 |
| Negro | 37 | 16 | * | 47 |
| Annual income under $3000 | 30 | 33 | 0.7% | 36 |
| Annual income over $3000 | 42 | 41 | * | 17 |
| Grade school education | 37 | 30 | * | 33 |
| High school education | 42 | 38 | * | 19 |
| College education | 32 | 58 | * | 10 |

* Less than 0.5 percent.
SOURCE: These figures come from a national sample-survey study by the Survey Research Center, University of Michigan, and were furnished the author through the Inter-University Consortium for Political Research.

Table 1 also illustrates the second respect in which the degree of mobilization of particular groups varies: the *intensity* with which their members support them. In the 1960 election a number of members (ranging from 10 percent to 47 percent) in every group did not provide even so minimum and undemanding a form of support as voting.

"Labor," "farmers," "businessmen," "veterans," "Catholics," and other such groups are by no means disciplined political armies ready to spring into action when their leaders give the command. Nor are they constant factors in political conflict. Like every political interest group, each contains members all of whom also belong to other groups. On a given issue some —but not all—of its members will approve of the group's political activities, and of those who do approve, some will participate actively and enthusiastically, while others will not lift a finger.

In certain societies under certain conditions, a few political interest groups may appear to approach 100 percent mobilization. In modern South Africa, for example, nearly all the "Afrikanders" (white residents of Dutch descent) have apparently given enthusiastic support to the drive for *apartheid* (total segregation of whites from Negroes and complete white supremacy). Such a situation usually means that the nation is dangerously near to civil war; but even in South Africa some Afrikanders are not unqualified advocates of *apartheid*.

### The Nature of the "National Interest"

References to the "national interest" (and the "general welfare") appear with great frequency in modern political discourse. Dictators often announce that this mass execution or that sacrifice of "butter" for "guns" is necessary for the "national interest." Political interest groups in democratic nations usually claim that their proposals are "in the national interest." For example, schoolteachers maintain that their demands for higher salaries and more school buildings (and therefore higher taxes) are "in the national interest," and not merely in the "special" interest of schoolteachers; and property owners demand lower taxes (and therefore more modest school budgets) on the ground that *this* is truly "in the national interest," and not merely in the "special" interest of property owners. Nor is there any reason to believe that one group is sincere in its concern for the national interest while the other group is not. In short, most groups appear to believe that governmental policies *should* be in the national interest; but they always disagree about what policy *is in fact* in the national interest. Each group appears to believe that whatever promotes its own "special" interest will also promote the "general" interest. A version of former Defense Secretary Charles Wilson's famous dictum, "what is good for General Motors is good for the nation," would seem to apply to every political interest group.[7]

How significant is the general agreement that governmental policies should be in the national interest? Is it merely a hypocritical mask political groups cynically don to disguise their purely selfish intentions? Or, since there is never general agreement about what the national interest is in actual situations, is this a mere verbalism, without effect on actual politico-governmental behavior?

In answer to these questions, the concept of national interest as a widely shared goal of governmental policy—however much the means of achieving that goal are disputed—is crucial to the very existence of a nation. The concepts "nation" and "society" suggest that their citizens *share* and hold in *common*. The fact that certain aggregates of human beings apparently do have—and *act* as though they have—certain common and shared interests is what enables us to call them "nations" or "societies."

If America's workers cared *only* for higher wages, businessmen *only* for

---

[7] Cf. Glendon A. Schubert, *The Public Interest: A Critique of the Theory of a Political Concept* (New York: The Free Press of Glencoe, 1960).

higher profits, Negroes *only* for an immediate end to all forms of racial segregation, and southern whites *only* for the eternal preservation of complete racial segregation, the four groups could hardly continue to live together peacefully as Americans. The fact is, however, that workers, businessmen, Negroes, and southern whites have—and act as though they have—a real interest in maintaining the particular modes of conducting political conflict that the American politico-governmental system provides. Each group stands to lose a great deal by destroying these modes and replacing them with civil war or dictatorship or decrees from some foreign army of occupation. Each group shares at least one interest in common with the nation's other groups, namely, that of preserving the society in which they live. The "national interest" in this sense is a goal sought by every group in conjunction with its "special" goals. When any major group ceases to regard the preservation of the society as in its best interest, then secession, dissolution of the society, and perhaps even civil war are likely to follow.

How is a nation to determine which specific governmental policies are in the national interest and which are not? Some people, including a number of political scientists, believe that this question can be settled scientifically. They believe that if well-trained and able experts, not identified with any of the nation's "special" interest groups, rationally examine the nation's needs, and, using scientific methods, study the effects of specific policies, they can remove this question from mere political controversy and determine exactly and beyond all reasonable doubt which policies are in the national interest.

Other people are firmly convinced that questions of this sort cannot be answered with any scientific certainty. They point out that experts rarely agree among themselves on questions of policy. They add that all policy decisions ultimately become choices among competing values, and that there is no *scientific* way of deciding matters of good and evil. Many of these people are understandably skeptical about the whole concept of the national interest. They are impressed by the facts that each interest group advances its special interests in the name of the national interest, and that there is no more unanimity among groups than among experts on the question of what specific policies are in the national interest. They conclude that "the national interest" is either merely a propaganda slogan interest groups use in their struggle for power or a meaningless verbalism.

The author fully agrees that the question of which policies promote the national interest cannot be settled scientifically, mainly because it ultimately turns on questions of value preferences which are not amenable to scientific analysis. The point is worth making in greater detail by means of the following example. Most of us regard our physicians as experts in their specialty. Suppose Doctor X advises his patient, Mr. Y, to stop smoking cigarettes, on the ground that if he does not he will considerably shorten his life. Suppose Mr. Y replies that he would rather have a shorter life and enjoy it than have a longer life that he would not enjoy. Now Dr. X is considerably more expert than Mr. Y on the effects of smoking on the length of Y's life span, but Mr. Y is equally expert (or inexpert) on the question of what constitutes the good life. Dr. X has no special competence as a physician to tell Mr. Y what he *ought* to regard as the good life. In other words, Y's decision in regard to cigarette smoking is basically a question of competing *values*, not a question of the laws governing the physical universe. Since this is also true of governmental policy decisions, there is also no scientific way of determining which policies are good or bad for the nation.

In short, the process of government should not be thought of as a process which should find perfect solutions to national problems and thereby still all disagreement and conflict. It should be thought of, rather, as a process by which a nation decides which proposals of its various groups shall, for the time being, be adopted as governmental policy and which proposals shall be rejected. In the chapter that follows we shall examine further this and other similarities in the governing processes of all modern nations.

# 2

# The Governing of Nations

In some respects the process of learning what it is to be a human being is not unmitigated joy. From the time of our birth each of us becomes a member of an increasing number of social organizations; and as we become aware of our membership in these organizations, we learn that each of them claims the right to make and enforce certain rules governing our behavior. We are born into a family, and our parents tell us that we must drink our milk, brush our teeth, keep our rooms neat, and not draw on the walls, break windows, or swear. We go to school, and our schoolteachers tell us that we must attend class, pass examinations, and refrain from shooting spitballs. We join a church, and our ministers tell us that we must attend services, say our prayers, and live according to certain ethical standards. We get a job, and our bosses tell us that we must do our work, obey orders, and refrain from giving away company secrets to competitors. And so it goes, throughout our lives.

Moreover, each of these organizations backs up its rules with some kind of *sanctions*—that is, penalties that can be imposed by rule makers upon those who violate their rules. Parents can spank us and send us to bed without supper; schoolteachers can keep us after school or send us to the principal; churches can expel us from membership; and bosses can fire us.

The older we get the more conscious we become of the rules and sanctions of another organization which claims authority over us—an organization which we call "the government." It orders us to stay in school until we are sixteen, sends the males among us "greetings" and a summons to military service, requires us to pay to it a certain proportion of our income in the form of "taxes," tells us where we can and cannot park our cars, and in general surrounds us with more rules than we can count. And if "the government" catches us violating its rules, it fines or imprisons us, or even puts us to death.

Government, in other words, is a very special kind of social organization —so special, in fact, that the discipline of political science concentrates largely on its operations and its role in various nations. This chapter discusses the nature of government, how it differs from other social organizations, and why nations have governments.

## The Nature of Government

### A Definition

The term "government" is commonly used in two related but distinct senses: it sometimes refers to a particular aggregate of *persons*, each with individual idiosyncrasies, vices, and virtues, performing certain functions in a particular society; and it sometimes refers to a particular set of *institutions* —a series of accepted and regular procedures for performing those functions. The definition we shall employ in this book includes both meanings: *a government is a body of persons and institutions that make and enforce laws for a particular society*. In a moment we shall distinguish "laws" from other kinds of rules governing human behavior.

As thus defined, government is undoubtedly one of man's oldest and most universal institutions. Some political philosophers, to be sure, have speculated about what life would be like in a "state of anarchy"—that is, in a society without a government; yet there is no recorded instance of an actual society, past or present, that has operated very long with no government whatever. Evidently men at all times and in all societies have felt that some sort of government is vital to life as they wish to live it.

Man's universal need for government has not, however, made all men at all times and in all societies establish the same *kind* of government. Indeed, one of the most striking facts about actual governments, past and present, is that no two have been exactly alike. They vary in complexity all the way from the simple chieftainships of the primitive Baganda tribes in Africa to the highly complex "pluralistic democracy" of the United States. They vary in the treatment of their peoples all the way from the mass executions and "brainwashing" of Red China to the gentle and benevolent "welfare state" of Sweden. Evidently, different societies feel they require different kinds of government to fulfill their particular needs.

In Chapters 4 and 5 we shall examine some of the principal respects in which modern governments differ from one another. Our present concern is to see how government differs from all other types of social organizations in modern society.

## How Government Differs from Other Social Organizations

### Comprehensive Authority over Involuntary Membership

The rules made by any particular social organization other than government apply, and are intended to apply, only to members of that organization. When the University of Illinois rules that all freshmen must take a course in personal hygiene, no one considers that this rule also applies to freshmen at Yale or Oxford or Slippery Rock Teachers College. If General Motors should decide to split its stock four-for-one, no one considers that Ford, United States Steel, or American Telephone and Telegraph must do the same thing. The rules of government, on the other hand, apply, and are intended to apply, to *all* members of American society. When Congress rules that every American with an annual income above a certain level must pay a portion of that income in taxes, no one thinks that this rule is not intended to apply to people who think income taxes stifle initiative, or who cannot afford to pay the tax *and* buy a new car, or who let payment slip their minds this year. When Congress says *every* American, everyone understands it means precisely that.

Membership in most social organizations other than government is, moreover, *voluntary*—that is, a person becomes a member of such an organization and thereby subjects himself to its rules only by deliberate choice and conscious act. One does not automatically become a Presbyterian at birth because his parents are Presbyterian or because he is born in a Presbyterian hospital. He can *officially* join the church only by going through such formal procedures as baptism and confirmation. Membership in a nation, however, is *involuntary*—that is, one initially becomes a citizen of a nation and subject to its rules without any deliberate choice or conscious act on his part. As we shall note in greater detail in Chapter 7, all nations officially regard as citizens either all persons born in their territories, or all children born of citizens, or some combination of both. Most nations provide for the official voluntary acquisition and abandonment of membership by adults, but the initial acquisition of membership in a national society is involuntary.

### Authoritative Rules

Rules made by various nongovernmental organizations are often in conflict with each other. A labor union may order its members to overturn cars and use clubs and fists to keep strikebreakers from crossing its picket lines, while the church of some of the union's members may rule that its communicants may not use physical violence at all. A college fraternity may order its members to spend all their time making decorations for the homecoming celebration, but the university may order its students to devote all their time to their studies. In most societies there is no clearly defined and generally accepted hierarchy among these organizations and therefore no cut-and-dried way of determining which organizations' rules shall prevail and which shall be ignored in situations of conflict. There is no universal agreement that a church is more important than a labor union or vice versa, so that each union member who is also a church member must decide for himself whether he will obey his church or his union.

The rules of government, however, are quite another matter; for in all nations these rules are generally recognized as *authoritative*—that is, they are generally considered to be more binding upon all the members of the society, church members and union members alike, than the rules of any nongovernmental organization. In case of conflict between the laws of government and the rules of any other organization, there will be general agreement that the former should prevail. If a particular religious group prescribes human sacrifice as part of its ritual, and the government forbids the taking of human life by any organization other than itself, most members of the society will regard the governmental prohibition as more binding than the religious prescription. If the local building code requires that brick walls must be at least twelve inches thick, and local engineers consider eight inches to be a far more reasonable safety standard, most of the town's citizens—including most of its engineers—will obey the twelve-inch requirement, however misguided they believe it to be.

### Legitimate Monopoly of Life-and-Death Sanctions

All this is not to say, of course, that all the rules of government are always obeyed by all the members of society. Every social organization has to deal with individuals who disobey its rules, and government is certainly no exception. All organizations deal with such individuals by imposing sanctions, but government differs from other organizations in the kind of sanctions it is authorized to impose. Nongovernmental organizations are authorized to withhold certain privileges, impose fines, and require certain penances. Their ultimate weapon, however, is expulsion. If a member of a fraternity, a church, or a labor union refuses to pay the fines or do the required penances, the most extreme penalty his organization can impose is expulsion from membership. Government can do all of these things to persons who disobey its rules, and it can also impose two additional sanctions which are forbidden to other organizations: it can imprison or execute violators of the law.

Although some nongovernmental organizations—for example, gangs of criminals—have sometimes been known to execute persons who violate their rules, only government has the *legitimate* power to do these things, that is, its monopoly of the power to do them is formally recognized in the nation's constitution and is regarded as right and proper by most of the nation's citizens, while the use of such sanctions by gangsters is generally regarded as improper and wrong.

### Overwhelming Force

All social organizations can muster some physical force to enforce their rules. At the very least they can enlist the fists of their members, and many of them can also, if the occasion calls for it, round up clubs, rocks, razors, knives, and perhaps even pistols, rifles, and submachine guns. Some organizations actually use physical force on occasion to gain their ends. No nation conducts its intergroup conflict entirely without violence.

Government is by no means the only organization that can and does use force to compel obedience to its rules, but it differs from other organizations in the *amount* of force it can muster. This difference is so great that we often think of government as monopolizing all physical force. Nor is this too far from being accurate, for the clubs and knives and pistols that nongovernmental organizations can use to pursue their objectives are feeble indeed by comparison with the police, armies, intercontinental missiles, and hydrogen bombs that governments can use to pursue their objectives. In short, governments have no monopoly of force, but they can usually muster a degree of force that is overwhelmingly greater than that available to nongovernmental organizations.

Despite its unique position among social organizations, government does not make the only rules that govern and limit men's behavior nor are its laws in all cases and in all situations the most powerful regulators. Some laws, such as those against speeding, are disobeyed far more frequently than other kinds of rules, for example the "custom" requiring men to wear modern dress rather than togas.

Later in this chapter, we shall describe the kinds of rules other than laws by which men live. First, however, we must note that the particular kind of governments and laws that will be our main concerns in this book are those which operate in the large modern societies generally called "nations."

## The Nature of Nations

### *The Modern "State System"*

Every human being lives in a number of political societies. He is part of several aggregates of persons, each of which has some kind of government that is authorized to make law for its particular society. In America most of us live in a *city* governed by a mayor and a council, a *county* governed by a board of supervisors, a *state* governed by a governor and a legislature, and also the *United States,* which is governed by the President and Congress.

These societies and their governments are formally related to one another in a hierarchy of authority: state governments can override certain kinds of decisions made by city and county governments, and the national government can override certain decisions made by the state governments. At the peak of this hierarchy stands the national government. No government has the legal and generally recognized right to override decisions of the national government of the United States, and the national governments of such countries as Great Britain, Soviet Russia, Canada, and China are equally supreme or "sovereign" in their own areas.

Political scientists use the term "state system" to denote this division of the world's population into a number of "nations," each of which has complete governmental authority within its particular area, and none of which recognizes a government superior to its own.[1] Chapter 22 is devoted to a discussion of the origins and consequences of the state system. At present, we shall confine ourselves to listing the main traits that distinguish "nations" from other kinds of societies.

### Earmarks of the Modern Nation[2]

### 1. A Definite Territory

Each of the world's nations is located in a particular area of the earth's surface, and has definite and generally recognized boundaries which do not overlap the area of any other nation. To be sure, the exact locations of mutual boundaries are sometimes disputed by adjoining nations, as in the case of China and India in the 1960's; but the *principle* of definite boundaries is accepted by all nations.

### 2. A Definite Population

Each nation regards only certain persons as its legal "citizens" or "subjects" and all others as "aliens" (see Chapter 7).

---

[1] Political scientists agree that there are about 126 nations in the world today. The number cannot be stated more exactly because of such societies as Andorra, San Marino, and the Vatican City State, whose claim to full nationhood is marginal. For the list of nations we shall employ in this book, see Table 2 in Chapter 4.

[2] Two leading works on the characteristics of modern nations with particular emphasis on the psychological phenomenon of nationalism are Hans Kohn, *Nationalism: Its Meaning and History* (New York: The Macmillan Company, 1955); and Karl W. Deutsch, *Nationalism and Social Communications: An Inquiry into the Foundations of Nationality* (New York: John Wiley & Sons, Inc., 1953).

### 3. A Government

Each nation has an officially designated set of persons and institutions authorized to make and enforce laws for all people within its territory.

### 4. Formal Independence

Each nation's government is "sovereign"—that is, it is formally recognized by other nations as having the exclusive right to make policy for the nation's territory and inhabitants. Thus each nation has supreme legal power over its own affairs and in this respect is the full equal of any other nation. Known in international law as the principle of "the sovereign equality of nations," this is a *legal* principle only. In terms of actual behavior some nations may be more subject to influence by foreign nations than others. If the United States strongly suggests that Guatemala adopt a certain policy, Guatemala is more likely to act on the suggestion than the United States is to act on a similar suggestion put to it by Guatemala. But *legally* speaking, Guatemala has as much power to make its own decisions as does the United States.

### 5. Nationalism

The psychological basis of the state system is nationalism—the citizens' love for and loyalty to their respective nations. For a great many of the world's inhabitants, nationalism is the highest loyalty, more compelling than loyalty to family, race, church, or economic class. The most striking evidence of nationalism's power over men's minds and behavior is the fact that wars, which are the supreme test of men's loyalties, are mostly fought among nations, not among races or churches or economic classes. When the United States has gone to war with Germany, American workers, Catholics, capitalists, and Lutherans have killed and been killed by German workers, Catholics, capitalists, and Lutherans.

Why do most Americans think of themselves primarily as Americans and secondarily as workers or capitalists or Catholics or Lutherans? What makes a particular aggregate of persons think of themselves as a *nation?* Social scientists are unable as yet to answer these questions satisfactorily. Most of them agree, however, that nationalism is found among peoples who display most, although not necessarily all, of the following traits.

IDENTIFICATION WITH THE NATIONAL TERRITORY. Not only does each nation occupy and rule over a particular territory, but most of its citizens to some degree psychologically "identify" with it. They have an affection for its physical characteristics—its rivers and lakes, mountains and plains, deserts and prairies—and these feelings are powerfully evoked by such sights and phrases as "the white cliffs of Dover," "the rock-bound coasts of Maine to the sunny shores of California," and" how quiet flows the Don."

**A COMMON HISTORY.** Most citizens of each nation are to some degree conscious of being part of a continuous historical entity, and this historical consciousness furnishes them with a strong reminder of their common identity and a powerful source of resolution to carry on in such a way that what their forefathers created "shall not perish from the earth." It apparently makes little difference whether the nation's history is, as in the case of the United States and Great Britain, largely one of success and domination or, as in the case of Poland, Eire, and Israel, largely one of defeat and oppression. Accordingly, most nations instruct their children in national history, and erect monuments and statues commemorating the great episodes and figures of the past.

**A COMMON LANGUAGE AND LITERATURE.** Most of us feel a certain kinship with persons who speak the same language we do in the same accent and idiom. When we meet someone who, as in the case of an American conversing with an Englishman, speaks substantially the same language but uses a different accent and idiom, we probably think of him as somewhat "foreign"; and when we meet someone who, as in the case of an American dealing with a Frenchman or a Swede or an Indonesian, speaks a tongue entirely different from our own, we probably think of him as *very* "foreign." Thus those who share a common language—and a common literature that transmits not only the nation's language but also its history, traditions, and customs—are likely to feel both a certain kinship with each other and a certain apartness from people who speak other tongues. There are, to be sure, some bilingual and trilingual nations, such as Canada and Switzerland; but they are exceptional, and most nations have one official language which is spoken by the great majority of their citizens.

**A COMMON CULTURE.** The citizens of each modern nation also share a particular culture. Most of them conduct their lives—courtship, marriage, child rearing, business, and recreation—according to the manner generally accepted and approved in their own nation. Their particular culture differs in at least a few respects from the culture of any other nation. Thus each citizen feels a certain kinship with his fellow citizens, whose way of life is similar to his own, and at the same time he entertains a certain feeling of strangeness and difference from citizens of other nations, who live somewhat differently.

**A DESIRE FOR POLITICAL INDEPENDENCE.** The foregoing traits do not produce full-fledged nationalism unless the people who share them also feel that their collective aspirations can be satisfied only by full political independence. Californians, Texans, and New Yorkers apparently feel that they are somewhat different from less fortunate folk; but their feelings do not result in any genuine nationalism, for they are content to remain under the government of the United States and do not agitate seriously for complete political independence. On the other hand the aspirations and demands of the people of India, Indonesia, and Ghana in the twentieth century could not be satisfied merely by improved standards of living or a stronger voice in the councils of the European nations who once controlled them. They could be satisfied only by complete political independence—by the recognition of their status as fully independent and sovereign nations and of their consequent right to make all their own political decisions without guidance or interference from any other nation. Only when the traits that a particular people share result in a demand for political independence can we accurately describe their collective feelings and aspirations as "nationalism."

### *"Developing" Nations*

The period since World War II has seen the greatest effusion of new nations in history. Table 2 in Chapter 4 shows that of the 126 nations listed, no fewer than 52 (41 percent) have achieved formal independence since 1945. Africa outdistances all other areas with 32 new nations, followed by Asia with 11, the Middle East with 5, and the Caribbean and Oceania with 2 each. So nationalism and the state system, far from dying out, are stronger forces in world politics today than they have ever been.

Political scientists generally call the new nations (and most of the older nations in Latin America, the Middle East, and Asia as well) "developing nations," as opposed to the "advanced nations" of Western Europe, the pre-1945 British Commonwealth, and the United States. Many writers in the Afro-Asian nations object to this usage, arguing that it falsely implies that there is a single standard of perfection aimed at by all nations which only the Western nations satisfy.[3] There is something in this criticism, but the term "developing nations" is now so widely used it would be pointless to coin another here. We need only note that the principal indices of "development" include such economic and social measures as per capita gross national product, number of persons per doctor, vehicle, telephone, and radio, and percentage of population literate. The main political measures include degree of competition for public office permitted, freedom and breadth of political communication, and success in articulating and aggregating the demands of interest groups.[4]

Social scientists have studied the developing nations intensively in recent years, but their findings are far too voluminous and complex to

---

[3] Fred R. von der Mehden, *Politics of the Developing Nations* (Englewood Cliffs, N.J.: Prentice-Hall, Inc., 1964), pp. 4–6.

[4] The most complete statement is the Introduction and Conclusion of Gabriel A. Almond and James S. Coleman, *The Politics of Developing Areas* (Princeton, N.J.: Princeton University Press, 1960).

*Figure 3.* Violence Is Not Unknown in the Most "Advanced" Nations: November 22, 1963. (Copyright © 1963 by Bill Mauldin. Reproduced by courtesy of Chicago *Sun-Times*.)

summarize in any detail here.[5] Some leading themes are as follows. The developing nations fully cover the whole range of forms of government (see Chapter 4), with such multiparty democracies as Israel and Chile, such one-party-dominant near democracies as Mexico and Malaysia, such one-party monopolistic dictatorships as Algeria and Ghana, and such nonparty traditional dictatorships as Ethiopia and Saudi Arabia. Many developing nations are beset, with varying degrees of severity, with the difficulty of converting the old anticolonial fervor into a new and effective

Freedom from Colonial Rule Does Not End All Conflict: Berber Rebels against Former Ben Bella Dictatorship in Algeria. (Wide World Photos, Inc.)

national unity; they must, as in the Congo and Algeria, pacify divisive factions ranging from irredentist objectors to armed secessionist rebels. All are struggling with the problems of national economic growth, industrial and agricultural modernization, and increasing literacy while moderating the differences—and hostility—between the relatively advanced cities and the primitive rural areas.

In short, the new nations are finding that when the last colonial overlord departs for London or Paris or Amsterdam their problems do not magically leave with him; indeed, they seem to multiply. They are learning what

---

[5] The leading works include Almond and Coleman, *op. cit.*; Rupert Emerson, *From Empire to Nation* (Cambridge, Mass.: Harvard University Press, 1960); John H. Kautsky, *Political Change in Underdeveloped Countries* (New York: John Wiley & Sons, Inc., 1962); Max F. Millikan and Donald L. M. Blackmer, *The Emerging Nations* (Boston: Little, Brown & Company, 1961); and Lucian Pye, *Communication and Political Development* (Princeton, N.J.: Princeton University Press, 1963).

the "advanced" nations have learned before them: that holding a nation together is every bit as arduous as establishing one.

# The Rules Men Live By

## What Holds a Nation Together?

### The Problem

When a particular group of people are caught up with the feelings of nationalism just described, they are likely to settle for nothing short of independence, and most groups that feel this way sooner or later achieve full nationhood. The fact that the citizens of a nation wish to live together as a nation does not impel them to abandon all conflict among themselves: living together is only *one* of the things each of the nation's groups wishes to do. Even if all the citizens agree that the nation should survive, they are bound to disagree about such vital matters as who among them shall be rich and who poor, who shall give orders and who receive them, who shall receive deference and from whom, and so on. Conflict—some form of struggle among persons trying to realize differing goals and opposing interests— exists, as we observed in Chapter 1, wherever human beings live together in a society; and modern nations are certainly no exceptions.

Every nation, accordingly, faces the imminent possibility of civil war and disintegration; for each constituent group in any nation wants to pursue its own "special" interests and realize its own particular goals as well as to advance the "national" interest and realize the common goal of preserving the nation. When any major group completely abandons its concern with the latter goal in its zeal to accomplish its particular purposes, the nation cannot long survive. Thus every nation faces the ever-present problem of survival in the presence of conflict among its constituent groups —to say nothing of threats to its independence by other nations.

### Some Unifying Forces

Few nations have perfectly and permanently solved the problem of internal conflict. Rebellion and civil war have occurred in many nations, including the United States; and some—for example, the British Empire and France in the eighteenth century, and Austria-Hungary, Spain, and China in the twentieth—have perished or undergone drastic revisions as a result. Yet most modern nations have solved the problem well enough to maintain at least their national identity and independence—a fact which appears all the more remarkable when we remember that each of them encompasses a wide variety of groups and interests and therefore a large volume of internal political conflict.

How have they done it? The most immediate and obvious answer is that, while most groups in most of these nations might have pursued their special interests in ways that would make their particular nation's survival impossible, they have not in fact done so. Why not? What forces, social and psychological, have impelled them to limit their pursuit of power in this manner?

To answer these questions fully, to describe all the forces that hold nations together, we should take into account just about every aspect of modern national societies: their ethnic composition, occupational and income differences, religious differences, general wealth or poverty, and a host of other factors. The unifying forces most relevant to the concerns of this book, however, are the rules by which citizens of modern nations live. In every modern nation precepts encouraging certain kinds of behavior, tolerating others, and prohibiting still others are superimposed on the citizens' inherent impulses and inclinations and place effective limitations on various aspects of their behavior, including the means they employ to pursue their special political interests.

Most Americans, for example, wear clothes, even on hot summer days when they might be more comfortable without them. Moreover, they wear "modern" clothes, not togas, loincloths, or sarongs. They eat with knives and forks rather than with chopsticks or their fingers, pay money for what they buy, drive on the right-hand side of the road, and refrain from eating human flesh or killing disobedient children. Some of what they do is governed by habit—that is, it never occurs to them to do otherwise. Much of what they do, however, is governed by rules—that is, they consciously feel that they ought to act in certain ways or that their associates will disapprove of them or that they will be punished if they act differently. Some of the rules by which men live are closely associated with government; others are not. Let us briefly examine each type.

### The Main Kinds of Social Rules[6]

#### Moral Precepts

Every human being to some extent directs his behavior in terms of some kind of moral code, a series of principles according to which certain kinds of behavior are right and good and others are wrong and bad. He may consciously bear in mind and try to obey such Christian "commandments" as

---

[6] For descriptions of the sources and effects of conduct-guiding rules other than law, see R. M. MacIver and Charles H. Page, *Society* (New York: Holt, Rinehart and Winston, Inc., 1949), Chs. 7–9; Eliot D. Chapple and Carleton S. Coon, *Principles of Anthropology* (New York: Holt, Rinehart and Winston, Inc., 1942), Chs. 12–16; and R. M. MacIver, *The Web of Government* (New York: The Macmillan Company, 1947), Chs. II, IV.

"Thou shalt not kill," "Honor thy father and mother," and "Do unto others as you would have them do unto you." Or he may adhere to such non-Christian "commandments" as "Never give a sucker an even break" and "Look out for number one first and everyone else second."

Part or all of any particular person's moral code may come from religious sources. The "commandments" may emanate from a church and have behind them some sort of supernatural sanction, such as a priest's warning that nonobservance will displease God and thus condemn the violator to the eternal fires of hell. Part or all of a person's moral code may also stem from nonreligious sources. The "commandments" may emanate from his philosophy of the good life and have behind them such nonsupernatural sanctions as his fear that violating them will bring highly undesirable personal and social results, or his inner conviction that "virtue is its own reward."

Whatever their source, moral precepts differ from other kinds of social rules in that those who obey them do so not because they fear some kind of retribution from other human beings, but rather because they believe that it is good to do so regardless of what others may think.

### Customs

Every person also directs his behavior to some extent according to what he thinks others expect him to do. For example, neither his church nor his private moral philosophy requires him to wear a business suit to the office instead of a toga or a monk's habit, or to leave a tip for the waitress at a restaurant, or to begin his letters with "Dear so-and-so" and close them with "Sincerely yours." Yet he regularly follows all these rules because he knows that if he does not, most of his associates will regard him as "peculiar"—and few people wish to be singled out and pointed to as "peculiar."

Customs, or, as some sociologists call them, "folkways" and "mores," are powerful regulators of human activity in all societies. According to anthropologists, they are the most powerful regulators of all in most primitive societies, and even in the more literate and "civilized" modern nations they play an important role. The reader can check the accuracy of this statement by asking himself how much of what he does and does not do is determined by his desire to avoid being regarded as "peculiar" rather than by what his church or his private moral philosophy tell him to do, or by his fear of being arrested.

### Law

The kind of behavior-limiting rules with which we are mainly concerned are those which collectively go under the name of "the law." In Chapter 20 we shall describe in detail the nature, sources, and types of law, but for our present purposes we need to understand just what "law" is in general and how it differs from moral precepts and customs.

The literature of political science, jurisprudence, and sociology offers many definitions of "law."[7] As we shall use the term in this book, however, *law is the body of rules emanating from governmental agencies and applied by the courts*. Law, therefore, differs from other kinds of social rules in that, unlike customs, it emanates from a specific governmental source, and, unlike moral precepts, it is regularly enforced by the courts. Law, in short, consists of *governmental* rules; and government, as we have seen, differs from all other rule-making social organizations in a number of significant respects.

## Why Nations Have Governments

### *Why Not Anarchy?*

In Chapter 1 we observed that political conflict exists wherever human beings live together in a society. Thus, no nation has a choice as to whether or not it will have political conflict; it has only a choice as to how that political conflict will be conducted. Its only option is in deciding what methods of promoting their causes conflicting groups may employ, what channels of communication and points of contact will be made available to them, and, perhaps most important of all, what methods will be used to resolve the various conflicts—that is, the processes by which the nation will determine which groups "win" and which "lose," and by which the "losers" will be induced to accept the verdict.

Any nation may choose the possible alternative of anarchy. That is to say, it could establish no authoritative and binding procedures whatever for settling these matters; it could let its groups conduct their political conflict in any manner they saw fit; and it could leave to the particular conflicting groups themselves the choice of a method for determining the "winners." In short, a nation could solve the basic problem of government by having no government at all. At first glance, such a solution seems very tempting indeed, for who among us has not sometimes dreamed of living in a society without tax collectors, traffic cops, and draft boards?

Yet, no nation has ever embraced anarchy as its established and permanent method of conducting political conflict. Why not? There appear to be two main explanations.

---

[7] For a convenient summary of various definitions, see Kenneth Redden, *An Introductory Survey of the Place of Law in Our Civilization* (Charlottesville, Va.: The Michie Company, 1946).

*"Oh, Pablo, you're not going back into politics!"*

*Figure 4.* In Some Nations Politics and Violence Are Often Synonymous. (Drawing by B. Wiseman; Copyright © 1956 The New Yorker Magazine, Inc.)

## The Desire for Authoritative Rules

In Chapter 1 we noted that most groups in modern nations have some values that can be satisfied only by rules applying to and binding upon *all* persons in the nation—that is, by *governmental* rules. Let us illustrate this point further with an example from perhaps the most bitter group conflict in current American politics. The National Association for the Advancement of Colored People (NAACP) and the persons for whom it speaks have their hearts set on achieving rights and opportunities for Negroes fully equal to those possessed by white persons. They long for the day when all decisions as to whether a particular Negro will get a particular job, be paid a particular wage, vote, hold public office, and so on, will be made strictly according to his personal abilities and qualifications, with no weight whatever being given to the color of his skin. They wish, in short, that Negroes be judged—as they feel white persons now are—as individuals, not as members of a particular ethnic group.

This goal can never be achieved, they believe, merely by attempting to persuade, one by one, every individual white American, every business firm, and every election official to forswear discrimination voluntarily; such a process would take forever, and they are not willing to wait that long. Nor are they willing to settle permanently for some version of the present situation, in which some employers and election officials discriminate against Negroes and others do not; such a solution would mean that some Negroes would always be second-class citizens.

The NAACP and its supporters feel that they will achieve their goal of equality only when American society enforces some kind of antidiscrimination rule applying to *all* Americans, including those who prefer discrimination and white supremacy. They regard anything short of such a rule as only a second-best solution, for which they may have to settle temporarily, but with which they will never be permanently and fully satisfied.

The antidiscrimination group believes, moreover, that such a rule must be genuinely binding—that is, it must be obeyed by all Americans and not merely by those who tend to approve of it. If it is not, then the group's goal of ending all discrimination everywhere in America cannot be achieved. Accordingly, they are unwilling to let each American decide for himself whether or not he will obey the rule. They demand that non-discrimination be embodied in law, which is generally regarded as a society's most solemn and authoritative manner for prescribing rules of conduct. They also demand that the society punish in some fashion persons who violate the law. That is why they fought so hard for the passage of the Civil Rights Act of 1964.

In short, most Americans who feel strongly that racial discrimination should be abolished in the United States believe that they can achieve their goal only by an antidiscrimination rule that applies to the whole society and is genuinely binding upon every American. Only government can adopt and enforce such a rule. By the same token, those Americans who believe that white supremacy must be maintained can achieve their opposite goal only by preventing the adoption and enforcement of such a rule. That is why they fought so hard against the 1964 Civil Rights Act. And so it is with the conflicting groups on many other issues in the United States and in all other nations, past and present. Every nation, in other words, contains groups that have goals which only governmental action can fulfill; so long as this continues to be the case, no nation will be willing or able to settle for anarchy.

### The Desire to Preserve the Nation

The desire of interest groups for general and binding rules does not automatically and in all situations lead to the rejection of anarchy and the establishment of government. After all, many of the world's nations also feel that certain rules of conduct should apply to and be enforced upon all of mankind. The Red Chinese, for example, would like to impose a Peking-directed communist politico-economic system on all the earth's peoples, while the Western democracies feel that any such communization of the world would mean the death of their most cherished values. Yet neither the communist nor the noncommunist nations clamor for the establishment of a world government with power to decide this issue authoritatively. Both sides prefer to conduct this and other issues in international politics in the context of the state system, which closely approaches a state of international anarchy.

There is no *a priori* reason why interest groups within a particular nation should not attempt to achieve their goals by the same means the world's nations now use. The NAACP, for example, might proclaim a no-discrimination rule and, by such means as destruction of property, torture, and assassination, attempt to force all Americans to obey it; and the white supremacists might resist with machine guns, poison gas, and hydrogen bombs.

The NAACP and its opponents *might* do these things, and yet for the most part they do not. Like most interest groups in most nations, they apparently prefer to pursue their objectives in the context of government, not anarchy. Why? The answer lies in the characteristics of political group conflict we observed in Chapter 1. Each member of both the antidiscrimination group and the white-supremacy group is also a member of many other groups. It is very unlikely, therefore, that either group could mobilize the all-out support of all its members for the "total war" that the tactics suggested above would bring on. Both groups, moreover, have a number of important interests and objectives in common. Both are part of American society and receive many benefits from it—e.g., more personal freedom, a higher standard of living, and more voice in the determination of governmental decisions than they could have in most other nations. Each group therefore has a considerable stake in preserving the United States. Each group knows that the nation could not survive if its political issues were regularly settled by civil war; in this imperfect world a nation that can no longer govern itself is not likely to pass into a state of blissful anarchy. It is far more likely to be conquered and governed by some other nation that *can* keep internal conflict under control.

In deciding what tactics they will pursue, the NAACP and their opponents—and, indeed, all interest groups in all nations—must make these decisions: they must calculate their chances of success in a possible civil war, and decide whether what they stand to gain from such a war is more valuable than what they stand to lose from the destruction of their nation.

Sometimes, groups in certain nations in particular situations choose anarchy and civil war. Violence, rebellion, and large-scale violations of law are by no means unheard of in human affairs, and in later chapters the role of these phenomena in politics and government will be discussed at greater length. Only in international "society" do anarchy and war appear to be generally accepted as proper and regular principles of organization. In most modern nations groups act most of the time as though they believe that preserving their particular nation is necessary to the kind of lives they wish to lead, and that some form of government, not anarchy, is the only method of settling political conflict that can preserve a nation. Seeing government in this light makes it easier for most persons to put up with revenue agents, traffic cops, and draft boards.

### The Main Task of Government

People prefer government to anarchy, then, because they want society-wide and binding rules, because they wish to preserve their particular nations, and because they feel government is a better bet than anarchy to accomplish these goals.

The main task of any government, whatever its form and in whatever nation, is to satisfy the social needs that call it forth: to make and enforce authoritative rules in such a way that the nation will hold together and remain independent. Different governments perform this basic task in different ways, but all governments continually face the challenge of determining the "winners" and "losers" on issue after issue in such a way that the latter will peacefully abide by the decision. In other words, the first job of the governing officials in any nation is to prevent war; and only when they are confident that this is being done can they afford to concentrate on other matters.

There is no single universal and proven method of accomplishing this task, no political snake oil that is guaranteed to prevent civil war in all nations under all conditions. Governments have traditionally relied upon combinations, varying greatly in emphasis from time to time and from government to government, of two basic methods for keeping the "losers" in line.

#### Compromise

A government may strive to make the content of its policies such that the "losers" may feel that life under the existing regime, while perhaps a far cry from their maximum desires, is at least bearable. Governments may encourage such an attitude by giving each group something of what it wants so that no group experiences *total* "defeat." This can be done only by withholding from the "winners" complete victory—in other words, by compromising the maximum demands of opposing groups. The resulting policy is likely to contain a number of logically inconsistent provisions and may even look downright ridiculous when judged by the canons of logical neatness. But a government is likely to be more concerned with preserving its existence than with logical neatness, and if the policy in question does the job, no one will care very much about its lack of symmetry.

The current conflict over racial segregation in southern public schools provides a classic example of the uses of compromise. Consider, for a moment, what is happening in this explosive and dangerous conflict. The extreme antisegregationists demand an immediate end to segregation, while the extreme white supremacists demand that it be continued permanently. Completely satisfying the demands of either group would mean total defeat for the other—and neither group is at present likely to accept such defeat peacefully. The civil war potential in this conflict is perilously high. How has our government handled this dangerous situation? In 1954 the Supreme Court ruled that segregation is unconstitutional. This was a major victory for the antisegregationists, but not a total victory; for the Court, after hearing suggestions on the matter for a year, chose as its method for ending segregation an order that local school boards show "good faith" in ending segregation in their districts. It also recognized that segregation must be abolished more slowly in some areas than in others by ordering the various federal district courts to proceed "with deliberate speed" to see that the local school boards comply with the order. Since 1955 segregation has been almost completely abolished in some states (e.g., Missouri and Maryland), abolished only in certain areas of others (e.g., Texas), and hardly touched at all in still others (e.g., South Carolina, Georgia, and Mississippi).

Thus the antisegregationists have received something but not all of what they want and also the strong hope of getting a great deal more. The white supremacists have received less but still some of what they want, mainly the hope that they will not be forced by outsiders to suffer an immediate, total revolution in their way of life. Neither group, of course, is ecstatically happy about the present situation; but both groups apparently feel that it is sufficiently bearable that there is no need to start a civil war to alter existing conditions. Our present policy toward segregation may not satisfy anyone's vision of perfect justice or logical symmetry, but it enables the nation to deal with this bitter issue by means other than civil war. This, from the standpoint of government, is all the justification it needs.

## Coercion

A government may also try to coerce the "losers" into abiding by its decisions. It may use propaganda to "sell" its policies to the "losers" in such a way that they will not think of themselves as "losers" at all. Dictatorial governments, e.g., Red China, the Soviet Union, and Nazi Germany, have placed heavy reliance upon this technique. Or, if the "losers" remain unconvinced by propaganda, a government may threaten them with fines, imprisonment, torture, and death. Coercive measures of the latter type have two main purposes: to convince potential rebels that the consequences of open rebellion are bound to be more disastrous than those of abiding by the despised policies, and to take out of circulation the "losers" who, undeterred by these threats, seek to become active rebels.

In all nations coercion is a powerful method of winning assent to governmental policies; and the Chinese Communists in recent years have given the world a terrible lesson in how brainwashing, torture, and mass executions can annihilate dissent—and dissenters. There is reason to believe, however, that coercion is not an absolute and irresistible weapon against all dissent under all conditions. Even the Red Chinese satraps apparently give some consideration to satisfying some of the demands of their subjects. All governments use *both* compromise and coercion as means of avoiding civil war, although they vary greatly in the reliance they place upon each method.

In the next chapter we shall review some of the major functions performed by modern governments. As we survey them, we should bear in mind not only that each of these functions has been undertaken to satisfy the demands of some group but also in opposition to the desires of another group. While every modern government performs many functions, the main task of any government is the determination and enforcement of its policies in such ways that its citizens can continue to live together as a nation.

# 3

## The Functions of
## Modern Governments

Since most of us do not hold public office, we know government mainly as a performer of certain "functions." Some governmental agencies build our primary and secondary schools, hire teachers and janitors, and require us to attend school until we are sixteen. Others compel the young men among us to spend some time in military service. Still others supervise our marriages and perhaps grant our divorces. Yet others license our automobiles, businesses, and dogs.

No one of us, however, has personally had experience with *all* the functions our governments perform. Hence we may be tempted, like the blind men who examined the elephant, to think of the functions of government with which we have had firsthand contact as constituting everything—or at least everything important—our governments do. No student of government should succumb to any such temptation; for one of the traits that makes government such a uniquely pervasive and significant institution in modern life is the incredible variety and dimension of the functions it performs. And in every modern nation one of the most durable and hotly disputed political issues is the perennial controversy over what functions government *should* perform.

The present chapter lists some of the functions most generally performed by governments the world over, notes some of the leading issues and points of view in the dispute over what functions government should perform, and outlines and accounts for the general role of government in modern life.

## What Governments Do in the United States

For better or worse, modern governments do just about everything. If one could compile a complete list of all the functions performed by all the world's governments today, that list would undoubtedly include activities which directly and powerfully affect just about every conceivable aspect of human life—marriage, the rearing of children, education, the production and distribution of wealth, religion, art, sport, and so on *ad infinitum.*

Assertions like these, however, are too broad and general to mean very much to most of us. They do not give us a vivid sense of the enormous

*The Law of Moses and the Laws of Today*

**Figure 5.** Modern Government Is the Biggest of All Businesses. (Fitzpatrick in the St. Louis *Post-Dispatch.*)

scale and almost endless variety of activities that governments perform. We shall, therefore, try to indicate the scope of government with a brief listing and classification of some of the major functions now performed in the United States by one or another of its various local, state, and national governments. The United States makes a convenient case study, for its governments perform somewhat fewer functions than do those of some nations (e.g., Sweden, Great Britain, and Denmark), and somewhat more than other nations (e.g., Switzerland). By modern standards, the following list is neither unusually long nor unusually sparse.

### PROTECTION OF PERSONS AND PROPERTY

1. Enforcement of contracts, and the granting and protection of copyrights and patents
2. Enforcement of safety standards in the construction of buildings, bridges, and roads, and provision for fire-prevention and fire-fighting services
3. Enforcement of safety standards in all forms of commercial transportation, and in such matters as the private operation of automobiles, airplanes, and boats
4. Regulation of threats to public morals by the control of liquor, narcotics, gambling, the exhibition of motion pictures, and the publication of books and magazines
5. The capture and punishment of murderers, thieves, and other criminal offenders
6. Aids to businessmen in the form of subsidies, tariffs, marketing advice and services, and price-maintenance laws in order to cushion the rigors and risks of going into business
7. Aids to farmers in the form of subsidies, tariffs, soil conservation, research, and marketing advice and services in order to increase productivity and maintain income against the hazards of the market
8. Enactment of antimonopoly laws, corporation income taxes, excess-profits taxes, and so on, in an attempt to prevent excessive concentrations of economic power
9. Levy of progressive income taxes on the rich and provision of relief and unemployment payments to the poor in an attempt to prevent extremes of individual wealth and poverty
10. Control of the volume of currency and credit, initiation of public works, control of prices, and so on, in order to prevent extremes of inflation and deflation
11. License of radio and television broadcasters and regulation of rates and services offered by such public carriers as trains, airplanes, ships, and buses to guarantee certain levels of service in transportation and communication
12. Provision of protection for the organization and operation of labor unions and management associations to guarantee "fair competition" in collective bargaining between labor and management.

Government As Mediator: In an Attempt to Head Off Threat-
ened Rail Strike in 1964, Secretary of Labor W. Willard Wirtz
Meets with Representatives of Both Unions and Carriers. Two
Days Later, Both Sides Agree to Delay Strike Fifteen Days.
(Wide World Photos, Inc.)

13. Provision of conciliation and mediation services for ending strikes and
    lockouts
14. Provision of protection against fraud in the sale and purchase of
    securities
15. Provision of an army, navy, air force, marine corps, and coast guard to
    protect American lives and property against foreign invasion

### DEVELOPMENT AND CONSERVATION OF NATURAL RESOURCES

1. Promotion and protection of wild life by limitations on the hunting of
   various kinds of wild game and fish, the restocking of depleted streams
   and lakes, and the provision of sanctuaries for species in danger of
   extinction
2. Enforcement of conservation regulations in the use of land, water,
   forest, mineral, and other resources
3. Construction and operation of dams to prevent floods and generate
   electricity
4. Development of atomic energy for civilian as well as military uses

### HEALTH AND SANITATION

1. Subsidization and conduct of medical research
2. Encouragement and subsidization of hospitalization insurance and pro-

vision of public hospitals and free medical care for the aged and indigent

3. Regulation of the training, licensing, and practice of medicine, nursing, and pharmacology
4. Control of the spread of infectious and epidemic diseases by such means as quarantine control
5. Enforcement of sanitary regulations in the production, distribution, and consumption of food
6. Enforcement of safety standards and labeling regulations in the manufacture and distribution of drugs

### PUBLIC ASSISTANCE AND SOCIAL SERVICES

1. Provision of training, hospitalization, and other special benefits for orphans, the deaf and blind, and disabled war veterans
2. Provision of placement services to assist people in locating jobs
3. Provision of old-age and survivors' insurance through social security and other retirement systems
4. Provision of special economic aid and redevelopment for depressed areas
5. Delivery of mail
6. Promotion of homeownership by guaranteeing private lending agencies against loss in the financing of home construction, so that these agencies will charge lower interest rates for their mortgages
7. Replacement of slum dwellings with subsidized low-rent housing for lower-income groups
8. Provision and subsidization of public libraries, museums, playgrounds, golf courses, public parks, monuments and historical sites, zoos, and so on

### EDUCATION

1. Construction and maintenance of classrooms, offices, laboratories, machine shops, and other physical facilities necessary for education
2. Provision of preparation, employment, and pay for teachers
3. Provision of loans, scholarships, and fellowships for students
4. Support of research in physical, biological, and social sciences
5. Regulation of school attendance by legislating compulsory school ages
6. Provision of various types of adult education programs

## The Debate over What Government Should Do

By no means every American, needless to say, is happy about the fact that American governments perform all the functions they do. Just about every function in the foregoing list was undertaken only after some debate between those who favored it and those who opposed it; for none of these functions, as we shall note in a moment, has the support of *every* American. Nor have the "losers" in these debates always accepted their loss quietly, cheerfully, and permanently. Some of them, indeed, have managed to secure a subsequent reversal of the initial decision and an abandonment by the government of the function they dislike.

A certain amount of the political controversy in any modern democracy, as we shall see in later chapters, is related to the forms and procedures of government. By far the largest proportion, however, centers on questions of what government should and should not do—in other words, over the functions it should and should not assume. Thus, most of the political arguments we hear and engage in at our dinner parties and over our back fences, read about in our newspapers, and see on our television sets are over such matters as whether the government should undertake or abandon hydrogen bomb tests, price supports for farmers, "socialized medicine," "foreign aid," and the like. To most of us this sort of controversy is the sum and substance of politics.

In what follows we shall not attempt anything so ambitious (and fool-hardy) as offering a final disposition of all arguments about the proper functions of government. We shall merely offer a few guideposts and warn-ing signs that may assist the reader in finding his own way through the mazes and difficulties of this enduring political dispute.

### Specific Issues and General Debate

#### The Specific Nature of Governmental Functions

Every "function" performed by a modern government consists of a series of specific activities to which, for the sake of convenience, we cus-tomarily give a general label. When we speak of "governmental regulation of private motorists," for example, we are referring to a series of episodes in which a policeman flags down a private motorist and gives him a ticket, after which a justice of the peace assesses a fine of so many dollars which the motorist promptly pays. When we speak of "governmental aid to foreign nations," we have in mind a series of episodes in which representa-tives of American government in such nations as Western Samoa, Brazil, and Turkey take money provided by American taxpayers and appropriated by Congress and give it to the officials of the foreign nations to buy such goods as food, tractors, and lathes. Our mental picture of the "functions of government" is likely to be more accurate if we bear in mind that each of the general labels pinned to the various "functions" refers to a series of specific activities.

#### The Specific Nature of Political Issues

As we noted in Chapter 2, everything that any government does—every policy it adopts and every function it performs—is undertaken in response to the demands of some political interest group and over the objections of other such groups. In other words, every governmental function is controversial; simply because a particular function *is* performed does not mean that everyone in the nation agrees that it *should* be performed. Some functions, of course, are more controversial than others. Far fewer people in the United States, for example, actively oppose free public education than actively oppose the Taft-Hartley Act or economic aid for foreign nations or racial integration in public schools. The point is that some Americans —for instance, the publisher of a Santa Ana, California, newspaper—oppose even free public education.

In the final analysis, therefore, all political conflict in the United States or any other nation is fought over *specific* issues—that is, over such issues as whether this particular person shall go to jail, or whether that particular corporation shall pay over part of its income to the public treasury, or whether that particular squadron of B-52's shall drop hydrogen bombs on Moscow. We may customarily refer to these issues in general terms, such as, respectively, "enforcement of criminal law," "the excess-profits tax," and "foreign policy." But it is well to remember that these general phrases refer to specific activities and issues, and that the payoff in politics is in the specific activities government performs, not in the general words we use to describe what government does.

### General Issues in Political Debate

Political debate in modern nations is to some degree conducted in terms appropriate to general ideological issues. For example, the advocates of progressive income taxes usually say something like this: "Such a tax makes for a more equitable distribution of income, and thus helps the nation avoid dangerous extremes of individual wealth and poverty." By the same token, its opponents usually reply in some such fashion as this: "Such a tax confiscates part of what a successful man earns and thus penalizes initiative and ability." Both groups may also argue about the proper size of the surtaxes on the upper-income levels, but they are likely to spend most of their energy in debating the more general question of whether *any* sort of income tax is desirable and just. So it is with just about all political debate—so much so, in fact, that there is a danger that we may focus our attention on these general issues so exclusively that we will forget that what really matters in politics is the specific, concrete activities that government does or does not perform

The most durable and frequently debated of these general issues is that defined by the British philosopher-politician Edmund Burke as "What the state ought to take upon itself to direct by public wisdom, and what it ought to leave, with as little interference as possible, to individual discretion."[1] In most of the democratic nations the debate over this perennial

---

[1] *The Writings and Speeches of Edmund Burke* (Boston: Little, Brown & Company, 1901), V, 166.

issue has revolved around the positions denoted by the terms *"laissez faire,"* "socialism," and "the welfare state." Each of these terms has two related but distinct meanings: each is a descriptive label applied to a certain general pattern of governmental activity, and each refers to an ideology according to which a government can best help its citizens achieve the good life. Let us now examine both the descriptive and ideological aspects of each of these three terms.

### Laissez Faire

#### As a Descriptive Term

The term *"laissez faire"* literally means "let it alone." It is generally used to refer to situations in which there is a minimum of governmental interference in the lives and activities of private citizens, particularly in their economic activities. In such situations the government provides the basic conditions for free competition among its citizens by maintaining law and order, enforcing contracts, protecting private property, and defending the nation against attack by other nations. Within these limits the government allows competition to function freely and unregulated. *It neither holds back the successful nor helps the unsuccessful.*

#### As an Ideology

The doctrine that "that government is best which governs least" was first enunciated in the seventeenth and early eighteenth centuries by such writers as the English philosopher John Locke and a group of French economists known as the "Physiocrats" (whose title meant something like "those who believe in rule according to nature"). Its most famous and influential exposition was made in *The Wealth of Nations,* a book published in 1776 by the Scottish professor Adam Smith. The case for *laissez faire* may be summarized as follows. Society, like the physical universe, is a rationally designed, sensible, orderly mechanism governed by natural laws. These laws of social order are, like the laws of physical order, knowable by human reason, and some of them—for example, the law that prices in a freely competitive market are determined by the interplay of supply and demand, and "Gresham's law" that bad money will drive good money out of the market—are already known. A nation that ignores or flouts these laws in shaping its economy will encounter disaster as surely as a person who ignores and flouts the law of gravity. If government attempts to regulate and restrict economic competition, hamper the efficient and successful, or help the inefficient and unsuccessful, it can only blunder like the proverbial bull in the china shop and upset the delicate but perfectly adjusted balance of the natural economic system, and the whole nation will suffer and be the poorer for it. The best economic policy a government can pursue, therefore, is to leave the economy strictly alone.

Adam Smith, like many other writers who have expounded the doctrine of *laissez faire*, was perfectly willing to accept certain deviations from this pattern. He believed, for example, that the government should not let any citizen starve no matter how inefficient he is and that the government should regulate production and consumption in whatever ways are necessary to make sure that its defense is adequate to ward off foreign attack. He added, however, that such deviations are justifiable only on humanitarian and nationalistic grounds; from the standpoint of strict *economic* efficiency, they are indefensible and should therefore be undertaken only when absolutely necessary.

## Socialism

### As a Descriptive Term

The term "socialism" resembles such terms as "democracy" and "science" in that, even as a purely descriptive term, it apparently means different things to different persons. It also resembles them in that it is highly charged with emotional connotations for many people: to many Europeans, for example, it suggests equality and justice, while to most Americans it suggests quite the opposite and, indeed, is often used as a "smear word" in political debate.

In this book, however, we shall use the term "socialism," as most political scientists do, to denote a situation in which a substantial portion of a society's economic productive machinery is governmentally owned and operated.

### As an Ideology

There are many varieties of socialist doctrine, and some socialists devote a great deal more energy to pointing out the ideological errors and organizational sins of rival brands of socialism than to criticizing *laissez-faire* capitalism. Despite the many and often bitter disagreements among themselves, however, all socialists have a sufficient number of common beliefs so that we may speak of "socialism" as a general ideology. Professor Hallowell defines those beliefs as follows:

> There are many varieties of socialism but all socialists agree that the principal source of evil in the world is the institution of private property and all, although in varying degrees, advocate the common ownership of all the means of production as the cure. All advocate the transformation of private property into public property and the division of the income from such property in accordance with individual needs.[2]

---

[2] John H. Hallowell, *Main Currents in Modern Political Thought* (New York: Holt, Rinehart and Winston, Inc., 1950), pp. 368–369.

### Socialists *versus* Communists

The main schism among modern socialists is that between "socialists" and "communists"; and the main disagreement between the two groups is over the question of *how* private property should be abolished and governmental ownership and operation of the economy established and maintained.

The "socialists"—including the adherents of such groups as the British Labour party, the French and American Socialist parties, and the West German and Scandinavian Social Democratic parties—place a high value upon democrcy as well as upon socialism. They hold that socialism can and should be brought about only by such democratic and peaceful means as the organization of socialist political parties, the victory at elections and the capture of control of democratic governments, and the peaceful adoption and enforcement of socialist economic policies. In recent years, indeed, their fervor for the abolition of private property has generally yielded to less doctrinaire and more pragmatic programs of piecemeal social reforms.

From its origins in the writings of Karl Marx and Friedrich Engels in the mid-nineteenth century to the death of Stalin in 1953, orthodox communist doctrine held that (1) true socialism can be established, as it was in Russia in 1917, only by violent revolution and the liquidation of unrepentant capitalists; (2) it can be maintained only by the dictatorship of the proletariat through monopoly of power by Communist parties; and (3) Soviet Russia must be the center and the Russian Communist party the commander of the world communist movement, and all Communist parties and policies in other nations must unquestioningly follow the Russian leader's "line."

During this period, accordingly, socialists and communists occasionally collaborated with each other against a common enemy, as in the "popular front" against Fascism in Western Europe in the 1930's. But most of the time they were in bitter conflict, for each saw the other as the betrayer of true socialism. Hence some of the communists' toughest opponents have been socialists like Willy Brandt, Mayor of Berlin and Leader of the German Social Democratic party in the 1960's, and Hugh Gaitskell, Leader of the British Labour party from 1955 to 1963.

### Schisms in Modern Communism

Since 1945 the monolithic, Moscow-commanded world communism of Lenin and Stalin has developed a number of deep, perhaps irreparable, fissures. In 1948 the Communist dictator of Yugoslavia, Marshal Tito, refused to accept Moscow's overlordship of Yugoslavian affairs, and Stalin expelled him and his party from the world movement. In 1949 the Chinese communists under Mao Tse-tung won complete control of mainland China, and launched a policy of radical collectivization at home, aggressive

## "And Stop Pinching Me"

*Figure 6.* World Communism Is No Longer Monolithic. From *Straight Herblock* (Simon & Schuster, 1964).

expansion abroad, and war-to-the-death with capitalism as the only proper course for communism. In 1953 Stalin died, and his eventual successor, Nikita Khrushchev, increasingly emphasized a policy of "peaceful coexistence" with the capitalist West—a policy endorsed by his successors, Brezhnev and Kosygin. In the late 1950's and early 1960's the differences between the Chinese and Russian versions of communism sharpened and deepened, and the attacks by each side on the other grew more open and virulent, culminating in an open break in 1963. Khrushchev's overthrow a year later removed many of the personal animosities exacerbating the quarrel, but by the mid-1960's it appeared that communism would never again be the monolithic world movement it had been before 1948.[3]

## The Welfare State

### As a Descriptive Term

The term "welfare state" has been widely used in political discourse only since the early 1940's and is, therefore, much newer than either *"laissez faire"* (which dates from the early 1700's) or "socialism" (which dates from about 1830). It is generally used to denote a situation in which the government provides all its citizens with certain guaranteed minimum aspects of the good life, such as formal education, medical care, economic security in old age, housing, and protection against loss of jobs or business.

A *"welfare state"* differs from a *"laissez-faire"* state mainly in that the latter guarantees to its citizens only the opportunity to compete with each other for the good things of life and does not make such a guarantee for those who cannot provide for themselves. A "welfare state," some of its opponents to the contrary, is not the same thing as "socialism." It may provide these minima by such socialistic means as, for instance, providing free public schools; or it may provide them by such nonsocialistic (and also non-*laissez-faire*) means as, for instance, giving—as in the "G. I. Bill of Rights"—government subsidies to veterans for attendance at privately owned and operated schools.

### As an Ideology

The advocates of the welfare state argue that every citizen ought to have these minimum conditions of the good life as a matter of right and

---

[3] For changes in the USSR after Stalin, see John A. Armstrong, *The Politics of Totalitarianism* (New York: Random House, Inc., 1961); and Howard Swearer, *The Politics of Succession in the USSR* (Boston: Little, Brown & Company, 1964). For the split between China and Russia, see William E. Griffith, *The Sino-Soviet Rift* (Cambridge, Mass.: The Massachusetts Institute of Technology Press, 1964); and Donald S. Zagoria, *The Sino-Soviet Conflict, 1956–61* (New York: Atheneum Publishers, 1964).

justice, and that no citizen should be denied them because he cannot finance them out of his own resources. They do not all agree, of course, on the exact minima that ought to be guaranteed or to what degree they should be guaranteed. Some, for example, would include complete medical care of the highest caliber, while others would include only hospitalization insurance. Some might include free public education for qualified students through the Ph.D. degree, while others would limit the guarantee to a high school diploma. They all agree, however, that the proper function of government is to provide every citizen with some degree of formal education and medical care even if this requires—as it usually does—that the rich be taxed to provide for the poor.

## The Role of Government in Western Nations

### *The Passing of* Laissez Faire

Whatever may be the relative merits of the three ideologies just summarized, it is clear that the functions actually performed by Western governments add up to something far more like the "welfare state" and/or "socialism" than *"laissez faire."*[4] In most European nations, indeed, even the general ideology and slogans of *laissez faire* have lost most of their support and are defended by only a few small "right-wing" political parties. Even the Conservative party of Great Britain, despite its (to Americans) somewhat misleading name, espouses a program that fully accepts such socialist measures instituted by the Labour party between 1945 and 1951 as public ownership and operation of coal mines, railroads, and medical services. No major group or political party in Great Britain or any European nation advocates a return to *laissez faire*.

The United States is one of the few modern nations in which the general ideology of *laissez faire* still commands a good deal of support. In America we still hear many people speak in favor of "free enterprise" and against government "regimentation" and "meddling" in business. These are leading themes of the post–1945 conservative movement in the United States, which has had considerable political success, culminating in

---

[4] For useful accounts of the rise of *laissez faire* in Western nations in the eighteenth century, its heyday in the first half of the nineteenth century, and its steady and universal decline since then, see Karl Polanyi, *The Great Transformation* (New York: Holt, Rinehart and Winston, Inc., 1944); D. W. Brogan and Douglas V. Verney, *Political Patterns in Today's World* (New York: Harcourt, Brace & World, Inc., 1963), Ch. 4; and Harry K. Girvetz, *From Wealth to Welfare* (Stanford, Calif.: Stanford University Press, 1950).

the presidential nomination (but not election) of Barry Goldwater by the Republican party in 1964.[5]

However, when we look behind the general pronouncements for "free enterprise" to see how Americans feel about the performance of specific functions by their government, we find that no major group in American politics seriously urges the sort of *laissez faire* expounded by Adam Smith. Many American businessmen, for example, urge the elimination or sharp reduction of such governmental *regulations* of business as minimum-wage and maximum-hour laws, excess-profits taxes, and price controls. But very few advocate the elimination or reduction of such governmental *aids* to business as protective tariffs, direct subsidies of the sort given to airlines and the shipping industry, and the many research and marketing services of the Department of Commerce. Many American farmers strongly oppose governmental regulation and restriction of crop yields, but very few advocate the total abolition of all such governmental aids to farmers as price supports, rural electrification, and the Department of Agriculture's research and marketing services. Few Americans *act* as though they long for the "free enterprise" of Adam Smith, in which each man tries for unlimited success and risks complete failure, and the government neither restrains the successful nor helps the failures. One writer has suggested that regardless of how most Americans may *talk*, they *act* as though they believe in "safe enterprise" rather than "free enterprise"—that is, they seem to prefer a reasonable and secure level of profits guaranteed by government subsidies and government regulation of "cutthroat competition" to being permitted to risk complete failure in the hope of unlimited success.[6]

The United States probably still has more "free enterprise" than any other major modern nation. But even here the ideology of *laissez faire* has lost its prestige to such an extent that few individuals and groups and no major political party openly argues that government should do *nothing* to prevent depressions or cushion business failures or put a floor under agricultural prices or feed the unemployed. The actual functions American governments perform, as we have seen, go far indeed beyond the functions which, according to the classical doctrine of *laissez faire*, they should perform.

---

[5] Among the leading statements of the conservative position are Frank S. Meyer, *In Defense of Freedom: A Conservative Credo* (Chicago: Henry Regnery Company, 1962); and William F. Buckley, Jr., *Up from Liberalism* (New York: Ivan Obolensky, Inc., 1959). But conservatism, like socialism, has schisms: for a different version see Willmoore Kendall, *The Conservative Affirmation* (Chicago: Henry Regnery Company, 1963).

[6] Cf. Nathan Robertson, "What Do You Mean, Free Enterprise?" *Harper's Magazine*, CXCVII (November, 1948), 70–75.

## *The Omnipresence of Government*

Most of us are primarily interested, understandably enough, in those aspects of society that appear to have the most direct and visible impact upon our own personal lives and fortunes. Accordingly, most of us have no trouble in paying considerable attention to such social institutions as courtship, marriage, parent-child relations, schools, churches, businesses, and the like. We have all had a great deal of direct personal experience with these institutions and feel, quite rightly, that they have a powerful effect on our lives.

By this same standard, most of us should find government downright fascinating; for what "they" do in Washington and in our state capitols and city halls profoundly affects even the most ordinary and uneventful life in all sorts of ways. Most of us are born in government-regulated hospitals and delivered by government-licensed doctors. The government protects us against certain kinds of treatment by our parents. We spend most of our childhood and youth in government-supported schools. Our marriages (and divorces) are established under close governmental supervision. We enter and leave business, engage in the professions, buy and sell property, and retire—all under a considerable body of governmental regulations. We may be ordered by government to serve in the nation's armed forces and even kill and die by the orders of governmental officials known as "military officers." When we have finally filled out our last form and paid our last tax bill, we are buried in a government-licensed cemetery, and our estate —minus a portion retained by the government for the inheritance tax—is handed on to our heirs by probate courts and government-licensed lawyers. In short, government plays a major role at just about every main juncture of our lives.

## *Some Reasons Why*

### The Impersonality of Life in Western Nations

Government has not always been so omnipresent in men's lives as it is in our time. In the eighteenth and early nineteenth centuries a great many men in all nations lived out their lives with only occasional direct contacts with police magistrates and tax collectors, and no contact whatever with draft boards or social security cards. Since the middle of the nineteenth century, however, the governments of all modern nations have steadily increased the volume and variety of their activities and have played a role of ever-growing significance in the lives of their citizens.

Most political scientists believe that the root-cause for this universal expansion in the role of government lies in the changing nature of society. The nations of the eighteenth and early nineteenth centuries were pre-

**SOCIAL SECURITY**
ACCOUNT NUMBER

654-21-4931

HAS BEEN ESTABLISHED FOR

Frank F. Smith

SIGNATURE  *Frank F. Smith*

FOR SOCIAL SECURITY PURPOSES • NOT FOR IDENTIFICATION

*a*

§ 14. **Town and city clerks to issue marriage licenses; form.** The town or city clerk of each and every town or city in this state is hereby empowered to issue marriage licenses to any parties applying for the same who may be entitled under the laws of this state to apply therefor and to contract matrimony, authorizing the marriage of such parties, which license shall be substantially in the following form:

State of New York,
County of...........................................
City or town of.....................................

Know all men by this certificate that any person authorized by law to perform marriage ceremonies within the state of New York to whom this may come, he, not knowing any lawful impediment thereto, is hereby authorized and empowered to solemnize the rites of matrimony between .................... of .................... in the county of .................... and state of New York and .................... of .................... in the county of .................... and state of New York and to certify the same to be said parties or either of them under his hand and seal in his ministerial or official capacity and thereupon he is required to return his certificate in the form hereto annexed. The statements endorsed hereon or annexed hereto, by me subscribed, contain a full and true abstract of all of the facts concerning such parties disclosed by their affidavits or verified statements presented to me upon the application for this license.

In testimony whereof, I have hereunto set my hand and affixed the seal of said town or city at .................... this

*c*

State of New York—Department of Taxation and Finance—Bureau of Motor Vehicles

**PASSENGER VEHICLE 1958 Registration**

Ann. Fee $

Fee Paid $

PLATE NO............
Do Not Write In Above Space

VALID FOR DESCRIBED VEHICLE TO MIDNIGHT JAN. 31, 1959

Print Name

Address     Street and No.
City or       (Residence, if Individual, Otherwise Business Address)
Post Office        Zone
                No.     State

| 5. Year and Make of Vehicle | 6. Type | 7. Cyls. | 9. Model No. |
| 10. Serial Number | 11. Engine or Identification No. | | 12. Weight lbs. |

(Sign Name in Full     (State if Partner, or Give Title
—in Regular Handwriting)     if Officer of Corporation)

*b*

**Registry of Deaths**

Section 33 of the Sanitary Code requires physicians "to make and preserve a Registry of Deaths."

Name of Deceased....................

Place of Death....................

(a) NEW YORK CITY: (b) Borough....................
(c) Name of Hospital or Institution
            (If not in hospital, give street and number.)

(d) Length of stay at place of death immediately prior to death

Usual residence....................

Date of death....................     Hour....................  A.M. / P.M.

Sex............Color............     Married Single / Divorced Widowed

Age............years............months............days     hrs............min. INTERVAL BETWEEN ONSET AND DEATH

Direct cause....................

*d*

**FORM 941** (Rev. Jan. 1957)
U. S. Treasury Department
Internal Revenue Service

# EMPLOYER'S QUARTERLY FEDERAL TAX RETURN

COPY FOR EMPLOYER

1. Federal Income Tax Withheld From Wages (If not required to withhold, write "None") . . . . $
2. Adjustment for preceding quarter(s) of calendar year. (Attach explanation. See instructions) . . $
3. Income tax withheld, as adjusted . . . . . . . . . . . . Enter Adjusted Total Here➔ $
   Federal Insurance Contributions Act Taxes (If no taxable wages paid, write "None")
4. Number of employees listed in Schedule A ............  5. Total taxable wages paid (from Item 21) $
6. 4½% of wages in Item 5 (2¼% employer tax and 2¼% employee tax) . . . . . . . . $
7. Credit or adjustment. (Attach explanation. See instructions) . . . . . . . . . . . $
8. F.I.C.A. taxes, as adjusted . . . . . . . . . . . . . . Enter Adjusted Total Here➔ $
9. Total taxes (Item 3 plus Item 8). If deposits of taxes are made, fill in Schedule B on other side . . . . . . . . $

# YOUR COPY

**IMPORTANT**
Keep this copy and a copy of each related schedule or statement.
Before filing the return be sure to enter on this copy your name, address, and identification number, and period for which the return is filed.

10. Type or print in this space employer's identification number, name, and address exactly as shown on original.     Return for Calendar Quarter (Enter quarter and year as on original)

*Figure 7.* Modern Government Plays a Wide and Varied Role in Our Daily Lives. The Documents Represented Above are (a) Social Security Card, (b) New York State Automobile Registration, (c) New York State Marriage License, (d) New York State Death Registry, and (e) Federal Tax Return for Employers.

dominantly rural, and most social relations among their citizens were conducted in direct and personal fashion. Most of our great-great-grandfathers lived on farms or in small hamlets.[7] They had a face-to-face acquaintance with most of the persons who most directly affected their lives—their neighbors, the people who bought their produce, those who sold them their equipment, seed, drugs, clothing, etc. In protecting themselves against maltreatment by their associates they relied to a considerable extent upon self-help. If someone with whom they dealt cheated or injured them, they often obtained redress by their own efforts rather than by appealing to some governmental official to intervene on their behalf.

The nations of our own time, on the other hand, have become predominantly urban, and most social relationships are indirect and impersonal. Many of us never see face-to-face most of the people who directly affect our lives, and we often do not even know the names of the people in the next apartment. Many of the men who make our cars, compound our drugs, buy our products, and bank our money live hundreds and even thousands of miles away, and most of them remain anonymous and faceless. The impersonality of modern life results not only from the sheer size of the communities in which most of us live, but also from the great complexity and the high degree of specialization of labor that characterize modern national societies.

To illustrate this point, let us consider an episode in the life of "John Doe," a typical American living in 1830, and compare it with a similar episode in the life of his great-great-grandson, "John Doe IV," living in 1966. John Doe feels a little out of sorts one day and decides he needs a "spring tonic" to pick him up. So he goes over to the next farm to see his neighbor, Ezra Roe, who makes and sells tonic, and buys a bottle. After a few swallows Doe becomes sick, however, and he knows Roe has cheated him. So he returns, demands his money, and when Roe refuses, uses his fists to convince Roe that he had better return it after all. Doe sees no reason to ask Judge Solon down at the general store to intervene, for he is used to handling such matters himself.

Five generations later, John Doe IV feels under par and goes to the corner drugstore to buy a bottle of Ezra Roe's Scientific Blood Reconditioner. He takes a couple of swallows, becomes sick, and learns from his

---

[7] The 1790 United States census reported that no city in the nation had a population of over 50,000, and that 95 percent of the people lived in areas of under 2500 population. The 1960 census, by sharp contrast, reported that only 36 percent of the population lived in rural areas, and that 27.5 percent lived in cities of over 100,000 population.

Even so, the United States is far more thinly populated than most Western European nations: we have 60 persons per square mile, compared with the Netherlands' 949, Belgium's 783, West Germany's 579, Great Britain's 563, Italy's 434, Switzerland's 365, France's 225, and Spain's 159.

doctor that he has a mild case of poisoning from impurities in the reconditioner. He feels like hitting the man who did this to him; but the person who compounded this particular bottle of reconditioner is one of 4000 workers employed by one of the twelve Roe Drug Corporation factories located in a city 800 miles away. John Doe IV simply cannot gain redress purely by self-help, and it never occurs to him to try. Living as he does in an impersonal society, he turns, instead, to government: he sues the Roe Corporation for damages and writes to his congressman urging that the pure-food-and-drug laws be tightened to prevent further damage.

### Government as the Main Gap-Bridger

This little story illustrates why government has come to play so pervasive a role in Western life. Most of us can never see, identify, or know most of the persons whose activities bear directly upon our lives. We therefore customarily turn to government to bridge the gap between them and ourselves. We are so accustomed to the intervention of government between us and our fellows that we hardly give it a thought.

Take, for example, the act of faith that we all commit when we do such an ordinary thing as taking a dose of aspirin. We ask the druggist for aspirin, pay our quarter, and take the pills. But how many of us are skilled enough at analytical chemistry to be sure merely by seeing and tasting the pills that they do in fact contain, as the label says they do, aspirin instead of arsenic or some other poison? Our great-great-grandfathers personally knew the men who compounded their drugs, but we have never seen and never will see the men who make our aspirin tablets. How, then, do we dare take the risks involved in swallowing them? The answer is that we know, without even bothering to think about it, that the men who make the tablets are checked by government inspectors and that the firm that manufactures and sells them is required by law, under heavy penalties, to state on the tin's label the contents of the pill and whether they are poisonous or dangerous. We do not have to be skilled analytical chemists to take aspirin safely, for the government protects us from our own ignorance and from the impersonality of life in our society.

Government, in short, is omnipresent in Western life because the conditions of Western society seem to demand it. It may still be true, as Dr. Samuel Johnson wrote two centuries ago, that

> How small of all that human hearts endure
> That part which Laws or Kings can cause or cure.

The fact remains, however, that, for good or ill, Western nations and the human beings who compose them have turned to "Laws or Kings" as the principal means for putting into effect whatever cures they think they have found or will find in the foreseeable future for "all that human hearts endure."

# 4

# Forms of Government

IN his *Essay on Man,* the eighteenth-century English poet Alexander Pope dismissed the subject of our present chapter with this widely quoted couplet:

> For forms of government let fools contest;
> What'er is best administer'd is best.

In the long sweep of human history, however, few persons have agreed with Pope. As long ago as the fifth century B.C. Greek scholars classified the governments they knew as either "monarchies," "aristocracies," or "democracies" and argued that these different "forms" represent significantly different ways of governing. A generation after Pope's death the English colonies in the New World fought a war for independence from the mother country, arguing in their Declaration of Independence that "whenever any Form of Government becomes destructive of" the ends of "Life, Liberty, and the Pursuit of Happiness," it is the "Right of the People to alter or to abolish it" and "to institute new Government, laying its foundation on such principles and organizing its powers in such form, as to them shall seem most likely to effect their Safety and Happiness." In our own time most of the world's peoples have been involved in wars, both "hot" and "cold," between something called "democracy" and something called "fascist dictatorship" or "communist dictatorship."

Evidently most people believe that significantly different ways of governing do exist. Evidently also most people believe that their particular nation's "form of government" so powerfully affects such basic values as individual freedom, social justice, and national independence that preserving it—or overthrowing it—is worth fighting and dying for. In the present chapter, we shall continue our introductory survey of the general themes and principal variations in politics and governments by considering what is

[ 59 ]

involved in classifying governments as to "form," describing some of the classifications men have found useful and outlining some of the social forces that incline different nations to adopt different forms.

# Classifying Governments

### What Is a "Form of Government"?[1]

#### It Is a Partial Description of an Actual Whole

Most of us often refer to the governments of the United States and Great Britain as "democracies," and the governments of Russia and Red China as "dictatorships." Let us consider for a moment what is meant by these labels. They do not mean that the governments of the United States and Great Britain are completely different from the governments of Russia and Red China; for we know that all four governments make authoritative rules, punish those who violate those rules, maintain armed forces, collect taxes, and so on. Nor do the labels mean that the governments of the United States and Great Britain are exactly alike; for we know that certain British public officials (e.g., the Queen and some members of the House of Lords) inherit their positions, while all American public officials are either elected or appointed to their jobs.

We know that to some extent the governments of all nations are alike, and yet no two governments are exactly alike in every detail. How, then, can we justify calling some of them "democracies" as though they were identical and distinguishing them from "dictatorships" as though the latter were also identical and completely unlike the "democracies"? The answer is clear: the labels mean that *in certain respects* the governments of the United States and Great Britain are essentially alike, and that *in those same respects* they differ significantly from the governments of Russia and Red China. The "form" of a particular nation's government is a label we apply to it in the light of our judgment of certain items selected from its unique total aggregation of laws, customs, and institutions. When we have labeled that government a "democracy" or a "monarchy" or a "federation," we have described it only partially, and many other valid statements may also be made about it.

#### It Is Based upon a Particular Principle of Organization

Granted that we describe a particular government's "form" in terms of only certain aspects of its total character, how then do we decide *which* of its many different aspects reveal its "form"? The answer is that we concen-

---

[1] Cf. Austin Ranney and Willmoore Kendall, *Democracy and the American Party System* (New York: Harcourt, Brace & World, Inc., 1956), pp. 18–22.

trate on those features we consider to be most relevant to the particular principle of governmental organization we have in mind when making the classification.

For example, the basic principle of organization involved in "democracy" is the location of the ultimate decision-making power in all the members of the community. Thus we classify the governments of the United States and Great Britain as "democracies" because we believe that in both nations governmental decisions are actually made in ultimate accordance with the wishes of their respective peoples, and not according to the wishes of small elites or dictators. The fact that the formal head of the American government is an elected President, while the formal head of British government is a hereditary monarch, is crucial when we are classifying the two governments according to another principle of organization (i.e., as "monarchies" or as "republics"); but it does not in itself make either government more or less democratic than the other.

When considering classifications of governments, therefore, we should bear in mind that agreeing upon a government's form according to any particular principle of organization tells us little or nothing about its form according to any other principle.

### Why Bother to Classify Governments?

Many cogent objections can be made to the whole business of classifying governments. For one thing, as we have pointed out, labeling a particular government a "democracy" or a "dictatorship" may tell us something about how that government operates, but it also leaves out a great deal; and there is a danger that once we have determined its "form," we will feel we know all about it that is worth knowing. The categories and their criteria are so simple and government reality is so complex that properly classifying "borderline" cases is next to impossible: e.g., it is easy to classify the United States and Great Britain as "democracies" and Russia and Red China as "dictatorships," but what about nations like South Vietnam or Brazil? Then again, the process of classifying governments is difficult at best and may be scientifically worthless. If, for example, we classify only in terms of formal constitutional arrangements, we cannot avoid this kind of problem: the written Constitutions of Albania, Bulgaria, Czechoslovakia, Hungary, Poland, Russia, and Yugoslavia expressly state that the nation's sovereignty resides in the people, and yet we know that the decision-making power in these nations is actually held by the leaders of their Communist parties. Shall we, then, ignore the realities and concentrate on the formalities, or vice versa? If we take the former course, our classifications will hardly be worth the effort it takes to make them. If we take the latter course, we may plunge into an endless labyrinth of trying to find out what the realities are and compressing them into simple "forms."

These objections are well founded and should be borne in mind. Yet most political scientists feel that the gains in analysis and understanding likely to accrue from a valid set of classifications are so great that we should not abandon the enterprise altogether. One of the necessary early stages in the development of any science is what may be called its "taxonomic" or "natural history" phase, in which "the facts . . . are immediately apprehended by observation, expressed in terms of concepts with carefully controlled denotative meanings by description, and systematized by classification."[2] Only when this job is well advanced can the science reach the stage of explanation and general-theory formation. However difficult it may be, therefore, classifying governments is an unavoidable task for political scientists.

## Some Leading Classifications of Governments

Since each "variable"[3] in governmental organization provides a potential basis for a "typology" or set of categories, it is not surprising that scholars have classified governments on all sorts of bases: e.g., "legitimate" and "usurped," "de jure" and "de facto," "theocratic" and "secular," and even "governments of laws" and "governments of men." We shall confine our attention to the four typologies that political scientists have used most frequently, and for each typology we shall state the particular principle of organization on which it is based and describe the resulting forms with examples of each.

### According to the Manner of Selecting the Formal Chief of State

Every nation has a public official who acts as the formal head of its governmental apparatus. He may or may not also wield actual power. Governments in which this official inherits his job because of some family relationship are known as *monarchies*, while those in which this official is selected by any means other than heredity are known as *republics*. Before the nineteenth century this classification was regarded as highly important, for the formal heads of governments usually exercised considerable power, and most kings were "absolute" monarchs in fact as well as in name. In

---

[2] F. S. C. Northrop, *The Logic of the Sciences and the Humanities* (New York: The Macmillan Company, 1947), p. 35.

[3] "Variable" is a technical term often used in the literature of the social sciences, and it will appear frequently in this book. As we shall use it, it denotes a particular characteristic of social situations and institutions which may appear in different degrees or forms in different situations and institutions.

our own time, however, most monarchs (e.g., those of Great Britain, Belgium, the Netherlands, Sweden, Norway, Denmark, and Japan) have become ceremonial and symbolic figures, and only a few (e.g., those of Saudi Arabia, Bhutan, Ethiopia, and Libya) still wield real power in the manner of Louis XIV or Ivan the Terrible. Consequently, the distinction between "monarchies" and "republics," while still valid, is now generally regarded as relatively unimportant.

As of 1966, thirty-five nations, including about 12 percent of the world's population, officially described themselves as "monarchies," "kingdoms," "empires," "dominions," "grand duchies," "principalities," and the like; the largest were Japan (population: 95,900,000) and Great Britain (population: 52,900,000). The remainder described themselves as "republics" or "people's republics."

### *According to the Formal Distribution of Power among the "Levels" of Government*

Every nation has a national government with authority over the entire nation and a series of local governments, each of which has authority over a particular subnational geographical area known variously as a "state" or "province," a "county" or "shire" or "department," a "borough" or "city" or "commune," and so on.

The written Constitutions of fourteen nations provide for *federal* government in which power is divided between the national government and certain local governments, each of which is legally supreme in its own sphere. In these nations the constitution usually delineates the areas over which the national government has authority and those areas in which the local governments are sovereign and prescribes that neither level is subordinate to the other. The United States, Switzerland, Australia, Canada, and West Germany are usually given as examples of nations in which the constitutional division of powers is paralleled by an actual division of authority. Such nations as Argentina, Mexico, Russia, Venezuela, and Yugoslavia, on the other hand, are regarded as "paper federations" only, since the local governments are actually subordinate to the national governments.[4] We shall discuss the peculiar nature and problems of federalism in Chapter 21.

The constitutions of all other nations provide for *unitary* governments, in which the national government is supreme over the other levels. It may permit local governments to exist and to conduct certain activities, but it has the full legal right to overrule them, and they are formally subordinate to it. The governments of Great Britain and France are usually given as examples of the unitary type.

---

[4] Amos J. Peaslee, ed., *Constitutions of Nations* (2d. ed.; The Hague: Martinus Nijhoff, 1956), I, 3–4.

A possible third category according to this principle of organization is *confederate* government, in which the central government is subordinate to local governments and exists and operates only by their sufferance. Most political scientists feel, however, that such arrangements leave the central government so little power that it cannot accurately be called a "government" at all, and that they are better described (as in the case of the United Nations) as types of "covenants" or "treaties" or "organizations" among sovereign governments rather than as a form of government.[5]

## According to the Actual Location of the Ultimate Ruling Power

### The Classical Typology

The first two classifications are, as we have noted, based upon purely formal principles of organization. Consequently, determining a particular government's form according to either principle, while easy to do, tells us little or nothing about the actual decision-making process in the nation in question. We have noted "monarchies" in which the monarch is actually a mere figurehead, and "federations" in which the local governments are actually entirely subordinate to the national government. Purely formal classifications have their uses, to be sure, but most students of government have been more concerned with a far more crucial question: Who actually possesses the nation's ultimate ruling power?

The oldest, most persistent, and most significant classification of governmental forms—and the most difficult to apply to actual governments—is concerned with this question. As early as the fifth century B.C. the Greek historian Herodotus classified all governments as either *monarchies* (government by the one), *aristocracies* (government by the few), and *democracies* (government by the many) and summarized the arguments for and against each form. A century later Plato revised this typology by adding that each of these forms has its degenerate version ("autocracy," "oligarchy," and "mob rule") in which the ruling class governs lawlessly and ruthlessly in its own selfish interest. Aristotle offered a somewhat revised version of Plato's set of categories.

### Modern Versions

This ancient typology has persisted in one version or another down to our own time. Some present-day political scientists argue that the diffi-

---

[5] Cf. K. C. Wheare, *Modern Constitutions* (New York: Oxford University Press, 1951), pp. 26–33.

culties of determining exactly where a nation's ultimate ruling power actually rests are so great that the accurate classification of actual governments as "democracies" or "oligarchies" or "autocracies" is impossible. Yet few political scientists are willing to entirely banish from the description and analysis of modern governments such classificatory terms as "democracy" and "dictatorship." In Chapter 5 we shall explore in some detail such questions as the essential nature of democratic government and how it differs from dictatorship and suggest a "spectrum-analysis" method for determining whether particular governments should be called "democracies," "near democracies," "near dictatorships," or "dictatorships."

For the purposes of our classifications of modern governments in Table 2 below, we shall place each government in one or another of these four categories according to our judgment of where its ultimate ruling power actually lies. We shall further subdivide the third and fourth categories into three subcategories each: (1) monarchical dictatorships, in which the dictator exercises actual power in his capacity as hereditary monarch; (2) republican dictatorships, in which there is no hereditary monarch and the dictator acquires power by some means other than heredity; and (3) communist dictatorships, which are organized as we shall describe in detail in later chapters.

### According to Formal Legislative-Executive Relations in the Democracies

Most political scientists agree that there are two main types of democratic government in the modern world. The government of the United States is of the *presidential* type, in which executive officers are prohibited from being members of the legislature and hold office for fixed terms regardless of whether or not the legislature approves of their actions. The governments of the Philippine Republic, Liberia, and all the Central and South American republics are also of this type. All other democratic governments are of the *parliamentary* type, in which, on the British model, the leading executive officers are required to be members of the legislature and hold office only so long as they command the legislature's "confidence." In Chapters 17 and 18 we shall examine further the nature and consequences of these two types of formal legislative-executive relations.

## Modern Governments Classified

In Table 2 we present our classification of the governments of modern nations according to each of the principles just outlined.

## Table 2.  Governments of Modern Nations

| NATION | APPROX. DATE OF ACQUIRING PRESENT NATIONAL STATUS | SELECTION OF FORMAL HEAD | FORMAL DIVISION OF POWER | ACTUAL LOCATION OF POWER |
|---|---|---|---|---|
| Afghanistan | 1747 | Kingdom | Unitary | Monarchical near dictatorship |
| Albania | 1912 | Republic | Unitary | Communist dictatorship |
| Algeria | 1962 | Republic | Unitary | Republican dictatorship |
| Andorra | 1278 | Republic | Unitary | Parliamentary near democracy |
| Argentina | 1811 | Republic | Federal | Presidential near democracy |
| Australia | 1919 | Commonwealth* | Federal | Parliamentary democracy |
| Austria | 1918 | Republic | Unitary | Parliamentary democracy |
| Belgium | 1830 | Kingdom | Unitary | Parliamentary democracy |
| Bhutan | 895 | Kingdom | Unitary | Monarchical dictatorship |
| Bolivia | 1825 | Republic | Unitary | Presidential near democracy |
| Brazil | 1822 | Republic | Federal | Presidential near democracy |
| Bulgaria | 1908 | Republic | Unitary | Communist dictatorship |
| Burma | 1947 | Republic | Federal | Republican dictatorship |
| Burundi | 1962 | Kingdom | Unitary | Parliamentary near democracy |
| Cambodia | 1953 | Kingdom | Unitary | Monarchical near dictatorship |
| Cameroon | 1960 | Republic | Federal | Parliamentary near democracy |
| Canada | 1919 | Dominion* | Federal | Parliamentary democracy |
| Central African Republic | 1960 | Republic | Unitary | Republican dictatorship |
| Ceylon | 1948 | Dominion* | Unitary | Parliamentary democracy |

## Table 2.  Governments of Modern Nations (continued)

| NATION | APPROX. DATE OF ACQUIRING PRESENT NATIONAL STATUS | SELECTION OF FORMAL HEAD | FORMAL DIVISION OF POWER | ACTUAL LOCATION OF POWER |
|---|---|---|---|---|
| Chad | 1960 | Republic | Unitary | Republican dictatorship |
| Chile | 1810 | Republic | Unitary | Presidential democracy |
| Communist China | 1949 | Republic | Unitary | Communist dictatorship |
| Nationalist China | 1949 | Republic | Unitary | Republican near dictatorship |
| Colombia | 1819 | Republic | Unitary | Presidential democracy |
| Congo (Brazzaville) | 1960 | Republic | Unitary | Presidential near democracy |
| Congo (Léopoldville) | 1960 | Republic | Federal | Parliamentary near democracy |
| Costa Rica | 1829 | Republic | Unitary | Presidential democracy |
| Cuba | 1899 | Republic | Unitary | Communist dictatorship |
| Cyprus | 1960 | Republic | Unitary | Republican near dictatorship |
| Czechoslovakia | 1918 | Republic | Unitary | Communist dictatorship |
| Dahomey | 1960 | Republic | Unitary | Republican near dictatorship |
| Denmark | 925 | Kingdom | Unitary | Parliamentary democracy |
| Dominican Republic | 1821 | Republic | Unitary | Republican near democracy |
| Ecuador | 1830 | Republic | Unitary | Presidential near democracy |
| El Salvador | 1839 | Republic | Unitary | Presidential near democracy |
| Ethiopia | 1000 B.C. | Empire | Unitary | Monarchical dictatorship |
| Finland | 1917 | Republic | Unitary | Parliamentary democracy |
| France | 8th cent. | Republic | Unitary | Parliamentary democracy |

## Table 2.   Governments of Modern Nations (continued)

| NATION | APPROX. DATE OF ACQUIRING PRESENT NATIONAL STATUS | SELECTION OF FORMAL HEAD | FORMAL DIVISION OF POWER | ACTUAL LOCATION OF POWER |
|---|---|---|---|---|
| Gabon | 1960 | Republic | Unitary | Republican near dictatorship |
| East Germany | 1949 | Republic | Unitary | Communist dictatorship |
| West Germany | 1949 | Republic | Federal | Parliamentary democracy |
| Ghana | 1957 | Republic | Unitary | Republican dictatorship |
| Greece | 1821 | Kingdom | Unitary | Parliamentary democracy |
| Guatemala | 1839 | Republic | Unitary | Republican near dictatorship |
| Guinea | 1958 | Republic | Unitary | Republican dictatorship |
| Haiti | 1804 | Republic | Unitary | Republican dictatorship |
| Honduras | 1838 | Republic | Unitary | Presidential near democracy |
| Hungary | 1918 | Republic | Unitary | Communist dictatorship |
| Iceland | 1918 | Republic | Unitary | Parliamentary democracy |
| India | 1947 | Republic | Federal | Parliamentary democracy |
| Indonesia | 1949 | Republic | Unitary | Parliamentary near democracy |
| Iran | 9th cent. B.C. | Kingdom | Unitary | Monarchical near dictatorship |
| Iraq | 1921 | Republic | Unitary | Republican near dictatorship |
| Ireland | 1921 | Republic | Unitary | Parliamentary democracy |
| Israel | 1948 | Republic | Unitary | Parliamentary democracy |
| Italy | 1861 | Republic | Unitary | Parliamentary democracy |
| Ivory Coast | 1960 | Republic | Unitary | Republican dictatorship |

## Table 2.   Governments of Modern Nations (continued)

| NATION | APPROX. DATE OF ACQUIRING PRESENT NATIONAL STATUS | SELECTION OF FORMAL HEAD | FORMAL DIVISION OF POWER | ACTUAL LOCATION OF POWER |
|---|---|---|---|---|
| Jamaica | 1962 | Dominion* | Unitary | Parliamentary democracy |
| Japan | 7th cent. B.C. | Empire | Unitary | Parliamentary democracy |
| Jordan | 1946 | Kingdom | Unitary | Monarchical near dictatorship |
| Kenya | 1963 | Republic | Unitary | Parliamentary near democracy |
| North Korea | 1948 | Republic | Unitary | Communist dictatorship |
| South Korea | 1948 | Republic | Unitary | Republican near dictatorship |
| Kuwait | 1961 | Kingdom | Unitary | Monarchical dictatorship |
| Laos | 1949 | Kingdom | Unitary | Parliamentary near democracy |
| Lebanon | 1943 | Republic | Unitary | Parliamentary democracy |
| Liberia | 1846 | Republic | Unitary | Presidential near democracy |
| Libya | 1951 | Kingdom | Unitary | Monarchical dictatorship |
| Liechtenstein | 1866 | Principality | Unitary | Parliamentary democracy |
| Luxembourg | 1841 | Grand Duchy | Unitary | Parliamentary democracy |
| Malagasy | 1960 | Republic | Unitary | Parliamentary near democracy |
| Malawi | 1964 | Republic | Unitary | Republican near dictatorship |
| Malaysia | 1963 | Republic | Federal | Parliamentary near democracy |
| Mali | 1960 | Republic | Unitary | Republican near dictatorship |
| Malta | 1964 | Dominion* | Unitary | Parliamentary democracy |
| Mauritania | 1960 | Republic | Unitary | Republican dictatorship |

## Table 2.　Governments of Modern Nations (continued)

| NATION | APPROX. DATE OF ACQUIRING PRESENT NATIONAL STATUS | SELECTION OF FORMAL HEAD | FORMAL DIVISION OF POWER | ACTUAL LOCATION OF POWER |
|---|---|---|---|---|
| Mexico | 1810 | Republic | Federal | Presidential near democracy |
| Monaco | 1860 | Principality | Unitary | Parliamentary near democracy |
| Morocco | 1956 | Kingdom | Unitary | Monarchical near dictatorship |
| Nepal | 1769 | Kingdom | Unitary | Monarchical near dictatorship |
| Netherlands | 1813 | Kingdom | Unitary | Parliamentary democracy |
| New Zealand | 1919 | Dominion* | Unitary | Parliamentary democracy |
| Nicaragua | 1838 | Republic | Unitary | Republican near dictatorship |
| Niger | 1960 | Republic | Unitary | Republican dictatorship |
| Nigeria | 1960 | Republic | Federal | Parliamentary democracy |
| Norway | 1814 | Kingdom | Unitary | Parliamentary democracy |
| Pakistan | 1947 | Republic | Unitary | Presidential near democracy |
| Panama | 1903 | Republic | Unitary | Presidential democracy |
| Paraguay | 1811 | Republic | Unitary | Republican dictatorship |
| Peru | 1821 | Republic | Unitary | Presidential near democracy |
| Philippines | 1946 | Republic | Unitary | Presidential democracy |
| Poland | 1918 | Republic | Unitary | Communist dictatorship |
| Portugal | 1147 | Republic | Unitary | Republican dictatorship |
| Rumania | 1878 | Republic | Unitary | Communist dictatorship |
| Rwanda | 1962 | Republic | Unitary | Parliamentary near democracy |
| San Marino | 4th cent. | Republic | Unitary | Parliamentary democracy |

## Table 2. Governments of Modern Nations (continued)

| NATION | APPROX. DATE OF ACQUIRING PRESENT NATIONAL STATUS | SELECTION OF FORMAL HEAD | FORMAL DIVISION OF POWER | ACTUAL LOCATION OF POWER |
|---|---|---|---|---|
| Saudi Arabia | 1927 | Kingdom | Unitary | Monarchical dictatorship |
| Senegal | 1960 | Republic | Unitary | Presidential near democracy |
| Sierra Leone | 1961 | Commonwealth* | Unitary | Parliamentary democracy |
| Singapore | 1965 | Republic | Unitary | Parliamentary near democracy |
| Somalia | 1960 | Republic | Unitary | Presidential near democracy |
| South Africa | 1919 | Republic | Federal | Parliamentary near democracy |
| Spain | 1492 | Republic | Unitary | Republican dictatorship |
| Sudan | 1956 | Republic | Unitary | Republican dictatorship |
| Sweden | 14th cent. | Kingdom | Unitary | Parliamentary democracy |
| Switzerland | 1291 | Republic | Federal | Parliamentary democracy |
| Syria | 1943 | Republic | Unitary | Republican near dictatorship |
| Tanzania | 1961 | Republic | Federal | Presidential near democracy |
| Thailand | 14th cent. | Kingdom | Unitary | Monarchical near dictatorship |
| Togo | 1960 | Republic | Unitary | Parliamentary near democracy |
| Trinidad and Tobago | 1962 | Dominion* | Unitary | Parliamentary democracy |
| Tunisia | 1955 | Republic | Unitary | Presidential near democracy |
| Turkey | 14th cent. | Republic | Unitary | Parliamentary near democracy |
| Uganda | 1962 | Kingdom | Federal | Parliamentary near democracy |
| Union of Soviet Socialist Republics | 1922 | Republic | Federal | Communist dictatorship |

### Table 2.    Governments of Modern Nations (continued)

| NATION | APPROX. DATE OF ACQUIRING PRESENT NATIONAL STATUS | SELECTION OF FORMAL HEAD | FORMAL DIVISION OF POWER | ACTUAL LOCATION OF POWER |
|---|---|---|---|---|
| United Arab Republic | 1922 | Republic | Unitary | Republican dictatorship |
| United Kindgom of Great Britain and Northern Ireland | 9th cent. | Kingdom | Unitary | Parliamentary democracy |
| United States of America | 1776 | Republic | Federal | Presidential democracy |
| Upper Volta | 1960 | Republic | Unitary | Republican dictatorship |
| Uruguay | 1825 | Republic | Unitary | Parliamentary democracy |
| Venezuela | 1830 | Republic | Federal | Presidential democracy |
| North Vietnam | 1954 | Republic | Unitary | Communist dictatorship |
| South Vietnam | 1954 | Republic | Unitary | Republican near dictatorship |
| Western Samoa | 1962 | Kingdom | Unitary | Monarchical near dictatorship |
| Yemen | 1918 | Republic | Unitary | Republican near dictatorship |
| Yugoslavia | 1918 | Republic | Federal | Communist dictatorship |
| Zambia | 1964 | Republic | Unitary | Presidential near democracy |

* Official head is the British Queen, represented by a governor-general.

SOURCE: For nations achieving independence before 1955, the information in the first, second, and third columns is drawn from Amos J. Peaslee, ed., *Constitutions of Nations* 2d ed.; (The Hague: Martinus Nijhoff, 1956), III, 794–804, Tables I and II. For nations achieving independence after 1955, the comparable information is taken from Walter H. Mallory, ed., *Political Handbook and Atlas of the World, 1965* (New York: Harper & Row, Publishers, 1965). The classifications given in the fourth column are the result of the author's judgment using the spectrum-analysis method described in Chapter 5. For the classification of certain nations the author also consulted the following area specialists, to whom he wishes to make grateful acknowledgment of their help: Latin America, Professor Charles W. Anderson; Africa, Professor M. Crawford Young; Asia, Professor Fred R. von der Mehden; and the Middle East, Professor C. Ernest Dawn.

# Social Influences on Forms of Government

## The Interrelations of Government and Society

### Government as an Aspect of Society

Students of politics have long been aware that government is an aspect of society and that it both shapes and is shaped by society. If we are to understand how a particular nation's government works and why that nation has that particular form of government, we must examine not only its formal governing institutions but also the society within which they operate.

The interrelations between British government and society furnish an illuminating illustration of this point. The British governmental system locates full governmental power in the House of Commons, which can dismiss any minister at any time for any reason, depose judges, abolish local governments, regulate succession to the throne, and do anything else it wishes—up to and including altering or abolishing any part of the British Constitution. No British court can overrule any act of Parliament as "unconstitutional." All decisions of the House of Commons are made by simple majorities: the will of as few as 50 percent plus one of the members present becomes the action of the whole House. Under normal conditions, moreover, a majority of the members belong to one or another of two political parties, Conservative and Labour. If we knew only these facts about the British system, we might well conclude that Britain must be perpetually teetering on the brink of civil war and that sooner or later (and probably sooner) the majority party will, in the pride and prejudice of its unlimited power, jam through some measure so disastrous to the interests of the minority party that revolution and civil war will soon follow.

Yet the British system, for all the formally unlimited power it gives the majority party, is, in fact, highly stable and revolution-resistant—far more so than, say, the systems of Vietnam and Argentina, despite the fact that their written Constitutions provide elaborate formal checks on majorities and safeguards for minorities. How can this be? The answer, according to most students of British government, is that British society is such that it simply never occurs to the majority party to try to impose anything totally unacceptable to the minority. For one thing, each party's leaders have more in common with their political opponents than with their own party's rank and file: unlike the general public, most have attended universities; most come from managerial, professional, or upper white-collar occupations; and all belong to the small and select group of political "insiders," to whom the world often appears different from what it appears to most "outsiders." Hence they share a great many common attitudes and values despite their differences in party allegiance.[6] For another, the deep

---

[6] Cf. W. L. Guttsman, *The British Political Elite* (London: MacGibbon & Kee, 1963); and Jean Blondel, *Voters, Parties, and Leaders* (Harmondsworth, Middlesex, Eng.: Penguin Books, Ltd., 1963).

conviction that certain things "are simply not done" is shared by all strata of British society from top to bottom—and crushing a formally defenseless minority is certainly one of those things. Then too, most Englishmen are deeply proud of their political system and would not dream of taking steps that might profoundly upset it and, in the manner of what Shakespeare called the "less happier lands" outside "this fortress built by nature for herself against infection," do something so un-English as starting a revolution!

The eighteenth-century political philosopher Thomas Paine believed that every nation is entirely free to discard its form of government and replace it with another at any time. Most modern political scientists feel that this is true in only the most superficial sense; for they believe that the kind of people who make up a nation's population and the structure of the society in which they live fix firm and enduring limits upon the kind of government the nation may have. The same considerations incline them to believe that a particular nation's form of government can be understood only against the background of the kind of society it has.

### The Concept of "Regime"

Some political scientists have suggested that the concept of "regime" is a better analytical tool than the concept of "form of government" for understanding the different ways nations govern themselves. A nation's "regime," as they use the term, includes such elements as its formal constitution and legal agencies, its extralegal or "informal" agencies like political parties and pressure groups, its nonpolitical economic and social structure, its belief system, and the basic characteristics of its people and the physical environment in which they live. "Regime" may be represented graphically as a series of concentric circles, as in Figure 8.

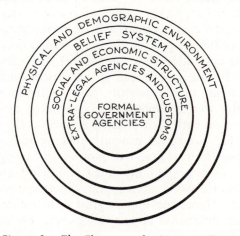

*Figure 8.* **The Elements of a Nation's "Regime."**

The concept of "regime" has not yet been fully worked out, and so we can talk only loosely of various "types of regime." We can, however, list and briefly describe some of the characteristics of a nation that most directly affect the nature of its society and the form of its government. We cannot yet say exactly how any particular factor influences a nation's form of government, but we can, as in the concluding pages of this chapter, draw attention to some of the main social variables that must be considered in any effort to understand why a particular nation has the kind of government it has.

### Some Leading Social Variables

#### 1. Territory

A nation's government can be influenced to some degree by the kind of territory the nation occupies. If its location—like Poland's—furnishes no natural barriers (mountains, rivers, or deserts) against military invasion, it may have to stress military preparedness in its governmental organization. If its territory—like that of Russia or the United States—is large in area, the government may have to make special provisions for dealing with the particular problems of various subnational regions.[7] Even the territory's climate and natural resources may make physical survival so difficult or so easy as to affect the shape of the government.

#### 2. Population

The populations of modern nations differ from one another in many ways, some of which may influence their forms of government. The size of a nation's population, for example, may well set limits upon the degree to which the citizens may directly participate in government.[8] The population's ethnic composition may affect the number and degree of the nation's intergroup conflicts and thus its "civil war potential." The population's literacy level and age distribution may affect the kind of role the people play in the governing process and also the kind of social-welfare services performed by the government.

#### 3. Economy

Karl Marx, the nineteenth-century ideological founder of modern communism, argued that a nation's religions, social customs, art, and form of government are simply reflections of its economic system. Noncommunist

---

[7] Russia has by far the largest area of any nation (an estimated 8,649,000 square miles) and Monaco the smallest (0.59 square miles). The United States, with 3,615,000 square miles, ranks third behind Russia and China.

[8] China has the largest population of any modern nation (over 700,000,000), and Andorra the smallest (5231). The United States, with over 190,000,000, ranks fourth behind China, India, and Russia.

social scientists have long since rejected Marx's thesis as an enormous over-simplification of the highly complex and multicausational phenomenon that is a modern nation's "regime." They also feel, however, that while a nation's economy is by no means the only factor that influences its form of government, it is nevertheless one of the more significant. A nation's technology and division of labor, for example, affect the number and variety of occupations and thus the number and variety of interests over which political conflict may take place. The general level of wealth and the disparity of incomes among different groups are bound to influence the nation's "civil war potential"; for, other things being equal, a great disparity in income is likely to generate bitter dissatisfaction among the poor and greatly reduce the chances for a united community presided over by a stable government. If, on the other hand, the general level of wealth and physical comfort is high—if even the poorer groups are well off compared with their counterparts in other nations—then they are less likely to start a civil war to improve their lot.

### 4. Social Structure

Broader still in its effect upon a nation's form of government is its social structure—which, as we use the term here, includes all the national attitudes and activities outside the strictly "political" and "economic" spheres. For example, the degree of stratification of the nation's population into upper, middle, and lower social or "deference" classes and the degree of mobility between the classes may greatly affect national unity and therefore the kind of government the nation can sustain. Then, too, the ways in which the people go about such basic life-activities as courtship and marriage, raising and educating children, worshiping, and communicating with each other all help to create a kind of *Gestalt* within which the government must operate. They also set limits on the kind of government the nation can operate successfully. We have already discussed how the British form of government must to some extent be explained in the light of the British social structure; the same general sort of considerations must be taken into account in the effort to understand any nation's form of government.[9]

### 5. Belief System

To some extent, the people of every nation share a common belief system, which consists of certain shared values (i.e., beliefs about the way things should be) and certain shared conceptions of reality (i.e., beliefs

---

[9] For excellent examples of the explanation of a nation's form of government in terms of its underlying social structure, see the shrewd and perceptive discussions of the American system by the British political scientist D. W. Brogan, *The American Character* (New York: Alfred A. Knopf, Inc., 1944), and *Politics in America* (New York: Harper & Row, Publishers, 1954).

about the way things are and about the relative effectiveness of various means for making things-as-they-are more like things-as-they-should-be). This does not imply that every citizen holds exactly the same values and beliefs as his fellows, but only that certain values and beliefs are shared by the great bulk of the citizens regardless of their particular social and economic classes or their ethnic and religious affiliations.

A nation's belief system, like an individual's, need not be and often is not a neatly arranged, logically ordered, and internally consistent set of propositions. It may well contain a great many logical inconsistencies and contradictions—such as the belief of so many Americans, noted in Chapter 3, in the logically contradictory ideologies of *laissez-faire* capitalism and the welfare state. The degree of diffusion of a nation's belief system as well as its logical consistency affects its form of government.

### 6. Social Tensions and Consensus

Every nation contains forces that make for national disintegration. They are usually described collectively as social tensions, which are the product of such social variables as the kinds and number of group conflicts among the populace, the degree to which group memberships are interlaced and overlapping, the degree of hostility among the competing groups, and the general national atmosphere of security or insecurity within which group conflict takes place. Every nation also contains forces that unify and preserve it by maximizing consensus—that is, by encouraging a general feeling among its citizens and groups that preserving the nation is at least as important as achieving their own "special" interests. In Chapters 1 and 2 we dealt with some of these forces in our discussion of the factors that limit, diffuse, and moderate group conflict and the factors that maximize nationalism.

In every nation the interplay of these two clusters of forces affects not only the "civil war potential" but also the kind of government the nation can operate. Probably more than any other social variable, the relative levels of social tensions and consensus determine whether a nation can maintain a genuinely democratic government. Dictatorships are free to use as much propaganda and physical force as may be necessary to force their peoples to accept the dictators' policies. But democracies, as we shall see in Chapter 5, must depend mainly upon freely given popular consent to public policies. Consequently, democratic governments can survive only in nations whose popular majorities refrain from trying to force unbearable policies upon minorities and whose minorities peacefully accept and abide by majority decisions. Only nations with relatively high degrees of consensus and low degrees of social tensions are likely to have popular majorities and minorities that regularly show such forbearance, and only nations of this sort can hope to operate genuinely democratic governments.

# What Difference Does It Make?

In Chapter 2 we noted that all governments—whether they be democratic or dictatorial, monarchical or republican, unitary or federal—are alike in many telling respects: they all have "sovereignty" over a particular territory and the persons in it; they all make rules regulating those persons' behavior; and they all fine, imprison, or execute rule violators.

In the present chapter we have briefly described some of the different ways in which different nations conduct these universal activities—that is, some of the principal "forms of government." And we noted the conviction of most men that their nation's form of government so profoundly affects such basic values as personal freedom, social justice, and national independence that preserving it—or overthrowing it—is worth fighting and dying for.

Communist political analysts insist that only the distinction between "capitalism" and "socialism" matters. But most political scientists in the noncommunist nations believe the choice between "democracy" and "dictatorship" is by far the most crucial. Accordingly, we shall conclude our preliminary survey of general themes and principal variations in modern governments by examining each of these forms in depth.

# 5

## Models of Democracy and Dictatorship

For a number of years the author has expounded to his classes in political science his conception of a model democracy. At the close of almost every such exposition something like the following colloquy has taken place.

STUDENT: Professor, it seems to me that the government of the United States differs from your idea of democracy in a lot of ways. For example, we have a lot of minority veto devices in our Constitution, such as judicial review and the two-thirds and three-quarters requirements for amendment. For another example, the equal representation of each state in the Senate regardless of population does not square with your idea of political equality. Furthermore, the government determines many of its policies without "consulting" the people. How about that?

TEACHER: What you say is quite correct.

STUDENT (*disturbed*): Well, does that mean that the United States is *not* a democracy?

TEACHER: If you mean by that question, does our government perfectly fulfill all of the requirements of a model democracy, the answer is that it does not—and neither does any other actual government in the world. But you must remember that this conception of democracy is a *model*, a construction of the imagination, and not a photographic description of any actual government.

STUDENT (*somewhat disgusted*): Well, if all you've been talking about is only a "model" and has no relation to any real government, why should we spin theories in a class in political *science*, which is supposed to deal with the *facts* of political life?

At this point the author has always found it necessary to offer an explanation of the nature and functions of a model democracy, and its application to the study of actual governments.

# The Nature and Role of Models in the Social Sciences

As we are using the term, a "model" is an intellectual construct of a particular mode of political organization fully and perfectly in accord with a particular principle.[1] Perhaps the best-known example of such a model is one widely used in economic analysis, that of the "free market." The free market is a mental picture of an economic system in which all exchange takes place by free bargaining among sellers and buyers in the marketplace, the only motive influencing human behavior is the universal desire to "buy cheap and sell dear," and the price of any commodity or service is determined solely by the interplay of supply and demand.

Now everyone, including economists who talk about this model, knows that no *actual* economic system has ever operated in perfect accordance with these principles. Men are, in fact, influenced by many motives other than their desire to buy cheap and sell dear—e.g., their (or their wives'!) desire to be "in fashion." Moreover, sellers often agree among themselves to "administer" prices regardless of supply and demand so that every seller can make a larger profit than he could under the conditions of unrestricted, cutthroat competition; and government in every nation, as we observed in Chapter 3, interferes in some fashion with the free interplay of supply and demand.

Why, then, do economists talk about this dream of a "free market economy" when no such system has ever existed? The answer is that they find it a highly useful device for isolating certain aspects of actual economies and studying their operation apart from all other aspects of those economies. The economist asks, "If an economy *were* organized in this fashion, what would be the effect on prices of variations in supply and demand?" He next observes what actually happens in a real economy when supply or demand changes. The differences between the effects indicated by the model and the effects actually observed gives him a rough measure of the nature and degree of influence of the supply-and-demand factor relative to other factors.

Using models, in other words, is one way social scientists can achieve something like the results physical scientists obtain with their technique of controlled experiments. The chemist in his laboratory, for example, can hold certain factors constant (e.g., molecular structure, volume, weight, or density), vary another (e.g., temperature), and observe the outcome. Variations in the results, he assumes, are caused by variations in the one changing factor, since all other factors have been held constant. The economist

---

[1] For a discussion of various meanings and uses of "models" in the social sciences, see Abraham Kaplan, *The Conduct of Inquiry* (San Francisco: Chandler Publishing Company, 1964), Ch. VII.

in his study, however, cannot manipulate human economies in this fashion. But he can *imagine* what would happen in a "free market economy" when supply is increased, observe what happens in actual economies when supply is increased, and by comparing the two sets of results, one imagined and the other observed, achieve increased understanding of the operation and influence of the factors of supply and demand relative to other factors.

Economists are noted for prefacing their comments on economic behavior with the phrase "other things being equal"—when in fact, as they know full well, "other things" are never "equal." Nevertheless they keep on thinking this way, because, like other social scientists, they have learned that using models is a highly useful technique for understanding the complexities of actual social institutions and situations.

### Normative versus Descriptive Models

In ordinary conversation we often mean by a "model" something worthy of imitation, an ideal to be sought: "He is a model boy," or "Her paper is a model of how to write an examination." This is what social scientists call a "normative" use of the term, since it equates the model with good and its opposite with bad.

We should be clear, however, that we are here using the term in a purely descriptive sense; it means, we repeat, an intellectual construct of a particular mode of political organization fully and perfectly in accord with a particular principle. Hence later in the chapter we shall talk of a "model of dictatorship" as well as a "model of democracy." And our normative preference that governments *should* follow the democratic model should not cloud our analytical judgment that some governments *do* follow the model of dictatorship.

### The Role of Models of Government

No actual government, as observed in Chapter 4, is organized according to a *single* principle. Every such government is a "historic compound" of many different organizing principles. The government of the United States, for example, is organized in accordance with the principles of "federalism," "separation of powers," "checks and balances," "popular sovereignty," "limited government," "majority rule," "minority rights," and a great many more. If we wish to determine whether or not it is a "democracy," we cannot do so on the basis of *all* its myriad institutions, laws, and customs, for many of these are not relevant to the question at hand. We must look only at those aspects of its total reality that are relevant. Our judgment concerning which particular aspects are relevant is inescapably determined by our conception of democracy, a conception that is necessarily an abstraction from the total realities of American or any other actual government.

A model of democracy or dictatorship, in short, performs two major functions. First, it provides us with the criteria of relevance by which to choose those aspects of an actual government we must examine in order to determine whether it should be classified as a "democracy." And second, the model provides us with a set of standards against which we can measure actual governments for the purpose of classification.

## Spectrum Classification of Actual Governments

### The Nature of Spectrum Classification

One more problem remains: if it is true that no actual government fully and in every respect measures up to, for example, our four-principle model of democracy, how can we legitimately call *any* such government a "democracy"? The answer is simple. If we think in terms of two mutually exclusive categories, "democracies" (actual governments which fully and in every respect correspond to our model) and "nondemocracies" (governments which in some respects fall short of the model), then all the governments in the world undoubtedly must be placed in the latter category. But if we think in terms of a *spectrum*, we can quite legitimately describe some actual governments as "democracies."

The familiar categories of "rich" and "poor" illustrate the principle of spectrum classification. We all use these categories every day, and nobody thinks we are talking nonsense when we describe this man as "poor" and that man as "rich." Yet, consider for a moment the reasoning that underlies these classifications. We could rank each person in the United States in increasing order of net worth. We would all agree that those at the top of any such list are "rich," and those at the bottom are "poor." But where would we draw the line between the two categories? Is it, say, exactly $10,000? If so, do we say that a man worth $9,999.99 is "poor" and that acquiring one more penny will make him "rich"? Clearly not. Yet the lack of a precise, arithmetic dividing-line between the categories does not prevent us—nor should it—from using the categories at all. They are, to be sure, "gross" categories in the sense that they are not as precisely defined and delimited as those in mathematics, but most of us regard them as useful all the same, particularly in describing persons at the two extremes of the spectrum.

### Spectrum Classification of Governments

This same kind of reasoning, with all its advantages and limitations, underlay our classification of actual governments in Table 2. Graphically, the spectrum may be pictured as in Figure 9.

To clarify the meaning of this kind of classification, the following comments should be noted.

First, one extreme of the spectrum was fixed by our model of democracy

—that is, by our mental picture of what a government would be like if it were organized in complete and perfect accordance with the principles of popular sovereignty, political equality, popular consultation, and majority rule (see below). The other extreme was fixed by our model of dictatorship —by our mental picture of what a government would be like if one man had effective ultimate control of all governmental machinery and policy making.

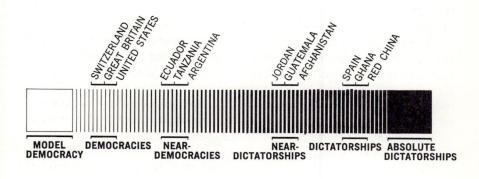

*Figure 9.* Spectrum Classification of Democracies.

Second, each government in the world was ranked according to the judgment of the author and the experts he consulted as to how closely its actual governing processes measure up to each model's requirements. To do this job perfectly, of course, would require at least two things: full knowledge of all the governing processes of all nations, and the ability to measure precisely and arithmetically how closely each government resembles one or the other of our two models. Obviously, the social sciences cannot offer either the requisite information or the precise measuring tools necessary to do the job perfectly. Consequently, the author's judgment of each nation's proximity to a model was based upon his general impressions, the validity of which can be checked only by their correspondence with the general impression of others using the same models as bench marks. The relative ranking of particular nations *within* each category is less important for the purposes of a loose classification of this sort than the question of whether or not they should be placed in that category at all. That is why we have chosen to present the complete classification in the tabular form in which it appears in Chapter 4 rather than in the spectrum figure that appears above.

This then, is how we have used our models. But let us be clear that the utility of the whole procedure depends most of all upon their adequacy. Accordingly, we shall devote the remainder of the chapter to outlining each model and explaining why it was chosen over other possible versions.

## The Essentials of Democracy

Try a little research project. Ask anyone you know whether he is for or against democracy. Read the political columns and editorials in your newspaper, and ask whether their authors think democracy is a good thing or a bad thing. Listen to the political commentators on television and radio, and ask the same question. Anyone who conducts this experiment will soon learn, if he does not know already, that just about everyone is for democracy and that most people believe that labeling a particular act or attitude or institution as "undemocratic" is to condemn it out of hand.

If you expand the focus of your study, moreover, you will learn that the popularity of democracy is by no means confined to the United States and the nations of Western Europe and the British Commonwealth. Even the communist nations describe themselves as "people's democracies," and judging by what they say, their inhabitants are as devoted to democracy as we are. The same things can be said of most of the developing nations as well, although many of them call themselves "guided democracies" or "collective democracies."[2]

These facts suggest that the word "democracy" has undergone a kind of political beatification in the sense that just about everyone in the modern world apparently believes that democracy is noble and good and that its enemies are ignoble and bad.

How, then, can anyone possibly say—as so many people on both sides of the Iron Curtain are saying today—that democracy is in grave danger from its enemies? How can democracy, which apparently has few enemies anywhere in the world, be in any kind of danger?

To learn the answers to these questions, carry your research project one step further. Try to find out exactly what the word "democracy" *means*. You will soon learn that it means a great many different things to different people, and that one man's "democracy" is frequently another man's "socialism" or "capitalism" or even "fascism" and "communism." You will discover, for example, that communists believe their one-party dictatorships to be the only *true* democracies and regard the regimes of the West as pseudodemocratic screens hypocritically masking "fascist-reactionary-capitalistic" realities. You will learn that *Il Duce*, Benito Mussolini, used to describe his fascist dictatorship as "the realization of true democracy," and that the Nazi propaganda chief Josef Goebbels proclaimed the regime of *Fuehrer* Adolf Hitler "the most ennobled form of a modern democratic state."[3]

---

[2] For the nearly universal popularity of "democracy" in the developing nations' official ideologies, see Fred R. von der Mehden, *Politics of the Developing Nations* (Englewood Cliffs, N.J.: Prentice-Hall, Inc.), Ch. VII.

[3] Cf. John D. Lewis, "The Elements of Democracy," *American Political Science Review*, XXXIV (June, 1940), at 467.

Suppose, however, that you dismiss the communist, fascist, and Nazi conceptions of "democracy" as too fantastic to be considered seriously, and confine your investigation to the meaning the word is given in the Western nations of today. You still will not be out of the woods, for even on our side of the Iron Curtain "democracy" means many different things to different persons. For example, the NAACP contends that "democracy" requires an end to racial segregation in American public schools, while the White Citizens' Councils argue that it is "undemocratic" for nonsouthern-ers to force desegregation upon southerners. In Great Britain some Labour ideologists argue that it is "undemocratic" to permit any man to accumu-late a great deal more wealth than his neighbors, while some of their Con-servative opponents reply that it is "undemocratic" to prevent an able man from accumulating and enjoying as much wealth as he can earn by his talents and labors.

In fact, there is no single definition of "democracy" on which almost all persons in the West agree. There are, instead, a great many definitions, each of which has its defenders and each of which differs in some respects from the others. Your study may, indeed, incline you to agree with the dry comment of the American historian Carl Becker that "democracy is a kind of conceptual Gladstone bag which, with a little manipulation, can be made to accommodate almost any collection of social facts we may wish to carry about in it."[4]

Later in the present chapter, we shall explain in some detail the mean-ing of the word "democracy" as used in this book and why that meaning has been chosen over its many competitors. Before we do so, however, let us briefly describe various meanings of the term that are most often encountered in present-day political discussions.

### The Communist Conception[5]

Communists insist that only the Soviet Union, Red China, and nations whose regimes are modeled on theirs can legitimately be called "democ-racies." They are aware, of course, that many persons regard the regimes of nations like the United States, Great Britain, and France as "democ-racies," but they reply contemptuously that all noncommunist regimes are merely false fronts thrown up by capitalists for the purpose of concealing the naked realities of fascism and capitalist exploitation from the masses.

The bone and marrow of the communist conception is the belief that

---

[4] Carl Becker, *Modern Democracy* (New Haven, Conn.: Yale University Press, 1941), p. 4.

[5] The best description and analysis of this matter is N. S. Timasheff, "The Soviet Conception of Democracy," *Review of Politics*, XII (October, 1950), 506–518. A useful discussion of the somewhat narrower communist conception of "people's democracy" is Ruth Amende Rosa, "The Soviet Theory of 'People's Democracy,'" *World Politics*, I (July, 1949), 489–510.

true democracy is a regime in which governmental policies and activities always advance the real interests and welfare of the proletariat. To a communist, then, "democracy" is solely a matter of *what* government does, the *content* of governmental policy. It has nothing to do with the *process* by which policy is made and enforced. Communists, in short, believe that democracy is government *for* the people (the proletariat) and not necessarily government *by* the people.

Proceeding from these premises, communists have no difficulty in justifying their one-party systems, their suppression of all political dissent, and their one-candidate-per-office elections. Nor are they impressed by the Western nations' freedoms of political organization and propaganda, or by the fact that Western voters can make real choices in elections, or by other Western paraphernalia of "pseudo democracy." During the present stage of proletarian development, the communists believe, only a specially trained and highly dedicated proletarian elite, the Communist party, is capable of determining just what policies will promote the real interests (definable, of course, only by the party) of the toiling masses. Whatever the Communist party does is, by definition, democratic. On the other hand, freedom of political organization and propaganda for non- or anticommunists is, again by definition, undemocratic: it permits capitalist exploiters to oppose, retard, and otherwise hamper "democratic" policies and perhaps even seize power.

Communists, of course, are quite willing that the proletarian masses outside the party (which, in Soviet Russia, constitute almost 97 percent of the population) should approve and support party policy, but they regard such approval and support as secondary and postponable objectives. The primary objective is for the most class-conscious and politically aware proletarians to seize power and use it for the benefit of their less advanced comrades. Once the party has carried out its reforms and once the masses have been properly "educated" (see Chapter 10), the proletariat will, as a matter of course, enthusiastically support the party. As Lenin himself put it:

> Seeing their interests satisfied, the masses will appreciate the Communist leadership, start supporting it and thus provide the solid foundation of recognition by the majority. *But this recognition can come only after the Communists have gained power, not before.*[6]

### Some Agreements and Disagreements among Noncommunist Conceptions

Outside the communist world, the term "democracy" has many different meanings. All is not sheer chaos and hopeless confusion, however, for a survey and comparison of these different meanings demonstrates that they share areas of agreement as well as of disagreement.

---

[6] Quoted in Timasheff, *op. cit.*, at p. 511, italics added.

## Areas of Agreement

Almost all noncommunists believe, contrary to the heirs of Lenin, that democracy is *at least* a form of government—that is, a particular way of arriving at governmental decisions. They agree, moreover, that a genuinely democratic government must have *at least* the following characteristics.

POLITICAL EQUALITY. In a democracy each of the members of the community must have the same legal and actual opportunity to participate in the governmental decision-making processes as every other member of the community, no more and no less. If, as in the communist regimes, certain persons (e.g., members of the party) have more such opportunities than others, the favored few are a "ruling class," and such regimes should be called "oligarchies" rather than "democracies."

GOVERNMENTAL RESPONSE TO THE POPULAR WILL. A democratic government does whatever the people want it to do and refrains from doing whatever they do not want it to do. To put the same idea in different words, in a democracy the people—not some elite of party members or businessmen or college professors—are the final judges of what is in the people's best interests. Democracy, in short, is government *by* the people.

MAJORITY RULE RATHER THAN MINORITY RULE. When the people disagree among themselves about what government should do and a decision must be made, the democratic way to decide is by majority rule. Each member of the community should register his wishes (by an election or a referendum or any of a variety of methods described in subsequent chapters), the results should be totaled, and public officials be mandated to act in accordance with the wishes of the greater proportion of the people (the majority) rather than the wishes of the lesser proportion (the minority). Many noncommunists believe that popular majorities in a true democracy must not adopt certain kinds of policies, but none argue that minority rule is a more democratic procedure than majority rule for determining which of the permissible policies government shall follow.

## Areas of Disagreement

The main differences among noncommunists about the proper meaning of "democracy" center about two basic issues.

"LIMITED" OR "UNLIMITED" MAJORITY RULE. Some noncommunists believe that popular majorities in a democracy must not do certain things: e.g., abridge the rights of individuals, such as those outlined in Chapter 8. So they contend that a true democracy must have certain institutional machinery, such as judicial review, to restrain majorities from ignoring or stepping across their proper limits. Other noncommunists contend that any limitation upon popular majorities other than one imposed by the majorities themselves and removable by other majorities at any time means minority veto power and therefore minority rule. We shall return to this issue in a moment.

"FORM OF GOVERNMENT ONLY" OR "WAY OF LIFE." Some noncommunists believe that democracy should be thought of solely as a form of government, a way of making public decisions, and not as directly concerned with the content of those decisions or with the purposes to which the power of government may be turned. Others, however, contend that the concept of "democracy," while it certainly includes a certain way of making political decisions, also includes other considerations as well—such as a certain kind of economic system, or a certain kind of relationship among the races, or a certain kind of religious philosophy. "Democracy" to such persons is more than merely a form of government. It is also a whole communal and/or personal way of life.

### A Working Definition of Democracy[7]

Let us recognize that neither science nor logic provides a way of proving that any particular conception of "democracy" is the only "correct" one—that is, one to which all men must adhere if they are not to be considered irrational or immoral. The proper meaning of "democracy," like that of any other word, ultimately depends on convention: that is, its validity depends upon the degree to which it is generally understood and accepted. Let us further recognize that many persons, communists and noncommunists alike, do not use "democracy" in exactly the sense in which we are about to define the term.

Recognizing these differences does not, however, exempt us from the obligation of selecting a particular definition. The term "democracy" cannot be avoided in discussing certain aspects of the governing of men. When we describe the political and governmental agencies and processes in the "democracies," we shall discuss the agencies and processes of certain nations and not of others. We shall have to decide which nations to include and which to omit on the basis of a particular conception of "democracy." Our discussion of modern government is likely to be clearer and more useful if we state at the outset what "democracy" means in this book

---

[7] The analysis of democracy given here is a somewhat revised version of that presented by the author in collaboration with Willmoore Kendall in *Democracy and the American Party System* (New York: Harcourt, Brace & World, Inc., 1956), Chs. 1–3. The author gratefully acknowledges the permission of Harcourt, Brace, & World, Inc., to borrow heavily from these chapters in the present analysis.

For some leading conceptions of democracy which to some degree diverge from that presented in the text, see Robert A. Dahl, *A Preface to Democratic Theory* (Chicago: University of Chicago Press, 1956); Henry B. Mayo, *An Introduction to Democratic Theory* (New York: Oxford University Press, 1960); Joseph A. Schumpeter, *Capitalism, Socialism and Democracy*, (2d ed.; New York: Harper & Row, Publishers, 1947); and Thomas Landon Thorson, *The Logic of Democracy* (New York: Holt, Rinehart and Winston, Inc., 1962).

and why that particular meaning has been chosen over others. In no sense, however, do we insist that our particular conception is the only one that is logically possible or morally permissible.

As we shall use the term in this book, *democracy is a form of government organized in accordance with the principles of popular sovereignty, political equality, popular consultation, and majority rule.* In order to understand what this definition means, let us briefly examine what is involved in each of its four basic principles.

## Popular Sovereignty

Briefly stated, the principle of popular sovereignty requires that the basic governmental decision-making power be vested in *all* the members of the community and not in any particular person or "ruling class." This principle is the nucleus of our conception of democracy, in the sense that the other three are logical elaborations of it. Let us therefore examine more closely its major elements.

(1) "SOVEREIGNTY." Political scientists have long argued about the proper content and usefulness of the concept of "sovereignty." Our purposes in using the term make it unnecessary to summarize or take sides in this debate, for we are merely repeating a point first made in Chapter 2: one characteristic of any modern nation is its possession of the full and exclusive legal power to make and enforce laws for the people within its territory and under its jurisdiction. Such a nation is, in a word, "sovereign" over its own affairs. Every sovereign nation, moreover, must locate its "sovereign power" somewhere in its politico-governmental structure. In a democracy it must be vested in all the members of the community.

(2) "VESTMENT IN THE PEOPLE." The principle of popular sovereignty does not, of course, require that all the people themselves directly make all the day-to-day decisions of government. Democracy, in other words, does not demand that dog licenses and parking tickets cannot be issued unless all the members of the community specifically consent to them—any more than a dictatorship implies that the dictator personally issue all licenses and tickets. The people in a democracy, like the dictator in a dictatorship, may "lend" or "delegate" any part of their decision-making power to legislators, executives, judges, or anyone else they wish. The people are sovereign so long as they, and not their delegates, have the power to decide such matters as what kinds of decision-making powers are to be delegated, to whom, under what conditions of accountability, and for what periods of time.

(3) "THE MEMBERS OF THE COMMUNITY." If democracy means "government by the people," then one may reasonably ask, "Who *are* 'the people'?" Are they, for instance, all the persons physically present at the

moment within the nation's borders—including infants, aliens, lunatics, criminals in prison, and so on? We have implied an answer to this question by stating that in a democracy power rests in all the *members of the community,* not in just anyone who happens to be around.

By what criteria, then, can we determine which persons may share this power? The criteria are suggested by the phrase "the members of the community." The term "community," for one thing, suggests something more than a mere aggregation of people. It suggests a group of persons somehow bound together, sharing common values, and experiencing some mutual overlapping of interests, feelings, and behavior. The term "member" implies a special kind of relationship between an individual and a group—a relationship which involves both the assuming of certain obligations to the group and the receiving of certain privileges from it.

By way of illustrating this point, a person's title to the privileges of voting and holding public office in modern democratic nations is determined by the community's judgment of both his ability and his willingness to fulfill the obligations of loyalty to the community and of obedience to its laws. Accordingly, children and lunatics in such nations are generally excluded from these privileges because they are judged incapable of understanding and performing the obligations of loyalty and obedience. Aliens and criminals in prison are generally excluded because they are judged unwilling to accept these obligations. One may, of course, disagree with the application of these criteria to certain classes of persons. Some people, for example, believe it is undemocratic to deny the vote to persons between the ages of eighteen and twenty-one or to persons who cannot read and write. The criteria of capability and willingness to assume certain obligations, however, are generally regarded in the democratic nations as the proper standards for determining what persons should and should not be regarded as part of "the sovereign people."

(4) "SOVEREIGNTY OF ALL THE PEOPLE." This element requires little comment, for where power is vested in one man the government is of the type described in Chapter 4 as a "dictatorship" or an "autocracy." Where it is vested in only part of the members of the community, the favored ones constitute a "ruling class," and the government is of the type we have described as an "oligarchy" or "aristocracy."

## Political Equality

The second principle of democratic government, political equality, requires that each member of the community have the same opportunity as his fellows to participate in the nation's governmental decision-making processes. This certainly means "one man, one vote," but it includes other matters as well. For instance, all citizens of the Soviet Union over the age of eighteen have the legally guaranteed right to vote, but they do not have political equality in our sense of the term. The fact they can vote for only one Communist-sponsored and -approved candidate for each office (see Chapter 13) deprives them of the opportunity to make genuine choices. Their right to vote, accordingly, gives them no real power over political decision. "In Russia," as one observer puts it, "everyone is equal; but some are more equal than others!" Certainly the Communist satraps who pick candidates are "more equal" than the ordinary Soviet voters who can only rubber-stamp the slate or "scratch" his ballot.

Political equality, as we are using the term, requires such guarantees as the following. Each member of the community must be able to vote and have his vote counted and given equal weight with every other vote cast. Genuine alternatives must be put before the voters so that they may make real choices. Each member of the community must have an equal chance to find out what the alternatives are and what arguments are made for and against each alternative. He must also have an equal opportunity to per-suade others—and to be persuaded by them—of the desirability of particular alternatives.

The principle of political equality is, of course, a logical consequence of the principle of popular sovereignty. If some members of the community have greater opportunities than others—if, for example, their votes are given double or triple weight, or if eligibility for public office is strictly limited—then they become a kind of specially favored "ruling class," which, according to the principle of popular sovereignty, is not permissible in a democracy.

The principle of political equality means equal political *opportunities* for all members of the community, not actual equal participation. In no known or imaginable democracy does every person actually participate to exactly the same degree as all others. So long as each member has a genuinely equal opportunity to participate to the degree he wishes and his individual capabilities permit, the requirements of political equality are satisfied.

## Popular Consultation

The third principle, that of popular consultation, has two requirements. First, a democratic nation must have some kind of institutional machinery whereby public officials learn what public policies the people wish made and enforced. And second, having ascertained what policies the people prefer, public officials must then put them into effect whether or not they feel those policies are wise. This principle, like that of political equality, is a logical consequence of the idea of popular sovereignty. If officeholders do what they, rather than the people, wish, they and not the people are the real sovereigns.

This principle is the most obvious point of difference between our conception of democracy and that of the communists. Communists, as we have seen, regard democracy as government *for* the people—government in which a special elite, the Communist party, decides what policies will best promote the "real" interests of the people. Popular approval of these policies is desirable but quite secondary to the objective of instituting the "right" kind of policies.

Our conception, on the other hand, regards democracy as essentially government *by* the people. Our principle of popular consultation requires that the question of which particular public policies will best promote the people's interests be decided ultimately by the people themselves and not by any "ruling class" of party leaders or college professors or scientists or priests or businesmen. According to our conception, the claim of a particular policy to the title "democratic" is determined by how it was made rather than by what its contents are. Policy content comes into the picture only when it directly affects the nature of the decision-making processes themselves.

## Majority Rule

THE NATURE OF THE PRINCIPLE. Our final principle of democracy is likely to be regarded as the most controversial of the four, and so we shall take special pains to explain its meaning, and why we regard it as essential to our conception of democracy.

When the people in a democracy unanimously agree that a particular policy should be followed, the principle of popular sovereignty clearly requires the government to follow that policy. Most governmental decisions in a democracy, however, eventually become choices among alternatives, each of which has its supporters among the sovereign people. In every such situation only one group can have its way, and the other group or groups must "lose." The problem that arises in all such situations is this: How should a democratic government, resting as it does on the principle that the basic decision-making power must be vested in *all* the members of the community, determine *which* of the disagreeing groups should carry the day?

The principle of majority rule requires that no governmental decision in a democracy may ultimately be made against the desires of popular majorities. When the people disagree on a particular issue, in other words, the government should act as the larger rather than the smaller number desire on that issue. This principle does not require that each and every governmental action be undertaken only after all the people have been consulted and a majority have specifically approved. The principle leaves it up to popular majorities to decide how they want various kinds of decisions made. A majority may, for example, wish to reserve for itself and

future majorities all governmental decisions, however minor they may be—
though no actual popular majority has ever done so. Or a majority may
wish to leave all such decisions up to certain elected and appointed public
officials and confine itself to deciding by periodic elections whether or not
those officials should remain in office. Or it may leave some decisions to
public officials and reserve others for direct popular decision by such means
as initiative and referendum (see Chapter 12). In short, so long as the
*procedures* used to make governmental decisions are at all times approved
by at least 50 percent plus one of the people and so long as the same
proportion of the people can at any time revise those procedures, the
requirements of the principle of majority rule are satisfied.

"LIMITED" MAJORITY RULE.[8] Some political commentators argue that
"unlimited" majority rule is incompatible with true democracy. They argue
that, in a true democracy, certain kinds of action must not be taken by
bare popular majorities. Such majorities, for example, must not destroy any
principles of democracy by such actions as transferring sovereignty from
the people to a dictator, or giving certain persons multiple voting power,
or prohibiting certain persons from expressing their political views, or
abolishing elections. Bare popular majorities must not destroy the kind of
liberties and due-process-of-law instruments guaranteed to individuals as
described in Chapter 8. Any nation in which a bare popular majority does
any of these things, these commentators contend, has no legitimate claim
to the title of "democracy." For these reasons, they conclude, "unlimited"
majority rule cannot be considered a principle of true democracy.

THE CASE FOR "UNLIMITED" MAJORITY RULE. Persons who, like the
present writer, believe that "unlimited" majority rule must be a principle
of democracy have no quarrel with the statements just made—as far as they
go. The next—and crucial—question is this: *How are popular majorities to
be prevented from destroying other democratic principles?* Some opponents
of "unlimited" majority rule do not answer this question directly but seem
to suggest two answers. First, popular majorities in a true democracy must
voluntarily restrain themselves from stepping over the line. And second,
when a popular majority in a particular nation fails to restrain itself and
does in fact destroy some of its institutions and guarantees, that nation is
no longer a democracy. Yet both of these propositions are entirely compatible with our conception of democracy and its principle of "unlimited"
majority rule—since they conceive of majorities as *self*-limited only.

---

[8] For lengthier expositions of the "limited majority rule" position, see Herbert
McClosky, "The Fallacy of Absolute Majority Rule," *Journal of Politics*, XI (November,
1949), 637–654; and Thomas Landon Thorson, "Epilogue on Absolute Majority Rule,"
*Journal of Politics*, XXIII (August, 1961), 557–565. For the author's reply to the latter,
see *ibid.*, pp. 566–569.

Other opponents of "unlimited" majority rule, however, contend that in a true democracy bare popular majorities must be limited by some agency independent of control by such majorities. These commentators argue that there must be some majority restraining institution, such as judicial review (see Chapter 6) or the requirement of "extraordinary" majorities (i.e., two thirds or three quarters as opposed to a mere 50 percent plus one) to take certain kinds of action. Such an institution must enable a minority to veto any action of a majority which the minority considers a threat to the sacrosanct institutions and guarantees.

In the debate over the appropriateness of such minority veto devices to a democracy the issue between the opponents and advocates of "unlimited" majority rule is most clearly joined. Those who, like the author, favor "unlimited" majority rule argue that such devices are incompatible with the principles of popular sovereignty and political equality. To give minorities the power to veto, they contend, is to give them the power to *rule*. Why? Because in any decision-making situation there are always a number of possible alternatives which might be chosen, and one of them is always that of continuing the status quo. A minority with veto power can, to be sure, choose *only* the status quo; but if it is large enough (i.e., if it commands one third plus one of the votes, or a majority of the Supreme Court), it can force the retention of the status quo over any alternative policy desired by the majority.

Such minority veto power is incompatible with the principles of popular sovereignty and political equality. A person who votes "No" counts for two or three times as much as a person who votes "Yes," in violation of the principle of political equality. Under such a system each person who opposes change and prefers the status quo has more political power than a person who desires change, and thereby those who prefer the status quo become something like a special "ruling class." Minority veto power, therefore, violates the principle of popular sovereignty.

For these reasons, then, our conception of democracy demands that no limitations be laid upon the power of bare popular majorities to take any governmental action they choose other than those imposed—*and removable*—by such majorities. But what if a majority in a particular nation chooses to give all power to a dictator, or to abolish all freedom of speech and press, or to deprive everyone but themselves of the right to vote? The answer is, of course, that as soon as such actions are taken that nation will cease to be a democracy. This does not mean, however, that locating the full *power* to take such actions in popular majorities is inconsistent with democracy; for surely even the power to commit suicide as a democracy must be part of the all-inclusive sovereign power which democracy, as we conceive it, locates in the people.

You may also ask, what if a particular majority chooses to set up judicial review or some other device to restrain future majorities? Under our conception this is perfectly compatible with majority rule and the other principles of democracy *provided* any future majority can at any time it wishes to do so abolish judicial review or any other majority restraining device by the same simple majority procedures by which the device was initially established.

The debate over the appropriateness of "unlimited" majority rule to democracy has to some extent been obscured by the fact that both sides have sometimes talked as though there were such a thing as *"the* majority"—a single, identifiable group of persons who stick together on issue after issue and continually beat down *"the* minority." The opponents of "unlimited" majority rule, for instance, have sometimes argued that "the majority" is made up of the more ignorant, prejudiced, and selfish members of the community who cannot be trusted to rule wisely in the interests of all. The defenders of "unlimited" majority rule have sometimes fallen into the same trap by arguing that "the majority" is composed of "common men" who, like Longfellow's village blacksmith, may not read books or use fancy words but make their decisions on the much sounder grounds of "practical experience" and "common sense."

Both sides, of course, are talking about something that does not exist. As we shall note in greater detail in Chapter 10, in reality every time one issue leaves the center of the political stage and is succeeded by another there is always some reshuffling of the individuals making up the various "opinion groups." Neither the majority nor the minority on any given issue is made up of exactly the same persons as the majority or minority on any other issue. When, for example, the issue of who should be elected President of the United States in 1964 was settled and was succeeded by the issue of "medicare," the majority group which had supported Johnson contributed some of its members to both the promedicare majority and the antimedicare minority. The minority group which had supported Goldwater also split on the new issue.

Actual majorities and minorities, in short, are (like "public opinion" in general) specific to particular issues, not permanent bodies whose members remain always the same on all issues. That is why we have specified that the only restraints on popular majori*ties* (not "the majority") compatible with democracy are those imposed by majorities on themselves and removable at any time without any restraint by minorities.

### The Advantages of This Conception of Democracy

We do not insist that the preceding conception of democracy is the only one logically possible or morally acceptable. We do, however, suggest that it has at least the following advantages.

### It Accords with the Historical Meaning of Democracy

The word "democracy" was first coined by the ancient Greeks in about the fifth century before Christ and was compounded of the words *demos* ("the people").and *kratos* ("authority"). Its original meaning was "authority in the people," and it became one element of the ancient tripartite classification of governments as democracies, aristocracies (authority in a few of the people), and monarchies (authority in one man). From then until World War I, "democracy" continued to be used by most persons in its original meaning. Only since 1918 has it been given the bewildering variety of meanings described at the beginning of the present chapter. Thus our conception of democracy, unlike many of its present-day rivals, closely accords with its generally accepted historical meaning.

The use of a word in a particular sense during most of its history does not, in itself, obligate us to retain its usage today. If some new meaning makes the word more useful in political discussion, and if the new meaning is generally accepted, we are well advised to abandon the old meaning in favor of the new. No other present-day conception of democracy, however, can claim either of these advantages. None of the newer meanings of the word, as we have seen, commands any general agreement. The fact that "democracy" now means many different things to different persons has greatly *reduced* its usefulness in modern political discussion. The advantages lost in abandoning the old meaning of the word obviously have not been replaced by corresponding advantages in adopting new meanings.

### It Accords with the Present-Day Areas of Agreement among Noncommunists

Our conception of democracy also has the advantage of incorporating —without going beyond—the elements of democracy which most present-day noncommunists agree should be included in any proper conception. The latter, as we noted above, agree that democracy is at least a form of government. They further agree that, as a form of government, it includes at least the principles of political equality, governmental response to the popular will, and majority rather than minority rule. They do not agree, however, as to whether democracy is more than just a form of government. Even those who maintain that it is also a "way of life" do not agree upon just what kind of social system, economic system, and personal attitudes and manners it requires.

It therefore seems reasonable to hope that our conception will provoke less disagreement among people on this side of the Iron Curtain than another, more ambitious conception might. We may even hope that, while many persons may believe our conception to be incomplete, few will feel that it contains elements which are incompatible with *any* defensible meaning of the word.

In any case, wherever it appears in this book, "democracy" will mean that form of government organized in accordance with the principles of popular sovereignty, political equality, popular consultation, and majority rule.

### "Democracy" and "Constitutionalism"

A "democratic" government, in our terminology, is not logically synonymous with a "constitutional" or "limited" or "free" government. The latter, as explained in Chapters 8 and 9, are governments in which the rights of man are formally and actually protected from abridgment either by public officials or by private groups. Such governments, in short, receive their titles as "constitutional" or "free" governments because of *what* they do and/or refrain from doing relative to these rights. A "democratic" government, according to our conception, receives its title because of the *processes* by which it reaches its decisions—not because of the content of its decisions.

It is theoretically possible for a benevolent despot to exercise his absolute decision-making power in such a way that all his subjects have full freedom of speech, press, and religion, and are guaranteed all their other individual rights. He might even promulgate a constitution formalizing these particular limitations on his activities, while reserving to himself the exclusive power to make all other political decisions. Such a government would certainly be "free" and even "constitutional," but it could not, under our definition of the term, be called "democratic." A "democratic" government, on the other hand, might have no written constitution and no formal guarantees of civil rights whatever and still be a "democracy," though hardly a "limited democracy."

This distinction between "democracy" and "constitutionalism," however, is more important logically than practically. Most of the nations we classified in Table 2 as "democracies" would certainly also appear on any list of "constitutional governments"; and none of the nations classified in that table as "dictatorships" would win a place on such a list. It therefore appears that most modern democracies have decided that one—though not the only—useful way of maintaining their democratic decision-making processes is to accept and formalize in constitutions the personal freedoms and immunities that make possible genuine political equality and popular consultation.

"Democracy" and "constitutionalism" are logically distinct. In practice, however, they are closely associated, and one rarely, if ever, comes across a government that merits one label but not the other.

# The Essentials of Dictatorship

## Origins of the Term

Explicating a model of dictatorship should take less time and argument than a model of democracy. The reason is clear. As we have seen, the word "democracy" evidently kindles such a pleasant emotional glow in most people the world over that they feel impelled to insist it applies best—perhaps exclusively—to whatever form or output of government they favor. Hence any effort to claim it for another form or output is always bound to encounter resistance and often resentment.

The word "dictatorship" has neither this popularity nor its attendant confusions. For most people it connotes something bad. Hence the much rarer disputes over its usage usually concern not what it means but whether it should be applied to this or that actual government.

The word "dictator" originated in the Republic of ancient Rome: when the city was threatened by foreign invasion or domestic rebellion and the Senate determined that the regular governing procedures were inadequate to meet the danger, they appointed a *dictator* and gave him, for a limited period, absolute power to use all of Rome's resources as he saw fit in order to save her. When the danger had passed, the dictator's power reverted to the Senate and the people, and, like the great Lucius Quinctius Cincinnatus, he returned to his former status of ordinary citizen. In the Republic's late years, however, ambitious politicians seized the title and powers of dictator by armed rebellion or intimidation of the Senate. For many centuries thereafter, accordingly, a "dictator" was generally thought of as one who seized and held absolute power by illegitimate means, as opposed to an "autocrat," who had equally absolute power but achieved it by such legitimate means as inheriting a throne.

## The Meaning and Varieties of Dictatorship Today

Political scientists have long since dropped the ancient distinctions, and now use the term "dictatorship" to denote a form of government in which the ultimate ruling power is held and exercised by one man with no effective responsibility to any other men or institutions. He may acquire his power, like the Emperor Haile Selassie of Ethiopia, by inheritance; he may, like the *Caudillo* Francisco Franco of Spain, seize it by armed rebellion; he may win it, like President François Duvalier of Haiti, by killing or jailing his rivals; or, like Adolf Hitler, he may use the procedures of democracy to gain a foothold and then eliminate all opposition. The essence of dictatorship, in short, is the *possession* of absolute and irresponsible power, not the manner of its acquisition.

Dictatorship thus conceived is a model in the same sense that democracy is a model: a full intellectual realization of a particular organizational principle, not a precise and complete description of any actual government. Hence just as there are degrees of democracy (i.e., degrees of approximation to the model), so there are degrees of dictatorship. In no actual government has one man actually controlled *all* governmental decisions by himself. All dictators from Julius Caesar to Joseph Stalin have had to rule by issuing orders to subordinates; those subordinates have had to interpret and implement his orders; and, as we shall see repeatedly in later chapters, any interpretation and implementation of an order necessarily creates an area of discretion effectively controlled by the subordinate, not his boss, whatever the organization charts may say.

So dictatorships, like democracies, are a matter of more or less, not of all or none. They range from the harsh totalitarian regimes of Red China and Albania and the Haitian terror of François Duvalier, through the post-Stalin "thaw" in the Soviet Union and its counterparts in Poland and Yugoslavia, to the relatively mild and permissive tutelary monarchies of Iran and Jordan.

### "Dictatorship" and "Totalitarianism"[9]

#### The Meaning of the Terms

Our terminology makes a distinction between "dictatorship" and "totalitarianism" analogous to that previously made between "democracy" and "constitutionalism." Democracy and dictatorship, as we are using the terms, are particular ways of *allocating* the ultimate power to make governmental policy. Constitutionalism and totalitarianism concern the limits or lack of limits on the permissible *exercise* of power.

A constitutional government, as we have seen, is one in which the rights of man are formally and effectively protected from abridgment either by public officials or by private groups. The essential trait of a totalitarian government is its effort to annihilate all personal privacy and claim every aspect of every citizen's life for the service of the nation's purposes as determined and interpreted by the Leader.

Most political scientists believe that the closest approaches to complete totalitarian dictatorship have been in fact Hitler's Germany, Stalin's Russia, and Mao's Red China, and in imagination the terrifying society depicted in George Orwell's novel *1984*. They regard this form of government as a twentieth-century Western invention quite different from older forms of

---

[9] The leading analyses of modern totalitarianism include: Hannah Arendt, *The Origins of Totalitarianism* (New York: Meridian Books, Inc., 1958); Carl J. Friedrich, ed., *Totalitarianism* (New York: Universal Library, 1964); and Carl J. Friedrich and Zbigniew Brzezinski, *Totalitarian Dictatorship and Autocracy* (2d ed., Cambridge, Mass.: Harvard University Press, 1965).

autocracy, such as the ancient despotism of Caligula, the oriental satrapy of Genghis Khan, the Renaissance tyranny of Cesare Borgia, or the absolute monarchy of Louis XIV. Each of these dictators had relatively limited political objectives, and demanded only that part of his subjects' lives and thoughts necessary to accomplish them. But the modern totalitarian regimes set no limits on either their objectives or the individual citizen's duty to sacrifice faithfulness to his religion, love of his family, and even the privacy of his thoughts to the Leader's demands.

### Essential Characteristics of Totalitarian Dictatorships

Two leading students of totalitarian dictatorships list six essential characteristics of this new kind of government:[10]

1. An official ideology covering all aspects of man's existence to which every member of the society must adhere, not only by outer form but by inner conviction
2. A single mass party, led typically by one man and consisting of a relatively small proportion of the total population, which acts as the official ideology's priesthood and the Leader's apostles and Janizaries
3. A system of terroristic police control based on modern technology
4. Nearly-complete monopoly of control by the Leader and party of all means of effective mass communication
5. Nearly-complete monopoly of all means of effective armed combat
6. Central control of the entire economy through bureaucratic coordination of all its hitherto private corporate entities

In strict logic "dictatorship" and "totalitarianism" are no more indivisible than "democracy" and "constitutionalism." Theoretically speaking, there could be a "totalitarian democracy"—indeed, this seems to be what the advocates of the "limited majority rule" position outlined above seem to fear will develop if popular majorities are unchecked. In fact, however, the modern world shows no example of a government which is both democratic and totalitarian. And while all totalitarian governments have been dictatorships of the most ruthless sort, most dictatorships, like their ancient and medieval predecessors, are not very totalitarian as we use the term.

## Conclusion

Our classification of actual governments as some variety of democracy or dictatorship is admittedly a tentative and imperfect operation at best. Given the present state of political science in such matters (see Chapter

---

[10] Friedrich and Brzezinski, *op cit.*, pp. 9–10.

24), it could hardly be otherwise. Yet, such a book as this, which seeks to describe the main processes of politics and government the world over, can hardly avoid talking about "democracies" and "dictatorships," nor would its author wish to do so.

We observed in Chapter 4 that anyone who talks of the "form" of an actual government necessarily does so by abstracting part of its total reality, and that the particular parts he chooses to investigate are determined by his conception of a "model" or "perfect" example of such a form of government. Anyone who uses the terms "democracy" and "dictatorship," therefore, does so on the basis of his conception of a perfect democracy and an absolute dictatorship; and anyone who describes an existing government as a "democracy" or a "dictatorship" does so by judging how that government's actual processes and institutions compare with his models.

Our purpose in this chapter has been to make as clear as we can what "democracy" and "dictatorship" mean when they appear in this book, why we have chosen these particular conceptions over their rivals, and by what line of reasoning we have come to describe some actual governments as "democracies" or "near democracies" and others as "dictatorships" or "near dictatorships." We now turn to the description and analysis of the main political agencies and processes in the nations whose governments we have labeled "democratic" and some of their counterparts in the nations whose governments we have labeled "dictatorships."

# part two

# The Constitutional Position of the Individual

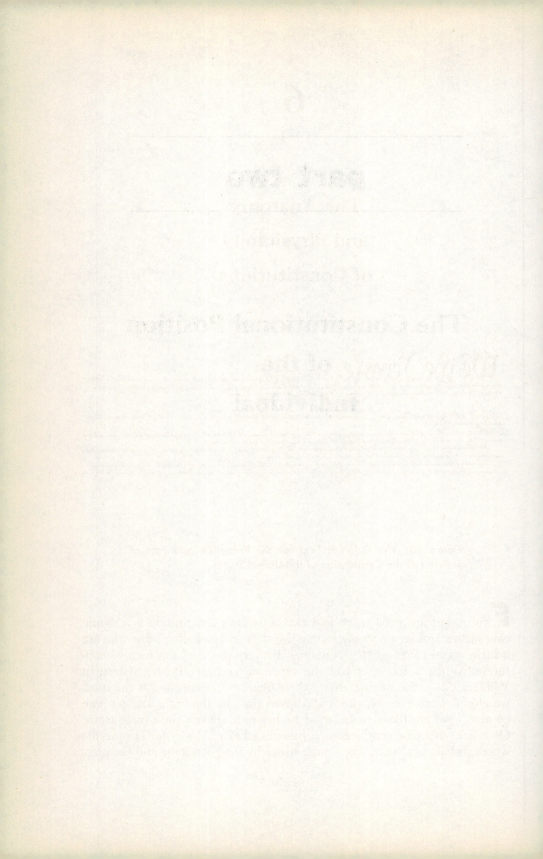

# 6

# The Anatomy and Physiology of Constitutions

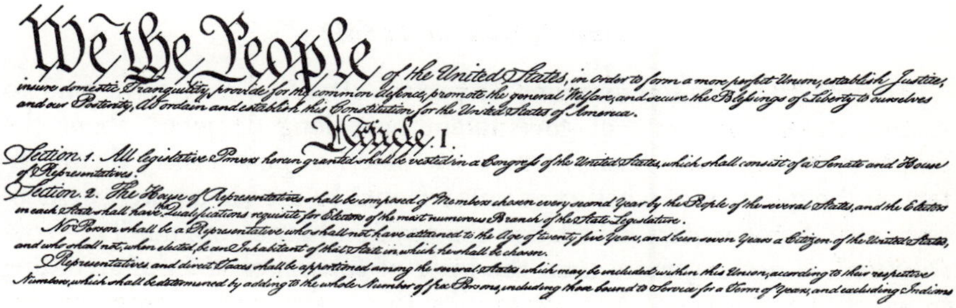
We the People of the United States, in Order to form a more perfect Union, establish Justice, insure domestic Tranquility, provide for the common defence, promote the general Welfare, and secure the Blessings of Liberty to ourselves and our Posterity, do ordain and establish this Constitution for the United States of America.

Article. I.

Section. 1. All legislative Powers herein granted shall be vested in a Congress of the United States, which shall consist of a Senate and House of Representatives.

Section. 2. The House of Representatives shall be composed of Members chosen every second Year by the People of the several States, and the Electors in each State shall have the Qualifications requisite for Electors of the most numerous Branch of the State Legislature.

No Person shall be a Representative who shall not have attained to the Age of twenty five Years, and been seven Years a Citizen of the United States, and who shall not, when elected, be an Inhabitant of that State in which he shall be chosen.

Representatives and direct Taxes shall be apportioned among the several States which may be included within this Union, according to their respective Numbers, which shall be determined by adding to the whole Number of free Persons, including those bound to Service for a Term of Years, and excluding Indians

***Figure 10*** **The Original Text for the Preamble and Part of Article I of the Constitution of the United States**

Few Americans need to be told that a nation's constitution is a significant element of its governing system. Most of us (including some who are a little vague about what it contains) are very proud of our own Constitution. When a foreigner like the nineteenth-century British statesman William Gladstone declares that "the American Constitution is the most wonderful work ever struck off at a given time by the brain and purpose of man," we are likely to feel that he has only spoken the simple truth. Or when the nineteenth-century French scholar Alexis de Tocqueville writes that he has "never been more struck by the good sense and the practical judgment of the Americans than in the manner in which they elude the numberless difficulties resulting from their Federal Constitution," we are likely to inquire indignantly how a *Frenchman* of all people presumes to comment on the "numberless difficulties" resulting from *our* Constitution.

By no means all the world's peoples, as we shall see, revere their constitutions as Americans do. Yet most political scientists believe that scrutinizing a nation's constitution is a useful way to begin the study of its governing system. In the present chapter, accordingly, we shall begin our description of the ways in which modern nations govern themselves by explaining what a constitution is, the different kinds of status constitutions enjoy in different nations, where constitutional rules may be found and what matters they deal with, and how constitutions grow and develop.

## What Is a "Constitution"?

### *Description or Ideal?*

Despite the long-standing and respectful attention they have paid to "constitutions," students of government have long disagreed about the proper meaning of the term. Perhaps the oldest dispute among them centers on the question of whether or not it should be used in a purely descriptive sense. Some writers have taken the position that a community's "constitution" is nothing more than the body of fundamental rules according to which it is governed. Any community that makes and enforces governmental policies in conformity with certain generally understood and accepted procedures, they feel, has a constitution of some sort. The fact that one may disapprove of a particular community's procedures, they hold, does not entitle him to dismiss that community as having no constitution whatever.

Another group of writers, however, have agreed with the eighteenth-century political philosopher Thomas Paine that only certain kinds of governmental rules and procedures deserve to be called "constitutions." In *The Rights of Man* (1791–1792), Paine argued that no community can properly be said to have a constitution unless it passes these tests: its people must consciously and deliberately establish its basic rules and (presumably) promulgate them in the form of a written document; this document must be generally regarded as antecedent to and therefore binding upon the community's government; it must define and thereby limit governmental authority; and any governmental action exceeding these limits must be generally regarded as an exercise of "power without right." Paine avowed that any government which, like Great Britain's, does not measure up to these standards, has nothing that deserves to be called a "constitution."[1]

### Written or Unwritten?

Paine's argument that the British have no constitution at all touched off a debate as to whether constitutions must be "written" or may also be "unwritten." Paine's position won many supporters in his own time, especially in the United States; and even today one occasionally encounters in newspaper editorials and elsewhere the argument that since Great Britain, unlike the United States and most other nations, has no single written document officially designated as its Constitution, the British are in the unhappy state—somewhat akin to that of a man in an automobile with a high-powered engine but no brakes—of having no constitution whatever.

Most students of government in Paine's time and since have agreed with his contemporary, Edmund Burke, that since the basic rules of British government are at least as well understood and generally obeyed as those promulgated in written Constitutions, the British constitution's title to the label of "constitution" is at least as good as that of any nation with a written document. In the nineteenth and early twentieth centuries many writers discussed learnedly and at great length the differences between "written" and "unwritten" constitutions (with the British constitution always providing the sole example of the latter type) and concluded, among other things, that the latter are more flexible but less stable than the former.

Most contemporary political scientists, however, pay little heed to this distinction. They agree with the argument first advanced by the British scholar-statesman James Bryce that this dichotomy is a distinction without a difference; for, as Bryce pointed out, all "written" Constitutions are unwritten in part, and parts of the "unwritten" British constitution are promulgated in official written documents.[2]

### Our Definition

As we shall use the term in this book, a constitution is *the whole body of fundamental rules, written and unwritten, legal and extralegal, accord-*

---

[1] One of Paine's contemporaries, Arthur Young, quipped that Paine talked "as if a constitution was a pudding to be made by a receipt": quoted in Charles H. McIlwain, *Constitutionalism Ancient and Modern* (Ithaca, N.Y.: Cornell University Press, 1940), p. 4.

[2] James Bryce, *Studies in History and Jurisprudence* (New York: Oxford University Press, 1901), Vol. I, Ch. 3.

*ing to which a particular government operates.*[3] The reader will note that this is a purely descriptive definition. We shall reserve the term "constitutionalism" to denote the ideals advocated by Paine, and we shall have more to say about them in a moment.

## The Status of Constitutional Rules

### *Superiority to Ordinary Law*

All modern nations have "constitutions" in the broad sense just presented.[4] Each nation's constitution, as our definition suggests, consists of a number of rules—rules requiring certain kinds of behavior, permitting others, and prohibiting still others. By no means all governmental rules, however, have constitutional status; for, as our definition also suggests, a nation's constitution is made up of *fundamental* rules—rules that occupy a special status, perform a special function in the nation's total governing system, and are generally regarded as superior to the rules of ordinary law. Some languages, indeed, actually have different words to distinguish between constitutional law and ordinary law. In German, for example, ordinary law is called *Gesetz*, while constitutional law is called *Grundgesetz* or *Verfassung*. In French the two types of rules are called respectively *loi* and *constitution*; and in Italian *statuto* and *legge*.[5] Constitutional rules are generally considered to differ from the rules of ordinary law in the following main respects.

### Constitutional Rules Are Regarded as More Fundamental

They establish and regulate the whole basic framework of government; they prescribe the matters with which the government may (and may not) deal, the agencies authorized to deal with them, the procedures which those agencies must follow, and the processes by which the members of the various agencies are selected. Constitutional rules, in other words, are generally regarded as more fundamental than the rules of ordinary law in the sense that a constitution applies to more general and significant matters than "law" and also fixes the limits of "law."

In some modern Constitutions, to be sure, one can find rules applying to matters whose claim to being regarded as fundamental in these senses

---

[3] This is a somewhat revised version of a definition given in Francis D. Wormuth, *The Origins of Modern Constitutionalism* (New York: Harper & Row, Publishers, 1949), p. 3.

[4] For purposes of distinguishing between "constitutions" in the broad sense in which we have defined the term and the written documents officially designated as "Constitutions," we shall in this chapter and throughout the book capitalize the latter term and use the former in lower case.

[5] Herman Finer, *Theory and Practice of Modern Government* (rev. ed.; New York: Holt, Rinehart and Winston, Inc., 1949), p. 117.

may seem very weak indeed. The Constitution of Afghanistan, for example, provides that "in Friday sermons the name of the King will be mentioned" (Art. 7). The Constitution of Peru requires that "there shall be at least one school in every place where the school-going population amounts to thirty pupils" (Art. 73), and the Swiss Constitution provides that "the bleeding of slaughter animals which have not been previously stunned is expressly forbidden" (Art. 25A). The point is, however, that while these rules may seem to outsiders to be petty and undeserving of constitutional status, the constitution makers of the nations involved apparently do not agree. It is they, and not their critics in other nations, who decide for their communities what is fundamental and what is not.

### Constitutional Rules Are Less Easily Changed

Most written Constitutions, as we shall see below, can be formally amended only by procedures more difficult and time consuming than those by which ordinary laws are adopted. This is intended to accomplish several purposes, one of which is to make the Constitution more difficult to change than ordinary law and therefore to make its rate of change slower than that of ordinary law. The same objective is accomplished even in those few nations (e.g., Great Britain and New Zealand) in which constitutional rules may be changed by the legislature through the same formal procedures it uses to alter ordinary laws. The legislatures of these nations know what is at stake when they are considering bills that involve constitutional change, and the historical record shows that they have not wrought such changes more rapidly or in greater number than have other nations. New Zealand, for example, has passed only about thirteen parliamentary acts tantamount to constitutional amendments since 1908, while Switzerland, with its far more elaborate formal amending procedure, has adopted as many as thirty-four amendments since 1874. In all nations constitutional rules are generally less easily changed than the rules of ordinary law.

### Constitutional Rules Are Regarded as More Binding

In most nations it is generally understood that any rule of ordinary law that in any way contravenes a constitutional rule has no legal standing and may not legitimately be enforced. The reasoning behind this prohibition runs thus: in the senses noted above, constitutions are fundamental and ordinary laws are derivative; what is derivative may not violate what is fundamental. The only legitimate way to adopt such law is to change the constitution so that it is no longer contravened by the ordinary law.

### *Maintaining Constitutional Supremacy*

If constitutional rules are generally regarded as more binding than conflicting rules of ordinary law, the question remains, *who decides* whether particular ordinary laws do or do not contravene the constitution? What agencies, in other words, maintain constitutional supremacy? The world's nations answer these questions by one or the other—but not both—of the following two institutional arrangements.

### By Judicial Review

Judicial review, as we shall use the term, is *the power of a court to render a legislative or executive act null and void on grounds of unconstitutionality.* Although some English judges in the seventeenth century claimed this power, it first became generally established and accepted in some of the American states in the late eighteenth century and was made a part of the national constitutional system by Chief Justice John Marshall's decision in the case of *Marbury v. Madison* (1803). During the nineteenth and twentieth centuries the institution of judicial review gradually spread to other nations, with the period after World War I being the time of its widest adoption.[6] As of 1956, the latest date for which complete information is available, the Constitutions of thirty-two nations expressly located this power in the courts; and in two additional nations the Constitution has been construed—as in the United States—so as to establish judicial review.[7] In several of these nations (e.g., Nicaragua, Portugal, and Syria) judicial review is a paper power only; for both the courts and the legislature do whatever the nations' dictators or ruling elites order, and it never occurs to the courts to attempt to exercise their formal powers. In several other nations (e.g., the United States, West Germany, and Japan), however, the courts can and do on occasion declare legislative and executive acts null and void on grounds of unconstitutionality, and their decisions are accepted and acted upon by their respective legislative and executive bodies and peoples. In Chapter 20 we shall examine further the operation and consequences of judicial review in such nations.

### By Agencies Other than Courts

As of 1956, the Constitutions of six nations expressly located the power of reviewing the constitutionality of legislative and executive acts in various popularly elected bodies, such as the legislature or the cabinet or some combination of the two. The remaining forty-six nations had no constitutional provisions or judicial declarations whatever on the subject. This does not mean that in these fifty-two nations no distinction whatever is made between constitutional rules and the rules of ordinary law, nor does

---

[6] David Deener, "Judicial Review in Modern Constitutional Systems," *American Political Science Review*, XLVI (December, 1952), 1079–1099.

[7] Amos J. Peaslee, ed., *Constitutions of Nations* (2d ed.; The Hague: Martinus Nijhoff, 1956). III, 840–849, Table VII.

it mean that in such nations the constitution is not regarded as supreme. It means rather that the duty of maintaining constitutional supremacy and the power to decide whether legislative and executive acts do, in fact, contravene the constitution rest in bodies other than the courts—the popularly elected legislatures and cabinets in the democracies, and the dictators in the dictatorships.

## Where Constitutional Rules May Be Found

The fundamental rules that comprise a nation's "constitution" in the broad sense may be found in some combination of the following four locations.

### The Written Constitution

Every nation, with the few exceptions noted above, possesses a written document which is formally and officially designated its Constitution. Despite their formally central position, however, the rules set forth in these documents may or may not occupy an important position in the total constitution of any given nation. We can discern at least the following three general patterns. The rules stated in the written Constitutions of the United States, the nations of the British Commonwealth and Western Europe, and a few Latin American nations are of high prestige and constitute the nucleus around which the total constitution is built. In such nations as Russia, Hungary, Albania, and Czechoslovakia, on the other hand, lip service may be paid to the written Constitution, but everyone understands that it may be set aside with no fuss or sense of wrongdoing whenever certain public officials decide that "reasons of state" require it— that is, whenever the officials feel that observing the rules will make it inconvenient for them to do something they want to do. In such nations as Paraguay, Nicaragua, the Dominican Republic, and Saudi Arabia the written Constitution is frequently ignored, its rules are violated, and it receives relatively little attention or respect.[8]

As we shall see below, political scientists describe nations of the first type (and also, despite its "unwritten" constitution, Great Britain) as having "constitutional governments." Nations of the latter two types, despite their written Constitutions, cannot claim this title, because in each

---

[8] J. Roland Pennock and David G. Smith suggest distinguishing between the "formal" and "effective" constitutions in such cases: *Political Science, An Introduction* (New York: The Macmillan Company, 1964), pp. 241–242.

the government and particularly the executive agencies are supreme over and are accorded more respect (or fear) than the Constitution.[9]

## Organic Laws

Few written Constitutions establish and outline the organization of *every* major agency of government. The gaps are usually filled in part by acts of the legislature—rules which, while adopted by ordinary legislative procedures, are nevertheless regarded as almost as important as the rules in the Constitution itself. These special legislative rules are usually called "organic laws." They differ from other kinds of laws in that they deal with the basic organization and procedures of the government rather than, as in the case of ordinary laws, with specific governmental policies.

The Constitution of the United States, for example, provides that "the judicial Power of the United States, shall be vested in one supreme Court, and in such inferior Courts as the Congress may from time to time ordain and establish" (Art. III, Sec. 1). Thus most elements of our national court system—the district courts, courts of appeal, the tax courts, the patent court, and so on—have been established by acts of Congress, beginning with the Judiciary Act of 1789. The Constitution also refers to "the executive Departments" but does not prescribe what departments there shall be or how they shall be organized; and all of the existing departments, from the Department of State (established in 1789) to the Department of Housing and Urban Development (established in 1965), have been created by acts of Congress. Despite their legislative rather than constitutional origin, these courts and executive departments are certainly a part of the American constitutional system; and it is scarcely easier to alter the legislation creating them than it is to amend the Constitution itself. The organic laws of most other nations enjoy this same special status.

## Judicial Decisions

Every written Constitution and organic law, as we shall see below, is necessarily couched to some extent in ambiguous language—that is, in terms whose application to specific situations is not agreed upon by all reasonable men. Many of the written parts of any constitution, in other words, must be interpreted. Every governmental agency in every nation therefore interprets the constitution every time it acts, for presumably it will do only what it believes it has the constitutional authority to do. Many of these interpretations are so obvious and uncontroversial that they go unchallenged. A few, however, become controversial; and in constitutional

---

[9] K. C. Wheare, *Modern Constitutions* (New York: Oxford University Press, 1951), p. 6.

governments many of the controversies over conflicting constitutional interpretations are fought out in cases at law. Thus, while the courts in such
nations have no monopoly on interpreting the Constitution and organic
law, they do deal with many of the controversies over such interpretations,
and their decisions are generally regarded as authoritative. In each of these
nations the decisions of most courts are written, collected, and published,
and these collections constitute another leading source of constitutional
rules.

Perhaps the outstanding example of a major constitutional institution
established by judicial decision rather than by a constitutional provision
or an organic law is the American institution of judicial review. The Constitution of the United States nowhere expressly authorizes the courts to
exercise this power, nor did any act of Congress do so before the year 1803.
In that year, however, the Supreme Court in the case of *Marbury v.
Madison* interpreted the Constitution in such a way as to give the courts
the reviewing power; this interpretation was subsequently accepted by the
other agencies of government and by the people, and judicial review
thereby became an established part of our constitutional system. Even
today, however, when the question arises, "Where is the national courts'
power of judicial review authorized?" the answer is, "In the decision in
*Marbury v. Madison.*"

### Customs

The first three varieties of constitutional rules are all expressed in written form and for that reason are relatively easy to find and deal with. The
fourth, however, is of a somewhat different nature. The category of "customary" constitutional rules includes all those regularized, clearly understood, and generally accepted and obeyed fundamental rules of government that are not written down in the same formal and official manner
in which written Constitutions, organic laws, and judicial decisions are
promulgated. The only written form in which these customs may be found
is in such nonofficial documents as constitutional commentaries by scholars
of jurisprudence, constitutional law, and political science. The fact that
these rules are not officially written down, however, does not make them
any less binding or authoritative than the other kinds of rules. Some persons find this difficult to believe, since they assume that "the law" is the
only really powerful regulator of governmental activity and believe that if
a particular procedure is not required by a written law it may or may not
be observed, depending on the whims of the persons involved at the
moment. A few examples of constitutional customs, however, should make
clear their authoritative and binding nature.

The Constitution of the United States expressly provides that the

## "We're Almost Ready To Take Off Again"

*Figure 11.* Sometimes Constitutional Customs Are More Advanced than Written Procedures. From *Straight Herblock* (Simon & Schuster, 1964).

President shall be elected by the Electoral College, the members of which shall be selected by the states in whatever manner the latter choose. The authors of the Constitution clearly intended the electors to choose the President according to their own individual judgments entirely free from popular pressure. Yet for over a hundred years all the electors have been pledged to vote for particular presidential candidates; and from 1789 to 1964, in no more than 8 instances of a possible 14,500 did an elector vote for someone other than the candidate to whom he was pledged.[10] Since all electors are now popularly elected, the Electoral College has become, in effect, a machine for rubber-stamping the choice of the American *people*.

Thus, in arithmetical terms, the machine has worked 99.95 percent of the time—which, to say the least, matches the record of compliance with written laws and Constitutions. Yet students often ask, "But what happens if an elector *does* violate his pledge?" The answer, based on the eight instances mentioned above, is that he is not subject to any national *legal* penalty, since neither the Constitution nor any act of Congress expressly requires him to honor his pledge. In only three states would any present defector violate a state law. Yet legal penalties, as we observed in Chapter 2, are by no means the only sanctions that can be imposed upon deviant political behavior; there are also such penalties as socially ostracizing him, smashing his political career, and in other ways convincing him he has done evil.

In short, we know that in only .05 percent of the opportunities to do so have electors violated their pledges. We know that even in the very special circumstances of the 1960 election—the closest election in the twentieth century, in which a number of embittered southern electors pledged to Kennedy might have bolted and thrown the election into the House of Representatives—the system worked almost perfectly, with only 1 defector out of 537 electors.[11] It therefore seems likely that the custom will, in the future as in the past, hold firm almost all of the time. It also seems likely that if it should break down and result in the election of a President whom a majority of the people oppose, the custom will swiftly become law (which possibility in itself undoubtedly inhibits some potential defectors). So "custom" though it be, it is as rigid and unyielding as any rule in our Constitution, organic laws, or judicial decisions.

The Constitution of Canada expressly authorizes the governor-general,

---

[10] Estes Kefauver, "The Electoral College," *Law and Contemporary Problems*, XXVII (Spring, 1962), 188–212, at 208–209. Three instances have occurred since World War II: in 1948 Preston Parks was a candidate for elector in Tennessee on both the regular Democratic ticket pledged to Truman and the Dixiecrat ticket pledged to Thurmond, and voted for Thurmond; in 1956 segregationist W. F. Turner, an Alabama elector pledged to Stevenson, voted for segregationist Alabama Judge W. B. Jones; and in 1960 Henry D. Irwin, an Oklahoma elector pledged to Nixon, voted instead for Senator Harry F. Byrd.

[11] The 8 Mississippi electors who voted for Byrd in 1960 ran as "unpledged" electors, and thus violated no pledge; the 6 Alabama electors who joined them had announced in advance that they would not support Kennedy and so, strictly speaking, they too violated no pledge.

who is the Queen's official representative, to appoint the ministers (i.e., the heads of the executive departments) and places no limitations on his choice. By custom, however, the governor-general—like the Queen in Great Britain and all "constitutional monarchs"—appoints only those persons whom the prime minister recommends, and it would never occur to him to do otherwise. Nor does the prime minister have an absolutely free hand in making his recommendations. He knows, for instance, that he is expected to recommend both French- and English-speaking persons, to provide for approximately equal representation from the provinces of Quebec and Ontario, and to make sure that the western provinces have some representation. These expectations are so firmly established and taken for granted that it would never occur to a prime minister to disappoint them.

The Constitutions of the United States and Canada authorize the lower houses of their national legislature to elect their own "speakers" (presiding officers) but say very little about the powers and duties of such officers. The speaker of the American House of Representatives, as we shall see in Chapter 17, has by custom become the principal active leader of the majority party in the House, while the speakers of the Canadian and British Houses of Commons are by custom removed from just about all connections with political parties and are almost completely nonpartisan officials. It would never occur to any speaker of either of these bodies to step out of the role that constitutional custom assigns him.

As these illustrations make clear, the rules involved in these customs are every bit as firmly established a part of the general body of constitutional rules as are the rules written down in the Constitution, organic law, and judicial decisions.

## The Contents of Written Constitutions

While the rules of written Constitutions are, as we have seen, by no means the only rules in any nation's constitutional system, they provide an obvious and often useful point of departure for studying any particular system. In some nations the written Constitution has high prestige and forms the nucleus around which the whole constitutional system is built. Even the nations that largely ignore their Constitutions do not junk them altogether. Apparently, even these nations feel that having such a document accomplishes some purposes, even if those purposes do not include regulating the actual conduct of the governing process.

Although there are almost endless variations in the detailed provisions of the world's Constitutions, the contents of most of them can be classified into one or another or a combination of the following main categories.

### Statements of Ideals

The bulk of most Constitutions is made up of legal rules intended to act as direct and more or less specific guides to and limitations on the behavior of public officials. Many Constitutions, however, also contain statements of general ideals and objectives. These are usually regarded as having no direct or specific application to particular agencies but are intended to set the tone and give the spirit of the whole document. To this extent, such Constitutions are more than collections of legal rules; they are also political manifestos or testaments.

These statements of ideals more often than not are located at the beginning of the Constitution, and they usually state by what authority the Constitution is established and for what purposes. The Preamble of the Constitution of the United States, for example, proclaims:

> We, the People of the United States, in Order to form a more perfect Union, establish Justice, insure domestic Tranquility, provide for the common defense, promote the general Welfare, and secure the Blessings of Liberty to ourselves and our posterity, do ordain and establish this Constitution for the United States of America.

Similar statements appear in the Constitutions of Brazil, Cuba, Finland, Korea, Liberia, the Philippines, and many of the American states.

Many of the Constitutions of the communist nations also describe, in rather tendentious terms, the circumstances of their origins. Thus, the Russian Constitution of 1936 proclaims:

> The political foundation of the U.S.S.R. is the Soviets of the Working People's Deputies, which grew and became strong as a result of the overthrow of the landlords and capitalists and the conquest of the dictatorship of the proletariat.[12]

And the Bulgarian Constitution of 1947 begins:

> Bulgaria is a People's Republic with a representative government established and consolidated as a result of the heroic struggle of the Bulgarian people against the monarcho-fascist dictatorship, and of the victorious national uprising of September 9, 1944.[13]

### Structure of Government

All Constitutions specify what major organs of the government shall exist, what kinds of persons shall be eligible to occupy positions in these organs, and how they shall be selected and retired. Many also outline the

---

[12] Ch. I, Art. 2, reproduced in Peaslee, *op. cit.*, III, 485.
[13] Ch. I, Art. 1, reproduced *ibid.*, I, 262. The Constitutions of Albania, Czechoslovakia, Hungary, Poland, and Rumania begin with similar statements.

organization of these agencies and, in broad terms, describe their proper relationships with one another.

## Distribution of Powers

Most Constitutions have a number of rules stating what the various governing officials are authorized to do. These "powers of government" may be distributed in one or both of the following two ways.

### Among Governmental Organs

The Constitution assigns to each governmental organ—the legislature, the executive and administrative agencies, and the courts—power to act upon certain matters. The Constitutions of the presidential democracies, as we observed in Chapter 4, do this according to the principle of "separation of powers": each "branch" of government is assigned certain powers and, by implication at least, is largely forbidden to exercise powers assigned to the other branches. The Constitutions of the parliamentary democracies, on the other hand, not only authorize the legislative bodies to supervise, regulate, and select the heads of the executive agencies but also allow them to supervise the courts as well. The 1926 Constitution of Saudi Arabia, by contrast, locates full power in the King and permits (but does not require) him to appoint such advisers and administrators as he wishes.

### Between Levels of Government

All federal Constitutions distribute powers between the national and local governments. This is done in several ways. The Constitution of the United States gives certain specific "delegated" or "enumerated" powers to the national government and "reserves" all the rest to the states. The Constitutions of Canada and India, on the other hand, have three lists of powers: those belonging exclusively to the national government, those belonging exclusively to the local governments, and those belonging to the two levels "concurrently." In most federal governments these lists can be formally altered only by joint action of both levels of government.

Some unitary Constitutions also list the powers of both levels of government, although these lists can be changed without the consent of the local governments. In most unitary governments, however, the powers of the local governments are stated in the organic law rather than in the Constitution.

## Rights of Individuals

Just about every Constitution declares that certain "rights" must be guaranteed to the persons within its jurisdiction. These rights are of two main varieties.

## Limitations on Government

The oldest and most familiar form of constitutionally guaranteed individual rights are lists of things which government may not do to individuals. The Constitution of the United States, for example, declares that Congress may not abridge any individual's freedom of speech, press, or religion, and that no state shall deny to any person the "equal protection of the laws." Most other Constitutions list a number of individual rights against government stated in much the same manner.

## Obligations of Government

Many of the more recent Constitutions add to these rights of individuals against government a number of positive obligations the government owes to every individual. The most common of these obligations are such guarantees as the right to work, the right to education, and the right to security in old age. Some Constitutions add rights which the framers of the American Constitution would hardly recognize as proper matters for constitutional guarantees. The Irish Constitution of 1937, for example, provides that "the State shall . . . endeavour to ensure that mothers shall not be obliged by economic necessity to engage in labour to the neglect of their duties in the home";[14] and the 1948 Constitution of Italy states that "the Republic favors through economic measures and other provisions the establishment of families and the fulfillment of their functions, with especial regard to large families."[15]

### *Amending Procedures*

Most Constitutions specify the procedures by which they may be formally amended. Very few modern Constitutions (that of New Zealand is an example) are "flexible" in the sense that they can be formally amended by the same procedures used to pass ordinary laws. Most Constitutions are "rigid" in that they can be formally amended only by special procedures which generally make the amending process more difficult than the ordinary legislative process. In his survey of modern Constitutions, K. C. Wheare found that the special amending procedures of the "rigid" Constitutions are intended to accomplish one or more of the following four main objectives.

First, to ensure that the Constitution should be changed only "with deliberation, and not lightly or wantonly." Every special amending procedure is intended to accomplish at least this end.

Second, to give the people an opportunity to express their views before

---

[14] Art. 41, Sec. 2, reproduced *ibid.*, II, 459.
[15] Art. 31, reproduced *ibid.*, II, 486.

a change is made. Some Constitutions (e.g., those of Ireland, Denmark, Australia, and Switzerland) require that all proposed amendments be approved by the voters in referenda before they may take effect. Other Constitutions (e.g., those of Belgium, the Netherlands, and Sweden) require that an amendment must first be approved by the legislature, the legislature must then be dissolved and a general election held, and the amendment must then be passed again in identical form by the new legislature. The Swiss Constitution (and the Constitution of some American states) permit the voters to initiate as well as ratify constitutional amendments.

Third, to provide (most federal Constitutions do) that the powers of the national and local governments cannot be altered by either level acting alone. In the United States, for example, there are two amending procedures, but the only one ever used provides that amendments must be proposed by a two-thirds vote of both houses of Congress and ratified by the legislatures or conventions of three fourths of the states. In Switzerland and Australia amendments proposed by the national legislature must be ratified by a majority of all the voters in nation-wide balloting and also by a majority of the voters in a majority of the cantonal or state governments.

Fourth, to safeguard the rights of certain linguistic, religious, and/or cultural minorities. The Swiss Constitution, for example, specifies that German, French, and Italian shall have equal status as the official languages of the federation; and the Canadian Constitution makes similar provisions for French and English.

## The Birth and Growth of Constitutions

### How Constitutions Begin

Since the constitutions of Great Britain, Bhutan, and Yemen have no single written document as their nucleus, we can only say that each constitution began when the nation achieved its nationhood; and it is difficult if not impossible to fix a specific date or point to a single historical episode as the "origin" of such constitutions. All other Constitutions, however, can be said to have had their origins at specific times.

#### The Circumstances

The nations with written Constitutions date the origin of their present constitutional systems from the time of the writing, promulgation, and ratification of their Constitutions. As Wheare points out, "If we investigate the origins of modern [written] Constitutions, we find that, practically without exception, they were drawn up and adopted because people wished to make a fresh start, so far as the statement of their system of government was concerned."[16] Some peoples have wished to make a fresh start because they have overthrown an old regime and wished to erect a new one on new principles. The first modern attempts at written Constitutions were of this type. After having overthrown the Stuart monarchy in England in the 1640's, Oliver Cromwell's "Roundhead" revolutionaries set to work to draw up a new Constitution for the realm. One, the Agreement of the People (1649), was rejected; but another, the Instrument of Government (1653), governed England until the restoration of the monarchy in 1660. More recent examples of this type are the French Constitution of 1789 and the "Weimar" German Constitution of 1919. Other peoples, living in neighboring communities, have wished to unite together under a new government, as in the case of the United States in 1787 and Australia in 1900, or have achieved independence and established a Constitution for the new government, as in the case of Ireland in 1921.

### Drafting

Whatever the circumstances in which these Constitutions have been written, however, each has been drafted by a particular body at a particular time. Various drafting procedures have been followed. In some instances the constituent body has been the legislature of the old government; in others it has been a revolutionary "junta" that has shot its way to the drafting power; in still others it has been a popularly elected special "constitutional convention"; in yet others it has been composed of representatives from governments who wish to join together in a federation; and in still others the king or dictator and his "palace guard" have written the Constitution without outside help.

### Ratification

Some Constitutions have not been formally ratified at all but have simply gone into effect by proclamation of their respective framing bodies. Others have been ratified by a referendum taken among the people. Still others have gone into effect when the federating governments have accepted them.

## *Methods of Constitutional Change*

### 1. Substituting Constitutions

No nation has been content to keep its constitution forever in exactly the same form in which it began. Many nations have, for one reason or another, become so dissatisfied with their written Constitutions that they

---

[16] Wheare, *op. cit.*, pp. 8–9.

have replaced them with new ones; and a considerable number have changed Constitutions several times. Of the sixty-seven nations shown in Table 2, Chapter 4, as having achieved their present national status before 1939, the present Constitutions of thirty-one have been adopted since 1945, twenty-four adopted theirs between 1900 and 1945, and only twelve adopted theirs before 1900. Thus, the Constitution of the United States, written in 1787 and put into effect in 1789, is the oldest written Constitution still in effect.

Most, although not all, Constitution substituting has taken place in these three historical periods: first, during the European liberal revolutions in the middle of the nineteenth century; second, during the period 1918–1920, in response to the changes in national status and forms of government wrought by World War I; and third, in the late 1940's as the result of the changes in national status and forms of government brought about by World War II and by the conquests of the communist movement in Eastern Europe and Asia.

## 2. Formal Amendments

Junking old Constitutions and replacing them with new ones is by no means the only—or even the most important—method of constitutional change. Another method is formal amendment of the established Constitution. In most nations this has been the least significant of the various methods of constitutional change. Most groups desiring such change have found other methods easier to use and equally productive of satisfactory results. Ascertaining how many times a particular Constitution has been amended, therefore, tells us very little about the full dimensions of constitutional change in that nation. For example, there have been twenty-four formal amendments to the Constitution of the United States, forty-eight to the Constitution of Switzerland, and only four to the Constitution of Australia. Yet no one concludes from these data that the constitutional system of Switzerland has changed far more than have the systems of Australia or the United States. To understand how much constitutional change has taken place in these or any other nations, we must look not only at the number of formal Constitutional amendments but at other indices as well.

## 3. Statutory Revision

Since a nation's organic law is, as we noted above, part of its constitutional system, any major change in such law is a constitutional change. For example, in 1789 the American Congress established the Department of War and in 1798 added the Department of the Navy. For the next century and a half these two agencies constituted the nation's military establishment. In 1947 and 1949, however, Congress demoted these two departments from cabinet rank, created a new agency, the Department of the Air Force, and placed all three under the authority of a brand-new executive department, the Department of Defense. Congress since 1789 has also created other executive departments, increased the size of the Supreme Court and altered its appellate jurisdiction, established such regulatory bodies as the Interstate Commerce Commission (1887) and the Federal Communications Commission (1934), and so on. All of these represented changes in our constitutional system at least as significant as, say, the Third, Eleventh, and Twelfth Amendments to the Constitution. The same observation may be made in connection with changes in the organic law of other nations.

#### 4. Judicial Revision

The power of the courts to interpret the Constitution necessarily involves the power to revise the constitution. For example, the Fourteenth Amendment to the Constitution of the United States specifies that "no State shall . . . deny to any person within its jurisdiction the equal protection of the laws." In the case of *Plessy v. Ferguson* (1896) the Supreme Court held that the laws in southern states requiring racial segregation in transportation (and, by implication, laws requiring segregation in all other areas as well) are not violations of this clause *if* the facilities provided each race are substantially equal to those provided for the other races. In the case of *Brown v. Board of Education of Topeka* (1954), however, the Court reversed this ruling and held that racial segregation *in itself* is a violation of the "equal protection" clause, and that all state laws requiring racial segregation in public schools are therefore unconstitutional. This decision, as many southern objectors quite correctly pointed out, changed the constitution almost as drastically as did the Fourteenth Amendment; but this was by no means the first time the Court had ever altered the constitution, nor will it be the last.

Perhaps the most striking example of the power of courts to change constitutional systems is provided by the contrast between Canadian and American constitutional development. The Canadian Constitution gives the provinces (Quebec, Ontario, and so on) a few specific or "delegated" powers and leaves all the rest to the national government. Yet the interpretation of the Constitution by the Judicial Committee of the British Privy Council (which held this power from 1867 to 1950) greatly whittled down national power and expanded the powers of the provinces. The Constitution of the United States, on the other hand, places the delegated powers in the hands of the national government and the reserved powers in the states. Yet the Supreme Court, by such devices as the doctrine of "implied powers,"[17] has so generously and broadly interpreted the national government's delegated powers that the whole balance of lawmaking power has shifted markedly away from the states. Thus it may be said that judicial interpretation has made the Canadian constitution more and more like the original American constitution, and vice versa. These judicial changes on both sides of the border are regarded by most political scientists as far more drastic revisions of the two constitutions than any wrought by formal amendments to either Constitution.

## 5. Change by Custom

We have already noted that the authors of the American Constitution intended the Electoral College system to remove the election of the President from popular pressure, and that the custom of popularly selecting electors pledged to candidates nominated by the national political parties has, without changing a word in the Constitution, converted the Electoral College into a machine for registering the people's choice for the presidency. This change in our constitutional system is at least as drastic as any brought about by the formal amendments.

Change by custom has altered the American constitutional system in several ways. Not only have customs changed the operation of parts of the Constitution in the manner just noted, but new customs have also changed old customs, and some have led to formal amendments. Before 1940, for example, it was generally understood that no President would serve more than two terms in office, and at least two presidential aspirants, U. S. Grant and Theodore Roosevelt, were rejected (by a political party and by the voters, respectively) in large degree because it was felt that their re-election would violate constitutional custom. In 1940 and 1944, however, President Franklin D. Roosevelt was elected to a third and fourth term; but the defenders of the no-third-term tradition managed, in 1951, to secure the adoption of the Twenty-second Amendment, which restored the old rule by prohibiting a President from serving more than two elective terms or a total of ten years in office. Thus a customary revision of the constitution in 1940 was again altered by a formal amendment to the Constitution in 1951.

---

[17] First laid down in the case of *McCulloch v. Maryland*, 4 Wheaton 316 (1819), this doctrine declares that the clause in Art. I, Sec. 8, which empowers Congress to make all laws "which shall be necessary and proper" for carrying into execution its delegated powers, means that Congress may pass any law which is "helpful" in executing its delegated powers and which is not expressly prohibited by the Constitution.

## Constitutions and the Individual

The data we have presented concerning the various forms and provisions of constitutions, written and unwritten, tell us a number of things worth knowing about how modern nations govern themselves. Yet beyond all the legalisms and formalities lie a number of deeper and more crucial questions. To what extent do modern constitutions limit and restrain governmental officials in their dealings with the people under their jurisdiction? By what means do they do so? What values and ideals are served where such limitations are effective and injured where they are not?

Where, in short, does the individual stand in relation to his nation and government and to all others? We shall deal with these urgent questions in the next three chapters, and we shall begin by describing what is meant by his status as a "citizen" or an "alien" and estimating what difference it makes to the way he lives his life.

# 7

## Citizens, Aliens,
## and Immigrants

In the modern state system, as we learned in Chapter 2, each person in the world has a definite legal status in relation to every independent sovereign nation. The status is usually that of citizen or alien, but there are also the hybrid statuses of the dual citizen, the stateless person, and the immigrant.

The purpose of the present chapter is to examine how each of these statuses is regarded by different nations, with a view to discovering not only their legal character but also their political and social consequences.

## Citizens

### The Meaning of "Citizenship"[1]

#### In Political Theory

The earliest basis for human association and organization was kinship—the tie of relationships based on common biological family trees or, in some cases, marriage or adoption. For many thousands of years in the dawn of man's history human beings were divided into clans or tribes, and "membership" in such groups was exclusively a matter of sharing kinship with the other persons in the group. In many present-day primitive societies kinship remains the basic principle of social membership and cohesion.

---

[1] See Charles H. Maxson, *Citizenship* (New York: Oxford University Press, 1930), Ch. 1; and H. Mark Roelofs, *The Tension of Citizenship* (New York: Holt, Rinehart and Winston, Inc., 1957).

The city-states of ancient Greece, however, introduced—without totally abandoning the kinship principle—a new basis for membership and cohesion: that of loyalty to a political society made up of persons who were not necessarily kinfolk. The "city," in other words, was to some extent a body of like-minded persons in the sense that they all stood in the same relationships of loyalty, obligations, and privileges to its institutions, traditions, and customs, and were not merely a body of kinship relatives. A "citizen" was a person who partook of these relationships, not merely someone's son or cousin or wife.

The modern conception of citizenship, which underlies and illuminates the legal rules we shall describe in a moment, stems from this ancient Greek attitude. In every modern nation citizenship implies a special status *not* automatically given to all persons who happen to be physically present within the nation's borders—a status that includes both obligations and benefits.

The basic obligation of citizenship is allegiance and loyalty to the nation. A citizen is expected to place his nation's interests and welfare above those of any other nation. When he knowingly and willfully works against his nation's interests for the benefit of some other nation, especially in time of war, he is guilty of treason. Treason, moreover, is everywhere regarded as one of the gravest crimes a person can commit, and convicted traitors are usually executed. The citizen's specific obligations stemming from this basic duty include such matters as obeying the nation's laws, paying its taxes, and serving in its armed forces when called upon to do so. (These obligations are not unique to citizens, however; as we shall see below, most nations also impose them on aliens.)

The citizen has two basic privileges: the ability, upon attaining what the nation regards as adulthood, to participate in its governmental decision-making processes by such means as voting and holding public office; and the right to the protection of his life and property by his nation at home or abroad. Thus, in most modern nations only a citizen may vote and hold public office, and only a citizen may legitimately call upon the government to intervene on his behalf when some foreign nation unjustly or unlawfully jails him or confiscates his property.

## In Law

The status of citizenship in international law is not at present entirely clear or universally agreed upon, but there is general agreement on at least the following propositions. In strict legal terms *"citizenship" means membership in a nation.* Some nations use the term "subject" or "national" as synonymous with "citizen," while others reserve the term "national" for persons who, while not full-fledged citizens, are nevertheless not citizens of any other nation and are under the legal protection of the nations claiming them as "nationals" (for example, before 1924 most American Indians were "nationals" but not "citizens" of the United States; but in that year Congress made them all citizens).

Each nation now decides for itself what persons are its own citizens, and no other nation or international body has the legal power to override its decisions. This basic rule may be subject to some limitations in international law (e.g., no nation could confer its citizenship upon every person in the world and have that act recognized and accepted by other nations or by international law),[2] but it remains the basic rule, and thereby creates a number of complications. For one thing, the nationality laws of most nations are highly complicated and contain a great many qualifications and exceptions. For another, basic nationality rules vary somewhat and their details vary greatly from nation to nation. It is impossible, consequently, to make more than a few general statements about the legal rules of citizenship that apply to all nations. A person who wishes to learn the details of any particular nation's rules must go to that nation's statute books, administrative regulations, and court decisions. In such a general survey as we are conducting here only the general rules and their most common variations can be described.[3]

What follows, therefore, is a description of the rules and variations governing the acquisition and termination of citizenship, concluded by a brief description of some of the major complications which stem from the fact that each nation legally determines for itself what persons are and are not its citizens.

### Acquisition of Citizenship

#### By Birth

Generally speaking, every modern nation prescribes that a person may acquire its citizenship either by birth or by naturalization. In determining which persons shall be considered its "native-born" citizens (i.e., those who acquire their citizenship because of the circumstances of their birth), each nation follows one or the other or a combination of the following two basic legal principles.

*Jus Sanguinis.* This rule, literally meaning "the law of blood," prescribes that *citizenship is determined by parentage*—that is, a person

---

[2] See the relevant discussion and cases in Manley O. Hudson, ed., *Cases on International Law* (3d ed.; St. Paul, Minn.: West Publishing Company, 1951), Ch. 4.

[3] The most complete collection of the rules of various nations for acquiring and losing citizenship is United Nations Legislative Service, *Laws concerning Nationality* (New York: United Nations Publication, 1954/1959). For a general discussion of the legal complications, see Paul Weis, *Nationality and Statelessness in International Law* (London: Stevens & Sons, Ltd., 1956).

acquires the citizenship of his parents regardless of the place where he is born. It is the older of the two principles and was the basic rule of the ancient Greek city-states and the Roman republic and empire. It became incorporated in the Napoleonic code (a codification and modernization of the principles of Roman law completed by the orders of Napoleon in 1804). It remains the basic rule of citizenship in those nations whose legal systems are based upon Roman rather than Anglo-Saxon law (see Chapter 20). A typical statement of it may be found in the Ethiopian Nationality Act of 1930, which declares that "any person born to an Ethiopian, man or woman, in Ethiopia or abroad, is an Ethiopian subject."[4]

*Jus Soli.* This rule, literally meaning "the law of place," prescribes that *citizenship is determined by place of birth*—that is, a person acquires the citizenship of the nation in whose territory and under whose jurisdiction he is born regardless of the citizenship of his parents. This principle originated in feudal England, where all ranks of society—serfs, peasants, freemen, and nobles alike—were regarded as legally attached to the soil on which they lived; a person born on soil whose title was granted by the King of England thereby acquired not only an economic relationship to the land but also a political relationship to the king and the realm. It remains the basic rule of citizenship in those nations whose legal systems are based upon Anglo-Saxon common law. A typical statement of it may be found in the first section of the Fourteenth Amendment to the Constitution of the United States, which declares that "all persons born . . . in the United States, and subject to the jurisdiction thereof, are citizens of the United States and of the State wherein they reside."

Nowadays only a few nations (e.g., Ethiopia, Finland, and Hungary) base their nationality laws solely on the principle of the *jus sanguinis*, and none entirely on the principle of the *jus soli*. Most use either the *jus sanguinis* somewhat modified by the *jus soli* (e.g., France, Italy, and Syria) or the *jus soli* somewhat modified by the *jus sanguinis* (e.g., Argentina, India, and the Soviet Union).

The nationality laws of the United States are an example of the last of these four types. In accordance with the *jus soli* rule in the Fourteenth Amendment, all persons born in the United States—with the exception of children born on foreign public ships in United States territorial waters, or to foreign diplomats, or to heads of foreign nations, or to enemies in hostile occupation of the nation, all of whom are considered to be not legally subject to United States jurisdiction—now automatically become American citizens. Congress has also added a number of circumstances in which, according to the principle of the *jus sanguinis*, citizenship is granted to children of American parents born outside American jurisdiction. For example,

---

[4] Reproduced in *Laws concerning Nationality*, p. 147.

a child born abroad of American parents automatically becomes a "native-born" American citizen if at least one of his parents had been physically present in the United States or one of its possessions prior to his birth. A child born abroad of parents one of whom is an American citizen and the other an alien is regarded as a native-born citizen if the citizen parent had been physically present in the United States or one of its possessions for ten years prior to the birth, and if at least five of these years were spent after the age of fourteen. Such a child will lose his citizenship, however, unless he comes to the nation before he is twenty-three and lives here for at least five continuous years between his fourteenth and twenty-eighth birthdays.

The overwhelming proportion of citizens of the United States, however, have acquired their citizenship either by birth within United States territory and being subject to United States jurisdiction or by naturalization.

## By Naturalization

PROCESSES. Every modern nation establishes its own processes of naturalization—that is, processes whereby it bestows its citizenship upon persons who have not acquired it by birth. These are usually people who were citizens of some other nation before their naturalization, but sometimes they are "stateless persons," who, as we shall see below, are legally the citizens of no nation.

Sometimes nations bestow citizenship upon all the inhabitants of a particular area, usually one acquired by purchase or conquest, without requiring individual applications by and examinations of such persons. This process is known as *collective naturalization,* and the United States used it to grant citizenship to the inhabitants of such acquired territories as Louisiana, Florida, New Mexico, Alaska, Texas, Hawaii, Puerto Rico, the Virgin Islands, and also (in 1924) to the Indian tribes within the United States.

The more common process, however, is that of *individual naturalization.* Each nation permits certain noncitizens to apply individually for naturalization. It specifies certain conditions they must satisfy, establishes procedures for determining whether or not they qualify, and, after ascertaining that they have passed all the tests, bestows citizenship.

REQUIREMENTS. The qualifications required vary considerably in detail from nation to nation, but most nations impose some version of the following general tests. *Residence:* the applicant must have lived in the nation for a certain period (e.g., one year in Great Britain, five years in the United States, twelve years in Switzerland) prior to his naturalization. *Familiarity with the language:* the applicant must have a certain minimum level of understanding of the nation's language. *Moral character:* the applicant must be of "good moral character," however that may be defined by the particular nation. *Understanding of the nation's political institutions:* some nations (e.g., the United States and Argentina) require the applicant to display a minimum level of understanding of the nation's political institutions, while others (e.g., Great Britain and Japan) do not. *Nonsupport of revolutionary organizations and doctrines:* some nations (e.g., the United States and Japan) require that the applicant neither believe in, advocate, nor freely belong to organizations that support opposition to organized government; while others (e.g., Great Britain and Canada) make no such requirement. *Oath of allegiance:* when the applicant has passed all other tests, he is finally required to take an oath of allegiance to the nation and thereby forswear allegiance to his former nation and all others. He then becomes a citizen.

THE STATUS OF NATURALIZED CITIZENS.   Most nations make no distinction whatever between the statuses of nativeborn and naturalized citizens. The Constitution of the United States, however, stipulates that only a native-born citizen may be elected President or Vice-President. A naturalized citizen may be elected to the Senate or the House of Representatives, but only after having been a citizen for nine years or seven years, respectively.[5] Otherwise, a naturalized United States citizen enjoys the same status as a native-born compatriot, although his citizenship may be terminated for reasons that do not apply to the native-born.

## Termination of Citizenship

### By Expatriation

Most nations, including the United States, have established two general kinds of procedures whereby citizenship may be terminated. The process of *expatriation* applies to native-born and naturalized citizens alike, whereas the process of *denaturalization* applies only to naturalized citizens.

A citizen provides the most common legal grounds for his expatriation when he voluntarily and knowingly takes an oath of allegiance to a foreign nation, renounces his allegiance to his own nation, votes in the elections of, or holds public office in, a foreign nation, serves in the armed forces of a foreign nation without the consent of his own nation, or commits treason. Many nations, again including the United States, usually deprive convicted felons of some political privileges, such as the right to vote and to hold public office; but they do not deprive felons of their citizenship unless they have been convicted of such crimes as treason or subversion.

---

[5] Art. II, Sec. 1; Art. I, Secs. 2 and 3.

## By Denaturalization

Many nations (including the United States) revoke the citizenship of a naturalized citizen for such causes as committing fraud or perjury in the naturalization process, or affiliating with a subversive organization within a certain period of time following naturalization.

## Some Complications in Nationality and Citizenship

### Dual Citizenship

Since each nation determines for itself who are and are not its citizens, it is quite possible for a person to be regarded as a citizen by two different nations. A number of people in the modern world are in just this position. Suppose, for example, a Yugoslavian couple move to the United States and have a child before they become United States citizens. According to the *jus soli* principle of the Fourteenth Amendment, their child is a native-born American citizen, and the United States will regard him as such. But the Yugoslavian Nationality Act of 1946 is based upon the *jus sanguinis* and provides that, regardless of where he is born, a child acquires Yugoslavian citizenship "if both his parents are nationals of the Federal People's Republic of Yugoslavia."[6] Thus, Yugoslavia will regard the child as a Yugoslavian citizen. Is he, then, an American or a Yugoslavian? The answer is that he is an American so far as the United States is concerned, a Yugoslavian so far as Yugoslavia is concerned, and (since the two nations have no treaty by which he can be awarded to one nation or the other by mutual agreement) a "dual citizen" so far as international law is concerned. If this child visits Yugoslavia after reaching the age of twenty-two and claims the benefits of Yugoslavian citizenship, he automatically loses his American citizenship unless he takes a special oath of allegiance before an American diplomatic or consular official within three years of his arrival in Yugoslavia.

By the same token, if an American couple have moved to Canada and made it their legal domicile without applying for Canadian citizenship and have a child in Canada, that child becomes a native-born American citizen by American law and a native-born Canadian citizen by Canadian law; he has, in effect, twenty-five years in which to chose which of the two citizenships he prefers to keep permanently.

Most dual citizens, especially those who have American citizenship as one of their two statuses and wish to keep it, are well advised to check with officials of the Immigration and Naturalization Service in the Department of Justice before they become twenty-five and before they travel or

---

[6] Reproduced in *Laws concerning Nationality*, p. 554.

vote or exercise any other privilege in the other nations which regard them as citizens.

## Statelessness [7]

The fact that each nation legally determines for itself what persons are and are not its citizens not only gives a number of persons dual citizenship but also leaves a number of others with no legal citizenship whatever. They are called "stateless," and in general they are persons who, for one reason or another, are not regarded as citizens by the nations in which they were born and have not yet acquired the citizenship of any other nation.

There are two main categories of stateless persons. The first is that of the *de jure* stateless—that is, persons who are not legally the citizens of any nation, either because at birth or subsequently they were not given any citizenship, or because during their lifetime they lost their citizenship and did not acquire any other. *De jure* stateless persons include (1) children born in certain *jus sanguinis* nations of stateless or unknown parents (some *jus sanguinis* nations grant citizenship to such children under certain conditions, but others apply the rule strictly and thereby leave the children stateless); (2) women who are citizens of a nation (e.g., Spain and Haiti) that deprives women of their citizenship when they marry aliens irrespective of whether they acquire new nationality by marriage or not, and who marry citizens of a nation (e.g., the United States, Great Britain, Argentina, and Yugoslavia) that does not automatically confer citizenship upon the alien wives of its citizens; (3) naturalized citizens who have lost their citizenship; and (4) persons who have been expatriated (see above) but have not acquired any other citizenship.

The second category is that of the *de facto* stateless. It includes persons who have left the country of which they were citizens, and no longer enjoy its protection and assistance, either because its authorities refuse to grant them assistance and protection, or because the emigrants themselves renounce it. In international law the status of *de facto* stateless persons differs appreciably from that of the *de jure* stateless, but in practice and in terms of human suffering they are equally miserable.

Most stateless persons in modern times are of the *de facto* variety. The Russian Revolution of October, 1917, for example, left in its wake over a million anticommunist escapees who had lost or renounced their Russian citizenship without acquiring another. The fascist regimes in Italy, Germany, and Spain before World War II produced nearly another million stateless escapees. The postwar formation of new nations and new regimes

---

[7] The most useful studies of stateless persons are Weis, *op. cit.*; and United Nations, Department of Social Affairs, *A Study of Statelessness* (New York: United Nations Publications, 1949).

in old nations has created the greatest flood of refugees in history. Over 2,000,000 persons fled the newly formed communist satellite regimes in Eastern Europe after 1945. Some 1,400,000 French, Italian, Greek, Cypriot, and Jewish residents of Algeria, Libya, Morocco, Tunisia, and Egypt became refugees after the new regimes took over. After Indonesia became independent in 1949 an estimated 250,000 Dutch and Eurasian residents became refugees. After the Russians crushed the Hungarian "freedom fighters'" anticommunist revolt in 1956, over 200,000 rebels fled. Fidel Castro's communist regime in Cuba drove over 160,000 refugees to the United States.[8]

The International Refugee Organization was created in 1946 to feed, clothe, house, and relocate such refugees; in 1951 the United Nations established a High Commissioner for Refugees who took over the IRO's operations. Both agencies urged traditional immigrant-receiving nations to relax their immigration restrictions to permit the entry of refugees with a view to their eventual naturalization, and most responded to a degree. From 1945 to 1954 the United States took in 338,000; Australia, 187,600; Canada, 174,500; Israel, 132,000; and Great Britain, 86,000.[9] A majority of the refugees have been permanently settled; but by the early 1960's there were still over ten million stateless refugees living in "DP" camps all over the world awaiting permanent settlement and citizenship—a bitter testimony to man's inhumanity to man.

The long-range problem of statelessness, with all the insecurity and fear it inflicts on its victims, will never be solved so long as international anarchy in the determination of citizenship continues—as it seems likely to do for some time to come.

## Aliens

Every modern nation must decide what to do about the aliens—persons who are not its citizens—under its jurisdiction. These aliens fall into one or the other of two general classes: temporary visitors, who leave their own nations for more or less specific purposes, and who intend to be gone for only a limited period of time; and resident aliens, who make a foreign nation their permanent home and intend to stay indefinitely, but who may or may not seek naturalization.

Such aliens have always posed problems for the nations receiving them,

---

[8] The most complete survey of the postwar refugee problem is Joseph B. Schechtman, *The Refugee in the World* (New York: A. S. Barnes and Company, 1963).

[9] These figures are taken from the Annual Reports of the High Commissioner for Refugees to the General Assembly, published by the United Nations, for the years 1952–1955.

but for many nations the technical revolution in transportation since the early nineteenth century has helped to multiply both the number of aliens and the problems they create. When crossing the Atlantic meant an expensive, uncomfortable, dangerous, and dreary voyage of months, few persons would undertake it unless they expected to remain on the other side the rest of their lives; hence many who wished to make a permanent change would decide it was not worth the bother. Now that a crossing is a relatively cheap, comfortable, safe, and pleasant voyage of a few days or a flight of a few hours, many people come for temporary visits as well as for permanent residence.

Although both types of aliens create similar problems for the nations receiving them, the two types are sufficiently different to justify separate consideration.

### *Temporary Visitors*

#### Who They Are and What They Want

Some of the types of persons who make temporary visits to foreign nations are diplomatic officials—ambassadors, ministers, attachés, and consuls—and their employees, who represent their nations abroad for limited periods of service; tourists, who wish to travel in foreign nations for recreation and culture; businessmen and entertainers, who wish to sell their goods and services in foreign nations; students, who wish to study in foreign schools, and teachers, who wish to teach in them; travelers, who merely pass through certain foreign lands in order to reach others or to return to their native lands; and crewmen of ships and airplanes, who spend time abroad in the course of their duties.

Most temporary visitors are tourists, and Americans in particular are inveterate tourists—so much so, that it is said that in "the season" (from June to September) of each year since 1945 there have been more Americans than Britons in Piccadilly Circus and Westminster Abbey, and more Americans than Frenchmen in the sidewalk cafes along the *Champs Elysées* or riding in the elevators of the Eiffel Tower.

#### The Governmental Problems That They Create

Most nations are delighted to welcome tourists, especially if they are willing and able to spend freely and thereby increase foreign exchange. But tourists, like all other temporary foreign visitors, are a mixed blessing for any government, for they create a number of problems. If, for example, a government wishes to control the number and type of persons it admits as potential permanent residents (see below), it must make sure that the temporary visitors do not remain indefinitely. If it wishes to exclude foreign spies, saboteurs, criminals, paupers, lunatics, subversives, and so on, it must make sure that they are not admitted even temporarily. If it wishes to secure for its own citizens traveling abroad the same rights and privileges granted to its foreign visitors, it must exercise some control over the latter.

### How Governments Deal with These Problems[10]

From the very origins of the modern state system until the outbreak of World War I, most Western nations had alternately adopted and abandoned systems of legal regulation applying to temporary foreign visitors several times. From the early nineteenth century to 1914 few nations imposed any such regulations. After 1918, however, all nations established a number of legal devices regulating the entry, stay, and exit of temporary foreign visitors, and such regulations now seem to be permanently established everywhere.[11]

The main devices used are as follows.

PASSPORTS.  A passport is a document issued by a nation to one of its citizens authenticating his identity and citizenship and authorizing him to travel in certain—but sometimes not all—foreign nations. Most nations require their citizens to obtain passports before they travel abroad; and by issuing passports only to certain persons a government can control both the nature and the number of its citizens who leave the country. Rigidly restricting the number of passports issued, for example, has been one, though not the only, device by which the communist nations have drawn the Iron Curtain between themselves and the rest of the world. Most nations grant entry only to those foreigners who bear valid passports, so that passports are one way of controlling entry as well as exit.

VISAS.  A visa is an official permission to enter or leave its territory granted by a nation to a foreign traveler, usually given in the form of a statement stamped on the traveler's passport. Some nations (the United States is one) require a traveler to display both a passport and a visa obtained in advance at a consular office abroad in order to enter. Other nations require passports but no visas, and a few require neither for visitors from certain favored nations. An entry visa, then, can be used as a device to control the number and nature of foreigners seeking entry, and an exit visa can be used to ensure that the foreign traveler seeking to leave has paid all necessary taxes and fees, complied with all laws, and so on.

---

[10] A useful though incomplete summary of various regulations imposed on temporary foreign visitors by the various nations is UNESCO, *Travel Abroad* (rev. ed.; Paris: UNESCO, 1953).

[11] A brief but illuminating history of such regulations is given in Egidio Reale, "Passport," *Encyclopaedia of the Social Sciences* (New York: The Macmillan Company, 1937), XII, 13–16.

HEALTH REGULATIONS. Many nations, including the United States, require all persons seeking entry, as well as their own citizens who have been abroad, to produce documents attesting to their immunization against such diseases as smallpox, typhoid, yellow fever, and cholera.

CUSTOMS AND CURRENCY REGULATIONS. In addition to the regulations intended to control the number and kind of persons who enter and leave, most nations also have a number of regulations designed to control the flow of trade and currency across their borders. Most nations, for example, limit the amount of foreign-purchased goods a traveler may bring in duty-free. Most nations, particularly those in short supply of foreign exchange, also restrict the amount of their own currency that may be taken out, either by their own citizens or by foreign visitors.

### The Selective Control of International Travel as an Instrument of Foreign Policy

Since the regulations outlined above permit a nation to control the number and nature of persons and goods entering and leaving its territory, they can be and often are used as instruments of foreign policy. A particular nation can demonstrate good will and friendship toward another by facilitating travel and trade between them; conversely, it can demonstrate its distrust of the other by making such interchange difficult or impossible.

All United States passports, for example, are now automatically valid for travel to any nation in the Western Hemisphere, Western Europe, and certain other areas; but at the present writing no American passport is valid for travel to Albania, Cuba, or the "communist-controlled parts of China, Korea, and Vietnam."

The Western European democracies will admit any American or citizen of most of the other NATO nations on his passport alone but require both passports and entry visas from citizens of the communist nations. The Soviet Union and the other communist nations require both passports and entry visas for the entry of all foreign citizens and also transit visas for travel across their territories. The citizens of most nations, in short, find it considerably easier to enter and travel in nations with whom their own government is friendly than in nations with whom it is unfriendly.

### The Legal Status of Aliens

Most nations make it considerably more difficult for a foreigner to enter as a prospective resident alien, with no restriction upon the duration of his stay, than as a temporary visitor. The reason for this is clear: most nations' resident aliens become permanent additions to their populations, and many also become naturalized citizens. Most nations wish to control both the size and the ethnic and occupational compositions of their permanent populations, and so they impose more stringent restrictions upon both the total number and the individual qualifications of persons admitted as resident aliens than they apply to temporary foreign visitors.

Persons seeking admission as resident aliens are usually called "immigrants," and in the concluding section of this chapter we shall survey the general kinds of policies and laws modern nations have adopted to regulate immigration. Our present concern is the legal status of resident aliens and temporary visitors in the nations to which they have been admitted.

### In International Law[12]

The legal status given to each nation's resident aliens is to some extent fixed by certain generally accepted rules of international law. The basic rules are these: each nation decides for itself what persons, if any, it will admit as resident aliens; once they are in residence the nation need not accord them the same privileges and rights its citizens enjoy, but it must guarantee its resident aliens a certain "minimum standard of justice" in the protection of their rights of person and property. The specific content of this "minimum standard of justice" is nowhere spelled out in detail, but it is generally considered to prohibit only the more flagrant departures from a rather elementary standard of "fair treatment." It certainly does not include all the niceties of the free nations' conception of "due process of law" described in Chapter 8. Whatever guarantees it does include, however, it is clear that international law requires every nation to provide the minimum standards to the aliens under its jurisdiction even if they are not provided for its own citizens! If Saudi Arabia, for example, subjects certain of its own citizens to peonage and something approaching slavery, it may not legally subject aliens to such conditions.

But what happens if, say, Saudi Arabia fails to provide this minimum standard of justice to a citizen of the United States? How can this person or the American authorities make Saudi Arabia obey the rules? The United States may use the alternative of subjecting all Saudi Arabian persons and property under its jurisdiction to various penalties until Saudi Arabia resumes obeying the rules. If this fails, the United States has recourse to whatever other legal machinery and forces are available for the enforcement of international law. The present nature and effectiveness of such machinery and forces are complicated and vexing matters with which we shall deal in Chapter 23.

### In National Law

Within the limitations laid down by international law most nations give the aliens under their jurisdiction a legal status somewhat different from

---

[12] A useful summary is given in J. L. Brierly, *The Law of Nations* (6th ed.; New York: Oxford University Press, 1963), pp. 276–291.

that of citizens. Aliens, for instance, are required to assume many but not all of the obligations laid on citizens. Like citizens, they are expected to obey laws and pay taxes, but, unlike citizens, they are often exempt from military service and jury duty.

Aliens in most nations, moreover, do not have all the rights and privileges granted to citizens. Aliens, unlike citizens, usually cannot vote or hold public office. They may (as the United States has required them to do since 1940) have to register with public authorities. Their freedom of movement within the nation may be more restricted than a citizen's. They may be barred from engaging in such occupations as law and medicine. Perhaps the most important difference, however, is the fact that, since aliens are legally resident in a nation largely because of that nation's sufferance and, unlike its citizens, have no *right* of residence, they may be expelled at any time for any of a variety of reasons. The attorney general of the United States, for example, has broad discretionary power to deport any alien who in his opinion intends to engage in activities "prejudicial to the public interest" or "subversive to the national security"; but no American citizen can be deported until he has first been deprived of his citizenship by expatriation or denaturalization (see above).

In time of war the persons and property of enemy aliens may be restricted more severely than those of other aliens; but even enemy aliens are, by international law, supposed to receive the minimum standard of justice required for the treatment of all aliens.

### The Special Status of Diplomats[13]

According to one of the oldest rules of international law, diplomatic agents dispatched by one nation to another must be accorded special privileges and immunities. This rule is considered to be the logical and necessary result of the fact that diplomatic agents represent sovereign nations, and no nation may legally interfere with the sovereignty of another. Diplomatic agents, accordingly, are legally immune from the criminal jurisdiction of the nation in which they are serving and largely immune from its civil jurisdiction. If the Russian ambassador to the United States or one of his official assistants committed a murder, he could not be tried or convicted by American courts. In such a case the American government would no doubt declare him *persona non grata* and demand that the Russians recall him, which, according to international law, the Russians would have to do. If on his return to Russia his government failed to prosecute him, the United States would likely regard this failure as an "unfriendly act." But the point is that American courts could not try him as they could try any other kind of alien charged with murder. If the British ambassador or one of his official

---

[13] See *ibid.*, pp. 254–267.

assistants refused to pay his debts, he could not be sued in an American court—although, again, American authorities could demand and obtain his recall.

# Immigrants

## The Nature and Direction of Migration

### Before World War II

An immigrant is a person who seeks entry to a foreign nation for an indefinite period of time and for the presumed purpose of permanent residence. The migration of such persons from Europe to other parts of the world, particularly the Western Hemisphere, began in the sixteenth century and has persisted ever since. Migration from the Far East did not begin until the nineteenth century but increased rapidly soon thereafter. Most migration has moved from thickly populated to thinly populated areas. The principal motive of migrants has apparently been their desire to improve their economic status, but many have also sought to get away from what they have regarded as oppressive political regimes.

The main direction of intercontinental migration before World War II is shown in Figures 12 and 13.

As these Figures show, Western Europe and particularly the British Isles were the main emigrant-sending areas in the nineteenth and early twentieth centuries, and the United States was by far the greatest single receiver of immigrants, followed at some distance by the nations of the British Commonwealth, Argentina, and Brazil.

The great volume of immigrants received by the United States before World War II is shown by the fact that between 1820 and 1940 a total

## Table 3.   Reception of Immigrants, 1945–1961

| NATION RECEIVING IMMIGRANTS | IMMIGRANTS RECEIVED | | TOTAL |
|---|---|---|---|
| | *1945–1953* | *1954–1961* | *1945–1961* |
| United States | 1,628,775 | 2,188,438 | 3,817,213 |
| Canada | 980,868 | 932,060 | 1,912,928 |
| Australia | 800,871 | 859,377 | 1,660,248 |
| Israel (including Palestine, 1945–1947) | 785,002 | 252,690 | 1,037,692 |
| Argentina | 690,424 | 205,118 | 895,542 |

SOURCE: These data are taken from the United Nations *Demographic Yearbooks* (New York: United Nations Publications, 1948–1962).

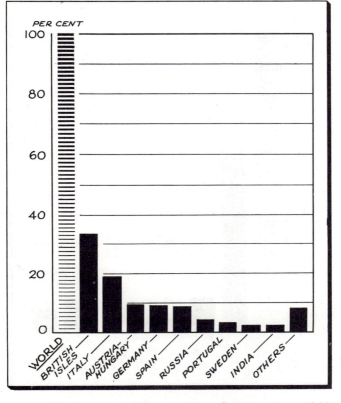

*Figure 12.* Sources of Intercontinental Emigration, 1846–1932.

of 38,290,443 were admitted.[14] They came in three great waves: the first, from 1820 to 1890, consisted mainly of persons from Great Britain, Ireland, Germany, and Scandinavia; the second, from 1890 to 1920, was made up principally of immigrants from Central and Eastern Europe, particularly from Italy, Austria-Hungary, and Russia; and the third and by far the smallest, from 1920 to 1940, was composed largely of ordinary immigrants from Italy, Canada, and Mexico, and refugees from the fascist regimes of Germany and Italy.

### Since World War II

Since the end of World War II in 1945 the basic prewar pattern of immigration has persisted, but, except in the United States and Australia, its volume has noticeably slacked off, as is shown in Table 3.

---

[14] Cf. William S. Bernard, Carolyn Zeleny, and Henry Miller, eds., *American Immigration Policy* (New York: Harper & Row, Publishers, 1950), Table 1 on p. 8.

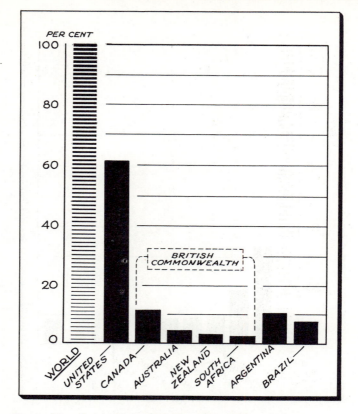

*Figure 13.*   Destination of Immigration, 1820–1930.

## The Regulation of Immigration in the United States

### 1. Immigration Policy before 1952

On a tablet at the base of the Statue of Liberty in New York Harbor are engraved these words:

> Give me your tired, your poor,
> Your huddled masses yearning to breathe free.
> The wretched refuse of your teeming shore.
> Send these, the homeless, tempest-tost to me.
> I lift my lamp beside the golden door!

These words are a poetic and accurate description of the immigration policy followed by the United States during the first century of its national existence. From 1783 until 1882 the national government freely admitted any and all foreigners who wished to make their homes here, and a number of states and private individuals even offered inducements to attract immi-

SEARCH FOR AN OPEN DOOR

*Figure 14.* World War II Refugees Have Found Few Wide-open Doors. (Copyright Low—London Evening Standard.)

grants. This policy, together with the attractiveness of the United States for so many Europeans and Asians, gave the nation its rank as the world's greatest immigrant-receiving country.

In the 1840's, however, a political movement of ever-increasing strength developed against admitting more Irish Catholics. Its adherents organized the secret Order of the Star Spangled Banner and were generally known as "Know-Nothings" since they were sworn to profess ignorance to any outsider who queried them about their order. After the Civil War the "nativists" were joined by the emerging trade-union movement—first the Knights of Labor and later the American Federation of Labor. The latter, though disavowing any prejudice against any ethnic or national group, sought to restrict immigration in an effort to reduce competition from cheap foreign labor, especially from the Chinese coolies who had been brought over in the 1860's and 1870's to help build the western railroads.

As a result of these pressures Congress enacted the Chinese Exclusion Act in 1882 and also prohibited the entry of such undesirable aliens as paupers, lunatics, and criminals. During the next four decades Congress added a number of other categories of inadmissible aliens.

## 2. The National-Origins Quota System after 1921

These selective regulations did not reduce the total volume of immigration, and the period from 1881 to 1920 produced the heaviest volume of immigrants in our history—a total of 23,465,374, primarily from Central and Eastern Europe.[15] From 1890 on an increasing number of Americans pressed for the adoption of a system of regulations that would not only drastically restrict the total number of immigrants but would also maintain the predominance of Western and Northern European influence in our population.

In 1921 this group won a great victory when Congress enacted the national-origins quota system that has been the basis of our immigration policy ever since. The 1921 acts have been amended a number of times, but the following basic provisions have been retained. The system, first, places limitations on the total number of immigrants that may enter each year; and, second, it sets a quota for each immigrant-sending nation, permitting each nation to send each year only the number of immigrants allowed by its quota. The quotas, moreover, are allocated in such a way as to maintain America's present ethnic composition: each nation's quota was set at the same percentage of the total number of immigrants as its percentage of the total American population was in the 1920 census.

## 3. The McCarran-Walter Act of 1952

In 1952 Congress revised and assembled in one piece of legislation all our immigration regulations. In certain respects the new law, the McCarran-Walter Act, liberalized immigration policy: it abolished all previous exclusions of immigrants from Asian nations, including China, though it assigned them very small quotas. It permitted the alien husbands, wives, and minor children of American citizens to enter outside the quotas assigned to their native countries. But it retained the basic machinery and underlying ideology of the national-origins quota system and designed the quota regulations so that the proportions of immigrants permitted from nations outside Western and Northern Europe were little if any larger than before 1952. President Truman vetoed the act mainly on the ground that it unduly discriminated against immigrants from such nations, but Congress passed it over his veto.

## 4. The Immigration Act of 1965

The national-origins quota system came under increasing fire after 1952. It was attacked on two main grounds: the nontransferability of the quotas unduly restricted the total number of immigrants, and the use of 1920 as the base discriminated against persons from central and eastern Europe while allowing unlimited entry to Latin Americans. Presidents Truman,

---

[15] *Ibid.*, p. 8.

Eisenhower, and Kennedy all vainly sought its repeal, but in 1965 President Johnson persuaded Congress to act. The new legislation eliminated the national-origins quota system entirely, authorized the admission of up to 350,000 immigrants per year, limited immigrants from any one country to 20,000 per year, put an annual ceiling of 120,000 on immigrants from all Latin American countries, and established a system of preferential admissions favoring persons with close relatives already in the United States and persons with special skills, talents, or education needed here. These provisions are among the world's most liberal.

### The Regulation of Immigration in Other Immigration-Receiving Nations

#### Canada and Australia[16]

Canada and Australia, as Figure 15 and Table 3 show, rank second and third respectively below the United States as the greatest immigrant-receiving nations both before and after World War II. Unlike the United

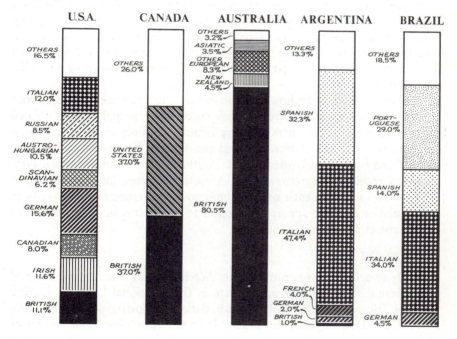

*Figure 15.* Ethnic Composition of Immigration to Principal Immigrant-Receiving Nations.

[16] The information in the text is drawn largely from *American Immigration Policy*, pp. 206–219.

States, however, neither of these nations has ever followed a policy of unrestricted immigration. From their national beginnings both Canada and Australia have imposed various restrictions on immigration intended to accomplish two main objectives: (1) to maintain the largely British ethnic composition of their populations, and especially to bar Asians; and (2) to attract mainly agricultural rather than industrial workers or members of the learned professions. In pursuit of the first objective Canada set up a system between the two world wars applying to immigrants from all nations except Great Britain and the United States, which distinguished between "preferred," "nonpreferred," and "other" countries. Immigrants from the "preferred" nations (those in Western Europe and Scandinavia) were admitted on terms similar to those applying to Great Britain. Immigrants from the "nonpreferred" nations (those in Central and Eastern Europe) were admitted only if they proposed to be agricultural workers or domestic servants. Immigrants from the "other" nations were admitted only by special permits, which were rarely given. Australia, as we learn in Chapter 9, has always pursued this first objective by firm adherence to its "white Australia" policy, which bars all Asian immigration. Both nations have sought the second objective by encouraging immigration of white agricultural workers, especially from Great Britain (and, in the case of Canada, also from the United States), through such measures as maintaining publicity agents abroad and paying part or all of the passage of desirable immigrants.

Since World War II, however, the immigration policies of both nations have changed somewhat. Pressure has successfully brought about revised restrictions which now encourage the increased immigration of industrial and professional workers from Central and Eastern Europe as well as from Great Britain and the United States. Neither Canada nor Australia, however, has relaxed its barriers against Asian immigrants, and neither seems likely to do so. While each nation is now making a serious effort to enlarge its population, neither apparently intends to permit any major alteration of its present ethnic composition.

### Argentina and Brazil[17]

Only two Latin American nations, Argentina and Brazil, have received any substantial number of immigrants in their national histories. During most of the nineteenth century both nations followed policies of unrestricted immigration; and the Preamble to the Argentine Constitution of 1853 even proclaimed the nation's desire to make itself a home "for all men

---

[17] See *ibid.*, pp. 219–231; William Lytle Schurz, *This New World: The Civilization of Latin America* (New York: E. P. Dutton & Co., Inc., 1954), pp. 228–234; and Robert D. Ochs, "A History of Argentine Immigration, 1853–1924," unpublished Ph.D. thesis in history, University of Illinois, 1939.

of the world who wish to establish themselves on Argentine soil." From the end of the nineteenth century onward, however, both nations placed an ever-growing number of restrictions upon immigration. First they excluded anarchists, diseased and disabled persons, gypsies, persons of bad moral character, and so on. Then they excluded certain immigrants on ethnic grounds, particularly Asians; and in 1934 Brazil adopted a national-origins quota system modeled upon that of the United States from 1921 to 1965.

In the years following World War II, however, both Argentina and Brazil have eased their restrictions upon immigration with a view to increasing their populations and especially to receiving European refugees with special industrial and professional skills. Like Canada and Australia, neither Argentina nor Brazil has relaxed its controls over the ethnic composition of immigration, and both nations have sought to encourage immigration from the European nations—mainly Italy, Spain, and Portugal—that have contributed most of their immigrants in the past.

## Israel[18]

One of the main, though not the only, reasons for the establishment of the nation of Israel in 1948 was the desire of Jewish "Zionist" leaders to provide a national home and haven for all Jewish refugees from oppression all over the world, whether by the fascists in Europe or the Arabs in the Middle East. As soon as the nation came into being, it adopted a policy of unlimited immigration for Jews. From 1948 to 1951 the Israeli government admitted over 700,000 refugees—a staggering total in view of the fact that Israel's total nonimmigrant population during that period was less than a million—and created a special government agency, the Absorption Department, to settle them and provide them with jobs.

Toward the end of this period, however, the Israeli government concluded that it simply could not feed, house, clothe, and find jobs for its immigrants if they continued to enter in such floods. And so in 1951 Israel put into effect a policy of selective immigration, admitting only those persons who could make an immediate contribution to the nation's economy—with the proviso that the new restrictions would apply only to immigrants from "countries in which there is no immediate danger to the Jewish population and from which Jews can freely emigrate." The government further announced that it wished to encourage immigration of Jews from Great Britain, South Africa, and North and South America.

The new immigration policy sharply reduced the volume of immigration from the annual range of 101,828 to 239,141 in the four years before the

---

[18] The author has found no general discussion of Israeli immigration policy, but the *Government Year Books*, published annually by the Israeli government, contain information on both policy toward and amount of immigration. The discussion in the text is taken from the volumes for the years 1952 to 1964.

policy went into effect to the rate of 23,375 in 1952, the first year the new policy operated. The rate has been stabilized at about the 1952 level since.

### Immigration Policy: A Summary

All the principal immigrant-receiving nations not only restrict the total number of immigrants permitted to enter each year but also control the kind of persons admitted. One of the main purposes of both kinds of restrictions in each nation is the prevention of any major alteration in the ethnic composition of its population. Whereas the ethnic controls imposed by the United States under its national-origins quota system are better known than those of the other nations—probably because more people wish to emigrate to the United States than to any of the others—the ethnic controls of the other nations have favored particular ethnic groups even more than have the American restrictions, as is shown by the data in Figure 15.

# 8

## The Rights of Man:

### *principles and problems*

We hold these truths to be self-evident, that all men are created equal, that they are endowed by their Creator with certain unalienable Rights, that among these are Life, Liberty and the Pursuit of Happiness. —That to secure these rights, Governments are instituted among Men, deriving their just powers from the consent of the governed,—That whenever any Form of Government becomes destructive of these ends, it is the Right of the People to alter or to abolish it, and to institute new Government, laying its foundation on such principles and organizing its powers in such form, as to them shall seem most likely to effect their Safety and Happiness.

THESE wingéd words are, of course, taken from the opening sentences of the American Declaration of Independence. Drafted mainly by Thomas Jefferson and adopted by the Continental Congress of the rebel American colonies on July 4, 1776, this document is probably the most widely known, succinct, and eloquent statement of the principles of the rights of man.

These principles were not, however, newly created by Jefferson and his fellow revolutionaries, nor did they lose their significance after 1783 when the colonies achieved their independence. As Jefferson himself later pointed out, the purpose of the Declaration was "not to find out new principles" but rather "to be an expression of the American mind" based upon "the harmonizing sentiments of the day."[1] Those sentiments grew from the colonists' devotion to a political philosophy whose ancient lineage we shall trace in a moment. And their significance in our own time is revealed when

---

[1] Quoted in Carl Becker, *The Declaration of Independence* (New York: Harcourt, Brace & World, Inc., 1922), pp. 25–26. This work is a classic statement of the nature and sources of the Declaration's underlying philosophy.

many men speak of the present struggle in world politics as basically a contest between the "free" and the "totalitarian" nations—that is, between nations who are devoted to the principles of the rights of man and attempt to realize them in their governing systems, and nations who are committed to other principles and show little or no concern for the protection of human liberty.

## What Is a "Civil Right"?

Most people closely associate, and properly so, the terms "civil rights" and "freedom." What, then, is freedom? As Roger H. Soltau points out:

> Originally to be free was not to be a slave, to have legal guaranteed control over one's person and this is still its essential meaning. To be free is not to be prevented from doing what one wants to do, and not being forced to do what one dislikes doing. Any limitation of this two-fold power is an interference with freedom, however excellent its motives, however necessary its action.[2]

Yet in every democracy, however constitutional or libertarian, all men's freedoms are, *by general agreement*, subject to many limitations. Many parents spank their children for using profanity, but no one considers the children's freedom of speech violated. Governments prohibit men from selling narcotics to high school pupils, but no one says the freedom to engage in the business of one's choosing has been wrongfully limited. Governments also prohibit devotees of one religion from murdering the followers of another, and yet no one protests that freedom of religion has been abridged. Evidently a man's "civil rights" include only *some* freedoms, but they are not a blank check to act as he pleases in all circumstances without any external restraint.

What kind of freedom, then, is a civil right? As we shall use the term in this book, it is *a constitutionally defined and governmentally protected area of freedom for individual persons*. Civil rights, as thus defined, fall into two general classes: (1) *limitations on government*, a series of things which government is forbidden to do to the individual, intended to preserve "those opportunities, the absence of which would deprive him of something essential"; and (2) *obligations of government*, a series of duties government is pledged to perform for the individual, intended to preserve "those liberties without which man cannot be at his best or give of his best—what is needful to the adequate development and expression of his personality."[3] Before we describe the specific areas of freedom generally

---

[2] *An Introduction to Politics* (London: Longmans, Green & Co., Ltd., 1951), p. 127.
[3] *Ibid.*, p. 135.

included in these two classes, however, we must first examine the underlying principles of the rights of man and take stock of some of the considerations that have impelled the free nations to establish and protect civil rights.

## "We Hold these Truths to Be Self-evident": Rights as Ends

### The Argument

Just about everyone who believes in governmental protection of human rights bases his conviction on one or the other or a combination of these two positions: (1) civil rights are ends in themselves, and their preservation is not only the main function of government but the very reason for its existence; and (2) civil rights, while not ends in themselves, are indispensable means to the creation and maintenance of the good life and the good society.

Nearly all those who argued and fought for civil rights in England and America in the seventeenth and eighteenth centuries did so on the basis of their deep commitment to the first of these two positions. Probably its most influential exponent was the English political philosopher John Locke. In the brilliant and widely read two treatises *Of Civil Government* (1690), Locke raised the central question, Under what circumstances and for what reasons should men obey the commands of government? The answer, he contended, must be based on the fact that men join together in civil societies and establish governments for only one reason: to better secure the personal rights to life, liberty, and property that naturally belong to all men equally simply because they are human beings. As he put it, "The great and chief end . . . of men uniting into commonwealths, and putting themselves under government, is the preservation of their property [i.e., their natural rights]."[4] When a government fails to preserve these rights and thereby ceases to serve the end for which it was created, Locke continued, the citizens have the right—indeed, the duty—to overthrow it:

> Whenever the legislators endeavour to take away and destroy the [rights] of the people . . . they put themselves into a state of war with the people, who are thereupon absolved from any farther obedience, and . . . have a right to resume their original liberty, and by the establishment of a new legislative (such as they shall think fit) provide for their own safety and security, which is the end for which they are in society.[5]

---

[4] John Locke, *Two Treatises of Civil Government* (Everyman's edition; London: J. M. Dent & Sons, Ltd., 1924), Ch. IX, p. 180.

[5] *Ibid.*, Ch. XIX, p. 229.

Locke's conviction that the sole end and justification of government is the preservation of human rights was shared by most of the rebel American colonists and became the basic argument of their Declaration of Independence. "Governments are instituted among Men," the Declaration proclaims, "to secure these rights"; and "whenever any Form of Government becomes destructive of these ends, it is the Right of the People to alter or to abolish it."

Locke's position was also affirmed by the Declaration of the Rights of Man and of the Citizen proclaimed by the revolutionary French National Assembly on August 26, 1789. "The aim of every political association," the French Declaration declares, "is the preservation of the natural and imprescriptible rights of man. These rights are liberty, property, security, and resistance to oppression. . . . Any society in which the guarantee of the rights is not secured, or the separation of powers not determined, has no constitution at all."[6]

### Its Philosophical Foundation: The Law of Nature

Locke and his disciples among the American and French revolutionaries were steeped in and committed to one of the oldest and most influential ideas in Western political philosophy: the doctrine of the law of nature. There have been several different versions of this doctrine. Natural-law philosophers have disagreed, for instance, about the source of the law of nature. Some have held that it consists of a series of more or less specific commands by God prescribing how individual men should behave and how societies and governments should be organized and operated; while others—notably Locke and his followers—have taken the view that God created nature and that the law of nature is in a general way implicit in the grand design He created rather than articulated in specific divine moral injunctions. Natural-law philosophers have also disagreed about the nature of the sanctions enforcing the law of nature. Some have held that a person or a society violating its moral commands will soon come to disaster on this earth as divine punishment for disobedience. Others have held that while retribution for such disobedience may not come in this life, it will surely come in the Hereafter. Still others have regarded natural law as solely a matter of how men and societies *should* behave; consequently they have not dealt with the question of divine or other sanctions by which men may be forced to obey its commands.

Natural-law philosophers, finally, have not all agreed as to precisely what rules of political behavior the law of nature prescribes. In the seventeenth and eighteenth centuries, however, most of them agreed that natural

---

[6] Reproduced in Herman Finer, *Governments of Greater European Powers* (New York: Holt, Rinehart and Winston, Inc., 1956), Appendix, p. ix.

law makes every human being the equal of every other human being in at least the sense that he has an "unalienable" right to whatever enjoyment of his own life, liberty, and property his personal capacities permit. They also believed that men cannot satisfactorily secure their rights in a "state of nature" (i.e., anarchy); for where each man must rely solely on his own strength to preserve his rights, there is always the danger that the physically strong may abridge the rights of the weak. To secure their rights, therefore, men enter into a "social contract" with each other whereby they agree to form a society and erect a government that, by pooling the strength of many individuals, will better protect the rights of each against threats either from outside or from within the society.

Some of these philosophers believed that, in actual historical fact, all societies were created by such a "contract" some time in the past. They apparently assumed the existence of many ancient versions of the famous episode in November, 1620, in which the Pilgrim fathers drew up and signed their compact in the cabin of the *Mayflower* anchored off the coast of New England. Others, however, used the "contract" as a rhetorical device for emphasizing their contention that the only rightful government is one based upon the freely given consent of its individual citizens and not upon any moral obligation of the living to perpetuate what has been passed on to them by the dead.

All of them believed, however, that any government, once established, which abridges the rights of man violates the law of nature and thereby loses all moral claim to obedience from its citizens. Securing the rights of man, in short, is *the* purpose of government, because that is what God and/or the law of nature commands.

## "The Best Test of Truth": Rights as Means

### The Decline of Belief in Natural Law

There is no doubt that for better or worse the doctrine of the law of nature has far fewer adherents in our own time than it had in 1776 and 1789. Under the influence of such more recent philosophies as utilitarianism, positivism, and pragmatism a great many philosophers and ordinary citizens have come to believe that such laws of nature as may exist are purely descriptive and not prescriptive or moral. They are, that is to say, only ways of describing certain recurring patterns of behavior: they tell us how physical phenomena—and perhaps human beings also—*do* behave, but they have and can have nothing to say about how men *should* behave. Thus, when modern man in his bewilderment and pain cries out to the heavens, "What should I do?" the only reply is the silent glittering of the stars millions of light-years distant.

Modern man can no longer rest the doctrine of the rights of man upon its original philosophic foundation. What has he left? Nothing, according to some philosophers. They argue that the only kind of values and beliefs that men will live by and, if need be, defend to the death are those which they believe are ordained by God and/or nature—that is, by some power greater than the mind and conscience of man himself. Men once believed that God and the law of nature command the protection of human rights, and so they fought and died to secure these rights. But modern man no longer believes that God or nature tells him clearly whether he should value human rights or anything else. He therefore cannot be counted upon to defend those rights, for he has no compelling philosophical reason nor psychological motive for doing so. The communists, on the other hand, believe deeply that history commands the destruction of all human rights and free institutions. Therefore, unless free men revive their traditional belief in God and nature as the source of human rights, the institutions and freedoms originally created by that belief may well follow it into the ash heaps of history.

### The Modern Argument for Civil Rights

If the argument just outlined is correct, the future of civil rights in the free nations looks bleak indeed, for there seems little likelihood that many modern men will return to their forebears' belief in a law of nature as their guiding principle. Some modern writers, however, reply to this argument by contending that the decline of belief in a moral natural law has not deprived the doctrine of human rights of all philosophical foundation nor stripped modern man of all reasons and motives to protect those rights. That doctrine, they believe, has instead come to rest upon a new philosophical foundation which, on the record, is at least as satisfactory as the old one. The new foundation, as they explain it, consists mainly of the following three basic ideas.

#### An Assumption: The Human Source of Human Values

The crucial issue of this debate is whether men in fact live by and fight for only those values and beliefs they believe are imposed upon them by some superhuman and extraworldly agency. Many modern philosophers argue, and ordinary citizens believe, that nature does not tell man how he should behave and that man himself must, therefore, be the basic source of his own values and moral beliefs. Is this enough? These philosophers believe that it is. They argue that the important test of moral beliefs is, after all, whether men act consistently and courageously in accordance with them, whatever may be their source. Talk, however moral and elevated in tone, is cheap. The "payoff" is how men *act*; not how they talk. Judged by this standard, men who invoke no supernatural agency as the source of their moral beliefs are not less moral nor less courageous than those who do. In the particular case of human rights, these writers submit, a great many modern men deeply believe in and fight for the preservation of such rights because they are human beings and because their personalities, life-experiences, and instincts make unbearable the thought of living in a world or a society in which human beings are considered no more precious than cattle or gold—because they believe in the supreme value of the individual.

### An Act of Faith: The Primacy of the Individual

Many modern defenders of the rights of man thus rest their case upon their belief in the supreme value of the individual. Stemming from such diverse sources as the ancient Graeco-Roman school of philosophy known as Stoicism (c. 300 B.C.) and more recent developments in the Jewish and Christian religions, this doctrine declares that all human beings, whatever their individual differences, are precious, and that each person has immense potentialities for good. A prime goal of all human societies should therefore be to permit and encourage to the fullest possible extent the growth of each person and the realization of his potentialities. All human institutions, including government, should be judged by the degree that they help or hinder the achievement of these goals. "Man," in short, "is the measure of all things"—especially of society and government. The main purpose of the latter is to provide him the most fertile and propitious environment possible for his full spiritual growth. Guaranteeing him the opportunity freely to form and express his own conscience is a prime element in such an environment.

But why should any man believe in and act upon these propositions if he does not believe that nature has ordained it so? The only possible answer, these writers reply, is that he must commit an act of faith. Anyone who commits an act of faith gives himself up to a certain conviction not because he can scientifically or empirically or even logically prove that it is "correct," but rather because he feels it must be true and because he does not wish to live in a world where it is not true. After all, these writers continue, the beliefs in the existence of God and in a moral natural law are also acts of faith, in the sense that there is no scientific-empirical proof that either exists. So, they conclude, the question for each individual is not one of choosing between an act of faith and philosophical certitude, but rather one of *which* act of faith he finds easier to make and live by. Many modern men have found it easier to accept on faith the preciousness of the individual than to choose to believe in a moral law of nature.

### A Pragmatic Consideration: The Best Test of Truth

Every nation, the modern defenders of civil rights add, wishes to pursue the policies best calculated to achieve whatever values it may hold. Discovering just which of the many policy proposals brought forth are best is one of the greatest problems before any government. Experience has shown that the most effective way to solve this problem is to permit the advocates and critics of each proposal to argue their ideas freely, for in the long run good ideas and good proposals will win public acceptance over bad ones.

The argument that the best test of truth is its ability to defeat falsehood in the competitive marketplace of ideas was first made by the English poet and pamphleteer John Milton, in his famous pamphlet *Areopagitica* (1644). In his attack upon efforts by the English government to suppress the printing of subversive literature, Milton argued:

> And though all the winds of doctrine were let loose to play upon the earth, so Truth be in the field, we do injuriously, by licensing and prohibiting, to misdoubt her strength. Let her and Falsehood grapple; who ever knew Truth put to worse, in a free and open encounter? . . . She needs no policies, nor stratagems, nor licensings to make her victorious; those are but the shifts and defences that error uses against her power.[7]

A more recent but equally eloquent statement of this pragmatic argument for civil rights is the famous dissent by Justice Oliver Wendell Holmes, Jr. in the case of *Abrams v. United States* (1919). In support of his view that Congress should suppress the advocacy of unpopular opinions only in conditions of extreme national danger, Justice Holmes wrote:

> But when men have realized that time has upset many fighting faiths, they may come to believe even more than they believe the very foundations of their own conduct that the ultimate good desired is better reached by free trade in ideas—that the best test of truth is the power of the thought to get itself accepted in the competition of the market; and that truth is the only ground upon which their wishes safely can be carried out. That, at any rate, is the theory of our Constitution. It is an experiment as all life is an experiment. Every year if not every day, we have to wager our salvation upon some prophecy based upon imperfect knowledge.[8]

And the same argument applies equally to the matter of determining the guilt or innocence of a person accused of crime.

### Which Position Is Correct?

Most present-day advocates of civil rights are convinced that the arguments just summarized are more than adequate and believe that one need not be committed to historic conceptions of natural law in order to believe

---

[7] *Areopagitica and Other Prose Works* (London: J. M. Dent & Sons, Ltd., 1927), pp. 36–37.

[8] Dissenting opinion in *Abrams v. United States*, 250 U.S. 616 (1919).

in and vigorously defend the rights of man. The really difficult theoretical and practical problem of civil rights, they are convinced, is not their philosophical justification so much as the construction of sensible and reliable standards for determining how far such rights may extend when they come into conflict with the needs of modern governments to preserve internal order, protect the rights of one group of private citizens against the aggressions of other groups, and defend national institutions and independence against the onslaughts of other nations and ideologies which have only contempt for both the idea and the practice of civil rights. We shall return to these problems in the next chapter.

The debate we have just summarized is one aspect of one of the oldest and most difficult problems in philosophy: What is and/or should be the source of the ultimate moral values of men and societies? This problem has engaged the attention and energies of the greatest philosophical minds for centuries and continues to do so in our own time. As we have seen, no general consensus, no single answer has yet emerged. It would therefore be highly presumptuous for the author to establish which of the two general positions outlined above is "correct." For the purposes of this book it is enough to recognize that these different positions exist and that different men have at least somewhat different reasons for wishing to preserve human rights.

## "Certain Unalienable Rights": The Formal Designations

What *are* the rights of man? What specific areas of individual freedom are defined and guaranteed by the various constitutions of modern nations? We may begin our answers to these questions by noting that every modern Constitution contains at least some formal guarantees of civil rights. Even the United Nations in 1948 adopted a Universal Declaration of Human Rights, which endorsed about as complete a list of human rights as has ever been compiled. This does not mean, of course, that each formal guarantee in each nation's Constitution—to say nothing of those in the UN Declaration—represents an actual right genuinely protected for the persons living under the particular authority. After we have reviewed the nature of the formal guarantees, we shall describe the nature and incidence of the legal machinery enforcing and the political and social forces supporting civil rights in modern nations, and thereby summarize the actual as opposed to the formal status of human rights in our time.

The mere presence of formally guaranteed rights in any nation's Constitution has at least this much significance: it indicates that the framers of the nation's Constitution have, for whatever reasons seemed sufficient to them, deemed it desirable to pay at least lip service—and perhaps more—

to the idea of the rights of man. For that reason they deserve the following listing.

**LIMITATIONS ON GOVERNMENT**

1. Protections of Belief and Expression[9]
   Religious worship*
   Speech*
   Press*
   Secrecy of Correspondence*
   Preservation of distinct subnational languages and cultures
2. Protections of Action
   Assembly*
   Petition*
   Suffrage*[10]
   Secrecy of votes
   Prohibition of slavery*
   Practice of chosen profession
   Privacy of domicile*
   Movement within and to and from the nation
   Organization of labor unions and trade associations
   Strikes
   Collective bargaining
3. Protections for Persons Accused of a Crime
   Prohibition of
       bills of attainder*
       ex post facto laws*
       guilt by association
       unreasonable searches and seizures*
       trial without indictment*
       double jeopardy for the same offense*
       coerced confessions*
       excessive bail and fines*
       cruel and unusual punishments*
       extradition for political crimes

---

[9] This list is derived from the author's survey of the various Constitutions reproduced in Amos J. Peaslee, ed., *Constitutions of Nations* (2d ed.; The Hague: Martinus Nijhoff, 1956), 3 vols. The asterisks indicate rights formally guaranteed by the Constitution of the United States.

To elaborate the full meaning of each of these formal guarantees would be a task far beyond the scope of the present chapter. The reader who wishes to find out more about their interpretation and application in American circumstances is advised to consult such works as Walter Gellhorn, *American Rights* (New York: The Macmillan Company, 1960); Thomas I. Emerson and David Haber, *Political and Civil Rights in the United States* (2 vols., 2d ed.; Buffalo: Dennis & Co., Inc., 1958); and any of the descriptions and analyses of the current American constitutional system.

[10] Some Constitutions guarantee universal suffrage. The American Constitution, through the Fifteenth and Nineteenth Amendments, prohibits the denial of the right to vote to any person on account of race, color, previous condition of servitude, or sex.

    capital punishment
    imprisonment for debt
Guarantee of
    writ of habeas corpus*
    "due process of law"*
    speedy and public trial*
    trial by an impartial jury*
    confrontation of hostile witnesses*
    subpoena power for the defendant*
    assistance of counsel*
    equality before the law or equal protection of the laws*

4. Protections of Property Rights
    Just compensation for private property taken for public use*
    Patents and copyrights*

**OBLIGATIONS OF GOVERNMENT**

1. To Provide Economic Assistance
    Work
    Equal pay for equal work regardless of sex, age, nationality, or caste
    Minimum wages
    Maximum hours
    Unemployment assistance
    Social security

2. To Provide Social Assistance
    Education
    Prohibition of child labor
    Protection of families, children, and motherhood
    Preservation of historical monuments
    Recreation and culture

### The Incidence of Various Formal Guarantees

As the above listing suggests, the world's Constitutions contain a wide variety of formally guaranteed civil rights. Some of these provisions seem strange to persons reared in the Anglo-American tradition: the provision in the Brazilian Constitution guaranteeing "the right of a woman to rest before and after giving birth, without prejudice to her employment and salary" (Art. 157, Sec. X), and the declaration in the Indian Constitution that "the State shall regard the raising of the level of nutrition . . . as among its primary duties" (Part IV, Sec. 38). Certain guarantees, however, appear in some version in most Constitutions. The incidence of the most frequently encountered guarantees is shown in Table 4.

As Table 4 demonstrates, the types of guarantees appearing most frequently are those which protect individuals against governmental interference with their freedom of thought, belief, and action and which require fair treatment for persons accused of crime. The types appearing less fre-

## Table 4.  Incidence of Formal Civil Rights
## Guarantees in the World's Constitutions

| RANK | TYPE OF GUARANTEE | PERCENTAGE OF CONSTITUTIONS IN WHICH IT APPEARS |
|---|---|---|
| 1. | Rights of individual liberty and fair legal processes | 88 |
| 2. | Freedom of speech and press | 83 |
| 3. | Property rights | 82 |
| 4. | Rights of assembly and association | 80 |
| 5. | Rights of conscience and religion | 80 |
| 6. | Secrecy of correspondence and inviolability of domicile | 79 |
| 7. | Education | 78 |
| 8. | Equality | 72 |
| 9. | Petition | 64 |
| 10. | Labor | 56 |
| 11. | Social security | 51 |
| 12. | Freedom of Movement | 47.5 |
| 13. | Health and motherhood | 47 |
| 14. | Nonretroactivity of laws | 35 |

SOURCE: Amos J. Peaslee, ed., *Constitutions of Nations* (2d ed.; The Hague: Martinus Nijhoff, 1956), I, 7.

quently are for the most part those which obligate the government to provide individuals with certain guaranteed minima of the good life. This distribution no doubt results mainly from the fact that only the newer Constitutions (i.e., those written since World War I) have raised guarantees of the latter type to the status of formal constitutional provisions. The older Constitutions, such as the American, confine themselves largely to guarantees of the former type and leave welfare-state guarantees to the statute books of ordinary law.

Whatever may be the verbal content of the civil rights formally underwritten by the world's Constitutions, however, we can assess their actual status only by surveying what social and political forces challenge and sustain them and with what results.

## Liberty's Challengers and Champions

### The Classical View: Government as Enemy

#### The Antigovernment Bias of the Early Constitutional Framers

We noted previously that most of the Constitutions written before World War I guarantee only rights of the individual against government. Their "bills of rights," that is to say, contain only lists of actions that government is prohibited from taking against the individual, such as abridging his freedom of speech and religion, or subjecting him to unreasonable searches and seizures, or forcing him to testify against himself, and the like. The classical meaning of a "civil right," in short, was something a government may not do to an individual person, and government was thought to be the only enemy of liberty.

This conception of civil rights was rooted in the conviction of John Locke and his disciples among the constitution makers of the eighteenth and nineteenth centuries that men are naturally free and that all governmental authority, being a special and artificial creation of man rather than a universal creation of nature, is inherently hostile to human freedom and must always be watched suspiciously and guarded against vigilantly.

Locke and his followers also recognized, however, that men's rights are unsafe in a state of anarchy; for where human aggressions are entirely unrestrained there is an ever-present danger that the strong will ride roughshod over the rights of the weak. Some kind of government, they believed, is indispensable for the protection of the rights of *all* men. Thus they faced a dilemma: the rights of man cannot be preserved without government; but government is also inherently hostile to those rights. The only way out of this dilemma, they believed, is to organize government so that it will maintain law and order without abridging human rights; and the only way to do that, they were convinced, is to organize it according to their version of the ancient doctrine of constitutionalism.

## "A Government of Laws and Not of Men": The Classical Doctrine of Constitutionalism

For more than two thousand years before the Continental Congress proclaimed the Declaration of Independence a long and distinguished succession of political philosophers argued that only constitutional government can be good government. A constitutional government, as the term has traditionally been used, is one whose range of activity is limited by certain generally accepted and understood basic and immutable principles. A nonconstitutional government, by contrast, is one whose range of activity is unlimited and whose decisions are made solely in accordance with the ever-changing whims and prejudices of the public-officials-of-the-moment. The contrast is succinctly put in the famous declaration of the Massachusetts Constitution of 1780 that its structure is dedicated "to the end that it may be a government of laws and not of men."[11]

Locke and his disciples converted this ancient doctrine to their purposes

---

[11] See pages 97, 99–100. Some leading accounts of the meaning, origins, and development of the ideal of constitutionalism are Charles H. McIlwain, *Constitutionalism Ancient and Modern* (Ithaca, N.Y.: Cornell University Press, 1940); Francis D. Wormuth, *The Origins of Modern Constitutionalism* (New York: Harper & Row, Publishers, 1949); and Carl J. Friedrich, *Constitutional Government and Democracy* (Boston: Ginn & Company, 1946).

by holding that all rightful governments must operate within limits specified by a Constitution. The Constitution, in turn, must firmly restrain governmental power by such means as the following: (1) listing the things government may not do (in a "bill of rights"); (2) carefully defining the areas in which it is authorized to act (in a list of "enumerated powers") and confining it strictly to such powers; and (3) establishing "separation of powers"—that is, distributing governmental power among three separate and mutually independent branches of government, the legislative, executive, and judicial. In this manner, the "constitutionalists" of the eighteenth century believed, the power of government could be restrained sufficiently to minimize its inherent danger for the rights of man.

### The Doctrine of Constitutionalism Today

It is not surprising that Locke and his followers should have regarded government as the sole enemy of human rights. The governments they lived under were of the *ancien régime*, founded on such principles as "the divine right of kings" and the privileges of royalty and nobility over peasants and yeomen. The actual violations of human rights they knew about—the suppression of antimonarchy speeches and pamphlets, the "star-chamber" jailing and torture of opponents of the regime, and the like—were all acts committed by agents of these authoritarian governments in the name of "royal prerogative" and "reasons of state." The only serious and visible threat to human rights in Locke's time was government; as a result his belief in the rights of man logically led him to the antigovernment doctrine of constitutionalism.

In modern times, however, the free nations have instituted governments whose decisions are made not by autocratic monarchs and their lackeys but by popular majorities and their representatives. Yet, despite this change, the doctrine of constitutionalism and the institutions implementing it have not lost any major ground. A great many citizens of the modern democracies feel that popular majorities may on occasion try to smash the rights of unpopular minorities, and that such tyranny must be guarded against no less vigilantly than tyranny by monarchs or aristocrats. They feel, in short, that constitutional government is quite as necessary for the preservation of human rights against the modern popular democracies as it ever was against the authoritarian governments attacked by Locke and Paine.

### The Special Role of the Courts

The various Constitutions of the American states and the national government written after 1776 were the first in modern times to attempt to put the doctrine of constitutionalism into practice. It soon became apparent that these new systems needed a "watchdog"—that is, some kind of agency whose special duty and prerogative it is to determine, in each instance where the question arises, whether or not the government or any branch thereof is exceeding its constitutional limits. In the United States it was decided that the courts rather than the legislatures or the executives should take over this role by assuming the power of judicial review. As noted in Chapter 6, however, some free nations with constitutional governments have assigned the "watchdog" function to their legislatures rather than to their courts; and some nations whose Constitutions formally establish judicial review actually have governments that are neither "free" nor "constitutional."

Whether or not they have the power of judicial review, the courts in all the free nations perform a special role in the protection of civil rights. This results from the fact that a great many—though not all—of the conflicts involving such rights are fought out mainly in cases at law. When, for example, a person is being tried for a crime, the court must not only determine his guilt or innocence but also decide whether his rights to a fair trial and due process of law are being preserved in such matters as the way in which the charges are framed, jury selection, admission of evidence, and proper provision for counsel. When a court is deciding a libel suit brought by plaintiff A against defendant B, it must determine whether in the special circumstances of the particular case A's right to his good name has been unduly unfringed by what B has written about him—or whether to punish B would be to abridge B's freedom of speech and press. In short, while the courts of only some free nations have the power to set aside laws as unconstitutional, the courts of all free nations necessarily have the power to interpret and apply in specific cases the laws and constitutional provisions guaranteeing civil rights. For this reason court decisions and judicial interpretations constitute a significant body of data for determining the actual status of civil rights in any free nation, whether or not its courts have the power of judicial review.

## The Modern View: Government as Enemy and Ally

### Nongovernmental Threats to Civil Rights

Most citizens of the modern free nations agree with their eighteenth- and nineteenth-century ancestors that human rights must be protected against certain kinds of oppressive governmental action. Unlike their forebears, however, they do not regard government as the only serious threat to those rights. They have come to believe that there are at least three additional kinds of threats, each of which is no less dangerous than governmental oppression—and each of which can be countered only by enlisting the power and authority of government to protect the individual.

The first is aggression against the rights of national citizens by local governments. A good deal of the conflict over civil rights in the United

American Negroes
Turned to the National
Government for
Protection of Their
Rights against Some
State Governments:
Birmingham, Alabama,
1963 (Wide World
Photos, Inc.)

States in recent years has arisen from the effort of certain state and local governments to impose racial segregation and white supremacy upon Negroes. The Fourteenth Amendment to the national Constitution makes Negroes, like other native-born or naturalized citizens, citizens of the United States first and citizens of the state wherein they reside second; moreover, it stipulates that "no State shall make or enforce any law which shall abridge the privileges or immunities of citizens of the United States. . . ." To secure their constitutional immunity against being forced to live as second-class citizens, the Negroes, particularly in the southern states, have turned to the national government as their principal ally against oppression by the state and local governments. In Chapter 9 we shall describe this conflict and its results in detail, but this brief mention should serve to illustrate the point that "government" is no longer thought of in Lockean terms as a monolithic whole threatening the civil rights of all; it has come to be thought of as an aggregation of many different levels and agencies, and some governments in a nation may well be the only instrument powerful enough to protect human rights against infringement by other of its governments.

The second kind of threat is aggression against the rights of private individuals by other private individuals. The rights of persons accused of crime to fair trials have many times been threatened by lynch mobs; in such situations the only effective protection of their rights lies in the ability and determination of the law-enforcement authorities to save these people from the mobs for the courts. The rights of Negroes or Jews to live in houses and neighborhoods they like and can afford are widely violated by "restrictive covenants"—private agreements among property owners to sell only to white gentiles; in these cases the right to decent housing can often be protected only by the passage and enforcement of "open occupancy" laws prohibiting such discriminatory agreements. The right of members of any racial and ethnic minority to equal opportunities with "WASP's" (white Anglo-Saxon Protestants) for jobs and promotions commensurate with their ability and training are often abridged by private employers' policies not to hire or promote them; if this is the case, then their employment rights can be secured only by the application of a fair employment practices law outlawing such discrimination. In all these situations government, far from being the enemy of human rights, is their chief defender.

In Chapter 3 we noted the nearly-universal acceptance in modern nations of the idea that every man has a right to at least the minimum conditions of a decent life for himself and his family, and the third kind of threat includes such ancient hazards as unemployment, poverty, old age, illness, and, above all, ignorance. Here, too, most modern men look to government, not as their enemy, but as their main hope for overcoming these hazards.

### Governmental Intervention against These Threats

Whether or not they have formally enshrined in their Constitutions this new conception of government as the protector of human rights, all modern democracies have clearly accepted the principle for many years and from time to time have brought new rights under governmental protection. We have seen that in the third area the principle of the welfare state and such of its guarantees as universal free public education and protection against starvation are so firmly established in all free nations that any effort to remove them is likely to be considered about as drastic an attack on the rights of man as a proposal to repeal, say, the constitutional guarantees of freedom of speech or fair trial.

A similar development has taken place in the first two areas. In the United States as early as 1866 and 1870, for example, Congress enacted laws penalizing any individual who "willfully subjects any person to a deprivation of any rights or privileges secured by the Constitution or laws of the

United States." For many years the enforcement of these laws was left in the hands of United States attorneys in various localities, and few persons were prosecuted for violating them. In 1939, however, Attorney General Frank Murphy established a Civil Rights Section in the Criminal Division of the Department of Justice and charged it with undertaking a more vigorous enforcement of the 1866 and 1870 laws. Since then the national government has played a more active part in protecting human rights. The greatest leap forward, however, came when Congress passed the Civil Rights Act of 1964, which commits the national government to full positive action to secure for all citizens full equality in their right to register and vote, to be served by private businesses offering public accommodations, to use public facilities, and to equal job opportunities. We shall discuss the act and its impact further in Chapter 9.

## Liberty's Hard Choices

It may be that "the price of liberty is eternal vigilance," but that is not its only price. We cannot begin to understand the difficult problem of securing the rights of man in a modern nation until we recognize that it consists of making hard choices among widely held but competing values. Let us illustrate by describing the two main kinds of choices government must make when dealing with human rights.

### Freedom versus Security

**The Problem**

One ever-recurring dilemma of government in a free nation arises from these facts: (1) most citizens value *both* freedom *and* security—freedom for the reasons outlined earlier in this chapter, and security—the governmental preservation of law and order—for the reasons outlined in Chapter 2. (2) But freedom and security are always in conflict, and whatever government does to promote one is likely to jeopardize the other.

By way of illustrating this point, consider the conflicting claims of freedom and security in this situation: A child is kidnapped and later found brutally tortured and murdered. The outraged townspeople demand that the murderer be arrested and punished immediately. The police turn up enough evidence to convince them that a tramp named John Doe is the murderer—but not enough to guarantee his conviction under the stringent rules of evidence used in American courts. So they arrest Doe "on suspicion" and "grill" him in an effort to make him confess, knowing that a confession added to the evidence they already have will be sufficient to convict him. But Doe refuses to confess. The police are convinced he is

Even a Person Accused of the Most Heinous Crime Deserves a Fair Trial: Dallas, Texas, November 24, 1963. (Photo copyright *The Dallas Morning News,* 1963.)

lying, and they know that giving him the "third degree"—beating him with a rubber truncheon or shining bright lights in his eyes while they question him until he breaks down or pressing lighted cigarettes on parts of his body—may force him to confess. The townspeople, meanwhile, fear that Doe will go free because of some "legal technicality," and this hideous crime will go unpunished. The question arises among them, Why not get a rope, drag him out of jail, and hang him to the nearest lamp post?

Now if security—punishing the guilty and deterring potential criminals— is the *only* value held by the townspeople and police, the question of what to do is easily answered: either beat a confession out of Doe or just string him up without a trial.

In authoritarian nations, where this *is* the prime value, the matter is beautifully (or horribly) simple. They believe that punishing the guilty is the only important consideration in justice; and if the government must murder hundreds of the innocent to make sure that none of the guilty escape, it is a price well worth paying.

In a free nation like the United States, however, punishing the guilty is only one of the values the people hold. The townspeople and police in the episode described above have no wish to hang Doe if he is innocent. So they have to choose which they value more, punishing the guilty or protecting the innocent. If they choose the former and torture or lynch Doe, they run the risk of punishing an innocent man; and if they choose the latter and give Doe all his constitutional rights to a fair trial, they run the risk of letting a murderer go unpunished.

The citizens of free nations, in short, are willing neither to sacrifice all security to absolute freedom nor to abandon all freedom for absolute security. In the free nations, accordingly, one of the ever-present problems of civil rights is determining in specific instances just where the line should be drawn between the inevitably conflicting claims of freedom and security.

## Some American Standards for Drawing the Line

Recognizing that this kind of decision must be made in all concrete instances in which the question of restraining human activity is involved, most of us would agree that such decisions should be made in accordance with the most just and sensible general standards that we can devise—and not according to the individual whims and caprices of the law-enforcement officers and judges involved in the case of the moment. The American Supreme Court has developed several general standards over the years, the best known of which apply to determining the circumstances in which speech and writing may be suppressed without violating the constitutional injunction in the First Amendment that "Congress shall make no law . . . abridging the freedom of speech, or of the press." The principal tests may be briefly summarized.[12]

CLEAR AND PRESENT DANGER. First laid down in the case of *Schenck v. U.S.* (1919), this ruling holds that speech and writing can be suppressed only when "the words are used in circumstances and are of such a nature as to create a clear and present danger that they will bring about the substantive evils that Congress has a right to prevent."[13] The words, that is to

---

[12] The reader who wishes more information than can be presented in these short summaries in the text about the nature and application of these tests is advised to consult such sources as the lucid short summary in James M. Burns and Jack W. Peltason, *Government by the People* (5th ed.; Englewood Cliffs, N.J.: Prentice-Hall, Inc., 1963), 135–137; and the more detailed summary in Gellhorn, *op. cit.*

[13] *Schenck v. U.S.*, 249 U.S. 47 (1919).

say, may be suppressed only when they clearly have the potentiality of inciting riot or assassination or subversion or the like, and when they are uttered in such circumstances as to make it likely that these things will shortly occur as a direct result. The presumption is clearly against suppressing speech, and the burden of proof rests with those who would suppress it. This test, with occasional departures, has been generally followed by the Court in free-speech cases since 1919.

GRAVITY OF EVIL. In its 1951 opinion upholding the conviction of eleven Communist leaders for conspiring to advocate violent overthrow of the government, the Court took a somewhat different position. It held that freedom of speech can be invaded whenever "the gravity of the evil, discounted by its improbability, justifies such invasion . . . as is necessary to avoid the danger."[14] In other words, if the evil that authority is trying to prevent would be very grave if it did come to pass, then words which might lead to it—even if the possibility is relatively slight—may be suppressed. Under this standard, then, the presumption is far more in favor of suppressing speech than it is in its "clear and present danger" predecessor. This later standard has been used by the courts in some cases since World War II involving the suppression of the advocacy of communist doctrines. In cases involving speech by persons other than Communists, however, the Court has generally, although not in every instance, adhered to the earlier standard; it has, for example, declared unconstitutional state laws and municipal ordinances censoring newspapers, prohibiting all picketing in labor disputes, and banning "sacrilegious" movies.

### Group versus Group

Many people try to resolve the dilemmas and escape the hard choices of liberty by declaring that "every man should be free to exercise his rights so long as they do not interfere with anyone else's rights." This aphorism has a comforting to-each-his-own air of justice and plausibility about it, and its popularity is not surprising. The only thing wrong with it, indeed, is that it seldom works. Why? Because in most situations government must deal with, securing the rights of one group of citizens inevitably abridges some rights of other groups.

For example, for a number of years Ollie McClung and his son owned and operated Ollie's Barbecue, a restaurant in Birmingham, Alabama, and seated and served only white customers at their tables. In 1964, however, Congress passed its revolutionary Civil Rights Act, Title II of which forbids private businesses offering public accommodations—including restaurants, hotels, and motels—to refuse service to any customer because of his race.

---

[14] *Dennis v. U.S.*, 341 U.S. 494 (1951).

Shortly after the act went into effect, a group of Negroes asked to be seated and served at Ollie's Barbecue. The McClungs refused, the Negroes sought an injunction to force compliance with the act, and it was eventually granted by the Supreme Court of the United States.[15]

Now, consider the clash of values and rights underlying the legal contest. On the one hand, the Negroes argued that for many years they had had to plan their trips through the South carefully because most restaurants and hotels would not serve them. This exclusion not only made travel wearying and unpleasant for themselves and their children, but it was a painful and humiliating badge of their second-class status. The McClungs, on the other hand, argued that the restaurant was their private property, and if they wanted to exclude Negroes—whether because they themselves wanted no Negroes around or because serving Negroes would drive white customers away—surely this was part of their right to manage their own property as they saw fit.

It is hard to escape the conclusion that both sides were right! To deny the Negroes seats in the restaurant was to abridge *their* right to be treated like other citizens and to make travel more difficult and humiliating for them than for whites. But equally, to force the McClungs to serve Negroes when they did not wish to was to abridge *their* right to manage their property in their own way. Consequently, neither side could freely exercise its rights without abridging the other's. There was no way on earth to fully secure the rights of both the McClungs and the Negroes. Congress, the Attorney General, and the Supreme Court had to choose, and choose they did. One may agree or disagree with their choice, but he cannot blink the fact that a choice had to be made.

## Civil Rights in the Political Process

### *Civil Rights Conflicts Are Political Conflicts*[16]

We are likely to understand better what is involved in conflicts over civil rights if we remember that they are *political* in nature. The fact that they are so often fought out largely (though never entirely) in courts of law, and the fact that some people mistakenly regard the judicial process as somehow not "political" in the same sense that legislative and executive processes are "political," may obscure their political nature. Yet, according to the analytical framework we are using in this book, these conflicts can-

---

[15] *Katzenbach v. McClung,* 379 U.S. 294 (1964).

[16] The point of view expressed here is a special application of the general position so ably presented in Jack W. Peltason, *Federal Courts in the Political Process* (New York: Random House, Inc., 1955). We shall take it up again in Chapter 20.

not be other than political. Every conflict over civil rights involves the question of governmental policy: should government restrict this person's or that group's freedom of action? And, as we saw in Chapters 1 and 2, every governmental action promotes some persons' goals and damages the interests of others.

If, for example, government enforces a policy of racial integration in public schools, it promotes the Negroes' goal of equal status and frustrates the southern whites' desire for segregation. If government bans the sale of "obscene" magazines or comic books, it promotes the cause of certain religious sects and groups of parents and damages the authors, artists, and publishers concerned. Should government enforce "open occupancy" laws, it would forward the claim of Negroes and Jews to equal housing opportunities and thwart the efforts of certain whites and gentiles to keep their neighborhoods "exclusive."

Thus the decisions as to what government shall do in these and all similar situations are, in our sense of the term, *political*. We should expect, therefore, that they will be made as all other political decisions are made— as the result of conflict among competing interest groups. Most of these groups will, to be sure, publicly defend their positions in terms of their "constitutional rights" rather than in terms of self-interest; and most of them will genuinely believe that "freedom of speech" or "due process of law"—quite apart from any crass considerations of self-interest—require that the decision be favorable to their points of view. This should not, however, conceal the fact that in civil rights matters, as in all other matters involving governmental policy, somebody stands to gain and somebody to lose. The student of politics and government will better understand any particular conflict over civil rights if he explores, in addition to the ideological aspects of the conflict, the question of who stands to win what and who stands to lose what.

### Some Consequences of This View

Viewing civil rights conflicts in this light may suggest that the processes by which they are conducted and the governmental decisions affecting them are essentially the same as the processes by which all other political conflicts are conducted and governmental decisions made. An approach to civil rights conflicts from this point of view may well provide an understanding and insight otherwise absent. Some persons, for example, feel that governmental policies (including court decisions) on civil rights matters should always be made in accordance with a set of clear and mutually consistent logical principles; and they are disturbed by the fact that such decisions do not always fit this pattern but seem instead to shift logical grounds from circumstance to circumstance and from time to time. It is easier to make sense of this situation if we recognize the political nature of civil rights conflicts, for we start with the assumption that particular decisions result not from ill will or temporary aberrations from rationality by judges and legislators but rather from the variations in nature and fluctuations of strength in the competing interests involved.

Another consequence of this view is that it makes us aware that in any given nation the particular processes by which these conflicts are conducted and the resulting civil rights of individuals determined are shaped by the same forces that shape the nation's other political conflicts and governmental policies. In other words, the general condition of civil rights in a particular nation depends largely upon such matters as the number and variety of its competing groups, the issues which differentiate them and set them in conflict with one another, the degree of overlapping membership, the degree to which the competing groups are mobilized, the number and strength of common interests and other unifying forces, the general level of physical wealth and its distribution among all groups, the degree of security from foreign attack, and all those other general factors affecting politics and government that were described in Chapters 1 through 4.

Even for those groups and nations who wish to "buy" it, the "price of liberty" varies for each group and each nation from issue to issue and from time to time. What "prices" are the free nations and their competing groups currently willing to pay? We shall see some of the answers to this question in the following chapter, which considers some of the principal challenges to civil rights in modern nations and some of the ways in which various nations have responded to them.

# 9

## The Rights of Man:

### *challenges and responses*

In every free nation the problem of preserving the rights of man in a world of international insecurity and intranational political conflict is both perennial and grave. Since 1945, and particularly in the United States, it has emerged from the relative quiet of the scholar's study into the forefront of political strife.

"Clergymen denounce Supreme Court's Ban on School Prayers." "Civil Liberties Union Charges Security Program Violates Constitutional Rights." "Senator Blasts Witnesses for Hiding behind Fifth Amendment." "Three Civil Rights Workers Murdered in Mississippi." Such headlines as these have been prominent in American newspapers since the end of World War II, and no American needs to be told that the current conflicts over civil rights questions are among the most acute problems with which the nation must deal.

The dilemmas every free nation faces in preserving human rights, as we observed in Chapter 8, unhappily cannot be solved by the pat formula that everyone should be free to do what he wishes so long as he does not abridge the freedom of others. For every governmental action involves coercing some people to do something or to refrain from doing something else. Unavoidably, every such action restrict's someone's freedom to some extent. Guaranteeing the Negroes' right to be served at a restaurant abridges the proprietor's right to manage his property. Protecting the Jehovah's Witnesses' right to seek converts by door-to-door canvassing abridges the heathens' right to privacy. Protecting a suspected criminal's privacy by prohibiting the tapping of his telephone handicaps police efforts to protect other people's right to security of life and property. So preserving freedom forces all free nations to make choices—hard choices, *political* choices.

The political conflict over human rights is therefore fought between group and group, not between "the individual" and "the government": it takes place not between all individuals on the one hand and an ever-threatening government on the other, but rather between the rights of one group and the conflicting rights of another.

Every time a particular group calls upon government to engage in some course of action or inaction, it challenges the civil rights of some other group. It is clearly impossible in the limited space of the present chapter to describe all the challenges to human rights and all the governmental responses to those challenges in all the modern free nations. So we shall have to limit our discussion to a survey of three areas of present-day political conflict in certain free nations that have received the most attention in the civil rights context: the conflict over church-state relations; the conflict over the handling of communist subversion; and the conflict over racial discrimination.

## Conflict over Church-State Relations

### Religious Toleration and Separation of Church and State

For the thousand years between the collapse of the Roman Empire and the beginning of the Protestant Reformation in the sixteenth century the idea that Christianity as interpreted and administered by the Roman Catholic Church was the only true religion was accepted by most men and all societies in Western Europe (though not, of course, in the rest of the world). Equally accepted was the church's "establishment," meaning the provision of governmental support for the church in the form of appropriations of public funds for church use, employment of governmental agencies for the suppression of heresy, and governmental appointment of high church officials.

The civil and international wars touched off by the revolts of Martin Luther, John Calvin, and their followers were fought mainly over the question of *which* church should be established, and few raised the question of whether *any* should be.

Some degree of establishment has remained to this day in a few Western nations. In Great Britain, for example, the queen is the official head of the Church of England and, on the advice of the prime minister, appoints its bishops and archbishops; but no Englishman is in any way forced to join or support the "established church." In Spain the Roman Catholic Church is closely allied with the *Caudillo's* government, and what few Protestants there are operate under a number of legal and social handicaps.

However, in most Western nations the twin ideas of religious toleration and separation of church and state have taken deep root—and stirred up political conflict. They were first advanced in the seventeenth and eighteenth centuries by such philosophers as John Milton, John Locke, and Voltaire, who argued that every man should be free to worship (or not worship) according to whatever doctrine, liturgy, and organization he chooses—though even Milton and Locke were unwilling to extend this freedom to anyone so beyond the pale as a Roman Catholic.

The men who wrote the Constitution of the United States were not only deeply imbued with these principles; they also faced the difficult practical problem of constructing an instrument of government for a nation that already had many different faiths. Accordingly, they gave the twin ideals of religious freedom first priority in the Bill of Rights: the first sentence of the First Amendment reads, "Congress shall make no law respecting an establishment of religion, or prohibiting the free exercise thereof. . . ." As the Framers saw it, religious freedom has two aspects: no governmental *interference* with the private individual's religious beliefs, and no government *support* for religion. Each, they believed, is necessary to the other; and only the two together constitute genuine religious freedom.

### How Separate Is Separate?[1]

In no free nation has there been any serious attempt to set up a particular denomination as the official church. Even the British have disestablished the Church of England in Wales and Northern Ireland, and, as we have seen, no Englishman is required to support any church in any way.

Most of the conflict over church-state relations in recent years has concerned governmental attempts to promote religion-in-general against atheism, agnosticism, and other forms of unbelief. Some have succeeded, some have not.

### 1. Tax Exemptions

In the United States financial contributions to churches are deductible from one's income tax; churches are themselves exempt from estate taxes, gift taxes, admission taxes, social security taxes, unemployment compensation taxes, and real and personal property taxes. This is clearly governmental support of religion, albeit indirect; yet there is no serious move afoot to repeal or invalidate such measures.

---

[1] For a complete recent review of the legal status of this question in the United States, see David Fellman, *Religion in American Law* (Boston: Boston University Press, 1965).

## 2. Sunday Closing Laws

Many states have laws requiring most kinds of business establishments to stay closed on Sundays. Originally enacted for religious reasons, they are now upheld by legislatures and courts mainly on the secular ground that it promotes the general welfare to set aside one day each week for family rest and recreation.

## 3. Education

By far the greatest area of controversy has been state support of religious education. Most European democracies fought out this issue in the late nineteenth and early twentieth centuries, with a general and nearly complete victory for the secularist forces opposing all forms of governmental support of religion in the state schools or the religious schools.[2] In the United States, however, it has remained in dispute well into the 1960's.

One issue is whether the national government may properly give financial support to religious schools, such as those operated by the Roman Catholic and Lutheran churches, where indoctrination in a particular denomination's beliefs is part of the educational program. This sensitive question has plagued both Congress and the courts, and the answer that seems to have emerged is that indirect aid—e.g., in the form of subsidizing bus transportation of pupils to and from school—is permissible because it is a benefit to the child, not support of religion.[3] Even so, a number of states refuse to provide such help because they feel it violates the separation principle.

The issue receiving the greatest attention in recent years has been whether a government may properly include any form of religious worship, however nondenominational, in the program of a public school. It has been fought out mainly in the courts, and the courts have given something short of a single consistent and unequivocal answer. In one leading case the Supreme Court has held that sectarian religious instruction may not be given during "released time" in school hours in school buildings even though the students' participation is voluntary.[4] In another case three years later the Court held that such instruction is permissible, even during regular school hours, if it is kept voluntary and if it is given outside school property in buildings supplied by the churches.[5]

One of the greatest storms was provoked in 1962 when the Court ruled that New York public schools could not have their pupils recite a short

---

[2] But in some nations, notably France, it remains a matter of bitter dispute even today: cf. Bernard E. Brown, "Religious Schools and Politics in France," *Midwest Journal of Political Science*, II (May, 1958), 160–178.

[3] *Everson v. Board of Education,* 330 U.S. 1 (1947).

[4] *Illinois ex rel. McCollum v. Board of Education,* 333 U.S. 203 (1948).

[5] *Zorach v. Clauson,* 343 U.S. 306 (1952).

nondenominational prayer as part of the school program even though no pupil was compelled to join in the prayer over his or his parents' objections.[6] And a year later the Court held that compulsory Bible reading in public schools is also unconstitutional.[7]

Predictably, these decisions evoked angry comments by a number of congressmen and clergymen that "someone is tampering with America's soul" and "they put the Negroes in the schools, and now they've driven God out." But after the rhetorical dust had settled, a number of religious leaders praised the decisions both on constitutional grounds and on the religious ground that true faith is better learned from the precepts and examples provided by the home and the church than from recitations required by public schools. The controversy soon cooled, and the net result seems to be that while the First Amendment continues to be read as requiring something short of absolute and total separation of church and state, there is a powerful constitutional presumption against any governmental support of religion. Only indirect aid given as part of a broad program of aid to all schools will be tolerated constitutionally or politically.

## Conflict over Control of Communist Subversion

### *The Problem*

#### The Nature of Communist Subversion

At least since the breakup of the anti-Nazi coalition immediately following the end of World War II, the free nations of the world have had to face the problem of deciding what, if anything, they should do to defend their free institutions and national independence against the onslaught of world communism. The problem arises both from the necessity of establishing military and diplomatic policies to counter the maneuvers of Soviet Russia and Red China and also from the need to adopt domestic policies against communist subversion at home. The determination of such policies, as we shall see, has become deeply involved with the problem of protecting political freedom.

OBJECTIVES AND STRATEGY. The freely proclaimed objective of communism in both its Moscow and Peking versions is nothing less than the establishment of communist regimes everywhere in the world. But, as we noted in Chapter 3, since the death of Stalin in 1953 world communism has increasingly divided over the question of what grand strategy to follow.

---

[6] *Engel v. Vitale*, 370 U.S. 421 (1962).
[7] *Abingdon School District v. Schempp*, 374 U.S. 203 (1963).

One group follows the Russian "coexistence" line as laid down by Khrushchev and continued by his successors: a thermonuclear war would destroy communism just as much as capitalism, and must be avoided; therefore, communism must coexist with capitalism until the latter, with a few helpful nudges from its enemies, eventually collapses from its own internal contradictions and the misery (so communist ideology insists) it brings its people. The other group follows the "hard" Chinese line: capitalism will fall only if Communists make incessant war on it everywhere, including thermonuclear war if it comes to that.

TACTICS. Whatever general strategy Communists advocate, however, they usually employ the tactics of internal subversion and sabotage, fomenting tension among ethnic groups and economic classes, placing men in governmental positions with access to secret military and diplomatic information, infiltrating noncommunist "progressive" political-action groups and trade unions, and so on.

In most noncommunist nations the Communist party has two sections, each of which does a particular job. The "open" party prints newspapers like *The Daily Worker* and *L'Humanité*, runs candidates for elective office, holds conventions, and in general acts as the face the party turns toward the noncommunist public. Its members make no secret of their Communist affiliations and claim that they are a political party like any other. But there is also a "secret" party, whose members try to conceal their Communist affiliations and have no public or admitted connection whatever with the "open" party. Communists in the "secret" party work as direct agents of the Russian or Chinese political and military apparatus, and, on orders from Moscow or Peking, perform the party's clandestine functions of espionage, sabotage, and infiltration of government agencies and noncommunist groups.

### Maintaining National Security

The "open" and "secret" Communist parties pose somewhat different kinds of threats to nations that wish to preserve their institutions against the communist assault. The "secret" party is perhaps the more serious threat. For one thing, its tactics of espionage, sabotage, and infiltration directly attack the free government's nerve centers. For another, its concealment behind many noncommunist protest movements makes efforts to detect it and stamp it out difficult and creates the real danger of crushing the civil liberties of those persons who dissent from the nation's orthodox political and social views but who are nevertheless genuinely loyal and noncommunist. The "open" party's activities, on the other hand, are relatively visible and easy to watch; in no free nation has the party ever won the majority of public support necessary to capture control of the government in a free election. Yet its connection with the "secret" party and its open advocacy of the overthrow of all free institutions also constitute a threat to those institutions.

### Anticommunist Operations and Political Rights

These Communist tactics create for all free nations a particularly difficult problem of reconciling freedom with security. On the one hand, most citizens of such nations deeply desire to defend their independence and preserve their free institutions; and they know that should the Communists win neither will survive. On the other hand, free men also wish to preserve the right to express preferences for political views and institutions different from the established ones.

Drawing a line between freedom and security so that each value receives its proper place is never easy. Drawing it when the detection and eradication of Communist subversion is at stake presents one of the most vexing problems faced by the free nations in our time. Let us now briefly review how three such nations—the United States, Great Britain, and France— have faced this dilemma.

## *Drawing the Line in the United States*

### The American View of the Communist Threat

Since 1945 most Americans have come to believe that the Communists and Communist-sympathizers in our midst constitute a very serious danger indeed to American institutions and independence. This conviction does not arise from any widespread fear of a Communist coup putting a commissar in the White House. The American Communist party has never had a membership of more than about 100,000; and since 1954, according to the Federal Bureau of Investigation, it has dwindled to less than 15,000. Most Americans are familiar with these facts, and few believe that native Communists are about to take over the government.

Most Americans are convinced that the real danger posed by native Communists stems from the fact that they are allies and agents of a great and hostile military power, the Soviet Union, and that they operate as its spies and saboteurs. The congressional and other investigations of the late 1940's and early 1950's convinced many Americans that a number of governmental employees—such as Alger Hiss and Henry Julian Wadleigh— had, because of their Communist affiliations, delivered military and diplomatic secrets to the Soviet espionage organization. Many also believe that the Russians developed the atomic bomb several years earlier than they would otherwise have done because of scientific secrets given them by such Communist sympathizers among scientists as Britain's Klaus Fuchs and America's Julius and Ethel Rosenberg. As a result of these disclosures most

Americans have come to believe that our native Communists are a "fifth column" which, in the event of war with the Soviet Union, could be as dangerous to our cause as the Nazi fifth columns were to the European democracies in World War II.[8]

### Governmental Attacks on Communist Subversion

The United States has long had a number of laws prohibiting espionage and sabotage, and these laws have been used to authorize such agencies as the Federal Bureau of Investigation and the military counterespionage services to ferret out and punish members of the "secret" party engaging in such activities. Few, if any, noncommunist Americans have argued that enforcing these laws constitutes a threat to civil liberties.

Most of the controversy over methods of dealing with Communist subversion has centered upon a number of recent legislative and executive acts, mostly by the national government, intended to restrict the advocacy of communist doctrines and other activities of the "open" party as well as the "secret" party. Briefly summarized, these acts are as follows.[9]

*The Smith Act* (1940). This law makes it a federal crime to advocate or teach the doctrine of violent overthrow of any government of the United States, or to organize or help organize any group that does these things, or to conspire to accomplish any of these ends. In 1949 eleven leaders of the "open" Communist party were convicted of violating this act, and in 1951 the Supreme Court sustained their conviction and upheld the constitutionality of the law.

*The Internal Security Act* (1950). This law establishes two classes of subversive organizations: "communist-action" groups (defined by the act as those which are substantially controlled by the Soviet Union and which operate primarily to advance the objectives of world communism); and "communist-front" groups (defined as those which are substantially controlled by a communist-action organization and primarily operated for the purpose of giving aid and support to the communist cause). The law requires both types of organization to register with the United States attorney general and institutes a five-man Subversive Activities Control Board to determine which organizations must register. It also disqualifies Communists from employment in nonelective federal offices and in defense plants,

---

[8] Cf. Harold W. Chase, *Security and Liberty: The Problem of Native Communists, 1947–1955* (Garden City, N.Y.: Doubleday & Company, Inc., 1955), Ch. 1.

[9] Useful summaries of the legislation, executive orders, and judicial interpretations outlined in the text may be found in Jack Peltason, *Constitutional Liberty and Seditious Activity* (New York: Carrie Chapman Catt Memorial Fund, Inc., 1954), pp. 31–45; Robert E. Cushman, *Civil Liberties in the United States* (Ithaca, N.Y.: Cornell University Press, 1956), pp. 167–207; and James M. Burns and Jack W. Peltason, *Government by the People* (5th ed.; Englewood Cliffs, N.J.: Prentice-Hall, Inc., 1963), pp. 148–152.

and requires that all Communist propaganda by mail and broadcasts be openly labeled as such.

*The Communist Control Act (1954).*  This law, without quite making it a crime to be a member of the Communist party, strips the party of just about all its legal rights and privileges (the party cannot appear on the ballot, have recourse to the courts, conduct business as a corporate entity, and so on). It also subjects "Communist-infiltrated organizations" (i.e., those under the control of Communists) to the same requirements and penalties imposed on "communist-action" and "communist-front" organizations by the 1950 Act.

*The Loyalty-Security Program.*  Since 1947 the national government has, by presidential orders and congressional acts, sought to exclude Communists and Communist sympathizers from federal employment. Two related but different requirements have been imposed: "loyalty," which involves the question of whether an employee values the interests and welfare of a communist or other foreign nation more than he does those of the United States; and "security," a broader requirement, which involves determining whether a particular person's holding a government job creates a danger to the military strength and national independence of the United States. Under the "loyalty" tests a person is denied employment only if he is deemed to have Communist affiliations or communist preferences. Under the "security" tests, on the other hand, a person is denied employment if, even though personally loyal, he is vulnerable to Communist pressure because of such traits as family connections, alcoholism, homosexuality, and other possible grounds for blackmail.

The loyalty-security program requires that every applicant for a position in the executive agencies be investigated to determine whether he is of doubtful loyalty or a security risk. The more "sensitive" the agency (i.e., the more it deals with secret military, intelligence, or diplomatic matters) and the more important the post, the more thorough is the investigation. If sufficient "derogatory material" (i.e., evidence suggesting disloyalty, drunkenness, homosexuality, or any trait that might make him vulnerable to blackmail and hence a poor security risk) is uncovered, the applicant is denied the job. The program also calls for the investigation of any employee suspected of these things and for his dismissal if in the judgment of his employing agency the suspicion proves to be well founded.

### The Position of the Courts

In 1951 the Supreme Court upheld the constitutionality of the Smith Act by using the "gravity-of-evil" test described in Chapter 8.[10] A later decision narrowed the act's application by construing it to cover, not the

---

[10] *Dennis v. U.S.,* 341 U.S. 494 (1951).

mere advocacy of some abstract doctrine of violent overthrow of government, but only to the making of plans and exhortations for such overthrow in the near future.[11] And another decision held that membership in an organization advocating violent revolution is punishable only if there is clear evidence that the accused "specifically intended to accomplish the aims of the organization by resort to violence." Mere membership in the Communist party, said the Court, is not sufficient evidence in itself.[12]

The Internal Security Act and Communist Control Act have also been upheld by the Court, although with the same narrow construction applied to the Smith Act. Various aspects of the loyalty-security program have been challenged, and the Court has generally upheld their constitutionality but construed them closely to confine their application to persons in sensitive agencies who *knowingly* join or support Communist-dominated organizations.[13]

In summary, then, the Supreme Court has upheld the constitutionality of the national legislative-executive attack on communist subversion; but in order to protect constitutional rights, it has limited the program's application and restricted some of its procedures.

### Drawing the Line in Great Britain[14]

#### The British View of the Communist Threat

The Communist party of Great Britain has never been able to muster more than about 60,000 members, and its membership has declined sharply since it reached its peak in 1943. The Communists have long sought a "united front" with the Labour party, but the latter has repeatedly refused any such alliance. The dangers of a Communist coup have seemed no more serious to Britons than to Americans.

Great Britain has also had, however, disclosures of Communist infiltration into governmental positions with access to secret military and diplomatic information. In the late 1940's the British public learned with considerable shock that some of its atomic scientists (e.g., Klaus Fuchs, Alan Nunn May, and Bruno Pontecorvo) had been giving secrets to Soviet Russia. Perhaps even more celebrated and shocking was the case of the

---

[11] Yates *v*. *U.S.*, 354 U.S. 298 (1957).

[12] *Scales v. U.S.*, 81 S.Ct. 1469 (1961).

[13] Cf. Burns and Peltason, *op. cit.*, pp. 155–156.

[14] A useful general survey of the status of civil rights in Britain is Harry Street, *Freedom, the Individual and the Law* (Harmondsworth, Middlesex, Eng.: Penguin Books, Ltd., 1953). A comprehensive survey of how Britain has handled the problem of its native Communists, and one that portrays British procedures approvingly, is H. H. Wilson and Harry Glickman, *The Problem of Internal Security in Great Britain, 1948–1953* (New York: Doubleday & Company, Inc., 1954). Most of the data, although not all of the conclusions, in the text are drawn from this survey.

two high-level Foreign Office diplomats, Guy Burgess and Donald Mac-Lean, who mysteriously vanished in 1951, and in 1956 dramatically revealed themselves in Moscow as employees of the Soviet Foreign Office working for "peace."

Thus, espionage and sabotage by native Communists exist in Great Britain as well as in the United States. Yet the British people have demanded and their government has taken far fewer and less drastic steps to combat it than has been the case on the other side of the Atlantic.

### Governmental Attacks on Communist Subversion

Great Britain has a number of laws which are not specifically aimed at Communists but which could be used by a government dead set on stamping out Communist subversion. The Incitement to Mutiny Act (1797) and the Incitement to Disaffection Act (1934) prohibit any effort to subvert the loyalty of members of Her Majesty's armed forces; and both acts have on occasion been used to prosecute persons distributing subversive political literature. The Official Secrets Act (1911) provides for the detection and conviction of spies, and the Emergency Powers Act (1920) authorizes the government to suspend all civil rights guarantees and declare martial law for a period of one month. Britain has, moreover, relatively few formal guarantees of civil rights—far fewer, for example, than the many provisions in the Constitution of the United States—and the British constitution permits such governmental activities as using evidence obtained by tapping private telephone lines, opening and inspection of private mail, and using the law of libel to suppress many kinds of criticism of public officials.

Despite its wide constitutional range of discretion, however, the British government has actually taken far fewer steps than has the American to inhibit the activities of native Communists. The military intelligence services have since World War I quietly gathered information and kept dossiers on the political beliefs of persons in administrative positions suspected of Communist sympathies, and the private mail of such persons has sometimes been opened and read by agents of these services. The government prohibited the publication of the Communist newspaper *The Daily Worker* in January, 1941, but allowed it to reappear in December, 1942.

The only major new British response to the postwar threat of communism has been the loyalty program for the civil service established by the Labour Government in 1948. Prime Minister Clement Attlee announced at that time that, for all civil servants below the policy-making level, there would continue to be complete freedom of political belief and activity, even of the communist variety. All civil servants in the professional, technical, and scientific grades, however, must satisfy certain requirements of loyalty that exclude Communists and Communist sympathizers. He added a number of civil rights safeguards in the enforcement of these standards: all investigations of individuals must be conducted in secret and the information gathered kept confidential; accused persons must have every opportunity to reply to the charges against them; and every effort must be made to transfer to "nonsensitive" positions all persons discharged from "sensitive" positions. From 1948 to 1955 these security measures were applied to about 17,000 out of over a million civil servants, and 152 were suspended for further investigation. Of these, 28 were reinstated, 72 were transferred, 20 resigned, 9 went on special leave, and only 23 were dismissed.[15]

The Burgess-MacLean affair (see above) caused the government to re-examine its security procedures, and in 1957 it announced that they had been tightened. At present a British civil servant is still less likely than an American to be removed for security reasons. But one who is lacks one major right enjoyed by his American counterpart: he cannot appeal to any court of law to review and possibly reverse the administrative agency's decision. His only resource is to get his M.P. to question the minister in Parliament; but the minister may, if he chooses, refuse to answer on the ground that to do so would endanger the national security.[16]

On balance, however, it must be said that the government of Great Britain has not attacked its native Communists as drastically or as vigorously as has the government of the United States. It has not altered the Communist party's status as a legally tolerated party, nor outlawed the advocacy of communist doctrines, nor stripped the party's members of their legal rights, nor required them to register with the government. It has not even barred Communists from all governmental employment.

Why, then, the difference between the anticommunist policies followed by the two nations? Some persons on both sides of the Atlantic answer this question by saying, "The British people and their representatives have not succumbed to the 'hysteria' and 'McCarthyism' that have swept the United States since World War II." Other persons in both nations answer it by saying, "Britons in government and out are asleep to the terrible and imminent threat of world communism to free institutions, and so have taken no effective measures to combat it." These statements, however, are respectively laudatory and denunciatory ways of describing the same basic fact: there is every reason to believe that the particular kind of government policy toward Communist subversion in each nation represents the judgment of its citizenry about the dimensions of the threat to free institutions posed by native Communists on the one hand and by anticommunist measures on the other. Americans and Britons alike, in other words, wish to preserve their freedoms; but they disagree about which threat is the greater and which response involves the least risk to human rights.

---

[15] Street, *op. cit.*, p. 222.
[16] *Ibid.*, pp. 224–230.

## *Drawing the Line in France*

### The French View of the Communist Threat

The threat of native Communists to free institutions is far greater and more obvious in France than in the United States or Great Britain. Communist party membership in the latter nations is under 25,000; but the French Communist party had as many as 800,000 dues-paying members in 1946, and while this figure has since declined to about 400,000, the party still has more dues-paying members than all other French parties combined! In the United States and Great Britain, moreover, the Communists have been able to elect almost no candidates to public office, national or local; but in all French general elections since World War II Communist candidates have received about one quarter of the total popular vote and many Communists have been elected to the national legislature. In the most recent such election (1962) they received 21.3 percent of the popular vote and elected 41 deputies, which made them the third largest party in the National Assembly.

The French Communist operation is powerful in a number of other ways. The party, for example, officially publishes no less than fifteen daily newspapers, fifty-one weeklies, and fifty-six periodicals—to say nothing of the "fellow-traveling" journals it controls. The nation's largest trade union, the CGT (*Confédération Générale du Travail*), is so tightly controlled by its Communist leaders that it is little more than a party agency. Much of the party's strength comes from the fact that over half of France's industrial workers support it, but it also has considerable electoral support from peasants in certain rural areas.[17]

Why are the Communists so much stronger in France than in the United States or Great Britain? There appear to be many explanations. For one thing, the Communists won control of much of the resistance movement during the years of German occupation in World War II and have managed to keep alive in the hearts of Frenchmen their reputation as "the party of 75,000 martyrs." Most observers, however, explain their strength mainly in terms of certain deep-seated ills in the whole French political, social, and economic structure. The divisions among the French people along economic-class, social-class, and ideological lines are deep and bitter; and in many respects there is no single, united French community at all but rather several French communities, each at war with the others. Then, too, a great many Frenchmen have never accepted the traditional Western

---

[17] Cf. Charles A. Micaud, "The Bases of Communist Strength in France," *Western Political Quarterly*, VIII (September, 1955), 354–366; and Roy C. Macridis, "France," in Roy C. Macridis and Robert E. Ward. eds., *Modern Political Systems: Europe* (Englewood Cliffs, N.J.: Prentice-Hall, Inc., 1963), p. 176.

idea of democracy described in Chapter 5. In the 1956 general election, the last under the Fourth Republic, not only did the Communists win a quarter of the votes, but the right-wing, anti-Fourth Republic "Defense-of-Tradesmen-and-Artisans" movement led by Pierre Poujade won 11 percent of the vote and fifty-three parliamentary seats—suggesting that well over one third of the French people rejected the whole idea of democracy. Many Frenchmen, moreover, are far more concerned with social and economic issues than they are with the preservation of French democratic institutions.[18] Whatever may be the reasons, however, it is clear that the Communist threat in France is both unmistakable and powerful, and recognized as such by most noncommunist Frenchmen.

### Governmental Attacks on Communist Subversion

For some time after the liberation in 1944 the noncommunist French parties made every effort to get along with the Communists. There were Communist ministers in the provisional governments following the war and in the first regular government under the new Constitution from 1946 to 1947. When the world-wide Cold War between communism and democracy began in earnest in 1947, however, all attempts at cooperation in France ended. In the spring of that year the Communist ministers left the government, and the Communists have been a major part of every opposition ever since. They have bitterly and often violently attacked all French efforts to join in the activities of the anti-communist world coalition (the Marshall Plan, the North Atlantic Treaty Organization, the European Defense Community, the war against communists in Indochina, and so on).

In their combat against these and similar actions by noncommunist French governments, the French Communists have used three main tactics: infiltrating the armed forces and the civil service, calling riots and general strikes to protest French support of the democracies, and engaging in espionage. Despite the great strength and wealth of the Communists, various noncommunist cabinets have attacked these moves in several different ways. In 1950 they removed as High Commissioner of the French Atomic Energy Commission Professor Frédéric Joliot-Curie, an open Communist sympathizer and winner of the Stalin Peace Prize, and a year later his wife, Mme. Irène Joliot-Curie, as a member of the Commission. In 1951 they suspended a number of civil servants for participating in a Com-

---

[18] Cf the diagnoses of the modern French political *malaise* in François Goguel, *France under the Fourth Republic* (Ithaca, N.Y.: Cornell University Press, 1952); Herbert Luethy, *France against Herself* (translated by Eric Mosbacher; New York: Frederick A. Praeger, Inc., 1955); and Raymond Aron, *France Steadfast and Changing* (Cambridge, Mass.: Harvard University Press, 1960).

munist demonstration against General Eisenhower's NATO headquarters in Paris.

Perhaps the best-known French attack on native Communist activities came in the early summer of 1952, when General Matthew B. Ridgway arrived in Paris to take over the command of NATO forces. The Communists launched a major protest demonstration, mustering approximately 2000 rioters. The police broke it up, and arrested 718 participants, including no less a person than Jacques Duclos, the Number Two leader of the party and a member of the National Assembly. Three days later police all over France raided Communist headquarters in a search for arms and documents showing Communist plans for subversion. The Communists, however, had apparently received advance warning of the raid, for the police found only a few caches of arms and a number of stoves still smoldering with the ashes of burned papers. A Paris appeals court later ordered Duclos's release on the ground that the police had violated his parliamentary immunity to arrest. The fact that M. Paul Didier, the presiding magistrate of the court, was a well-known supporter of many Communist "peace" movements did not make his decision any the less binding.

In summary, then, the threat from native Communists is far stronger and more visible in France than in the United States or Great Britain. This makes governmental restraint of Communist subversion at one and the same time more imperative and more difficult in France than in either of the other two nations. Despite the French Communists' great voting strength and wealth and also despite the traditional French distrust of any kind of governmental interference with political activity, the French government has taken more drastic steps to restrict Communist activities than has the British.

There is no reason to believe that the Communists have had any greater success in espionage and sabotage in France than in the other two nations. But an American observer, E. Drexel Godfrey, Jr., feels that French Communists may well have already accomplished their long-range objective of weakening democracy in France so that it will collapse with one good shove from the outside. As he says:

> Years of bombast fired at the "criminal Republic" and all its works have added imperceptibly to the Frenchman's normal disdain for government in any form, and particularly for the government in power. . . . The real winner in the struggle that has been going on since Liberation may be the grey hosts of complete political irresponsibility and disaffection from public life.[19]

---

[19] "The Communist Presence in France," *American Political Science Review*, L (June, 1956), 321–328.

### Controlling Communist Subversion: Conclusion

A growing number of leaders in the free nations have come to believe that recent developments in world communism have rendered the old certainties of the Cold War less certain, and question whether the policies based on them are relevant to present-day conditions. They point to the "thaw" in the Soviet Union after Stalin's death, the increasing Russian emphasis on "coexistence," the apparent moderation in tactics and possible alteration of objectives of Communist parties in most of the free nations, and, above all, the repeated and bitter clashes between the Russians and the Red Chinese. They conclude that these developments at least suggest the possibility that Russian-style Communists are becoming, or will become, tolerable participants in free societies and not, as heretofore, their implacable enemies.

Other Western leaders insist that the post-Stalin developments have in no way affected the basic nature of communism or lessened its danger to free institutions. Accordingly, they argue that if the free nations drop their guard in any way, freedom will perish.

Clearly, any free government's analysis of this question will largely determine its view of how far it should go to control Communist subversion at home. But the free nations' most learned and shrewd experts on world communism disagree among themselves about the correct analysis. Hence no government can be *certain* that its policy is based on an accurate diagnosis of what its domestic Communists intend. So any line of attack on Communist subversion—including the line of no attack at all—involves grave risks for the rights of man. Every policy is inevitably a gamble—and a gamble for the highest stakes men play for.

## Conflict over Racial Discrimination

### "An American Dilemma": The Conflict in the United States

#### The Drive for White Supremacy

"Racial discrimination" means placing handicaps on all members of a particular racial group solely because of their race and without regard to their individual characteristics: e.g., barring any Negro, no matter how intelligent or well prepared, from attending a university; or prohibiting any Jew, no matter how pleasant or cooperative, from buying a house in a "restricted" neighborhood. It is one of the oldest and most often encountered aspects of man's inhumanity to man. Wherever men of different races have been thrown together in the same society, at least some members of the dominant race have attempted to discriminate against members of another race or races—Gentiles against Jews, whites against Negroes, Occi-

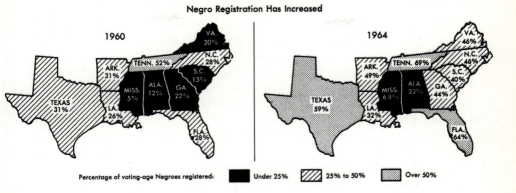

Negro Registration Has Increased

Percentage of voting-age Negroes registered:  ■ Under 25%   ▨ 25% to 50%   ▧ Over 50%

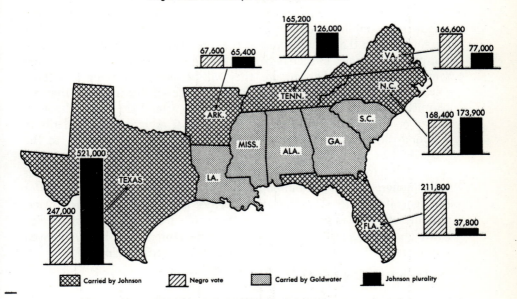

Negro Vote Was a Major Factor in Johnson Total

▧ Carried by Johnson   ▨ Negro vote   ▨ Carried by Goldwater   ■ Johnson plurality

*Figure 16.* Southern Negroes and the Right to Vote. (Copyright by *The New York Times,* November 22, 1964. Reprinted by permission.)

dentals against Orientals, Anglo-Saxons against Latins, Africans against Indians, and so on. In most societies the conflict over discrimination has become political: i.e., the group favoring discrimination has tried to embody its desires in governmental policy, while the antidiscrimination group has resisted and tried to secure governmental help to prevent discrimination by private groups.

The United States, as we shall see, certainly has no monopoly on the practice of racial discrimination, governmental or private. But discrimination against Negroes in America has, whether fairly or not, received more attention and comment, both here and abroad, than have its counterparts in other nations.

The drive for discrimination against Negroes in the United States is conducted by white persons who believe in establishing and maintaining "white supremacy." These "white supremacists" live and exert political pressure in all parts of the nation, but they are found in the highest concentration and are the most powerful in the Deep South states of Alabama, Georgia, Louisiana, Mississippi, and South Carolina. Their most prominent official spokesmen are certain white residents of these states, and their main formal organizations are the White Citizens' Councils, the Society for the Preservation of the White Race, and a revived Ku Klux Klan.

Briefly summarized, the white supremacists' position is as follows: Negroes are *racially* inferior to whites in intelligence, morality, civic-mindedness, stability, maturity, and so on. This is no fault of theirs; they are simply born that way. So long as they are "kept in their place," Negroes can play useful roles in society by performing many of the menial jobs that must be done; and what is more, they will be happiest playing only those roles. But if Negroes are not kept in their place—if, for instance, they are permitted to vote and hold public office or to attend the same schools as whites or to hold the same jobs as whites—their inherent racial inferiority will drag down the whole community, whites, Negroes, and all, to the Negroes' low level. The worst catastrophe that can occur is the intermarriage of Negroes and whites, for the children produced by such alliances will "mongrelize" the whole population with disastrous consequences for the general welfare. Consequently, Negroes must be kept in their place, and any effort to raise any or all of them to a higher place must be vigilantly guarded against. To this end the white supremacists have employed a number of devices, some of which we shall describe below.

### The Drive for Racial Equality[20]

Opposed to the white supremacists are a number of Americans, both Negro and white, who are trying to secure for Negroes the same legal, social, and economic rights and opportunities now enjoyed by whites. Their position may be briefly summarized: Negroes are human beings. They are also American citizens and are therefore fully entitled to the same rights

---

[20] Among the better recent accounts of the Negro rights movement are Alan F. Westin, *Freedom Now! The Civil-Rights Struggle in America* (New York: Basic Books, Inc., 1964); Oscar Handlin, *Fire-Bell in the Night: The Crisis in Civil Rights* (Boston: Little, Brown & Company, 1964); and Arnold M. Rose, ed., "The Negro Protest," *Annals of the American Academy of Political and Social Science*, Vol. CCCLVII (January, 1965).

and privileges as all other American citizens. Whether or not a particular Negro shall vote, hold public office, get a job, attend a school, or practice a profession should be determined according to his individual capabilities, not by the color of his skin. To give Negroes anything less than this kind of equal opportunity with whites is to deny them not only their constitutional rights, as guaranteed in the Fourteenth Amendment, but their basic rights as human beings.

The equal-rights movement is organized into six main groups which agree on these objectives but differ somewhat in tactics, as the following groupings suggest.[21]

### The "Legalists"

The oldest group is the National Association for the Advancement of Colored People (NAACP), founded in 1909. It has consistently emphasized pressure on Congress and constitutional challenges to discrimination in the federal courts, and it has won many notable legislative and judicial victories, some of which we shall describe in a moment.

### The "Educationists"

The National Urban League, founded in 1910, stresses interracial educational programs in local communities aimed at breaking down segregation and discrimination, particularly in housing and employment. It operates as much in the North as in the South. The Southern Regional Council (1944) is a group of southern whites and Negroes working together to overcome racial prejudice by education; in recent years it has also undertaken a program of Negro voter education.

### The "Activists"

In recent years a number of equal-rights advocates have felt that the victories of the other organizations, while welcome, are being achieved at too slow a pace. Accordingly, they have organized three groups committed to the idea of using such direct-action techniques as picketing, demonstrations, "sit-in's," boycotts, and the like. The Congress of Racial Equality (CORE), organized in 1941 by James Farmer, was the first such group; in its first decade it operated mainly in the North, but since the early 1950's it has been very active in the South as well. The Southern Christian Leadership Conference, founded by Dr. Martin Luther King, Jr., in 1957, uses Gandhian nonviolent resistance tactics for the same goals; its activities have won not only a number of victories over segregation in southern cities but also the 1965 Nobel Peace Prize for Dr. King. The Student Nonviolent

---

[21] For more complete descriptions see Rose, *op. cit.*, pp. 97–126, especially the article by James H. Laue at pp. 119–226.

Co-ordinating Committee (SNCC) was originally founded in 1960 to keep the various student "sit-in" groups in communication, but more recently it has devoted most of its efforts to organize Negro registration, voting, and education drives in the Deep South.

### Some Areas of Conflict

Both sides, then, are well organized and deeply committed to their profoundly clashing goals. Their conflict has been perhaps the most bitter and explosive issue in American politics for many years. It has been particularly acute in the following areas.

VOTING. Since the Reconstruction period immediately following the Civil War, the white supremacists in the South have attempted by one device or another—poll taxes, literacy tests, "grandfather clauses," and the "white primary" are examples—to keep Negroes from exercising the voting rights granted them by the Fifteenth Amendment. However, the Twenty-fourth Amendment, ratified in 1964, outlaws state requirements of poll taxes for voting in federal elections; and the Supreme Court has held unconstitutional all discriminatory devices: i.e., those which keep well-qualified Negroes from voting because of their race while permitting otherwise unqualified "poor whites" to vote. The result has been that Negroes are voting in ever-increasing numbers in southern elections, although many are still barred from the polls by such informal and extralegal devices as intimidation and violence. The use of such measures partially explains why 64 percent of the Negroes cast no ballots in the 1956 elections and why in most southern states a far smaller proportion of legally eligible Negroes than whites even get their names on the rosters of registered voters.

EDUCATION.[22] For many years white supremacists have insisted that under no conditions must Negroes be permitted to attend the same schools as whites, arguing that the Negroes' intellectual inferiority will be a drag on the educational development of white pupils if the two races are educated in the same classes. Immediately after the Civil War most states, southern and nonsouthern alike, had constitutional or statutory prohibitions requiring racial segregation in public schools.[23] In the succeeding decades, however, most nonsouthern states repealed them, and twenty-two states adopted constitutional or statutory provisions specifically prohibiting such segregation.

---

[22] An excellent account of the background of the Brown decision is Robert J. Harris, *The Quest for Equality* (Baton Rouge: Louisiana State University Press, 1960). The Southern Education Reporting Service provides the most up-to-date information about the progress of school desegregation.

[23] These were included in several "Jim Crow" laws requiring racial segregation in a number of areas; cf. C. Vann Woodward, *The Strange Career of Jim Crow* (New York: Oxford University Press, 1957).

The present crisis in this long-standing conflict began in 1954. In that year a total of nineteen states (four of them outside the South) and the District of Columbia legally required racial segregation in their public schools. On several occasions these laws had been challenged in the Supreme Court as violations of the clause in the Fourteenth Amendment which provides: "No State shall . . . deny to any person within its jurisdiction the equal protection of the laws"; but the Court consistently upheld them, following the "separate-but-equal" rule first laid down in 1896 that segregation in itself is not a denial of equal protection so long as equal facilities are afforded both races.[24] In the early 1950's, however, the NAACP under the leadership of its principal constitutional lawyer, Thurgood Marshall, again challenged the constitutionality of state school-segregation laws by asking the Court to abandon the old "separate-but-equal" formula. In a unanimous opinion written by Chief Justice Earl Warren in the case of *Brown v. Board of Education* the Court did just that by holding that racial segregation *in itself* is a denial of equal protection regardless of the facilities provided; and in 1955 the Court ordered the federal district courts to proceed "with all deliberate speed" to see that local school boards complied with the ruling.[25]

The Brown decision has by no means ended all school segregation. The border states (Delaware, Kentucky, Maryland, Missouri, Oklahoma, and West Virginia) and the District of Columbia have abolished segregation almost completely; the "upper-South" states (Arkansas, Florida, North Carolina, Tennessee, Texas, and Virginia) have proceeded with much more deliberate speed, and by the mid-1960's there are still many enclaves of segregation in all; and the Deep-South states of Alabama, Georgia, Louisiana, Mississippi, and South Carolina have admitted only tiny fractions of their Negro children to unsegregated schools—and then only under the strongest pressure from the federal government. And in many northern cities the concentration of Negroes in certain residential areas and the drawing of school district boundaries has continued the long-practiced *de facto* segregation.

The principal technique of the most unyielding southern segregationists has been what may be called "local nullification," which includes the refusal of local school boards to integrate voluntarily—or of state legislatures to permit the local boards to integrate. However, the federal government has directly intervened with United States marshals and even troops to enforce court desegregation orders in, for example, Little Rock, New Orleans, and Oxford, Mississippi. These interventions have increased the segregationists' anger, for they seem to be the most flagrant violations of

---

[24] *Plessy v. Ferguson*, 163 U.S. 537 (1896).
[25] *Brown v. Board of Education*, 347 U.S. 483 (1954); and 349 U.S. 294 (1955).

states' rights and recall the bitter memories of federal armies of occupation in the Reconstruction era following the Civil War. This anger was manifested in 1964 when Senator Barry Goldwater, who had publicly denounced such violations of states' rights, carried the five Deep-South states—the first Republican to carry four of them since the 1870's.

It seems clear, then, that for better or worse the complete racial integration of public schools North and South will take a number of years. The Court's 1954 decision, in short, was a signal—but far from total—victory for the racial-equality forces.

HOUSING.  For many years Negroes (and, to a lesser extent, Jews) have been denied equal opportunities for housing by the private device of "restrictive covenants." These are agreements among white property owners that they will not sell their houses to Negro buyers, thereby ensuring segregation of the races in residential areas. These covenants used to be embodied in formal contracts among property owners, and had a particular owner violated the covenant by selling to a Negro he could have been sued in the courts for breach of contract. In 1948, however, the Supreme Court struck a powerful (though not mortal) blow at restrictive covenants by declaring that while they are not in themselves unlawful, they cannot be enforced by any court of law, state or federal, on the ground that such enforcement would make the courts parties to the covenants and thereby violate the Fourteenth Amendment.[26]

In a great many white residential areas, of course, restrictive covenants are still highly effective in preventing Negroes from moving in; for they are regarded as "gentlemen's agreements," and while the 1948 decision removed all legal sanctions supporting them, the desire of white property owners to retain the esteem of their white neighbors remains a powerful social and psychological force sustaining them. Hence many civil-rights leaders believe that government must take positive action against private discrimination. A number of cities and some states have adopted "open occupancy" laws which make it illegal to refuse to sell or rent property to anyone because of his race. In 1962 President Kennedy signed an executive order forbidding racial discrimination in the sale or rental of housing owned or operated by the federal government, but only about 25 percent of the new housing market was covered by it. In the area of housing, too, Negroes are thus substantially better off today than they were in the 1940's, but still far from their goal of complete equality.[27]

---

[26] In the case of *Shelley v. Kraemer*, 334 U.S. 1 (1948). This decision was further extended in *Barrows v. Jackson*, 346 U.S. 249 (1953).

[27] Cf. Davis McEntire, *Residence and Race* (Berkeley: University of California Press, 1960).

EMPLOYMENT. Negroes have long been the most economically depressed ethnic group in America. The only jobs open to most have been those in low-paying manual labor or domestic service. Many civil-rights leaders believe that the key to unlock all other doors now closed to Negroes is to upgrade them economically by improving their training for more skilled and better-paying jobs and by making sure that qualified Negroes have a fair chance to get those jobs. So they have pressed for the enactment of "fair employment practices" laws prohibiting discrimination in hiring and promotion because of race. A number of states have adopted such laws, but many are loosely drawn and others laxly enforced, so they have helped somewhat but not enough. Moreover, few applied to trade unions, which sometimes refuse to let Negroes join and earn the union card necessary for so many jobs.

PUBLIC ACCOMMODATIONS. White supremacists have long sought to keep Negroes from using the same public services and accommodations as whites—from riding in the same parts of trains and buses, sitting in the same parts of theaters, using the same restaurants, golf courses, swimming pools, barbershops, and so on. For a time some twenty-odd states actually had "Jim Crow" laws requiring such segregation, but they were deemed unconstitutional after the Brown case dropped the "separate-but-equal" formula. Another twenty or so states adopted laws prohibiting racial discrimination by private businesses offering public accommodations or in any publicly owned and operated facility. But many of these laws were enforced little or not at all, Negroes were commonly refused service, and civil-rights leaders came to feel that only action by the federal government would ever guarantee equal access.

### The Civil Rights Act of 1964

As we have seen, the conflict over Negro rights began to play a major role in American politics right after World War II, and the racial-equality groups scored a number of victories—notably the school desegregation decision of 1954. In 1963, however, a series of ugly incidents in Birmingham, Alabama—particularly unrestrained police brutality in breaking up Negro picket lines, and the bombing of a church causing the death of several Negro children—escalated the conflict to a new and dangerous level of rancor and violence.

At this point President John F. Kennedy decided that the time had come for truly full-scale federal intervention to secure Negro rights and to end the small-scale but increasingly bitter civil war. In mid-year he asked Congress to enact by far the most sweeping federal civil-rights legislation since Reconstruction. His proposals met determined opposition from most southern congressmen and from a number of northern conservative advocates of states' rights. Moreover, his assassination in November put into the White House the first Southerner to hold the Presidency since 1869. So the fate of the civil-rights bill—and the whole future of the conflict—seemed very much in doubt.

But the new President, Lyndon B. Johnson, gave the bill the top priority in his program. His unmatched skills at congressional leadership, supplemented by the support of a number of leaders of both parties in Congress—notably Democratic Senate Whip Hubert Humphrey and Republican Senate Minority Leader Everett Dirksen, brought off the legislative miracle: the bill was passed by the House of Representatives in February and by the Senate in July.

For some time to come the Civil Rights Act of 1964 will be the principal legislation guaranteeing Negroes' rights. Its main provisions are as follows.

(1) VOTING RIGHTS.  Title I reinforces the federal government's authority to secure Negroes' voting rights. It prohibits state election officials from using different registration standards and procedures for Negroes and whites, and authorizes the attorney general to intervene wherever he detects a violation of these rules. It is reinforced by the 1965 Voting Rights Act.

(2) PUBLIC ACCOMMODATIONS.  Title II forbids racial discrimination in the serving of customers by all private businesses providing public accommodations—hotels, motels, restaurants, gasoline stations, theaters, sports arenas, and the like.

(3) PUBLIC FACILITIES.  Title III prohibits racial discrimination in all publicly owned and operated facilities: parks, libraries, swimming pools, golf courses, and so on.

(4) SCHOOL DESEGREGATION.  The act seeks to accelerate school desegregation by offering financial and technical assistance to schools trying to desegregate, and by authorizing the attorney general to proceed directly against school boards refusing to desegregate, thereby removing the burden of enforcement from the victims of discrimination, where it had rested since 1954.

(5) EQUAL EMPLOYMENT OPPORTUNITIES.  Title VII forbids private employers to practice racial discrimination in hiring or promotion. It also forbids labor unions to exclude anyone from membership because of his race. These rules will be enforced by an Equal Employment Commission empowered to hear and investigate charges of discrimination, and by the attorney general, who is authorized to force compliance if voluntary efforts and state and local laws fail.

(6) WITHHOLDING FEDERAL FUNDS.  Title VI authorizes the executive

agencies to withhold funds from any federally financed program in any locality where racial discrimination is practiced in defiance of the law.

Many observers feared massive resistance to the new law, particularly to the public accommodations section in the Deep South. But, to the surprise of everyone and to the relief of most, there was immediate and general voluntary compliance in all parts of the South. Pockets of resistance remained here and there, but in the main the law was voluntarily obeyed without intervention by federal executive agencies. Thus most observers feel that President Johnson did not exaggerate when he called the act "an historic step forward for the cause of human dignity in America."

### The Problem in the Republic of South Africa[28]

#### Its Dimensions

The United States is by no means the only free nation in which a major political group is pressing for a governmental policy of white supremacy. Most Australians, for example, have long regarded their nation as "a white island in a colored sea," and since its origins as a nation Australia has consistently followed a "white Australia" policy supported by all parties. This policy has prevented racial conflict by simply prohibiting nonwhite immigration and thus restricting the nonwhite population to a tiny fraction of the total.[29]

Even Great Britain, long considered a model of racial equality, has had its troubles. The great influx of Negro West Indians and Asiatic Pakistanis in the 1950's led to the formation of racial ghettos in several big cities, race riots in the Notting Hill Gate area of London, and such ugly slogans in political campaigns as "If you want a nigger neighbour, vote Labour," which is supposed to have cost Labour's prospective foreign secretary, Patrick Gordon Walker, his seat at Smethwick in the 1964 general election. It also led to the passage in 1961 of the Commonwealth Immigrants Act, which ended the free entry of West Indians and Pakistanis.

The drive for governmentally enforced white supremacy has come closest to total victory in the Republic of South Africa, which presently has a population of about 17,000,000, of whom 3,600,000 are of pure European descent, 1,500,000 are "colored" (of mixed native and European descent), and 11,400,000 are of pure native or Bantu descent. Most of the

---

[28] Among the best discussions are Gwendolen M. Carter, *The Politics of Inequality* (2d ed.; New York: Frederick A. Praeger, Inc., 1959); Leopold Marquard, *The Peoples and Policies of South Africa* (3d ed.; New York: Oxford University Press, 1962); and Edward Roux, *Time Longer than Rope* (2d ed.; Madison: University of Wisconsin Press, 1964).

[29] Cf. Alexander Brady, *Democracy in the Dominions* (2d ed.; Toronto: University of Toronto Press, 1952), pp. 143–147.

Europeans are highly conscious of their status as a small white minority among a large native majority, and their feelings are reinforced by the knowledge that on the whole continent of Africa there are only about 5 million Europeans compared with 260 million natives.

From the time of the earliest white settlements, most Europeans in South Africa—the Afrikaners (settlers of Dutch descent) and the British-descended settlers alike—have been acutely conscious of the *Swart Gevaar* ("black menace" in Afrikaans, the language of the Dutch-descended South Africans) and have resolved to maintain the *baaskap* (literally "boss-ship") of white men over black. Their fears and resolution were clearly expressed in a 1955 statement by Eric H. Louw, then South African foreign minister:

> If we were to give [the natives] equality of franchise, then even-tually the white man would be outvoted, and the non-Europeans would have control. The present laws which are for the purpose of keeping the races separate, allowing each race to develop along its own lines in its own areas—those laws would all be swept away. European and Bantu would live together. There would be miscegenation, and in another 100 years, or even earlier, South Africa would become a coun-try with a large mixed population.[30]

## The Policy of *Apartheid*

For many years the white rulers of South Africa have pursued the policy of *apartheid* ("separateness"). The long-range goal of this policy is com-plete separation of the natives from the Europeans, with each race living in its own special areas but with ultimate governmental power over all areas and races remaining exclusively in white hands. Most white South Africans, however, regard the achievement of this goal as two or three hundred years away; and so as a short-range policy *apartheid* generally means as com-plete segregation of the races as possible with white supremacy maintained in all aspects of life. Among its leading legal manifestations may be men-tioned the following.

SEPARATION. The Population Registration Act of 1950 provides for the classification and registration of the entire South African population into three categories: European, native, and "colored." Each person must be ticketed and photographed and must carry an identity card showing to which of the three races he belongs. The ultimate goal is the compilation of a complete "Book of Life" containing the racial classification of every South African. The Group Areas Act of 1950 empowers the government to designate particular areas for exclusive occupancy by particular races, and

---

[30] From a copyrighted interview in *U.S. News & World Report,* XXXIX (July 22, 1955), 58–63.

the Native Resettlement Act authorizes the forcible relocation of natives from their present living areas to native "reserves." Every native must carry an identity card, and if he wishes to travel or live outside his reserve he must show on demand a "pass" authorizing him to do so. Since 1950 the government has actually moved several hundred thousand natives in accordance with this legislation, but at present less than half of the natives live in reserves. Those who do are required by the government to follow their ancient forms of tribal government and chieftainships even though many feel these forms are outmoded and wish to adopt more modern procedures.

EDUCATION. The South African government now controls all native education and for the most part follows a policy of providing education appropriate only to the traditionally primitive culture and technology of the Bantus. Prior to 1957 a few "coloreds" and natives attended South Africa's universities. The Separate Universities Education Act of 1957 ended all that: all nonwhites are barred from attending any of the regular universities, and a "Bantu College" has been established for each nonwhite ethnic group: one for the Xhosa, another for the Zulus, another for the Sotho, another for the coloreds, and so on. None of these are independent colleges, but are administered directly by government departments to make sure that the right things are taught.

POLITICAL PARTICIPATION. In only one of the five provinces, the Cape Province, have natives and coloreds ever been allowed to vote for members of the national Parliament. The Representation of Natives Act of 1936 confined the natives to voting only for seven members of Parliament, each of whom had to be a European. In 1956 the coloreds were deprived of the right to vote for members of Parliament other than the seven "native representatives." But in 1960 the Cape Province natives and coloreds were deprived of even these rights, and the "native representatives" were abolished.

OCCUPATIONS. Natives in South Africa have long been informally barred from engaging in any occupation higher or better paid than domestic service and unskilled labor. The Industrial Conciliation Act of 1954 placed the power of the government behind this discrimination by authorizing the minister of labor to determine at his own discretion what occupations are open to members of the various races.

PUBLIC SERVICES AND ACCOMMODATIONS. Complete racial segregation in such areas as transportation, hospitals, cemeteries, restaurants, and theaters has long been practiced by the private individuals who manage them. The Separate Amenities Act of 1953 made such segregation compulsory.

## Political Conflict and Constitutional Revision

Only a few South African whites (including the well-known novelist Alan Paton) support the tiny Liberal party, which advocates a policy of gradual racial integration and equality. The great bulk of the European population and the parties they support believe in some form of *apartheid*, although there has been sharp conflict among them over the pace and proper means of establishing it. This conflict has been fought out mainly between the two leading political parties: the Nationalist party, now led by the Prime Minister Hendrik Verwoerd, and the United party, formerly led by Field Marshal Jan Christiaan Smuts, and now headed by Sir de Villiers Graaff.

The Nationalists replaced the United party in power in the general election of 1948 and since then have pressed for drastic measures of *apartheid* at a pace more rapid than their opponents have thought proper. They have controlled Parliament ever since, and in their resolute effort to establish *apartheid* and to stamp out all effective opposition to it they have pushed the nation well along the road to totalitarianism, although not yet quite all the way. The major milestones in this movement have been the following.

In 1951 the Nationalist Government forced through the Suppression of Communism Act, which not only empowers the government to jail all "Communists" and suppress all "communist" doctrines but also defines "communism" as any doctrine or scheme "which aims at bringing about any political, industrial, or economic change within the [Republic] by the promotion of disturbance or by the threat of such acts," or ". . . which aims at the encouragement of feelings of hostility between the European and non-European races in the [Republic]."[31]

In 1951 the Nationalist Government drove a bill through Parliament to strike the coloreds from the common roll of voters in Cape Province (see above), but the five-man Supreme Court of Appeals unanimously declared it unconstitutional. The Nationalists then adopted a bill making Parliament itself a High Court with final authority to interpret the Constitution, but the Supreme Court also declared this unconstitutional. After three years of searching for ways of getting around the Court, the Nationalists found one: in 1955 they passed a bill enlarging the Court from five to eleven; the Nationalist prime minister appointed as the six new judges men known to be faithful supporters of the Nationalist program. Thereafter the Court caused them no trouble.

In the years following, the Nationalists passed the "ninety-day law,"

---

[31] Quoted in John Gunther, *Inside Africa* (New York: Harper & Row, Publishers, 1955), p. 540.

which empowers the government to arrest anyone it wishes and hold him in house or village arrest without having to bring him to trial. Under this provision Chief Albert Luthuli, winner of the 1960 Nobel Peace Prize, has been confined to his village in Natal for years. The Nationalists in 1962 also enacted the General Law Amendment (Sabotage) Act which gives a very broad definition of sabotage and makes it an offense punishable by death. Most observers now feel that there is no legal or political barrier in the path of any policy of *apartheid* the Nationalists may wish to enact.

### The Future of Apartheid

In 1955 the Nationalist Government appointed a special commission, headed by Professor F. R. Tomlinson, to study the problem of implementing *apartheid* more rapidly. In 1956 the government accepted the commission's report as the basis of its future policy, which has come to be known as the "Bantustan" policy. It proposes to press on with the development of seven exclusively native areas (three of which—Swaziland, Basutoland, and Bechuanaland—are British protectorates and would have to be handed over by the British to South Africa, a most unlikely prospect), and that money be spent to develop these areas to make possible mass relocation of the natives. The Promotion of Bantu Self-Government Act of 1959 established the first "Bantustan" under the new policy. The government, however, has announced that it will not spend its funds for development of these areas and that any development funds must come from the natives themselves. An American commentator, Gwendolen M. Carter, has suggested that, since there is no possibility that the natives can ever provide out of their own resources anything remotely approaching what is needed, it is unlikely that the "Bantustan" policy will be fully implemened in the foreseeable future.[32] If she is correct, for some time to come *apartheid* in South Africa will continue to mean governmental policies of segregation and white supremacy, and not a complete separation of the two races.

# The Rights of Man: A Summary

In this and the preceding chapter we have tried to portray the problem of the rights of man in the modern world as one that has not only its philosophical and legal aspects but its political side as well. Specifically, we have made the following observations.

---

[32] Gwendolen M. Carter, "The Consequences of *Apartheid*," *Annals of the American Academy of Political and Social Science*, CCCVI (July, 1956), 38–42.

1. The term "civil rights" refers both to certain things governments are constitutionally prohibited from doing to individual persons and also to certain duties governments are constitutionally obligated to perform for individual persons.

2. Although every present-day Constitution contains at least some formal guarantees of civil rights, modern nations can be divided into two classes: the "free nations," in which most persons value highly the protection of these rights and insist that their governments preserve them; and the "authoritarian nations," in which the preservation of civil rights is far outranked by other and conflicting values.

3. In the free nations most people are committed to the idea that civil rights should be preserved either because they are regarded as ends in themselves or because they are thought of as indispensable means for creating and maintaining the good society.

4. The problem of preserving civil rights in the free nations is best understood by recognizing the fact that the conflict over human freedom takes place between group and group, not between "the individual" and "the government." Guaranteeing the freedom of one group usually means abridging the freedom of another. The basic question of freedom is not whether there shall be any at all, but rather what kind of freedom shall be preserved and for whom.

5. One great challenge to civil rights in the free world is the problem of how to control subversion by native Communists without abridging the rights of free speech, free press, and due process of law for noncommunist dissenters from the established order. The United States, Great Britain, and France have each attacked this problem in a different way; and no one can say authoritatively which of the three solutions is best.

6. The free nations of the world are faced with another challenge to civil rights: the conflict over racial segregation and white supremacy. In the United States the groups pressing for equal rights for Negroes have recently won a series of impressive victories but are still far from fully achieving their ultimate goal of complete equality. At the same time white-supremacy groups in the Union of South Africa, with ever-increasing vigor and success, have smashed all efforts to secure anything approaching equal rights with whites for persons classified as natives or coloreds.

What does it all add up to? Essentially this: the question eternally facing all free nations is not whether they shall have absolute freedom for all or none whatever but rather which freedoms they shall guarantee to which groups and at what social costs. No free nation has answered this question perfectly, if indeed it can be answered perfectly. But seeking more satisfactory answers to benefit ever-increasing proportions of their citizens is surely one of the most crucial and difficult tasks all free nations face.

# part three

## Political Agencies
## and
## Processes

# 10

## Public Opinion:

### *nature and determinants*

Most of us in the Western world are accustomed to think that public opinion plays a significant role only in a democracy. Yet this view is far too parochial. As one of the greatest political scientists of our time put it:

> Governments must concern themselves with the opinions of their citizens, if only to provide a basis for repression of disaffection. The persistent curiosity, and anxiety, of rulers about what their subjects say of them and their actions are chronicled in the histories of secret police. Measures to satisfy each curiosity by soundings of public opinion are often only an aspect of political persecution; they may also guide policies of persuasion calculated to convert discontent into cheerful acquiescence. And even in the least democratic regime opinion may influence the direction or tempo of substantive policy. Although a government may be erected on tyranny, to endure it needs the ungrudging support of substantial numbers of its people.[1]

For these reasons, in both democracies and dictatorships the cultivation of public opinion is a major preoccupation of most powerful political groups. In the democracies political parties, candidates, and pressure groups spend millions bombarding us ordinary citizens with television "spots," billboard displays, newspaper advertisements, bumper-sticker slogans, and the like, all intended to nudge public opinion in the desired direction. A "public relations counsel" sits at the elbow of many a public figure advising him how to cultivate "a good public image." Commercial polling organizations are hired by newspapers to issue frequent reports on how the public views the parties, candidates, and issues of the moment.

---

[1] V. O. Key, Jr., *Public Opinion and American Democracy* (New York: Alfred A. Knopf, Inc., 1961), p. 3.

[ 205 ]

But dictatorships are also much concerned with public opinion. Their ministries of propaganda (or "public education" or "public information") spend millions to whip up enthusiasm for what the dictators want to do. And their secret police spend as much ferreting out and destroying clandestine efforts to oppose the dictator's policy.

So all governments and all political groups treat public opinion as a mighty force. But just what *is* it? What forces shape it? How can we be sure what public opinion calls for on this or that matter of public policy? These questions have long fascinated students of politics, and in this and the succeeding chapter we shall review some of their findings.

## Public Opinion in the Democracies

By way of introduction, let us sketch a picture of the opinion processes in an imaginary democracy and then call attention to some of their main characteristics.

Imagine a New England town with a total citzenry of fifteen members. Members A, B, and C have farms on the town's north road and propose that the town pave it; A and B feel very strongly about it, but C is less worked up. D, E, and F, who own farms on the south road, feel discriminated against and oppose any such move, although F is less angry about it than the other two. G, H, and I are merchants who feel that paving the road will mean higher taxes, so they plan to oppose it—unless doing so means the loss of A, B, and Cs' business. J and K are widows living on income from real estate, and they too oppose such a move because of the higher taxes it will bring, but they consider it unladylike to be too openly political. L and M, the town's odd-jobs men, own no farms, pay no real-estate taxes, dislike the persons who do, and could not care less about the whole matter. N and O, the town's ministers, have parishioners on both sides, feel that no moral or religious issue is involved, and decide it would be prudent to stay out of the fight.

At the town meeting A moves that the north road be paved. A, B, and C vote Yes; D, E, F, G, H, I, J, and K vote No; L and M don't even bother to attend the meeting; and N and O, while present, do not vote. Thus A's motion is defeated, 8 votes to 3. Then A has an inspiration: he moves that *both* the north and south roads be paved, and that they be officially named after the late husband of J. On this second proposal, A, B, and C again vote Yes, and are joined not only by D, E, and F but also by J and by N (the late Mr. J was one of N's favorite parishioners). Only G, H, I, and K vote against it, and the proposal carries by a vote of 8 to 4.

What then, can we say about the nature of "public opinion" in this imaginary democracy? For one thing, on neither issue did *all* the town's members express an opinion. For another, not all the members of any side felt equally strongly about the matter. And for yet another, when the first issue was replaced by the second, there was a reshuffling of the individuals composing the "pro" and "con" groups. While both issues may be said to have been decided in accordance with "public opinion," it is inaccurate to picture the latter as a body of attitudes on all issues held by all fifteen members of the community constituting an entity known as *the* public. How, then, should we picture "public opinion"?

## A Definition

The literature of social science offers many different definitions of "public opinion." In this book we shall use V. O. Key's: *public opinion consists of those opinions held by private persons which governments find it prudent to heed.*[2]

In this definition an "opinion" is any expression of a private person's attitude on a political issue, and an "attitude" is any preference, idea, or other notion about what government should or should not do that is expressed in any manner by which others can be made aware of its content—including such methods as words conveyed in speech or writing, gestures, facial expressions, making *X*'s on ballots, and holding up hands. "Public opinion" is the sum of all those opinions of which governmental officials are to some degree aware and which they take into account in deciding what official action they should or should not take.

According to this definition, then, "public opinion" is specific to particular political situations and issues; it is not a body of ideas on all issues held by all the members of the community known as *the* public. Each issue produces its particular constellation of opinion groups, always including one which expresses no opinion whatever (every "public opinion poll" that queries a cross section of the populace on a particular issue always discovers that some of the responses have to be classified as "don't know" or "don't care"). From issue to issue there is always some reshuffling among the individuals composing the various opinion groups: some of the "pros" and "cons" on one issue reverse sides or become "don't cares" on the next; and some of the previous "don't cares" now take sides.

## Dimensions of Public Opinion

Political scientists find it useful to think of public opinion as having two dimensions: *direction* and *intensity*. The direction dimension measures the quality of being for or against some party, candidate, or policy; and the intensity dimension measures how strongly a person or group of persons feel about their directional preferences.[3] In terms of actual political conflict, each dimension is just as important as the other: e.g., if 60 percent

---

[2] *Ibid.*, p. 14.
[3] Cf. Robert E. Lane and David O. Sears, *Public Opinion* (Englewood Cliffs, N.J.: Prentice-Hall, Inc., 1964), pp. 6–9.

of the voters prefer Johnson and 40 percent Goldwater, and all feel strongly enough to vote, Johnson wins by a 3–2 margin; but if only half of the Johnsonites and all the Goldwaterites care enough to vote, Goldwater wins by a 4–3 margin. History, indeed, records many victories of small but intensely motivated groups over larger but more apathetic opposition.[4]

So political candidates and public officials need to know not only what people prefer but how strongly they prefer it. Academic opinion analysts try to measure both dimensions by arraying individuals along *scales* of preference rather than classifying them all as either "pro" or "con." For example, in 1960 the Survey Research Center of the University of Michigan asked a national sample of adult Americans how they felt about this statement: "The government in Washington should stay out of the question of whether white and colored children go to the same school." Of their 1954 "respondents," 747 (38 percent) agreed, 796 (41 percent) disagreed, 129 (7 percent) were not sure, and the remainder (14 percent) had no ascertainable opinion. In short, a slight plurality for federal intervention.[5] But when both the intensity and the direction of their responses are recorded, as in Figure 17, the situation looks quite different.

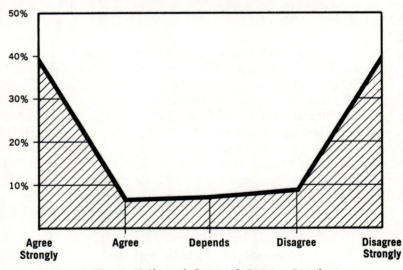

*Figure 17.  A U-Shaped Curve of Opinion Distribution.*

"The government in Washington should stay out of the question of whether white and colored children go to the same school." DATA SOURCE: Survey Research Center, University of Michigan, 1960. Percentage base excludes those with no opinion.

[4] Robert A. Dahl has illuminated the difficulties the intensity factor introduces into such conceptions of majority rule as that presented in our Chapter 5: *A Preface to Democratic Theory* (Chicago: University of Chicago Press, 1956).

[5] These data are furnished by the Inter-University Consortium for Political Research, which is based at the University of Michigan.

Figure 17 presents a classic example of a U-shaped curve, which reveals a pattern of high conflict. Most persons have opinions, most of those who do feel strongly, and those who feel strongly are more or less evenly split between the two extreme positions. Hence proposals for federal intervention against school desegregation will be strongly pushed and hotly opposed, and the political system's capacity to resolve the dispute peacefully will be taxed far more than if most persons were clustered in the middle categories of intensity and preference.

## Some Characteristics of Public Opinion

Public opinion has been studied intensively in a number of democracies, and out of these studies have emerged several findings which may be briefly summarized as follows.

### Consensus and Conflict

Suppose the 27,175,000 Americans who voted for Barry Goldwater in 1964 were deeply convinced that Lyndon Johnson would ruin the nation. Surely they would not quietly permit the disaster to happen; they would launch a rebellion to save America by putting Goldwater in his place. These suppositions are not idle fancies. Armed rebellion against election winners is common in many nations: Venezuela, for example, became an independent republic in 1821, but the first freely elected President to serve out his full term in office and be succeeded by a freely elected successor was Romulo Betancourt (1959–1964)—138 years after the nation's birth! Nor need Americans feel superior to the hot-blooded *latinos*: in 1860–1861 eleven southern states refused to accept the election of Abraham Lincoln, and the result was the bloodiest civil war in history.

Democracy requires that minorities peacefully accept the decisions of majorities. But such minority acquiescence depends in good part upon majority forbearance: majorities must not try to impose on minorities policies the latter find so unbearable that they would rather fight, however hopelessly, than submit. Democracy, in a word, requires a substantial degree of *consensus* to limit its conflicts and cool its passions.[6]

If most political issues divided public opinion in the U-shaped manner shown in Figure 17, it is difficult to see how consensus could be maintained and democracy survive. But the public opinion studies show that in fact a great many issues produce J-shaped curves of the sort shown in Figure 18, which makes clear that there is substantial consensus among Americans on actively helping foreign contries to resist communism.

Studies of public opinion in the United States and other democracies

[6] For an extended exposition of this view, see Austin Ranney and Willmoore Kendall, *Democracy and the American Party System* (New York: Harcourt, Brace & World, Inc., 1956), Ch. 3.

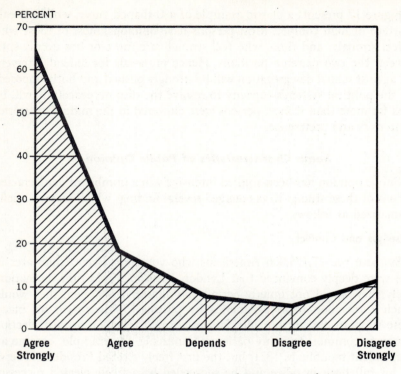

*Figure 18.* A J-Shaped Curve of Opinion Distribution.

"The United States should keep soldiers overseas where they can
help countries that are against communism." DATA SOURCE: Research
Center, University of Michigan, 1960. Percentage base excludes
those with no opinion.

have shown that this kind of J-curve consensus exists on many political
issues, while U-curve conflicts are relatively rare. There is good reason to
believe that democracy requires neither perfect consensus nor sharply
defined conflict but rather conflict *within* consensus. Conflict without consensus means civil war, but consensus within conflict means no choices to
be made, no public interest or participation in politics, and social and political stagnation. As the social theorist Talcott Parsons sums it up, in a
healthy democracy

> divisive tendencies are controlled by being placed in the context of the
> hierarchy of solidarities . . . so that the cleavages that develop tend to
> be toned down and muted on their own level and referred to higher
> orders of integration for resolution.[7]

[7] In Eugene Burdick and Arthur J. Brodbeck, eds., *American Voting Behavior* (New
York: The Free Press of Glencoe, 1959), p. 100.

## Information

Public opinion studies in the democracies have consistently shown that most citizens have little information on which to base their opinions. For example, in 1956 the Survey Research Center asked its respondents' opinions on a variety of issues and then asked them to describe what the government was actually doing on each matter. The "no opinion" groups ranged from 10 to 30 percent of the sample; the groups holding opinions but unfamiliar with what the government was doing ranged from 10 to as high as 39 percent; and those who both held opinions and knew what the actual governmental policy was ranged as high as 78 percent but fell as low as 45 percent.[8] In their five-nation study Almond and Verba asked respondents to name the national leaders of the principal parties in each country and to identify the heads of as many ministries or executive departments as they could. The responses are tabulated by country in Table 5.

### Table 5.  Ability to Name Party Leaders and Governmental Ministers, by Nation

Percentage of total samples who could

| NATION | NAME FOUR OR MORE PARTY LEADERS | NAME NO PARTY LEADER | NAME FOUR OR MORE MINISTERS | NAME NO MINISTER |
|---|---|---|---|---|
| United States | 65 | 16 | 34 | 28 |
| Great Britain | 42 | 20 | 34 | 23 |
| West Germany | 69 | 12 | 40 | 20 |
| Italy | 36 | 40 | 23 | 53 |
| Mexico | 5 | 53 | 21 | 47 |

SOURCE: Reprinted from Gabriel A. Almond and Sidney Verba, *The Civic Culture* by permission of Princeton University Press. Table II, p. 96.

## Involvement and Sense of Efficacy

Many college students, teachers, and graduates are likely to cluck their tongues at the generally low level of information shown in Table 5. After all, they assume, politics is terribly important these days, even the most ordinary citizen in a democracy has the power to influence the course of policy, and so people must be pretty lazy or stupid or both to know as little as they do. But these assumptions are not universal truths. To a great

---

[8] Angus Campbell, Philip E. Converse, Warren E. Miller, and Donald E. Stokes, *The American Voter* (New York: John Wiley & Sons, Inc., 1960), Table 8–1, p. 174.

many people politics is far less important than finding a job, getting married, raising a family, and a lot of other basic personal concerns. Hence in any democracy only a fraction of the citizens are highly involved in politics, most are only somewhat involved, and a fair proportion are involved little or not at all. For example, the 1960 American presidential election was the closest in this century; yet when the Survey Research Center asked its respondents how interested they were in the outcome, only 38 percent replied "very much" and 25 percent replied "not much"; and only 63 percent of the age-eligible voters actually voted.

College people—particularly those who study political science—are especially apt to overlook this. For them politics *is* interesting, and so they acquire a lot of information; but they are mistaken to assume that everyone is—or should be—as interested and knowledgeable as they. Public opinion studies have generally shown that the most educated people are the most involved politically mainly because they tend to have a stronger sense of political efficacy than the less educated. That is, more of them believe that their opinions and votes are the final determinants of public policy and that elections in particular and politics in general do matter a lot.[9]

### Stability and Change

One of the more puzzling traits of public opinion is that opinions on some questions seem to zig or zag almost overnight (for example, the metamorphosis of the Russians from our "gallant allies" in 1945 to our "godless enemies" in 1946), while on others it changes, if at all, at a glacial pace (for example, the high stability of party preferences discussed in Chapter 14).

Why the difference? Public opinion analysts find this a highly complicated question, and they are far from having a complete and definitive answer. Part of it, however, is the degree to which the opinion is "structured." If it concerns a matter on which most people have held opinions for a long time, few are likely to change their views; for, other things being equal, the longer a person holds a view the more intensely he feels about it.[10] On the other hand, if it concerns a new question on which most people have no strong views, their opinions will be more amenable to change. Hence in the United States opinion on such long-standing and emotion-arousing issues as recognition of Red China or federal intervention to secure Negro rights will, in Key's metaphor, have a "high viscosity" and

---

[9] For evidence of this pattern in the United States, see *ibid.*, p. 479; for its operation in other nations, see Gabriel A. Almond and Sidney Verba, *The Civic Culture* (Boston: Little, Brown & Company, 1965), Ch. VI; and Seymour Martin Lipset, *Political Man* (New York: Doubleday & Company, Inc., 1960), Ch. VI.

[10] For the operation of this principle in the intensification of party identifications, see Campbell, Converse, Miller, and Stokes, *op. cit.*, pp. 161–164.

flow into new channels turgidly if at all, while opinion on such new and generally unexciting issues as private ownership of communications satellites or fair trade laws is likely to move and change more freely.[11]

## Latency

Political leaders regularly have to decide whether a contemplated action is politically safe. Often they can discern no clear public opinion on the matter at the moment, so they are forced to estimate how the public will respond if the action is taken. Thus they must act, in political scientist Carl Friedrich's phrase, according to "the law of anticipated reactions." But the estimation of the nature and possible consequences of latent public opinion is exceedingly difficult. How many people now silent and unconcerned will be aroused if the action is taken? Will most of them approve or disapprove? Will their concern flare up and then die away in a few weeks, or will it persist and grow stronger? Will they translate their feelings into votes for or against a particular party or leader, or will they give them no partisan interpretation? Even the best public opinion polls are poor instruments for estimating the degree and direction of activation of latent opinions. But while the opinion analyst can and should explore this difficult question slowly with ever more scientifically rigorous methods, the politician has to deal with it every day with whatever tools he has at hand. For latent public opinion may become active, and active public opinion is bound to provide some guidelines for, and set some limits on, what political leaders can do with political safety and governmental effectiveness.[12]

# Some Determinants of the Political Opinions of Individuals

As a force acting in politics (see Chapter 1), a political opinion is always a *group* opinion. It is, that is to say, a policy preference held and advanced by a number of persons jointly, never one pushed by one lone and isolated individual. But no political group has any existence or "oversoul" or "group mind" that is above and beyond and independent of the individual human beings who are its components. So the study of public opinion involves the study of the individual's political psychology.

A person's political opinions, like any of his other opinions, are made up of the interplay of his "values" (his notions about what things are good and bad) and his "reality perceptions" (his notions about the way the universe really works). So an obvious starting point for understanding how

---

[11] Key, *op. cit.*, pp. 235–242.
[12] *Ibid.*, pp. 282–287.

political opinions are formed is to examine the factors affecting the selection of values and reality perceptions in individuals. Such an examination, of course, is the business of philosophy, psychology, and sociology, as well as of political science. It raises one of the most difficult of all questions, "Why do human beings think and act as they do?" We obviously cannot, within the limited scope of this chapter and this book, present a thorough and detailed analysis of this whole complex question. But we can and shall briefly outline some of the principal factors which modern social scientists believe affect the formation of individuals' political opinions.[13]

### Biological Nature and Needs

We may begin by borrowing James Davies' formula for picturing how a person acquires his opinions and determines his behavior: $B = f(SO)$. This is simply a shorthand way of saying that "behavior is a function of the interaction of the situation and the organism."[14] To look at the organism first, it is clear that one of the most powerful drives affecting human behavior is the individual's desire to maintain his biological existence (although this is by no means his only desire). To satisfy this desire at even the minimum level of bare existence he must eat, sleep, clothe and shelter himself, defend himself against attacks by animals and by other human beings, and against the onslaughts of nature in the form of floods, fire, hurricanes, and so on. Most persons also wish to engage in sexual relations, reproduce themselves, and protect their mates and offspring. Moreover, most persons wish to achieve these goals at a level beyond that of bare existence: they wish to live in comfort and enjoy pleasure. So they are likely to favor policies they believe will help achieve these good things for themselves and their families and oppose policies they believe will prevent or make difficult their achievement.

### Psychological Processes

Our formula of human behavior says it results from the *interaction* of the situation and the organism. Accordingly, one of the critical factors in behavior is the person's neurological-mental-psychic apparatus for receiving, ordering, and interpreting the stimuli he receives from the external situation and translating them into action. One useful way to think of this apparatus is to say that each person carries in his head a "cognitive map" of the physical and social world in which he lives. This "map" has three main elements. First, it includes many *perceptions*—"signals" of sight,

---

[13] Two recent explorations-in-depth by political scientists are James C. Davies, *Human Nature in Politics* (New York: John Wiley & Sons, Inc., 1963); and Robert E. Lane, *Political Ideology* (New York: The Free Press of Glencoe, 1962).

[14] Davies, *op. cit.*, pp. 2–3.

sound, touch, taste, and smell from the outside world that provide the raw material for his picture of what the world is like. Second, it includes *conceptualization*—the mental categories into which he sorts his perceptions and relates them to each other in a way that enables him to give them meaning. And third, it includes *affect*—the emotional coloring of good or bad with which he endows the patterns of meaning he has created.

## Perception and Cognitive Dissonance

Students of political psychology have found many variations in people's cognitive maps. In the matter of perceptions, for example, they have found that people do not invariably receive and record political signals as a photographic plate receives and records light waves; rather, their perceptions are powerfully affected by the nature and degree of "cognitive dissonance" the signals arouse.[15] For example, if person A hears person B, whom he admires, advocate position X, which A already agrees with, well and good; but if B advocates position Z, which A opposes, there is painful "dissonance" between A's admiration of B and his opposition to Z. And he may resolve the dissonance and ease the psychological pain by simply blocking out the signal that B advocates Z. A striking illustration of just such blockage is provided by a famous study of voters in Elmira, New York, in the 1948 presidential election. A leading issue in that election was the Taft-Hartley Act, which restricted certain labor union practices; many people held strong views on the act, and the two leading candidates repeatedly took strong opposing stands on it: Republican Thomas Dewey for the act, and Democrat Harry Truman against it. The investigators asked their

### Table 6. Cognitive Dissonance in Elmira Voters, 1948

| PERCENTAGE OF THOSE WHO THINK THE CANDIDATE IS FOR THE TAFT-HARTLEY ACT | DEWEY VOTERS | | TRUMAN VOTERS | |
|---|---|---|---|---|
| | *For the* Act | *Against* the Act | *For the* Act | *Against* the Act |
| Dewey | 96 | 54 | 85 | 95 |
| Truman | 27 | 43 | 40 | 10 |

SOURCE: Reprinted from Bernard R. Berelson, Paul F. Lazarsfeld, and William N. McPhee, *Voting* by permission of The University of Chicago Press. Copyright 1954 by the University of Chicago Press. Chart CII, p. 221.

---

[15] The leading exposition is Leon Festinger, A *Theory of Cognitive Dissonance* (New York: Harper & Row, Publishers, 1957).

Elmira respondents' own views on the act, their voting intentions, and their perceptions of how the candidates stood on the act. By sorting their responses into various groups, they discovered some interesting results, as summarized in Table 6, which shows that almost all the voters whose views of the act were in fact shared by the candidate they preferred correctly perceived his stand (96 percent and 95 percent); but large proportions of those whose views were opposed by their favored candidates simply blocked out the dissonant signals and saw their man as holding a position he did not in fact hold (54 percent and 40 percent). In short, many persons' cognitive maps are not photographically exact reproductions of the external world; they are perceptually touched up so as to make them easier to live with.

### Levels of Conceptualization

The day after the 1964 American presidential election, the San Diego *Union* editorialized, "The vote for Senator Barry Goldwater indicated that four out of ten Americans are sincerely and devotedly conservative." By the same reasoning, the vote for Johnson showed that six out of ten Americans are sincerely and devotedly liberal, but the *Union* neglected to add this. But both propositions rest upon the assumption that Americans are highly ideological—that they see politics as a conflict between liberalism and conservatism and determine their opinions and votes according to the ideology they adhere to.

This assumption has been largely discredited by social science research. In 1956, for example, the Survey Research Center asked its respondents a series of open-ended questions about what they liked and disliked about the parties and candidates. They found that only 12 percent of their sample replied in terms that could be called "ideological" in even the broadest sense of the term. The most common type of conceptualization, characteristic of 42 percent of the sample, was what the SRC labeled "group benefits" (e.g., "The Democrats are for the workingman," "The Republicans are for big business"). Another 24 percent gave "nature-of-the-times" answers (e.g., "Times are good so why change parties?"; "Republicans cause depressions"). And the remaining 22 percent had no issue content in their conceptualizations (e.g., "I Like Ike"; "I'm a Democrat").[16]

In short, in both perception and conceptualization the cognitive maps of most Americans differ significantly from those underlying the discussion of politics in newspaper columns, magazine articles, television commentaries, and political science classes. It therefore behooves those of us who receive most of our signals from these sources to refrain from assuming that the world of politics looks to everyone about as it looks to us.

---

[16] Campbell, Converse, Miller, and Stokes, *op. cit.*, Ch. 10.

### *Physical Environment*

One major external influence on human beings' political opinions is the physical conditions in which they live. If, for example, climate, soil, and resources make biological survival difficult, men are likely to view proposals for governmental policy in a perspective different from that held by persons living in areas where the physical environment makes biological survival easy. If a particular nation's physical location makes it easy to invade, its people are likely to view issues of foreign policy and national defense differently from the way such issues are viewed by persons living in a nation difficult to invade.

One recent school of political analysis, generally known as "geopolitics," holds that any nation's basic foreign policy is determined entirely by the necessities of its geographical position and that its citizens have no real choices in making such policy.[17] Most political scientists, however, believe that this point of view greatly oversimplifies the policy-making process. They contend that, while a nation's physical environment undoubtedly exerts a considerable influence over the kind of policies it adopts, it is only one of a number of influential factors.

### *Group Membership and Pressures for Conformity*

#### The Nature of the Process

Another general category of external pressures on the political opinions of individuals are those exerted by various social groups. Some of these groups—notably pressure groups and political parties—make conscious efforts to influence political opinions not only of their own members but of nonmembers as well. Chapters 15 and 16 describe the nature and opinion-influencing operations of these groups.

Here, however, we are concerned with the influence of social groups of which the individual is himself a member. Chapter 1 noted that *every person in modern society belongs to a great many "categoric" groups*—that is, aggregates of persons with whom he shares at least one characteristic, such as sex, age, race, occupation, religion. We further noted that some categoric groups are also "interest" groups—that is, groups whose members are conscious of their shared characteristics, regard themselves as having certain common goals arising from those characteristics, and to some extent direct their behavior accordingly. Finally, some interest groups are "political" in the sense that to some extent they pursue their goals by seeking to influence governmental action.[18]

---

[17] A leading exposition of this point of view is Halford J. Mackinder, *Democratic Ideas and Reality* (reissue of the 1919 edition; New York: Holt, Rinehart and Winston, Inc., 1942).

[18] See pages 11–16.

A number of social psychologists have investigated this aspect of the opinion-forming process. Some of them have focused mainly upon the influence of "primary groups"—that is, groups whose members have regular face-to-face contacts. Others have studied the broader and more impersonal "categoric" groups mentioned above. These investigators have concluded that primary groups generally have a more direct and powerful influence on the opinions of their members than do larger and more impersonal groups, but that the latter also have considerable influence on the opinions of most persons.

Perhaps you might find it valuable to descend from these dizzying heights of theory and polysyllabic words for a moment and check these generalizations with your own experience. Summon to your mind a picture of the persons with whom you have most of your day-to-day contacts—your parents, fraternity brothers and sorority sisters, sweethearts, friends, and so on. Then ask yourself this question: Are my opinions about most things, including politics, pretty much like their opinions—or do my opinions sharply differ from theirs on many matters? Each of us who asks and honestly answers this question about himself will learn that the social psychologists are talking not about "other people" but about *us!*

Just how does this all come about? By what processes do we form pretty much the same opinions as the other members of the "primary groups" to which we belong? Investigations and experiments conducted by social psychologists reveal that the process works as follows.[19]

In every social group, and particularly in every primary group, there are certain pressures working for uniformity of opinion among its members, pressures which operate on each individual member and powerfully affect his opinions, political and otherwise. This pressure arises from such sources as the following. (1) Membership in particular groups to some extent limits the stimuli a particular person receives and, therefore, affects his ideas of what the world is really like. A Ku Klux Klansman in Mississippi, for example, is likely to be confronted with somewhat different facts about racial segregation and prevailing interpretations of those facts than is a Unitarian minister in Vermont. Hence the Klansman and the minister are likely to have somewhat different opinions about such matters as the intelligence of Negroes and the degree to which Negroes in Mississippi are unhappy about segregation. (2) Most persons desire the acceptance and approval of their associates and wish to be regarded as "regular" and "okay" rather than as "peculiar" or an "oddball." Many social psychologists believe that this desire, far more than any "patriotism" or "love of

---

[19] The leading studies are George C. Homans, *The Human Group* (New York: Harcourt, Brace & World, Inc., 1950); Sidney Verba, *Small Groups and Political Behavior* (Princeton, N.J.: Princeton University Press, 1961); and Robert T. Golombiewski, *The Small Group* (Chicago: University of Chicago Press, 1963).

democratic ideals," accounts for the high physical courage under fire shown by so many soldiers. (3) If a person values highly his membership in a particular group, such as his family or his fraternity or his church, and derives many personal satisfactions from it, he may well feel that if he holds an opinion sharply different from that held by most of the other members, the group might expel him or disintegrate altogether and thereby deprive him of the satisfactions its brings.

Sometimes these group pressures are brought to bear on individuals through the medium of communications by certain members of the group who are given a kind of "sergeant-at-arms" function. Sometimes they are brought to bear by informal communications between the individual and other members of the group holding no such official position. Chapter 11 describes some of the processes of social and political communication. The strength of these pressures on any particular individual depends upon a number of factors, including the importance of membership in the group to his own personal satisfactions, the number and strength of counter-pressures exerted by other groups of which he is also a member and which have conflicting goals, the amount of pressure brought to bear on him by the group, and so on.

## Some Types of Influential Group Memberships

Social scientists generally agree that "primary" groups have a more powerful influence than the more impersonal "categoric" groups upon the political opinions of their respective members. Most primary groups, however, are segments of particular categoric groups. One useful way to describe the more influential types of group membership, accordingly, is to consider pairs of related primary and categoric groups as follows.

FAMILIES AND ETHNIC GROUPS. The first group in which most of us become conscious of our membership is the family. Many of our values, reality perceptions, thinking and acting habits, and so on, we receive from our parents, brothers, and sisters. We often hear, indeed, that most persons "inherit" their party affiliations and political attitudes from their parents. In Chapter 14 we shall see how much truth there is in this allegation.

Most families are formed largely or exclusively on blood relationships and are, therefore, parts of particular ethnic groups. An "ethnic group," as social scientists use the term, is an aggregate of persons who share a common ancestry and certain special social customs and behavior patterns. The most often-discussed ethnic groups are the "races" (white, Negro, Mongoloid, and so on), but the term also includes groups of persons who stem from particular areas and nations (e.g., Scandinavians, Latin Americans, Polish-Americans, and Italian-Americans). Social scientists believe that the political opinions of most persons are to some extent influenced by their memberships in particular ethnic groups, but the influence is less strong than that of families. The degree of ethnic-group influence appears to be greatest among members of minority groups (e.g., Negroes and Jews in the United States, Afrikanders in South Africa) which feel themselves threatened by larger groups.

FRIENDS AND AGE GROUPS.   The second group in which most of us become conscious of our membership is our circle of friends and playmates. Most of us desire the approval of and are strongly influenced by the opinions of our friends as well as our parents, not only in childhood and adolescence but in adult life as well.

Who are our friends? The old maxim "Birds of a feather flock together" applies to most of mankind. Most of our friends, that is to say, are persons very much like ourselves: they live in the same general kind of neighborhood, attend the same general kind of schools and churches, come from similar economic levels and social classes, and often work at the same general kind of jobs. Most of our friends are also close to us in age. As we all know, a perennial complaint of older people is that they "cannot understand the younger generation," and a perennial fear of older people is that young people's passion for, say, the singing of Rudy Vallee, Frank Sinatra, or the Beatles (depending on which generation is "young" at the moment) shows that they have no taste or even morality. Much of our literature is focused upon the conflict of the old and the young, and most social scientists agree that membership in particular age groups has some influence upon most persons' opinions.

CONGREGATIONS AND RELIGIOUS GROUPS.   Most of us begin to attend Sunday school at an early age and later join church youth organizations and become members of congregations. Most religions are deeply concerned with both values and conceptions of the nature of the universe, and most churches try to indoctrinate their communicants with their particular slants. There is no doubt that the attitudes of most persons on many matters are powerfully influenced by their membership in particular congregations and religious groups.

Many churches, moreover, make official pronouncements on certain political issues and have, to some extent, a direct influence on the political opinions and behavior of their communicants. Nations that encourage a particular religion and/or restrict or ban other religions (e.g., Spain and certain Latin American nations) give the favored religion a particularly influential role in the formation of political opinions and public policy. But even in nations, like the United States, that have no officially "established" or favored religion, the churches have a significant influence upon the political opinions of a great many persons.

SCHOOLMATES AND EDUCATIONAL GROUPS. Modern nations vary greatly in the amount of formal education their citizens receive, but in most of them both the proportion of persons attending school and the average time spent in school are increasing year by year. The United States census estimated that in 1962 18 percent of the population of the United States had at least some college education, 64 percent had some high school education, and 98 percent had some grammar school education. All three percentages will doubtless be higher in the 1970 census reports. The opinions of most Americans, therefore, are exposed to the influence of both schoolmates and schools.

The purposes of education in all nations, democracies and dictatorships alike, include not only instructing the young in some of the technical skills and techniques they need to perform a useful role in society (e.g., the ability to read and write, count, and perhaps to drive automobiles and run machine lathes), but also indoctrinating them in the political values and reality notions the nation favors. In the United States the schools are committed to educating their pupils in the principles of democracy and "the American way," just as in the Soviet Union the schools are committed to educating Soviet youth in the principles and attitudes of communism. In all nations the schools are generally considered to be such important shapers of opinion that they are perennial subjects of controversy. We are all familiar with the periodic clashes in this or that part of our country over the issue of whether the schools are indoctrinating the young in the *proper* values and beliefs. We have all read or heard about charges that the schools are teaching "socialism" or "atheism" or are "apologizing for business exploitation" or "propagandizing for one-worldism," and so on. Since most schools in most modern nations, democracies and dictatorships alike, are governmentally rather than privately owned and operated, what the schools do and how they should do it are always political issues, and the schools are always subject to pressures, some of them powerful, from public officials, parents, pupils, teachers, churches, economic pressure groups, and so on.

WORK ASSOCIATES AND OCCUPATIONAL GROUPS. Most adults spend half or more of their waking hours working at their jobs. In terms of the sheer volume of face-to-face contacts, accordingly, their immediate work associates constitute one of their most important primary groups, and social scientists have discovered a high degree of uniformity in the opinions, political and otherwise, of such groups.

All work-associate groups are also segments of the larger and more impersonal "occupational groups"—college professors, retail merchants, carpenters, unskilled laborers, farm operators, business executives, and "white-collar" office workers. As we shall see in Chapter 14, however, the evidence suggests that membership in this kind of categoric group has less influence on political opinions than does membership in many of the other categoric groups we have discussed.

NEIGHBORS, INCOME GROUPS, AND SOCIAL CLASSES.   The remaining kind of primary group of which most of us are conscious is that of our neighbors —the persons who make their homes in our particular immediate residential area. Social scientists have long observed that most neighborhoods are composed of people who are similar in a number of different respects. Most of the persons living in a particular neighborhood, that is to say, are likely to be of the same or similar ethnic groups, religious groups, educational levels, and income levels.

They are also likely to be members of the same "social class"—a concept that requires some definition and explanation. According to Karl Marx and his communist disciples, a "class" is strictly and solely a group of persons holding a particular position in the process of production, and only two such classes exist: the *bourgeoisie*, who own the instruments of production and exploit persons who operate them; and the *proletariat*, who operate but do not own the instruments of production and are exploited by the bourgeoisie. The Marxist conception of classes proclaims a sharp distinction and irreconcilable hostility between the two classes and sees all politics as a struggle between them for total domination.

Non-Marxist social scientists, however, use the concept of "class" in quite a different sense. They see society as divided into many more classes than just two and conceive of each class as based upon a number of differentiae, including such matters as ethnic affiliations, length of family residence in the nation and in the local community, educational level, income, prestige of occupation, and so on. Since most of these factors are difficult to measure and express in arithmetical terms, the boundaries of each class are indistinct and the classification of particular individuals is often difficult. The one generally used criterion of class membership that is relatively definite and measurable is that of wealth and income level, but few, if any, non-Marxist social scientists consider it to be the *sole* factor determining social class.[20] Whatever their particular definitions of class, however, most social scientists agree that class membership has a powerful influence upon the political opinions of most persons.[21]

---

[20] For a brief but lucid explanation of the non-Marxist social scientists' concept of "class," see John W. Bennett and Melvin M. Tumin, *Social Life, Structure and Function* (New York: Alfred A. Knopf, Inc., 1948), Ch. 25.

[21] Cf. Richard Centers, *The Psychology of Social Classes* (Princeton, N.J.: Princeton University Press, 1949); Lipset, *op. cit.*, Chs. VII–IX; and Robert R. Alford, *Party and Society* (Chicago: Rand McNally & Company, 1963).

## Political Socialization and Change

In recent years public opinion analysts have grouped the many forces and processes shaping people's political attitudes under the general heading of "political socialization." We cannot present their findings in detail, but we can report some highlights.[22]

Most persons acquire their first political attitudes very early in life—by the age of five years or even younger. By age seven or eight most have party identifications. By early adolescence most have views on a number of political issues. Up to this point their political socialization is like their religious socialization: they absorb their views from their parents and hold them, not as independent choices made from surveys of the available alternatives, but as part of their solidarity with their families. Hence young people almost always say "*We* are Republicans" and "*We* are Methodists," rarely "*I* am a Republican" or "*I* am a Methodist."

Most persons retain their original attitudes through high school and, if they are among the minority that go on, through college as well. In a small minority of instances adolescents and young adults rebel against their parents' views and adopt opposing ones, but, as Lane and Sears point out,

> political rebellion is not an integral part of that constellation we think of as "adolescent rebellion." The rebelling adolescent is much more likely to rebel in terms which are more important to his parents, such as in his dress, his driving, his drinking, his obedience of the law, his behavior, and so forth. Only in rather rare instances does it have political effects as well.[23]

The higher levels of education in the democracies do have some tendency to make people more tolerant of heterodoxy, but their main effect, as we have seen, is to increase the sense of political efficacy and involvement. The most common form of directional change among adults is wives changing their views to fit their husbands'. Politics is less important to most women than to most men, and in many cultures it is thought unfeminine to hold strong political views of any sort, let alone views contrary to the husband's. So rather than jeopardize their marriages for something as peripheral and unfeminine as politics, women change sides.

In short, very few persons change the direction of their political opinions as they grow older. Rather, they hold their original views with increasing intensity, apparently not because they grow more irascible with age (though they may!) but because the longer they hold an opinion the more identified they become with it. Of the few who do change, some do so for

---

[22] The most complete summary is Herbert H. Hyman, *Political Socialization* (New York: The Free Press of Glencoe, 1959).

[23] *Op. cit.*, p. 25.

purely personal reasons: they get married, they move to new neighborhoods, they get new jobs, they move from one social class to another, and the new environments produce new attitudes. But the evidence is that the direction of such changes is evenly divided: as many conservatives become liberals and as many Democrats become Republicans as the other way around.

In a few periods of great social upheaval there have been massive switches of party affiliations: for example, in the United States in the 1850's with the demise of the Whigs and the rise of the Republicans, and in the early 1930's when the Democrats replaced the Republicans as the majority party; in Great Britain in the early 1920's when the Labour party replaced the Liberals as the second major party; and in France in the late 1950's when the fragmented loyalties of the Fourth Republic became massive support for De Gaulle. But such occasions are rare, and on most political issues of high visibility and general saliency most persons' opinions in the democracies remain highly stable.

## Public Opinion in the USSR[24]

### The Role of Public Opinion in Communist Ideology

#### The Relations between the Party and the Masses

According to the ideology of communism, "democracy" is government *for* the people (the proletarian masses) in which policies are made by the Communist party for the benefit of the masses, and in which approval of those policies by the masses is a desirable but secondary consideration. The "elite" character of the party is openly and proudly proclaimed by Communist leaders, and they confine party membership to the small segment of the population they consider to be most "class conscious," intelligent, and skilled in the principles of Marxism-Leninism. That they succeed in keeping the party's membership relatively small is shown by the fact that the present membership of the Soviet Russian Communist party is about 4 percent of the total Russian population.

According to communism's great prophet Lenin, the party must avoid either of two equally grave mistakes: putting into effect only those policies that accord exactly with the present state of mass opinion, or those policies that are so far beyond what the masses can understand and accept that they become unenforceable. The proper objective for the party, said Lenin, is to

---

[24] The leading analyses are Alex Inkeles, *Public Opinion in Soviet Russia* (Cambridge, Mass.: Harvard University Press, 1950); and Frank S. Meyer, *The Moulding of Communists* (New York: Harcourt, Brace & World, Inc., 1961).

make policies far enough ahead of mass feelings as to induce progress and yet not so far ahead that they cannot be enforced.

The task of the party and its agents, therefore, is twofold: to sound out the feelings of the masses in order to learn what policies are possible at any given moment, and to mold public opinion in such a way that ever more "advanced" policies become possible. We shall describe in a moment the agencies they have developed to accomplish these tasks.

### Samokritika and Party Policy

Persons on our side of the Iron Curtain sometimes make the mistake of thinking of the Soviet Union as a place in which no critical or adverse comment of any kind is ever publicly made about public policies or officials. Not only is this a somewhat misleading picture of what goes on in Russia, but it overlooks the peculiar communist institution of *samokritika* ("self-criticism"). This institution is defined by the Soviet *Political Dictionary* as "exposing the deficiencies and errors in the work of particular persons, organizations, and institutions on the basis of a free, businesslike discussion by the toilers of all the problems of economic-political life . . . [and] developing the ability to see, to uncover, to acknowledge one's mistakes and to learn from them."[25]

"About three more men and we would have large-scale production."

Rohac (Bratislava)

"Comrade Chairman, the tractors are ready to work "
"Fine, the spare parts are over there in the stall."

Ludas Matyi (Budapest)

*Figure 19.* Communist Cartoons Show *Samokritika*-type Humor. (YEAR 1965, Encyclopedia News Annual.)

All Communist leaders, from Lenin to Kosygin and Brezhnev, have stressed the desirability of *samokritika*. As it actually operates, this institu-

---

[25] Quoted in Inkeles, *op. cit.*, p. 197.

tion means that the masses are permitted—indeed, encouraged—to voice publicly certain kinds of criticisms of certain kinds of policies and public officials. The masses are not, for example, permitted to attack the Communist regime in any way, or to attack the party's policies, or to criticize the top leaders of the party—for criticisms of that sort give aid and comfort to the "enemies of the people" and are therefore treasonable. The ground rules appear to permit the masses to criticize the execution of policies by minor public officials. Thus the ordinary workers at a collective farm would certainly be hustled off to a slave-labor camp if they publicly argued that the whole idea of collective farms is bad; but they are often smiled upon if they contend publicly that the manager of the farm is inefficient, or that there is too much red tape, or that the farm is not fulfilling its quotas, because of a lack of enthusiasm among the workers.

On a few occasions, moreover, the party has permitted and encouraged public discussion of the merits of policies themselves. Two notable examples of such debated policies were the marriage-divorce-abortion laws and the staggered five-day week.[26] For the most part, however, *samokritika* is strictly limited to the execution of policies rather than to their content.

### The Agitation-Propaganda Operation

#### Communist Conceptions of Agitation and Propaganda

For the reasons already mentioned, Communist leaders place great emphasis on "educating" the masses so as to generate enthusiastic and active support for the party's policies. The amount of money spent for these purposes, indeed, is second only to that spent on national defense. In organizing its "educational" activities, the party makes a sharp distinction, unknown to most noncommunist political analysts, between "agitation" and "propaganda." Propaganda, as the Communists use it, refers to the indoctrination of party members and nonparty intellectuals in the principles of Marxism-Leninism. It involves lengthy discussions and considerable reading and, in general, is aimed only at those persons whom the party considers eligible to join the proletarian elite. Agitation, on the other hand, means presenting a few simple ideas to the great masses of people in as dramatic a fashion as possible so as to inspire them to behave as the party wishes. The ideas are kept few and simple because of the Communist conviction that the masses cannot understand very many or very complex ideas.

#### Techniques of Mass Persuasion

The basic responsibility for the entire gigantic agitation-propaganda operation belongs, significantly enough, to a party agency rather than to a

---

[26] J. A. Brown, Jr., "Public Opinion in the Soviet Union," *Russian Review*, IX (January, 1950), 37–44. See also Merle Fainsod, *How Russia Is Ruled* (rev. ed.; Cambridge, Mass.: Harvard University Press, 1963), pp. 211–212.

# "To Give You An Idea How Effective It Is—We're Beginning To Believe It Ourselves!"

*Figure 20.* Government Propaganda, Both for Foreign and Domestic Consumption, Plays a Major Role in the Communist System. (Drawing by Herblock, from *The Herblock Book,* Boston: Beacon Press, 1952.)

formal governmental agency. The Department of Propaganda and Agitation of the Central Committee of the All-Union Communist Party of Bolsheviks (commonly known as *agitprop*) makes all policies concerning the operations of the various communications media and supervises their execution by the various agencies administering each medium.

BOLSHEVIK AGITATORS.   The Communists believe that face-to-face communication is more effective than mass communication in bringing about the desired attitudes in the masses—in any case a considerable portion of the masses are illiterate. Consequently the Communists rely more heavily upon their "agitation" apparatus than upon any of the mass media. There are now well over 3 million "Bolshevik agitators," a ratio of about one agitator to every sixty-five adults. These agitators are picked by the party from its rank-and-file members, the most promising members of the Komsomols (the Communist youth organization), and nonparty intellectuals. Performing the task of agitation is considered to be one of the most valuable services one can render the party, and so to be chosen an agitator is a high honor. The party tries to place at least one agitator in every government agency, factory, collective farm, military unit, and so on. Each agitator is charged with explaining party policies to the nonparty masses in his particular agency, whipping up enthusiasm for them, and also reporting back to his superiors the kind of reception those policies receive and the general attitudes of the masses. The main technique of the agitator is to lead "discussions" with his fellow workers, but he is also expected to convince them by the example of his own actions as well as by words. For instance, if the party decides that all tractor factories must increase their output by 10 percent, the agitators in that factory are expected to increase their own personal productive efforts and output and so provide a good personal example for their co-workers. If some workers in the discussions set up by the agitators grumble, "Increasing our output is all well and good, but how can we do it as long as we have to bother with the red tape our manager insists on?" the agitators are expected to report this complaint to their superiors. In this fashion, the Bolshevik agitators are both "educators" of the masses and also reporters of the current state of mass opinion.

NEWSPAPERS.   Although the Communists place their heaviest reliance upon agitation, they also use the media of mass communications. Of these, newspapers are the most important. The number of newspapers and their size of total circulation have increased enormously in Soviet Russia since tsarist days, for they now cover just about every part of the Soviet Union. The two greatest national papers, from which all regional and local newspapers take not only their general directions but also much of the specific material they print, are *Pravda* (the official organ of the Central Committee of the party) and *Izvestia* (the official organ of the Supreme Soviet, the formal national governing body).

The task of the Soviet press, of course, is not to "present the news" in any Western sense of the term but rather to explain and arouse enthusiasm for the party's policies and to serve as a channel for *samokritika*. The latter function is accomplished mainly through letters-to-the-editor columns, which take up a considerable portion of the space of every Soviet newspaper. The "educational" function is performed by such methods as straight exhortations to the masses, and, above all, reporting the "news" and "events" both inside and outside the Soviet Union in such a way as to build in the mass mind the picture of the world that the party leaders wish the masses to have.

RADIO. Most persons on this side of the Iron Curtain think of a "radio" as a receiving apparatus which has no direct or exclusive connection with any particular broadcasting station and which is capable of receiving signals from a number of different broadcasting stations. The owner of the set, therefore, has some option about which programs he listens to. This is not what "radio" means to most Russians. Over 80 percent of the "radio" receivers in the Soviet Union are wired directly to particular broadcasting transmitters and can receive signals only from those transmitters. Most persons with a receiver, therefore, have access to only one set of programs. These direct-wired receivers are located not only in homes but also in such public gathering places as communal dwellings and dormitories, factories, barracks, offices, public squares, and the like. The content of the programs, closely controlled by the party, consists of such "cultural" matters as symphonic music and such "educational" matters as "news" and political comment, instruction in both technical matters and political ideology, and literary and dramatic programs, all of which are used to promote Communist political ideas.

MOTION PICTURES. The other prominent medium of mass communication—motion pictures—is used exclusively for political, technical, and cultural instruction, and not for "entertainment" in the Western sense.

### Contrasts between the Democratic and Communist Opinion Processes

"Public opinion" of a sort does exist in the USSR, as it does in any dictatorship. The essential differences between such opinion and the processes whereby it is formed and their counterparts in the democracies consist in the different roles of government in the two systems.

In the democracies, as we shall see, the government (i.e., persons who officially hold public office) is at one and the same time both a participant in the policy-making process with preferences of its own and also the agency which determines and registers the outcome of the contest over public policy among all the competing groups. Government is therefore only one of the political groups that have access to the media of communication, and its policy preferences are by no means the only ones that are circulated. Hence its desires are not the only factor that has a direct and powerful influence upon the formation of public policy.

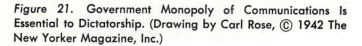

*"I think I may say, without fear of contradiction . . ."*

*Figure 21.* Government Monopoly of Communications Is Essential to Dictatorship. (Drawing by Carl Rose, © 1942 The New Yorker Magazine, Inc.)

In the communist dictatorships, on the other hand, the government has a legal monopoly over all the media of mass communications and also a great many advantages in controlling the face-to-face media. The only issues that are genuinely "controversial," therefore, are those on which the government allows "controversy" (see the examples given above). Only on these issues can "public opinion" in anything like the democratic sense be said to exist.

There is much evidence to suggest, however, that the Communists have been far from completely successful in molding the opinion of the masses to the party's purposes. The outstanding recent case in point is the revolt of the Hungarian masses against their native and Russian overlords in 1956. This revolt demonstrated conclusively that, despite their monopoly of all the mass media and their near monopoly of the face-to-face media for over a decade, the Communists did not succeed in stamping out all opposition to the regime, and that a considerable body of opinion counter to official opinion did exist in Hungary. Even in the USSR itself, the recurring "purges" of plays, movies, books, and even music, and frequent bitter criticisms by the party of the way the mass media are doing their jobs, suggest that the party knows that some of the Russian masses hold opinions other than those it prescribes.[27] Indeed, one of the most remarkable aspects of the post-Stalin "thaw" in the late 1950's and 1960's was the party's decision to conduct public opinion polls along semi-Western lines to determine how the masses are reacting to current lines of policy!

## Conclusion

These, then, are some of the more prominent processes and influences involved in the formation of political opinion in modern democracies and dictatorships. In the next chapter we shall complete our survey of public opinion by describing the nature and media of political communication and by assessing the value of public opinion polls as devices for learning what the content of opinion is at any given moment.

---

[27] Cf. Inkeles, *op. cit.*, pp. 318–323.

# 11

## Public Opinion:

### *communication and*

### *measurement*

The "communication" and "measurement" of "public opinion" is an immediate and practical concern in our daily lives. Most of us, for example, have at one time or another tried to induce our parents to let us use the family automobile. We have learned, sometimes the hard way, to make our requests when our parents are in a pleasant and receptive mood (e.g., just after we have mowed the lawn or washed the dishes, or just after Dad has obtained a raise, or Mother has won a bridge prize) and not when they are in an unpleasant mood (e.g., before they have had their morning coffee or just after we have brought home a bad report card). So we have developed certain ways of "measuring" the state of opinion of this particular "public."

We have all tried to figure out, moreover, the kinds of arguments (if any!) that are most likely to get results, and no doubt have learned that, in some situations, the smart thing is to say nothing at all but just look woebegone and ill-treated.

Every political party and pressure group in a democracy faces essentially the same necessities. Each group wants certain things from the voters and/or public officials, and in order to get them the group's leaders need to know both what public opinion is at the moment and how to move it along in the direction they desire.

The present chapter examines the nature and processes of political communication, its role in the formation of public opinion, the problem of measuring public opinion, and the manner in which public opinion polls try to solve this problem.

# Political Communication

## *The Nature of Communication and Its Role in Politics*

*Communication is the transmission of meaning by the use of symbols.* It is, in other words, the process whereby a person or group of persons tries to make another person or group aware of its feelings about a particular matter. Communication in this broad sense can be transmitted in many different ways—by pictures, music, mathematical signs, gestures, facial expressions, even physical blows. The most common form of communication in human society, however, is the use of oral and written verbal symbols we call "language."

As Professor Albig correctly points out, "Underlying all social process and all societal forms is the transfer of meaning between individuals. Social life can exist only when meaningful symbols are transferred from individual to individual. Group activities of any sort are impossible without a means of sharing experiences."[1]

Certainly communication plays a significant role in politics and in the process of forming political opinions, for it is the basic process by which political groups are formed and seek to influence public policy.[2] The fact that some people are rich and others are poor, for example, has no political significance in itself. By talking and reading, however, a poor person learns that some of his fellows are also poor but others are not; he learns that he is a member of a particular economic group which is different from and, to some extent, opposed to another economic group. By talking and reading some members of each group decide that they want the government to follow policies favorable to their interests. And by talking and reading—and perhaps also by cartoons, billboards, parades, and other nonverbal means—they try to induce public officials to adopt those policies.

Communication, in short, is the main catalytic agent by which the static social characteristics of men are transformed into the dynamic processes of political conflict.

## *The Elements of Political Communication*

The nature and role of political communication is most easily understood if we consider its constituent elements separately.

---

[1] Reprinted by permission from *Modern Public Opinion*, by William Albig, p. 33. Copyright, 1956, by McGraw-Hill Book Co., Inc., New York.

[2] Political scientist Karl W. Deutsch has developed a stimulating "cybernetic" model of political systems as communications structures in *The Nerves of Government* (New York: The Free Press of Glencoe, 1963). This is a special political application of a general social theory advanced by mathematician Norbert Wiener, *Cybernetics* (2d ed.; New York: John Wiley & Sons, Inc., 1961).

## 1. The Communicator

All groups that consciously try to influence governmental policy, and some that have no such conscious purpose, are political "communicators." The main types of communicators in the modern democracies are political parties and pressure groups, whose organization and activities are described in detail in Chapters 15 and 16. However, many governmental agencies in many of the democracies also try to influence the opinions of persons outside the formal structure of government. Several agencies in the national government of the United States, for example, maintain "public relations" or "public information" bureaus which print and distribute pamphlets, send out speakers, and otherwise try to create public support for their programs.[3] In the USSR (see Chapter 10) this is a major activity of government, which has a monopoly of all the media of mass communications and tries to achieve a near-monopoly of all face-to-face communications as well.

## 2. The Message: "Propaganda" versus "Education"

Every political communicator has a "message"—a series of communications intended to induce others to develop opinions favorable to the goals of the communicator. Much of the social science literature on the communication process has concentrated upon this particular aspect, and much has been made of the distinction between two types of communication: "propaganda" and "education."

The term "propoganda" was first used in the seventeenth century to describe a new effort by the Roman Catholic Church to "propagate" its faith and was formalized in 1622 when Pope Gregory XV created the College of Propaganda, a committee of cardinals. It retained its largely religious connotations until World War I, when it not only took on a mainly political meaning but also acquired for a great many people a number of odious moral connotations because of the "propaganda" efforts of each side, but particularly the Allies, to influence the American attitude toward the war. Since that time many persons have thought of "propaganda" as a certain *way* of influencing opinions—a way marked by such reprehensible practices as selecting and distorting facts, using emotional rather than rational and logical appeals, and discouraging critical examination of the nature of the message. Persons who use the term in this fashion generally contrast it with "education," which they regard as the presentation of the whole truth solely for the general benefit of the whole society rather than for the selfish benefit of the "educator."[4]

---

[3] Cf. James L. McCamy, *Government Publicity* (Chicago: University of Chicago Press, 1939).

[4] Albig, *op. cit.*, pp. 291–301, and Ch. 15. See also A. M. Lee and E. B. Lee, eds., *The Fine Art of Propaganda* (New York: Harcourt, Brace and Company, 1939).

Many present-day students of political communication, however, have largely abandoned this distinction. They feel that "propaganda" has become merely an epithet and "education" a "God-word," and that "propaganda" has come to mean communications by a group whose objectives you do not approve while "education" means the communications of a group you like. Such students speak only of "communications" and not of "propaganda" or "education."

### 3. The Medium of Transmission

The message must be transmitted to some receivers if it is to have any political significance, and a later section of this chapter deals with the nature, organization, and relative effectiveness of the most prominent communications media in the democracies.

### 4. The Receivers

A particular message by a particular communicator over a particular medium is received only by certain persons, not by all the members of the community. As we shall see below, the nature of the receivers has a significant influence upon the political effects of any communication.

### 5. The Responses

The responses include whatever effects the communication has upon the attitudes and actions of its receivers—effects which, as we shall see below, vary greatly from situation to situation.

## The Media of Political Communication

The media of political communication are usually divided into two categories: the "mass media"—those in which each message is aimed at large numbers of receivers, and in which there is no face-to-face contact between communicator and receivers; and the "face-to-face" media—those which carry messages to only a few receivers at a time, and in which there is face-to-face contact between communicator and receivers. Let us review the status of each of these types of media in modern nations.

### *The Mass Media*

### 1. Newspapers

In dictatorships, such as the Soviet Union, all mass media, including newspapers, are government-owned and -operated monopolies used to persuade the masses to support government policies with enthusiasm. In democracies a few papers, such as *L'Humanité* of Paris, are owned and operated by political parties mainly as agencies for drumming up electoral support. Most newspapers, however, are privately owned and operated and are run mainly for the same reason that every other kind of private business is run: to make profits for their owners.

Newspapers get their revenue partly from subscriptions but mainly from advertising, which accounts for from 65 to 90 percent of their total income. Increasing circulation is, therefore, a prime goal of all papers, for increased circulation not only brings in more revenue but also attracts more advertisers. This necessity inclines newspapers to print material they feel will hold reader interest and not unduly offend present and potential advertisers. No paper other than a rich man's plaything or the "house organ" of a political party can afford to print only what its editor thinks the readers ought to read; it must print what he thinks the readers want to read, and this has a great deal of influence in determining what is regarded as "news." In addition to news, moreover, most papers print a substantial number of "features"—comics, recipes, fashion notes, bridge columns, and so on.

Most newspapers also print material avowedly intended to influence the political opinions of their readers, mainly in the form of unsigned editorials and signed political commentaries by "columnists." The evidence suggests that such material is considerably less than irresistible. In both the United States and Great Britain, for example, almost every voter regularly reads a newspaper, and the great bulk of American and British newspapers editorially favor the Republican and Conservative parties respectively; yet the Democratic and Labour parties, despite their usual lack of editorial support (the 1964 presidential election was a major exception), continue to win their share of the elections.

We should not, however, leap to the conclusion that newspapers have *no* significant effect on public opinion. Many observers believe that most people get their notions about what is going on in politics mainly from what they read in the news columns of their newspapers, and that these notions fix the basic direction of their opinions. Thus, while a reader may not be impressed or convinced by editorials in his newspaper arguing that an incumbent governor is a great man and should be re-elected, he may well be impressed by news stories describing corruption and inefficiency in the administration and draw quite different conclusions from those the editors intend. The effect of newspapers on public opinion is no less powerful because it comes indirectly through news stories rather than directly through editorials.

Newspapers have a larger audience than any of the other mass media. In the United States, for example, approximately 90 percent of all adults regularly read at least some part of a daily newspaper. For basic economic reasons the largest number of newspapers and the largest audiences are found in nations with the highest rates of per capita wealth, industrial development, and literacy. Over 80 percent of the total newspaper circulation in the entire world is in Europe and North America.[5]

Since World War I there has been a marked trend toward increasing concentration of newspaper ownership and control in all the democracies and particularly in the United States. While total circulation has greatly increased during this period, the total number of papers has actually decreased. This has resulted from increases in the number of newspaper mergers and in the number of "chain" newspapers (papers in different cities owned and operated by one firm, such as the Scripps-Howard and Hearst "chains"). Some observers fear that a continuation of this decline in newspaper competition will make impossible the free access to this important medium of communication that democracy requires, although as yet, they feel, the concentration of ownership and control has not gone far enough to create a "clear and present danger."[6]

## 2. Television and Radio

The United States is the only nation in which most radio and television broadcasting is privately owned and operated. This does not mean, however, that broadcasters in the United States have a completely free hand. The Federal Communications Commission (FCC) closely regulates both kinds of broadcasting, using its licensing power as its main weapon. Every broadcasting station must obtain an FCC license before it can operate, and each license comes up for renewal roughly every three years. In order to qualify for a new or a renewed license the broadcaster must live up to a number of FCC standards and rules. Perhaps the FCC's most famous political rule is that which requires a station which grants free time to a political party to give equal free time to all opposing parties. However, a station may *sell* to any party whatever time the party can afford without furnishing the opposition equal time. The FCC also controls such matters as the operating frequency and power of broadcasting stations, their legal and financial relations with the networks, the proportion of "live" to "recorded" material presented, and the like. The commission has exercised little if any direct political censorship, but it has had considerable effect upon the content of programs as well as upon the financial and legal structure of the broadcasting industry.[7]

In the other democracies part or all of the radio and television broad-

---

[5] "Mass Communications and Their Audiences in Other Counties," in Wilbur Schramm, ed., *The Process and Effects of Mass Communication* (Urbana: University of Illinois Press, 1954), pp. 74–83.

[6] Raymond B. Nixon, "Trends in Daily Newspaper Ownership since 1945," *Journalism Quarterly*, XXXI (January, 1955), 13–14.

[7] Murray Edelman, *The Licensing of Radio Services in the United States, 1927 to 1947* (Urbana: University of Illinois Press, 1950).

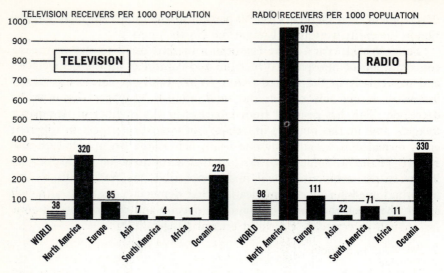

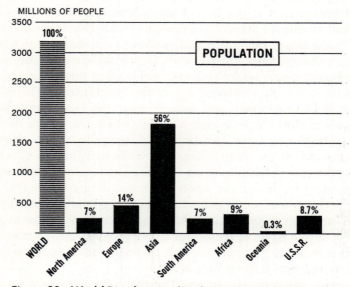

*Figure* 22.  World Distribution of Radio and Television Receivers.

casting stations are governmentally owned and operated. In Denmark, for example, all broadcasting is conducted by a government-owned and -operated monopoly. In Sweden broadcasting is also controlled by a monopoly, but one in which both the government and private interests participate.[8]

---

[8] See Albig, *op. cit.*, Table 23 on pp. 471–472.

The systems of greatest interest to most Americans, however, are those of Great Britain and Canada.

Great Britain has a mixture of publicly and privately owned broadcasting. The .British Broadcasting Corporation (BBC) was chartered as a "public corporation" by the government in 1927, but is not itself directly owned or controlled by the government as is its Danish counterpart. Its board of governors is appointed by the queen on the advice of the prime minister, but its members are not "political" in the partisan sense, and they make policies without any direct control by any regular governmental agency. Every owner of a radio or television set must purchase a license from the post office, and the revenue is returned to the BBC. The BBC gets the remainder of its revenue from the sales of its weekly publication, the *Radio Times*. Most BBC programs are planned and broadcast centrally and relayed over a series of local and regional stations, although some local and regional variations in programming are permitted. In general the programs of the BBC are designed with relatively less concern for what the viewers and listeners want and more concern for what the broadcasters think they should have than in the United States. The BBC also has a rule of "equal time" for partisan broadcasts.

In 1954, Parliament authorized private television (but not radio) broadcasting for commercial profits. It established a body somewhat comparable to the American FCC, the Independent Television Authority. The ITA owns and operates the transmitting stations, but the programs are produced by private program companies under contract to the ITA. There are now fifteen such companies, most of them organized on a regional basis. Some are controlled by motion-picture interests, others by newspapers, and others by general investors. Advertisers do not directly "sponsor" programs as in the United States, but purchase time in between programs when a series of advertisements are broadcast—singing commercials and all.[9]

The Canadian system is a hybrid version of the British and American. The Canadian Broadcasting Corporation (CBC), chartered as a public corporation in 1936 on the BBC model, gets its revenue mainly from the sale of licenses for receiving sets. Canada, however, has a small population spread over a large geographic area, which means a relatively large number of broadcasting stations required per listener and viewer. As a result the CBC has found the revenue from set licenses insufficient to support its operations, and so it has permitted the construction and operation of privately owned stations. The CBC sells these stations many of their programs and thus increases its revenue. About 80 percent of all broad-

---

[9] An up-to-date and concise description of the British system of broadcasting is given in *Britain, An Official Handbook, 1964* (published by the Central Office of Information), pp. 480–488.

casts, however, are "sustaining" (i.e., not commercially sponsored). The CBC, like the American FCC, also regulates the operations of private broadcasting stations through its power to grant and renew broadcasting licenses. The CBC requires that it shall have a monopoly of all network broadcasting, though it permits local stations, both public and private, to broadcast a certain number of nonnetwork programs.

Like newspapers, radio and television are found in the highest concentration in the more wealthy and literate nations. Since the early 1920's there has been a tremendous increase in the coverage of radio and the size of its audience. For instance in the United States only 300,000 homes had radio sets in 1922; 57 million homes had sets in 1964. In 1922 there were only 286 broadcasting stations; in 1964 there were 3,937 AM stations and 1,172 FM stations. The other Western democracies have not achieved figures of these dimensions, but they too have greatly increased radio coverage since the early 1920's.[10]

Since the early 1950's there has been almost equally phenomenal growth in television coverage in the United States. At the end of World War II television was still mainly a laboratory plaything. By 1964 about 96 percent of all American families lived in areas in which television signals could be received, and 90 percent of all homes had television sets.[11] The growth of television, however, has not driven radio out of business. In the other democracies television has not yet expanded at anything like the rate it has grown in the United States, and in those nations radio is still an important medium. Even in the United States, moreover, daytime radio has continued to hold much of its audience, and only evening radio has lost most of its audience and therefore most of its commercially sponsored programs.

The proportion of time given to the presentation of news and political commentary is somewhat smaller in the United States than in the other democracies, but nowhere is it more than 10 percent of the total broadcasting time.[12] Radio and television nevertheless play a significant role in the formation of political opinions. A number of studies have shown that while more people read parts of daily newspapers than regularly listen to radio or watch television, the latter get considerably more total hours of attention per day than do the newspapers. These studies reveal, moreover, that most people trust the accuracy and impartiality of news presentation over radio and television more than they trust what they read in their newspapers. The two electronic communications media, accordingly, are important sources of popular notions concerning world affairs and as such have a powerful impact upon the formation of public opinion.

---

[10] Albig. *op. cit.*, pp. 400–441.
[11] *Statistical Abstract of the United States, 1964* (Washington, D.C.: Bureau of the Census, 1964), Table 714, p. 521.
[12] Albig, *op. cit.*, Tables 20–22, pp. 447–451.

### 3. Motion Pictures

In all the democracies motion pictures are produced mainly by private firms, although government agencies occasionally issue "documentary" films. Only in the dictatorships is all film production monopolized by the government. In the democracies, however, the movie business is not only regulated in its financial and organizational aspects but is also subject to a greater degree of censorship than are newspapers and broadcasting. Some of this censorship is self-imposed (in the United States according to the rules of the industry's famous "production code"), and some is imposed by various national and local governmental agencies. Both types of censorship are intended mainly to prevent the showing of "obscene" and "salacious" material, and there is little direct political censorship.

The movie industry of the United States is by far the largest in the world. It has a capital investment of over $3 billion and employs over 160,000 people. American films, moreover, are widely shown outside the United States: over half the feature films shown in Europe, Central and South America, and Africa are made in the United States.

Generally speaking, movies have the third largest audience of the various mass media. In the United States that audience constitutes from 50 to 60 percent of the adult population. The proportion is somewhat lower in the other democracies, but even in these nations movies have larger audiences than any medium except newspapers and radio.[13]

Even more than radio and television programs the movies produced in the democracies are intended to entertain audiences and thereby make money for their producers, rather than to sell a particular political point of view. Direct and obvious political propaganda in movies is therefore very rare. This does not mean, of course, that movies have no effect whatever upon the political opinions of those who watch them. Most observers agree that the reality perceptions of many moviegoers are strongly affected by what they see, and that this in turn has a powerful impact on their political views. Perhaps the most striking illustration of this point is the impact of American movies upon attitudes toward the United States in the nations where they are shown. The picture of American life and society presented in Hollywood's products is, indeed, almost the only source of information about the United States that citizens of many nations have. This thought may make American readers shudder, but there seems to be little doubt of its truth. Some persons complain that the rather rosy and optimistic picture of life usually painted by the movies is both artistically and politically wrong, and they often argue that "the movies should be more like life"—to which others sometimes reply, "Nonsense. Life should be more like the movies!"

---

[13] *Ibid.*, Ch. 19.

### 4. The Minor Media

The other mass-communications media are "minor" in the sense that they make regular contact with far smaller proportions of the population than do newspapers, broadcasting, and motion pictures. Magazines have the largest audience of any of these media, followed by such others as books (which are read by about 30 percent of the adult population of the United States), pamphlets, billboards, posters in buses and trains, the "legitimate theater," and so on. The influence of the minor media on politics, however, is probably greater than the size of the audience suggests. Books and magazines, for example, are most heavily "consumed" by persons the social psychologists call "opinion leaders" (see below). Nevertheless, none of these media has either the audience or the general impact of the three major mass media.[14]

## The Face-to-Face Media

### General Nature

We have noted that every person belongs to a number of "primary groups," made up of persons with whom he regularly has direct face-to-face contacts, such as his family, his work associates, his schoolmates, his "lodge" brothers, the members of his congregation and the like. A generation ago, the social psychologists Kurt Lewin and Muzafer Sherif launched the study of the effect of membership in such groups on the formation of opinions, and a considerable body of generalizations based on empirical studies of specific groups has subsequently been developed. For our purpose the most significant of these generalizations are the following.[15]

Every member of a primary group is subject to a number of pressures tending to make his opinions conform to those of his associates. For one thing, he is likely to read the same newspaper, watch the same television programs, and see the same movies as his fellows, and so his reality perceptions tend to be the same as theirs. For another, he may dread the possibility of being regarded as "bull-headed" or "peculiar" by his associates. Then too, whenever he expresses an opinion contrary to those of his associates, some of them may try to "straighten him out," and he may learn that the price of clinging to his views is the ending of friendly relations with the other members of his group—a price most persons are

---

[14] The most complete description of these media is in Frederick C. Irion, *Public Opinion and Propaganda* (New York: Thomas Y. Crowell Company, 1950), Ch. 7

[15] See the discussion of primary-group influences on opinion in Chapter 10.

unwilling to pay. In this manner face-to-face communications exert a powerful influence upon the political opinions of most of us.

### The Role of "Opinion Leaders"

Many social scientists believe that in every primary group and local community there is a person or a few persons who act as political "opinion leaders." The opinion leader is more interested in politics than are his fellows. He gathers political news and commentary from the mass media in much greater volume than they, and so has many, more facts and arguments ready at hand. He usually initiates and sustains political conversations where the others in the group would not bother. Because he knows and cares more than the others, they customarily look to him for guidance in political matters. And, except on the rare occasions where his views run counter to views they hold strongly, they tend to accept his conclusions and preferences. Hence on most matters he is by far their most influential political communicator, and thus acts as an unofficial democratic analogue of the Bolshevik agitator (see Chapter 10).[16]

In short, the process of political communication is a two-step flow. First, the mass media broadcast their political messages to a largely unreceptive audience far more interested in relaxation and entertainment than in politics, but the signals are picked up loud and clear by a small attentive public of opinion leaders. Second, the opinion leaders pass on the messages —or at least revised versions of them—by personal conversation around the dinner table or at the shop or across the back fence. Hence the influence of any mass medium on opinion cannot be measured merely by determining the size of its audience. It is equally important to know who is in the audience.

## Communication and Public Opinion

What, then, has social science learned about the interrelations of communication and public opinion in politics? The most generally accepted conclusions can be summarized by portraying them as a "two-way street."[17]

---

[16] The most thorough exposition of this phenomenon is Elihu Katz and Paul F. Lazarsfeld, *Personal Influence* (New York: The Free Press of Glencoe, 1955).

[17] The point of view taken here has been advanced by, among others, Bernard Berelson, "Communication and Public Opinion," in Schramm, *op. cit.*, pp. 342–356; V. O. Key, Jr., *Public Opinion and American Democracy* (New York: Alfred A. Knopf, Inc., 1961), Ch. 15; and Joseph T. Klapper, "What We Know about the Effects of Mass Communication: The Brink of Hope," *Public Opinion Quarterly*, XXI (Winter, 1957–1958), 453–474.

### The Effect of Public Opinion on Communication

Most of the studies summarized here have been concerned with the effect of communication on public opinion. However, the influence also works the other way. The communicator, that is to say, does not address his audience in a social vacuum, nor are they formless lumps of social clay he can mold into any shape he wishes. They already have certain attitudes and values, some of which are strongly held. If his messages run clearly and strongly counter to those attitudes, not only will he win no converts, he will be lucky if they even listen. To some extent, therefore, every communicator must tell the people what they want to hear lest he lose his audience altogether. We have already seen how this necessity affects the content of the various mass media in the democracies, with radio, television, and movies particularly careful to tiptoe around "controversial subjects" and heavily emphasize "entertainment" within the generally accepted ideas of what is funny, beautiful and diverting.

### The Effect of Communication on Public Opinion

Some people apparently believe that propaganda is an absolute weapon. They see man as a bundle of psychological reflexes he cannot control; hence if a skilled propagandist taps the right reflex in the right way, he can make the masses do anything he wishes, from buying a particular brand of soap to voting for a particular candidate.

Now let us admit that the great success of the advertising industry and the ability of dictators like Adolf Hitler and Mao Tse-tung to mobilize the masses fanatically behind them lends a certain credibility to this view. But social science research has shown it to be largely spurious. Sociologist Bernard Berelson sums up what we have learned about the effects of communication on opinion and behavior thus: "Some kinds of *communication* on some kinds of *issues*, brought to the attention of some kinds of *people* under some kinds of *conditions*, have some kinds of *effects*."[18] Each of the italicized words in this sentence refers to a significant variable in the process, each of which may appear quite different in different circumstances.

#### The Kind of Communication

A communication may have "reportorial" or "editorial" content or both. Though most attention has been directed to the latter, the evidence suggests that reportorial content is more effective in influencing opinions. If you tell a man, "The Communists want to overthrow our government," he may or may not be impressed; but if you tell him, "The Communists have just murdered the mayor and blown up the city hall," you are likely to get a more active response.

---

[18] *Op cit.*, at p. 345.

Another aspect of the communication that has long concerned social scientists is the relative effectiveness of the various media. Their research indicates that the more personal and direct the medium of communication the more effective it is likely to be.[19] The superiority of the face-to-face media in this regard, according to one study, results from the following characteristics.[20]

1. They are nonpurposive. Face-to-face political discussion comes up casually in the course of ordinary everyday conversation, and the receiver cannot "turn it off" as he can a television set. Most persons, moreover, tend to "consume" propaganda over the mass media only for opinions with which they already agree and not for opinions counter to their own. They cannot so easily control the content of personal conversations.
2. The communicator can be flexible when encountering resistance. He can shape and alter his arguments in quick response to the observed reactions of his auditors. The mass media, on the other hand, can alter their messages much more slowly even if, as is not often the case, they know exactly how their audience is reacting.
3. They provide immediate and personal rewards for compliance or punishment for noncompliance. They can, in other words, take advantage of the general human desire to be liked by one's associates. The propagandist on radio or television, or the political columnist or editorialist in the newspaper, is a remote and impersonal figure to most of his auditors, and they therefore have no particular desire to be liked by him. Hence, they do not have the personal reason to respond favorably that an associate would have.
4. Their pressures may be exerted by a trusted and intimate source whom the receiver knows, not by some remote and impersonal—and therefore less trustworthy—"pressure group."

As a result of these factors not only are the face-to-face media generally more effective than the mass media, but the more direct mass media, such as radio, television, and the movies, appear to be more effective than newspapers and books, which depend mainly upon the printed word. Most political parties and pressure groups are fully aware of the advantages of face-to-face communication and try to organize their campaigns accordingly.

### The Kind of Issue

Communication is most effective on new and unstructured issues—those on which no strong opinions already exist. Most of us are more likely to accept strong judgments, favorable or unfavorable, of persons and groups

---

[19] Cf. Joseph T. Klapper, "The Comparative Effects of the Various Media," in Schramm, op. cit., pp. 91–105.
[20] Paul F. Lazarsfeld, Bernard Berelson, and Hazel Gaudet, The People's Choice (2d ed.; New York: Columbia University Press, 1948), Ch. XVI.

we know little or nothing about than of those we feel we know well. For example, if you tell a railroad president "All politicians are crooks!" he may well agree; but if you tell him that "X railroad is the most inefficient in the world," he will probably reply that the situation has too many complex and hard-to-assess factors to justify any such extreme statement. On the other hand, if you make both statements to a politician, he will probably enter qualifications and reservations to the first and heartily agree with the second.

Communication, moreover, is likely to be more effective on issues which the receiver regards as relatively unimportant than on those he believes to be crucial. He may have views on both kinds of issues, but his opinions on what he regards as important issues are likely to be far more strongly held (and therefore less changeable) than his opinions on issues that seem to him unimportant.

### The Kind of People

Obviously a communicator can affect the opinions only of those who receive his message. Thus, persons who consume relatively few mass communications are less likely to be affected than those who spend a lot of time reading, listening to a radio, or watching television. On the other hand, persons who do a lot of reading, listening, and viewing are likely to be better informed and less easily influenced than persons who devote less time to communications media. Strongly predisposed persons, in short, are less likely to be influenced by communications than weakly predisposed persons.

### The Kind of Conditions

A communicator who has a monopoly over the media of communications is obviously in a better position to influence opinion than one who has to worry about large-scale counterpropaganda. This, of course, explains why ruling groups in the Soviet Union and the other dictatorships are careful to control the media of communications as much as they possibly can. It also explains why the model of democracy outlined in Chapter 5 requires free access to communications media, and it accounts for the concern some observers have expressed over the tendencies toward increasing concentration of ownership and control of the mass media in the modern democracies. Most observers agree, however, that this tendency has not yet gone so far as to create anything approaching a monopoly situation; and, in any case, the effectiveness of mass communications is limited by the other factors we are considering here.

### The Kind of Effects

Berelson argues that the long-range effects of communication are more significant than its short-range effects. Among the former he includes such matters as providing definitions for key political terms, giving the receivers of communications their basic picture of what the world is like, emphasizing and perpetuating certain social values, and so on.

The short-range effects of communications, as observed, for example, in political campaigns, appear to be as follows.[21] The most infrequent effect is *conversion:* inducing persons actually to switch their opinions from one side of an issue to the other. A more commonly obtained effect is *reinforcement:* affirming the preferences of receivers already favorably disposed and giving them a supply of arguments with which to counter propaganda for the other side. The most frequent effect is *activation:* making persons on your side regard their preference as important enough to take some kind of action to advance it, such as voting, contributing money, attending meetings, and so on.

### Communication and Public Opinion: A Summary

Communication, then, is only one aspect, albeit an important aspect, of the total opinion-forming process. Public opinion cannot be formed without it, and it is a major weapon of every group that desires to influence governmental policy. Communication is not, however, an absolute and irresistible weapon for any such group, even the ruling class of a communist or other dictatorship. Its effectiveness depends upon a great many variables, by no means all of which can be controlled by the communicator. Thus, any attempt to understand the opinion-forming process in any nation must certainly include a study of the nature and operation of the various media of communications, but it must consider many other factors as well.

# Public Opinion Polls and the Measurement of Opinion

### The Problem of Measuring Public Opinion

Men have long been concerned with discovering what public opinion *is* on various issues. Even in the Soviet Union (see Chapter 10) the Communist party feels it must be aware of the state of mass opinion at any given moment so as to determine how far ahead of that opinion its policies may go. Hence its "agitprop" apparatus has the job of measuring as well as molding public opinion.

The problem of measuring public opinion has been of far greater concern in the democracies. Democracy, after all, means government acting

---

[21] *Ibid.,* Chs. VIII–X.

in accordance with the desires of popular majorities. If genuine democracy is to exist, there must be some way of learning how popular majorities feel about political issues—for if government does not and cannot know what those feelings are, it can hardly act in accordance with them.

Some democratic philosophers, most notably Rousseau, have dreamed of a "plebiscitary" democracy, i.e., one in which the majority will on each and every issue is always clear and by some kind of continuous machinery for ascertaining it determines whatever action the government takes. No actual democracy, including the famed New England town meetings and the Swiss cantonal *Landsgemeinden*, has ever been organized along these lines. The principal official devices for sounding public opinion in the modern democracies have been either indirect and periodic, such as representation and elections, or direct and periodic, such as the initiative and referendum (all these institutions are described in Chapters 12 and 13).

Modern social science has developed a device which some theorists believe is capable of both direct and continuous measurement of public opinion—the "sample survey" or "public opinion poll." No government has yet adopted such polls as part of its official policy-making apparatus (although a number of governmental agencies conduct polls to give them some idea of how the land lies), but polls have come to occupy a central position in the analysis and measurement of public opinion. We shall, therefore, conclude our description of the opinion process in the democracies by describing the nature, techniques, problems, and role of public opinion polls.

### The Nature of Public Opinion Polls

#### What Is a "Public Opinion Poll"?

In the broadest sense of the term, a "public opinion poll" is any effort to ascertain public opinion on a matter by directly asking certain members of the public what they think and taking the views of this "sample" to represent what the whole public or "population" (the accepted technical jargon) thinks. In this broad sense it includes everything from conducting elections and referenda to asking friends or passers-by on the street.

The term, however, is most generally used to denote a particular kind of procedure: determining the views of a scientifically selected "cross-section" sample and taking them to represent the views of the whole public. Polls in this sense are conducted by commercial pollers all over the world, including such famous firms as the American Institute of Public Opinion (headed by Dr. George Gallup) in the United States, and its counterpart organizations in a number of European and Asiatic nations. They are also conducted by academic pollers, such as the Survey Research Center of the University of Michigan and the National Opinion Research Center of the University of Chicago.

### "Straw Votes": The Polls' Predecessors[22]

As early as 1824 a Pennsylvania newspaper sent some of its reporters to ask voters how they intended to vote in that year's presidential election. Ever since then newspapers and magazines have tried to sound opinion, especially on elections, by sending out reporters and/or mailing out questionnaires to their subscribers or the general public. In most of these "straw votes" no particular effort is made to direct questions at a "cross section" of the public, and those who conduct them rely mainly upon getting as large a number of respondents as possible to ensure accuracy. Most of these "straw votes" are concerned only with opinion within a particular area, and few attempt to sound opinion over the entire nation.

Perhaps the best known of all the "straw votes," however, was national in scope. From 1916 through 1936 the *Literary Digest* magazine investigated the state of public opinion not only as it bore upon the outcome of presidential elections but also upon a number of other political issues. The *Digest* mailed ballots to its subscribers, to people listed in the telephone directories, and to automobile owners. By the 1930's they were mailing out over 20,000,000 ballots and getting back over 5,000,000 answers —a truly enormous "sample." By this procedure they were able to predict correctly the outcome of all the presidential elections between 1916 and 1932, and their success in doing so was one of the major reasons for the magazine's wide circulation. In 1936, however, came the *Digest's* famous Armageddon. On the basis of its poll in that year the magazine predicted that Governor Landon, the Republican candidate, would win with 59 percent of the popular vote and 370 electoral votes, but in the actual election he lost by landslide proportions, getting only 41 percent of the popular vote and a mere 8 electoral votes. The failure of the *Digest* by so wide a margin made the magazine a national laughingstock, and in less than a year it went out of business altogether.

### Development of Representative Sample Surveys

The method of sounding public opinion by interviewing small but carefully selected representative samples of the public has been used in consumer research and marketing since the early 1920's. It was first applied to the measurement of political opinions on a national scale by Dr. George Gallup in 1934, and in 1935 he founded the American Institute of Public Opinion. At about the same time two other pollers, Elmo B. Roper, Jr., and Archibald Crossley, launched similar operations. Just as the 1936 election witnessed the collapse of the *Literary Digest* poll, it saw the emergence and first popular success of the new-style pollers. The latter not only correctly predicted the outcome of the election; they also explained

---

[22] See Claude E. Robinson, *Straw Votes: A Study in Political Prediction* (New York: Columbia University Press, 1932).

publicly, in advance, that the *Digest* would fail because its sample was heavily overloaded with upper-income people attached to the Republican party, whereas their own samples, while much smaller than that of the *Digest*, represented each voting group in its proper proportion. The combination of their success in predicting the election's outcome and the plausibility of their basic approach got the new polls off to an excellent start, and, with a few setbacks here and there (notably in the 1948 election), they have flourished ever since.

At present over twenty democratic nations have private organizations that conduct public opinion polls in the Gallup manner. Most of them are affiliated with his American Institute of Public Opinion and are often referred to as the "British Gallup Poll," the "Norwegian Gallup poll," and so on. Most are members of the World Association for Public Opinion Research.

The polls have reached their greatest development in the United States. In fact, polling is becoming something like a big business. The commercial polling organizations together now gross upward of $100 million a year. Most of their research is done on consumer and marketing problems on contract for manufacturers, and the results are not published. Part of their revenue, however, comes from polling opinion on political questions and selling the results to newspapers, and it is in this aspect that most of us know the polls. Private polling has also become an important campaigning device for political parties and candidates at the national and state levels and in many local communities as well. Both the Democratic and Republican national committees maintain public opinion experts to analyze published polls and conduct private ones; and the polls and analyses of Louis Harris played a key role in the strategy and success of John F. Kennedy's drive for the Democratic nomination and the presidency in 1960.[23]

In addition to commercial polls a number of polls are operated by universities for the purpose of studying the opinion-forming process. Some government agencies also conduct polls to sound public opinion on policies and operations. The most extensive use is made by the Department of Agriculture, which has a Division of Special Surveys as part of the Bureau of Agricultural Economics charged with investigating public opinion on farm problems, farm programs, and related issues. Polling was also used extensively in World War II by the Office of War Information to check on the success of its propaganda program.[24]

---

[23] See Lewis A. Dexter, "The Use of Public Opinion Polls by Political Party Organizations," *Public Opinion Quarterly*, XVIII (Spring, 1954), 53–61; and Theodore H. White, *The Making of the President, 1960* (New York: Pocket Books, Inc., 1961), *passim.*

[24] H. H. Remmers, *Introduction to Opinion and Attitude Measurement* (New York: Harper & Row, Publishers, 1954), Ch. 9.

### How the Polls Work[25]

There is some variation in detail in the procedures used by the various polls, but they all use the same four basic procedures and operate according to the same basic principles.

#### Drawing the Sample

The basic premise on which the polls operate is that the opinions of a properly drawn sample may be taken, within certain well-established margins of "sampling error," as the opinions of the entire population. Thus the utility of a sample is determined not by its size but by its *representativeness:* a relatively small sample truly representative of the population is far more useful than a much larger sample which, like the *Literary Digest's*, is not representative. The first step in conducting a poll, therefore, is to draw a representative sample. This can be done, the pollers believe, with relatively few individuals. The Gallup and Roper polls, for example, generally use national samples of only 3500 to 5000 persons out of a national adult population of 114,000,000.

The particular persons in the sample are usually selected by one or the other or a combination of the following two procedures.

1. "STRATIFIED-QUOTA." The pollers select certain characteristics of the population, such as sex, age, size of community, income, and so on, and construct their samples in such a way that each characteristic appears in the sample approximately as often as it does in the population. The difficulty with this method is that by stratifying according to these characteristics the pollers have predetermined that the characteristics selected play significant roles in shaping opinions when they may not at all. Hence more and more pollers are using the second procedure.

2. "PROBABILITY." The objective in drawing a probability sample is that every member of the population will have just as good a chance of being selected as any other member, so that there will be no systematic bias in any particular direction or directions. The procedure for accomplishing this involves a number of operations too technical to be described here, but it is fair to say that they are all aimed at making the selection of sample members as completely random as possible.

#### Phrasing the Questions

The next step is to phrase the questions the respondents will be asked. The main object is to avoid "leading questions," since such questions will affect the answers and thereby distort whatever picture of public opinion emerges. The problem of designing the right kind of question has received

---

[25] A useful short introductory manual is Charles H. Backstrom and Gerald D. Hursh, *Survey Research* (Evanston, Ill.: Northwestern University Press, 1963).

a great deal of attention from the pollers, and while it has not yet been perfectly solved, most pollers agree that considerable improvements have been made.

### Getting the Answers

The next step is to get answers from the respondents. Sometimes the pollers use mailed questionnaires, since it is by far the cheapest method. The preferred method, however, is personal interviews. The Gallup organization, for example, normally employs a total of from 250 to 300 interviewers in a national poll, a ratio of one interviewer to each 15 to 20 respondents. Interviewing of this sort requires certain special skills, since it is necessary to avoid all "interviewer bias"—distortion of the answers due to such factors as the effect of the interviewer's personality on the respondent, the latter's desire to appear well in the interviewer's eyes, and so on. Considerable study has been made of proper interviewing techniques, and most interviewers are trained in these techniques before they are sent out.

### Coding and Interpreting the Answers

Ideally all answers should be tabulated so that each person's opinion on a particular issue can be treated as a mathematical unit equivalent to all other opinions on that issue, since only opinions of this sort can be statistically analyzed and manipulated. Thus, answers to Yes-or-No questions or to questions about preferences among political parties and candidates are the easiest with which to deal. Answers to questions about issues are usually ranged along scales allowing for variations between the two extreme answers on each question. The actual coding, sorting, and interpreting process has been greatly expedited by the use of International Business Machines card-punch and card-sort machines and electronic computers, which are now generally used at this stage of the operation.

### Some Questions about the Polls

For a number of years the polls have been the subject of a great deal of discussion, not only by social scientists but by the general public as well. Although they have won general acceptance and approval in most quarters, they are still somewhat controversial and have both their critics and defenders. The debate over them appears to center about the following main questions.

### How Accurate Are They?

Perhaps the most frequently asked question about the polls is whether or not they accurately report the state of public opinion on the questions with which they deal. So far no entirely satisfactory method has been developed to check the accuracy of their reports on public opinion con-

# "Now, About Predictions For Next Year — "

*Figure 23.* Their 1948 Failure Only Temporarily Lowered the Polls' Prestige. (Drawing by Herblock, from *The Herblock Book,* Boston: Beacon Press, 1952.)

cerning "issues"—questions of whether the government should or should not follow this or that policy. Pre-election polls, however, have the great advantage of being checkable by actual election returns; and whereas such unpredictable factors as the weather on Election Day may influence the actual voting figures, most persons believe that the best method yet developed of checking the accuracy of the polls in general is to see how successful they are in predicting the popular vote in elections.

By this standard, then, how accurate are the polls? Their record in predicting the outcome of American presidential elections is shown in Table 7.

Table 7 reveals that the major polls have correctly forecast the outcome of seven of the eight presidential elections they have dealt with, and all failed to predict President Truman's re-election in 1948—a failure which has received about as much publicity as all their correct predictions put together.

## Table 7.   Some Recent Presidential Polls

| YEAR | ACTUAL DEMOCRATIC VOTE | GALLUP POLL | ROPER POLL | CROSSLEY POLL |
|------|------------------------|-------------|------------|---------------|
| 1936 | 60.2% | 53.8% | 61.7% | 53.8% |
| 1940 | 54.7 | 55.0 | 55.2 | . . . |
| 1944 | 53.8 | 53.3 | 53.6 | 52.0 |
| 1948 | 49.4 | 44.5 | 37.1 | 44.8 |
| 1952 | 45.0 | 46.0 | 43.0 | 47.0 |
| 1956 | 42.0 | 40.5 | 40.0 | . . . |
| 1960 | 49.4 | 49.0 | 47.0 | . . . |
| 1964 | 61.3 | 61.0 | . . . | . . . |

SOURCE: The figures for 1936–1960 are reprinted by permission from *Government by the People*, 5th ed., by James M. Burns and Jack W. Peltason, p. 244. Copyright 1963 by Prentice-Hall, Inc., Englewood Cliffs, N.J. Figures for 1964 are added by the author.

Most observers agree that this and other evidence indicates that on the whole the record of the polls in predicting election results has been very good indeed and is far better than the record of "straw votes" or the "hunches" of politicians and political commentators. Some of the polls' critics, however, argue that the polls' success in predicting the outcome of elections is no sign that they are equally capable of revealing the state of public opinion on other kinds of issues. When dealing with the latter type of questions, the critics charge, the polls are subject to two great limitations. First, they have no satisfactory way of measuring the *intensity* of the opinions of their respondents. This, the critics believe, is a crucial deficiency, since in the actual opinion-forming process the intensity with which various opinions are held is a factor of great importance in determining the outcome of the struggle among groups holding those opinions. The pollers are aware of this deficiency and are presently engaged in developing ways and means of overcoming it, although no entirely satisfactory way of measuring intensity has yet been found. The second limitation, according to the critics, is the *irresponsibility* of the respondent's opinions. They argue that a man may give one answer to a question when he knows that the only likely result of his answer is to contribute one more unit to a polling organization's IBM cards, and quite another answer to the same question when he knows that his answer will have a direct and immediate impact upon policy formation and political events. Thus the interview situation is artificial and contrived, and opinions reported therein may or may not have a close correspondence with the respondents' real opinions. The pollers also recognize this difficulty, feel that it is even more difficult to overcome than the problem of measuring intensity, but agree that it is not insoluble.

### How Much Influence Do They Have?

Ever since modern pollers began to achieve their present prominence and prestige, a number of persons have asked just how much influence the polls actually exert on the policy-making process. In the main they have been concerned with two questions. First, do public officials read the polls' results and make their policies accordingly? There is every reason to believe that most public officials do read the results, but there is little direct evidence on the question of whether what they read influences what they do. Such evidence as there is suggests that polling results for many public officials is one, but by no means the only, factor in influencing their decisions (see Chapter 12). The second question is, Is there a "bandwagon" effect of polling results on the voters? Do a lot of undecided voters or voters with weak preferences read the pre-election polls and decide that they might as well be on the winning side? Here too there is little direct evidence, but such evidence as there is suggests that if there is such an effect, it operates on a small proportion of the voting public.

### How Much Influence *Should* They Have?

Next to the question of the polls' accuracy, the question most often raised about them is that concerning how much influence over the formation of public policy they *should* have. Some pollers argue that the polls should have a strong influence on policy formation. Dr. Gallup, indeed, has argued that the polls have made possible a sort of continuous national "town meeting," and that public officials should be guided by what the polls reveal about the state of public opinion on the issues before government.[26] Some critics, notably the political scientist Lindsay Rogers, argue that such a national town meeting is neither possible nor desirable. Not only are the polls inaccurate and misleading, Rogers contends, but the

---

[26] George Gallup. *Public Opinion in a Democracy* (Princeton, N.J.: The Stafford Little Lectures, published by Princeton University, 1938), p. 15.

whole idea of direct democracy is nonsense in a modern nation because of the great complexity and difficulty of the problem its government faces and because of the ignorance of rank-and-file citizens.[27]

Most political scientists consider both views far too extreme. The polls, they believe, are here to stay, not as the key element of the machinery of democratic government but as valuable aids and supplements in solving one of democracy's most vexing problems: the problem of linkage.

## Linkage

Why should a survey of political science, such as this book, devote one twelfth of its space to an analysis of public opinion when the subject is so well covered in sociology and social psychology? The answer is clear. In Chapter 5 we declared that the essence of democracy is government in accordance with the people's wishes, and in Chapter 10 we observed that even dictatorships must pay some heed to public opinion. For the political scientist, then, the final and most significant aspect of public opinion is its linkage with the processes of government—that is, the interaction of public opinion and governmental agencies in the formation and execution of governmental policy.

There is little dispute among democratic theorists about what the linkage should be in an ideal democracy: everyone agrees that public officials should be aware of what popular majorities approve and disapprove and that they should never act contrary to those wishes. But the political scientist and the public official face a host of difficult problems in trying to find out what the linkages between government and public opinion are in any democracy, how far short of the ideal they fall, and what can be done to improve them.[28]

Public opinion polls are the latest device used by the democracies for dealing with the linkage problem, and most have found them useful to a degree. Nowhere, however, do they play more than an advisory role to the institutions officially or quasi-officially charged with ascertaining and implementing public opinion. These include representation, elections, direct legislation, political parties, and pressure groups. We shall devote the next five chapters to describing how these institutions operate in modern governments and to estimating their contribution and limitations in the solution of the linkage problem. We shall begin with representation, the oldest and most fundamental of them all.

---

[27] Lindsay Rogers, *The Pollsters* (New York: Alfred A. Knopf, Inc., 1949).
[28] Key's description and analysis of these problems is both impressive and discouraging: *op. cit.*, Chs. 16–20.

# 12

## Theory and Practice of
## Political Representation

Iᴛ is hard to imagine how we could live our lives without making frequent use of some form of "representation"—that is, using one thing to stand in the place and be taken as the equivalent of another thing. We hand a television dealer a mere piece of paper known as a "check," and in return he gives us a 21-inch electronic miracle of home entertainment. School teachers all over our land daily lead their pupils in a ceremony in which they pledge allegiance to a piece of cloth called a "flag." We go to church and eat a wafer of bread and sip a glass of wine, while our minister tells us that we are consuming the Body and Blood of Jesus Christ. The very language we use employs "words"—scratchings on paper and vibrations in the air—to "represent" objects, persons, and ideas.

Much of what man does, in short, he does by "representation" rather than directly.[1] This is particularly true of the processes by which he governs himself. Some kind of political representation—that employed in the making and enforcing of governmental policy—performs a prominent role in all modern governments, democracies and dictatorships alike. In the democracies, however, political representation is in some sense a key institution; for it is, in Sir Ernest Barker's apt metaphor, the principal "conduit or sluice by which the waters of social thought and discussion are brought to the wheels of political machinery and set to turn those wheels."[2]

---

[1] For a comprehensive and searching analysis of the political and nonpolitical meanings and uses of "representation," see Hanna Fenichel Pitkin, *The Concept of Representation* (Berkeley: University of California Press, 1966).

[2] Sir Ernest Barker, *Reflections on Government* (London: Oxford University Press, 1942), p. 39.

In the present chapter we shall describe the general nature of political representation, outline the leading theories about its proper organization, and summarize the organization and problems of political representation in the modern democracies.

## The General Nature of Political Representation[3]

As we shall use the term, "political representation" means the performance of governmental functions by certain members of the community, known as "representatives," in the place and on behalf of other members of the community, known as "constituents." The functions performed by representatives are of the following two main types.

### The Instrumental Function

To some extent representatives are expected to *do* certain things on behalf of their constituents, and thereby to act as the latter's instruments for getting those things done. In their instrumental capacity, accordingly, representatives pass laws, issue decrees, make speeches, render judgments, declare wars, make peace, and so on. Some theorists consider their actions representative if they accord with what the constituents believe should be done, while others insist that the actions must be in the constituents' best interests. In either case, the instrumental is the more obvious of the two functions of representation, and the literature of political science abounds with discussions of such questions as which members of the community should have the power to choose representatives, what devices should be used to let the representatives know what their constituents want, how the representatives can be held to account for what they do or fail to do, and so on. We shall return to these questions in a moment.

### The Symbolic Function

In addition to *doing* what his constituents want him to do, the representative is also to some extent expected to *be* the kind of person his constituents want him to be. There is good reason why this should be so. Political man is only in part a calculator of material advantages or disadvantages anticipated from this or that governmental policy. He is also

---

[3] In addition to Pitkin, *op. cit.*, useful discussions of political representation are given by Alfred de Grazia, *Public and Republic* (New York: Alfred A. Knopf, Inc., 1951); and Warren E. Miller and Donald E. Stokes, *Representation in the American Congress*, to be published by Prentice-Hall, Inc.

a creature of personal loyalties and emotional needs, many of which are satisfied by symbolic rather than material rewards. Flags snapping in the breeze, military bands playing national anthems, stirring speeches by prime ministers and presidents—none of these make men materially richer, but, like rituals in all human organizations, they satisfy deep-seated psychic needs.[4]

The illustrations of symbolic representation in both democracies and dictatorships are endless. In 1956, for example, a great many Americans voted for President Eisenhower not so much ʼbecause they approved his Middle Eastern policy or his stand on farm price supports but simply because they "liked Ike"—that is, because they felt he was a good man who looked and acted as a President should. For another, the phenomenal popularity of France's President de Gaulle by no means stems solely from approval of his specific policies; it rests in good part upon the fact that for many Frenchmen he incarnates the great France of Joan of Arc and Louis XIV, not the squabbling and petty France of the Third and Fourth Republics.[5] Party politicians in all democracies know that they had better not run candidates known to be dope peddlers or murderers, and if the electorate includes large numbers of voters of, say, Irish extraction, they had better see to it that there is a fair sprinkling of McCormacks and Kennedys on the ticket along with the Saltonstalls, Bellottis, and Goldbergs.

Most students of dictatorship believe that symbolic representation is an important element in the strength of successful dictators. To many Italians for many years, for example, the very person of Benito Mussolini incarnated their vision of themselves as stern, aggressive, and martial Romans rather than lazy, ineffectual, pasta-devouring *paisani*. To many Germans for many years Adolf Hitler personified the idea of the *Herrenvolk*—a German people destined to establish the overlordship of "Aryan" civilization over all mankind. Much of Latin American politics is dominated by *personalismo*—the devotion of segments of the population to this or that *caudillo*, not so much because of his policies but because of the kind of man they think he is.

In short, in all nations and in all forms of government the representative is expected both to *be* the kind of person who symbolizes his constituents' values and aspirations and to *do* the things best calculated to achieve their goals.

---

[4] For a stimulating discussion of this point, see Murray Edelman, *The Symbolic Uses of Politics* (Urbana: University of Illinois Press, 1964).

[5] Cf. Philip E. Converse and Georges Dupeux, "Eisenhower et de Gaulle: les généraux devant l'opinion," *Revue française de Science politique*, XII (March, 1962), 54–92.

# The Proper Organization of Representation: Leading Issues

For many centuries most men in most societies have agreed that some kind of representation is a necessary and significant part of any satisfactory governmental structure. They have widely disagreed, however, over just what kind of representative system is best. The proper organization of representation has, indeed, been one of the most disputed issues in the political literature written since the early Middle Ages. The main issues in this ancient and persistent debate may be summarized as follows.

## What Should Be Represented?

### 1. Interests

In most Western nations during most of the Middle Ages the dominant idea was that the great "estates" of the realm should be represented in the assemblies advising the king (e.g., the English Parliament, the French Estates-General, and the Spanish Cortes). Described in modern terminology, the "estates" were the great interests of the realm. They included the church, the feudal nobility, and the "commons" (the counties and towns); and their spokesmen were, respectively, the "lords spiritual" (the top levels of the church hierarchy—candinals, archbishops, and bishops), the "lords temporal" (the top levels of the nobility—barons, earls, counts, dukes, and so on), and the knights and burgesses of the counties and towns. Each "estate" was thought of not as a collection of individual human beings but rather, again in modern terminology, as an *interest*.

All the "lords spiritual" and "lords temporal" were qualified to attend meetings of the assemblies, but the knights and burgesses making up the "House of Commons" or the "Third Estate" were a different matter. Since the interest they represented was that of certain *places*, the medieval "shires" (counties) and "boroughs" (towns), the knights of the shires and the burgesses of the towns selected particular persons from their ranks in their areas to go to the assembly and speak for them.[6]

There are several present-day versions of this medieval idea. Most familiar to Americans is the organization of the United States Senate and the upper houses of many state legislatures to represent certain governmental units (states, counties, townships) equally regardless of their differing populations. A similar principle operates in the organization of such other legislative bodies as the Australian Senate and the Swiss Council of

---

[6] See Maude V. Clarke, *Medieval Representation and Consent* (London: Longmans, Green & Co., Ltd., 1936).

States, and, in a somewhat diluted form, in the Canadian Senate and the West German *Bundesrat*.

A number of recent social theorists have advocated another modernization of the medieval ideal, in a form generally called "functional representation." They contend that the significant units of the modern community are not its individual citizens but rather the basic "interests" or "functions" of its citizens. Hence the representative system should be organized to represent them directly and efficiently rather than, as at present, indirectly and inefficiently. One version of the functional representation doctrine was set forth in the early 1920's by the British political theorist G.D.H. Cole (who subsequently abandoned it). Briefly summarized, Cole's argument ran as follows. How, he asked, can a legislator who is himself, say, a lawyer, a Catholic, a veteran, and a white man possibly represent those of his constituents who are businessmen, workers, Protestants, Jews, nonveterans, Negroes, and so on? The answer, of course, is that he cannot, and that such constituents simply go unrepresented. He concluded:

> The essentials of democratic representation . . . are, first, that the represented shall have free choice of, constant contacts with, and considerable control over, his representative. The second is that he should be called upon, not to choose someone to represent him as a man or as a citizen in all the aspects of citizenship, but only to choose someone to represent his point of view in relation to some particular purpose or group of purposes, in other words, some particular *function*. All true and democratic representation is therefore *functional* representation.[7]

Another version of this position was set forth in 1931 by Pope Pius XI in his encyclical *Quadrigesimo Anno*. A basic object of representation, he declared, should be to "abolish conflict between classes with divergent interests, and thus foster and promote harmony between the various ranks of society." Thus, instead of the present division between labor and capital that cuts across industrial and functional lines there should be a combination of workers and employers within each industry to promote the welfare of the whole industry and all persons engaged in it.[8] One version of the Pope's ideas later appeared in the "corporative" representative bodies of Italy and Portugal, which are described below.

A number of democratic nations have established certain advisory bodies directly representing various functional groups. Only one democratic

---

[7] G. D. H. Cole, *Guild Socialism Re-stated* (Philadelphia: J. B. Lippincott Company, 1920), pp. 32–33. For a more recent statement of this position, see Fritz Nova, *Functional Representation* (Dubuque, Iowa: William C. Brown Company, Publishers, 1950).

[8] Cf. John H. Hallowell, *Main Currents in Modern Political Thought* (New York: Holt, Rinehart and Winston, Inc., 1950), pp. 681–684.

nation, however, has incorporated this principle in the organization of its legislative assembly. The Constitution of Ireland provides that the upper house of the Parliament, the Senate, shall represent certain interests or functions rather than individual persons. Of its sixty members, eleven are named by the prime minister, six by the nation's universities, and the remainder are elected by the lower house of Parliament from panels of candidates representing the functional areas of literature, art, and education; agriculture and fisheries; labor; industry and commerce; and public administration and social services. From 1922 to 1936 the Senate possessed the power to delay bills passed by the lower house, but Prime Minister de Valera and his supporters contended that it was unreasonable to give a body not directly responsible to the voters the power to upset the programs of a legislative body and executive that are so responsible. In 1936, accordingly, the Constitution was amended so as to deprive the Senate of all power to veto or delay bills passed by the lower house. Since then the Irish Senate, while still nominally a legislative house, has become, in fact, nothing more than an advisory body.[9]

Two authoritarian nations have introduced the principle of functional representation in one of their legislative bodies and thereby established what they called "corporate states." In 1926 the fascist regime of Mussolini established twenty-two "corporations," each representing a particular industry, such as glass and ceramics, textiles, and water, gas, and electricity. Each corporation was composed of delegates from the official employers' organization and employees' organization for its industry, delegates from the Fascist party, and a few technical experts. Each corporation was supposed to plan all production for its industry so as to promote the common interests of its owners, workers, and consumers. In 1930 the National Council of Corporations was created to supervise their activities. In 1939 Mussolini abolished the Chamber of Deputies, the lower house of Parliament which had been organized along traditional democratic lines, and replaced it with the Chamber of Fasces and Corporations. The new legislative house was composed of delegates from the top echelons of the Fascist party and National Council of Corporations, and so the reconstituted Parliament had no members whatever directly elected by individual voters.[10] From the democratic point of view, however, this change made little difference. The old Chamber of Deputies had been little more than a claque for the orations of the *Duce*, and the new Chamber of Fasces

---

[9] The fullest account of the nature and problems of the Irish Senate is Donal O'Sullivan, *The Irish Free State and Its Senate* (London: Faber & Faber, Ltd., 1940).

[10] The best description of the organization of the Italian "corporate state" is G. Lowell Field, *The Syndical and Corporative Institutions of Italian Fascism* (New York: Columbia University Press, 1938).

and Corporations served the same purpose. The post-Mussolini regime abolished his "corporate state" (and, for that matter, the *Duce* himself) and restored the Chamber of Deputies in its traditional democratic form.

The other "corporate state" is still in existence. The Portuguese Constitution of 1935, written under the direction of that nation's dictator, Dr. Oliveira Salazar, established a parliament consisting of a National Assembly, based on traditional democratic forms (if not realities), and a Corporative Chamber composed of representatives of such groups as local governing units and industrial, agricultural, commercial, financial, cultural, and religious organizations. Neither body can override any policy decision made by Dr. Salazar, but the Corporative Chamber is supposed to "advise" both the dictator and the National Assembly on bills that are under consideration. Dr. Salazar has formally proclaimed a "Decalogue of Principles for the New State," in the course of which he expounds the ideas underlying the Portuguese system of representation as follows.

> The welfare of the collectivity transcends—and includes—the welfare of the individual. In the New State the individual exists socially, as member of a group, which may be natural, as the family; or professional, as the corporation; or territorial, as the municipal council—and it is in this social quality that all his necessary rights are recognized. . . . The nation is represented not by artificial groups or ephemeral parties but by real and permanent elements in national life.[11]

## 2. Persons

In Chapters 16 and 17 we shall note that most modern democratic governments provide for at least indirect representation of interests either through the formal establishment of advisory councils or the informal operations of pressure groups. But (with the exception of the upper houses in the federal legislatures mentioned above) they base their official lawmaking representative bodies on a theory of representation going back at least as far as England's Civil War in the mid-seventeenth century. This theory, which some have called "liberal" and others "democratic," holds that the basic political units of the community are its individual citizens, that each should be represented equally with every other, and that the *sine qua non* of a democratic government is that its representatives are responsive to the wishes of the people. Representation, in other words, must be organized according to the principles of popular sovereignty, political equality, popular consultation, and majority rule (see Chapter 5). But how? That is the second great issue of representation.

---

[11] Quoted in S. George West, *The New Corporative State of Portugal* (London: The New Temple Press, 1937), pp. 13–14.

### How Should Persons Be Represented?

## 1. Virtual Representation

Many theorists argue that the best way to run a government is to select the ablest members of the community, give them the leading governmental offices, and allow them freedom to make policy in an atmosphere of calm and reasoned consideration of the community's best interests rather than force them always to consider whether this or that policy will be popular with the ignorant and unstable mob. But how can such an elite be prevented from ruling in its own selfish interests rather than in the interests of the people? The answer, some say, is that if a nation recruits its ablest citizens for its ruling class, they will have a sense of duty and devotion to the nation that will make them put its interests before their own. In this way the people will be "virtually" represented, which is much better than being directly represented.

Two main versions of this doctrine may be noted. The first was advanced by the famous Irish politician and writer of the eighteenth century, Edmund Burke. He argued in 1792 that while only a very small segment of the British people could actually vote for members of the British Parliament, that body nevertheless "virtually" represented their "real" interests very well:

> Virtual representation is that in which there is a communion of interests, and a sympathy in feelings and desires, between those who act in the name of any description of people, and the people in whose name they act, though the trustees are not actually chosen by them. . . . Such a representation I think to be, in many cases, even better than the actual. It possesses most of its advantages, and is free from many of its inconveniences; it corrects the irregularities in the literal representation, when the shifting current of human affairs or the acting of public interests in different ways, carry it obliquely from its first line of direction. The people may err in their choice; but common interest and common sentiment are rarely mistaken. But this sort of virtual representation cannot have a long or sure existence, if it has not a substratum in the actual. The member must have some relation to the constituent.[12]

Burke's theory of "virtual" representation, as the concluding sentences in this quotation make clear, retains an element of the democratic idea that the constituents should have some kind of direct control over their representatives, however attenuated it may be. Fascist and communist ideologists, however, have gone far beyond Burke's theory by dismissing all kinds of direct control by the people over their "representatives."

Representation, according to the fascist and Nazi political theorists of

---

[12] *Works* (Boston: Little, Brown & Company, 1871), IV, 295.

the 1920's and 1930's, is nothing more than the process whereby the leader whips the masses into line behind the policies *he* knows are in the national interest. The democratic idea that representation requires consulting the masses about their policy preferences is ridiculous. For, as Adolf Hitler himself pointed out, "the political understanding of the great masses is not sufficiently developed for them to arrive at certain general political opinions by themselves and to select suitable persons." One of his leading disciples added:

> [The masses are] the instrument on which the political leader must play. Insofar as he gets the right notes out of that instrument—that is, has the confidence of the people in his leadership—he gets therewith the indispensable basis for the activity of his political leadership. *But a people can never lead itself.*[13]

The communist theory of representation is nearly identical with the fascist theory. The communists regard the party as "representative" of the proletarian masses in the sense that it works only for the masses' welfare and knows far better than the masses themselves what policies are best for this purpose. With the communists as with the fascists and the Nazis, therefore, "representation" involves no procedures whereby the masses can replace the members of the ruling elite or directly control it in any other way. Quite the contrary; for, according to communist theorists, if the masses were armed with such powers, they would probably use them to put in the saddle an elite that would exploit the proletariat. To communists, Nazis, and fascists a "representative system" should consist of devices whereby the masses are "educated" and their enthusiasm is mobilized for policies made and enforced by the ruling class. The "elections" and "plebiscites" held in such nations (see Chapter 13) have only the most superficial resemblance to elections and referenda in the democracies.

## 2. Direct Representation

Most democrats hold that representation must be direct: that is, each citizen must have the power to elect one or more representatives, those representatives must hold office for only limited terms, and at the end of their terms the voters must be able to deny them re-election. In this way the representative's responsibility to his constituents will be direct rather than "virtual," and the citizens will not be dependent on the representatives' *noblesse oblige* to keep the representative assembly responsive to the community's desire.

---

[13] Both statements are quoted in René de Visme Williamson, "The Fascist Concept of Representation," *Journal of Politics*, III (February, 1941), 29–41, emphasis in the original.

### How Should Representatives Be Selected?

Most democrats agree upon at least two basic principles of representation: the units represented should be persons, not areas or interests; and persons should be represented directly, not "virtually." But they are divided on the other great issues. One of the most contentious is how representatives should be selected. Some democrats stand by some form of the "single-member district" or "majority" system, while others advocate some form of "proportional" representation. We shall summarize both points of view and outline both systems in Chapter 13.

### How Should Representatives Be Apportioned?

As we shall see in Chapter 13, the United States, Great Britain, and most of the democracies modeled on them use some form of the single-member district system. In such a system the nation (or state or province) is divided into a series of geographical subdivisions known as "districts" or "constituencies," each of which normally elects one member of the representative assembly. "Apportionment" is the process of drawing the constituencies' boundaries and thus allocating representatives and political power among the nation's regions and interest groups. And the problem of achieving fair apportionment to some degree vexes all the Anglo-American democracies.

In Great Britain, Parliament has established four nonpartisan boundary commissions (one each for England, Scotland, Wales, and Northern Ireland) to review constituency boundaries every ten to fifteen years and make recommendations for their revision. The commissions' recommendations are accepted and sometimes revised by the ruling political party and made into law by an act of Parliament. Under this system a sweeping redistribution of seats was made in 1948 and a minor one in 1955; another is due in the late 1960's.[14]

In the United States, the Constitution stipulates that each state, regardless of population, shall have two members of the Senate, but leaves it up to Congress to allocate seats in the House of Representatives. Under the present law, after each national census (taken every decade from 1790 on) Congress determines how many representatives each state shall have, but allows each state's legislature to draw the boundaries for its congressional districts. Since the state legislatures also determine their own districts, they collectively play the key role in the nation's apportionment.

Fair apportionment is difficult in any single-member district system because a number of competing principles have legitimate claims, and it is impossible to satisfy them all. The most obvious and in some sense the

---

[14] The authoritative account is D. E. Butler, *The Electoral System in Britain since 1918* (2d ed.; Oxford: Clarendon Press, 1963).

# "You Can't Say We're Denying Your Right To Vote"

*Figure 24.* Malapportionment of Legislatures Denies Political Equality. (From *Straight Herblock,* Simon & Schuster, 1964.)

most basic is the "principle of *equal electorates,*" according to which each constituency should have the same number of citizens as every other. Any deviation from this standard means a violation of the basic democratic principle of political equality (see Chapter 5): if District A has a population of 500,000 and District B one of only 250,000, then each resident of B has twice as large a share of the nation's lawmaking power as any resident of A. In the "reapportionment revolution" it has wrought since 1962, the United States Supreme Court has held that the principle of equal electorates must be the primary rule governing the apportionment of both houses of all state legislatures[15] and the United States House of Representatives.[16] Even minor deviations are constitutionally permissible only when "based on legitimate considerations incident to the effectuation of a rational state policy."

What might qualify as such "legitimate considerations"? The Court has yet to say, but in most modern democracies they include at least the following. *Coincidence with local government boundaries:* since it is much cheaper and easier to have elections administered by local government authorities, it is desirable to make national constituency boundaries coincide with those of local governments; hence congressional districts and parliamentary constituencies are usually formed by combining counties or metropolitan wards rather than by creating entirely new subdivisions without regard to existing local government boundaries. *Protection of incumbents:* since the new boundaries are drawn up by incumbent legislators, they are usually drawn so as to minimize the number of incumbents whose districts are radically changed. *Gerrymandering:* no matter how equal the districts' populations may be, it is always possible for the dominant political party to draw their boundaries so as to make the most effective use of its votes and waste the opposition's. The basic technique is to concentrate large blocs of opposition voters in a few districts and distribute large blocs of favorable voters more broadly. Successful gerrymandering results in, say, two opposition candidates regularly elected by margins of ten to one, and five of the dominant party's own candidates regularly elected by margins of three to two. The most faithful application of the other principles will not prevent gerrymandering; the main safeguards against it are the dominant party's feeling that it had better show some restraint lest the opposition take revenge at some future date, and, above all, the insistence of the voters that apportionment not be used to give one party an unfair advantage over the other.[17]

### What Is the Proper Relation between the Representative and His Constituents?

The oldest and most debated dispute among democrats is over the proper relation between the representative and his constituents. Two distinct positions on this issue were fully stated by the late eighteenth century, and most subsequent expositions of both have been restatements of the originals.

---

[15] *Baker v. Carr,* 369 U.S. 186 (1962); *Reynolds v. Sims,* 12 L. ed. 2d 506 (1964).
[16] *Wesberry v. Sanders,* 376 U.S. 1 (1964).
[17] An instructive review of how these conflicting principles were juggled in the American states in the early 1960's is Malcolm E. Jewell, ed., *The Politics of Reapportionment* (New York: Atherton Press, 1962).

## 1. The Mandate Theory

Some theorists, such as John Lilburne and Jean-Jacques Rousseau, have argued that the proper function of the representative assembly in a democracy is not to make policy on its own but only to register the dominant policy preferences of the assembly's constituents. They start from the premise that the ideal method of popular consultation is the face-to-face assembly of all the community's members. Since this method is impossible in a spacious and thickly populated nation, the next best thing is for the members of the community to express their will through representatives. So long as the representative assembly confines itself to registering its constituents' views, representation involves no significant departure from democracy. But when the assembly starts making policy on its own, either in ignorance or in defiance of its constituents' desires, it becomes a kind of oligarchy. As William Paterson put it during the American Constitutional Convention of 1787, "What is the principle of representation? It is an expedient by which an assembly of certain individuals chosen by the people is substituted in place of the inconvenient meetings of the people themselves."[18]

A logical corollary of Paterson's idea is the argument that the representative may rightfully act only on the basis of a *mandate* from his constituents to present their views, not his, in the representative assembly. If they wish him to support a proposal he feels is wrong, he must either swallow his objections and vote the way they wish, or resign and give way to a representative who will. Under no circumstances should a representative vote contrary to his mandate. If he does not know his constituents' desires on an issue, he should go back home and find out what they want before he votes.

## 2. The Independence Theory

In 1714 a British Member of Parliament, Antony Henry, received a communication from his constituents asking him to vote against the budget of that year. He is reputed to have replied:

> GENTLEMEN: I have received your letter about the excise, and I am surprised at your insolence in writing to me at all.
> You know, and I know, that I bought this constituency. You know, and I know, that I am now determined to sell it, and you know what you think I don't know that you are now looking out for another buyer, and I know, what you certainly don't know, that I have now found another constituency to buy.
> About what you said about the excise: may God's curse light upon

---

[18] Quoted in Max Ferrand. *Records of the Federal Convention of 1787* (New Haven, Conn.: Yale University Press, 1937), I, 561.

you all, and may it make your homes as open and as free to the excise officers as your wives and daughters have always been to me while I have represented your rascally constituency.[19]

Certainly no one could accuse Mr. Henry of undue pandering to his constituents, but most advocates of the independence theory of representative-constituents relations have chosen somewhat softer words. They have argued that the kind of representative system advocated by Rousseau and Paterson is neither possible nor desirable in a modern nation. The problems facing a modern government are so complex and difficult that they can be understood and dealt with intelligently only by persons who make it a full-time job. Constituents must necessarily spend most of their time and energy on earning a living and cannot possibly acquire the necessary information and understanding as well as can the representatives, for whom pondering problems of government is a full-time job. The representative assembly must therefore make and not merely register policy if the nation is to avoid disaster. This need not convert democracy into a kind of legislative oligarchy, for the power to decide who shall sit in the legislature is still the basic power to rule; and under this theory that power is retained by the constituents.

A logical corollary of this position is the proposition that the representative should exercise his judgment on public affairs *independently*, without regard to what his constituents think. If at the end of his term they feel he has used his power badly, they can defeat him for re-election. But while he is in office, his views, not theirs, should determine his votes.

The best-known exposition of the "independence" theory is that made by Edmund Burke (see above) in 1774. In that year he was elected to the House of Commons from the city of Bristol, and immediately thereafter he wrote and circulated a pamphlet in which he told his constituents what they should and should not expect from him as their representative. The essence of his position is presented in the following quotation.

[The constituents'] wishes ought to have great weight with [the representative]; their opinions high respect; their business unremitted attention. . . . But his unbiased opinion, his mature judgment, his enlightened conscience, he ought not to sacrifice to you, to any man, or to any set of men living. . . . If government were a matter of will upon any side, yours, without question, ought to be superior. But government and legislation are matters of reason and judgment, and not of inclination; and what sort of reason is that in which the determination precedes the discussion, in which one set of men deliberate and another decide, and where those who form the conclusion are perhaps three

---

[19] Quoted in Peter G. Richards, *Honourable Members* (London: Faber & Faber, Ltd., 1959), p. 157.

hundred miles distant from those who hear the arguments? . . . Parliament is not a *congress* of ambassadors from different and hostile interests, which interests each must maintain, as an agent and advocate, against other agents and advocates; but parliament is a *deliberative* assembly of *one* nation, with *one* interest, that of the whole— where, not local purposes, not local prejudices, ought to guide, but the general good, resulting from the general reason of the whole.[20]

Which of the two positions is correct? It is unlikely that we can here settle in a sentence or two a debate that has been going on for two hundred years, but we may make at least these observations. Complete independence, whatever may be its desirability on other grounds, certainly is inconsistent with our conception of democracy, which requires governmental *response* to the desires of the citizens. On the other hand, complete mandating is simply not possible, because on many issues that come before legislators their constituents have no clear or strong views at all, and the legislator has no effective way of finding out what they are. What modern legislators actually *do* is a matter we shall take up in Chapter 17.

## The Organization of Representation in the Democracies

As we have learned from the foregoing, by no means all democrats agree as to just what kind of representative system is best for democracy. It is not surprising, therefore, that no democracy's system is organized strictly in accordance with any one of the principles we have outlined above. The representative systems of most democracies, indeed, are based upon several principles, some of which are logically inconsistent with others.

Table 8 (pages 272–273) outlines the methods used to select the main representative officials of the modern democracies.

### *Legislators*

#### Selection of Legislators

In every modern democracy all the members of at least one house of the national legislature are directly elected by popular vote. In some democracies, as Table 8 reveals, some legislators are selected by means other than direct popular election. All the members of the Canadian Senate, for example, are appointed for life by the governor-general on the

---

[20] "Address to the Electors of Bristol, November 3, 1774," in *Works*, II, 95–96, emphasis in the original.

## Table 8. Selection of Representatives in the Democracies

| Nation | LEGISLATORS | | | | CHIEF OF STATE | | | HEAD OF GOVERNMENT | |
|---|---|---|---|---|---|---|---|---|---|
| | All Directly Elected | Some Indirectly Selected | Plurality System | PR[a] | Directly Elected | Elected by Legislature | Hereditary or Appointed | Directly Elected | Confidence of Legislature |
| Australia | X | | X | | | | X | | X |
| Austria | | X | | X | | X | | | X |
| Belgium | | X | | X | | | X | | X |
| Canada | | X | X | | | | X | | X |
| Ceylon | | X | X | | | | X | | X |
| Chile | X | | | X | X | | | X | |
| Colombia | X | | | X | X | | | X | |
| Costa Rica | X | | X | | X | | | X | |
| Denmark | | X | | X | | | X | | X |
| Finland | X | | | X | * | | | | * |
| France | | X | X | | X | | | ** | |
| West Germany | | X | X | X | | X † | | | X |
| Greece | X | | X | | | | X | | X |
| Iceland | X | | | X | | X | | | X |
| India | | X | X | | | X | | | X |
| Ireland | | X | | X | | X | | | X |
| Israel | X | | | X | | X | | | X |
| Italy | | X | | X | | X | | | X |
| Jamaica | X | | X | | | | X | | X |
| Japan | X | | X | | | | X | | X |
| Lebanon | X | | X | | | X | | | X |

**Table 8. Selection of Representatives in the Democracies (continued)**

| Nation | LEGISLATORS | | | | CHIEF OF STATE | | | HEAD OF GOVERNMENT | |
|---|---|---|---|---|---|---|---|---|---|
| | All Directly Elected | Some Indirectly Selected | Plurality System | PR | Directly Elected | Elected by Legislature | Hereditary or Appointed | Directly Elected | Confidence of Legislature |
| Liechtenstein | X | | | X | | | X | | X |
| Luxembourg | X | | | X | | | X | | X |
| Malta | X | | X | | | | X | | X |
| Netherlands | | X | | X | | | X | | ‡ |
| New Zealand | | X | X | | | | X | | X |
| Nigeria | | X | X | | | X | | | X |
| Norway | X | | | X | | | X | | X |
| Panama | X | | | X | X | | | X | |
| Philippines | X | | X | | X | | | X | |
| San Marino | X | | | X | | X | | | X |
| Sierra Leone | | X | X | | | | X | | X |
| Sweden | | X | | X | | | X | | X |
| Switzerland | | X | | X | | | § | | § |
| Trinidad and Tobago | X | | X | | | | X | | X |
| United Kingdom | | X | X | | | | X | | X |
| United States | X | | X | | ‖ | | | ‖ | |
| Uruguay | X | | | X | # | | | # | |
| Venezuela | | X | | X | X | | | X | |

ᵃ Proportional representation.

* In Finland, the chief of state is the President of the Republic, who is indirectly elected by an electoral college. He has a number of independent powers, and shares with the prime minister the job of head of government.

† The President of India, indirectly elected by an electoral college (members of the national legislature and of the state legislatures), has no power as head of government.

‡ The Netherlands does not permit ministers to be members of the legislature; hence the prime minister is not in quite the same position as his counterparts in the orthodox parliamentary democracies.

§ In Switzerland the chief of state is the President of the Swiss Confederation, a title automatically conferred upon the Chairman of the Federal council. This seven-man body is elected by the legislature for four-year terms, and the chairmanship rotates by seniority once each year. This body is also the "head of government," and so Switzerland has a plural political executive.

‖ The President of the United States, who is both chief of state and head of government, is formally elected by an electoral college but actually elected by popular votes.

# The executive in Uruguay consists of a nine-man Federal Council, selected by direct popular vote for four-year terms. One member is each year designated by the others to act as president. It is a plural executive similar to the Swiss except that it is directly elected.

** Under the Constitution of the Fifth Republic (1958) the chief of state is the President of the Republic, who is directly elected by popular vote. For his unique position, see Chapter 18.

advice of the prime minister. Some members of the Indian Council of States are appointed by the president and the others are elected by the legislatures of the various states. All members of the Swedish upper house are selected by special electoral colleges. Most legislative bodies of this type (see Chapter 17) have little or no real power, and in all the democracies the bulk of the lawmaking power formally rests in the bodies whose members are directly elected by the voters.

### Representation of Local Governing Units

In some democracies one of the legislative houses is intended to represent certain units of local government rather than individual persons. All the federal democracies, for example, constitute the upper houses of their national legislatures in this manner: the United States Senate has two members from each state, the Australian Senate ten from each state, and the Swiss Council of States two from each canton and one from each half-canton. The Canadian Senate's structure somewhat reflects population differentials among the provinces (Quebec and Ontario each has twenty-four senators, and no other province has more than six). The West German *Bundesrat* is organized similarly although the members of both bodies are nevertheless intended to represent the provinces and *Länder* as such rather than individuals. Even some of the unitary democracies represent local governing units in one house of the national legislatures. In Burma and the Netherlands, for example, the provinces derive all their formal power by grant from the national government; yet the upper houses of the legislatures of both nations are composed of equal numbers of representatives from each province.

### Average Size of Constituencies

Most advocates of direct popular representation feel that the total number of constituents in each representative district should be kept as small as possible so that the representatives may maintain personal contacts with their constituents. They feel that this consideration is of special importance in the nations using the single-member district system, since each constituency has only one representative to speak for it. This ideal is also held, however, by most advocates of multiple-member districts and "proportional representation."

Most modern democracies have discovered that the increase in size of their populations during the past century has made the price of living up to the ideal of small constituencies that of constantly enlarging the memberships of their legislative bodies. The first American House of Representatives in 1789, for example, had 65 members, 1 for every 30,000 persons. The present House has 435 members, 1 for every 446,000 persons —and if the original ratio had been maintained, the House would now have no less than 6,467 members! The United States, like most other democracies in recent years, has decided that ever-growing legislative assemblies do even more damage to proper democratic representation than do ever-growing constituencies, and so it has followed the policy of putting a ceiling on the total membership of the assembly and allowing the constituencies to continue to grow in size. Table 9 shows the populations of the average constituencies in various modern democracies using single-member districts.

### Table 9.  Size of Legislative Bodies and Population of Constituencies

| NATION | SIZE OF ASSEMBLY | PER CONSTITUENCY AVERAGE POPULATION |
|---|---|---|
| Australia | 124 | 88,000 |
| Canada | 265 | 71,000 |
| Ceylon | 151 | 70,000 |
| Costa Rica | 45 | 30,000 |
| France | 465 | 103,000 |
| West Germany | 499* | 224,000 |
| Greece | 300 | 28,000 |
| India | 500 | 899,000 |
| New Zealand | 80 | 32,000 |
| Nigeria | 320 | 116,000 |
| Philippines | 102 | 296,000 |
| United Kingdom | 630 | 84,000 |
| United States | 435 | 446,000 |

* Of these, 247 are elected from single-member districts, the rest by proportional representation.

As Table 9 shows, India and the United States, both using single-member district systems, have by far the largest constituencies of any of the modern democracies. Since they also have by far the largest total populations of any of the nations listed, they can reduce the size of their constituencies only by greatly enlarging the size of their legislatures. Apparently, both nations have decided that holding the size of their constituencies down to the level maintained by the other democracies is not worth the price of having legislative bodies with thousands of members.

The figures in the second column of Table 9 are, of course, only averages. In most of the nations there are considerable variations in constituency populations. In the United States, for example, congressional districts range in size of population all the way from 182,845 (the Second District of South Dakota) to 951,527 (the Fifth District of Texas).[21] There are also great discrepancies among the districts within particular states. In Maryland, for example, the First District has a population of 243,570 while the Fifth District has one of 711,045. In Arizona, for another, the Third District has 198,236 while the First has 663,510.

The United States is by no means the only democracy in which such disparities exist. In the 1964 general election, constituencies for the British House of Commons ranged from 24,280 (Ross and Cromarty) to 90,996 (Epping).[22] And in Canada before the 1952 redistribution, constituencies for the Canadian House of Commons ranged from 21,202 (Brant) to 95,942 (St. James).[23]

In the United States pressures by the Supreme Court and in most other democracies the efforts of boundary commissions (see above) will minimize the variations in size among legislative constituencies; but so long as standards other than the principle of equal electorates are also applied in drawing district boundaries, some discrepancies will be inevitable.

### Executives

In most modern democracies, then, the directly elected legislative body is regarded as the basic element of the legal representative system. In addition to such bodies, however, each democracy also has certain other elements, including certain executive officials. Every democracy (see Chapter 18) has two top executive positions: a chief of state, who acts as the formal apex of the nation's governmental structure and may or may not exercise power over policy making; and a head of government, who directs the people and agencies in command of the actual decision-making apparatus. In the presidential democracies, such as Chile, Costa Rica, Venezuela, the Philippines, and the United States, both of these positions are occupied by a president who is elected, directly or indirectly, by a nation-wide constituency. In all other democracies these positions are held by different officials selected in different ways. In the "constitutional monarchies," such as Australia, Belgium, Sweden, and the United Kingdom, the chief of state is either a hereditary monarch or an official appointed by such a monarch to act in his behalf. In the "parliamentary republics," such as Austria, Ireland, and Italy, the legislature elects a president who performs approximately the same functions as a constitutional monarch. In all the democracies except the presidential democracies, Switzerland, and Uru-

---

[21] U.S. Bureau of the Census, *Congressional District Data Book (Districts of the 88th Congress)* (Washington, D.C.: Government Printing Office, 1963), pp. 465, 483.

[22] R. L. Leonard, *Guide to the General Election* (London: Pan Books, Ltd., 1964), Table 4, p. 35.

[23] Robert M. Dawson, *The Government of Canada* (Toronto: University of Toronto Press, 1947), p. 369.

guay (the latter two nations have "plural executives"), the head of government is a prime minister formally appointed by the chief of state but actually holding the job because he has the approval of a majority of the members of the directly elected legislative body.

### Judges

In all the democracies except the United States and Switzerland (see Chapter 20), judges are appointed rather than elected and, therefore, do not directly represent the people. In a number of states of the United States (but not in the national government) and in Swiss cantons judges are directly elected and, therefore, directly represent the voters.

### Appointed Administrative Officials

In every democracy the great bulk of the public officials are appointed administrative officials or employees who, by definition, do not directly represent the people. One of the great debates in modern democratic political theory (see Chapter 19) is over the questions of how "representative" these administrators actually are, how "representative" they should be, and what institutional arrangements are best calculated to achieve the proper degree of "representativeness."

### Advisory Bodies Formally Representing Interest Groups

A number of modern democracies have certain formal devices for directly representing interest groups in the governmental policy-making process. In the United States, for example, the bar associations in a number of states are directly represented on the bodies that select judicial nominees, the medical associations are directly represented on the bodies that license physicians, and the architectural associations are directly represented on the bodies that license architects. Many administrative agencies maintain advisory boards made up of representatives named by the organized interest groups most directly affected by the particular agencies' activities.[24] In Great Britain representatives of labor, management, and "the public" usually sit on the governing boards of the various nationalized industries.

A few democracies have established more general advisory bodies representing their nations' main economic interests. The best-known example is the French Economic and Social Council, established by the Constitution of 1946. The council is composed of representatives named by national

---

[24] The most complete description of this type of direct interest representation in the United States is Avery Leiserson, *Administrative Regulation: A Study in Representation of Interests* (Chicago: University of Chicago Press, 1942).

organizations of workers, employers, farmers, civil servants, and various other interest groups. It is empowered to consider bills before the National Assembly, either by request or upon the council's own initiative. However, it can only make recommendations, which the National Assembly may or may not accept. The council has no power to veto, amend, or even delay a bill, and is therefore a purely advisory body. It is used mainly as a source of information both on technical matters and on the opinions of the various interest groups; and it appears to have some influence on policy-making in France, though hardly a decisive one.[25]

In every modern democracy, however, the representation of interest groups is accomplished mainly by the informal and extralegal processes of "lobbying" and "propaganda" conducted by "pressure groups" and working through and with the traditional democratic devices for representing individual citizens. These processes are examined in greater detail in Chapter 16.

## Direct Legislation

### *Rationale*

Some democratic theorists, as observed previously, have always regarded *any* system of representation as a more or less unsatisfactory method of popular consultation. Rousseau, for example, argued that representation in any form inevitably distorts public opinion to some degree; for, he declared, when one person's ideas are passed through the mind of a second person and expressed by the latter, they always come out looking somewhat different from the way they looked when they went in—an observation with which anyone who has ever read a set of examination papers will heartily agree! If this be so, Rousseau and his followers have argued, we cannot permit representation to be the sole method for finding out what the people want. At the very least we must supplement it with some device that expresses the popular will directly and without "interpretation" by any intervening agency.

Many persons believe that the New England town meeting or the Swiss *landsgemeinde* is the ideal device for this purpose, and some believe that public opinion polls can also do the job. But town-meeting procedures are possible only in small local communities, and too many people have too many doubts about the polls' ability to measure genuine public opinion accurately to turn the job of popular consultation over to the pollers. Consequently, most persons who have reservations about repre-

---

[25] Cf. Edward G. Lewis, "The Operation of the French Economic Council," *American Political Science Review,* XLIX (March, 1955), 161–172.

sentation hold that some form of "direct legislation" is a necessary part of the machinery for democratic popular consultation. Few advocates of direct legislation have ever argued that it should replace representative assemblies entirely but have proposed it as a necessary supplement for such assemblies, always available for the people to use whenever they feel that the legislature is not accurately expressing their desires.[26]

### Organization

Two main devices are generally classed under the general heading of "direct legislation."

1. *The Initiative.* This device enables voters to initiate a law or constitutional amendment by their own direct action without any action by the legislature. The general procedure is this: a group of voters desire a particular law or constitutional amendment that the legislature is unwilling to pass; they circulate a petition bearing a statement of the proposed action; when they have secured the required number of legitimate signatures (in some instances a flat number, in others a certain percentage of the votes cast at the most recent general election), their proposal is placed on the ballot at the next general election; if it receives the necessary majority (in some instances a simple majority, in others a two-thirds majority), it becomes law.

2. *The Referendum.* This is a device whereby the voters approve or disapprove a law or constitutional amendment proposed by the legislature or a constitutional convention. The most common procedure is the compulsory referendum, by which the proposal is automatically referred to the voters by the initiating body and does not become law until and unless it is approved by the required majority. A few governments also have the optional referendum, whereby the legislature may if it wishes refer a proposal to the voters.

By far the most common form of direct legislation in modern democracies is the constitutional referendum. Roughly half of the democracies listed in Table 8, including Australia, Austria, Denmark, Ireland, and Japan, require popular approval of constitutional amendments proposed by their legislatures or constitutional conventions. A few more require a popular referendum if a proposed amendment is approved by less than a designated proportion (two thirds or three fifths) of the legislature. The national government of the United States has no direct-legislation proce-

---

[26] Most of the literature advocating direct legislation was written in the "Progressive Era" in the United States from the early 1890's to World War I. Two leading expositions of the position outlined in the text are Nathan Cree, *Direct Legislation by the People* (Chicago: A. C. McClurg & Company, 1892); and William B. Munro, ed., *The Initiative, Referendum, and Recall* (New York: Appleton-Century-Crofts, Inc., 1912).

dures of any sort, but they are widely used by the states: all but one have the compulsory constitutional referendum, thirteen have the constitutional initiative, twenty-two have the optional legislative referendum, and twenty have the legislative initiative.[27]

The oldest system of direct legislation in the modern democracies is that of Switzerland, which used the constitutional referendum as early as 1802. Certain Swiss cantons (the local governing units corresponding to the American states) adopted the constitutional and legislative initiative and referendum in the 1830's, and the national government incorporated the compulsory constitutional referendum in its Constitution in 1891. The Swiss system has long been regarded as the model by advocates of direct legislation, and it remains the most extensive system employed by the national government of any modern democracy.[28]

### Results and Evaluation

A number of studies have been published on the operation of direct legislation in Switzerland, in the German Weimar Republic (from 1919 to 1933), and in the American states.[29] They all make similar observations. Initiative and referendum elections usually draw substantially smaller proportions of the eligible voters than are drawn by elections of public officials. The voters generally vote down measures intended to increase taxes or limit public expenditures and generally approve measures authorizing public works and limiting the size of public debts. The campaigns for and against most measures are conducted mainly by organized interest groups rather than by spontaneous opinion groups of citizens. Extensive use of direct legislation has tended to weaken the authority and prestige of representative bodies and has also noticeably increased the number and complexity of the decisions the voters are called upon to make.

There is no general agreement, however, upon whether the net effect of direct legislation has been good or bad. In recent years no democracy has added any of these procedures to its lawmaking processes, and at least one (West Germany) that used to have direct legislation has now abandoned it. Most observers would probably agree with the judgment of two

---

[27] Clyde F. Snider and Samuel K. Gove, *American State and Local Government* (2d ed.; New York: Appleton-Century-Crofts, Inc., 1965), pp. 14, 169, 173.

[28] See Felix Bonjour, *Real Democracy in Operation* (Philadelphia: J. B. Lippincott Company, 1920), pp. 30–39; and William E. Rappard, *The Government of Switzerland* (Princeton, N.J.: D. Van Nostrand Company, Inc., 1936), pp. 66–70.

[29] The most comprehensive surveys are Harold F. Gosnell and Margaret J. Schmidt, "Popular Law-Making in the United States, 1924–1936," *Proceedings of the New York State Constitutional Convention, 1938*, VII, 313–315; and Herman Finer, *Theory and Practice of Modern Government* (rev. ed.; New York: Holt, Rinehart and Winston, Inc., 1949), pp. 562–567.

American political scientists that the actual results of direct legislation have neither confirmed the predictions of disaster made by its early opponents nor justified the predictions of democratic utopia made by its early advocates.[30]

## Conclusion

Whatever may be their relative merits, representation rather than direct legislation remains the principal formal machinery for popular consultation in all modern democracies, and the election of legislators and (in some but not all democracies) executives and judges is the principal formal and direct device the people have to express their desires about what government should and should not do. The next chapter describes the main legal methods used by the modern democracies to conduct elections, and the three chapters that follow examine the roles of the voters, political parties, and pressure groups in animating and operating the legal machinery of representation.

---

[30] Joseph G. LaPalombara and Charles B. Hagan, "Direct Legislation: An Appraisal and a Suggestion," *American Political Science Review*, XLV (June, 1951), 400–421.

# 13

## Choosing Representatives:
## Suffrage, Nominations,
## and Elections

Abraham lincoln's northern political opponents, and they were many, called him a dictator. Look at what he has done, they said: in clear defiance of the Constitution he has suspended the writ of habeas corpus, clapped his political adversaries in jail, raised an army, withdrawn money from the Treasury, and started a war, all without even asking Congress for prior authorization.

Lincoln's supporters replied that he had certainly used the emergency powers of the presidency to their fullest, but he was no dictator. Why? Because in the elections of 1862 and 1864 the voters had a chance to throw first his supporters and then Lincoln himself out of office. Any public official who can be turned out of office in a compulsory and free election, they declared, is no dictator; for so long as such elections are held, the people, and not the President or any other public official, retain the ultimate ruling power as democracy requires.

Most democrats then and now agree that this distinction between a strong democratic executive and a dictator is both valid and important. They recognize that in all modern democratic nations the sole or principal institutional device by which the sovereign people control their government is the election of its top officials. The process of elections, accordingly, plays a role of high significance in the organization of modern democracies.

The ideals of democracy require that elections be organized in such a way that all the members of the community have the opportunity to participate, that they be confronted with genuine alternatives from which to choose, and that whatever choices they make are binding on the government. The present chapter's survey of electoral processes, accordingly, will describe the modern democracies' main answers to these basic questions.[1]

1. Who may vote?
2. How are alternatives placed before the voters?
3. How are their choices made and registered?

After describing the organization of elections in the democracies, we shall describe the very different purposes and organization of elections in a communist dictatorship.

# Deciding Who May Vote: The Suffrage

## The Suffrage and Democracy

### The Principle of Universal Suffrage

Democrats have long agreed that "democracy" means at least a form of government in which the basic ruling power is vested in all the members of the community. The only suffrage rules consistent with this principle, they have also agreed, are those of universal suffrage and political equality: each member of the community must have one vote but no more than one vote.

The principle of universal suffrage, however, has never required that *everyone* in the community must have the right to vote. No democratic nation, for example, has ever permitted ten-year-old children to vote, and no democratic theorist has ever called such exclusion undemocratic. Most democracies also exclude aliens, lunatics, and criminals in prison, and few democrats feel that such rules violate democratic principles.

As a democratic ideal, in other words, the principle of universal suffrage requires that every *member* of the community, and not every person physically present within the community, must have the right to vote. Only persons who have demonstrated both their ability and their willingness to assume the obligations of loyalty to the community and obedience to its laws are generally considered to be full-fledged members of the community and therefore entitled to vote in its elections.

### The Historical Democratization of the Suffrage

The history of suffrage rules has been essentially the same in all modern democratic nations. In each, one kind of restriction after another has been abandoned and consequently ever-greater proportions of the

---

[1] A thoughtful discussion of these processes in modern nations is W. J. M. Mackenzie, *Free Elections* (New York: Holt, Rinehart and Winston, Inc., 1958).

population have been successively included in the electorate. In all the nations here considered this trend has reflected an increasing commitment among persons already possessing the franchise not only to the principle that all members of the community should have the vote but also to an expanding conception of what persons should be considered full-fledged members.

In the first American election under the new Constitution in 1789, for example, only about one out of every thirty adults was eligible to vote! Women, were the largest single group of ineligibles but most of the states also excluded slaves and males owning no property or paying no taxes, and a few states even excluded adherents of certain religions. Through the succeeding decades, however, the restrictions were gradually removed one by one. All religious qualifications were removed by the early nineteenth century, and by the end of the Civil War in 1865 most states had removed all property-owning and taxpaying requirements. The Fifteenth Amendment to the national Constitution (1870) prohibited the denial of the right to vote "on account of race, color, or previous condition of servitude"—although even in our time, nearly a century later, some southern states, in defiance of this constitutional injunction still use non-legal and indirect means to bar Negroes from the polls simply because they are Negroes. The final major legal step came in 1920 with the adoption of the Nineteenth Amendment, which prohibited denial of the right to vote "on account of sex" and thereby admitted women to full voting equality with men.

In the other democracies the story has been substantially the same: the gradual elimination of religious, property-owning, and taxpaying requirements in the nineteenth century, and the adoption of woman suffrage in the twentieth. New Zealand, for example, adopted woman suffrage as early as 1893 and Norway in 1913. France and Italy, on the other hand, did not adopt it until 1946, and Switzerland has not yet adopted it.

### Current Suffrage Requirements

The main qualifications required of voters in the modern democracies are summarized below.

CITIZENSHIP. Most democratic nations permit only their own citizens to vote but make no distinction in this regard between native-born and naturalized citizens. This requirement rests upon the conviction that only persons who are loyal to the nation and prefer it to all others should be permitted to vote in its elections. The possession of citizenship is generally regarded as the best formal indication of such loyalty.

AGE. Just about every society requires each of its members to attain a certain minimum age as a prerequisite for his full participation in community affairs, on the ground that infants and children are incapable of such participation. Most primitive societies, for example, have special rites and ceremonies for the induction of young persons into adulthood and full membership in the society. So it is in the modern democracies, each of which requires that its citizens reach a certain minimum age before they can vote.

Every such age limit, of course, is arbitrary in the sense that it cannot take account of the fact that different individuals mature at different ages. In all such nations, however, the difficulties of conducting individual "maturity examinations" are generally regarded as greater than the possible injustices resulting from applying one minimum-age requirement to all. The most common minimum-age limit is twenty-one years. The lowest limit is eighteen years (e.g., in Brazil, Israel, Uruguay, and the American States of Kentucky and Georgia), and the highest is twenty-five (e.g., Denmark). In most nations the rule is uniform for all voters, but Italy permits only persons over twenty-five to vote for senators and makes all persons over twenty-one and married men over eighteen eligible to vote for deputies!

RESIDENCE. Most democracies also require a voter to have lived in the nation and/or his particular voting district for a certain period of time (e.g., in Illinois a voter must not only have lived in the state for a year prior to the election in which he wishes to vote but also for ninety days in the county and for thirty days in the voting district in which he seeks to vote).

REGISTRATION. In order to prevent such election frauds as "voting the graveyard" and "repeaters" (see below), most democracies take steps to supply the officials in each election district with a full roster (usually called a "register") of all eligible voters against which the names of persons asking for ballots can be checked. Some registration systems are "permanent," in that once the roster is compiled it is kept up to date by dropping ineligible individuals and adding eligible ones. Others are "periodic," in that at regular intervals the entire register is scrapped and a new one drawn up.

The most significant distinction among registration systems is the location of the responsibility for compiling the register. At one end of the scale stand Great Britain and most European democracies, which require the registering officer to make periodic door-to-door canvasses of his district and enroll any eligible person who is not already on the register. The United States stands at the other end: most states require each would-be voter to assume the initiative by coming to the registering officer's office and making application for registration; only a few permit or encourage door-to-door canvassing and registration in the home or in the neighborhood. Hence in the United States most voters must take the initiative on two occasions: during the registration period and then again on Election Day. In Britain and most other democracies the voters must take the initiative only on Election Day. Most analysts believe this is one of the main causes for the relatively lower voting turnouts in the United States.[2]

OTHER REQUIREMENTS. In addition to these four basic requirements, some democracies add others. Some (e.g., Brazil, Chile, and Great Britain) exclude certain public officials and members of the nobility. Others (e.g., the Philippines, Brazil, and some American states) exclude persons who cannot read and write. Still others (e.g., Australia and South Africa by law and some American states by extralegal practices) exclude members of certain races. Switzerland, as we noted above, still excludes women. Most democracies exclude lunatics and convicted felons. In Great Britain, for example, it is sometimes facetiously but accurately said that the vote is denied to "criminals, idiots, infants, and peers (members of the nobility)!"

Of all these special requirements, however, only those barring members of certain races disqualify substantial portions of the adult population, and the suffrage rules of most modern democracies, accordingly, come very close to satisfying the democratic ideal of universal suffrage.

### Nonvoting and Compulsory Voting

Locke, Rousseau, Jefferson, and other early advocates of democracy apparently assumed that once the members of a community are given the legal right to vote they will exercise it as a matter of course at every opportunity. The evidence indicates, however, that the actual voting turnouts in the modern democracies do not measure up to this ideal. Table 10, for example, shows the percentage of legally eligible voters actually voting in recent general elections in a number of democratic nations.

Table 10 shows that in terms of the age-eligible citizens who actually voted, only India had a lower turnout rate than the United States. But a fair comparison of the American rate with others must take into account the fact that in the United States a substantial number of persons of voting age are discouraged from voting because of their race, many others are temporarily disfranchised because of moving just before the election, and still others fall afoul of our demanding registration laws. The American Heritage Foundation, a nonpartisan get-out-the-vote organization, has estimated that when we exclude such persons from our calculations, the turnout rate of those not excluded nor discouraged from voting runs more like 71–73 percent—a figure which approaches that in most British Commonwealth nations.

---

[2] This is Mackenzie's judgment, *ibid.*, pp. 117–118; and it was confirmed by the President's Commission on Registration and Voting Participation in its Report of December 20, 1963.

## Table 10.   Voting Turnouts in Recent General Elections

| NATION | DATE | PERCENT OF VOTER TURNOUT |
|---|---|---|
| Australia | 1961 | 95 |
| Austria | 1962 | 93 |
| Belgium | 1961 | 92 |
| Canada | 1962 | 79 |
| Costa Rica | 1962 | 81 |
| Finland | 1962 | 84 |
| France | 1962 | 72 |
| West Germany | 1961 | 88 |
| Greece | 1961 | 84 |
| India | 1962 | 53 |
| Ireland | 1961 | 71 |
| Israel | 1961 | 81 |
| Norway | 1961 | 79 |
| United Kingdom | 1964 | 77 |
| United States | 1964 | 61 |

SOURCE: The figures for all nations except the last two are taken from D. E. Chapman, *A Review of Elections, 1961–1962* (London: The Institute of Electoral Research, 1964). The U.K. figures are from the *Times House of Commons, 1964* (London: The Times Office, 1964), p. 246; and the U.S. figures are from *The World Almanac, 1965* (New York: The World-Telegram and Sun, 1965), p. 40.

Many of democracy's well-wishers regard any nonvoting as both a disgrace to democracy's fair name and a threat to its survival. A number of political scientists, accordingly, have studied the causes of nonvoting (which we shall discuss in Chapter 14) and recommend such remedies as making registration easier, reducing the frequency of elections and the number of elective offices, get-out-the-vote drives by civic organizations and advertising councils, and—that analgesic for all social ills—education.

The most drastic remedy, however, is compulsory voting, pioneered by Belgium (1893), the Netherlands (1917), and Australia (1924). The Australian law, as a representative example, specifies that every person eligible to vote must, within twenty-one days of becoming eligible, apply to the registrar of voters in his voting district for enrollment. If he fails to do so, he is fined. After each election the returning officer sends to each person on the roster who did not vote a form on which the nonvoter must explain why he failed to vote. If he offers what the law allows as a valid excuse (e.g., illness or religious scruples) and if the returning officer verifies his excuse, no penalty is imposed. But if he offers no excuse or an invalid or untrue excuse, he is fined.

Some nations (e.g., Brazil and Uruguay) have adopted compulsory-voting laws but have not enforced them. Others have both adopted and enforced such laws and have seen the average turnouts in their elections increase markedly thereafter (e.g., from 70 to 95 percent in Belgium, and from 64 to 94 percent in Australia). There is, however, no general agreement among political scientists—or, for that matter, among Belgians and Australians—as to whether the *total* effect of compulsory voting has been beneficial. Some commentators argue that it has greatly increased the volume of thoughtless and irresponsible votes and enlarged the "automatic anti" vote. Others feel that compulsion, by lessening nonparticipation, has also lessened indifference and thereby aided democracy.[3]

The most we can say is that in the few democracies that have adopted compulsory voting there is no powerful sentiment to abolish it, and that most modern democracies depend upon other agencies, notably their political parties (see Chapter 15), to get their voters to the polls.

## Providing Choices: Nominations and Candidate Selections

### The Recruitment of Candidates

**Process**

Most free elections involve voters choosing among competing "candidates"—persons legally eligible for the offices contested whose names are printed on the official ballots (or, on rare occasions, written in by the voters). Hence the first step in the conduct of free elections is the process by which out of the many citizens eligible for the offices emerge the very few who actually appear on the ballot—a process we may generally call "candidate recruitment." This general process, in turn, has two major parts: the first is *nomination*, which includes the legal proceedings by which eligible persons are formally designated "candidates" and have their names accepted by public authorities for printing on the election ballots. As we shall note below, these legal procedures vary substantially from one democracy to another, but in one significant respect they are all alike. In elections for all but the most minor offices they are preceded and dominated by extralegal activities of political parties which we shall call *candidate selection* and which constitute the second part of candidate recruitment.

Some kind of candidate recruiting process precedes elections in just

---

[3] For a general survey, see Henry J. Abraham, *Compulsory Voting* (Washington, D.C.: Public Affairs Press, 1955).

about every organization in which elections are held. When football teams elect their captains, for example, it is customary for various members of the teams to talk over the possibilities informally and settle upon particular players they will support. When the American Political Science Association is about to elect a new president, the outgoing president appoints a nominating committee that selects someone for this honor and presents his name to the entire association, which then invariably proceeds to elect him.

Both these procedures are similar to that in which the National Convention of the Republican party in 1964 decided that the party's presidential candidate would be Barry Goldwater rather than Nelson Rockefeller or William Scranton, although Goldwater's nomination, of course, involved a decision by a highly organized party, while the former examples are decisions by smaller "factions" and committees. In all three instances part of the electorate met in advance of an election and decided which of the many persons legally eligible for the elective post they would support— which person, in short, would be the *candidate* of their particular faction, committee, or party.

### Significance

In a democracy every voter has the legal right to vote for any legally eligible person he wishes for any office. In practice, however, he does not have such complete freedom and could not use it if he had. In the United States, for example, about 115 million persons presently fulfill all the legal qualifications for the presidency. Suppose that every voter had been required to choose among all these persons in 1964. If he wished to be fair to all of those eligible, he would have had to learn the personal qualifications and position on issues of every one! This is obviously impossible. No human being can even perceive the nature of each of 115 million alternatives, let alone make an intelligent choice among them. But no such impossible task actually confronted the voters in 1964. The various political parties, by making their nominations, had reduced the alternatives from 115 million to about 10. Since we have a two-party system, most voters were faced with choosing between only the two alternatives of Goldwater and Johnson. The major parties' nominating processes, accordingly, reduced the number of alternatives before the voters from 115 million to 2.

Most of us can learn the personal qualifications and political opinions of two candidates and can make a meaningful choice between them. Hence the process, which reduced the number of potential presidents from 115 million to 2, made it possible for the voters to make a meaningful choice between the "finalists." Surely it was as significant a part of the total process for selecting the President as the general election in November, in which the voters reduced the number of potential Presidents from 2 to 1.

For these reasons, therefore, the nominating process not only plays a crucial role in the selection of elected officials but is also an indispensable mechanism for enabling the voters in a democracy to participate meaningfully in selecting those who govern.

### Formal Nominating Procedures

It is clear from the foregoing that candidate selection by the parties is clearly the most important part of candidate recruitment. Yet the parties' activities are restricted and influenced by the legal nominating machinery within which they must operate. So before we discuss those activities (which we shall in Chapter 15), we shall briefly review the principal formal nominating procedures in modern democracies.

#### In the United States

In several respects the laws regulating nominations in the United States differ sharply from comparable laws in other modern democracies. For one thing, American laws on the subject are far more elaborate and detailed than those of any other democracy. Most of them are enacted and enforced by the states rather than by the national government, and so their details vary considerably from one state to another. Every state, however, regulates in rather minute detail most nomination procedures.

THE UNIQUE DIRECT PRIMARY. Perhaps the sharpest contrast between American formal nominating procedures and those in other democracies lies in the unique use of the "direct primary" in the United States. This is a system in which nominations are made in government-supervised elections *directly* by the voters themselves rather than indirectly by such representatives of the voters as party leaders or conventions. Its stated purpose, indeed, is to remove the control of nominations from party "bosses" and place it in the hands of the "rank-and-file party members." Every one of the fifty states uses it for making some nominations, and most states require it for all.

In general, the direct-primary system is designed to ensure that nominations shall be made as nearly as possible in the same manner as that in which regular elections are conducted. Thus, any qualified person who wishes to receive a particular party's nomination for a particular public office may file with election officials a petition containing his name, address, the nomination desired, and the signatures of a legally designated number of party members. When the filing period has elapsed, the election authorities print ballots for each party containing the names of all persons who have petitioned for each office. On "primary day" the members of each party go to the polls and, under the same conditions of secrecy as those prevailing at regular elections, mark their preferences for each nominee for each office. The persons who receive the largest number of votes for each office on each party's ballot are then certified as that party's official nominees, and their names and party designations are then printed on the ballot for the ensuing general election.

The only major differences among the direct-primary systems of the various states are those relating to the eligibility of voters in the primary of a particular party. Some states use the *closed primary*, in which the voter publicly states his party affiliation and, if challenged, must pass some kind of test of his party membership (usually by taking an oath that he is a party member). Other states use the *open primary*, in which the voter makes no public statement of his party affiliation and may vote in the primary of whichever party he chooses.

Most observers agree that the general use of the direct primary has had a profound effect upon the nature of politics and political parties in the United States, although there is no general agreement upon just what effects it has had or whether its total effect has been good or bad. Some observers believe it has accomplished its main purpose of "democraticizing" the nominating process by giving ordinary voters the power to overrule party leaders. Others contend that, since the leaders control the primaries, there has been no real change. Some commentators believe that the direct primary has lessened the amount of conflict between the parties and has thereby increased the incidence of one-party areas in the United States; others argue that it is one of the main causes for the decentralization, lack of cohesion, and absence of discipline characteristic of American political parties.[4]

One thing is clear: there is little disposition within the United States to abandon the direct primary, and little disposition in the other democracies to adopt it.

OTHER PROCEDURES. As we noted above, some nominations in the United States are made by procedures other than the direct primary.

*Caucuses.* A "caucus" is a small face-to-face gathering of like-minded persons usually held in secret for the purpose of agreeing on what nominees and policies they will support. The oldest and most informal of all nominating procedures, it is presently used only for a few minor offices.

*Conventions.* A nominating convention is an assembly of delegates picked in some fashion by the members of a party to represent them in the selection of the party's nominees. This system was the dominant American nominating procedure in the nineteenth century and still is used

---

[4] Cf. the discussion of these questions in Austin Ranney and Willmoore Kendall, *Democracy and the American Party System* (New York: Harcourt, Brace & World, Inc., 1956), pp. 281–283; and V. O. Key, Jr., *American State Politics: An Introduction* (New York: Alfred A. Knopf, Inc., 1956), Chs. 4–6.

by some states (e.g., New York and Indiana) to select nominees to various state and local offices. The best-known nominating conventions, of course, are the national conventions of the major parties, which meet every four years to pick the parties' presidential and vice-presidential nominees and to write their national platforms.

*Petitions.* In some states an aspirant to certain public offices can get his name printed on the general election ballot merely by filing a petition signed by a legally designated number of voters. This procedure is used mainly for nominations to such local offices as school-board members, for which nonpartisan elections (i.e., elections in which no party designations appear on the ballot) are held, but sometimes also to enable new parties and small parties to get their candidates on the ballot.

### In Other Democracies

The formal nominating procedures of the other democratic nations are, as already noted, far simpler than those used in the United States. Two principal methods are currently in use.

PETITIONS. The formal procedure for becoming a candidate for the British House of Commons is simplicity itself. Persons legally eligible are any British subject or Commonwealth citizen who is over twenty-one years of age and who is not a peer, a High Court judge, a member of the permanent civil service, a clergyman of the Church of England, the Church of Scotland, or the Roman Catholic Church, or a convicted felon. Any eligible person who wishes to become a candidate secures from election officials an official nomination paper, on which he states his name, address, occupation, and the constituency in which he wishes to "stand." The form must also be signed by two electors of the constituency acting as "proposer" and "seconder," and by eight other such electors as "assenters." When completed, the form must be filed with the returning officer, along with a deposit of £150. This deposit will be forfeited to the Treasury if in the ensuing election the candidate fails to poll more than one eighth of the total votes cast in his constituency. The purpose of the deposit requirement is to discourage frivolous and "nuisance" candidacies, and it appears to have accomplished its purpose rather well. When these minimal requirements have been met, the candidate's name is placed upon the ballot (without a party designation) for the forthcoming election.[5]

Approximately the same procedure is followed in such other democracies as Canada, France, Japan, and New Zealand.

PARTY-LIST DESIGNATIONS. In most nations using some form of the party-list system of proportional representation (see below) the authorized

---

[5] A. N. Schofield, *Parliamentary Elections* (2d ed.; London: Shaw & Sons, Ltd., 1955), pp. 124–142.

agency of each recognized political party (usually a party executive officer or committee) draws up a list of candidates for each constituency and presents it to the election authorities. When the latter have verified the names and eligibility of the names on each list, they are placed on the ballot without further ado. In some nations using this system (e.g., Brazil and Israel) this is the only way a candidate can get on the ballot. In other nations (e.g., Chile, Denmark, and Finland) groups ranging from fifty to one hundred independent voters can also, by petition, nominate single candidates or lists of candidates. In general, however, the initiative in the formal nominating procedures of nations using the party-list system is mainly or exclusively in the hands of party officials and agencies.

## Making Choices: Elections

### Election Administration

#### The Timing and Frequency of Elections

In the presidential democracies, such as the United States, Chile, and the Philippines, the terms of the president and members of the legislative body are fixed by constitutional provisions, and elections for these offices are held at regular intervals fixed by law. In the United States, for example, the term of the President is fixed at four years, the terms of senators at six years, and the terms of representatives at two years. Consequently, a presidential election must be held every four years, a general election for representatives every two years, and an election for one third of the members

Election Official in Swaziland Examines Posters Used to Help Tribesmen Vote. Each Candidate Is Known by a Symbol, Like a Clock, and Only Symbols Are on Ballots for Illiterate Voters. (Wide World Photos, Inc.)

of the Senate every two years. Special elections to fill the places of deceased or resigned senators or representatives may be held at other times, but the timing of all general elections is fixed by law.

The situation is more fluid in the parliamentary democracies. The British constitution, for example, requires that a general election for all members of the House of Commons (and therefore, in a sense, for all members of the ministry and cabinet) must be held at least every five years. Unlike the presidential democracies, however, the British can hold a general election at any time before the five-year period has expired if the prime minister asks the monarch to dissolve Parliament and hold new elections. In conditions of national emergency, moreover, a majority of the House can extend the life of a particular Parliament beyond the normal five-year period. To illustrate how this system works, we need only recall that a general election was held in Britain in 1935, but when the next one came due in 1940 the nation was fighting a desperate war, and so Parliament was continued for each of the next five years. After the defeat of Germany in 1945 a general election was held, and the new Parliament lived out its full statutory life. The general election of 1950 returned a Labour majority too small to govern effectively, and so in 1951 Prime Minister Attlee asked the king to dissolve Parliament. The new election returned a Conservative majority which governed until 1955, when the Conservative leaders called a new election which returned their party to power. The same kind of formal flexibility obtains in the other parliamentary democracies.

Some political scientists believe that much of what is objectionable in American elections results from the fact that their timing is determined by the calendar rather than by the current state of public opinion and party conflict. If, they argue, public opinion is up in arms about some mistake public officials have made, there is no effective way the people can "turn the rascals out" if an election does not happen to be scheduled at the time. If, on the other hand, an election happens to fall in a period of political quiet and public apathy—which not infrequently happens in the United States—then the party leaders have to campaign with all sorts of foolish and extravagant charges ("The Democrats coddle Communists!" "The Republicans care nothing for the common man!") in an effort to rouse the voters from their torpor. In either case, these writers argue, it is sheer coincidence if Election Day in the presidential democracies happens to arrive when the people really want an election.[6]

This may well be so, but we should also recognize that the power of dissolution is used sparingly in most parliamentary democracies and that

---

[6] Cf. Pendleton Herring, *The Politics of Democracy* (New York: Holt, Rinehart and Winston, Inc., 1940), p. 290.

it gives the party in power a substantial advantage over the opposition. Two recent British examples show this clearly. In 1956 the Conservative Government of Great Britain joined with France in a surprise attack upon the Egyptians to regain control of the Suez Canal; they were forced to withdraw, and in early 1957 their leader, Anthony Eden, suddenly retired because of ill health. If an election had been scheduled then, they might well have lost. As it was, they were able to defer it until their standing had improved; they actually increased their majority in the autumn of 1959. Most observers believed the Conservatives would have to call the next general election in the spring of 1964, but the polls all showed them running far behind the Labour party. So they put off the election until almost the last moment possible under the law, and, in the autumn of 1964, lost power to Labour by only the narrowest of margins. Thus flexible elections have their problems too.

### The Secret Ballot

In the eighteenth and nineteenth centuries many democratic theorists believed that voters should register their preferences publicly rather than privately. Even so eminent a democrat as John Stuart Mill argued that in most circumstances secret voting is undesirable, on the ground that

> . . . the duty of voting, like any other public duty, should be performed under the eye and criticism of the public; every one of whom has not only an interest in its performance, but a good title to consider himself wronged if it is performed otherwise than honestly and carefully.[7]

Before the middle of the nineteenth century no democratic nation tried to guarantee the secrecy of the vote. One widely used procedure was that in which each voter simply came before the election officials and announced, in the presence of anyone who cared to listen, which candidates he preferred. A growing number of reformers, however, condemned this procedure on the ground that it exposed voters to intimidation and bribery and thereby made genuinely free voting impossible. They won their first success in 1856, when the British colony of South Australia adopted a system of voting that soon came to be known as the "Australian ballot." One of its basic features was the requirement that votes be cast and counted in such a way that no one could tell how a particular person had voted. At the present time every democratic nation has adopted this requirement, and guaranteeing the secrecy of the ballot is one of the main objectives of election laws and administration in all such nations.

---

[7] John Stuart Mill, *Utilitarianism, Liberty, and Representative Government* (Everyman's Library ed.; London: J. M. Dent & Sons, Ltd., 1910), p. 300.

## Some Problems in Democratic Elections

### Fraud

One prime objective of a democratic election is to register clearly and accurately the voters' free choices among the various candidates. Any flaws in election laws and administration that prevent the full achievement of this objective are therefore a matter of great concern for democracy's well-wishers.

One of the most publicized kinds of deviation from this standard is fraud—the illegal manipulation of voters, ballots, and the counting process by certain persons or groups for the purpose of winning more votes than they could otherwise gain. The history of every modern democracy contains many instances of election fraud, and some commentators regard fraud as one of the gravest threats to the health of democracy. Election-riggers in various nations over the years have developed a bag of tricks far too complicated to be described in their entirety here, but among the more widely used methods of fraud are such operations as "padding the register" (putting fictitious names on the roster of eligible voters), intimidation and bribery of voters, "stuffing the ballot box" (introducing large numbers of fraudulent ballots into the count), altering and spoiling ballots during the counting process, and falsely reporting the count. Most democratic nations have enacted laws to prevent such practices, but their efficacy depends not only upon how diligently they are administered by election officials but also upon how much the general public insists that they be enforced.

No one can say precisely how much fraud prevails in the elections of any particular democratic nation, let alone in all the democracies. Most students of the subject have concluded, however, that the incidence of fraud has greatly declined in the past century and that a very small proportion of the elections in any modern democracy are marred by any large-scale fraud.[8]

### Representativeness

Even if all fraud is removed from election administration, the problem still remains of establishing the kind of electoral system best calculated to clearly and accurately register the voters' preferences. Few problems of modern democracy have been debated so extensively as that of just what kind of electoral system is conducive to the best representation. Modern

---

[8] Unfortunately, the most recent systematic estimate of the incidence of fraud in American elections is Joseph P. Harris, *Election Administration in the United States* (Washington, D.C.: The Brookings Institution, 1934), pp. 37–75, 316–320, 377–382. For a more recent but briefer estimate, see V. O. Key, Jr., *Politics, Parties, & Pressure Groups* (5th ed.; New York: Thomas Y. Crowell Company, 1964), pp. 636–638.

democratic nations have adopted a wide variety of electoral systems as solutions to this problem. Each system has its advocates and its critics, and in the following section we shall describe how each of the principal systems operates, and offer an estimate of their actual political effects.

## Principal Electoral Systems[9]

The following discussion summarizes the three major types of election systems: majority systems, semiproportional systems, and proportional systems.

### Majority Systems

Most readers are probably familiar with the two types of majority systems, those simply requiring pluralities and those requiring absolute majorities, since both are used in Anglo-America.

#### Requiring Pluralities

SINGLE-MEMBER CONSTITUENCIES.    The most common version of the "majority" system is the single-member-constituency plurality system, which is employed for elections to such bodies as the American House of Representatives, the British House of Commons, the lower houses of the parliaments of the nations listed in Table 8, and many state, provincial, and local legislative bodies in the United States and the nations of the British Commonwealth. Under this system each constituency elects only one member of the legislative assembly at each election. The voter votes directly for one individual candidate, usually by marking an X in the box printed beside his name. When the votes are counted, the candidate receiving the largest number of votes (i.e., a "plurality") is declared elected. Hence some commentators call this the "first-past-the-post" system.

MULTIMEMBER CONSTITUENCIES (THE "BLOCK VOTE" SYSTEM).    In elections for members of the Turkish National Assembly and certain state and local legislative assemblies in the United States, Canada, and Great Britain the following method is used. Each constituency elects two or more representatives at each election. Each voter is permitted to vote for as many candidates as there are posts to be filled from his constituency. The candidates receiving the highest pluralities are declared elected.

---

[9] Two comprehensive surveys are Mackenzie, *op. cit.*; and Enid Lakeman and James D. Lambert, *Voting in Democracies* (London: Faber & Faber, Ltd., 1955). The descriptions in the text are drawn largely from these works.

### Requiring Absolute Majorities

Some democrats are disturbed by the fact that the plurality systems just described make possible the election of public officials, who, in races with three or more candidates, have received less than an absolute majority of the votes and who therefore have more of their constituents registered against them than for them. To correct this situation and to guarantee that every elected representative shall have the approval of more than half the voters, one or the other of the following alternatives has been adopted by a few democratic governments.

THE PREFERENTIAL BALLOT.    This system, which is now used for election to the Australian national House of Representatives and to four Australian state parliaments, instructs the voter to mark the candidates in the order of his preference by placing numbers rather than X's in the boxes beside their names. If no candidate receives a majority of first-place preferences on the first count, the candidate having the least first-place preferences is "dropped," and his ballots are redistributed according to the second-place preferences on each. The redistribution of votes in this manner is continued until one candidate's pile of ballots, made up of his original first-place ballots and the second- and third-place choices of the candidates dropped, constitutes an absolute majority of all the ballots cast. He is then declared elected.

THE SECOND BALLOT, OR "RUNOFF" ELECTION.    In the direct primary elections of the dominant Democratic party in nine southern American states the following system is used. The voter casts his ballot for one candidate by the usual procedure of marking an X beside the candidate's name. If no candidate receives an absolute majority of the votes in the first election, a second or "runoff" primary is held, usually about a month later, between the candidates who finished first and second in the first election. Since only two candidates are running in the second election, one is bound to get an absolute majority.

The most common "majority" system, however, is the single-member-constituency plurality system, and it is this system, as we shall see below, at which the advocates of "proportional representation" have directed most of their critical fire.

## Semiproportional Systems

### The Single Nontransferable Vote

Under this system, which is now used for the election of members to the lower house of the Japanese Diet, each constituency returns two or more members at each election. Each voter, however, is permitted to vote for only one candidate. The purpose of the Japanese system is to prevent the majority of the voters in any constituency from electing all its repre-

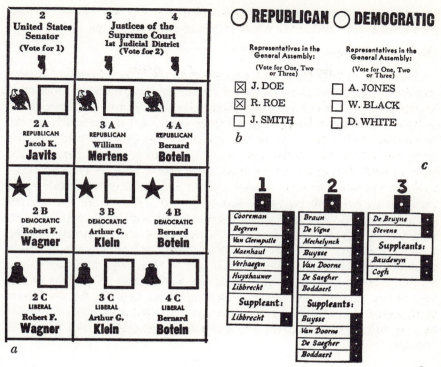

| Mark order of preference | Names of Candidates |
|---|---|
| | **BROWN** (John Brown, of 52, George St., Bristol, Merchant). |
| | **JONES, JOHN** (John Jones, of 5, Mary St., Bristol, Retired Teacher). |
| | **JONES, WILLIAM DAVID** (William David Jones, of 10, Charles St., Bristol, Merchant). |
| | **ROBERTSON** (Henry Robertson, of 8, John St., Bristol, Builder). |

### INSTRUCTIONS TO VOTERS

VOTE BY PLACING:

the figure 1 in the space provided opposite the name of the candidate who is your first choice; *and further (if you so desire)*

the figure 2 opposite the name of the candidate who is your second choice; *and further (if you so desire)*

the figure 3 opposite the name of the candidate who is your third choice; *and so on as far as you may choose.*

Figure 25.   Ballots for Four Major Electoral Systems: *a,* The "Majority" System (United States Senate); *b,* Cumulative-vote System (Illinois House of Representatives); *c,* Party-list System (Belgian Chamber of Representatives); *d,* Preferential Ballot (British Borough Council).

sentatives and guarantees a certain amount of minority representation from each constituency and in the whole House of Representatives.

### The Cumulative Vote

Now used only in elections for members of the Illinois House of Representatives, this system provides for the election of three members from each legislative district. Each voter has three votes, but he may distribute them as he wishes: that is, he can cast all three votes for one candidate, or cast one-and-one-half votes each for two candidates, or cast one vote each for three candidates. The purpose of the system is to guarantee the minority party in each district one of the three seats, and it achieves this end effectively. If the minority party in each district nominates only one candidate (and few are foolhardy enough to nominate more), the majority party must get more than 75 percent of all the votes cast to win all three seats, for each vote for the minority candidate (which gives three votes to his cumulative total) cancels out three votes for the majority candidates (each of which gives each of the three candidates one vote to their respective cumulative totals). Thus any minority party that can muster over 25 percent of the vote in any election can be sure of electing its one nominee for the House of Representatives.[10] The same system was once used in elections for members of British school boards but was abandoned early in the twentieth century.

## *Proportional Systems*

### Rationale

Since the middle of the nineteenth century a number of democratic theorists have argued that the majority systems make impossible the achievement of genuinely democratic representation, and have proposed that all such systems be replaced with some kind of "proportional representation" (or "PR" for short). Briefly summarized, their case runs as follows.[11]

A truly democratic representative assembly should be to the political divisions in the nation as a map is to the territory it represents or a mirror to whatever is placed before it (these metaphors recur frequently in the pro–PR literature). Thus the representative system should ensure that every point of view held by some members of the community will have its

---

[10] Cf. George S. Blair, *Cumulative Voting* (Urbana: University of Illinois Press, 1960).

[11] For a thorough summary and analysis of the case presented for PR, see Hanna Fenichel Pitkin, *The Concept of Representation* (Berkeley: University of California Press, 1966), Ch. 5. Perhaps the leading advocacy is Clarence G. Hoag and George H. Hallett, *Proportional Representation* (New York: The Macmillan Company, 1926).

spokesmen in the assembly, and the proportion of supporters of each in the assembly should be the same as its proportion of adherents in the community.

The majority system is incapable of providing such an assembly. Everywhere it is in force the majority party gets more assembly seats than its share of the total popular vote warrants, and all other parties get fewer seats than their shares of the vote entitle them to. Morover, the majority system forces upon the population a two-party system, since third and fourth parties have little or no chance of electing any members of the assembly. The legislatures that result from this kind of party system can express the many shades of public opinion no more accurately than a black-and-white photograph can represent the many colors and shades of the real world. Hence any picture they present of the state of public opinion is bound to be grossly distorted.

Then, too, in a truly representative system every member of the community should be directly represented in the assembly. Each voter, that is to say, should be able to point to at least one member of the assembly and say, "My vote helped put him there, so he represents me." But under the majority systems all the persons who vote for losing candidates have no such direct representative, and so their votes are wasted and they go unrepresented.

For these reasons, then, the majority systems should be replaced with some kind of "proportional system"—one in which no votes are wasted and in which all points of view are represented according to their relative strength in the electorate.

The proportional systems now used in modern democratic nations are variations of two basic types.

## Party-List Systems

All these systems treat political parties as the basic units for which fair representation is sought. They all use multimember constituencies, in which voters are confronted with lists of candidates nominated by the leaders or executive committees of the various parties (see above). The counting process is designed to distribute seats in the legislative assembly as nearly as possible in accordance with each party's share of the total popular vote.

Party-list systems differ from each other only in the degree of freedom they give the voters to register their preferences for individual candidates as well as for whole party lists. In this regard the following main subtypes are presently employed.

NO CHOICE AMONG CANDIDATES. In the election for members of the Israeli *Knesset* (Parliament) the entire nation is one huge constituency electing all 120 members. Any party which can muster the signatures of 750 eligible voters can submit a list of candidates up to the number of 120, and it can arrange them in whatever order it wishes. Each party has a separate ballot paper, and the voter selects the paper of his chosen party and deposits it in the ballot box. There is no way he can either indicate his preference for particular candidates on his party's list or for candidates on the lists of other parties. Whatever number of seats each party is entitled to according to its percent of the total popular vote are filled by the candidates at the top of its list.[12]

Israel is the only democratic nation currently using this particular type of party-list system, but it was also used for elections to the German *Reichstag* from 1919 to 1933, the Czechoslovakian parliament from 1919 to 1938 and from 1945 to 1948, and the French National Assembly in 1945 and 1946.

LIMITED CHOICE AMONG CANDIDATES.   Under this type of party-list system the voter may vote either for one party's list in its entirety, or for a limited number (from one to four—the specific limits vary from nation to nation) of individual candidates within a particular list. If he chooses the latter course, he indicates his desire to move his preferred candidates to the top of his favored party's list, and if a majority of the voters voting for a particular party list indicate a preferred order of candidates other than that specified by the party, whatever number of seats it is entitled to are filled by the candidates in the order indicated by the voters rather than in that chosen by the party leaders. In elections for the Belgian Chamber of Representatives, the Danish *Folketing,* and the Second Chamber of the Dutch parliament, the voters are permitted to indicate a preference for only one candidate. In elections for the Norwegian *Storting,* both houses of the Swedish parliament, and the First Chamber of the Dutch parliament, the voters are permitted to indicate preferences for from two to four candidates.

"PANACHAGE": FULL FREEDOM OF CHOICE AMONG CANDIDATES.   Under this type of party-list system each voter has as many votes as seats to be filled from his particular constituency, and he may distribute those votes as he wishes. He may, if he desires, register several votes for a particular candidate, or one vote each for different candidates. He may also vote for particular candidates on several party lists. In the counting process the votes are totaled for all candidates on each list, and seats are allotted to each party in accordance with its proportion of the total votes for all lists. Each party's quota of seats in each constituency is then filled by the party's candidates receiving the largest number of votes, the second largest, and so on. This system is now used in elections for the Swiss National Council

---

[12] Marver H. Bernstein, *The Politics of Israel* (Princeton, N.J.: Princeton University Press, 1957), pp. 80–92.

and a number of cantonal councils, and in elections for the parliament of Finland.

## The Single Transferable-Vote System

All party-list systems, as we have seen, operate on the assumption that the voter is most interested in supporting a particular political party. All single-transferable-vote systems operate on the contrary assumption that voters are more interested in individual candidates than in parties and should be given maximum freedom to indicate their preferences for individuals.

Each constituency elects several members to the legislative assembly, and any individual can get on the ballot by petition either with or without a party designation. The voter indicates his order of preference among the various candidates, much in the manner of the preferential-ballot systems described above, by marking numbers in the boxes beside their names. In the counting process the ballots are first sorted according to the first-place choices for each candidate. Then an "electoral quota" is figured according to one or another of various formulas.[13] If no candidate has enough first-place choices to fill the quota, the candidate with the least first-place choices is dropped and his ballots are redistributed according to the second-place choices on each. This process of dropping the low man and redistributing his ballots according to their second (or, as the case may be, third, fourth, and so on) choices is continued until a sufficient number of candidates have reached the quotas and are declared elected.

This system is now used for the election of members of the Irish *Dail*, the Senate of Northern Ireland, the Australian Senate, the South African Senate, particular houses of the parliments of the Australian states of Tasmania and New South Wales, and for some city councils in the United States.

## *The Political Effects of Electoral Systems*

Both the majority systems and the proportional systems have strong partisans among present-day democratic theorists.[14] We have already summarized the main arguments for PR, and we should note here that its critics reply that, wherever it has been tried, PR has given rise to multiple-party systems, deepened ideological fissures, and lowered consensus. It has also, they say, made every government a weak coalition of quarreling and

---

[13] The formula favored by most advocates of this system is

$$\frac{\text{total votes}}{\text{total seats} + 1} + 1 = \text{quota}$$

[14] The leading exponents of PR are listed in footnote 11 above. Its leading critics include F. A. Hermens, *Democracy or Anarchy?* (Notre Dame, Ind.: The Review of Politics, 1941); Herman Finer, *Theory and Practice of Modern Government* (rev. ed.; New York: Holt, Rinehart and Winston, Inc., 1949), pp. 556–558 and Ernest Barker, *Reflections on Government* (London: Oxford University Press, 1942), pp. 78–81.

mutually suspicious parties, and it has failed to elicit popular mandates on the immediate and practical political issues of the day.

In a work of this sort we cannot present the full case for each side, let alone decide which has the better of the debate. But we can and shall make certain observations about what actual political effects these two types of election systems have had on the politics of the nations that have tried them.

Most of the nations using the majority system have two-party systems, and in such nations the majority party almost always gets a substantially larger proportion of the elective public offices than its arithmetical share of the popular vote would seem to warrant. On the other hand, most of the nations using some kind of PR have multiple-party systems and coalition governments. The relative virtues and vices of each type of party system pose difficult and complicated questions, which are dealt with in Chapter 15. In any case, however, no one can say with full certainty that the majority systems *cause* two-party systems and the PR systems *cause* multiple-party systems. All we know is that the two phenomena frequently but not invariably appear together.[15]

Most of the democratic structures erected since World War II, such as those in Japan, West Germany, Italy, and Israel, have adopted PR. One nation (Greece) first adopted it and later (1952) replaced it with a majority system. Few, if any, of the Anglo-American nations now using majority systems are seriously considering adopting PR. Whatever may be the respective merits of the two systems, therefore, it is clear that in the foreseeable future neither is likely to become *the* democratic method for electing representatives.

## Nominations and Elections in the Soviet Union[16]

### *Formal Procedures*

At first glance the formal nominating and electing procedures in Communist Russia appear to justify Stalin's famous boast that Russia's Constitution is "the most democratic in the world." Every Soviet citizen over the age of eighteen can vote, and there is no legal or actual disfranchise-

---

[15] Two leading expositions of the position that PR tends to produce multiple-party systems while majority systems encourage two-party systems are Maurice Duverger, *Political Parties*, trans. by Barbara and Robert North (New York: John Wiley & Sons, Inc., 1959), pp. 216–255; and E. E. Schattschneider, *Party Government* (New York: Holt, Rinehart and Winston, Inc., 1942), pp. 69–84. For a contrary position, see Leslie Lipson, "The Two-Party System in British Politics," *American Political Science Review*, XLVII (June, 1953), 337–358.

[16] A useful short description is given in W. W. Kulski, *The Soviet Regime* (4th ed.; Syracuse, N.Y.: Syracuse University Press, 1963), pp. 67–72.

# "We Now Bring You More Late Election Returns"

*Figure 26.* In Communist Elections Reality Differs from Formality. (Drawing by Herblock, from *The Herblock Book*, Boston: Beacon Press, 1952.)

ment of any person on grounds of race, religion, property, or sex. Voting turnouts, moreover, are far higher than the best that the democracies can boast: in the 1962 election for members of the Supreme Soviet (the national legislature), for example, a staggering 99.95 percent of all the eligible voters actually voted! Even the most optimistic get-out-the-vote organizations in the Western democracies must despair of ever matching this figure.

When, however, the Western democrat looks a little closer at the formal procedures and actual conduct of Soviet nominations and elections, he can only conclude that they add up to a process that has little if any correspondence with the democratic ideals of popular selection of representatives and popular control of public officials.

### Nominations

The Supreme Soviet is a bicameral body, and the members of each house are selected by pluralities from single-member constituencies. The election laws state that nominations of candidates for these posts may be made by Communist party organizations, trade unions, cooperative societies, youth organizations, cultural societies, and such work units as factories and collective farms. When such a group has met and agreed upon a candidate, it must submit his name and the minutes of the nominating meeting to the local election commission, which, fifteen days after the end of the period for submitting candidates, prints the candidates' names on the ballot. How could nominating rules be simpler or more democratic?

### Elections

After a campaigning period of about two months the election is held. The voter goes to the polls and receives a ballot from the local election officials. The ballot, to be sure, contains the name of only one candidate, but if the voter wishes to do so, he can retire to a partitioned area, cross out the candidate's name (he is not permitted to write in another name), fold his ballot so that no one can tell what he has done (!), and drop it in the ballot box. If he approves of the candidate on the ballot, he merely drops his ballot in the box without further ado. Then the votes are counted, the official candidates declared elected, and *Pravda* and *Izvestia* announce that the national "ticket" of the "bloc of Communist party and nonparty candidates" has won by a landslide of over 99 percent of the votes—a plurality that must excite the envy, if not the wonder, of many a Western party leader!

## The Role of the Communist Party

In our earlier descriptions of various aspects of the Soviet regime we have learned that the formal procedures act as the instruments and agencies whereby the Communist party, operating from its position as the only legal party in Soviet Russia, rules the nation. So it is with Soviet nominations and elections.

To begin with, the party has members in every trade union, cooperative society, cultural organization, collective farm, and factory. It requires

CHOOSING REPRESENTATIVES: SUFFRAGE, NOMINATIONS, AND ELECTIONS

very little imagination to figure out what happens in these "nominating" organizations when a party member proposes a candidate or opposes candidates suggested by nonparty persons. Most nominations, as a matter of fact, are made in mass meetings in factories and on collective farms rather than in private meetings of the various associations, and when the party members in attendance have made known their views—as they always do—the matter is settled. If the machinery should happen to slip up somewhere and present some election commissions with *two* nominations, the party also has members on every such commission; and in the fifteen-day period before the ballots are printed the commissions can and do eliminate all conflict.

The evidence strongly suggests, in fact, that the party exercises close control over nominations. For example, the membership of the party is only about 4 percent of the whole population, but over 80 percent of the members of the Supreme Soviet are party members. Even nonparty deputies are carefully selected to represent such major elements of their areas as workers, farmers, old and young, women, the intelligentsia, and so on. And no nonparty candidate, we may be sure, is *anti*party!

The voter's ability to register dissent by scratching out the name of the official candidate (remember, he cannot write in the name of some other person) means very little in practice. If he goes to the partitioned area and returns with a folded ballot, there can be little doubt about what he has done—and little doubt about how such action will be regarded by the authorities.

Despite the fact that the election results are a foregone conclusion as soon as the candidates are named, the campaigning is quite as noisy and energetic as it is in the most hard-fought contests in the Western democracies. For a full two months the voters are flooded with radio speeches, newspaper stories and editorials, pamphlets and broadsides, and door-to-door campaigning by "agitators" (see Chapter 10). Mass meetings and parades are held several times weekly, and in general a tremendous effort is made to get out 100 percent of the voters.

### Why Do They Bother?

To those of us accustomed to the procedures of the Western democracies the whole elaborate Soviet nominating-campaigning-electing procedure seems pointless and ridiculous. That is because we, in our democratic blindness, think of nominations and elections as methods by which a truly sovereign electorate chooses among the many rivals for public office and political power, and it is hard for us to understand why the Communists bother to go through the motions of democracy when they know they have—and *want* to have—rule by the party elite rather than by the masses.

When we view the matter from the Communist point of view rather than our own, however, it makes a kind of sense. Elections are first and foremost a device for mobilizing the masses' approval and enthusiasm for the party's policies while giving them the feeling—however spurious it may seem to democratic eyes—that they are participating in the nation's governing processes. They also provide the regime with a façade of democratic legality which may be useful in its dealings with other nations—e.g., Algeria and Ghana—with a strong desire to cloak the hard realities of dictatorship in the respectable garments of democracy.[17] And, minute though they may be by democratic standards, the tiny variations in the number of abstentions and negative votes may provide a useful barometer for detecting changes in public opinion.[18]

In short, the purpose of democratic candidate recruitment and elections is to establish popular *control* over public officials. The purpose of Communist nominations and elections is to create popular *support* for policies and leaders already determined by the party oligarchs. In few other institutional comparisons is the contrast and distance between the Western and Communist conceptions of "democracy" so apparent.

---

[17] Cf. Merle Fainsod, *How Russia Is Ruled* (rev. ed.; Cambridge, Mass.: Harvard University Press, 1963), pp. 381–383.

[18] Vernon V. Aspaturian in R. C. Macridis and R. E. Ward, eds., *Modern Political Systems: Europe* (Englewood Cliffs, N.J.: Prentice-Hall, Inc., 1963), p. 511. For an interesting analysis of Polish elections as "barometers" in this sense, see Jerzy J. Wiatr, "Elections and Voting Behavior in Poland," in Austin Ranney, ed., *Essays on the Behavioral Study of Politics* (Urbana: University of Illinois Press, 1962), pp. 244–251.

# 14

## Voting Behavior

I N every modern democracy votes are basic units of political power. When all is said and done, the groups that mobilize the larger numbers of voters in support of the policies and public officials they favor get the larger shares of what they want out of politics. If a man has every quality necessary to be a great President except the ability to make people vote for him, his other qualities will not make him *any* kind of President. A political party may have the most intelligent and foresighted program possible, but if it cannot convince the voters, its program will never become public policy. A pressure group may lobby so skillfully that it lines up everyone in the legislature on its side, but should the voters throw those legislators out of office at the next election, its lobbying efforts may well have gone for naught. Even the power of money, sometimes mistakenly regarded as an "absolute weapon" in politics, ultimately depends upon its ability to produce votes.

Most party politicians and pressure-group leaders know these political facts of life. For them the whole question of what makes voters vote as they do is a matter of the most vital concern. No doubt few political leaders think of themselves as having anything so fancy as a "working theory of voting behavior." Each of them, however, has just that in the form of a number of practical rules of thumb which guide his campaigning operations: voters get more stirred up *against* persons and issues than for them; people vote mainly to advance their own economic self-interest; if a district has a lot of Polish and Italian voters, some Polish and Italian candidates ought to appear on the ticket.[1]

---

[1] For a summary of some of the party leaders' ideas about what makes voters tick, see Austin Ranney and Willmoore Kendall, *Democracy and the American Party System* (New York: Harcourt, Brace & World, Inc., 1956), pp. 340–344.

Despite its obvious importance in the decision-making processes of democracy, few social scientists before World War I made any but the most casual efforts to study voting behavior. In 1924, however, the American political scientists Charles E. Merriam and Harold F. Gosnell published a pioneer study of the causes of nonvoting.[2] Since then a considerable body of literature has been published on nonvoting and many other aspects of voting behavior. As a result voting behavior (or political behavior" as it is sometimes misnamed—see Chapter 24) has become not only a full-fledged "field" of political science but, by general agreement, one of its most advanced. And while the bulk of the work has been done on American voters, there are also a number of excellent studies of British, Finnish, French, German, Italian, Norwegian, and Swedish voters.

In the present chapter we shall summarize their principal findings.

## Dimensions[3]

Political scientists picture voting behavior as having two principal categories illustrated on the preference dimension shown in Figure 27.

The horizontal axis in Figure 27 represents the voter's *preference*—that is, the degree of his approval or disapproval of particular political parties, candidates, laws, policy proposals, or whatever. The seven categories shown in Figure 27 are those used by the Survey Research Center of the Univer-

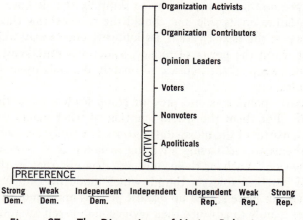

*Figure 27.* The Dimensions of Voting Behavior.

---

[2] Charles E. Merriam and Harold F. Gosnell, *Non-Voting* (Chicago: University of Chicago Press, 1924).

[3] This discussion closely follows that in Hugh A. Bone and Austin Ranney, *Politics and Voters* (New York: McGraw-Hill Book Company, Inc., 1963), pp. 4–6.

sity of Michigan for measuring American voters' attitudes toward the major parties in our two-party system. However, similar scales can be constructed (they would need many more categories) for measuring the voters' preferences in multiple-party systems by arranging the parties on some kind of Left-Right continuum (see Chapter 15).

The vertical axis represents the voter's *activity*—that is, what, if anything, he does about his preferences. Its six categories are usually defined as follows. (1) *Organization activists* are persons who regularly devote substantial time and energy to working in political parties or in pressure groups, such as party leaders and precinct captains, and pressure group leaders and lobbyists. It is estimated that no more than 1 percent of the adult population in most democracies belong in this category.[4] (2) *Organization contributors* occasionally donate money, do volunteer campaign work, or otherwise actively lend a hand. Perhaps 5 percent of adults may be classed here. (3) *Opinion leaders,* as we saw in Chapter 11, are persons who regularly "talk politics" with their family, friends, and work associates, and thus have a noticeable impact on the formation of political opinion; around 25 percent of adults fit this description. (4) *Voters* are persons who cast ballots in most elections but do nothing more to support their preferences; this describes around 35 percent of adults.[5] (5) *Nonvoters* seldom or never vote, but still have some trace of interest in political affairs; they make up around 30 percent of the adult population. (6) *Apoliticals* have no discernible knowledge of or interest in politics; they constitute perhaps 4 percent of adults.

How, then, are adults in modern democracies generally distributed along these axes and why? Let us see.

## Intervening Variables

In any democracy the aspect of voting behavior that first concerns both practicing politicians and political scientists is the *result*—how many people vote and which way—because this is the point at which the voters make their most direct and powerful impact on the governing process. Hence voting studies take the voters' preferences and activity as their main "dependent variable"—that is, the set of varying effects whose causes they wish to understand and explain.

---

[4] Robert E. Lane, *Political Life* (New York: The Free Press of Glencoe, 1959), pp. 52–56, presents estimates of the proportion of adults generally found at each level of activity.

[5] The proportions in the last three categories obviously vary widely from one democracy to another (see Table 10, Chapter 13). The figures in the text are rough estimates of the "average" proportions in most democracies.

Now voting behavior is a species of the genus *Public opinion*. As we saw in Chapters 10 and 11, a great many "independent variables" affect men's political attitudes and behavior—their biological natures and needs, psychological makeups, perceptions, conceptualizations, memberships in secondary and primary groups, communications received, and so on. Should we, then, simply say that these factors also explain voting behavior, and let it go at that?

The most distinguished study of American voting behavior says no.[6] Its authors point out that when you ask a person why he voted the way he did in a particular election, he is not likely to reply, "Because I have a high socioeconomic status" or "Because I live in a metropolitan area" or "Because my daddy told me to." Rather he will probably say, "Because I am a Democrat" or "Because I want to stop the Communists from taking over the country" or "Because Goldwater is trigger-happy." In other words, most persons see their own votes as the products of their opinions of the parties, the issues, and the candidates rather than as automatic responses to their social statuses. Hence these pychological factor *intervene* between the voters' general life situations and their votes or failure to vote in particular elections.

If this is so, we need to understand not only the ultimate independent variables of men's biopsychological natures and social statuses but also the intervening variables of their party identifications, issue orientations, and candidate orientations.[7]

## *Party Identification*

### Meaning

Party identification is "the sense of general attachment or belonging which an individual feels toward a given party."[8] Thus it is an inner psychological attitude, not an overt organizational attachment such as party membership (see Chapter 15). Political scientists usually measure party identification by asking their respondents questions comparable to the Survey Research Center's standard, "Generally speaking, do you usually think of yourself as a Republican, a Democrat, an independent, or what?"— and, to those replying "independent," the follow-up question, "Do you think of yourself as closer to the Republican or Democratic party?" According to their responses, they can be put into one or another of the seven categories illustrated on the preference dimension shown in Figure 27.

---

[6] Angus Campbell, Philip E. Converse, Warren E. Miller, and Donald E. Stokes, *The American Voter* (New York: John Wiley & Sons, Inc., 1960), Ch. 2.

[7] *Ibid.*

[8] Angus Campbell and Henry Valen, "Party Identification in Norway and the United States," *Public Opinion Quarterly*, XXV (winter, 1961), 505.

## Development

On the basis of the evidence so far compiled, it appears that party identification is the first attitude most persons acquire in their political socialization: as we saw in Chapter 10, by age seven or eight most Americans will tell an interviewer, "We [that is, the respondent's family] are Republicans (or Democrats)." Evidently, then, we acquire our initial party identifications, like our religious preferences, mainly from our parents as aspects of our identifications with our families. The more united are the parents in their party preferences and the more vocal they are about them, the more likely are their children to hold the same preferences the rest of their lives.[9] In most persons these early preferences are likely to grow stronger through life as a result of the general principle, noted in Chapter 10, that the longer one maintains identification with any group the more intense becomes his attachment to it. On the other hand, where, as in France, the usual family relationship has no room for political discussion by the parents with or in front of the children, fewer people have stable long-run party identifications.[10]

## Fluctuation

Another reason for the lower incidence of stable party identifications in France is the fact that the parties themselves have been less stable than in many other democracies: the parties of the Third Republic (1870–1940) disappeared in the Vichy regime (1940–1944), reappeared in somewhat altered form with some new names in the Fourth Republic (1946–1958), and have undergone more reshuffling in the Fifth Republic (1958— ). Moreover, in the Fourth Republic some parties (the RPF, Social Republicans, and Poujadists) were purely "flash" parties: they emerged, fought one or two elections, and disbanded. So in recent years France has offered fewer durable parties with which Frenchmen could form lasting identifications than most other democracies have provided their citizens.

In the United States, however, the present party alignment has lasted since 1854; in Great Britain and Norway since 1900; in Switzerland since 1919; in Canada since 1918; and so on. In such countries party identifications tend to be noticeably stronger and more stable than in France, but some fluctuation takes place nevertheless. According to the Survey Research Center, some Americans switch parties for personal reasons: a woman mar-

---

[9] For American evidence, see Campbell, Converse, Miller, and Stokes, *op. cit.*, pp. 146–149. For British evidence, see Richard Rose, *Politics in England* (Boston: Little, Brown & Company, 1964), pp. 61–63.

[10] Philip Converse and Georges Dupeux found that where 91 percent of American respondents had some idea of their father's party, only 29 percent of their French respondents did; "il ne disait rien à ses enfants" was a reply often heard in France: "Politicization of the Electorate in France and the United States," *Public Opinion Quarterly*, XXVI (spring, 1962), 11–13.

ries a man with an opposing party loyalty and shifts hers to keep peace at home; a man achieves a socioeconomic status higher than his father's, or moves to a new neighborhood and switches to the party predominant in his new environment; and so on. Politically, however, the significant phenomena are the rare fluctuations in which massive numbers of voters switch from one party to another and thereby change the parties' balance of electoral power. This certainly happened in the United States from 1930 to 1936 when many Republicans became Democrats,[11] in Great Britain in 1918–1924 when many Liberals switched to Labour or the Conservatives, and in France after 1958 when many former supporters of the Left, Center, and Moderate Right parties became supporters of the new Gaullist party, the UNR.

## Distribution

Party leaders and candidates are naturally most concerned with the distribution of party identifications, since this is one of the prime (though not the only) factors controlling their chances of winning elections. Table 11 shows, by way of illustration, recent distributions in a two-party democracy and a multiple-party democracy.

### Table 11.   The Distribution of Party Identifications in the United States and Norway

United States, 1962 (1237 respondents)

| DEMOCRATS | | | | REPUBLICANS | | |
|---|---|---|---|---|---|---|
| Strong | Weak | Independent | Independent | Independent | Weak | Strong |
| 24% | 24% | 8% | 8% | 6% | 17% | 13% |

Norway, 1957 (587 respondents)

| LABOR | | LIBERAL | | CHRISTIAN | | AGRARIAN | | CONSERVATIVE | |
|---|---|---|---|---|---|---|---|---|---|
| Strong | Weak | Strong | Weak | Strong | Weak | Strong | Weak | Strong | Weak |
| 21% | 24% | 4% | 13% | 6% | 4% | 6% | 9% | 5% | 8% |

SOURCE: The American figures come from the Survey Research Center, University of Michigan, and are provided through the Inter-University Consortium for Political Research. The Norwegian figures come from Angus Campbell and Henry Valen, "Party Identification in Norway and the United States," *Public Opinion Quarterly,* XXV (winter, 1961), Table 2, p. 517.

---

[11] Cf. Campbell, Converse, Miller, and Stokes, *op. cit.,* pp. 149–160.

Table 11 shows several things of political importance. First, in the United States the Democrats are clearly the majority party: 56 percent of the respondents express some degree of preference for them, to only 36 percent for the Republicans. This means the Democrats enter any national election with a long head start, and it takes powerful short-range counter-vailing forces, such as Eisenhower's great personal popularity in the 1950's, to overcome their lead. In Norway, the Labor party has almost a majority of the population (45 percent to all the others' 55 percent). This means that the only way to prevent a Labor government is for all the other parties to combine behind one government excluding Labor. The difficulty of this is shown by the fact that from 1945–1965 Labor formed the government all the time except for twenty-eight days in 1963; but it lost again in 1965.

Table 11 also shows that Norwegians have somewhat stronger party attachments than Americans: 42 percent express strong identifications, compared with 37 percent of the Americans.[12] We shall note some consequences of this in a moment.

### Impact

As we noted previously, in most modern democracies the most visible contestants in politics today are the same political parties (or at least parties bearing the same labels) that have been prominent for periods ranging from sixty years to over a century.[13] In such nations the parties constitute "virtually the only interesting political objects that are surely perceived by the quasi-totality of the population."[14] Hence party identification serves as most persons' principal device for making order and sense out of the flood of political events, personalities, issues, charges, and countercharges flowing at them from the communications media. That is to say, the one thing most of us are sure of is that we are Democrats or Republicans; when in doubt—as we often are—about this issue or that candidate, we can still make a choice by the simple and psychologically comfortable device of going along with our party's position or candidate.

So it is not surprising that political scientists have consistently found powerful associations between intensity of party identification and most other aspects of voting behavior. For example, the most partisan among us are also the most interested in and best informed about political affairs, the most likely to vote, and the most likely to try to influence others to vote.

---

[12] In France in 1958, by contrast, 10 percent refused to give the interviewers their party preferences. Of the remainder, only 60 percent identified themselves with a party or even a general *tendance* such as "left" or "right": Converse and Dupeux, *op. cit.*, p. 9.

[13] The principal exceptions are the new democracies, such as Ceylon, India, Israel, and Nigeria, and nations which have recently replaced dictatorial regimes with democratic, such as France, West Germany, Italy, and Japan.

[14] Philip E. Converse, "Information Flow and the Stability of Partisan Attitudes," *Public Opinion Quarterly*, XXVI (winter, 1962), 582.

The least partisan are quite different. We are all familiar with the inspiring picture of the Independent as the ideal citizen—a man who is deeply concerned with civic affairs, acquaints himself with the facts about the issues and candidates, and makes his decision on each according to a careful examination of its merits, his thinking uncontaminated by loyalty to party labels. Without commenting on whether good citizens *should* be like this, we must recognize that the voting studies have found that only a tiny fraction of self-styled Independents fit this ideal. Quite the contrary: the typical Independent is far less interested in politics than the strong partisan, he knows much less about the issues and candidates, he cares little about how elections come out, and he is much less likely to vote. His independence, in short, results from plain apathy, not from a high-minded rejection of partisanship.[15]

Party identification, then, has the most powerful impact of the three intervening variables. Yet it is obviously not the sole determinant of voting behavior: if it were the Republicans would never win a presidential election, when in fact they have done splendidly in every election since World War II except that of 1964. To some degree this can be explained by the countervailing effects of the other two intervening variables.

### Issue Orientation

A political "issue" is a question about what government should do or not do and about which people disagree. Much of what we hear about politics in our newspapers or over TV—especially during election campaigns—describes interparty (and often intraparty) disputes over issues: Senator A says that the United States should use atomic weapons against the Communists in Southeast Asia, while Senator B says that we should get out of the area altogether. Thus some people—such as most readers of this book—who pay considerable attention to discussions of politics in the mass media assume, quite erroneously as we saw in Chapter 11, that everyone else is as interested as they are and knows as much about issues as they do. Consequently, students of political science, like many political commentators, tend to exaggerate the influence of issues on the mass electorate.

Why "exaggerate"? The authors of *The American Voter* correctly point out that in order to have a measurable impact upon a voter's behavior, an issue must fulfill three conditions. First, it must be cognized in some form—that is, the voter must be aware of its existence and have some kind of opinion about it. Second, it must arouse enough intensity of feeling to make him take it into account in deciding how to vote. And third, he must

---

[15] Cf. Campbell, Converse, Miller, and Stokes, *op. cit.*, Ch. 6.

perceive that the issue position of a particular party or candidate is nearer his own than the opposition's. Only when an issue fulfills all three conditions for large numbers of voters can it exert significant influence on the outcome of an election.[16]

The voting behavior studies have generally found that the persons for whom issues are most likely to fulfill all three conditions are those with the strongest party identifications. And they, in turn, are likely to derive their issue positions from the stands their parties take—or, as we saw in Chapter 10, if their parties and candidates take issue positions contrary to their own, many of them simply will ignore that fact and continue to think that the party they favor takes the issue positions they favor.[17]

The main consequence of this pattern is the general rule that the more ideological the parties and the larger the proportion of the voters strongly identified with them, the more likely are people's issue stands to be predictable from their party identifications. This association is weaker in the United States, where the major parties, to say the least, espouse less clear and consistent ideologies than do those in many other nations. It is stronger in Great Britain, where the parties are more ideological than in the United States but less so than in many European democracies.[18] And it is still stronger in nations such as Norway, in which a number of durable parties have for many years expounded quite different social philosophies and taken widely divergent stands on public issues. To illustrate, the Campbell-Valen study asked both Norwegian and American respondents whether they thought there are any important differences in what the respective sets of major parties stand for. Forty percent of the Americans thought the Democratic and Republican parties are about the same, but only 11 percent of the Norwegians saw no important ideological differences among their five major parties. The intranational comparisons are also suggestive: among the Americans, only about a third of the strong party identifiers saw no differences between the parties, compared with almost half of the weak identifiers. Among the Norwegians, only 2 to 6 percent of the strong identifiers saw no differences, compared with 12 to 17 percent of the weak identifiers.[19]

All this is not to say that all the voters in all democracies acquire their views on issues merely as by-products of their party identifications, or that issue orientation has no independent effect on voting behavior. Clearly this is not the case; for example, a good many Democrats in 1952 were sick of the Korean War, blamed their party for getting us into it, and voted

---

[16] *Ibid.*, pp. 169–171.

[17] Cf. pages 215–216.

[18] Cf. Jean Blondel, *Voters, Parties, and Leaders* (Harmondsworth, Middlesex, Eng.: Penguin Books, Ltd., 1963), pp. 75–87.

[19] Campbell and Valen, *op. cit.*, Table 2, p. 517.

Republican to get us out.[20] And comparable examples from other elections and other nations are easily found. But it is to say that party identification acts as a kind of filter through which most voters most of the time perceive and evaluate political issues. Hence it is a more powerful influence on their behavior than what remains of issue orientation when all partisan coloring is removed.

### Candidate Orientation

Candidate orientation consists of the voters' attitudes toward the candidates' personal qualities considered apart from their party affiliations or stands on issues. To illustrate, if a man votes for Lyndon Johnson because Johnson is the Democratic candidate, party identification is the prime factor; if he votes for Johnson because he approves Johnson's stand on the 1964 Civil Rights Act, issue orientation is most evident; but if he votes for Johnson because he feels Johnson is an experienced, mature, and prudent leader (perhaps seen in contrast with "trigger-happy" Barry Goldwater), candidate orientation is the prime factor.

Candidate orientation is most powerful where the voters can vote directly for the occupant of a high office, and choose between well-publicized candidates. Where the office seems less important, the candidates are less visible, or the voting is indirect, candidate orientation is less powerful. Accordingly, it is at its strongest in elections for the office of chief executive in the presidential democracies. For example, the Democrats have been the majority party in the United States since the early 1930's. Yet in 1952 and 1956 Republican Dwight Eisenhower won near-landslide victories, in 1960 Republican Richard Nixon almost won, but in 1964 Republican Barry Goldwater got a substantially smaller share of the vote than might have been expected from party identifications. Most election analysts agree that in 1952 the Democrats' lead was overcome by popular dissatisfaction with the Korean War (issue orientation) and by the great popularity of Eisenhower as an experienced world leader, a man of peace with a lovable personality, and a man well above ordinary politicians (candidate orientation). In 1956 his popularity was even greater. In 1960 many Republican Catholics voted for John Kennedy and even more Protestant Democrats voted against him, both groups because of his Roman Catholicism. And in 1964 many Republicans voted against Goldwater because they thought he was reckless in foreign policy and reactionary in domestic.

Elsewhere in the Western Hemisphere the personalities of such recent presidential candidates as Eduardo Frei (Chile), Romulo Betancourt (Venezuela), and Janio Quadros (Brazil) have had comparable impacts on the outcome of presidential elections. And, despite the fact that he was

---

[20] Cf. Angus Campbell, Gerald Gurin, and Warren E. Miller, *The Voter Decides* (New York: Harper & Row, Publishers, 1954), Ch. XII.

not originally elected directly, the personality of Charles de Gaulle has played a critical role in French elections—as well as in world politics—since 1958.

Candidate orientation is generally of less significance in the parliamentary democracies, where prime ministers are not directly elected (see Chapter 18). To be sure, the personalities of such party leaders as Harold Wilson and Sir Winston Churchill in Britain, Sir Robert Menzies in Australia, John Diefenbaker in Canada, and Konrad Adenauer in Germany have attracted voters to (and repelled them from) their parties. But most voters in the parliamentary democracies vote for the *parties* of their choice with little regard to individual personalities; hence candidate orientation is less significant than in the presidential democracies.[21]

But direct election by no means automatically produces high candidate orientation. In many American states the voter first makes his choice —usually with some confidence—for President, Congress, governor, and members of the state legislature; but then the long ballot confronts him with choices for state secretary of state, treasurer, comptroller of public accounts, attorney general, and superintendent of public instruction; but he is not through yet, for then come choices for county supervisor, clerk, treasurer, sheriff, auditor, clerk of the circuit court, coroner, superintendent of schools, justices of the peace, sanitary commissioners, park commissioners, and recorder of deeds. By the time he gets down to the contest for recorder of deeds, even the most conscientious voter is likely to say to himself, "I don't know either of these candidates, I don't know what the recorder of deeds does, I can't imagine it makes any difference which man holds the office, and I'm tired!" So he either leaves the contest unmarked or votes for the candidate of his party knowing absolutely nothing else about him. Direct elections for such offices, we may say with confidence, seldom elicit high candidate orientation! Here as elsewhere, party identification remains the most powerful psychological variable intervening between the voter's behavior at elections and the wider context of politically relevant events, institutions, and communications in which he lives.


## Patterns of Voting:
## The Behavior of Electorates

Psychologists study voting behavior because it helps them understand human attitudes and behavior in general. Sociologists study it to learn more about the general effect of status and group affiliations on social structure and change. Both disciplines have made invaluable contributions to our

---

[21] For British evidence on this point, see Mark Benney, A. P. Gray, and R. H. Pear, *How People Vote* (London: Routledge & Kegan Paul, 1956), pp. 158–159.

understanding of how and why men vote. But political scientists study the behavior of individual voters in order to understand the behavior of electorates, for their object is to comprehend the forces affecting the outcome of elections, which, as we have seen, are the democracies' principal devices for holding government responsible to the people.

Voting studies in various democracies have unearthed a number of patterns in the behavior of electorates which tell us a good deal about the operation of democracy in the modern world. We shall conclude this chapter by outlining some of the principal patterns.

### Some Correlates of Preference

#### Social Status

The factor most generally associated with voters' preferences in all democracies is their social status, which includes such items as their incomes, occupations, and educations—in short, their unequal shares in their societies' good things. In all modern democracies upper-status persons tend to prefer the parties of the "right"; lower-status persons, parties of the "left."[22] But in no democracy does either group give *all* its votes to a single party; everywhere some upper-status voters support left-wing parties, and some lower-status voters support right-wing parties.

Thus in the United States a majority of the more advantaged vote Republican and of the less advantaged vote Democratic. In Great Britain the same is true of the Conservatives and Labour, respectively. In Japan the middle and upper classes favor the Liberals, while the lower support the Socialists.[23] In Finland the support of the Communist and Social Democratic parties on the one hand and the Agrarians and Conservatives on the other follow similar patterns.[24] And the continental European parties have comparable class bases.

#### Region

In no modern democracy are all the classes, occupations, and religious affiliations in the population evenly distributed over the whole country. Rather, each nation has a number of geographical regions, each of which is populated more by some types of people than by others. As a result, the

---

[22] In Chapter 15 we shall say more about the meaning of the "left-right" scale as applied to political parties. The most complete documentation of this general point is Seymour Martin Lipset, *Political Man* (New York: Doubleday & Company, Inc., 1960), Ch. VII. See also Robert R. Alford, *Party and Society* (Chicago: Rand McNally & Company, 1963).

[23] Chitoshi Yanaga, *Japanese People and Politics* (New York: John Wiley & Sons, Inc., 1964), p. 275.

[24] Erik Allardt and Yrjö Littunen, eds., *Cleavages, Ideologies, and Party Systems* (Turku: Transactions of the Westermarck Society, 1964), X, 102, Table 2.

*"I wonder if we aren't approaching the income bracket to start voting Republican."*

*Figure 28.* Categoric-group Membership Is Not Necessarily a Cause of Voting Behavior. (Drawing by Doris Mathews, from *Bounty,* July 1956.)

parties' electoral support is never evenly distributed throughout the nation; each party has its enclaves of solid support and its political deserts. In the United States, for example, the Democrats dominate most of the southern and border states, and most of the big cities of the North, while the Republicans draw much of their support from northern small and medium-sized towns and from big-city suburbs. In Great Britain, Labour's support is concentrated in the big cities, mining areas, and depressed rural areas of Scotland, Wales, and the North of England; the Conservatives draw heavily from big-city suburbs and the prosperous middle-sized towns and rural areas of the South and West of England. In West Germany the

Christian Democrats' strength is drawn mainly from Westphalia, the Rhineland, the Saarland, and Bavaria, while the Social Democrats depend mainly on West Berlin, Hamburg, Bremen, and Lower Saxony.[25]

Thus in most modern democracies national party competition results not so much from even competition in all regions as from the competition of each party's one-party regions with the others'. So mapping a nation's electoral geography is usually indispensable to understanding its politics.

### Religion

Some democracies have parties more or less directly tied to particular religious faiths: the Christian Democrats in West Germany and Italy (Roman Catholic), and the Netherlands' Catholic People's Party (Roman Catholic), Anti-Revolutionary Party (Calvinist), and Christian Historical Union (other Protestant) are examples. They get most of their support from their coreligionists, although not all their coreligionists support them.

Other democracies, such as the United States and Great Britain, have no such religious parties, and yet the adherents of particular faiths tend to support particular parties. In the United States since the early 1930's substantial majorities of Roman Catholics and Jews have usually supported the Democrats, while smaller but distinct majorities of Protestants have supported the Republicans. And, as we have seen, John Kennedy's Roman Catholicism played a major role in the 1960 presidential election. In Great Britain the members of the Church of England have generally supported the Conservatives, while Labour has drawn heavily from Nonconformists (Protestants other than Anglicans), Jews, and nonbelievers.

These tendencies are pale reflections of the religious wars that racked Europe until the middle of the seventeenth century, but they do indicate that for many persons religious affiliations are still a major influence on voting preferences.

### Ticket-splitting

Strictly speaking, a "split ticket" is any ballot on which a voter has not voted for all the candidates nominated by one party. The structure of the American governmental system has always invited ticket-splitting: the institutions of federalism and separation of powers provide the voters at most elections with a number of different executive and legislative offices to be filled and lists of party candidates to choose from at the national, state, and local levels. This, of course, is in sharp contrast with the situation in the parliamentary democracies, particularly those with "plurality"

---

[25] Uwe W. Kitzinger, *German Electoral Politics: A Study of the 1957 Campaign* (Oxford: Clarendon Press, 1960), p. 281.

election systems, which usually require the voters to vote for only one office (e.g., a member of a legislative body) at any given election. The 1964 elections provided some dramatic illustrations of this American phenomenon: in Rhode Island, only 19 percent of the voters voted for Republican Goldwater for President, but 61 percent voted for Republican Chafee for governor; in Massachusetts, the Republicans got only 24 percent of the vote for President, but won the governorship with 50.5 percent of the vote; and in Michigan the Republicans got only 34 percent of the vote for President but 56 percent for the governorship. Senator Goldwater's extreme unpopularity outside the Deep South admittedly exaggerated the incidence and degree of ticket-splitting, but such behavior is common in American elections.

The most thorough study of who splits tickets and why was made by the Survey Research Center in the 1952 and 1956 elections. The main results of their analysis are shown in Table 12.

Table 12 shows some interesting patterns. For one, it shows that a sizable segment of the American electorate crossed party lines in both elections (about one third in 1952, and about two fifths in 1956). For another, it shows that an increasing number of northern Eisenhower voters voted for Democratic congressional candidates, while an increasing number of southern Eisenhower voters voted for Republican congressional candidates. Both trends have significant implications for the future of American politics.

What kinds of persons split their tickets? The SRC could find only one significant correlation between socioeconomic characteristics and split-ticket voting: the highest incidence of straight-ticket voting was among the Stevenson voters living in the metropolitan areas (where the Democratic "machines" are powerful) and among Eisenhower voters in the metropolitan suburbs. They found a larger number of motivational correlations. The least split-ticket voting was found among those persons for whom all three intervening variables pointed in the same partisan direction. Of the three, strong party identification was more highly correlated with straight-ticket voting than were strong issue partisanship or strong candidate partisanship. They concluded that ticket-splitters are of two basic types: the "indifferents," who care little about how the election comes out but who have some interest in a local candidate or wish to grant the request of a friend; and the "motivateds," who have strong but conflicting feelings about the parties, issues, and candidates. Very few, however, are civics-book "independents" with strong feelings about the issues and candidates but no preferences as between the parties.[26]

---

[26] Angus Campbell and Warren E. Miller, "The Motivational Basis of Straight and Split Ticket Voting," *American Political Science Review*, LI (June, 1957), 293–312.

**Table 12.  Distribution of Straight- and Split-Ticket Voting in the 1952 and 1956 Elections**

| | North | | | | South | | | | TOTAL | |
| | VOTED FOR EISENHOWER | | VOTED FOR STEVENSON | | VOTED FOR EISENHOWER | | VOTED FOR STEVENSON | | | |
| | 1952 | 1956 | 1952 | 1956 | 1952 | 1956 | 1952 | 1956 | 1952 | 1956 |
|---|---|---|---|---|---|---|---|---|---|---|
| Voted straight ticket | 66% | 56% | 70% | 68% | 17% | 34% | 95% | 96% | 66% | 61% |
| Voted straight except for President | 1 | 6 | — | — | 39 | 31 | — | — | 4 | 6 |
| Voted straight except for senator or congressman | 2 | 3 | 4 | 3 | 4 | 2 | 3 | 2 | 3 | 3 |
| Voted straight at national level, straight for opposite party at state and local level | — | — | — | — | — | 6 | 1 | — | — | 1 |
| Voted straight at national level, split at state and local level | 23 | 20 | 18 | 21 | 4 | 6 | 1 | 2 | 18 | 17 |
| Voted split ticket at both levels | 8 | 15 | 8 | 8 | 36 | 21 | — | — | 9 | 12 |

SOURCE: Angus Campbell and Warren E. Miller, "The Motivational Basis of Straight- and Split-Ticket Voting," *American Political Science Review*, LI (June, 1957), 293–312.

## Some Correlates of Activity[27]

### Social Status

Perhaps the most universal pattern of voting behavior is that high-status persons are more active than those of low status. This is most evident in the matter of voting and nonvoting: study after study in many different democracies has shown substantially higher proportions of nonvoters among low-income groups than high, among grammar-school educated than high-school, among high-school educated than college, among "blue-collar" manual workers than those in professional and managerial occupations, and—most striking of all—among Negroes (including those whose right to vote is as well protected as anyone's) than whites.

At first glance this seems strange. After all, government is as great a weapon for the disadvantaged to change the *status quo* as for the advantaged to preserve it; and a number of members of certain depressed groups —e.g., the Irish and Italians in the United States in the nineteenth century—have found politics an excellent way of improving their individual statuses. Yet the disadvantaged generally use politics far less than the advantaged. Why?

Lipset suggests that part of the reason lies in the fact that the low-status groups have poorer access to information than the high-status, and so are less likely to know how useful government can be. Moreover, he says, the low-status occupations are less likely than the high-status to produce persons with the skill in organizing and the free time necessary for political leadership. And low-status persons are less likely than high-status to join voluntary social associations which increase political awareness and stimulate plans to take political action.[28]

The Survey Research Center, however, suggests that nonvoting and other forms of low political activity stem basically from low levels of political involvement and feelings of low political efficacy. The middle-aged Negro laborer living on Chicago's South Side who only reached the fifth grade and has never voted and never expects to simply does not care how elections come out. He says it makes no difference whether a Democrat or a Republican occupies the White House or the governor's mansion, and he feels that little people like him have no influence on what government does or does not do. Whatever "they," the big boys, decide he and his will have to live with. On the other hand, the middle-aged white executive living in Evanston who went to college and regularly votes sees politics quite

---

[27] Lipset, *op. cit.*, Ch. VI, is the most comprehensive cross-national survey.
[28] *Ibid.*, pp. 190–203.

differently: he feels that his vote does have some effect on what government does, and that voting is a way of making the world a little more like what he wants it to be.[29]

### Sex

In every democracy women vote less and are otherwise less active politically than men. These sexual differences are most pronounced among the lower educational groups and almost disappear for the college-educated, but in most social groups in most democracies distinctly fewer women than men vote. The differences seem to result in part from the fact that care of home and children restricts women's ability to get out and vote. But a more powerful cause appears to be the persistent and widespread idea, held by both men and women, that politics is a rough and dirty man's affair, and getting involved in it is somehow unfeminine. Thus one woman respondent told an interviewer, "Woman is a flower for men to look after," not to get mixed up in politics; and another, "I have never voted, I never will. . . . A woman's place is in the home"; and yet another, "Voting is for the men."[30] Such notions tend to disappear among women who have been college-educated, but they maintain a strong hold on the attitudes of the less educated of both sexes in most nations.

### Age

The frequency of student political demonstrations, marches, rallies, protests, and riots all over the world seems to suggest that young people are far more excited about politics than their elders. Yet the voting studies show quite the contrary. Generally speaking, the proportion of voters to nonvoters is lowest among persons who have just attained voting age. It increases in each successively older group through the thirties, forties, and fifties, and reaches a peak among persons in their early sixties. After that it declines, evidently for reasons of failing health and lower physical mobility. The Survey Research Center explains this finding in terms of the general rule, noted previously, that the longer a person holds a particular preference the more strongly he feels about it. Hence persons in their forties and fifties have simply had a longer time than those in their twenties to develop strong attachments to parties and other political groups. And this appears to bring the world into sharper perceptual and emotional focus for them than for their younger compatriots. Moreover, as people grow older they get jobs, marry, raise children, accumulate property, and in these and other ways acquire stakes in society that make governmental action more obviously important for their personal lives and fortunes than in their earlier years.[31]

---

[29] Campbell, Converse, Miller, and Stokes, *op. cit.*, Ch. 17.
[30] Quoted in Lane, *op. cit.*, pp. 210–211.
[31] Cf. Campbell, Converse, Miller, and Stokes, *op. cit.*, pp. 493–498.

## Cross Pressures and Concurring Pressures

A voter's behavior may be pictured as the end product of a number of different "pressures"—that is, of various social and psychological influences inclining him to act in certain ways. As we have seen, strong Democratic identification urges him to vote and vote straight Democratic; strong admiration for the Republican candidate suggests he should temporarily abandon his party and vote for that candidate; poverty and a low educational level incline him to apathy and nonvoting; a high income and a college education incline him to high involvement and voting; and so on.

Often these pressures concur; that is, each inclines him in the same direction as the others and they reinforce each other synergetically. But some voters are sometimes "cross-pressured"; that is, some pressures push them toward voting for the Democrat, but others pull them toward voting for the Republican. The Survey Research Center studied the effects of cross pressures and concurring pressures on voters in the 1952 presidential election. They determined each of their respondent's partisan positions on party identification, issue orientation, and candidate orientation, and put each into one or another of the following motivational-pattern categories.

DDD: pro-Democratic in all three factors (5.6 percent of the sample).

DDR: pro-Democratic in two factors, but pro-Republican in one, usually pro-Eisenhower (6.2 percent of the sample).

DRR: pro-Democratic in one factor, usually party identification, while pro-Republican in the others (6.5 percent of the sample).

RRR: pro-Republican in all three factors (8.5 percent of the sample).

DD?: pro-Democratic in two factors, but neutral in one (14.4 percent of the sample).

D?R: pro-Democratic in one factor, neutral on another, and pro-Republican on the third; often Democratic in party identification, neutral on issues, and pro-Eisenhower (15.4 percent of the sample).

RR?: pro-Republican in two factors, neutral in the third (13.4 percent of the sample).

D??: pro-Democratic in one factor, usually party identification, and neutral in the other two (15.0 percent of the sample).

R??: pro-Republican in one factor, neutral in the other two (9.9 percent of the sample).

???: neutral in all three factors (5.1 percent of the sample).

The levels of activity of each of these categories is shown in Table 13.

Two main conclusions may be drawn from the data in Table 13. First, as partisanship declines (down each side of the triangular matrix) the level of participation also declines. The more partisan a person is, in other words, the more likely he is to vote and otherwise support the side he favors, and the least partisan group (???) has the lowest level of participa-

### Table 13.   Relation of Political Participation
### to Motivational Patterns

POLITICAL
PARTICIPATION*                                MOTIVATIONAL PATTERNS

| | DDD | DDR | DRR | RRR |
|---|---|---|---|---|
| High | 29% | 29% | 35% | 46% |
| Medium | 54 | 52 | 50 | 50 |
| Low | 17 | 19 | 15 | 4 |

| | DD? | D?R | RR? |
|---|---|---|---|
| High | 32% | 20% | 40% |
| Medium | 41 | 49 | 47 |
| Low | 27 | 31 | 13 |

| | D?? | R?? |
|---|---|---|
| High | 16% | 19% |
| Medium | 44 | 49 |
| Low | 40 | 32 |

| | ??? |
|---|---|
| High | 10% |
| Medium | 38 |
| Low | 52 |

SOURCE: Angus Campbell, Gerald Gurin, and Warren E. Miller.
*The Voter Decides* (New York: Harper & Row, Publishers, 1954),
Table 11.1, p. 158.
  * "High" participation means voted and also made some other
contribution to the favored candidate's cause; "medium" means
voted but did nothing else; and "low" means did not vote.

tion. Second, the participation-levels of the persons on the Republican side
of the matrix are higher than those of the persons on the Democrat side.
Partisan Republicans, in other words, have higher levels of participation
than partisan Democrats.

The preferences of the persons in each of these categories of motivational patterns are shown in Table 14.

The data in Table 14 reveal pretty much what we should expect: that
the most partisan groups are the most solidly for their respective candidates, that, as partisanship declines, the division within each group becomes
more even, and that the least partisan group (???) is the most evenly
divided.

The figures in Tables 13 and 14 confirm one of the most significant
and generally held beliefs of students of voting behavior. This is the generalization that where all the "pressures" upon a particular voter concur
(that is, where all his demographic characteristics and motivations point
toward the choice of a particular party or candidate), the chances are very

### Table 14.  Relation of Presidential Preference to Motivational Patterns

PRESIDENTIAL
PREFERENCE                                    MOTIVATIONAL PATTERNS

| | DDD | DDR | DRR | RRR |
|---|---|---|---|---|
| Eisenhower | 7% | 29% | 81% | 98% |
| Stevenson | 93 | 69 | 17 | 1 |
| Other, or none | — | 2 | 2 | 1 |

| | DD? | D?R | RR? |
|---|---|---|---|
| Eisenhower | 18% | 50% | 94% |
| Stevenson | 78 | 48 | 6 |
| Other, or none | 4 | 2 | — |

| | D?? | R?? |
|---|---|---|
| Eisenhower | 28% | 81% |
| Stevenson | 64 | 15 |
| Other, or none | 8 | 4 |

| | ??? |
|---|---|
| Eisenhower | 39% |
| Stevenson | 40 |
| Other, or none | 21 |

SOURCE: Angus Campbell, Gerald Gurin, and Warren E. Miller. *The Voter Decides* (New York: Harper & Row, Publishers, 1954), Table 11.2, p. 160.

high both that he will vote and that he will vote for the indicated party and candidate. Conversely, the more a particular voter is subject to "cross-pressures" (that is, where some of his demographic characteristics and motivations point in one direction and others point in the other direction), the less likely he is to vote at all and the less predictable is the direction of his vote if he casts one.

For example, if in a particular campaign we find twenty white doctors living in small towns in Illinois who earn over $10,000 a year, are Protestants, regard themselves as strong Republicans, fervently believe that the government should cut taxes and get out of social-welfare activities, and think the Republican candidate is a fine man, we can predict with high confidence that nineteen or twenty of them will vote and that they all will vote Republican. If, on the other hand, we find twenty Irish Catholic office workers living in the Chicago suburbs making $4500 a year who regard themselves as Democrats, favor extending social security but oppose "open occupancy" and like the Republican candidate, we know that as many as four or five of them will not vote at all, and that those who do will be more or less evenly divided in their preferences.

By the same token, if a man's parents, wife, friends, neighbors, and work associates all agree that the Democrat should win, he is likely to vote and vote for the Democrat. But if his father and neighbors are pro-Democratic, while his mother and wife are pro-Republican and his friends and work associates are also split, the resulting "cross-pressures" will tend to make him "withdraw" from the situation psychologically by expressing no preferences of his own and by staying away from the polls on Election Day.

In our capacity as voters, in short, each of us is subject to a great many demographic and psychological influences, some of which we understand and some of which we do not. When all these influences impel us in a particular direction, we are likely to move and move in that direction, but when they work against each other and push us this way and that, we may only wander about in circles. So long as this continues to be true, the art of political navigation and manipulation for the party and pressure-group leaders who wish to steer us will remain the uncertain and undependable rule of thumb "dead reckoning" that it has always been in a free society.

# 15

# Political Parties
# and Party Systems

O<small>NE</small> of the most influential books in contemporary political science begins with the following declaration.

> It should be stated flatly at the outset that this volume is devoted to the thesis that the political parties created democracy and that modern democracy is unthinkable save in terms of the parties. As a matter of fact, the condition of the parties is the best possible evidence of the nature of any regime. The most important distinction in modern political philosophy, the distinction between democracy and dictatorship, can be made best in terms of party politics. The parties are not therefore merely appendages of modern government; they are in the center of it and play a determinative and creative role in it.[1]

Extreme as such statements may once have seemed, an ever-growing number of political scientists accept them as an accurate assessment of the crucial role of political parties in modern governments, democracies and dictatorships alike. Several recent studies, indeed, have been written on the premise that we can gain more insight into the essential nature of any nation's political and governing process by examining the nature and role of its party system than by concentrating mainly on its formal-legal governing apparatus.[2]

---

[1] E. E. Schattschneider, *Party Government* (New York: Holt, Rinehart and Winston, Inc., 1942), p. 1.

[2] For example, Sigmund Neumann, ed., *Modern Political Parties: Approaches to Comparative Politics* (Chicago: University of Chicago Press, 1956); Maurice Duverger, *Political Parties: Their Organization and Activity in the Modern State*, translated by Barbara and Robert North (New York: John Wiley & Sons, Inc., 1954); Avery Leiserson, *Parties and Politics* (New York: Alfred A. Knopf, Inc., 1958); and Thomas Hodgkin, *African Political Parties* (Harmondsworth, Middlesex, Eng.: Penguin Books, Ltd., 1961).

The present chapter, then, in describing the nature and role of political parties in both democracies and dictatorships, deals with one of the most significant of all the aspects of modern government.

## Characteristics of Democratic Political Parties

### What Is a "Political Party"?[3]

Politics, as we have stated repeatedly in this book, is essentially a contest among human groups for influence over the policies of government. Several different types of groups engage in political competition, including such "unorganized interest groups" as consumers, and such "organized interest groups" and "pressure groups" as the American Medical Association. Each type of group, moreover, pursues its objectives by methods that differ somewhat from those used by other types. Each, accordingly, plays a somewhat different role in the democratic governing process.

Political parties are a particular kind of political group. What kind are they, and how can we tell them from the other kinds?

For our purposes, *a democratic political party is an autonomous organized group that makes nominations and contests elections in the hope of eventually gaining and exercising control of the personnel and policies of government.*[4] It differs from a group like consumers in that it is organized. It differs from a group like the American Medical Association mainly in that it nominates candidates directly—that is, its selections go on the ballots bearing the party's name either formally or informally. Pressure groups, as we shall see in Chapter 16, resemble parties in that they often contest elections by endorsing candidates, raising money, issuing campaign propaganda, even ringing doorbells; but most of them are mainly concerned with what government does, while parties are equally or more concerned with who occupies public office. The "who" and "what" of government, of course, are not completely different things, but only analytically separable aspects of the same thing. The distinction we are making here stems from the parties' generally greater emphasis upon the "who" aspect. The clearest manifestation of this emphasis and the main feature that distinguishes a party from a pressure group is the fact that parties formally make nominations in their own names, while pressure groups do not.

---

[3] The definition in the text is one answer to this difficult question. For others, see V. O. Key, Jr., *Politics, Parties, & Pressure Groups* (5th ed.; New York: Thomas Y. Crowell Company, 1964), pp. 163–165; Frank J. Sorauf, *Political Parties in the American System* (Boston: Little, Brown & Company, 1964), pp. 12–15; and Neil A. McDonald, *The Study of Political Parties* (New York: Doubleday & Company, Inc., 1955), Ch. 1.

[4] Austin Ranney and Willmoore Kendall, *Democracy and the American Party System* (New York: Harcourt, Brace & World, Inc., 1956), p. 85.

A democratic political party differs from a totalitarian "party," such as the Chinese Communist party or the Ghanaian Convention People's party of Kwame Nkrumah, in that it accepts the democratic framework of government, is content to pursue its goals within the framework's limits, seeks to defeat but not exterminate opposing parties, and strives for victory by such accepted democratic methods as making nominations and contesting elections. In the concluding section of this chapter we shall describe the many significant respects in which the totalitarian parties are not really like "parties" at all in the democratic sense but are more like political armies bent on total conquest and annihilation of all opposition. Our present concern, however, is with the similarities and differences among the democratic parties only.

## Activities of Democratic Parties

### Making Nominations

From the standpoint of the nation and the parties both, making nominations is the most important of all party activities. The nominating process, as noted in Chapter 13, plays a crucial role in the selection of public officials, and the fact that parties in all the democracies have a near monopoly on making formal nominations gives them a great deal to say about the shape of governments and their policies. As Professor Schattschneider points out, "The parties frame the question and define the issue [as to who shall occupy public office]. In doing this they go a long way toward determining what the answer will be."[5]

The nominating process is no less crucial for the external success and internal control of the parties themselves. For one thing, the ability to make *binding* nominations—that is, nominations that are regularly accepted and supported by most of the party's workers and members—is one of the prime requisites for electoral success. For another, the control of the party's nominations is the principal stake of power fought for by the various factions and leaders of any party that has a good chance of winning elections. He who controls the party's nominating process controls many other things: he names the persons who officially speak for the party before the electorate; he selects and phrases the party's official policies; he presides over the distribution of whatever good things in patronage and power may come to the party as the result of winning elections; and, in the last analysis, he determines what kind of party it is going to be. Most party leaders and workers, accordingly, feel that winning intraparty struggles with opposing factions over nominations is at least as necessary for their purposes as winning interparty contests in elections for public office.

---

[5] Schattschneider, *op. cit.*, p. 51.

To find the locus of power within any democratic party, therefore, we must discover what leaders and factions control its nominations.

### Contesting Elections

Having made their nominations, most democratic parties exert some effort to get their candidates elected. There is great variation among the types of parties, however, both in the amount of financial and personnel resources they can throw into election campaigns and also in the importance they place upon electoral victory as a goal. At one extreme of the scale, the major American parties together now spend over $200 million in presidential campaigns on such vote-getting operations as door-to-door canvassing, television and radio speeches and spot announcements, mass rallies, pamphlets and comic books, billboards, lapel buttons, and the like.[6] At the other extreme, some minor American parties and a number of European parties spend practically no money at all and confine their campaigning to a few street-corner speeches and telephone calls.

Political scientists generally agree that in most democracies party campaigning is the principal organized activity that arouses popular interest in elections and stimulates the citizens to vote. We learned in Chapter 14 that the more partisan a person the more likely he is to vote and to participate in politics in other ways, and the least partisan persons are the least active. If maximum participation in the election of public officials is as desirable as most theorists of democracy believe it to be, then political parties deserve a large measure of praise—which they do not always receive—for encouraging such participation more effectively than does any other social organization.

### Organizing Government

Every modern democratic government requires a great deal of organization. If each of a government's tens of thousands of public officials acted entirely on his own without any consultation or cooperation with any of the others, chaos and near anarchy would surely result. In Chapters 17 to 21 we shall describe some of the more prominent official intragovernmental organizations that give modern democratic governments order and direction, but we should recognize here that official agencies do not by any means do the job alone. In every modern democracy the successful candidates of most political parties form some kind of intragovernmental party organization. For just one example, the legislators belonging to a particular party usually join together in a "caucus" or "conference," select "policy committees" and "floor leaders," determine who shall serve on which

---

[6] The authoritative analysis of the costs of American presidential campaigns is Alexander Heard, *The Costs of Democracy* (New York: Anchor Books, 1962).

legislative committees, and consult together on matters of legislative policy and strategy. In this fashion the parties backstop the formal organization of the legislature with an informal organization based on some similarity of political objectives and outlook and thereby help to give the legislature a measure of order and direction.

We shall describe below the considerable variation among different types of parties in the cohesion, discipline, and direct impact on public policy of their intragovernmental organizations. The point made here is that most groups of successful party candidates set up some kind of party organization that has some impact on the government's operations.

### Ancillary Activities

Many democratic parties carry on a number of activities in addition to the three basic operations listed above. They hold a number of social affairs —banquets, picnics, "socials," and so on—at which the rank and file can mingle with the leaders. They establish youth organizations to mobilize persons newly entering the electorate and to recruit workers and leaders. Some parties sponsor boy-scout groups, summer camps, and adult-education classes in such nonpolitical subjects as foreign languages. Some publish daily newspapers and other periodicals. Some even organize and finance the funerals of deceased party members. The lives of many Europeans, indeed, are touched by political parties at almost every major juncture: they are named after one of their party's heroes, attend party schools as well as public schools, join party-sponsored children's and youth groups, receive wedding gifts from the party, do most of their socializing at party affairs, join party-sponsored trade unions, and are laid to rest at party-organized funerals. This is less true in the United States, but many Americans know their political parties as more than merely nominating and electioneering bodies.

## *Party Membership*

### "Members" and "Supporters"

Being a "member" of an organization usually means something different from being a "supporter." The loyal Green Bay Packers fan who attends all the games, cheers his side and jeers the opposition, and offers free (though unheard) advice to the coach is certainly a team supporter, but no one would call him a member. Membership implies both the assumption of obligations to the organization and guaranteed direct access to its decision-making processes.

If this is correct, then the sample-survey respondent who tells an interviewer "I am a Democrat" but never contributes money, rings doorbells, addresses envelopes, attends rallies, or makes any contribution to the party other than occasionally voting for its candidates is, like our Packers fan, a supporter rather than a member.

In most democracies other than the United States there is a formal distinction between party members and supporters. One becomes a member by making formal application and having it acted upon favorably by some party council or leader; he is obligated to pay annual party dues; and he usually receives some formal evidence—often a "party card" of some sort—of his membership.

But not in the United States. In each of the fifty states the qualifications for party membership are defined by law so as to control who can vote in a particular party's direct primary elections (see Chapter 13). To qualify as, say, a Republican in the "closed" primary states, a qualified voter must publicly state his party preference to a registration official, and then receives the Republican primary ballot. The laws usually permit a party representative to challenge his good faith, but he needs only to swear an affidavit of his sincerity, and there the matter ends. Hence such challenges are issued so rarely that the voter's self-designation is really the sole determinant of his membership. In the "open" and "blanket" primary states he can vote in the primary of whichever party he chooses without even having to state his choice publicly. Accordingly, in all American states the Democratic and Republican parties are unique among the world's parties in that neither has any effective control of its own legal membership, and there is no formal distinction between a "member" and a "supporter."

Many political scientists believe this to be one of the major causes of the American major parties' decentralization, low cohesion, and lack of clear and consistent programs. Whatever may be the truth of this charge, it is significant that in at least three states (California, New York, and Wisconsin) some adherents of both parties have tried to overcome the debilitating effects of loose legal membership and organization by aping parties in other democracies. They have established dues-paying party "clubs" that operate outside the legal machinery which they try to strengthen and guide by supporting particular candidates in primaries and assuming the main burden of raising funds and campaigning.[7] But in most states a party "member," in law and in fact, continues to be anyone who so designates himself.

### "Members" and "Militants"

Despite the fact that party membership means more than self-designation in most democracies, by no means all the members of any party are equally involved, active, or influential in party affairs. As in any

[7] Cf. James Q. Wilson, *The Amateur Democrats* (Chicago: University of Chicago Press, 1962); Leon D. Epstein, *Politics in Wisconsin* (Madison: University of Wisconsin Press, 1958), Ch. 5; and Ralph A. Straetz and Frank J. Munger, *New York Politics* (New York: New York University Press, 1960), pp. 21–23.

organization of people, some members—whom we may call the party's "militants" or "activists"—feel particularly strongly about the party's cause, devote a good deal of time and energy to its operations, and consequently have most of the say about what it does. This universal trait of parties is part—but only part—of what the Swiss political sociologist Robert Michels meant by his famous "iron law of oligarchy," and no political scientist would deny that it fits the facts. But Michels also went on to argue that these "oligarchies" of militants always operate with no effective check by their rank and file and that they act to advance their own selfish interests, not the general interest of the party and all its members.[8] Now the latter propositions do not flow inexorably from the first; indeed, most political scientists agree that they do not fit the facts.

To give just one illustration, membership in the British Conservative party is open to anyone "who declares his or her support of the party's objects" and pays dues equivalent to 35 cents a year to his local Conservative constituency association. The average membership of these associations is around 5000, but only a fraction—estimated at 1 to 3 percent—are continually active in association affairs. Most of the time these few dominate the associations' only important business, selecting the party's parliamentary candidates for their constituencies. But on a number of occasions the usually quiescent rank-and-file members have rebelled against the militants' choices and have replaced them with others.[9] So what operates here is no "iron law of oligarchy," but rather what might be called a "tendency toward the uneven distribution of influence"—which is quite a different matter.

## "Direct" and "Indirect" Members

Most democratic parties are like the British Conservatives in that membership is "direct"—that is, each member joins the party directly and not through some intermediary body. But the membership of some parties is to some extent "indirect"—that is, the parties are in part federations of organized interest groups, and any member of an affiliated group is automatically a member of the party. For example, the British Labour party has many thousands of individual members who directly join local Labour associations (called "constituency Labour parties") and pay annual dues just like their Conservative counterparts. But also most of Britain's trade unions are directly affiliated with the Labour party at the national level, and many local union branches are also affiliated at the constituency level. Part of every union member's dues goes directly into the Labour party's

---

[8] Robert Michels, *Political Parties; A Sociological Study of the Oligarchical Tendencies of Modern Democracy*, translated by Eden and Cedar Paul (New York: The Free Press of Glencoe, first published in 1915, reprinted in 1949).

[9] Cf. Austin Ranney, *Pathways to Parliament* (Madison: University of Wisconsin Press, 1965), Ch. 3.

coffers unless he specifically requests that they be withheld. This process is known as "contracting out," and relatively few union members bother to do it even if they support the Conservatives! In the party's annual conferences each union has a vote proportional to the number of its members who do not contract out. Thus, many union members become Labour party members indirectly because of their union membership.[10]

Similar relationships characterize some other socialist parties, such as the Belgian Socialist party, and some Catholic parties, such as the Austrian People's party and the Belgian Social Christian party, which are federations of Catholic workers' unions, peasants' associations, industrialists' organizations, and so on. But direct attachment by individuals unmediated by other organizations remains by far the most common form of democratic party membership.[11]

### Party Organization

#### Intragovernmental and Extragovernmental Structures

In all democracies most officials elected with a common party label form some sort of organization for mutual consultation on policy and strategy. A few of the smaller European parties have only this kind of organization, and are little more than tiny collections of legislators who insist on retaining their ideological purity and reject all compromise and alliance with the larger parties. Only by courtesy can they be called "parties" at all.

Since making nominations and contesting elections are highly important to democratic parties, most maintain organizations outside government for purposes of nominating and campaigning for candidates. Many parties shape their extragovernmental organizations to fit the electoral structures in which they must operate, and maintain some kind of organization for each district which elects one or more major public officials. In the United States, for example, we elect a President and a Congress for the nation, a governor, legislature, and some other executive officers for each of the states, a board of supervisors for each of our counties, and a council for each of our cities. To maximize their chances of winning elections at each of these levels, each major party holds a quadrennial national convention, maintains a national committee, a congressional and a senatorial campaign committee, a state central committee in each state, a county committee for each of the counties in which it has any strength at all, and a city committee for each city in which it has a chance to win elections. There are also a large number of congressional-district committees, judicial-district committees, and so on.

---

[10] The most authoritative account is Martin Harrison, *Trade Unions and the Labour Party since 1945* (London: George Allen & Unwin, Ltd., 1960).

[11] Cf. Duverger, *op. cit.*, pp. 5–17.

Most democratic parties are similarly organized. The British Conservative, Labour, and Liberal parties maintain organizations in the parliamentary constituencies, combine them in regional federations, hold annual conferences, and maintain executive committees to administer party affairs between conferences. The Canadian major parties are an amalgam of British and American practices, since they add to the British system organizations at the provincial level and formally select their national party leaders at national conventions organized along American lines. The major French parties (except the Communists) have local "sections" in the towns and villages, combine them into federations at the department level (see Chapter 21), and have national congresses and executive councils comparable to those of the British parties. The same is true of the leading West German, Italian, and other European and Scandinavian parties.

European Communist parties are organized somewhat differently. Carrying on the old Bolshevik tradition of the "soviets," their basic unit is the "cell." This was originally supposed to have an occupational rather than a geographic base, with each cell including all party members who worked in a particular factory, office, government bureau, ship, or whatever. But the Communists have found it increasingly necessary to add "area cells" to the old "work cells" to accommodate party members who are not concentrated in particular work units—e.g., doctors, lawyers, small merchants. Today over three quarters of all Communist party members are organized in area cells rather than work cells. It seems that, willy-nilly, the Communists have had to copy their bourgeois rivals to function effectively.

## Conflict between the Intragovernmental and Extragovernmental

In most democratic parties some degree of conflict between the two types of organization is endemic and occasionally sharp. One of the most bitter clashes in recent years took place in the British Labour party. In 1960 the party's annual conference adopted a resolution declaring the party's policy to be one of unilateral abandonment of nuclear weapons and withdrawal from alliances using them—e.g., the North Atlantic Treaty Organization. But the party leader, Hugh Gaitskell, and most of the parliamentary party refused to accept this directive. They continued to support NATO and British possession of nuclear weapons, and worked hard in the unions and constituency organizations to get the extraparliamentary party to reverse itself. Their efforts were rewarded when the annual conference of 1961 dropped the unilateral nuclear disarmament policy and adopted Gaitskell's position.[12]

---

[12] The story is well told and the general problem of conflict between the parliamentary parties and their mass supporters outside is brilliantly analyzed in Robert T. McKenzie, *British Political Parties* (2d ed.; New York: Frederick A. Praeger, Inc., 1964), Ch. X.

Some French parties provide examples of even sharper disjunctions between the intragovernmental and extragovernmental organizations. In France a clear distinction is made between the *groups* (collections of deputies meeting together in single "caucuses" or *bureaux*) and the *partis* or *militants* (nominating and campaigning organizations operating outside the National Assembly). Some *groups*, such as the Communists, Socialists, and the *Mouvement Républicain Populaire* (MRP), correspond in both name and policy to their *partis* outside the National Assembly. Others, notably the Gaullist *Union pour la Nouvelle République* (UNR), remain primarily *groups* with little or no extragovernmental organization. The UNR reflects its great leader's distaste for party politics by having its deputies campaign for election on the simple platform of loyalty to *le grand Charles*—which in 1962 was enough to elect 231 of 482 deputies, almost a clear majority.[13]

Even in the United States clashes between governmental and extragovernmental party organizations are not unknown. For example, after the 1956 election the Democratic National Committee established an Advisory Council to make official party pronouncements on policy. However, the party's leaders in Congress, House Speaker Sam Rayburn and Senate Majority Leader Lyndon Johnson, refused to join the council or to consider its declarations in any way binding upon the Democratic majorities in Congress.[14] And similar efforts by Republicans outside Congress since the electoral debacle of 1964 have met similar rebuffs from Republican congressional leaders.

It seems, then, that some tension between the intragovernmental and extragovernmental organizations is inevitable in most democratic parties.

## Differences among Democratic Parties

### In Selectivity of Membership: "Mass" Parties and "Cadre" Parties

Left to their own devices, most democratic parties have no desire to enroll every Tom, Reginald, and François in their organizations. They prefer to restrict their memberships to persons they know can be counted on to do the party's work well, participate intelligently in making its decisions, accept cheerfully the decisions made even if they disagree, and—above all—

---

[13] Roy C. Macridis, in Roy C. Macridis and Robert E. Ward, eds., *Modern Political Systems: Europe* (Englewood Cliffs, N.J.: Prentice-Hall, Inc., 1963), pp. 171–172, 196, 224.

[14] Cornelius P. Cotter and Bernard C. Hennessy, *Politics without Power: The National Party Committees* (New York: Atherton Press, 1964), Ch. 11.

not to talk about the party's internal affairs in public. In other words, they prefer a devoted, knowledgeable, and responsible *cadre* to an apathetic, ignorant, and irresponsible *mass*. Hence while they always try to increase the number of their supporters, they are far more concerned with the quality than the quantity of their members.

However, the socialist parties produced in Western Europe by the enfranchisement of manual workers in the late nineteenth and early twentieth centuries have taken a different tack. Their first object was to educate the workers to prepare them for taking control of the government and economy, and they had no rich persons or corporations to call on for party funds. Consequently they held repeated membership drives and established highly democratic party constitutions both to attract and involve as wide a membership as possible.[15]

Legally speaking, the American direct-primary laws force the Democratic and Republican parties to be the most "mass" in the world. Yet in most parts of the nation their affairs are in fact managed, not by the millions of legally registered party "members," but by small cadres of party activists. Moreover, even the European socialist party leaders grow less interested every year in maximizing their memberships. For party funds they now count far more on contributions by labor unions than on those by individual members; to get the vote out they increasingly rely on the mass media rather than on local enthusiasts; and they are not eager to invite the sort of elbow-joggling a large mass membership is prone to (as in the British Labour party—see above).

It appears, then, that the heyday of the mass party is over, and that most democratic parties will become more and more of the cadre type in fact if not in form.

### In the Nature and Role of Ideology: "Missionary" Parties and "Broker" Parties

Every democratic party appeals to the voters with some sort of platform or program—that is, a set of statements about how its candidates will use governmental power if elected. But some are more ideological than others. The term "political ideology" implies a basic and wide-ranging philosophy encompassing convictions about such matters as what ultimate values are most worth achieving, the fundamental nature of human life and politics, and the proper relations of means to ends. In this sense, the Communist Manifesto of 1848 was a highly ideological program, while the Democratic National Platform of 1964 (or any other year) was not.

Democratic parties vary greatly in both the nature of their ideologies and the roles their ideologies play in shaping party attitudes and operations.

---

[15] Cf. Duverger, *op. cit.*, pp. 62–71.

## "I Have The Same Trouble"

*Figure 29.*    Neither American Major Party Espouses a Particular Clear and Consistent Ideology. (Drawing by Herblock, from *The Herblock Book,* Boston: Beacon Press, 1952.)

At one extreme of the scale stand a number of European parties and some American parties—parties that we shall call the "missionary" type. As an example, let us consider the Socialist Labor party of the United States. Founded in the second half of the nineteenth century, this party is committed to what may be called noncommunist Marxism. That is, its members believe that true Marxism (as opposed to what they believe to be its outrageous perversion by Lenin and Stalin), with its explanation of history and society in terms of class conflict between the bourgeoisie and the proletariat and its goal of the victory of the proletariat and the classless society, provides the key not only for understanding what society is now but also for setting the objectives toward which men should strive. The Socialist Laborites are convinced that they have history and the truth on their side. In their electioneering activities they seek not votes as such but *converts*. If at any given time they realize that their ideology runs counter to the beliefs of a majority of the electorate, they will not alter it to make it more popular—any more than, say, Christian churches will abandon their doctrines of the Trinity and the Virgin Birth in order to increase their membership by catering to skeptics. If the party's ideology is unpopular with the voters, then it is the voters who must change, not the ideology. The ideology is *true*, and no part of it may be altered or soft-pedaled in any misguided effort to gain popularity. The party's strategy for winning power, if indeed it has any such goal, is gradually to convert the masses over many decades or even centuries, if need be. In this sense, then, the Socialist Labor party is a "missionary" party. So too are many European parties, whose ideologies we shall describe below, and such other American parties as the Socialist Workers party. Some European parties, such as the Democratic Socialist and Christian Democratic parties (see below) are not above occasionally trimming their ideological sails to make themselves more attractive to the voters, but even so they are much more "missionary" in character than the major parties in the Anglo-American nations.

At the other extreme of the scale stand the Democratic and Republican parties of the United States. If either of them has an "ideology" as defined above, no one has ever been able to state it satisfactorily. The Republican party contains liberals and internationalists, sometimes known as "moderate Republicans," and conservatives and isolationists, sometimes known as "Goldwater Republicans"; but neither faction can establish a claim to being the only "real Republicans." The Democratic party contains southern conservatives and white supremacists, northern liberals and antisegregationists; but neither faction can set itself up as the only "true Democrats." Each party directs its appeals at and draws electoral support from every major interest group in the nation. Rather than attempting to convert a majority of the voters to a rigid and never-changing ideology, each party seeks to find out what each interest group wants and then tries to throw together some kind of program that will attract the maximum support of a maximum number of groups. Success is measured not by the ideological consistency and devotion of its program, leaders, and supporters, but by the number of elections it wins.

The American major parties, in short, are "brokers" among the conflicting demands of the nation's interest groups. A. Lawrence Lowell coined this description of their nature in the early years of this century and added:

> The process of forming public opinion involves . . . bringing men together in masses on some middle ground where they can combine to carry out a common policy. In short, it requires a species of broker-age, and one of the functions of politicians is that of brokers. . . . If politicians are brokers, party is the chief instrument with which they work.[16]

The other democratic parties of the world can be ranged along a scale between these two extremes. The Liberal and Progressive-Conservative parties of Canada, for example, are almost as nonideological as the American major parties. The British, Australian, and New Zealand Conservative and Labour parties have somewhat more clearly defined ideologies, but they too are essentially "broker" parties. The "centrist" parties of France, such as the UNR, the MRP, and the Radical Socialists (who are accurately described as "neither radical nor socialist"), fall somewhere in the middle of the scale. The left-wing and right-wing parties of most European democracies fall nearer the "missionary" extreme. Later in this chapter we shall describe the European multiple-party systems and the main ideologies espoused by their leading parties.

### In Social Composition of Leadership and Support

In the kinds of persons who become their leaders and who provide their electoral support, the "broker" parties tend to be *cross sections* of their communities and the "missionary" parties tend to be *segments*. In Chapter 14 we observed that in the United States and Great Britain each of the major parties draws at least some electoral support from every major ethnic, occupational, religious, economic, and educational group in their respective communities, and the same is true of the major parties in Canada, Australia, and New Zealand. In each nation, to be sure, each major party usually draws more heavily from some groups than others, but no "broker" party can accurately be described as a rich man's party or a Catholic party or a white man's party.

This cross-sectional character of "broker" parties is also reflected in the nature of their leadership. In the United States, for example, both the Republicans and the Democrats include in their local, state, and national

---

[16] *Public Opinion and Popular Government* (New York: David McKay Company, Inc., 1914), pp. 61–64. Compare this view with the Almond-Coleman conception of interest groups as the "articulators" of narrow interests and political parties as the "aggregators" of these interests into general policies with which all groups can live: Gabriel A. Almond in Almond and Coleman, eds., *The Politics of the Developing Areas* (Princeton, N.J.: Princeton University Press, 1960), pp. 33–45.

committeemen and chairmen and in their slates of candidates Jews and Gentiles, Catholics and Protestants, lawyers, businessmen, farmers, trade unionists, and so on. In Great Britain many of the leaders of the Conservative and Labour parties are graduates of the great "public schools" (Eton, Harrow, Winchester, Marlborough, and so on) and of Oxford and Cambridge universities. The Conservative party, to be sure, draws more leaders and electoral support from businessmen than the Labour party does, and the latter draws more heavily from trade unionists; but neither party monopolizes the support or supply of leaders from either group.[17]

The "missionary" parties, on the other hand, tend to draw almost all their electoral support and leadership from particular segments of the community and hardly make a dent in other segments. The European Communist parties, for example, get their votes and leaders almost entirely from the working class, depressed farmers, and a few intellectuals, and draw hardly at all from middle-class groups. The Liberal parties (see below) draw almost exclusively from middle-class groups, and the Catholic parties receive little or no support or leadership from Protestants.

"Broker" parties, then, tend to be "cross-sectional" in their leadership and electoral support, while "missionary" parties tend to be "segmental." These tendencies have a significant effect upon the differing nature of party conflict in the nations where the different types of parties prevail.

### In Centralization

We noted above that every party has some kind of national organization and a number of intermediate and/or local organizations. Democratic parties differ sharply, however, in the distribution of intraparty power among the various levels of organization. Their differences in this regard are most clearly revealed in the varying locations of control over nominations.

From this point of view the American major parties are the most decentralized in the world. Their main national organizations, the quadrennial national conventions, nominate only the candidates for President and Vice-President—and even they are usually controlled by shifting and temporary coalitions of state and local organizations and leaders.[18] Each candidate for United States senator is nominated by a state direct primary or convention, and candidates for representatives by congressional-district primaries or conventions. If the national leaders of either party object to a particular

---

[17] See Jean Blondel, *Voters, Parties, and Leaders* (Harmondsworth, Middlesex, Eng.: Penguin Books, Ltd., 1963), pp. 56–59; and W. L. Guttsman, *The British Political Elite* (London: MacGibbon & Kee, 1963), Chs. 1, 4, 8–10.

[18] The most comprehensive description of American national party conventions is Paul T. David, Ralph M. Goldman, and Richard C. Bain, *The Politics of National Party Conventions* (Washington, D.C.: The Brookings Institution, 1960).

congressional nominee as not being a "true Democrat" or a "real Republican," they are helpless to block his nomination if he has the support of the local organization and/or local primary voters. On several occasions, most notably when Franklin D. Roosevelt tried to "purge" anti–New Deal Democrats in the primaries of 1938, a popular national party leader has attempted to prevent unacceptable local candidates from receiving his party's nomination. Not only did every such effort fail when the national leader was unable to enlist the help of the local organizations, but in all instances the very attempt was regarded by many voters and party leaders as a serious violation of the basic rules of American political morality.[19] Thus, in the Democratic and Republican parties alike, the power over nominations, which is the highest stake in any democratic party's internal game, rests in a congeries of state, county, and district organizations and leaders. It is, in a word, highly decentralized. Later we shall see to what extent this is true of other powers in American parties.

The United States is not the only democracy with some decentralized major parties. The French Radical Socialists have long been a loose federation of local associations and federations which, in Duverger's words, "resembles an incoherent agglomeration of associations linked by vague and variable bonds, resultant upon hidden intrigues, rivalries between cliques, struggles amongst factions and personalities."[20] A number of European conservative parties are similarly decentralized. In Switzerland all the major parties, with the possible exception of the Socialists, are organized mainly in the cantons,[21] and the national parties are, even more than in the United States, more or less loose alliances of local parties. There are no outstanding national party leaders, but only cantonal leading figures who are generally unknown to most people outside their own bailiwicks.[22] In the Scandinavian countries candidates for the national legislatures are selected by local committees or conventions in the districts in which they are to run, and the national party leaders can only advise as to who should and should not be elected.[23]

However, most democratic parties are somewhat more centralized in their nominating procedures and other activities. In Great Britain, for example, the Conservative and Labour constituency associations select the parliamentary candidates, but both parties' national agencies have the

---

[19] For a fuller account of these "purge" efforts, see Ranney and Kendall, *op. cit.*, pp. 286–289.

[20] Duverger, *op. cit.*, p. 42.

[21] These are subnational governing units comparable to but more powerful than the American states; see Chapter 21.

[22] Roger Girod in Erik Allardt and Yrjö Littunen, eds., Cleavages, *Ideologies, and Party Systems* (Turku: Transactions of the Westermarck Society, 1964), X, 132–133.

[23] Dankwart A. Rustow in Sigmund Neumann, ed., *Modern Political Parties* (Chicago: University of Chicago Press, 1956), p. 171.

power to veto unacceptable selections. The Conservatives have in fact used their power very sparingly and Labour somewhat more often, but both are certainly more centralized than the parties mentioned in the preceding paragraph.[24] Canadian parties, despite their federal form of organization, nominate their candidates in much the same way.[25] And in most European nations using the party-list form of proportional representation (see Chapter 13) national party agencies select the candidates on their lists and determine the order in which they appear. So decentralization, while far from unknown in democratic parties, is less common than centralization.

### In Discipline

In any organization of people "discipline" includes whatever means are available to the group's leaders for inducing the members to act according to the lines laid down by the leaders. The whole concept of "discipline," then, implies some kind of hierarchical or "chain-of-command" relationship among the group's members.

The leaders of every democratic political party have at least some discipliary weapons for controlling the actions of the party's workers and members, but these weapons vary widely in nature and effectiveness. The President of the United States, for example, can, if he wishes, hand out certain "patronage" appointments to faithful supporters in his party and withhold them from recalcitrant party members; or he can make his public support of his fellow partisans in their bids for election dependent upon their support of his policies; or he can even try to "purge" them in the party's primaries. None of his weapons are very effective, however: he can rarely bring off a "purge"; there is only so much patronage available; and many congressmen from his party do not need his support to be elected, and know it. Hence presidential "discipline" in either American party is a matter of little more than persuasion, pleas, and cajolery, and every President, as even Franklin Roosevelt and Lyndon Johnson learned, must expect a considerable amount of opposition to his policies from members of his own party.

A British prime minister or leader of the Opposition is in a stronger position. Every member of his party in Parliament knows that when "the whip is laid on" (i.e., when the party leader notifies the members they are expected to vote in a particular way on a particular bill), he disobeys at his political peril. The prime minister (and, potentially, the leader of the Opposition) controls the distribution of ministerial offices; and since the ordinary M.P. cannot, as in the United States, rise to power and influ-

---

[24] Cf. Ranney, *Pathways to Parliament*, Ch. 10.

[25] Cf. John Meisel, *The Canadian General Election of 1957* (Toronto: University of Toronto Press, 1962), pp. 120–124.

ence by seniority, the only path to political success is paved with the leader's good will (see Chapter 18). Also, as we have seen, the national party agencies, which the leader controls, can veto the renomination of a rebel M.P. and thereby effectively deny him his parliamentary seat.[26] But the leader's greatest power is the fact that the British parliamentary system gives governmental authority to the majority party team. When that team can no longer muster a parliamentary majority, it must give way to the Opposition team. Hence any M.P.'s vote against his own party is, in effect, a vote to put or keep the other party in power. It is not surprising, then, that in Britain party discipline is widely (though not universally) regarded as a virtue.[27]

Most of the "missionary" parties of Europe and Scandinavia locate in their national leaders the power to expel from the party members of the national legislature who refuse to vote according to the "party line." Such expulsion is somewhat less likely than in Britain to deny the expelled legislator his legislative seat, but it does exclude him from participation in the party's decision-making processes. It is, therefore, a somewhat less powerful disciplinary weapon than those held by British party leaders, but far more powerful than any available to American party leaders.

### In Legislative Cohesion

These differences in centralization and discipline are reflected in the different degrees of cohesion displayed by various democratic parties. As the term is normally used, a party's "cohesion" is the extent to which its members in public office vote alike on leading issues of public policy. Thus, a party whose legislative members always vote alike on every issue is said to have perfect legislative cohesion and a party whose legislative members divide fifty-fifty on every issue is said to have no legislative cohesion whatever.

Many political scientists believe that its degree of legislative cohesion is one of the most significant of all indices of a party's nature, since, they say, it reveals the extent to which the party as a party influences the formulation of public policy.[28]

---

[26] In 1948–1949 the Labour party's National Executive Committee expelled from the party five rebel M.P.'s. All five stood for re-election in 1950 and were soundly defeated by regularly approved Labour candidates. No Conservative M.P. has been disciplined in this fashion since before World War II.

[27] This point is well made by Leon D. Epstein in several articles; see, particularly, "Cohesion of British Parliamentary Parties," *American Political Science Review*, L (June, 1956), 360–377.

[28] Cf. Schattschneider's statement, after describing the relatively low cohesion of American parties in Congress, that this is *"the most important single fact concerning the American parties.* He who knows this fact, and knows nothing else, knows more about American parties than he who knows everything except this fact."—*Op. cit.*, pp. 131–132, italics in the original.

Democratic parties vary widely in legislative cohesion. The major British parties are among the most cohesive, as evidenced by the fact that each of them can usually count upon all of its members in the House of Commons to vote as the party leaders desire. On those few occasions in which some members cannot go along with the leaders' policies (as, for example, in 1956, when a number of Conservative members of Parliament could not support their leaders' move to withdraw British armed forces from the Suez area), the dissenters are more likely to abstain from voting than to vote against their leadership. At the other extreme, a number of small French parliamentary *groups* split internally on almost every public issue and therefore have little or no legislative cohesion. The other democratic parties fall somewhere between these two extremes. The larger French, Scandinavian, and German parties, for example, are almost, but not quite, as cohesive as British parties; the American major parties in Congress are less cohesive than either, but considerably more cohesive than the smaller French *groups*; and in the various American state legislatures the parties cover almost the whole range of cohesion.[29]

These, then, are some of the major respects in which democratic political parties differ from one another. Their differences are also expressed in the types of party systems prevailing in modern democratic nations, and we now turn to a brief description of the nature and political consequences of the various types.

## Types of Democratic National Party Systems

When analyzing and comparing political parties in various modern democracies, political scientists often speak of "party systems." This term is used to denote certain general characteristics of party conflict in particular democracies, and "party systems" can thus be classified according to a number of different criteria. On the basis of the factors described in the foregoing section, for example, we can speak of "ideological" party systems and "broker" party systems, or "centralized" and "decentralized" party systems. Most political scientists, however, emphasize the criterion of the number of parties that regularly secure substantial portions of the votes and public offices—on the premise that this variable has the most direct and powerful impact upon the general character of the nations' governing processes.

Based upon this criterion, then, we may classify the party systems of modern democratic nations into two main types.

---

[29] For the data underlying these generalizations, see Ranney and Kendall, *op. cit.*, pp. 391–395; and Malcolm E. Jewell, "Party Voting in American State Legislatures," *American Political Science Review*, XLIX (September, 1955), 733–791.

### *Multiple-party Systems*

#### Definition

A multiple-party system is one in which three or more—usually more—parties regularly share substantial portions of the votes and public offices, and in which a single party rarely, if ever, wins a majority of either.

#### Distribution and Characteristics

Multiple-party systems are characteristic of the democratic nations of Western Europe and Scandinavia. In each of these nations at least three, and usually as many as five or six, parties regularly win enough votes and legislative seats to be called "major" parties. Hardly ever does a single party win a majority of the legislative seats, and so the nations' cabinets and ministries are composed of coalitions of several parties rather than the representatives of any single party.

#### Leading Party Ideologies

Most of the major parties in these nations are more of the "missionary" than the "broker" type. The names of the parties, of course, vary somewhat from one nation to another, but the following main party ideologies can be found in most or all of the multiple-party systems.

COMMUNISM.   At the extreme "left" of the ideological scale[30] stand the Communist parties, whose ideology and structure we shall describe at the end of this chapter.

DEMOCRATIC SOCIALISM.   One long step to the right of the Communists stand the democratic socialist parties, which espouse some brand of noncommunist Marxist socialism somewhat similar to that of the American Socialist Labor party (see above). Every European democracy has such a party, and among the more powerful are the Norwegian Labor party, the Swedish and Danish Social Democratic parties, the French and Belgian Socialist parties, the West German Social Democratic party, and the Austrian Socialists.

CHRISTIAN (CATHOLIC) DEMOCRACY.   The ideology of "Christian democracy" stems from the doctrines promulgated by Pope Leo XIII in the encyclical *De rerum novarum* (1891) and by Pope Pius XI in another

---

[30] Although they have no precise definitions, the terms "left" and "right" are so commonly used in descriptions of political ideologies and conflict that they deserve a brief explanation. The ideological scale is constructed in terms of the degree of "socialism" particular parties espouse. "Socialism," too, has no very precise meaning, but as we are using the term here it refers to government ownership and operation of economic enterprise. In this sense the more sympathetic toward socialism a particular party is the more "left" it is, and the more sympathetic to private property it is the more "right" it is.

encyclical *Quadrigesimo anno* (1931). It holds that while capitalism works many unjust hardships upon the workers, socialism is the wrong solution. Employers and employees should remember that they are all children of God and that spiritual redemption and purity rather than material wealth should be the goal of society. In order to promote this end wealth should be distributed more equitably, and employers and employees should form partnerships for the mutual distribution of profits. Economies should be reconstructed in such a way that the excessive individualistic materialism of capitalism and the excessive collectivistic materialism of socialism will be replaced by a cooperative commonwealth in which the twin material barriers to spiritual well-being of excessive poverty and excessive wealth will be removed. In France, Belgium, West Germany, Switzerland, and Italy, each of which has many Catholics, some kind of Christian Democratic party has been established. The most powerful are the Italian Christian Democratic party and the West German Christian Democratic Union, but such others as the French MRP and the Belgian *Parti Social Chrétien* are often prominent in the governing coalitions of their respective nations. The Christian Democratic parties do not all interpret the papal encyclicals in exactly the same way, and, in fact, can be scaled from "left" to "right" with the MRP standing toward the "left" and the Italian Christian Democrats toward the "right."

LIBERALISM. In European politics "liberalism" was originally a doctrine calling for the individual's liberation from the domination of both church and state, with its ideals rooted in the attitudes of the Enlightenment and the French Revolution. The conflict between church and state, particularly over the control of education, was a leading issue in nineteenth-century European politics, and the liberal parties were generally either the first or second party.[31] Twentieth-century European politics, however, is focused mainly on economic issues, and the liberal parties have become "middle-roaders" between the socialists and the right-wing parties. Generally today they are no better than the fourth or fifth largest parties. Among the better-known liberal parties are the French Radical Socialists, the Belgian Party of Liberty and Progress, the West German Free Democrats, the Swedish Liberals, and the Swiss Radical Democrats.

DEMOCRATIC CONSERVATISM. A number of right-wing European parties accept and defend the democratic form of government but argue that all the modern tendencies toward socialism, the welfare state, and other basic revisions of their nation's traditional social-economic systems should be halted or reversed. Leading examples of such parties are the French Inde-

---

[31] Cf. Guido de Ruggiero, *The History of European Liberalism*, translated by R. G. Collingwood (London: Oxford University Press, 1927).

pendents, and the Conservative and Agrarian parties in the Scandinavian nations.

ANTIDEMOCRATIC CONSERVATISM.   Other right-wing European parties not only wish to return to the social-economic systems of generations ago but also advocate more or less drastic revisions in their nations' governmental systems in order to destroy majoritarian democracy and return to older ways of governing. These changes, however, are sought only by peaceful and constitutional means. Examples of such parties are the Austrian Independents and the Italian Monarchists.

ANTIDEMOCRATIC RADICALISM.   At the extreme right of the European ideological spectrum stand the parties who advocate a total destruction of democracy and are willing to use any means that will achieve this end. They are the heirs of Mussolini and Hitler, and while they do not use the term themselves, most of them may accurately be described as "neofascist." They include such parties as the Italian *Movimento Sociale Italiano* and the French Union and French Fraternity party, which, under the leadership of Pierre Poujade, had an unsavory but brief career from 1954 to 1958.

### Political Consequences

The multiple-party systems have both their critics and their defenders among political commentators. Their critics charge them with producing unstable and ever-changing governments, splitting their communities into hostile and uncompromising ideological camps, failing to elicit clear popular mandates on the issues of the day, and, as a result of all these traits, weakening democracy's ability to survive. Their defenders claim that multiple-party systems accurately reflect the various shades of public opinion in their nations and thereby more nearly realize the ideals of democracy than do the two-party systems in the Anglo-American nations.

The author has no intention of trying to award a final decision in this debate but feels that any such decision must at least take into account several important considerations.

Political and governmental instability is not an inevitable result of any multiple-party system. The systems of Belgium, West Germany, and the Scandinavian nations, for example, normally produce governments that are quite as stable as any in the two-party nations. It seems highly unlikely, moreover, that the structure of their party systems is the sole or even the main cause for the deep ideological divisions within certain European nations. Most students of French politics believe that the proliferation of French parties is the *result* of ideological fissures in the French nation produced by far more basic factors than a particular kind of party system. This is not to say, of course, that multiple-party systems are more desirable than two-party systems, but only to suggest that a nation's party system is only one cause, and in many instances not the most important one, of the nature of its basic political conflict.

## Two-Party Systems

### Definition

A two-party system is one in which only two parties regularly win substantial portions of the votes and public offices, and in which the major parties to some degree alternate in having a majority of both. Under this definition one party can have a substantial lead over the other, as, for example, in the United States, where from 1932 to 1964 the Democrats won seven of nine presidential elections and fifteen of seventeen congressional elections. But all along the Republicans have controlled a number of state legislatures and governorships, and have always been thought to have at least a chance of winning control of the national government. Hence the customary description of the American party system as "two-party" is quite proper.

Two-party systems also contain a number of "minor parties," which nominate candidates and contest elections (five put up presidential candidates in 1964), but rarely if ever win more than a tiny fraction of the votes or elect any candidates (the five together got less than one tenth of 1 percent of the votes).

### Distribution and Characteristics

Two-party systems are generally characteristic of the English-speaking democracies, including the United States, Great Britain, New Zealand, Australia, and Canada.[32] A few other democracies, such as Colombia, are also usually put in this class. Despite their many individual differences in detail, the major parties in all these nations are similar in five basic respects.

1. They tend to be of the "broker" rather than the "missionary" type. Some (e.g., the various labor and socialist parties) have somewhat more definite ideologies than others (e.g., both American parties and the various conservative parties), but all are more concerned with winning elections here and now than with eventually converting the whole population to pure and uncompromising ideologies.
2. They tend to draw their leadership and electoral support from all elements of their communities rather than from particular segments thereof.

---

[32] The latter two are questionable. Australia really has a "three-party system," but since 1949 the Liberal and Country parties have campaigned together against the Labor party and, when successful, have formed coalition governments. The Canadian Liberals won 129 seats in the 1963 election to the Progressive Conservatives' 96, but still needed help from the minor parties to form a government.

*Figure 30.*   Elections under Three Types of Party Systems.

3. They direct their appeals for votes at all major interest groups. The American Republicans and British Conservatives, for example, never say to organized labor, "We stand for business first, last, and always, and if we get into power we intend to destroy the unions! If you don't like it, take your votes elsewhere!" Rather they say, "We stand for the welfare of *both* business and labor, neither of which will benefit from a victory by our opponents. If you want fair and decent treatment for labor and management alike, vote for us instead of for them." Thus their programs and platforms are not as clear and internally consistent as the programs of the "missionary" parties, for they are designed to appeal to many interests, some of which are incompatible with others, with a view to landing as many votes as possible.

4. They are moderate parties. They try to put forth programs that will not unduly antagonize any major element of the electorate and will try to avoid or postpone taking a clear stand on any truly "hot" issue on which the community is sharply divided. Moreover, any unreconstructed extremist in the ranks of either major party must either moderate his views as the price of retaining his position in the inner circles of the party (e.g., Aneurin Bevan in the British Labor party) or maintain his extreme position and be isolated from most other party leaders (e.g., Huey Long in the Democratic party and Joseph R. McCarthy in the Republican party).[33]

5. They tend to be a good deal alike in their basic views and specific programs. They agree generally on the basic form of government and on the general direction of public policy. Thus, when one replaces the other in power, there is seldom a drastic shift in governmental policy. This does not mean, however, that they are identical and that the voters have no real choice; for they usually disagree about the *pace* at which certain policies should be adopted and implemented, and often on many of the details of such policies. Consequently, most voters believe that the parties are sufficiently different to warrant a preference for one over the other.

The American major parties, as we have seen, are considerably more decentralized than their counterparts in the other two-party systems; but otherwise the major parties in all the two-party systems are essentially similar.

### One-Party Systems in the Democracies

For almost a century no Republican has been elected to any state-wide office in South Carolina. In most elections no Republican has even bothered to run, and on those rare occasions when one did he got less than 5 percent of the votes. The Democrats have done better in Vermont, but

---

[33] Cf. Samuel Lubell's discussion of the fates of Bevan, Long, and McCarthy, in *Revolt of the Moderates* (New York: Harper & Row, Publishers, 1956), Ch. 3.

not much: since the Republican party was founded in 1854, the Democrats have won state-wide offices only three times and have never held more than a small fraction of the seats in the legislature. The Welsh coal mining constituency of Ebbw Vale for decades has given the Labour candidates majorities of 75 percent or more. A number of working-class districts in Paris, Lyons, and Lille regularly give comparable majorities to the Communists. In India the Congress party has never won less than 72 percent of the contests for seats in the lower house of Parliament.

In short, every democracy has a number of what can only be called one-party systems. But they differ from the one-party systems of the totalitarian nations in the vital respect that the dominant parties' existing and potential rival parties are not outlawed nor are their ideologies and programs suppressed. They have substantially the same opportunities as the dominant parties to win votes and office, but, for a variety of reasons, they have little success.

Hence, whether multiple-party, two-party, or even one-party, the differences among the various types of democratic parties and party systems look small indeed when compared with the wide gulf between all democratic party systems and the one-party systems of the dictatorships.

## The One-Party Systems of the Dictatorships

Dictatorship is as old as government itself. Dictatorship conducted through the medium of a single all-powerful "political party," however, is an invention of the twentieth century.[34] These regimes can be classified into three main types: the communist one-party systems of the Soviet Union, Red China, and their satellites; the fascist one-party systems of Spain and Portugal, which have survived the fascist regimes of Mussolini and Hitler in Italy and Germany; and the one-party systems adopted by a number of new nations in Africa and Asia. We shall briefly describe the characteristics of each type.

### Some Common Characteristics[35]

#### Differences from Democratic Systems

All democratic parties, including even those of the "missionary" type, cherish democratic government at least as much as they cherish achieving their particular social and economic aims. Accordingly, they tolerate the existence of opposing parties, use only peaceful and democratic methods

---

[34] Cf. Carl J. Friedrich and Zbigniew K. Brzezinski, *Totalitarian Dictatorship and Autocracy* (rev. ed. Cambridge, Mass.: Harvard University Press, 1965), Ch. 3.

[35] Cf. Duverger, *op. cit.*, pp. 255–280.

to pursue their goals, and accept the voters' verdicts as given in elections. Essential to all democratic party systems, in other words, is the general acceptance of the idea of the *loyal opposition*—the conviction that while opposing parties may be misguided and committed to incorrect ideologies and policies, they are nevertheless loyal to the nation and thus have a right to engage in its politics.

Communist and fascist parties, whether monopolizing the field in a dictatorship or contending with other parties in a democracy, bear no more than a superficial resemblance to democratic parties. Essentially they are like armies in combat, and many of them, indeed, openly use military terms ("vanguard," "phalanx," "spearhead") to officially describe themselves and their operations. An even more apt analogy is that between totalitarian parties and a militant religious order. Every totalitarian party arises from and is committed to a kind of secular religion, each with its sacred texts (*Das Kapital, Mein Kampf*), its prophets (Marx and Lenin, Hitler,) its total explanation of the nature of society (dialectical materialism, the destiny of the Aryan race), and its ethical system (the end justifies the means). The party is its priesthood and its evangelizers. Yet in one sense opposition is indispensable to a totalitarian party; for to justify its military organization and the fanatical devotion it demands of its members, a communist or fascist party needs a mortal enemy (e.g., the capitalists or the Jews) with whom it is locked in a struggle to the death.

### The General Role of Totalitarian Parties

Many of us in the democratic world are puzzled as to why communist and fascist dictators bother with the pseudodemocratic trappings of political parties at all. When we look a little closer at the totalitarian parties, however, we can see that they perform several roles of vital importance for their masters.

In the nations in which they are the sole legal party, totalitarian parties perform two main functions. First, they provide a tightly knit, well-organized, and fanatically devoted oligarchy to operate the nation's formal governing structure in the manner demanded by the party's satraps. Second, they provide a useful psychological and organizational bridge between the nation's masses and its rulers—a bridge that older, more aristocratic oligarchies lacked and consequently found themselves more vulnerable to revolts by the masses.

In the nations in which they are not in power but contend with other parties, totalitarian parties act as the spearhead of their movements' wars against the established systems of government.

In these and other respects, then, communist and fascist parties are essentially alike. In order to see in what respects they differ, let us briefly examine the structure of each type of one-party system.

## Communist One-Party Systems

### The Communist Conception of the One-Party State

The one-party system of Communist Russia is the oldest and still the most powerful of all such systems, and it has served as the model not only for all other communist systems but also for many aspects of the fascist systems. Since 1918 the Communist party has been the only legal party in Russia. All attempts to form rival parties are officially regarded as treason, and the 1936 Constitution describes the party as "the vanguard of the working people" and "the leading core of all organizations of the working people, both public and State" (Article 126).

How do the communists justify permitting only one party to exist in what they claim is the most "democratic" government in the world? According to the doctrine enunciated by Stalin and his disciples, every political party represents a class. In nations where several classes exist, several political parties must also exist; but in Soviet Russia only the working class exists, and so only one party—the Communist party—is needed to represent it. Any other party could only oppose the interests and welfare of the proletariat, and that, of course, would be counterrevolution and treason. Thus "true democracy" (i.e., government in the interests of the workers) can permit only one party.

### The Structure and Composition of the Party

The Russian Communist party presently has about 10 million members, or about 4 percent of the Russian population. This does not mean, of course, that communism is "unpopular" in Russia: the party is designed to be an elite, not a mass organization. Thus, a Russian citizen can become a party member only after having been recommended by three party members of at least three years' standing and after having successfully passed the many tests of a year's candidacy. Periodic purges, moreover, enable the leadership to eliminate all members who are deemed "inactive" or "politically incorrect." Lenin originally intended the party to be composed mainly of manual workers, but such persons now constitute only about one fifth of its membership, and over half of the party's members come from the "intelligentsia."[36]

The basic units of party organization, once called "cells," are set up in such places as factories, collective farms, and military units. Above them are placed a series of city committees, industrial and agricultural committees, and regional and territorial committees. Heading up the whole

---

[36] Merle Fainsod, *How Russia Is Ruled* (rev. ed.; Cambridge, Mass.: Harvard University Press, 1963), Ch. 8.

party is the national Party Congress, which is supposed to meet every four years but has not always done so (no Congress was held from 1939 to 1952, for example). The Congress nominally chooses the Central Committee, now made up of 175 full members and 155 "candidates" (alternates). The Central Committee chooses various committees, of which by far the most powerful (and the actual ruling oligarchy of Russia) is the Presidium, now composed of 11 full members and five alternates.

Communist ideologues have made much of the principle of "democratic centralism," which calls for full and free discussion within the party before a decision is made, but closed ranks and no criticism of a policy once it has been adopted. In practice, however, "democratic centralism" has meant that the party's rulers—Stalin himself before his death in 1953, and the Presidium since then—make the decisions, and their decisions are binding on all the lower party echelons, who may criticize only those few matters permitted by the ruling oligarchy.

Closely allied with the party structure are a number of auxiliary organizations characteristic of all one-party systems. They include the secret political police (now called the KGB) charged with detecting and disposing of all dissenters, deviationists, "Trotskyite reptiles," and other enemies of the regime. They also include the various youth organizations, all intended to indoctrinate the young with the attitudes of communism and pick out the more able for future positions of party membership and leadership. The main youth organizations are the Little Octobrists (ages seven to ten), Young Pioneers (ages ten to fifteen), and the Komsomols (Young Communist League, ages fourteen to twenty-eight).

### The Role of the Party

Like all totalitarian parties in power, the Russian Communist party is first of all a ruling oligarchy, "the government of the government," "a state within a state." Every major legislative, executive, administrative, and judicial agency of the formal government has its parallel party organization, which animates and operates its particular formal agency in such a way that the whole government does just what the party leaders want it to do.

By its agitation-propaganda operations (see Chapter 10) the party also keeps a check on the state of mass opinion in order to learn what policies are possible at the moment and to keep that opinion moving along so that ever-more "advanced" policies can be successfully put into operation with a minimum of physical coercion and terror.

The party, in short, is the brain and nervous system of the Soviet leviathan. One who knows the party structure and operations but not the formal structure knows far more about how Soviet Russia is governed than one who knows the formal structure but not the party.

### Communist Parties outside Russia

The Communist party of the Soviet Union was the first Marxist party to win and keep power in a nation. For thirty years, accordingly, its prestige among the world's Marxists was unmatched, and it was the unchallenged leader of the world communist movement.[37] In 1919 Lenin and Trotsky established the *Comintern* (Communist International) to organize and coordinate the world movement, but in 1943 Stalin abolished it (the other Communist parties had no say in the matter) as a gesture of good will to his democratic allies in the war against fascism. He revived it under the name of *Cominform* in 1947 as part of his strategy in the Cold War against his former allies, but Khrushchev abolished it in 1956 as part of his program of "de-Stalinization."

In all the nations outside the Soviet Union in which they seized power, the Communists established one-party regimes more or less closely modeled on the Russian system.[38] In the democratic nations in which they have failed to win power, the Communists maintain two types of organization. The first is the "open party," which publicly reveals its membership, nominates candidates and contests elections, sometimes tries to form "popular fronts" with other left-wing parties, and generally assumes the guise of a contender for electoral success just like the democratic parties. They have been most successful in France, where since 1945 they have regularly won about a quarter of the popular vote, have more dues-paying members than all the other parties combined, and are by far the largest single party in the National Assembly. The Communists have been almost as successful in Italy, where since 1945 they have regularly won from one fourth to one third of the popular vote and about one fifth of the legislative seats.

The second, and from the democratic point of view even more dangerous, type of communist organization is the "secret party." This organization keeps its membership and operations as secret as possible, attacks the existing regimes by such methods as espionage, sabotage, assassination, infiltration of trade unions, and political strikes, and in general operates as the local arm of the Russian military and intelligence apparatus.

Whether inside or outside Soviet Russia, or whether "open" or "secret," Communist parties have, for the reasons outlined above, only the most superficial resemblance to democratic political parties. They have, however, many significant similarities with their supposed mortal enemies, the fascist parties.

---

[37] As we pointed out earlier (pages 50–52), it no longer enjoys this position.
[38] Cf. Andrew Gyorgy, "Satellite Parties in Eastern Europe," in Neumann, *op. cit.*, pp. 284–301.

## Fascist One-Party Systems

### The Fascist Conception of the One-Party State

In its pre-1945 Italian and German versions, fascism, like communism, was a kind of secular religion at war with all other ideologies. It, too, had its sacred texts and prophets, its total explanation of society, and its ethical system. It, too, regarded the party as the priesthood of true believers charged with spreading the doctrine and liquidating infidels. The fact that fascism deified the Nation and the Race while communism glorifies the Class should not obscure the essential similarities of the two movements.

Their organizational similarities are even more striking. In both Mussolini's Italy from 1922 to 1945 and in Hitler's Germany from 1933 to 1945 the fascist parties (the Fascist party in Italy and the National Socialist German Workers', or "Nazi," party in Germany) were made the only legal parties in their respective nations. In each nation the party's structure paralleled the structure of the formal government and became the actual governing body. As in the communist one-party systems, accordingly, the fascist parties acted both as ruling mechanisms and as agencies for generating mass support for the policies formulated by the leader.

### The Structure and Composition of Fascist Parties

In the organization of the fascist parties the *Führerprinzip* (leadership principle) was *formally* more prominent than it has been in communist ideology, although in practice neither Hitler nor Mussolini dominated their parties and nations more completely than Stalin dominated his. Both the Fascist and Nazi parties were organized like armies, with the *Duce* and *Führer* as their absolute overlords and the black-shirted *Fasci di Combattimento*, brown-shirted "storm troopers," and black-uniformed "elite guard" as their "shock troops" (all these being official titles of the various party organizations).

The main channel for entering each fascist party was its youth organizations: the Italian GIL for persons from the ages of six to twenty-one, and the German Hitler Youth for young persons. Both parties conducted periodic purges (including the murderous Nazi "blood purge" of 1934) to eliminate all but the most fanatically devoted members, and both were, like the Communist parties, intended to be elites rather than mass organizations.

The Fascist and Nazi parties, like the Communist parties, declared war, *total* war, on the democratic world. In the *Götterdämmerung* of 1945 the fascist parties and their leaders were crushed in total defeat. The war between the Communist parties and their democratic foes, however, continues in our own time—sometimes "cold" and sometimes "hot," but always, as the Communists see it, a war without a peace treaty or even an armistice.

### One-Party and Modified One-Party Systems in Developing Nations[39]

#### The One-Party Systems

A few developing nations, notably Ethiopia, Libya, and Saudi Arabia, make no pretense of governing by popular selection of public officials, and so they neither need nor have political parties. But most at least go through the motions of popular elections, and many honor their substance as well.[40]

About a quarter of the developing nations have one-party systems fashioned more or less closely after communist or fascist models.[41] In each, only one party is legally permitted, and efforts to form opposition parties are considered acts of treason. The official party is usually the post independence version of the politico-military movement which won the nation's independence from colonialism, and it is usually dominated by one man: for example, Ahmed Ben Bella and the Algerian National Liberation Front, Prince Norodom Sihanouk and the Cambodian People's Social Community, and Kwame Nkrumah and the Ghanaian Convention People's Party. The dictator generally uses the party, as the fascists and communists do, for several purposes: to advance national unity by stamping out all opposition, to mobilize popular enthusiasm behind his program, to give the masses an invigorating if spurious sense of participation in government, and to find out how far he can push his program before popular resistance makes it unworkable.

When outsiders criticize these systems, the dictators and their party lieutenants usually reply with the classical fascist and communist arguments. The official party, they say, represents the nation, and opposition to it is opposition to the nation—i.e., treason. Quarreling parties and contested elections would only divide the people and make the nation easy prey for its colonialist enemies. And, they conclude, even if party competition might conceivably be tolerable in a time of peace, plenty, and security, that time is not yet.

#### The Modified One-Party Systems

In other developing nations[42] party competition is legally tolerated, and parties other than the national-liberation party organize, nominate some

---

[39] Some useful discussions are Gwendolen Carter, ed., *African One-Party States* (Ithaca, N.Y.: Cornell University Press, 1962); Gabriel A. Almond and James S. Coleman, eds., *The Politics of Developing Areas* (Princeton, N.J.: Princeton University Press, 1960), pp. 40–41, 286–294, 479–481; and Fred R. von der Mehden, *Politics of the Developing Nations* (Englewood Cliffs, N.J.: Prentice-Hall, Inc., 1964), Ch. IV.

[40] Von der Mehden estimates that 29 out of the 83 nations he considers have democratic two-party or multiple-party systems: *op. cit.*, pp. 61–64.

[41] Von der Mehden identifies 21 such nations, including Algeria, Cambodia, Ghana, Guinea, Liberia, and Tunisia: *ibid.*, pp. 56–59.

[42] Von der Mehden puts 12 nations in this class: *ibid.*, pp. 59–60.

candidates, contest some elections, and win a few seats in the national legislature. But the national liberation party regularly wins most of the votes and offices and monopolizes governmental power. Hence most conflicts over public policy are fought out, as in the one-party states of the United States, within the dominant party, not in contests between it and the opposition parties.

The two leading examples of such party systems are those of India and Mexico. The Indian National Congress was founded in the 1920's under the leadership of Mahatma Gandhi and Jawaharlal Nehru to bring together all Indians in a movement for independence from British rule. Since independence was achieved in 1947, its successor, the Congress party, has regularly won three quarters of the seats in elections for the national House of the People, and its leaders have always formed the Nation's government. It has been opposed by a variety of small parties espousing communism, socialism, communalism, capitalist enterprise, and so on; but, while these parties together have usually won over half the popular votes, their fragmentation and inability to coalesce has perpetuated the Congress party's dominance.[43]

The Mexican revolution of 1910 was followed by two decades of political confusion and instability, which were finally ended in 1929 with the establishment of a national party uniting all of Mexico's major groups and interests. The party underwent several reorganizations and changes of name, but in 1946 it adopted its present name, the Party of Revolutionary Institutions (PRI), and organization. Since then it has been opposed by the PAN (Conservative), PPS (Marxist), and PARM (dissident PRI) parties, but has won all presidential elections by overwhelming margins and held over 80 percent of the seats in Congress.[44]

The Indian and Mexican systems and their counterparts in Bolivia, Gabon, Malaysia, and elsewhere provide a highly significant alternative to the full competition of the two-party and multiple-party democracies and the repression of all competition and dissent in the dictatorial one-party systems. Whether this "third way" can be a permanent mode of conducting political conflict no one can yet say; but it certainly offers other new and struggling nations a way out of what many see as an impossible choice between too much party competition and none at all. For this reason if for no other, it deserves as much careful study as scholars have lavished upon other kinds of party systems.

---

[43] The Indian system is well described in Myron Weiner, *Party Politics in India* (Princeton, N.J.: Princeton University Press, 1957).

[44] The Mexican system is thoroughly covered in Robert E. Scott, *Mexican Government in Transition* (Urbana: University of Illinois Press, 1959).

## Conclusion

The political party is perhaps the greatest organizing agency of modern government. As we have seen, democracies and dictatorships alike depend on their parties to perform the crucial task of generating the policies, selecting the leaders, and arousing the popular support that enables government to operate in a thickly populated modern nation. The differences in the kinds of party systems that perform this task account for much of the differences between the democracies and the dictatorships. Thus, the editor of an outstanding recent survey of political parties concluded his book with much the same judgment with which Professor Schattschneider began his:

> Hesitation and doubt . . . reflect widespread uncertainties as to the true nature and direction of the revolution in our time. Above all, however, this revolution challenges our ingenuity to articulate workable programs, to organize functioning movements, and to put them to constructive action—weighty responsibilities which rest primarily with the people's great intermediaries: the political parties.[45]

---

[45] Sigmund Neumann, "Toward a Comparative Study of Political Parties," in Neumann, *op. cit.*, p. 421.

# 16

## Pressure Groups
## and Pressure Politics

Suppose you are a Negro living in Mississippi. Suppose that from your early childhood you have learned that there are some things colored folks like you can't do. You can't move out of the colored part of town, you can't get a high-paying job, you can't use the white folks' restaurants, golf courses, swimming pools, or theater seats, and you can't even register to vote. Of course you have to *give* just like the white folks—you have to pay taxes and go into the army when the draft board calls you. But you can't *get* what they do, and if you try to you are soon known as an "uppity nigger" who needs to be "put in his place"—and that is very dangerous indeed.

Then one day you look at your children and it suddenly hits you hard that they are in for the same second-class life you have had. That is just too much to bear, and you decide to do something about it. What can you do? Well, you can ask the white folks to give you a little better job and your children a little better education; but even if they will, that is not enough. You want nothing less than full status as an American citizen with all the rights and opportunities you know that means for the white people.

You know some of your friends feel the same way, so you get together with them and organize a group to fight for your cause. How can the group set about achieving its goals? One thing it might do is to form a political party and try to elect its own candidates to Congress and the state legislature. But you all know this is hopeless. The Democratic and Republican parties so monopolize elections that no minor "single-issue" party, such as

[ 365 ]

a Negro rights party, can hope for much success. Forming such a party, moreover, will probably isolate your group from the main channels of political power. So you may well decide to join a "pressure group" like the National Association for the Advancement of Colored People (NAACP) or the Congress of Racial Equality (CORE).

The point we are making is that "pressure politics" is one—but only one—kind of technique which a political group may use to pursue its objectives. Human beings in any society belong to several different types of groups, some of which play significant roles in the governing process (see Chapter 1). The main types, we repeat, are "categoric groups" (aggregates of individuals sharing one or more common characteristics—e.g., Negroes); "interest groups" (categoric groups whose members are conscious of their common characteristics and who, to some extent, direct their behavior so as to promote the values or "interests" arising from their shared characteristics—e.g., persons opposed to racial discrimination); and "organized interest groups" (interest groups whose members consciously organize and cooperate to promote their common interests). A political party, therefore, is one kind of organized interest group, and a "pressure group," such as the NAACP, is another. A pressure group differs from a political party mainly in that its tactics do not include nominating candidates as its own official representatives.

Pressure groups, in short, are only one of several types of political groups. When we say, as in Chapter 1, that "politics is a struggle for power among interest groups," there is a danger that this statement will be taken to mean that politics is exclusively a struggle for power among *pressure* groups. It is important to bear in mind that we are advancing no such proposition; for, as we have learned in the preceding chapters, "unorganized interest groups" like the consumers, and also political parties play significant roles in the process of government. Thus, pressure politics should be thought of not as the whole of politics but as a particular kind of tactics by which some political interest groups in every modern democratic nation pursue their objectives—a method, moreover, that a great many such groups have found more useful than forming political parties or depending solely upon the good will of other interest groups and public officials.

What, then, are the main types of pressure groups in the modern democracies? How are they organized? How do they try to induce governments to adopt policies they favor and reject policies they oppose? What factors affect the success obtained by various groups? What impact have pressure groups upon the formation of public policy? Are they beneficial or injurious to democratic government? The task of the present chapter is to suggest some answers to these questions.

## Leading Types of Pressure Groups

Although every modern democratic nation has a number of pressure groups, those in the United States have received by far the most attention from political scientists. Most of our discussion in this chapter, accordingly, will deal with American experience, although we shall introduce examples from other democracies wherever the literature makes it possible.[1] American politics contains a number of local pressure groups and national "single-issue" or "ad hoc" pressure groups, such as the National Council against Conscription, but we shall confine our description to the main types of groups commonly found in national politics and organized on a relatively permanent basis. Merely to list, let alone describe, all such groups in any one democracy would fill a much bulkier volume than this, and so we shall confine ourselves to a brief description of the major types and give a few of the more prominent examples of each.

### Business

Most modern democracies have two main types of business pressure groups. The first includes those which purport to speak for the interests of business-as-a-whole rather than for particular industries. In general such groups work for such policies as keeping government expenditures and taxation as low as possible, limiting government regulation of business, restraining trade unions, and subsidizing business and protecting it from the rigors of unrestrained competition. An outstanding American example is the National Association of Manufacturers (NAM), which, in recent years, has spent hundreds of thousands of dollars annually in its fight for measures like the Taft-Hartley Act and against measures like price control. Another leading American example is the Chamber of Commerce of the United States. The British counterparts of these groups are the Federation of British Industries, the National Union of Manufacturers, and the Association

---

[1] There is now a vast literature on pressure groups in many nations. The most general comparative study dealing with the advanced nations is Henry W. Ehrmann, ed., *Interest Groups on Four Continents* (Pittsburgh: University of Pittsburgh Press, 1958). Comparative descriptions of pressure groups in various developing nations are in Gabriel A. Almond and James S. Coleman, eds., *The Politics of the Developing Areas* (Princeton, N.J.: Princeton University Press, 1960). Two works on the United States are Harmon Zeigler, *Interest Groups in American Society* (Englewood Cliffs, N.J.: Prentice-Hall, Inc., 1964); and Donald C. Blaisdell, *American Democracy under Pressure* (New York: Ronald Press Company, 1957). Two works on Great Britain are Samuel E. Finer, *Anonymous Empire* (London: Pall Mall Press, 1958); and Allen Potter, *Organized Groups in British National Politics* (London: Faber & Faber, Ltd., 1961). A comparable work on France is Jean Meynaud, *Les Groups de Pression en France* (Paris: Armand Colin, 1959).

of British Chambers of Commerce. The French versions are the *Confédération Nationale du Patronat Français* and the *Petites et Moyennes Enterprises*.

The second general type of business pressure groups includes those which speak for particular industries and which are sometimes in conflict with each other as well as with labor and consumers. American examples of such groups are the American Petroleum Institute, which has so successfully defended the oil producers' bonanza of the "depletion allowance" in taxation; and the Association of American Railroads, which battled the St. Lawrence waterway project for so long and which presently urges "more equitable" taxation of trucks and buses. British examples include the British Iron and Steel Federation, the Newspaper Proprietors' Association, and the Road Haulage Association. One of the most powerful anywhere is the French *Confédération Générale des Viniculteurs,* the wine and alcohol distillers' group whose successful fight against former Premier Mendés-France's efforts to limit the consumption of alcohol was considered to be one of the main causes of his fall from power in 1955.

Even in nations far more "socialistic" than the United States business pressure groups are large and powerful.

### *Labor*

Conflict between employers and employees over such matters as wages, hours, working conditions, and control of industrial policy making has been prominent in every nation with a capitalist economy and a democratic government. Only in the fascist and communist dictatorships has there been "labor peace." The basic form of labor organization in this conflict, of course, has been the trade union. Thus, every modern democracy has one or more national federations of trade unions: the American Federation of Labor–Congress of Industrial Organizations (AFL–CIO) in the United States, the Trades Union Congress in Britain, and in France the *Confédération Générale du Travail* (CGT), the *Confédération Française des Travailleurs Chrétiens* (CFTC), and the *Force Ouvrière.*

The American labor movement, much to the despair and disgust of many socialist ideologists, has emphasized pressure politics over labor party activity far more than have its counterparts in most of the other democracies. Toward the end of the nineteenth century the Knights of Labor, the first national union, participated in the formation of the People's party (the "Populists"). The demise of the party after the election of 1896, however, inclined most labor leaders to go along with the advice of Samuel Gompers, the first president of the American Federation of Labor, that workers should avoid identification with any political party and should "reward your friends and punish your enemies" in both major parties. Hence the present-day AFL–CIO, while contributing much money and many votes to the Democratic party, has remained quite separate from it and completely rejects any notion of founding a labor party on British or European models.

The European tradition has been quite different. In most nations the labor movement and the socialist movement have been closely intertwined from the start, and most European trade unions are committed to the idea of a socialist labor party of some variety as the best way of advancing the common cause. The unions also to some degree act as independent pressure groups, but they have chosen to place their main emphasis on party activity. Thus, as we saw in Chapter 15, the British Trades Union Congress (TUC) is closely associated with the Labour party, and most major unions are directly affiliated with the party at the national and local levels. The bulk of the party's funds, workers, and votes are contributed by the unions, and a good many union-sponsored M.P.'s man the parliamentary party.[2]

French labor organizations are even more closely associated with political parties. The CGT, for example, is completely dominated by the Communist party, and is often referred to as the party's "industrial wing." The CFTC is almost as closely associated with the *Mouvement Républicain Populaire* party, and the *Force Ouvrière* with the Socialist party.

In short, "bread-and-butter unionism" (i.e., a policy of seeking only such immediate and practical goals as higher wages, shorter hours, and union security) continues to be the basic policy of the American labor movement, while European workers pursue the more ambitious goals of socialism and labor control of the economy. The differing emphases of American and European unions on pressure politics and labor party activity, in turn, are direct consequences of their differing objectives.

### Agricultural

In many modern democracies farmers, like businessmen, have established two main types of pressure groups. One type claims to speak for agriculture as a whole and presses for such policies as providing governmentally guaranteed floors under farm prices, protecting domestic farmers against competition from foreign crops, and government subsidization of such services as farm electrification, farm credit, and soil conservation. The leading American pressure group of this type and one of the most powerful of all our national pressure groups is the American Farm Bureau Federation. Its smaller but far from impotent rival is the National Farmers' Union. The leading British farmers' group is also called the National

---

[2] The authoritative account is Martin Harrison, *Trade Unions and the Labour Party since 1945* (London: George Allen & Unwin, Ltd., 1960).

Farmers' Union, and the French version is named the *Confédération Générale de l'Agriculture.*

In the United States there are also a number of special "commodity" pressure groups. The National Cooperative Milk Producers' Federation and the American Soy Bean Association are particularly well known because of their struggle over the passage and repeal of the special federal tax on oleomargarine, in which the protax "big butter-and-egg men" finally lost out to the antitax "oleo interests." Also prominent is the National Wool Growers' Association, which recently won; a unique and highly advantageous form of government protection for the incomes of wool producers.

The overrepresentation of rural areas, which is to some extent characteristic of the legislature in every democracy, contributes heavily to the power of farmer pressure groups. Thus, in all democratic nations they are more successful than one would expect from looking only at the proportion of farmers to the rest of the population or at the proportion of their contribution to the national income.

### *Professional*

In every modern democracy such leading professionals as doctors, lawyers, architects, and teachers have organized pressure groups to defend and promote their economic and other interests. The American Medical Association, for example, has secured the passage of laws regulating medical education and the use of the title "doctor of medicine" and restricting the power to prescribe certain drugs to persons who possess this title. In recent years it has doggedly fought efforts to establish "socialized medicine" (i.e., national compulsory hospitalization and medical-care insurance). The British Medical Association was unsuccessful in its campaign to block the Labour Government's program of socialized medicine (in the strict sense of medical care directly subsidized and administered by the government) but has had a great deal of influence on the program's administration. The American Institute of Architects has obtained laws in most states restricting the title of "architect" to persons who have passed examinations over the content and grading of which the institute exercises considerable influence. The American Bar Association and its affiliated state bar associations exert a similar influence over the examinations by which the states admit persons to the practice of law, and in a number of states the bar associations also have a great deal to say about the selection of judges. The American Federation of Teachers (a union affiliated with the AFL-CIO) and the American Association of University Professors press for better pay for teachers and oppose governmental interference with academic freedom. Even the American Political Science Association, through its executive director in Washington, conducted an arduous but ultimately successful campaign to have political science included as one of the social sciences eligible for government research and fellowship support through the National Science Foundation.

### Veterans

In the United States, as Professor Key drily observed, "every war has been followed by the establishment of a society of veterans to bring pressure for the creation of conduits from the Federal Treasury to the pockets of the veterans."[3] One of the earliest of all American pressure groups was the Society of the Cincinnati, an organization of former officers of Washington's army founded in 1783 to make sure that revolutionary veterans received their due from the newly independent government. For many decades after the Civil War the Grand Army of the Republic, an organization of Union veterans, had great success in its efforts to induce the national government to give generous pensions to old soldiers and was one of the most powerful pressure groups of its time. The most successful veterans' group of our own time is the American Legion, founded after World War I. The Legion, with over 3 million members, has not only pressed, with considerable success, for pensions and bonuses for veterans of both world wars but has also secured the adoption of the "veterans' preference" rule whereby veterans are given special consideration over nonveterans in obtaining federal civil service jobs. Smaller and less powerful than the Legion but nevertheless of some influence are such organizations as the Veterans of Foreign Wars, the American Veterans of World War II ("Amvets"), and the American Veterans Committee. Veterans' pressure politics in Great Britain are carried on by the British Legion, and in Australia by the Returned Soldiers' League.

### Religious

Many religious denominations are deeply concerned with such political issues as religious instruction in public schools, the regulation of child labor, the dissemination of information about birth control, and the censorship of books, newspapers, magazines, and motion pictures. In order to make their positions more effective such religious pressure groups have been organized in the United States as the Legion of Decency, the National Catholic Welfare Conference, the Council for Social Action of the Congregational Churches, the Federal Council of Churches of Christ in America, the American Bible Society, and the Woman's National Sabbath Alliance.

---

[3] V. O. Key, Jr., *Politics, Parties, & Pressure Groups* (5th ed.; New York: Thomas Y. Crowell Company, 1964), p. 106.

### Ethnic

A number of minority ethnic groups, particularly in the United States, have established pressure groups to push governmental policies protecting them against hostile attacks and establishing full economic, social, and political equality with all other ethnic groups. Outstanding examples are the NAACP, CORE, and the Southern Christian Leadership Conference, whose objectives and policies we described in Chapter 9. The White Citizens' Councils and the Society for the Preservation of the White Race are also examples, though on the opposite side of the fight.

### Reform

Our final category includes a number of groups, each of which is organized by persons of different economic, occupational, religious, and ethnic affiliations to urge the adoption of various governmental reforms. The prototype of such groups, and one of the most successful pressure groups in American history, was the Anti-Saloon League. Founded in 1893, this organization was far more influential than its parallel group, the Prohibition party, in securing the adoption of the Eighteenth Amendment and the Volstead Act outlawing the manufacture and sale of intoxicating beverages, and for three decades exerted great power over many national congressmen and state legislators.[4] Present-day examples of such groups in the United States are the American Civil Liberties Union, which seeks to publicize and prevent all encroachments upon the Constitutional freedoms of individuals and groups; the League of Women Voters, which has urged a number of governmental reforms in the interests of efficiency and democracy; and the National Municipal League, which has advocated such reforms as the short ballot, proportional representation, and the city-manager form of municipal government. In Great Britain the Fabian Society has enlisted a number of prominent intellectuals in drives not only for socialism but also for a number of more specific reforms, such as reapportionment of the House of Commons and reduction of the power of the House of Lords. Also influential in British politics have been the Society for the Prevention of Cruelty to Animals and the Society for the Prevention of Cruelty to Children.

The foregoing list, needless to say, includes the names and policies of only a tiny fraction of the leading national pressure groups in the modern democracies, but it should serve to indicate the great number and variety of such groups. Our main concern, however, is not with the many differ-

---

[4] An early and classic study of pressure politics in America is Peter Odegard, *Pressure Politics: The Story of the Anti-Saloon League* (New York: Columbia University Press, 1928).

ences among pressure groups but rather with their common characteristics and the role they play in modern democratic politics. We now turn, accordingly, to a consideration of the various ways in which such groups apply "pressure" to the policy-making agencies of their respective nations.

## The Weapons of Pressure Politics[5]

### *Organization*

"Let's get organized!" This cry is usually heard in any group of persons who have decided to pursue some common goal collectively. Most of us realize that a basic weapon in any such group's armory is that of organization—that is, deciding what tasks are to be done, assigning them to particular members, selecting leaders and allocating decision-making power, and so on. An organized group has one great advantage over an unorganized group: It has a far better chance of mobilizing all its resources and placing their whole weight behind the drive for its objectives, and it thereby minimizes the wasted effort and the working at cross-purposes that often handicap unorganized groups.

Pressure groups are organized in several different ways. The National Association of Manufacturers and the American Institute of Architects, for example, are "unitary" in that their decision-making power is, both formally and actually, centralized in their national officers and boards of directors, and one becomes a member directly of the national body. The AFL–CIO and the American Farm Bureau Federation (AFBF), on the other hand, are "federal" in that their powers and functions are formally divided between their state and local constituent groups and their national officers and directors, and one's membership in the national body is derived from his membership in a constituent group. The "federal" organizations are often less cohesive than the "unitary," and both the AFL–CIO and the AFBF sometimes encounter "rebellions" from one or another of their constituent bodies.

Most pressure groups are formally organized along democratic lines, with annual national conventions of representatives from the constituent groups empowered to set policy by majority vote. In practice, however,

---

[5] The classic formulation of the general group structure of politics, and one of the most influential works of twentieth-century political science, is Arthur F. Bentley, *The Process of Government* (Chicago: University of Chicago Press, 1908), subsequently reprinted in 1935 by the Principia Press of Evanston, Illinois. A major reformulation of Bentley's position with special emphasis on the organization and operations of pressure groups in the United States is David B. Truman, *The Governmental Process* (New York: Alfred A. Knopf, Inc., 1951). Another useful theoretical study of groups in politics illustrated by a case study is Earl Latham, *The Group Basis of Politics* (Ithaca, N.Y.: Cornell University Press, 1952). Zeigler, *op. cit.*, Blaisdell, *op. cit.*, and Key, *op. cit.*, also have detailed discussions of pressure-group tactics.

many such groups are largely run by small national bureaucracies. The American Medical Association, for example, locates its formal decision-making power in a House of Delegates, most of whose members are elected for two-year terms by the state medical associations. The House of Delegates appoints a board of trustees to govern between its annual sessions, and in practice this board controls most of the national association's decision making and sets most of its policies.[6] So it is with many other formally "democratic" pressure groups.

### Lobbying[7]

Many legislative chambers have adjoining "lobbies" in which legislators and their guests can informally and unofficially meet and talk. From this practice has emerged the term "lobbying," which refers to direct efforts by representatives of pressure groups to persuade public officials to act as the groups wish them to act. Legislators are still the main targets of lobbying, but executives, administrators, and even judges are also regularly and frequently approached.

As Truman points out, the first prerequisite for successful lobbying is *access*—the ability to get a hearing at one or more of the government's key decision-making points. Any group which consistently fails to get a serious hearing at any such point can hardly expect much success. The access of any particular group depends upon several factors, such as its general prestige and social position, and the reputation and skill of its lobbyists at dealing with public officials. Thus, for example, a Roman Catholic cardinal or archbishop is more likely to have access to committees of the Massachusetts legislature than is a representative of the Jehovah's Witnesses, and a lobbyist whom the legislators have long known as a reasonable, practical, well-informed, and friendly person is more likely to get a serious hearing than one with a reputation of being cantankerous or ignorant or merely a "do-gooder."[8]

Having gained access to one or more decision-making points, the lobbyist can employ a variety of techniques of persuasion. He can make a formal presentation marshaling facts, figures, and arguments so as to present his group's position in the most favorable light. He can suggest that if the legislator or executive turns him down dire consequences will follow at the next election, and he can reinforce this threat by stimulating

---

[6] Cf. Oliver Garceau, *The Political Life of the American Medical Association* (Cambridge, Mass.: Harvard University Press, 1941).

[7] The most comprehensive analysis of lobbying at the national level is Lester W. Milbrath, *The Washington Lobbyists* (Chicago: Rand McNally & Company, 1963).

[8] Cf. Truman, *op. cit.*, pp. 264–270.

a flood of telegrams, postcards, and letters from the official's constituents. He can offer to trade his group's support for some pet project of the legislator or executive in return for the latter's support of his group's proposal. This practice is a variety of "logrolling," which is conducted among lobbyists as well as among lobbyists and public officials. The lobbyist can even offer a bribe, either directly in the form of cash, mink coats, or deep freezers, or indirectly in the form of the promise of a well-paid private job for the public official after he leaves office. The bribe method, however, has become so generally disapproved and therefore so dangerous that it is used far less frequently today than it was a century ago.

Lobbying is still the main weapon of most pressure groups, but the changing nature of society and government in the modern democracies has forced many such groups to place increasing emphasis on other weapons as well.

### Mass Propaganda

In the nineteenth century most pressure groups concentrated on lobbying and paid little or no attention to mass public opinion. Commodore Vanderbilt's famous statement "The public be damned!" whether or not he actually made it, expressed the view widely held in his time that since the public's attitude toward the objectives of pressure groups did not seriously affect their chances of success, it was a matter of little importance. But in our own time the opinions of the general public—whether they be "pro," "con," or "don't care"—have a direct and powerful influence upon the success of any political group.

Most modern pressure groups are well aware of this fact. Accordingly, they cultivate mass public opinion by a wide variety of "public relations" operations and spend many hundreds of thousands of dollars each year in their efforts to create "favorable climates of public opinion" for their objectives. We are all familiar, for example, with the so-called "institutional advertising" in magazines and newspapers of a group like the Association of American Railroads, whose cartoons and "ads" are intended to sell us not railroad tickets but the idea that governmental tax policies unfairly discriminate against railroads in favor of trucks and buses. Anyone who has visited a doctor's office since the late 1940's has noticed that the piles of magazines on the reception room tables have been joined by stacks of pamphlets and cartoons opposing "socialized medicine." Frequently both unions and employer groups use full-page newspaper advertisements to plead their respective causes in strikes.

In short, the old-fashioned "lobbyist" and "wire-puller" has been joined, and in some pressure groups superseded, by the modern "public relations counsel."

## *Working inside Political Parties*

Lobbying, needless to say, is likely to be far more successful with favorably predisposed public officials than with those who are indifferent or hostile. Since political parties nominate most candidates for public office and thereby largely determine what kinds of persons holding what views shall occupy the formal positions of governmental power, no major pressure group can afford to ignore the internal operations of the parties. In Great Britain and the European democracies, as we have seen, most pressure groups are closely associated with particular parties and make relatively little effort to influence the policies and candidates of opposing parties. In the United States, however, the relatively amorphous and protean character of the major parties tends to keep the major pressure groups from openly and completely identifying themselves with either party. Rather, they try to secure the nomination of sympathetic candidates and the adoption of favorable planks in the platforms of *both* parties. Any particular group may work harder in one party than the other (e.g., the NAM in the Republican party and the AFL–CIO in the Democratic), but no group is as completely identified with either party as, say, most British trade unions are with the Labour party.

The AFL–CIO, for just one example, sends spokesmen before the platform committees of both parties' national conventions. It encourages its rank-and-file members not only to vote for prolabor candidates in the primaries of both parties but also to become precinct committeemen, delegates to party conventions, and even candidates for public office. Its representatives are particularly influential in the platform-writing and candidate-selecting activities of the national Democratic conventions. Neither party, indeed, is likely to nominate a presidential candidate regarded as totally unacceptable by the AFL–CIO, or, for that matter, by the AFBF, the NAACP, or any other pressure group that is generally believed to have the power to swing large blocs of voters from one party to the other.

## *Electioneering*

Most American pressure groups pay homage to the idea of "keeping out of politics," but this means only avoiding any open and complete identification with any particular political party and eschewing third-party activity. It certainly does not mean having nothing to do with electioneering. Some pressure groups work hard to secure the election of sympathetic candidates over hostile ones. They make endorsements, contribute both money and workers to the favored candidates' campaigns, propagandize their own members and the general public, help turn out the voters on Election Day, and generally perform all the election-contesting tasks of political parties.

An outstanding example of such activity is "COPE," the AFL–CIO's Committee on Political Education, which in recent years has been one of the largest and most effective campaigning organizations in the nation.

No pressure group can "deliver" anything like the entire vote of its membership to any particular candidate or party. One of the main reasons for this is the fact that in any area in which a particular group has a large number of members both parties are careful not to nominate candidates clearly and violently hostile to the group's interests. In the 1952 and 1956 elections, for example, COPE and its predecessors "delivered" only slightly over half of the union member vote to the Democratic candidate. But in 1964, when COPE campaigned against Republican Barry Goldwater, who was widely believed to favor a national "right-to-work" law and require the "open shop" in all labor contracts, over three quarters of the union member vote went to the Democrats.

### Strikes

The term "strike" usually refers to a collective work stoppage by a group of industrial workers, but, as we shall see, it can also refer to work stoppages by other elements of the community for political purposes. In the United States most labor strikes are conducted for nonpolitical reasons: that is, they are intended to make employers grant such nonpolitical demands of workers as labor contracts providing higher wages, shorter hours, better working conditions, union security, and so on. In many European democracies, on the other hand, labor strikes are sometimes used for political purposes—that is, to force the government to adopt or reject certain policies, or even to overthrow the existing form of government. In France, for example, the Communist-dominated CGT (see above) has called a number of strikes since 1945 for the avowed purpose of preventing the French government from participating in such anticommunist measures as the Marshall Plan, the European Defense Community, and the North Atlantic Treaty Organization. The "syndicalist" theorist Georges Sorel advocated the "general strike" (a complete work stoppage by all workers) as the best means for overthrowing capitalism and establishing his brand of socialism, and in some European and Latin American nations general strikes have been used to drive certain public officials and sometimes whole governments out of power.

A less familiar but equally important form of strike are the instances in which French and Italian farmers have destroyed their produce in an effort to compel their governments to treat farmers more favorably. Perhaps the most amusing instance of an unusual strike was that conducted by the French customs inspectors in 1947. In an effort to make the government raise their wages, these employees put on a two-hour "zeal strike": they

enforced to the letter *every* customs law and regulation and thereby unleashed a storm of protests by tourists that did much to induce the ministry
to grant the wage demands. Apparently work "speed-ups" can sometimes
be as effective as work stoppages![9]

### Violence

All pressure groups, as we observed in Chapter 2, can muster at least
some physical force—the fists of their members, çlubs, rocks, razors, and
even firearms—to accomplish their ends. Intergroup political conflict in
the democracies is normally conducted with little or no violence, but large-
scale outbreaks are not unknown. In the United States, for example,
employers have on occasion used "goon squads" of strikebreakers to break
up picket lines with clubs, tear gas, and even rifles; and labor unions have
sometimes responded with methods as extreme as assassination and bomb
throwing. Race riots occasionally flare up, and sometimes public officials
are beaten up, kidnapped, and even murdered. Even in the United States
we have had a major civil war.

Violence plays an even more prominent role in the politics of some
other nations. In France, for example, street riots and small-scale civil wars
appear to be endemic, and in many Latin American nations assassinations,
revolutions, and *coups d'état* (blows of state) are common methods for
trying to bring about social and political change. Most political scientists
believe that the frequency and degree of domestic violence is a significant
index of a nation's political health, but no nation conducts its political
conflict exclusively by peaceful and nonviolent means.

### Nonviolent Civil Disobedience

In his leadership of the movement for Indian independence from
British rule, Mahatma Gandhi developed a technique for political action
which has had a major impact on the Western world. He called it *satyagraha*, and its Western version is generally called "nonviolent civil disobedience."[10] Its leading American theorist and practitioner is the Rever-
end Martin Luther King., Jr., and it has provided the dominant philosophy
and the main line of tactics for much of the American Negro rights
movement.

---

[9] New York *Times*, May 9, 1947, p. 10.

[10] The theory and practice of *satyagraha* are described in Joan V. Bondurant, *Conquest of Violence: The Gandhian Philosophy of Conflict* (Princeton, N.J.: Princeton
University Press, 1958). A famous early American individualist version of the same doctrine is Henry David Thoreau's *Of Civil Disobedience* (1849), in which he explained
why he refused to pay taxes to support the Mexican War, which he regarded as an
outrage on justice.

Nonviolent Civil Disobedience Has Been a Major Tactic in the Negroes' Drive for Equal Rights: James Farmer, CORE's National Director, Was Carried by Police from Sit-in at New York World's Fair on Opening Day. (Wide World Photos, Inc.)

As Gandhi and Dr. King have both practiced and preached it, civil disobedience requires that pressure groups first explore all the possibilities of negotiation and arbitration with their opponents and the government. When, and only when, these have failed, they should issue an ultimatum explaining exactly what they are going to do and why. Then they employ various tactics to make things inconvenient for their opponents without using violence or doing them bodily harm and to commit their own members to the cause more deeply by making sacrifices for it. These tactics include economic boycotts, noncooperation with governmental authorities in such ways as refusing to pay taxes or send children to schol, and peaceful disobedience of whatever laws—for example, traffic regulations or prohibitions against parades and picketing—they feel appropriate. A tactic which has become familiar to newsreel viewers in several nations is what Gandhi called *dharna*—sitting down in streets, corridors of public buildings, airport runways, and other channels of movement. When public authorities enforce the laws with the usual methods of arrest and imprisonment, the members of the group must offer no resistance, but, in Dr. King's words, "testify with their bodies" to the justice of their cause. The ultimate object is not only to win support from neutral outsiders, but eventually to convert the opponents themselves.

The tactics of civil disobedience have scored many impressive victories. They contributed much to the winning of Indian independence. And there is no doubt that the contrast between the Negroes' peaceful demonstrations for their rights and the often brutal measures of suppression taken by southern white sheriffs and troopers—Birmingham and Selma, Alabama, are but two examples—touched the hearts of a great many theretofore apathetic northern whites and won their wholehearted support for the Negroes' cause.

Nonviolent civil disobedience, then, has joined the wide variety of weapons any pressure group can use in its struggle to make public officials pursue the policies it favors and reject the policies it opposes. But in every nation some groups are far more successful than others in getting what they want. What factors, then, determine "who gets what, when, and how"?

## Factors Affecting the Success of Pressure Groups

### Size

A pressure group's sheer size is obviously one factor affecting its ability to get what it wants. Other things being equal (which, as we shall see, they never are), the groups with many members are likely to be more successful than groups with few members, simply because the former represent many votes and the latter few votes. From this standpoint, therefore, the AFL–CIO is more likely than the American Association of University Professors to force the wages of its members upward, the American Legion is more likely than the American Veterans Committee to get its particular veterans' program adopted, and the AFBF's campaign for flexible farm price supports is more likely to succeed than the National Farmers' Union's drive for fixed price supports.

Political success, however, by no means invariably comes to the larger groups. In politics as in boxing, basketball, and football it is the *good* big man, not any big man, who always wins over the good little man. Thus, the remaining factors in our list all bear upon what makes a pressure group "good."

### Social Status

One of the major contests in post-1945 American politics has been the clash over national compulsory health insurance. The fight against such legislation has been conducted mainly by the American Medical Association, and the campaign for it mainly by the AFL–CIO. At first glance this would seem to be a highly unequal contest: the AMA has only about 180,000 members and the AFL–CIO over 15 million. Yet, as so often happens in democratic politics, the Davids have frequently defeated the Goliaths. How can this be?

Part of the explanation surely lies in the great social prestige of the medical profession and its spokesmen in the AMA. Most Americans feel that the doctor is not only a man of great learning, high skill, and eminent respectability but also a person selflessly dedicated to alleviation of human suffering. Many Americans, by contrast, regard the trade unionist as a rather uncouth, lazy, and ordinary person dedicated only to getting as much money as possible for as little work as possible. Whether or not either attitude is justified by the facts is irrelevant; the point is that for many Americans who are themselves neither doctors nor union members the social prestige of doctors and the AMA is notably higher than that of unionists and the AFL–CIO. Hence, the doctors' "access" is at least as good as that of the unions'; moreover, man for man, they command far more deference than the unions from society in general and thus find it easier than the unions to acquire political allies and support. The same factor does much to explain the success of such other relatively small pressure groups as the American Institute of Architects, the Daughters of the American Revolution, the American Humane Society, and the Izaak Walton League of America.

### Cohesion

One of the most common events in democratic politics is the defeat of a large but internally divided or apathetic pressure group by a small but cohesive and energetic group. In politics as in war ten who work closely together are more powerful than a hundred who cooperate loosely or not

## "I Think He Should Have A Choice of Doctors"

*Figure 31.* Internal Division in Pressure Group Weakens Its Effectiveness.

at all. Recognizing the value of group cohesion, however, is far easier than achieving it. The membership of every pressure group, as we learned in Chapter 1, "overlaps" with that of several other groups. Each of its members, that is to say, belongs to several other groups, and some of the latter have objectives and make demands that are in conflict with those of the group in question. Accordingly, one factor that powerfully affects the group's cohesion is the "heterogeneity" of its members—that is, the sheer number and variety of the other groups to which they belong. Another is the extent to which these other groups make demands that conflict with those of the group in question. Still another is the relative importance which each person attaches to his membership in this group or that. And yet another is how much danger each group's members consider it to be in at the moment.

Take, for example, the situation of the AFL–CIO in the 1956 presidential election. The union strongly urged the election of Adlai Stevenson as the more liberal and prounion of the two candidates, and its political arm COPE spent a great deal of money and effort toward that end. Yet a number of AFL–CIO members thought of themselves as Republicans; others believed Eisenhower was better able than Stevenson to prevent the Middle Eastern and Hungarian crises from involving the nation in World War III; and still others regarded the Republicans as more likely than the Democrats to lower taxes. Each of these unionists had to decide whether an Eisenhower victory would place the union movement in so great a danger as to outweigh its advantages for maintaining peace and lowering taxes. Judging by the election results, a great many decided these questions in favor of Eisenhower rather than as the AFL–CIO leaders had recommended. If the union had achieved perfect or nearly perfect cohesion among its 15 million members, it might well have elected Stevenson; but, as so often happens with so many pressure groups, the conflicting loyalties and attitudes of many of its members greatly reduced its effectiveness in this situation.

### Leadership

A pressure group's effectiveness, like an army's, also depends to some extent upon the quality of its leadership. A large and well-equipped army led by a John Pope or an Ambrose Burnside may well be routed by a smaller and poorly equipped army led by a Robert E. Lee; but when a U. S. Grant takes command of the larger army, victory for it becomes merely a matter of time. So it is in politics.

The leader of any political group must perform both internal and external functions for his group. Internally, he must make suggestions about such matters as who shall do which jobs and who shall make which decisions; he must appeal to the membership to support the group's policies and maintain its cohesion; he must oversee the punishment or expulsion of rebellious individuals or factions; and he must encourage the emergence and preside over the training of lower-echelon leaders and his own successor. Externally, he must initiate the group's strategy and tactics in its struggle with the opposition; and he must "represent" the group in its dealings with other groups and the general public, not only in the sense of being its spokesman but also in the sense of being the kind of person who symbolizes to outsiders the human qualities of the group. If he is widely regarded as a loud-mouthed, ignorant, untrustworthy person, his group will suffer accordingly; but if most outsiders think of him as a reasonable, well-informed, and honest man-of-his-word, his group will acquire allies and friends much more readily.

What kind of person makes a good political leader? Political scientists and psychologists have long pondered this question. For many years the "personality-trait" explanation was popular, according to which the successful leader is a man who possesses certain personal qualities (an attractive appearance, intelligence, vigor, dedication, and so on) that would make him a leader in any kind of group.[11] Recent social science, however, favors a more "situational" explanation, according to which leadership is not a thing possessed by certain favored individuals but a *relationship* among leaders and followers that depends upon the nature of the group, its objectives, and the sociopolitical environment within which it operates. Thus, men who successfully lead baseball teams or trade unions might well be unable to lead religious orders or scientific associations.[12] Modern social science, accordingly, cannot provide a full explanation of what makes a good leader that applies to all groups in all situations. There is no doubt, however, that skill of leadership is one of the prime factors affecting the success of any pressure group.

### The Politico-governmental Environment

As the foregoing discussion implies, the organization, tactics, and chances of success of any pressure group are powerfully affected by the politico-governmental system in which it operates; and the variations in these systems among the democracies do much to account for the differences in the structure and impact of their pressure politics.

The politico-governmental system of the United States, for example, is more decentralized than those of most of the other modern democracies. Not only are the political parties decentralized and relatively uncohesive (see Chapter 15), but the formal government is decentralized as well:

---

[11] For a summary of this view of leadership, see Ralph M. Stodgill, "Personal Factors Associated with Leadership: A Survey of the Literature," *Journal of Social Psychology*, XXV (1948), 35–71.

[12] For a fuller explanation of this point of view, see Alvin W. Gouldner, ed., *Studies in Leadership* (New York: Harper & Row, Publishers, 1950); and Lester G. Seligman, "The Study of Political Leadership," *American Political Science Review*, XLIV (December, 1950), 904–915.

power is divided between the national and state governments, and power within the national government is widely dispersed among such agencies as the President, his cabinet members, administrative officials, committees and leaders in each house of Congress, the various federal courts, and so on. Hence, the American system provides a great many points of access, and different groups make their most effective bids at different points of the system. Labor groups, for instance, have generally had more success in winning support from the President than from Congress. Veterans' groups, on the other hand, have done better in Congress than with the President. Before 1964, filibusters and threats of filibusters in the Senate (see Chapter 17) blocked all attempts to get antisegregation laws through Congress, but the antisegregation forces (see Chapter 9) won a number of signal victories in the Supreme Court's decisions outlawing racial discrimination in voting, housing, and education. Thus, the very multiplicity of points of access created by our decentralized politico-governmental system has done much to determine the special nature of American pressure politics.[13]

For many years political commentators talked as though pressure groups were a unique and somewhat reprehensible feature of the American system and averred that no such things existed, for example, in Great Britain. Recent scholarship has made it clear, however, that "even if compared with American examples, pressure groups in Britain are numerous, massive, well-organized, and highly effective" and that it may well be that "at the present time pressure groups are more powerful in Britain than in the United States."[14] The main differences between American and British pressure politics stem from the greater centralization of the British parties and governmental structure. British parties are highly centralized, disciplined, and cohesive, and a pressure group has far less chance than in the United States to win the support of some of a party's legislative members over the objections of its leaders. Hence British pressure groups, as we noted above, work more closely with the party leaders and are more closely associated with particular parties than are their American counterparts. The British governmental structure concentrates most decision-making power in the national government rather than in the county or borough governments; and within the national government power is concentrated mainly in the cabinet and a few key ministries and administrative bodies. There are, accordingly, fewer points of access in Britain than in the United States, and once a pressure group in Britain has gotten its way at one of these points, it is far less likely than in the United States to lose out at some other point. Beer puts it thus:

---

[13] Cf. Truman, *op. cit.*, pp. 322–327, 507–508.
[14] Samuel H. Beer, "Pressure Groups and Parties in Britain," *American Political Science Review*, L (March, 1956), 1, 3.

Not only do interest groups enjoy a greater degree of concentration, but the government with which they deal also is more highly centralized than ours: greater power to exert pressure is linked up with greater power to act. Whether that power to act will be used or not will depend on various factors. . . . Usually—this is the point to press— if you can bring over the Minister and the Chancellor of the Exchequer you have not much else to worry about. Compare the position of the American pressure group which, if it wants positive action, must win its battle at many different points—committees in both houses, the presidency, the secretary, the bureau chief. It is no wonder that our pressure politics is so much noisier and less tidy than Britain's.[15]

The studies of pressure groups in other democracies suggest that in general they resemble British more than American practices; but the main thing they show is that pressure groups play significant roles in the politics and government of all modern democracies.

## The Role of Pressure Groups in Democratic Government

### *Their Legal Position*

Freedom of organization and political action is generally considered to be an essential principle of democratic government. Hence, the Constitutions of most modern democracies guarantee the right of their citizens to organize associations for the purpose of advancing by peaceful and honest means whatever ideals and interests their members hold dear. The Constitution of the United States guarantees "the right of the people peaceably to assemble, and to petition the Government for a redress of grievances" (First Amendment); the Constitution of the West German Republic declares that "all Germans have the right to form associations and societies" except those "the objects or activities of which conflict with the criminal laws or which are directed against the constitutional order or the concept of international understanding" (Article 9); and the French Constitution of 1946 declared that "everyone may defend his rights and interests by trade-union action and may join the union of his choice" (Preamble). Most democracies, indeed, have provided some form of direct "functional" representation of pressure groups in the formal governmental structure by such devices as economic councils, interest-group membership on administrative advisory boards and public corporations, and so on (see Chapter 12).

This does not mean, of course, that in every democracy any pressure

---

[15] *Ibid.*, p. 9.

*Figure 32.* Pressure Groups Influence Foreign as well as Domestic Policy. (Drawing by Herblock, from *The Herblock Book,* Boston: Beacon Press, 1952.)

group is legally free to pursue any objective by any means it sees fit. Most democracies prohibit such tactics as bribery, violence, libel, slander, and intimidation, and prosecute in criminal actions any pressure-group representative who employs such tactics. Most democracies, as we shall see in Chapter 19, deny associations of public employees the right to strike.

The United States has gone further than most democracies in its efforts to regulate the lobbying activities of pressure groups. The Federal Regulation of Lobbying Act (1946), for instance, requires every individual, association, and corporation seeking to influence legislation to register and file quarterly reports with designated officials of the House and Senate. These reports must contain such information as the specific legislative bills in which the lobbyist is interested, the amount of financial receipts and names of those contributing over $500, and the amount and the names of those to whom expenditures of over $10 are made. Several states have adopted similar legislation. These acts have produced a considerable body of information about the nature and dimensions of lobbying, but whatever expectations their authors may have had that forcing lobbying out into the open would "shame" it out of existence have been sadly disappointed.[16]

Congressional committees occasionally launch investigations of lobbyists and their methods. An outstanding instance came in 1956 when Senator Francis Case (Republican of South Dakota) announced that he had been offered a $2500 "campaign contribution" by officials of the Superior Oil Company as an inducement to vote for a bill freeing natural-gas producers from federal regulation. The Senate appointed a special committee under Senator John McClellan (Democrat of Arkansas) to investigate this situation, and as a result of its inquiry the officials in question were indicted for violating the lobbying laws. No general revision of these laws was made, however.

### Impact on Policy Formation

#### What Is It?

There is little doubt that pressure groups have a powerful impact upon the policy-forming processes of every modern democracy. They are not, of course, the only political groups that have such an impact. In every democracy political parties have some influence on the shape of public policy, and in many democracies they have a more direct and obvious influence than the pressure groups have. In Chapters 17–21 we shall see that the many formal agencies of government are more than mere collections of robots whose activities are entirely controlled by such extragovernmental forces as pressure groups and parties. The point to bear in mind here, however, is that pressure groups have a significant impact upon public policy in every modern democracy.

#### What Should It Be?

Some commentators have argued that the present power of pressure groups is highly dangerous to the welfare of democracy. They say that "group organization is one of the perils of our times," that "there is no escape from the pressure of organized power," and that only the political

---

[16] Cf. Milbrath, *op. cit.*, Ch. XVI; and Belle Zeller, "The Regulation of Pressure Groups and Lobbyists," *The Annals*, CCCXIX (September, 1958), 94–103.

parties, not the pressure groups, can act as "the principal rallying point for the great public interests of the nation."[17] Pressure politics undoubtedly has acquired a bad name in some quarters because of the widespread belief that pressure groups represent only "narrow, special, and selfish interests" and that the more powerful they are the less consideration will be given to the "national interest."

Other commentators reply that since there is no objective, scientific test by which a democracy can determine the exact content of the "national interest" and the precise policies which promote it, both its content and its policies are best determined by a "pluralistic" process of peaceful discussion, negotiation, and compromise among political parties, legislators, executives, administrators, judges—*and* pressure groups. So long as the political climate is such that no pressure group or party becomes a fanatical political army determined to exterminate all its competitors, and so long as all these groups have overlapping rather than mutually exclusive memberships, "democracy under pressure" will retain its health and its ability to adapt its policies to meet the ever-changing demands of ever-changing social, economic, and political conditions. Pendleton Herring puts it this way:

> Democracy provides us with an ideal under which experimentation with institutions and negotiation among interests is tolerated and justified. We are not forced to believe in unity; we may glory in diversity. It is enough if we achieve a working union of interests, ideas, institutions, and individuals. If we would formulate and execute constructive national long-range policies under our democratic ideology, we must face a period of change, of experimentation and of danger. Yet face it we must.[18]

One thing is clear: the right of citizens to organize and advance their ideals and interests by peaceful methods of discussion and negotiation is an essential principle of democracy. It is the basic justification not only for permitting the existence of pressure groups but for tolerating political parties as well. In any nation in which it is guaranteed, pressure groups, like political parties, will continue to be organized and to play a significant role in the policy-making processes of democracy.

---

[17] The first two quotations are given in Truman, *op. cit.*, p. 501. The third is from E. E. Schattschneider, *Party Government* (New York: Holt, Rinehart and Winston, Inc., 1942), p. 206.

[18] Pendleton Herring, *The Politics of Democracy* (New York: Holt, Rinehart and Winston, Inc., 1940), pp. 420–421.

# part four

## Governmental Agencies
## and
## Processes

# 17

## The Legislative Process

In this chapter and the next four we shall consider the Western democracies' principal official governing agencies and processes—"official" in the sense that they are formally established by constitutions and laws and are generally regarded as parts of "the government" in contrast with the "extragovernmental" and "unofficial" agencies and processes we have dealt with in the preceding section.

## Official Governmental Agencies and Processes: An Introduction

### "Official" and "Unofficial" Elements of the Governing Process

During the nineteenth century most American political scientists wrote as though they believed the official agencies to be the only aspects of government worth considering. Constitutions, laws, legislatures, executives, judges—these, they believed, were, strictly speaking, the real "stuff" of government, and they regarded such phenomena as public opinion, communication, voting behavior, pressure groups, and even political parties as either peripheral or irrelevant. Thus, one of the most eminent political scientists of the time, John W. Burgess, wrote his two-volume survey of world governments, *Political Science and Comparative Constitutional Law* (1890), without even mentioning parties, pressure groups, or public opinion.

Beginning in the 1870's, however, a new school of "realists" arose in American political science, including such scholars as Woodrow Wilson,

Theodore Dwight Woolsey, Henry Jones Ford, and A. Lawrence Lowell. They proceeded from the premise that the official structure of government is, by itself, little more than a lifeless collection of legal machinery, and it is precisely such unofficial agencies as public opinion and political parties that animate it and enable it to govern. These unofficial agencies, they concluded, are the core of the governing process, and students of government should focus on them rather than on constitutions, laws, and legal doctrines.[1]

Present-day political scientists certainly follow the lead of these scholars in studying the unofficial and informal aspects of government, as the preceding section of this book indicates. They generally believe, however, that *both* the official and unofficial agencies play significant roles in the total process of government, and that we can understand how that process operates in any nation only by examining the nature, activities, and interrelations of both types of agencies.

Specifically, most contemporary political scientists justify the study of the formal aspects of government on the following main grounds. First, the formal structure of government provides the framework within which the "extragovernmental" groups conduct their conflict and constitutes the principal agency for stating authoritatively "who gets what, when, and how." Therefore, we cannot fully understand the process of government if we totally ignore its official structure any more than we can fully understand, say, the game of football if we ignore its official rules and consider only such informal matters as coaching techniques, the relative advantages of the T-formation and the single-wing, and the won-and-lost records of the teams. The rules, in other words, to some extent make the game what it is and provide certain limits within which coaches, offensive formations, and teams must operate. So it is in politics.

Second, the official agencies and public officers are not merely mechanical devices for registering the relative strength of the extragovernmental groups. They are themselves political groups, with political interests and lives of their own. Their activities are influenced not only by the pressures applied to them by extragovernmental pressure groups and political parties but also by their own special institutional natures, interests, and needs. In this chapter and later ones, accordingly, we shall consider the special institutional lives and interests of legislatures, executives, administrators, and judges as well as their relations with extragovernmental pressure groups and parties.

Contemporary political science, in short, is concerned with the *total*

---

[1] For an illuminating discussion of the changing nature of American political science, see David Easton, *The Political System: An Inquiry into the State of Political Science* (New York: Alfred A. Knopf, Inc., 1953), Ch. 6.

process of government—a process that may usefully be considered as having both official and unofficial agencies and processes. In the preceding section of this book we focused mainly on the unofficial aspects, and in the present section we shall consider mainly the official aspects. In both sections, however, we should remember that we are dealing with different aspects of one human process, and that our differentiation of them, while useful for analytical and pedagogical purposes, does not exist in the "real world" of society and government.

## The Doctrine of "Separation of Powers"

### Its Origins and Influence

Suppose the municipal council of your city passed an ordinance requiring, say, the innoculation of all dogs against rabies. Suppose the mayor and chief of police then announced, "We think this is a bad regulation, and we refuse to enforce it." Surely most of us, including many who object to the ordinance, would feel that the mayor and chief of police were acting wrongly. Why? Because we would feel that *making* the laws is the council's job, and it is up to the mayor and police to enforce them regardless of their personal convictions.

Suppose, again, that a citizen of your state were arrested for grand larceny. Suppose the governor then stated, "This poor man will not get a fair trial from the courts, so I will try him myself." Again, most of us would strongly object, on the ground that trying persons accused of crime is the job of the courts, not the governor's.

Most of us, in other words, accept, and operate from, the belief that each agency of government has its own proper "powers" and that it should not try to exercise the "powers" of any other agency.

However fundamental and self-evident this may seem to us, it is relatively new in man's thinking about government. Until roughly the seventeenth century few political theorists tried to separate the governing process into "legislative," "executive," and "judicial" components. To them government was one continuous process, and the only significant variations in it from society to society were in the matters of who governs and how he or they govern.

The institutions of government prevalent before the seventeenth century reflected this idea. The Ecclesia, the Council of Five Hundred, and the "courts" of Periclean Athens, for example, all made rules, apprehended suspected offenders, determined their guilt or innocence, and administered punishment, and no one raised the question of whether these bodies were "legislatures" or "executives." The Roman Senate performed many "judicial" as well as "legislative" functions. The great medieval assemblies, such as the English *Curia Regis* and Parliament, the French *parlements*, and the

Spanish *Cortes*, were also at one and the same time "judicial" and "legis-lative" agencies—the official title of the larger English assembly, indeed, was "the High Court of Parliament."

In the seventeenth and eighteenth centuries, however, a group of influential political theorists, including Locke, Montesquieu, Rousseau, Jefferson, and the authors of the *Federalist* papers, developed a new conception of the governing process. This new conception was in part a description of how the governing process does work and in part a doctrine about how it should work. It remains the basis for the belief widely held in the United States and some other modern democracies that legislatures should legislate, executives execute, and judges adjudicate.

### Its Content[2]

The most thorough and influential exposition of this point of view—and one of the most influential books about government ever written—was *L'Esprit des Lois*, published in 1748 by the French political theorist Montesquieu. Briefly summarized, his argument ran as follows.

The two significant elements of the governing process are the individual citizens and the official governmental agencies. In a properly run community the citizens establish a constitution which does three things. First, it stipulates what the whole government may do and may not do—that is, it states what "powers" the government shall have (e.g., to collect taxes, declare war, protect private property). Second, it establishes certain governmental agencies and provides a procedure for selecting their members. And third, it allocates certain powers to each agency.

The whole power of any government is, like Caesar's Gaul, divided into three parts, each substantially distinct from the others. There is the *legislative* power, which is the power to *make* the laws; the *executive* power, which is the power to *enforce* the laws; and the *judicial* power, which is the power to *interpret and apply* the laws to individuals whom the executive has charged with violating them. Thus, whatever any public official does in his official capacity is lawmaking, law enforcement, or law interpretation and application.

Like many of his contemporaries, Montesquieu believed that government is an eternal threat to men's liberties; yet, anarchy and lawlessness also threaten them. How, then, can we maintain a government strong enough to maintain law and order without allowing it to grow so strong as to become tyrannical? The answer, Montesquieu and his successors believed, is to give each of government's three basic powers to a separate

---

[2] For a more detailed description of the doctrine's origins, influence, and content, see Herman Finer, *Theory and Practice of Modern Government* (rev. ed.; New York: Holt, Rinehart and Winston, Inc., 1949), Ch. 6.

and independent governmental agency. When all three agencies or "branches" act in concert, government can do what it must do, but no single branch can ever control the whole power of government, and hence no president or legislature or court is ever able to use the whole power of government to work its particular way heedlessly and without restraint. Any concentration of powers in a single agency is tyrannical, no matter whether that agency be an elected and responsible representative assembly or an irresponsible hereditary monarch. Only a genuine *separation* of powers protects the liberties of men against the aggressions of government. Thus James Madison spoke for all the Founding Fathers when he wrote in the 47th *Federalist* paper:

> No political truth is certainly of greater intrinsic value, or is stamped with the authority of more enlightened patrons of liberty, than that . . . the accumulation of all powers, legislative, executive, and judiciary, in the same hands, whether of one, a few, or many, and whether hereditary, self-appointed, or elective, may justly be pronounced the very definition of tyranny.[3]

## The Institution of "Checks and Balances"

Madison and the other authors of the American Constitution believed that the most effective method for keeping the three powers of the new government truly separate requires two devices. First, no person must be allowed to serve in more than one branch of government at a time: Article I, Section 6 declares that "no Person holding any Office under the United States, shall be a Member of either House during his Continuance in Office." Hence if the Attorney General wishes to be a senator from New York, he must resign his executive position; and if the senator from Minnesota wishes to be Vice-President, he must resign his Senate seat. Second, each branch must be given a number of "checks" by which it can keep the other branches in proper "balance." Thus, Congress is empowered to check the President by impeaching him, withholding appropriations for his executive and administrative agencies, and withholding approval of the appointment of certain of his subordinates; and it is empowered to check the Supreme Court by controlling the latter's appellate jurisdiction and by withholding approval of the appointment of its new members. The President is empowered to check Congress by vetoing its acts and to check the Supreme Court by his initial appointment of its new members. The Supreme Court can check both Congress and the President with its power of judicial review.

---

[3] *The Federalist*, ed. by Max Beloff (New York: The Macmillan Company, 1948), pp. 245–246. For Montesquieu's similar argument, see *The Spirit of the Laws*, translated by Thomas Nugent (New York: Hafner Publishing Company, 1949), Bk. XI.

We should note, however, that most of the world's democracies have neither accepted the doctrine of separation of powers nor installed the American style of checks and balances. Of the thirty-nine nations classified in Table 2, Chapter 4, as full-fledged democracies, only seven are of the presidential type; the other thirty-two are called "parliamentary democracies" because their Constitutions vest in their parliaments some kind of ultimate control over all three kinds of power and the agencies exercising them. Yet even in these democracies, as we shall see in this chapter and the next three, there is a kind of working "separation of functions" in the sense that most observers speak of their legislative, executive, and judicial functions as being performed by different governmental agencies rather than as all being performed by a single agency.

The Constitutions of the presidential democracies, however, formally establish the principle of separation of powers according to which each of the three basic powers is given mainly to a particular "branch" of government, and no "branch" is supposed to interfere with the others' powers. In its purest form, the principle requires the inclusion of a "distributing" clause, such as Article XXX of the Massachusetts Constitution of 1780:

> In the government of this Commonwealth, the legislative department shall never exercise the executive and judicial powers, or either of them: The executive shall never exercise the legislative and judicial powers, or either of them: The judicial shall never exercise the legislative and executive powers, or either of them: to the end it may be a government of laws and not of men.

The Constitution of the United States contains no such clause, but it specifies that "all legislative powers herein granted shall be vested in a Congress" (Art. I), "the executive Power shall be vested in a President" (Art. II), and the "judicial power . . . shall be vested in one supreme Court, and in such inferior Courts as the Congress may from time to time ordain and establish" (Art. III).

In many contemporary nations the Constitution formally allocates two or all three of these basic powers to a single agency. In Saudi Arabia, for example, King Faisal is the nation's lawgiver and chief judge as well as its chief executive. In the parliamentary democracies the principal executive and legislative powers are exercised by the prime ministers and their cabinets.

### The Doctrine Today

Most contemporary political scientists regard Montesquieu's classification of the powers of government as an inadequate and misleading description of the activities in which its agencies engage. They recognize that in all modern democracies no agency sticks exclusively to the job formally assigned to it. Legislative bodies often conduct executive activities (e.g., in their investigations of wrongdoing in government, schools, and trade unions). Courts often make laws (e.g., in their "interpretations" of Constitutions and statutes). Executive and administrative agencies often make and interpret laws as well as enforce them (e.g., in making "administrative regulations" and in holding "hearings" to determine whether licenses for radio and television broadcasting should be granted, renewed, or revoked).

A few political scientists have attempted to preserve the traditional conception in the face of this situation by, for example, calling the judicial activities and powers of executive agencies "quasi-judicial." Most, however, have concluded that the adjectives "legislative," "executive," and "judicial" should be thought of only as convenient tags for identifying particular governmental agencies, and their utility depends strictly upon a general agreement as to which tags should be pinned to which agencies. The tags, in other words, are not regarded as accurate and complete descriptions of what their agencies actually do.[4]

In the present chapter, accordingly, we shall consider those agencies generally called "legislatures." In describing the "legislative process" we shall deal with the principal activities and processes that operate within and through these bodies. We shall not be concerned with the question of whether these activities and processes are truly "legislative" in the orthodox sense of the term. In short, for the purposes of this chapter, *any* function performed by an agency generally called a "legislature" is a "legislative function"; and we shall proceed from the same premises in our subsequent chapters on the executive, administrative, and judicial processes.

## The Functions of Legislatures

### Statute Making

Perhaps the most obvious and certainly one of the most important functions of modern democratic legislatures is making statutes. We have chosen the term "statute making" over the more commonly used term "law-making" because it more accurately describes what legislatures actually do. The term "law" refers to any kind of behavior-regulating rule that officially emanates from a definite governmental source. The rules officially established by legislatures, which are generally known as "legislative acts" or "statutes," certainly constitute an important segment of any democracy's total body of law; but the latter also includes such elements as judge-made

---

[4] Cf. Finer, *op. cit.*, Ch. 7.

rules of "common law" and equity, and the more significant executive and administrative "decrees" and "regulations." Legislatures, in short, monopolize statute making but not lawmaking.

### Constituent

Most democratic legislatures have certain powers over the establishment and amending of their nations' Constitutions. Many Constitutions were originally drawn up by legislative bodies, and every legislature is authorized to play some role in making formal amendments. In some democracies (e.g., Great Britain and New Zealand) the national legislature is the sole agency authorized to amend the constitution. In many others (e.g., Australia, Switzerland, and France) the normal amending process is for the legislature to propose amendments and the voters to ratify them in referenda. In still others (e.g., the United States) amendments are proposed by the national legislature and ratified by state legislatures or conventions. Most democratic legislatures have considerably altered and added to their constitutions by statutory enactments (e.g., those in the United Sates establishing the inferior federal courts, the executive departments, and the regulatory commissions).

### Electoral

Most democratic legislatures play a significant role in selecting certain public officials who play leading parts in the "executive." The outstanding instances are the indirect "elections" of prime ministers by the legislatures of the parliamentary democracies. These legislatures do not, of course, ever ballot for various "candidates" for this office; but every time they vote on a "confidence" question (see Chapter 18), they are, in effect, holding an election to determine whether the incumbent prime minister shall be "re-elected" or defeated.[5] Some commentators, indeed, believe that this has become the main function of the legislatures in these democracies.

Even in the presidential democracies the legislatures have some electoral powers. The Constitution of the United States, for example, provides that in cases in which no candidate for President or Vice-President receives a majority of the electoral votes, the House of Representatives, with each state casting one vote, shall choose the President from among the top two or three candidates, and the Senate shall choose the Vice-President in a somewhat different manner. No President or Vice-President has been selected by these procedures since 1824, but Congress retains its electoral powers against the day when they may be used again.

---

[5] Inter-Parliamentary Union, *Parliaments* (New York: Frederick A. Praeger, Inc., 1962), pp. 238–262. This volume is a useful, though formalistic, survey of the organization and functions of legislatures throughout the world.

### Financial

In every modern democracy the legislature holds the basic official financial power: it determines the nature and amount of taxes, and all public monies may be spent only as the result of legislative appropriations. Like so many other legislative functions, the main initiative in and direction of governmental finance has passed from the legislature to the executive in most democracies, and most legislatures merely revise and alter budgets proposed by executive officials rather than draw up their own *de novo*. How much revising and amending particular legislatures do depends upon the degree of control over them their nations' executives have achieved—a matter we shall consider later in this chapter.

### Executive

In addition to acting upon executive budgets, most democratic legislatures also pass upon certain other executive proposals. In most democracies, for example, international treaties are negotiated by the executive but must be approved by the legislature before they become effective. In the United States the President appoints various kinds of officials (e.g., federal judges, cabinet members, heads of administrative agencies, and ambassadors) "by and with the Advice and Consent of the Senate" (Art. II)—that is, the appointments are only provisional or "interim" until approved by a majority of the Senate.

### Judicial

Some legislatures also perform judicial functions. The Constitution of the United States, for example, provides that the House of Representatives may "impeach" any civil officer of the national government (including the President, the Vice-President, cabinet members, and judges), and any person so impeached must be tried by the Senate, with a two-thirds vote necessary for conviction. The House has impeached a total of twelve officers since 1789, nine judges, one President (Andrew Johnson), one senator, and one cabinet member. Of these only four, all judges, were convicted and removed from office, but President Johnson escaped conviction in 1868 by the bare margin of one vote.

Similarly, the French National Assembly can indict the President of the Republic and the ministers for treason and other crimes and misdemeanors, although officers so indicted are tried by the High Court rather than by a legislative body. The British House of Lords has lost most of its other powers but continues to be the nation's highest court of law. Most of the Lords' judicial work and all of its work as a court of appeals is performed in the name of the whole House by a small group of ten to fifteen legal experts, including the Lord Chancellor, the nine Lords of Appeal in Ordinary (or "law lords"), and other members of the House who have held high judicial office (e.g., former Lord Chancellors).

### Investigatory

The investigating function of legislative bodies has received much publicity in recent years, especially in the United States, because of such congressional "probes" as those of the McCarthy and Jenner committees into subversion in government and elsewhere in the late 1940's and early 1950's, of the Kefauver committee into the interrelations of organized crime and politics in the early 1950's, and of the McClellan committee into labor union affairs in the early 1960's. American legislatures, however, have no monopoly on this kind of activity. The British House of Commons, for example, establishes four or five "select" committees each year for the purpose of digging up information desired by the House on matters not covered by the "standing" committees. These select committees hold hearings, subpoena witnesses and records, and often submit reports that inspire changes in existing legislation or administrative practices or both. While the British, unlike the Americans, conduct much of their governmental investigations by Royal Commissions (bodies composed of both legislators and outsiders), the select committees nevertheless perform a significant role in the shaping of legislative and administrative policy.

### Informing

Some legislative investigations are conducted mainly to uncover information necessary for new legislation. A great deal of this activity, however, is intended mainly to inform other governmental agencies, extragovernmental bodies, and the general public about what is going on in the nation. The McCarthy and Jenner investigations of subversion, for example, were not mainly intended to provide the basis for new anticommunist legislation, but rather to determine whether the legislation already on the books was being enforced by the administration. The McClellan committee, by investigating Jimmy Hoffa's administration of the Teamsters' Union, intended, as Senator McClellan repeatedly stated, mainly to acquaint the union's rank and file and the AFL–CIO national leadership with the nature and extent of the Teamsters' leaders' dishonesty, in the hope that the unions might clean their own house.

Such investigations, then, are one aspect of the legislative function of informing the public, and legislative debate is another. In many legislatures party lines are so rigid that legislative debate hardly ever changes a member's vote. Yet debate provides the main forum in which the rights and wrongs of the issues are aired. It therefore performs much the same function of informing and activating public opinion that election campaigns are supposed to perform. Thus the debate in the British House of Commons, while it almost never changes legislative votes, sometimes changes the opinions of those who elect the members of the House, and some observers describe it as "a continuing election campaign." If an informed and enlightened citizenry is indeed one of the prime requisites for a healthy democracy, informing the public is far from being the least significant of the legislature's functions.

## The Structure and Organization of Legislatures

### *The Number of Houses*[6]

Of the thirty-nine nations classified in Table 2 as democracies twenty-six have bicameral (two-house) legislatures and thirteen have unicameral (one-house) legislatures. Although there are some variations in the structure of the bicameral legislatures, most of them are organized in a substantially similar fashion. One of the two houses, generally referred to as the "lower house," has the larger membership, and its members have the shorter terms of office and are elected, under one or another of the systems of representation described in Chapter 13, by the widest franchise. Examples of such houses are the American national House of Representatives, the British House of Commons, the French National Assembly, and the Swiss National Council. The other house, generally referred to as the "upper house," has the smaller membership, and its members have longer terms of office and are selected in various ways. The members of the American Senate, for example, are elected by the voters in state-wide constituencies for six-year terms; some members of the British House of Lords inherit their positions, and others are appointed for life by the monarch on the advice of the prime minister; the members of the Canadian Senate are appointed for life by the governor-general on the advice of the prime minister; and the members of the Austrian Federal Council are elected by the legislatures of the various *Länder* (provinces).[7]

Why should a nation establish two legislative houses rather than one? Historically there have been two main reasons. First, all the federal democracies have felt it necessary to give their subnational "sovereignties" equal representation in the national legislature: hence, the establishment of, for

---

[6] Cf. K. C. Wheare, *Legislatures* (London: Oxford University Press, 1963), Ch. 8.

[7] Norway's procedures are unique: the voters elect a 150-member *Storting*, which then proceeds to choose 38 of its members to serve in a second chamber, the *Lagting*; the remaining 112 are called the *Odelsting*.

## "Hope You Didn't Take Anything Personally—The Fact Is We Don't Even Get Along With Each Other"

*Figure 33.* The Two Legislative Houses Often Fight Each Other as well as the Executive. (From *Straight Herblock,* Simon & Schuster, 1964.)

example, the United States Senate with two members from each state regardless of its population or wealth. Perhaps an even more important reason, and one which has operated in both federal and unitary nations, has been the desire to provide a check upon the lower houses. The latter have been presumed to be closely in tune with popular appetites and passions and have, therefore, been regarded as dangerous to the nation's stability and welfare. Many nations, accordingly, have at one time or another established higher property and age qualifications for those who elect members of the upper house than for voters who elect members of the lower, and a few nations still retain these special franchise requirements.

In recent years a number of democracies have formally or informally abandoned bicameralism, mainly on the ground that it is a barrier to the full realization of democracy in the sense that full governmental power is not located in the representatives of popular majorities. A few (e.g., Denmark and New Zealand) have officially abolished their upper houses. Many more have stripped them of their powers so drastically that they are now little more than advisory bodies, and the lower houses have become, for all practical purposes, unicameral legislatures. For example, until the nineteenth century the British House of Lords was in many respects more powerful than the House of Commons. After the democratization of the Commons in 1832, however, the powers of the Lords began to slip away. The Parliament Act of 1911 stripped them of all but a few delaying powers, and an act of 1949 reduced their powers still more. At the present time, accordingly, the House of Lords is in effect merely an advisory and delaying body, with little or no formal legislative power. Most observers feel that it performs a useful function as a revising and suggesting body, but the British Parliament has become in practical operation a unicameral legislature. The same thing has happened to a greater or lesser degree to the upper houses in most of the other unitary democracies, e.g., the French and Irish Senates. Only in some of the federal democracies (e.g., in the United States and Switzerland, but not in Canada or Australia) does the upper house retain powers equal or superior to those of the lower house.

## Presiding Officers

### Selection

Every legislative body has a number of officers, including such positions as clerk, sergeant at arms, chaplain, and postmaster. The most significant and powerful officials are the presiding officers, only a few of whom acquire their position as the result of holding some other public office, such as the Vice-President of the United States, who presides over the Senate (possibly because the Founding Fathers wanted to give him something to occupy his time other than inquiring after the President's health every morning). Most presiding officers, however, are selected by the legislative bodies from among their own members (e.g., the speaker of the American House of Representatives, the speaker of the British House of Commons, and the president of the French National Assembly).

### Formal Powers and Functions

In their official capacities the presiding officers of all democratic legislatures have substantially the same powers and functions. They "recognize" legislators who wish to speak, put motions to the assembly to vote on, rule on points of parliamentary order and procedure, supervise the referring of bills to committees, sometimes appoint the members of the various committees, and in general direct and guide the body's formal operations.

### Partisanship and Party Leadership

It seems reasonable to expect that since the presiding officer of a legislative body has considerable control over who gets heard and what gets done, he should be fair to *all* the body's members, parties, and points of view, and thereby give each an equal chance to get its policies adopted. In order to ensure such fairness, the speaker of the British House of Commons has been purged of all party connections. The leaders of the principal rival parties agree on a candidate and always select a member who, though he has been a member of a party, does not have a reputation for violent partisanship; and more often than not he is elected unanimously. After his election the speaker completely divests himself of all connections with political parties and clubs and never takes part in debate. In general elections he sometimes runs without opposition, and in every other conceivable way is removed and insulated from partisan politics to the end that he may be completely impartial in his dealings with all parties and all members.[8]

The speaker of the United States House of Representatives (and of most other American legislative bodies) provides a striking contrast. Not only is he openly and avowedly partisan (e.g., there is certainly no tradition that he shall run unopposed for re-election in his district), but he is, in fact, the principal leader of the majority party in the House and one of the main leaders of his party in the nation. Some foreign observers of American government find it hard to believe that a speaker can at one and the same time successfully perform the two quite different jobs of neutral presiding officer and partisan leader. Yet most American speakers seem to do just that, for seldom does the minority party complain about the speaker's unfairness and seldom does the majority party complain about his ineffective party leadership.[9]

The presiding officers of the other democratic legislatures fall somewhere between the British and American extremes of neutrality and partisanship, but most of them follow the British model more closely.[10]

---

[8] Cf. W. Ivor Jennings, *Parliament* (London: Cambridge University Press, 1939), pp. 54–65.
[9] Cf. William J. Keefe and Morris S. Ogul, *The American Legislative Process* (Englewood Cliffs, N.J.: Prentice-Hall, Inc., 1964), pp. 265–270.
[10] Cf. Wheare, *op. cit.*, pp. 22–29.

## *Procedures*

### Rules

Democratic legislatures conduct their business largely according to rules of their own making, limited only by a few constitutional requirements, such as those requiring records of their proceedings and a quorum to conduct business. There are, of course, many variations in detail among the rules followed by various legislative bodies, but most of them model their rules more or less closely on the procedures of the "mother of parliaments," the British House of Commons. The familiar *Robert's Rules of Order,* according to which so many nongovernmental organizations operate (or are supposed to operate), are a kind of distillation of the procedures most generally followed by democratic legislative bodies the world over.

### Public Bills and Private Bills

Most democratic legislatures distinguish between "public bills" and "private bills." A "public bill" is one which applies to the whole population and which is intended to promote the general welfare: e.g., a tax law, or a military draft act, or a law against kidnapping. A "private bill," on the other hand, is one which applies to and is intended to promote the welfare of a particular person or locality: an appropriation of money to a person in compensation for property damage or personal injury, or a bill admitting a particular alien into the nation outside the regular immigration laws, or a bill appropriating money to improve the harbor at Porkville, Anystate, or the like.

Most democratic legislatures have established somewhat different procedures for handling public bills and private bills. In the British House of Commons, for example, private bills are filed with the "Examiner of Petitions for Private Bills" and with the government department most immediately concerned. Interested persons are invited to testify, and all bills that are opposed go to a private-bills committee, which holds hearings and makes recommendations that are almost always accepted by the whole House. The purpose of this procedure and similar procedures in other legislatures is to keep private bills from clogging up the regular legislative machinery and thereby blocking the consideration of more important questions.

### The Main Steps in Handling Public Bills

Despite their differences in details of procedure, most democratic legislatures put a public bill through a number of similar steps before it becomes law.

INTRODUCTION.	In most legislatures any member may introduce a public bill either by giving it a "first reading" on the floor and moving its adoption, or, as is the case in both houses of Congress, merely by dropping it in the "hopper" at the clerk's or secretary's desk. This formal equality in the right to introduce bills, however, is somewhat misleading. Many democratic legislatures, e.g., the British House of Commons, make a formal distinction between "Government bills" (those introduced by a minister on behalf of the ministry or "Government") and "private member's bills" (those introduced by an ordinary member on his own behalf). Only the former are likely to be passed: the "Government" introduces about 85 percent of all public bills in Great Britain and about 95 percent of all public bills passed are "Government bills."[11] No such formal distinction is made in Congress, but a bill generally known to be an "administration bill" (i.e., one desired by the President and pushed by his spokesmen in Congress) has a better chance of passage than does one which lacks this kind of backing.

CONSIDERATION BY COMMITTEE.	Later in this chapter we shall describe the structure, personnel, operations, and general role of legislative committees in the legislative process. In the present context the important point is that in most democratic legislatures bills are referred to and considered by committees *before* they undergo any general consideration and debate by the whole house. Committees, therefore, have a great deal to say not only about the content of bills but also about what bills will even have the chance to become laws. In the British House of Commons, however, bills are referred to committee *after* the stage of general debate and *after* their basic policies and most of their details have been established by the whole house (which means, in actuality, by the "Government"). British legislative committees, unlike those in most other democratic legislatures, are, in Professor Finer's words, "lowly handmaidens to help clean up amendments."[12] The nations of the British Commonwealth generally follow British practices in this regard, but the United States and most European democracies assign their legislative committees a far more decisive role, as we shall see in a moment.

GENERAL DEBATE.	The few bills fortunate enough to survive the "screening" process of the committee stage are then "reported" back to the whole house in their original or some altered form and are given a "second reading" (which usually means only that the presiding officer or the clerk

---

[11] Herman Finer, *Governments of Greater European Powers* (New York: Holt, Rinehart and Winston, Inc., 1956), p. 383.

[12] *Ibid.*, p. 116.

announces the number and title of the bill about to be considered, not that anyone literally reads the entire contents of the bill). At this point all the legislators have their chance to express their views about the basic policy questions involved in the bill, and also to offer amendments to it. If the bill passes this stage its chances of final passage are excellent.

FINAL PASSAGE. After general debate has been held and all proposed amendments have been accepted, rejected, or revised, the bill is given its third and final "reading," and the question is put whether the whole bill, as amended, should be passed. An affirmative vote means that so far as the particular house is concerned the bill is now law.

CONSIDERATION BY CONFERENCE COMMITTEE. In many nominal two-house legislatures, as we learned above, the upper house has merely the power to suggest amendments and to delay a bill passed by the lower house. Where this situation prevails, after the delaying period has elapsed and after the lower house has accepted or rejected the upper house's suggested amendments, the bill moves on to the next and final stage regardless of any further objections by the upper house. But where, as in the United States, both houses have coordinate legislative power, each bill must pass both houses in identical form before it can move on to the final stage. When the two houses disagree on the wording of a bill, whether it be over a minor matter of detail or a major question of policy, and neither house is willing to accept the other's version, the differences between them must be ironed out and the bill worded in a manner acceptable to majorities in both houses. This arises in about one third to one half of all the bills that pass both houses of Congress and in the case of just about every major public bill.

In all genuinely bicameral legislatures this necessary ironing-out process is accomplished by some version of the American "conference committee," which operates as follows. The presiding officer of each house appoints from three to nine members to represent the house as "conferees." The two sets of conferees constitute the conference committee, which meets in secret session and, in most cases, works out a version of the bill on which all or most of the conferees can agree. Usually this is a compromise between the versions of the two houses, but on rare occasions the committee will write a substantially new bill. When they have reached an agreement, the conferees report to their respective houses. The reports may not be amended, but must be accepted or rejected in their entirety—and usually they are accepted, for the good and sufficient reason that most members of both houses know that if the conference committee's version is not accepted, they will probably get no bill at all.

Conference committees, accordingly, have a great deal of power over the final content of legislation—so much so that some observers refer to them as "the third house of Congress." Some such institution, however, is inevitable in any genuinely bicameral legislature.[13]

SUBMISSION TO THE EXECUTIVE. After the legislature has officially passed a bill in its final form, it is submitted to some executive agency for official promulgation and inclusion in the collection of statutes in force. In the parliamentary democracies the executive—either the monarch or the president—has no choice but to accept the legislature's bill and declare it law. In the presidential democracies, however, the president can veto the bill, and if he does so it can become law only if repassed by both houses with a two-thirds majority in each. This will be further discussed in Chapter 18.

### Legislative Committees[14]

#### Structure

Every democratic legislative body establishes committees of its members to perform various functions, and they appear to be a universal response to two main needs. First, the sheer size of most legislatures prevents them from handling effectively questions of detail and wording. Most legislatures have several hundred members, and, as men in all organizations, governmental and otherwise, have learned, hundreds of men simply cannot deal effectively with matters of detail and wording, but must confine themselves to considering broad questions of policy. Second, the sheer number of bills introduced necessitates some kind of "screening" process to weed out the few which deserve serious consideration. In an average session of Congress at the present time, for example, from 10,000 to 12,000 bills are introduced —obviously far too many to receive serious consideration—and only about 500 to 1000 are passed.

In the United States and most European democracies most of the "screening" is accomplished by legislative committees. In the United States they are organized as follows. Each house of Congress maintains a number of *standing committees* (those which are considered to be permanent) established along subject-matter lines: Agriculture, Appropriations, Armed

---

[13] The authoritative analysis of conference committees in the American Congress is Gilbert Y. Steiner, *The Congressional Conference Committee* (Urbana: University of Illinois Press, 1951). For comparable practices in other nations, see *Parliaments*, pp. 185–189.

[14] A general survey of committee procedures and powers is in *Parliaments*, pp. 141–151. For their role in the United States, see Keefe and Ogul, *op. cit.*, Ch. 5; and Daniel M. Berman, *In Congress Assembled* (New York: The Macmillan Company, 1964), Chs. 6–8.

Services, Foreign Affairs, and Education and Labor are examples. They range in size from nine to fifty members, and include members of the majority and minority parties in approximately the same ratio the two parties have in the whole house. Nominally the members of each committee are elected by the whole house, but actually the leaders of each party (assembled in its "committee on committees") determine which of their legislators shall sit on which committees. In making their selections the leaders are bound by a series of informal but nonetheless powerful rules: e.g., all previous members of a committee must be reappointed if they so desire, every major area and interest must have a spokesman on a committee that deals with matters affecting it, and so on.

The *commissions* of the French National Assembly are in some respects similar to American legislative committees. The outstanding French variation is the institution of the *rapporteur* (reporter). As each bill is received by a particular *commission*, it appoints one of its members as *rapporteur* for that bill, in which capacity he takes the lead in studying it, in preparing the *commission's* report on it, and in defending the *commission's* position in the debate in the whole Assembly.

The British House of Commons, in contrast with American and French procedures, maintains only four "alphabet" standing committees (so called because they are officially designated Committees A, B, C, and D, rather than as Armed Forces, Agriculture, and so on), and a fifth Standing Committee on Scottish Bills. The British and French committees, as we shall see in a moment, are far less powerful than their counterparts in most other legislatures.

In addition to standing committees, democratic legislatures from time to time establish *select committees*, which make special inquiries into and recommendations on particular questions of the moment and dissolve when they have done their jobs (e.g., the select committee of the United States Senate which in 1954 recommended the censure of Senator Joseph McCarthy for "conduct unbecoming a senator," and the various select joint committees which in the 1940's investigated the causes of the Pearl Harbor disaster). The genuinely bicameral legislatures sometimes establish *joint committees*, composed of equal representation from each house, to supervise certain matters (e.g., the Joint Committee on Atomic Energy created to supervise the Atomic Energy Commission's administration of the nuclear-fission program).

### Activities and Power

Most legislative committees conduct two main types of activities. The first is disposing of bills referred to them by the whole house. A powerful committee (see below) has a wide range of choice in deciding how to dispose of a particular bill: it may merely deposit it in a special hollow cylindrical "file" and forget about it, and this appears to be the fate of most bills in most committees; or it may immediately report the bill in its original form back to the whole house with a recommendation "that it do pass"; or it may decide to work the bill over before making any recommendation. If the committee chooses the last course, it may hold hearings at which representatives of various interested groups are invited to testify. When the hearings are over, the committee may go into "executive" (secret) session and rewrite the bill as little or as much as it sees fit, up to and including deleting everything but the title and substituting an entirely new bill!

The last type of committee activity includes all projects the committee undertakes on its own initiative. It may decide to draw up and have a member introduce a brand-new bill of its own. It may decide to investigate, in the manner described above, possible wrongdoing in the executive, administrative, or judicial agencies, or in schools, trade unions, athletics, and the like.

The power of legislative committees over the general legislative process varies considerably among modern democracies. At one extreme stand the committees of the American Congress and state legislatures, which are the most powerful in the world. Not only do they receive bills before general debate and before the basic policy decisions have been made, but they can and often do make major decisions on basic policy as well as on matters of detail and wording. "Little legislatures," Woodrow Wilson called them, and the phrase is as apt today as it was when he wrote it in 1885.

At the other extreme stand the committees of the British House of Commons. They do not receive bills until after their "second reading"—that is, after the basic policy decisions have been made; and they are authorized to make alterations and amendments only on minor matters of detail. Since they do not specialize in particular areas of legislation, they develop no particular *expertise* or vested interest in any policy area. And their members are subject to strong party discipline both inside the committees and out. Hence the committees play a relatively unimportant role in the British legislative process.

Under the Third and Fourth Republics the powers of the French *commissions* resembled American more than British practices. De Gaulle's Constitution of the Fifth Republic, however, deliberately set out to cut down their power and thus reduce the fragmentation characteristic of the National Assemblies before 1958. The number of *commissions générales permanentes* (standing committees) was reduced from nineteen, each corresponding to a particular legislative area, to six nonspecialized committees on the British model. They now can only suggest changes to the Government, and it is the Government's bills—not the committees' amendments and counterproposals as under the Fourth Republic—that come before the whole Assembly for debate and final action.[15]

The power of legislative committees in the other democracies falls between these extremes. On the one hand, the committees' reports usually serve as the basis for debate and action in the whole legislature, and the committees have considerable power to redraft and amend the bills originally submitted to them. On the other hand, in most parliamentary democracies the Government's control of the legislature's calendar and the political parties' control of their members' votes is such that the committees can rarely impose on the Government a bill it does not want.[16]

In short, in most democracies legislative committees play a significant role in the legislative process, although nowhere are they quite as powerful as in the United States.

### Debate, Filibusters, and Cloture

One view of the legislative process sees the general-debate stage as the one in which most of the crucial decisions are made. It envisions a series of situations in which various members of the legislature try by their speeches to convince the others to vote as they recommend, and in which the most persuasive speakers carry the day. Needless to say, this is not an entirely accurate picture of how legislatures actually make decisions. It assumes not only that most of the legislators are present during the debate, and listen carefully to it, but also that they are subject to no pressures or influences other than their own personal views—and neither assumption, as we shall see, is justified by the facts in most modern democratic legislatures.

In most legislatures some members—always holding minority views—have at one time or another used debate not to convince anyone but to block action. This technique, called "the filibuster," generally refers to the action of some minority member or members holding the floor and making marathon speeches consisting of reading aloud from cookbooks, the Bible, or the manual of arms. The purpose? To delay or entirely prevent the vote on a bill the filibusterers oppose and know the majority will pass if a vote is taken; they know that if they can filibuster long enough, the pressure of the house's other business will necessarily force the majority to give in and shelve the controversial bill so that other things can get done.

During the nineteenth century, for example, the Irish Nationalist minority of the British House of Commons frequently delayed the business of the House by long harangues in an effort to force the other members to

---

[15] Roy C. Macridis in Roy C. Macridis and Robert E. Ward, eds., *Modern Political Systems: Europe* (Englewood Cliffs, N.J.: Prentice-Hall, Inc., 1963), p. 215.
[16] *Parliaments*, pp. 145–151.

# "Sure — I'm For Equalizing Things"

*Figure 34.* Filibusters Are a Weapon of Minorities. (From *Straight Herblock,* Simon & Schuster, 1964.)

grant Irish independence just to get rid of the nuisance. In many European legislatures today Communist minorities seize every opportunity to filibuster against all anticommunist proposals. In the United States Senate in 1964 the Southern minority filibustered for seventy-five days against the Civil Rights Bill before its supporters were able to force a vote.

Most democratic legislatures, accordingly, have found it necessary to adopt some kind of *cloture* rule to enable a majority to end debate, take a vote, and get on with other business.[17] The basic form is "simple cloture," whereby at any point in the debate a member may move that "debate now end and the question be put." Such a motion is itself undebatable, and if it receives the required majority (usually a simple majority, but in some legislatures and in *Robert's Rules of Order* a two-thirds majority), debate must cease and a vote be taken immediately on the main motion. Subsidiary forms of cloture are the "guillotine," which is an advance ruling that debate on particular sections of a bill may last only so long and then a vote must be taken; and the "kangaroo," which permits the presiding officer to decide in advance which amendments to a bill may be debated at all. Both, however, are backed up by simple cloture, which is the basic weapon of any legislative majority against filibusters.

Perhaps the most famous filibusters have taken place in the United States Senate. Under Rule XXII, as adopted in 1917 and revised in 1949 and 1959, debate can be stopped only if two thirds of the senators present and voting assent. The result is that any thirty-four senators—usually a smaller number is required—can block any bill.

The reader should understand, however, that legislative policy is influenced in the Senate far more by *threats* of filibusters than by actual filibusters, which rarely take place. The authors and sponsors of every bill have to consider the possibility of a filibuster when planning its content and their floor strategy. As Senator Clinton Anderson (Democrat of New Mexico) put it during the 1949 debate over changing Rule XXII:

> I am not suggesting that the filibuster is the regular order of the day on this floor. It does not have to be. However infrequently the hammer on the filibuster gun is drawn back and cocked, this veto power of the minority over the will of the majority is, as all of us well know, a factor never overlooked in legislative drafting, appropriations, strategy, and tactics in the Senate of the United States. It affects and conditions every piece of legislation from the time it is a twinkle in the eye of its parent through every stage of gestation and birth.[18]

### Party Organization

#### Principal Agencies

In every democratic legislature almost every member is elected as the nominee of a political party. In every legislature the members of each party form some kind of organization to consult on matters of policy and strategy so as to advance their common cause most effectively. Although these

---

[17] Finland and Sweden are among the few modern democracies which still have no formal procedure for limiting legislative debate.—*Ibid.*, p. 153.

[18] *Congressional Record*, Vol. 95, Part 2, p. 1589 (March 2, 1949).

legislative party organizations vary in detail somewhat from nation to nation and from party to party within a particular nation, most of them include some version of each of the following principal agencies.

THE CAUCUS. The most inclusive of the agencies is some form of the "caucus," an assembly of all the party's members in the particular house. The American versions are called "conferences" or "caucuses"; the British and dominion versions, the "parliamentary parties"; the French versions, "*groupes*"; and so on. Their main function is to select their party's legislative leaders, although occasionally some of them also decide what stands their members should take on particular legislative issues.[19]

THE EXECUTIVE COMMITTEE. The caucus usually selects a few of its members as a kind of "executive committee" or "board of directors" and authorizes them to determine the party's stand on legislative issues and to select the tactics by which the party will pursue its objectives. The American versions are called "steering committees" or "policy committees"; the British and dominion versions, the "leadership" or "the cabinet" and "the shadow cabinet" (see Chapter 18); the French versions, the "party executive"; and so on.

THE FLOOR LEADERS. The caucus also selects one of its members as its official floor leader and main spokesman. The American versions are called "the majority leader" and "the minority leader," depending on whether the particular party has a majority of the seats; the British equivalent is called the "party leader" and, depending on his party's share of the seats, holds the official position of either "prime minister" or "leader of Her Majesty's Loyal Opposition."

THE WHIPS. Finally, the caucus or leader selects a few members to act as assistant leaders, generally known as "whips."[20] Their functions are to inform the rank-and-file members of the leadership's decisions about policy and strategy, to make sure that the members vote and vote correctly on key legislative issues, and to transmit to the leaders information about whatever dissatisfactions and resentments the members may have.

### Power and Role

We learned in Chapter 15 that the legislative party organizations' discipline and cohesion vary widely among democratic parties. On any scale

---

[19] In many multiple-party democracies a group must have a minimum number of members (ranging from three in the Israeli *Knesset* to fourteen in the French National Assembly) to enjoy the privileges granted to recognized party groups.

[20] This widely used term is of British origin, and is derived from the "whippers-in" used in fox hunting to keep the hounds from straying from the scent.

the British parliamentary parties stand near the "high" end. The majority party picks the prime minister and accepts his appointments to the cabinet and the ministry. These leaders, in turn, exercise near-absolute control over the proceedings and decisions of the House of Commons, and also constitute the British executive. Organized opposition, moreover, is monopolized by the minority party's organization and "shadow cabinet," which not only keep up a running fire of criticism and opposition to the majority party's policies but stand ever ready themselves to become the Government when the voters decide to give them a majority of the seats. As a result, British government is more completely a *party* government than any other in the democratic world in the sense that party organizations and operations are the very core of its legislative and executive processes.

Nearest the "low" end of the scale stand a few of the smaller center and right-wing parties of the multiple-party democracies. Their members ordinarily feel little internal obligation and no external compulsion to vote or act together; hence they are little more than aggregations of independent legislators who happen to bear the same formal party label.

The Democratic and Republican parties in Congress stand between the two extremes. On matters of personnel (e.g., electing the presiding officers and allocating committee positions) they are quite as cohesive as their counterparts in London. On most issues of public policy they are less cohesive than the British parties but far more so than the French Radical Socialists or Independents. To illustrate, since the late 1940's the AFL–CIO has kept score on how every senator and representative has voted on issues of particular concern to organized labor. Its summary for the period 1947–1960 shows that 71 percent of the votes cast by Democrats in both houses supported labor-liberal positions, while only 27 percent of those cast by Republicans did so. It also shows that some Democrats (e.g., Byrd and Robertson of Virginia) were as conservative as the most conservative Republicans, and that some Republicans (e.g., Javits of New York and Kuchel of California) were almost as liberal as the most liberal Democrats. In short, on most key issues in Congress most Democrats oppose most Republicans, but each party has a few mavericks who vote mostly with the opposition.[21]

We also learned in Chapter 15 that in centralization, discipline, and cohesion the dominant parties in most democracies fall on the scale somewhere between the British and American parties. But in any democracy the parties' power over their legislative members' votes and actions determines the role of party in the nation's legislative process. And it also provides much of the milieu for the individual legislator's public life. Let us see how.

---

[21] Keefe and Ogul, *op. cit.*, pp. 276–281.

# Legislative Ways of Life

For our present purposes legislators in modern democracies may usefully be divided into two general types. First is the "party man," exemplified by the ordinary "back-bench" member of the British House of Commons: a legislator subject to such strong party discipline that, except under the most unusual circumstances, he feels compelled to vote as his party whips direct. Second is the "independent operator," exemplified by the ordinary member of the United States Senate or House of Representatives: a legislator whose subjection to party discipline is sufficiently weak that he can, if he wishes, feel safe in voting contrary to his whips' requests.

## The Party Man[22]

### Life in the House

The basic features of legislative life for the ordinary British back-bencher are two: practically speaking, his vote belongs to his party's leaders, not to himself; and for him, as for all his peers, legislative success consists of appointment to ministerial office by those same leaders. Hence, if he is ambitious, whatever he does as a back-bencher must not convince his leaders he is not of ministerial caliber. And even if he has no hope of reaching ministerial rank,[23] he has little freedom to use his *vote* to gain other goals.

What, then, can he do? For one thing, he can speak in parliamentary debates. If he is good at it, he may win the leaders' approval necessary for advancement to ministerial office; and even if he does not, he may still enjoy the House's applause and favorable notices in the newspapers. For another, he can keep the ministers on their toes by asking sharp questions in question time (see Chapter 19). For still another, he can rise to eminence in his party's committees of back-benchers and through them exert substantial influence on the leaders. He can put down motions, which may cause some public stir. He can introduce private members' bills, a few

---

[22] The most complete recent description of the British back-bencher is Peter G. Richards, *Honourable Members* (London: Faber & Faber, Ltd., 1959). Other useful works include S. E. Finer, H. B. Berrington, and D. Bartholomew, *Backbench Opinion in the House of Commons, 1955–1959* (London: Pergamon Press, 1961); and Roland Young, *The British Parliament* (London: Faber & Faber, Ltd., 1962).

[23] The odds are against him. Philip Buck's study of parliamentary careers from 1918 to 1959 showed that only 32 percent of Conservative and 24 percent of Labour M.P.'s reached ministerial rank: *Amateurs and Professionals in British Politics, 1918–59* (Chicago: University of Chicago Press, 1963), p. 9.

of which may even pass. And there is always the possibility, however remote, that by abstaining or threatening to abstain from voting in a major crisis he may bring down an unwanted Government (as in the unseating of the Chamberlain Government in 1940) or reverse a disastrous Government policy (as in the Suez crisis of 1956).

Thus, by American standards, the British back-bencher's position is not impressive. His vote is not his own. He has little independent power to put pressure on administrators. He is paid very little (the equivalent of about $5000 per year), and most M.P.'s have to earn outside incomes in addition. But he is by no means a complete cipher. He belongs to one of Britain's most exclusive clubs (and about the only one in London with guaranteed parking space for his car!); he is an insider in the nation's most fascinating game; and being an M.P. may be highly useful in his career as a journalist or lawyer or businessman. Hence, relatively few M.P.'s retire voluntarily, and many defeated in general elections try again and again to win their way back. Evidently, then, even the party man who never rises to ministerial rank finds other and sufficient satisfactions in being a legislator.

### Relations with Constituents

Since the ordinary back-bencher does not control his parliamentary vote, he has no individual "voting record" for his opponents to attack or his supporters to praise. But in his constituency he is much more than merely a name with a party label. He is expected to provide a number of local services, and if he does them well he can play a significant role in constituency affairs. While the institution of ministerial responsibility (see Chapter 18) prevents him from exerting pressure on civil servants in the American sense, he can explain local problems and dramatize local needs by speeches in the House and private representations to ministers. Most M.P.'s regularly hold "surgeries" in their constituencies—that is, announced office hours during which they are available for any constituent to visit, express his views, and make requests. If the M.P. finds merit in a constituent's claim, he can call it to the relevant ministry's attention, although he can go no further. The conscientious M.P. graces with his presence local festivals, celebrations, and ceremonials. And when his constituents so request, he procures them tickets of admission to the Strangers' Gallery to watch the House in session, and invites them to tea on the handsome terrace overlooking the Thames. An M.P. who shirks his local duties is more likely to find himself in trouble with his constituency party organization than with the voters, but the point is that his local obligations are an important—and often wearying—part of his public life. In some respects, then, he has many of the independent operator's burdens with few of his powers.

## The Independent Operator

### Life in the House[24]

The American congressman operates in quite a different milieu. He owes his nomination and renomination to local organizations and voters, and no national party agency can veto it. His chances of re-election may be marginally affected by the success and support of his national party leaders, but they depend mainly on what the local voters think. Not only do his leaders have little effective power to punish him for deviant voting, but a reputation for "independence" and "refusal to submit to party dictation" may well be worth thousands of votes in his district. Moreover, a vote against his party's "line" is in no sense a vote to put the other party in control of Congress or the presidency—fixed terms and separation of powers take care of that. Hence, his vote belongs to him, and he can use it as he wishes to promote whatever values he chooses. He may voluntarily decide to "go along" with his party on most issues—a majority of congressmen, as we have seen, do just that. But the fact that his party cannot effectively *order* him to vote this way or that makes his position very different from a British M.P.'s.

How do American legislators use their heady independence? Most political scientists have answered this question in terms of the different roles different legislators choose (or are forced) to play. Barber's study of Connecticut freshman legislators, for example, distinguishes among the "spectators," "advertisers," "reluctants," and "lawmakers." For another, the Wahlke-Eulau-Buchanan-Ferguson study of legislators in California, New Jersey, Ohio, and Tennessee identifies several sets of roles: in their representational functions legislators are "trustees," "politicos," or "delegates"; in their dealings with other legislators they are "inventors," "brokers," or "tribunes"; and in their dealings with pressure groups they are "facilitators," "neutrals," or "resistors." White's and Huitt's studies of the Senate distinguish between the "members of the inner club" and the "outsiders."[25] The common theme running through all these studies is that each legislator is impelled by his own psychological makeup, his perceptions of the legis-

---

[24] Many major studies of American legislators have been made in recent years. Those on Congress include Donald R. Matthews, *U. S. Senators and Their World* (Chapel Hill: University of North Carolina Press, 1960); and Charles L. Clapp, *The Congressman: His Work as He Sees It* (Washington, D.C.: The Brookings Institution, 1963). Those on state legislators include John C. Wahlke, Heinz Eulau, William Buchanan, and LeRoy C. Ferguson, *The Legislative System* (New York: John Wiley & Sons, Inc., 1962); and James David Barber, *The Lawmakers* (New Haven: Yale University Press, 1965).

[25] William S. White, *Citadel: The Story of the U.S. Senate* (New York: Harper & Row, Publishers, 1956); and Ralph K. Huitt, "The Outsider in the Senate: An Alternative Role," *American Political Science Review*, LV (September, 1961), 566–575.

lative process in the capitol and the electoral process in his district, and his goals and ambitions to choose a certain role; and the role he chooses determines both his actions and his effectiveness.

Let us illustrate with a not-so-hypothetical case study, which we may entitle "The Education of Senator X."

Mr. X, a brilliant and idealistic young liberal, is elected to the United States Senate from a midwestern state. Justly proud of his speaking ability and burning with a zeal to push the liberal legislation for which he campaigned, he makes his "maiden" speech a few days after having been sworn in and in the ensuing weeks follows it with a number of speeches on a wide variety of topics. All his speeches are eloquent, witty, and receive favorable notice in the press, but somehow the other senators do not seem to be persuaded by them—even the other liberals. So Senator X begins to accept a number of outside speaking engagements, in the course of which he makes a number of references to the stubbornness of the conservative senators, the lack of leadership among his fellow liberals, and the inertia and sloth of the Senate itself. His name appears in the headlines with increasing frequency, and his mail indicates that the folks back home think he is wonderful. But it seems that the more popular he becomes outside the Senate, the less ability he has to get things done inside the Senate. He introduces many intelligently drafted and worthy major bills, but most of them never even get out of committee.

Finally, in desperation, he goes to Senator Y, his party's floor leader, and asks him, "Why can't I get anything done in this outfit? What am I doing wrong?" Senator Y replies, "Look, X, you are doing just about everything wrong. A couple of days after you had been sworn in you made a major speech. During your first six months you sounded off—at length—on every major issue that came up. Then you started shooting your mouth off outside the Senate and had the gall to say a lot of nasty things about some individual senators and the Senate itself. And now you keep introducing bills on every subject under the sun. Frankly, X, the boys think that you are a blow-hard and a publicity hound. They think you don't know what you are talking about most of the time, and no matter how good the bills you introduce may be, the fact that you introduced them is, as far as most of the boys are concerned, reason enough to dump them. That's the way it is."

Senator X, of course, is stunned and angry. But while he is as eager as the next man to be a hero to the folks back home, he also wishes to see his liberal legislation pass the Senate. So he decides to make a few changes in the light of Senator Y's comments. First, he picks four subjects—agriculture, civil rights, foreign affairs, and taxation—and speaks only on legislation in those areas. Second, he carefully prepares each speech, shows himself to be thoroughly conversant with all the facts and figures in each area, and confines himself to no more than one major speech on each major bill in each of his chosen areas. Third, he sharply reduces his outside speaking commitments and refrains from any direct criticism of the Senate or its individual members. Fourth, he makes a point of frequently seeking the advice of Senators A, B, and C, who are older senators and chairmen of some key committees, and does several chores for each of them. Finally, he introduces only one or two major bills at each session.

After a while X notices that when he speaks in the Senate not only do the others listen but some of them even quote him in their own speeches. His bills begin to receive serious and friendly consideration, and most of them are passed in some form or other. Other senators begin to come to him for advice. Finally, Senator Y stops him in the lobby one day and says, "X, you've straightened out just fine these past months, and all the boys on both sides of the aisle think you're okay. In fact, you are in line for the next vacancy on our policy committee, so keep it up!" As X walks away feeling very pleased, he thinks to himself that learning how the Senate really works involves a lot more than memorizing the Senate rules and the committee structure—and he only wishes he had started his education a little sooner.

### Relations with Constituents[26]

Senator X, like every American congressman and most British M.P.'s, cannot concentrate solely on the game with his fellow legislators; for the voters back home are the final arbiters of his political success.[27] So he has to perform a number of services for them. Moreover, his local chores are even more important for him than for an M.P.: his personal electoral fortunes are less tied to his party's than are the M.P.'s; and, unlike the M.P., he *can* exert direct pressure on executives and administrators. Hence failure to get results are more likely to count against him than against the M.P. when re-election time rolls around.

There is an even greater difference. Since the congressman controls his own vote he makes an individual voting record which may play a major role in his effort to get re-elected. In Chapter 12 we outlined several theories about how a democratic legislator *should* determine his vote; now it is time to ask how American congressmen actually *do* make up their minds.

---

[26] A rigorous and imaginative study is Warren E. Miller and Donald E. Stokes, *Representation in the American Congress,* to be published by Prentice-Hall, Inc.

[27] This fact of life is ignored in Allen Drury's best-selling novel, *Advise and Consent* (New York: Pocket Books, Inc., 1962) which tells its story of senatorial decision-making as though there were no voters and all the senators held office for life.

In their study of the United States House of Representatives, Miller and Stokes consider three possible explanatory models: the Burkean independent legislator, the Rousseauan constituency delegate, and the responsible-party team player. To discover which, if any, best fits American congressmen, they interviewed a sample of 116 representatives and a sample of the voters in each of their districts. They found that on most issues most constituents, as we would expect (see Chapter 10), "are almost totally uninformed about legislative issues in Washington." Moreover, few voters know anything more about their representative than his party label, and for most his voting record is a total mystery.[28]

Miller and Stokes conclude that

> no single tradition of representation fully accords with the realities of American legislative politics. The American system is a mixture, to which the Burkean, instructed-delegate, and responsible-party models all can be said to have contributed elements. Moreover, variations in the representative relation are most likely to occur as we move from one policy domain to another.[29]

On civil rights issues, most representatives voted according to their constituents' views *and* their own, which usually coincided. On social welfare issues their votes conformed with their parties' stands more nearly than with their constituents' views. And on foreign policy issues they conformed more nearly to their own views than to either their constituents' or their parties' views.

It appears, then, that the independent legislative operator is not so independent after all. If his constituents hold strong views on a salient issue, he may not flout them if he wishes to keep his seat. He has fellow legislators whose cooperation he needs to get anything done. He has friends and supporters, in organized pressure groups and out, whose help he needs to continue in office. He has a party to which he feels some loyalty and obligation even if its leaders cannot "purge" him as in Britain. And he himself is not a mere aggregation of external pressures; he is a human being with values, perceptions, and goals. Lacking the confining but simplying all-powerful party cues of the M.P., he has the freedom—and necessity—to balance the many forces bearing on him so as to arrive at votes which he, and everyone important to him, can live with.

---

[28] Significantly, however, this was not true where a particular issue was highly salient. One of their districts was the Arkansas Fifth District, which, in 1958, featured a hot contest between segregationist Dale Alford and moderate Brooks Hays, won by Alford. *All* the respondents interviewed knew both candidates' stands on segregation.

[29] Warren E. Miller and Donald E. Stokes, "Constituency Influence in Congress," *American Political Science Review*, LVII (March, 1963), 45–56, at p. 56.

# The Changing Role of Modern Legislatures

### *Their Loss of the Initiative*

The authors of the traditional conception of government noted at the beginning of this chapter believed that the legislature both should and would be the main policy-making agency in any properly organized government. After all, they reasoned, statutes and public policy are one and the same thing, and since the legislature will originate, amend, and pass all statutes, it will necessarily monopolize the making of public policy.

Contemporary political scientists agree that, setting aside the question of whether modern democratic legislatures *should* play such a role, the fact is that they do not. In every modern democratic nation during the past century the legislature has increasingly lost its power of initiative in statute making to the executive and administrative agencies. In the United States, for example, an ever-larger proportion of the major public bills are conceived, drafted, and pushed by the President and his advisers in the executive and administrative agencies. In Great Britain and the dominions the prime minister, cabinet, and ministry not only originate almost all major public bills, but, even more than in the United States, control what happens to those and other bills in the legislature. In many continental European democracies executive agencies are less powerful than in the United States or in Great Britain and the dominions, but their weakness means that the initiative in legislation has passed to the administrative agencies rather than returned to the legislature. Chapter 18 examines this world-wide development in greater detail from the standpoint of the changing role of the executive, but the description of modern democratic legislatures is incomplete without at least a discussion of this significant deviation from their traditional role.

### *Their Growth as Checkers, Revisers, and Critics*

It would be a great mistake to conclude from the foregoing that the legislature plays *no* role of significance in modern democratic government. It certainly does play such a role, but a different one from that which the traditional doctrine envisions.

While they have lost their power as initiators of policy to the executive and administrative agencies, modern democratic legislatures have greatly increased their power and activities as checkers, revisers, and critics of policies initiated by others. After all, they still retain their formal statute-making powers, which means that for a great many of his most-desired policies (e.g., taxes, appropriations, treaties, and statutes of all types) the executive must obtain the legislature's consent. Where, as in Great Britain and the dominions, the cabinet's control of the legislature through the

# "Leaving Religion To Private Initiative Is Un-American!"

*Figure 35.* The Popular Stereotype of Legislators Is Not Flattering. (From *Straight Herblock*, Simon & Schuster, 1964.)

majority party is at maximum strength, the executive appears to be able to ram through whatever policies it wishes. Yet rebellions within the majority party are always a possibility, and defeat by the voters at the next election is an even greater possibility. Hence, no British or dominion cabinet can or does totally ignore resentments and discontent within its own party or sharp criticisms by the opposition—especially those which appear to represent the feelings of substantial portions of the electorate or powerful pressure groups. In Great Britain and the dominions, while the objections and misgivings of the legislature cannot force the executive to change its policies, they can and often do make the executive come to believe that a certain amount of trimming of sails and altering of course will make for a much smoother governmental passage.

In those countries such as the United States and most European democracies where the executive's party control over the legislature is weaker than in Britain and the dominions, the legislature's revising and critical functions are even more prominent. The President of the United States may initiate and propose most major pieces of legislation, but he must expect most of them to emerge from Congress in more or less altered form, and he will find that he cannot get some of them at all. He operates his administration, moreover, in the constant presence of congressional investigations drawing public attention to the mistakes of this executive officer and the peculations of that administrator, objecting to this contract and that appointment, and in general disabusing him of any notion he may have that he and he alone has a mandate to run the whole government and make whatever policy he wishes.

In short, no American President, British or dominion prime minister, or European premier, has to be reminded that there still is a legislature to be dealt with; he is only too well aware of it.

And who, after all, is to say that the modern legislature's present role of criticizing, revising, and checking the executive and the administration does not constitute as valuable a contribution to the health of democracy as the role of monopolizing policy making assigned to the legislature by our forefathers?

# 18

## The Executive Process

**H**ow many of the following can you name: the President of the United States; the senators from your state; the congressman from your district; the speaker of the House; the majority and minority leaders in both houses of Congress; the governor of your state; the state legislators from your district; the majority and minority leaders of both houses of your state legislature?

If you are like most Americans you know who the President is, and you can probably also name your governor and perhaps one or two of your senators; but if you know the names of the others you can consider yourself exceptionally knowledgeable.

The fact that you know more about the top executives than about the top legislators does not, however, mean that you are a poor citizen; it means that for you, as for most Americans (and for most citizens of the other modern democracies) executives are, so to speak, the "glamour boys" of government. The purveyors of news over the mass media talk far more about them than about individual legislators (with the rare exceptions of a Huey Long or a Joseph McCarthy) because they think executives are more "newsworthy"—that is, you and I are presumed to be more interested in hearing about executives than about legislators.

The fact that in most democracies executives normally receive more public attention than other types of officials is both a result and a cause of the changing roles and positions of the executive and legislative agencies. In Chapter 17 we noted that in most democratic nations the legislature has to a large degree lost its traditional policy-initiating role and has become largely a checker, reviser, and critic of policies initiated by the executive. In the present chapter we shall take up the other side of this story: the general expansion of executive power and influence which has taken place in most modern democracies including the United States.

Before we begin this survey we must recognize that in the modern democracies officials generally called "executives" perform two principal and distinct roles. The first is the role of the "chief of state"—that of acting as the nation's official ceremonial head and spokesman for its whole governmental structure. The second is the role of "head of government"—that of acting as the leader of the officeholders who for the moment propose, direct, and enforce the nation's public policies. In the parliamentary democracies each role is performed by a distinctly different official or group of officials, while in the presidential democracies both are performed by the same official.

Since the executive's role as head of government has the greater impact on the policy-making processes of modern democracy, we shall devote most of our attention to it in this chapter. The chief-of-state role is by no means insignificant, however, and so we shall begin by briefly surveying what it involves, how it is performed, and who performs it.

## The Executive as Chief of State

### Principal Types

#### Hereditary Monarchs

As the data in Table 8 show, the chief of state in eighteen modern democracies is a hereditary monarch—a person who inherits his position by primogeniture[1] from his deceased parent who held it before him and who performs its functions either directly (as, for example, in the case of the British Queen, the Belgian and Scandinavian kings, and the Japanese Emperor) or indirectly through a personal representative known as a "governor-general" (as, for example, in the British dominions of Australia, Canada, and New Zealand).

As recently as the nineteenth century many hereditary monarchs not only were their nations' formal chiefs of state but also played a prominent role in policy making, and a few were absolute dictators. Even today government in the monarchies mentioned above is formally conducted largely in the name of the monarch: the British Queen, for example, formally opens and dissolves Parliament, gives her assent to all acts of Parliament before they become law, appoints all ministers, and awards all peerages and other

---

[1] That is, the ancient rule of inheritance whereby the first-born has first claim on the deceased parent's estate.

honors. Yet the Queen, like her fellow sovereigns in the other nations considered here, does all of these things only on the advice of her ministers, who in turn are selected by Parliament and, through the latter, by the voters. Hence, political scientists call these nations "constitutional monarchies" or "limited monarchies," and regard them as full-fledged democracies. Only in the "monarchical dictatorships," such as Saudi Arabia, Libya, and Bhutan (see Table 2) do the present-day monarchs play a role remotely approaching the policy-making dominance of such "absolute monarchs" of yore as Henry VIII of England and Louis XIV of France.

"Constitutional monarchs," in short, are chiefs of state only, in which capacity they perform functions we shall describe in a moment.

### Elected "Monarchs"

The nineteenth and twentieth centuries have seen most absolute monarchs toppled from their ancient pinnacles of power and many of them replaced with democratic regimes. In the "constitutional monarchies" this has been accomplished by stripping the monarchs of all policy-making powers and leaving them only ceremonial functions. Other nations have entirely abolished their monarchies and replaced them with republican regimes formally headed by some kind of elected official, usually known as the president. These nations may be divided into two groups. The first includes those which have given their presidents *only* the chief-of-state role and have thereby made them into what may be called "elected monarchs." Eight of the democracies listed in Table 8 fall in this class. Of these, three (Austria, Iceland, and Ireland) directly elect their presidents by popular vote, and five (e.g., West Germany and Italy) elect them indirectly by legislative ballot or special convention. In all eight, however, the president acts only as chief of state and performs approximately the same functions as a constitutional monarch.[2]

### Elected Heads of Government

The seven presidential democracies listed in Table 8 vest chief-of-state functions in an elected president who also acts as the head of government in the sense noted above. The outstanding instance of such an official is, of course, the President of the United States, but the same dual role is also performed by presidents in Chile, Venezuela, and the Philippines, for example. In all these nations the fact that the same person performs both of these two quite different roles gives rise to a number of complications, some of which are described below.

---

[2] The President of France in the Fifth Republic, as we shall see below, does not easily fit into either of these categories.

## Collegial Executives

In all modern democracies but two the executive powers and functions are divided between two officials, as in the parliamentary democracies, or concentrated in one official, as in the presidential democracies. Switzerland and Uruguay, however, vest both functions in collegial bodies. In Switzerland the executive functions are performed by a seven-member Federal Council, selected every four years by the two houses of the national parliament meeting in joint session. The parliament also selects a member of the council as President of the Confederation, who serves for one year, and the office rotates by seniority among the members of the council.[3] In Uruguay the executive functions are vested in a nine-member National Council, six of the majority and three of the minority party, appointed for terms of four years by the two houses of the legislature in joint session. The presidency is rotated annually among the members of the majority party in the council. In both nations the ceremonial functions are accomplished by whatever member of the collegial executive happens to be president at the moment, but the policy-directing functions are performed by the whole body.

### *Principal Functions*

## Symbolic and Ceremonial

In Chapters 1 and 2 we learned that one of the great problems facing the people of every modern democratic nation is that of maintaining a society and a government in which the myriad interest groups can freely pursue their conflicting special objectives and yet continue to live together as one nation under one government. We observed that every democracy faces the ever-present possibility of civil war and disintegration, and that every democracy also contains certain social forces and institutions that make for national unity and consensus. In the final analysis, we concluded, the citizens of the United States, like those of any democracy, will continue to live together in this fashion only so long as they think of themselves as *Americans* as well as Negroes or rich people or workers or whatever.

Every nation has a number of symbols and ceremonies which help to remind its citizens of their nationhood and their common achievements and aspirations. No American needs to be told of the significant role in this regard played by the Stars and Stripes, the Pledge of Allegiance, or the Fourth of July; and every other nation has their equivalents. Most citizens

---

[3] Christopher Hughes, *The Parliament of Switzerland* (London: The Hansard Society, 1962), Chs. VII, IX.

of every democracy apparently feel the need to include among these symbols a person who officially incarnates their nationhood and on certain great occasions speaks for the whole nation both to the nation itself and to the outside world.

This is the main reason why every nation, democracies and dictatorships alike, has an official chief of state (usually, though not in every instance, a single official), and it gives rise to the functions he is supposed to perform. When, for example, a member of the armed forces is due to receive the nation's highest decoration—the Congressional Medal of Honor or the Victoria Cross—the President or the Queen pins it on. When the nation pays tribute to its war dead, it is the President or the Queen who lays the wreath on the Unknown Soldier's tomb. When the Red Cross or the Boy Scouts or some other worthy enterprise needs a boost, the President or the Queen speaks in its behalf and is photographed subscribing to it. In these and many other ways the President and the Queen personalize and humanize that sometimes grim abstraction "the government" and remind the citizens of their common heritage and hopes. Let only him who is without emotions and scorns all loyalties and patriotism say that these symbolic and ceremonial functions of the chief of state are insignificant!

### "Reigning"

Constitutional monarchs and elected "monarchs" perform largely but not exclusively ceremonial and symbolic functions. In addition to these duties they also "reign"—that is, provide the formal channel through which governmental power is passed in a peaceful and orderly way from one person or set of persons to another. In any of the parliamentary democracies, for example, when the prime minister leaves office and must be replaced by another, the chief of state formally accomplishes the transfer by "summoning" the new man and charging him with the responsibility of forming a new "Government." In the great majority of such occasions in Great Britain and the dominions the monarch has no option but must "summon" the leader of the party that controls the lower house of the legislature. Yet British monarchs have occasionally made real choices, the most clear instance of which occurred in 1957 when the prime minister and Conservative party leader Sir Anthony Eden resigned. Since the Conservatives held a majority in the House of Commons, Queen Elizabeth had to replace Eden with another Conservative, but the party had never indicated whether it wished Eden's successor to be Harold Macmillan or R. A. Butler. After private consultations with her personal advisers, the Queen "summoned" Macmillan, and he became the new prime minister. She is widely believed to have played a similar role in the choice of Lord Home over Butler in 1963.

## Separation and Combination of Roles

During the Korean war President Harry Truman was scheduled to award a posthumous Congressional Medal of Honor to one of our servicemen through his father, but the father refused to accept it saying "Harry Truman isn't fit to honor my son." This episode dramatized the disadvantages of combining in one executive officer the two quite separate roles of chief of state and head of government; obviously, the serviceman's father was not saying that the United States itself was unfit to honor his son, but only that the individual Harry Truman—who was not only President of the United States but also the head of the Democratic party, "that man who got us into the war," a Fair Dealer, and many other things *political*—was objectionable. In other words, the father objected to the head of government, not to the chief of state—but both officials were wrapped up in the same Missouri package!

The President Is Chief of State: Irish President Eamon de Valera Is Escorted by President and Mrs. Johnson to a State Dinner in the White House during the United States-Born Leader's Visit to the United States. (Wide World Photos, Inc.)

Radio and television networks face the same kind of problem. When an American President speaks free of charge over a national hookup on some public issue and the opposition party demands equal free time to reply, the networks have to decide whether the President was speaking as the chief of state or as the leader of his party. If he was speaking in the former capacity the opposition's demand is nonsense, but if he was speaking as a partisan, fair play and the Federal Communications Commission's rules require that the opposition party be given equal time.

It is illuminating to recall in this regard that when such British monarchs as Charles I and George III took an active part in policy making and strove to become the heads of their governments, they were widely and openly criticized—and indeed, Charles I was executed! Now that such monarchs as Frederik IX and Elizabeth II are chiefs of state only, they are largely beyond any kind of public criticism and certainly are in no danger of losing their heads! Occasionally recent British monarchs and their consorts have been criticized for making "political speeches" (i.e., speeches advocating certain policies) but this only means that the particular individuals may have stepped outside their proper roles, not that the roles are, as in the United States, intermingled and confused.

Professor Finer sums up the advantages of assigning the two roles to different officials thus:

> As a father-image, or an impersonation of the romantic, says the psychoanalyst, king or queen stands scatheless, the noble father or mother, while the politicians may be vilified and scourged. This duality is politically comfortable. On the one hand, politics might be red in tooth and claw; on the other, royalty reminds the nation of its brotherhood amid their conflicts. The silk gloves are something to be thankful for.[4]

Being chief of state is of considerable assistance to the President of the United States in his role as head of government. In the United States as in all modern democracies it is the latter role of the executive which most powerfully affects the making of public policy.

### The Executive as Head of Government: The Three Principal Types

Every modern democracy has an executive officer who in some fashion performs the role of head of government. The manner in which the role is performed, however, varies considerably among the different democracies. Hence, a useful way to describe the modern democratic executives as heads of government is to divide them into the following three principal types.

### 1. The President

In the seven presidential democracies the role of head of government as well as that of chief of state is performed by a president. This officer cannot be a member of the legislature and is elected, either indirectly by an "electoral college" as in the case of the presidents of Finland and the United States or directly by the nation's voters as in the case of the presi-

---

[4] Herman Finer, *Governments of Greater European Powers* (New York: Holt, Rinehart and Winston, Inc., 1956), pp. 189–190. See also Dermot Morrah, *The Work of the Queen* (London: William Kimber & Co., Ltd., 1958).

dents of Brazil, Chile, Costa Rica, Liberia, and the Philippines. He holds office for a legally fixed term whether or not he commands the "confidence" of the legislature. The President of the United States is the oldest and best-known example of such an official and remains the prototype for the others.

## 2. The Prime Minister

In all the parliamentary democracies the role of head of government is performed by a leader formally designated by the chief of state for the post but actually selected because he has the approval of a majority of the legislature. He has no fixed tenure of office but depends upon his continuing ability to command the "confidence" of a legislative majority. When that majority votes "no confidence" in him, he must resign, and the chief of state must replace him with some other leader whom the legislature will support. In Great Britain, the dominions, and the other parliamentary democracies with strong national two-party systems the prime minister is normally the leader of the party holding a majority or plurality in the lower house of the legislature. The British prime minister is the prototype of such an officer.

## 3. The Premier

A number of European democracies, as we observed in Chapter 15, have multiple-party systems and so no legislator can be the leader of *the* majority party as the British Prime minister is. In such democracies the role of head of government is performed by a leader who is formally designated as such by the chief of state. These officers have various official titles, such as "chancellor" (West Germany) or "premier" (France). We shall use the term "premier" to cover all such officials. He is chosen because he can head up a coalition "Government" made up of leaders of several parties and supported by the latters' members in the legislature. When one or two of these parties decide to withdraw their support, the premier's "Government" falls and he is replaced by another premier whom a majority of the legislature will support. Consequently, although the premier's position is formally very similar to that of the prime minister, his actual power and influence are considerably weaker—so much so, in fact, that it is useful to consider all such officers as constituting a different type from the prime ministers of Great Britain and the dominions. The French premiers of the Third and Fourth Republics are the prototypes, although their present status and relation to the French President is a somewhat complicated matter that we shall take up later.

We shall now consider in greater detail the nature of each of these three types of executives and the differing roles they play in their nation's governing processes.

# The President as Head of Government

## *The Development of the Office*

### The Intentions of the Founding Fathers

The members of the American Constitutional Convention in 1787 were well aware that many of their compatriots were extremely suspicious of executive power and that the weak governorships in many of the new state Constitutions resulted from this suspicion. But the Founding Fathers, unlike some of their contemporaries, were equally suspicious of an all-powerful legislature and felt that some kind of reasonably strong executive would be needed to check Congress. Everyone knew, moreover, that George Washington, the most venerated American of his time, would occupy whatever executive office was created.

Accordingly, they intended the office of President of the United States to be something closely approaching what they understood the British king to be—that is, George III with the corruption and the hereditary principle removed. As Clinton Rossiter sums up their views, "The President was to be a strong, dignified, nonpolitical chief of state and government. In a word, he was to be George Washington."[5]

### The Expansion of the Presidency since 1789

The presidency of Lyndon B. Johnson in the 1960's is a radically different office from the presidency of George Washington and John Adams in the 1790's. The modern President is not only a partisan official, but the number-one leader of one of the nation's two great political parties. Rather than acting merely as an adviser to and restrainer of Congress, he is the principal source of the major public bills Congress considers and is often called our "chief legislator." He and his advisers dominate the formulation and conduct of our foreign policy, and in times of national crisis the President becomes what some scholars have called a "constitutional dictator." Finally, what he does concerns many more people than just Americans; for he is regarded as the leader of the free world in its struggle with its communist antagonists, and what goes on in the White House is of almost as much concern in London and Paris—and, for that matter, in Moscow and Peking—as it is in New York and Chicago.

The story of how and why the presidency of the 1960's has come to be so much more powerful than the presidency of the 1790's is too lengthy and complex to be related in its entirety here. However, most political scientists believe that the expansion of the presidency has resulted from two

---

[5] Clinton Rossiter, *The American Presidency* (New York: Harcourt, Brace & World, Inc., 1956), p. 60.

main causes.[6] First, the democratization of the office resulting from the conversion of the Electoral College system into a machine for the popular election of the President (see Chapter 6) has made him the only public official (except the Vice-President, who doesn't count) elected by all the nation's voters. Every President since Andrew Jackson has to some degree regarded himself as holding a special "mandate from the people" to work in their behalf, and this has greatly enhanced the powers of the presidency and inclined many occupants of the office to exercise them vigorously—for the most part with the full and enthusiastic approval of a majority of voters. Second, the United States has grown from an agricultural nation of 4 million people to an industrial nation of nearly 200 million and from a third-rate power to the most powerful nation in the world. This has increasingly forced problems of foreign policy, international relations, and war and peace to the forefront of popular and governmental concern; and since the President has always dominated the handling of such problems, their increasing importance has greatly added to his power and prestige.

Some commentators have suggested that this expansion of presidential power is the consequence of the unfortunate fact that the office has been held by a number of persons greedy for power rather than by the modest constitutional types envisioned by the Founding Fathers. The evidence suggests, however, that this is a highly superficial explanation. For one thing, executive power has also expanded considerably in a great many local governments in the United States, and many mayors, city managers, and governors have increased their power much in the manner of the President.[7] For another, as we shall observe at the end of the present chapter, similar expansions of executive power have taken place in most of the other democratic nations. It is, in short, a development characteristic of most of the democratic world, and not unique to the American presidency.

Whatever may be the causes of the presidency's expansion, there is no doubt that it has become perhaps the most powerful elective office in the modern world.

### The Roles of the President[8]

#### 1. Chief of State

The first role of the President of the United States is that of chief of state, in which capacity he performs symbolic and ceremonial functions

---

[6] Cf. Rossiter, *op. cit.*, Chs. 3–4; and Norman J. Small, *Some Presidential Interpretations of the Presidency* (Baltimore: The Johns Hopkins Press, 1932).

[7] Cf. Leslie Lipson, *The American Governor, From Figurehead to Leader* (Chicago: University of Chicago Press, 1939); and Coleman B. Ransone, Jr., *The Office of Governor in the United States* (University: University of Alabama Press, 1956).

[8] An unusually thoughtful and influential study of the presidency in action is Richard E. Neustadt, *Presidential Power* (New York: John Wiley & Sons, Inc., 1960).

The President as Head of Government: President Johnson Gives One of the 72 Pens He Used in Signing the Civil Rights Bill in the White House in 1964 to Roy Wilkins of the National Association for the Advancement of Colored People. (Wide World Photos, Inc.)

similar to those of all chiefs of state. Although the combination of the chief-of-state and head-of-government roles in the presidency gives rise to a certain amount of confusion, that combination also gives the President a kind of majesty that assists him considerably in his head-of-government capacity. As Sidney Hyman points out,

> Though he is sharply judged by the memories of his predecessors, his size seems to grow larger and clearer because he stands in their place. . . . Most important of all, he can lend his personal style to proud imitation by millions of people in private stations; he can bind the aspiration of the nation to the upward leap of his individual conscience, and infuse his own compassion into the national mind. He is, or can be, the essence of the nation's personality. In him, many things can flower—or decay.[9]

---

[9] The American President (New York: Harper & Row, Publishers, 1954), p. 13.

## 2. Chief Executive

The President is formally responsible for most of the agencies charged with enforcing and administering acts of Congress and decisions of the national courts. The "Hoover Commission" studying the reorganization of the executive in the 1950's found that President Eisenhower was responsible in one way or another for the work of 9 major departments, 104 bureaus, 108 services, 460 offices, 631 divisions, and a host of other agencies, which together employed one out of every sixty-two civilians in the nation (by contrast with one out of every two thousand in Washington's day).[10]

For many years the President's principal assistance in supervising administrative agencies came from the heads of the executive departments, of which there are now ten: State; Treasury; Defense; Justice; Post Office; Interior; Agriculture; Commerce; Labor; and Health, Education, and Welfare. From the early 1790's these officers have regularly met together with the President and advised him not only on matters of administration but on matters of legislation and other policy making as well. In their collective advisory capacity they are known as the President's cabinet. Some Presidents have been strongly influenced by their cabinets, while others have consigned theirs to a distinctly secondary role. Abraham Lincoln, for example, used his cabinet as little more than a sounding board for his own ideas, while Eisenhower regarded his cabinet as one of his most important advisory bodies.[11]

Over the years the cabinet has increasingly become a policy-advising body rather than an administration-supervising agency, and recent Presidents have turned more and more to other agencies to assist them in their mammoth task of overseeing the administrative agencies. In 1939 Congress established a new agency, the Executive Office of the President, for this purpose. It now has over 1200 full-time employees, and includes such agencies as the White House Office, the National Security Council, the Council of Economic Advisers, the Office of Emergency Planning, and the Bureau of the Budget.

The presidency in short, is no longer something the individual President carries around under his hat. It has become an agency headed by the President but composed of a great many officers and employees performing a wide variety of tasks in the President's name, only a small fraction of which can he personally supervise. Chapter 19 further discusses the consequences of this situation.

---

[10] *Ibid.*, pp. 9–10.
[11] Cf. Richard F. Fenno, *The President's Cabinet* (Cambridge, Mass.: Harvard University Press, 1959).

### 3. Chief Diplomat

The President has always dominated the formulation and conduct of our foreign policy. He is the sole official channel of communications with foreign nations, and by receiving or refusing to receive official emissaries from foreign nations he alone determines whether or not the United States officially "recognizes" their governments. He and his representatives negotiate all international treaties and agreements. The Constitution requires that all treaties be approved by a two-thirds vote of the Senate, but recent Presidents have concluded a great many "executive agreements"—international agreements made by the President on his own authority and not referred to the Senate for ratification. Their importance is shown by the fact that the Supreme Court has refused to make any clear or major distinction between them and regular treaties ratified by the Senate with regard to which are more binding and which are, within the meaning of the Constitution, the "law of the land."[12]

### 4. Commander in Chief

The Constitution makes the President the commander in chief of all our armed forces. The framers of the Constitution wrote this clause mainly to establish the cherished principle of civilian supremacy over and control of the military, and some wartime Presidents (e.g., Lincoln and the second Roosevelt) have taken a very active role in planning strategy and even directing troop movements, while others (e.g., Madison and Wilson) have left such matters entirely to professional soldiers. The main significance of the commander-in-chief clause lies in the power it has given the President to threaten or even wage war even if Congress has not authorized it. Thus in 1950 President Truman ordered our armed forces to resist the North Korean and Chinese Communist attack on South Korea. For two years we fought a "police action" in Korea that was not a "war" only because Congress did not formally declare it such. A decade later in 1962 President Kennedy ordered the armed forces to "quarantine" Cuba from further shipments of Russian missiles even if it meant sinking Russian ships and starting a thermonuclear war with the Soviet Union. Yet a century of comparable actions by previous Presidents backed up by the Supreme Court's approval left no doubt that both Presidents were acting fully within their constitutional powers.[13] Hence, few can doubt that the power to

---

[12] Cf. *U.S. v. Belmont*, 301 U.S. 324 (1937).

[13] The leading case in point is *Durand v. Hollins*, 4 Blatch 451 (1860). For a discussion of the Court's position and an account of other episodes in which Presidents used force abroad without prior authorization by Congress, see Edward S. Corwin, *The President: Office and Powers* (3d. ed.; New York: New York University Press, 1948), pp. 241–49.

choose between war and peace—surely one of the greatest powers in any government—now lies with the President rather than with Congress.

## 5. Emergency Leader

In the spring of 1861, when he was faced with the secession of a number of southern states and the imminent collapse of the Union, Abraham Lincoln ordered Fort Sumter to be provisioned and reinforced, knowing full well that his action would precipitate civil war. After Sumter had been fired on, Lincoln—on his own authority and with no prior authorization by Congress—proclaimed a naval blockade of southern ports, summoned the state militia to active service, spent government money on war matériel, suspended the writ of habeas corpus, and in general simply ignored constitutional restraints on his power. Lincoln knew he had violated the Constitution by these actions, but in a letter to one of his critics he explained why he had done so:

> I felt that measures otherwise unconstitutional might become lawful by becoming indispensable to the preservation of the Constitution through the preservation of the nation. Right or wrong, I assumed this ground, and now avow it. I could not feel that, to the best of my ability, I had even tried to preserve the Constitution if, to save slavery or any minor matter, I should permit the wreck of the government, country, and Constitution all together.[14]

Lincoln believed, in other words, that any government must have an "emergency power"—the power to do whatever is necessary to save the nation in a time of crisis. Since the President can act more swiftly than Congress, this power must necessarily be his. Lincoln's re-election in 1864 and his subsequent elevation to something like national sainthood suggest that the people in his time and since have not only approved of Lincoln's "taking over" in this crisis but have demanded that his successors do the same in other crises. Thus, subsequent Presidents have at various times intervened in strikes, closed the banks, suspended stockmarket operations, ordered troops to suppress domestic disorders, and in general acted as the nation's protector of the peace." There is no doubt that in any future crisis —a great depression or an atomic war—most Americans will look to the President, not Congress, to lead them out of the wilderness.

## 6. Party Leader

The President is also either the chief Democrat or the chief Republican. The American national parties, as we observed in Chapter 15, are mainly devices for nominating and electing a President, to a smaller degree agencies for staffing the administrative agencies, and to a still smaller degree

---

[14] Letter to A. G. Hodges, April 4, 1864, quoted in Louis Brownlow, *The President and the Presidency* (Chicago: Public Administration Service, 1949), p. 58.

The President Carries an Enormous Burden: John F. Kennedy during the Cuba Crisis, 1962. (Wide World Photos, Inc.)

agencies for organizing Congress and guiding its activities. In all of these operations the President is the leader of one of the two contesting parties. He names the chairman of his party's national committee and, if eligible for re-election, dominates its national convention. Through his power of appointment he is the main dispenser of patronage. Through his appeals to party loyalty and his promise of support of his party's congressmen in their campaigns for re-election he exerts some influence over Congress. In none of these capacities is he as powerful as the national leaders of the parties in most other democracies, but he certainly comes much nearer to being the national leader of his party than any other person. No matter how strongly he may wish to be "nonpartisan" and "the President of the whole people," he sooner or later finds that he is forced to act in a partisan matter. For example, President Eisenhower at first wished to avoid any heavily partisan campaigning in the 1954 congressional elections, but the pleas of his fellow Republicans for help became so strong that he wound up not only issuing a public blanket endorsement of all Republican candidates against their Democratic opponents but personally campaigning more actively than any President had ever done in an "off-year" election.[15]

### 7. Chief Legislator

In his own executive capacity the President can make a great deal of "law" as we have defined the term: he can issue proclamations, directives, ordinances, regulations, and orders, all of which are at least legally binding on those to whom they apply and enforceable in the courts. He is generally regarded as our "chief legislator," however, mainly because he has taken over most of the initiative in the nation's statute-making process (see Chapter 17). Most of the major public bills passed by Congress are now originally conceived and drafted by the President's advisers in the cabinet and the administrative agencies and are steered through Congress by the President's supporters there.

This does not mean, of course, that Congress supinely does whatever the President wishes—far from it. More often than not Congress revises the President's requests more or less drastically and not infrequently turns them down entirely. It does mean, however, that in so far as the American system provides a single source and supervisor of an over-all legislative program, the President, and not any congressional agency, does the job.

The legislative relations between President and Congress are more often in the nature of a contest than a Quaker-meeting effort at compromise. Since Congress retains the formal power to enact statutes and make appropriations, it is far from helpless in this perennial contest. Over the years, however, various Presidents have fashioned a number of weapons which have done much to overcome Congress's constitutional advantages. Five of them are worthy of mention.

---

[15] Cf. Robert J. Donovan, *Eisenhower: The Inside Story* (New York: Harper & Row, Publishers, 1956), Ch. 20.

**CONVINCING CONGRESSMEN.** During his service as floor leader of the Senate Democrats (1953–1960) Lyndon Johnson won the reputation of being one of the most skilled legislative leaders in history. In his first years as President (1963–1966) he matched—many think excelled—Franklin Roosevelt's record of inducing Congress to adopt his programs, including such major and controversial measures as the Civil Rights Act of 1964, the Voting Rights Act of 1965, "Medicare," and the "War on Poverty." Most observers of Johnson's leadership believe that his basic method is convincing congressmen that it is in the nation's interest and their own to vote for his measures. He accomplishes this by such techniques as talking to them (the White House phone is in constant use), doing them favors and reminding them of favors done, knowing the politics and needs of their states and districts, and knowing whom to press, when, how hard, and how often. Johnson's phenomenal success suggests that the President's best way of winning his legislative contest with Congress is to keep it from being seen as a contest. But when Congress refuses to be persuaded, he, like other Presidents, has four other recourses.

**THE VETO AND THREAT OF VETO.** The Constitution provides that if the President vetos an act of Congress (i.e., refuses to assent to it) it becomes law only if repassed by two-thirds majorities in both houses. Since 1789 only about 16 percent of all vetoes of public bills have been overridden by Congress, and so the veto has been a powerful negative weapon.[16] It has also become a positive weapon, since many a President has let it be known through his spokesmen in Congress that if thus and such a provision is retained in a particular bill, he will veto it and has often thereby induced Congress to eliminate the objectionable provision. The effectiveness of this weapon is limited, however, by the fact that he does not have the power of "item veto"—that is, he must either approve or veto a bill in its entirety and cannot veto particular items while approving the rest. This has led to the practice of "riders," whereby Congress attaches an item the President opposes to a bill (e.g., an appropriations bill) he cannot afford to veto. Even so, however, his veto power is a powerful weapon of legislative leadership.

**PATRONAGE.** The President may, if he wishes, appoint to administrative positions persons favored by his supporters among his fellow partisans in Congress and withhold such favors from his opponents. Franklin D. Roosevelt used this technique with great success early in his first term. His successors, however, have used it much less, mainly because they have had

---

[16] Edward S. Corwin and Louis W. Koenig, *The Presidency Today* (New York: New York University Press, 1956), p. 88.

fewer patronage jobs at their disposal ("merit-system" regulations, described in Chapter 19, have increasingly reduced their number).

PARTY LEADERSHIP. To some extent every President since McKinley has used his position of party leadership to induce Congress to follow his wishes, and some, notably Woodrow Wilson, Franklin Roosevelt, and Lyndon Johnson, have used it with considerable success. As we noted in Chapter 15, however, the President can remove a recalcitrant congressman from his position only by defeating him in a state or local primary. Only a few Presidents have tried to do this, and they succeeded only on the rare occasions in which they were able to gain the support of the local party organization.[17] Consequently, the President's party leadership is one of the weaker weapons in his armory.

APPEAL TO PUBLIC OPINION. Rightly used, the President's most powerful weapon against balky legislators is a direct appeal to the people to pressure their congressmen to support his program. Most Presidents have considered it a weapon of last resort, to be used only when all others have failed. If the President is more nearly in tune than Congress with popular demands and if his appeal to them is skillfully made, Congress can hardly resist him—for such an appeal hits congressmen where they are most vulnerable, in the ballot box. But if they are nearer the popular temper than he, or if his appeal is ineptly made, or if he makes too many appeals on too many issues, he loses his audience and his appeals fall on deaf ears. The trick is knowing when and how and on what issues to make an appeal.[18]

### The Power and Problems of the President

The President has several advantages over the prime minister and many advantages over the premier (see below) as head of government. For one thir_3, his independent constitutional position (the fact that he is not elected by nor formally responsible to Congress aside from the seldom-used device of impeachment) and his independent constitutional powers (e.g., as chief executive, sole channel of communications with foreign nations, and commander in chief) enable him to make and enforce many kinds of policy without even consulting Congress, let alone obtaining its approval. For another, his position as chief of state gives him a kind of prestige denied to any prime minister or premier. For still another, the many roles he plays reinforce each other and add to his over-all dominance of the policy-making process; for, as Professor Rossiter points out,

---

[17] For a review of the various presidential "purges" of balky congressmen, see Austin Ranney and Willmoore Kendall, *Democracy and the American Party System* (New York: Harcourt, Brace & World, Inc., 1956), pp. 286–289.

[18] Cf. Pendleton Herring, *Presidential Leadership* (New York: Holt, Rinehart and Winston, Inc., 1940), pp. 68–69.

He is a more exalted Chief of State because he is also Voice of the People, a more forceful Chief Diplomat because he commands the armed forces personally, a more effective Chief Legislator because the political system forces him to be Chief of Party, a more artful Manager of Prosperity because he is Chief Executive.[19]   ,

Yet, there are many limitations on his power within which he must play his role as head of government. The Constitution limits him to two elected terms in office, and when Congress and his fellow partisans know that he cannot be President after a certain date, his legislative and party leadership inevitably declines in strength. The Constitution also locates large areas of independent power in Congress and the Supreme Court. When Congress denies him the legislation and appropriations he desires, he cannot, like a prime minister, "dissolve" Congress and get one more to his liking. The Supreme Court can declare his actions unconstitutional (e.g., the Court's decision against President Truman's seizure of the steel mills in 1952), and though he may threaten to "pack" the Court, the widespread belief in an "independent judiciary" may well frustrate his plans. He can never count upon either solid or energetic support for his policies from his partisans in Congress or elsewhere. Despite his formal position as chief executive, as we shall see in Chapter 19, he cannot even be sure that his orders to his administrative subordinates will be carried out as he wishes.

The presidency, in short, has become the key institution of the American system of government. But while the system allows him many opportunities to persuade, it gives him little chance to command and be sure he will be obeyed. Here is testimony from one who knows:

In the early summer of 1952, before the heat of the campaign, President Truman used to contemplate the problems of the General-become-President should Eisenhower win the forthcoming election. "He'll sit here," Truman would remark (tapping his desk for emphasis), "and he'll say, 'Do this! Do that!' *And nothing will happen.* Poor Ike—it won't be a bit like the Army. He'll find it very frustrating." . . . Long before he came to talk of Eisenhower he had put his own experience in other words: "I sit here all day trying to persuade people to do the things they ought to have sense enough to do without my persuading them. . . . That's all the powers of the President amount to."[20]

So while we have placed Atlas's burden on our President's shoulders, we have also severely limited the ways in which he can carry it. Are other types of democratic executives better off? Let us see.

---

[19] Rossiter, *op. cit.*, p. 25.
[20] Neustadt, *op. cit.*, pp. 9–10.

# The Prime Minister as Head of Government[21]

## *The Formation of the British Executive*

The British executive is composed of three interrelated but distinct sets of officials, the prime minister, the ministry, and the cabinet; and it is formed as follows.

First, the monarch "summons" one of her subjects and asks him to become prime minister and form a "Government."[22] In most instances the monarch has no option but must pick the designated leader of the party holding a majority of the seats in the House of Commons, although, as we

The Prime Minister.
(Wide World
Photos, Inc.)

noted earlier, on a few occasions in which the majority party has not designated a leader the monarch has exercised some real choice. The prime minister must not only be a member of Parliament, but, since 1902, a member of the House of Commons.

The prime minister automatically becomes First Lord of the Treasury (a sinecure with no administrative duties), and then proceeds to fill the other executive posts by making recommendations to the monarch, which

---

[21] Useful accounts of the British executive include W. Ivor Jennings, *Cabinet Government* (London: Cambridge University Press, 1959); Herbert Morrison, *Government and Parliament* (London: Oxford University Press, 1960); and Byrum E. Carter, *The Office of Prime Minister* (Princeton, N.J.: Princeton University Press, 1956).

[22] In the technical parlance of Great Britain, the dominions, and many other parliamentary democracies, the term "the Government" is roughly synonymous with the American term "the Administration" and refers to all the officials in the ministry and cabinet discussed in the text.

are invariably followed. These posts include: (1) the ministers—the heads of the twenty-four[23] executive departments or "ministries" (e.g., Foreign Office, Home Office, Defence, and Education), and several additional ministers, some without departmental duties (e.g., the Lord Privy Seal and the Chancellor of the Duchy of Lancaster) and some with (e.g., Economic Secretary to the Treasury, Minister of State in the Foreign Office); (2) the "parliamentary secretaries" who serve in various departments as deputies to the minister; (3) several "law officers" (e.g., the Attorney General and the Solicitor General); and (4) the "whips" (see Chapter 15). All of these executives, amounting to about one hundred officers in all, plus the prime minister together make up the "ministry" or "Government."

In making his recommendations to the monarch, however, the prime minister by no means has an absolutely free hand. In the first place, with rare exceptions every member of the ministry must be a member of Parliament, and most of the important ministers must be members of the House of Commons. Note that this rule is the direct opposite of the rule in the presidential systems which prohibits anyone from holding both a seat in the legislature and an executive post at the same time. In the second place, most members of the ministry and all the important members must be leaders of the majority party—except in the case of "coalition" or "national" Governments (i.e., all-party) such as those established during times of crisis (e.g., 1895–1905, 1915–1922, 1940–1945). In the third place, the prime minister must find a place for the other top parliamentary leaders of his party regardless of how he feels about them personally, and also must make sure that no major faction of his party feels left out.

The ministry rarely or never meets and deliberates as a body. This kind of activity is left to the cabinet, which consists of those members of the ministry whom the prime minister regularly invites to meet together and consult with him as a body. Its size and composition change from time to time in accordance with his desires, but in normal times the cabinet has from eighteen to twenty-three members and includes all the top ministers both with and without departmental duties. It has thus been called "a select committee of Parliament," but could better be described as "a committee of the top leaders of the majority party."

### The Status, Functions, and Powers of the Cabinet

Some commentators on the British system emphasize the convention according to which the cabinet, like the ministry and the prime minister, remains in power only so long as it "commands the confidence" of the House of Commons—that is, so long as the House does not vote down any measure which the cabinet regards as important or pass a motion of

---

[23] As of 1965; the number has varied as new ministries have been established and old ones abolished from time to time.

"no confidence" in the whole cabinet or any of its members. This emphasis, however, is misleading. Since 1894 only three prime ministers and cabinets have resigned because of adverse votes in the House (Rosebery in 1895, Baldwin in 1924, and Chamberlain in 1940), and the discipline and cohesion of British parties are so strong that such episodes, which can occur only as the result of rebellions within the majority party, are highly unlikely. This does not mean that the cabinet can or does totally ignore the feelings of the House, but it does mean that any cabinet with a reasonably large party majority behind it in the House can count on as much of its full statutory five-year tenure in office as it wishes.

Although a number of its members have administration-supervising duties, the cabinet is almost exclusively a policy-making and legislation-designing body. Its members and their advisers think up, draft, and present to Parliament most of the major public bills introduced therein. They defend the Government's policies in parliamentary debate, guide the Government's legislation through the various stages of Parliament's law making processes, decide what amendments to accept and what to reject, and in general control what Parliament does.

The dominance of the cabinet over Parliament is far greater than that of the President over Congress. There are many reasons why this is so, some of which, e.g., the great cohesion and discipline of British parties, we have already mentioned. We should mention an additional reason: the prime minister's power to dissolve the House. Although there is some doubt about the full extent of this power, it is generally agreed that if at any time the prime minister asks the monarch to dissolve the House before its five-year term has expired, the monarch must do so. When she does, a general election must be held forthwith to elect a new House. This means, of course, that if the House should happen to kick over the traces and deny the prime minister and cabinet some item of legislation, they need not meekly resign. They can ask for a new election and, through their influence over who may and may not run as the party's official candidates (see Chapter 15), make it very difficult for the rebels in their party to be re-elected. Most observers believe that these two powers of the party leaders—to dissolve Parliament, and to withhold the party label from rebellious M.P.'s—are the basic and almost irresistible weapons of control the cabinet holds over the House of Commons.

### The Role of the Prime Minister

Not so long ago it was fashionable to say that the position of the prime minister in the cabinet and ministry is that of *primus inter pares* ("first among equals") and that his position is much like that of the chairman of the board of directors of a business corporation. Most present-day commentators, however, feel that while this may have been true years ago, the modern prime minister has become the dominant figure within the cabinet and the ministry and, therefore, within the whole British system of government. He and not the cabinet has the power to ask the monarch to dissolve Parliament and to appoint and dismiss ministers, judges, and diplomatic representatives. He and not the cabinet represents Britain at international conferences "at the summit" among other heads of government. And it is he who determines who shall sit in the cabinet, not the cabinet who determines who shall be prime minister.

The present dominance of the prime minister is the result of three main factors. First, the increasing centralization, discipline, and cohesion of British political parties have given their leaders, one of whom is always prime minister, increasing control not only over the parties' rank and file but also over the parties' second-echelon leaders who make up the cabinet and the ministry.[24]

Second, the combination of universal suffrage and modern mass communications has increasingly converted British general elections into contests for the office of prime minister. The campaigns are centered mainly about the personalities and qualifications of the two rival party leaders, who carry the bulk of the campaigning for their respective parties. Most people vote for or against one of these two men as well as for or against the party he leads. As Lord Robert Cecil put it:

> I should say that if you really looked into the real principle of our constitution now, it is purely plebiscital, that you have really a plebiscite by which a particular man is selected as Prime Minister, he then selects the Ministry himself, and it is pretty much what he likes, subject to what affects the rule that he has to consider—namely, that he must not do anything that is very unpopular.[25]

Finally, the same kind of economic and military crises that have, as we saw previously, taken power away from the collegial body of Congress and given it to the President as a one-man "emergency leader" have also taken power away from the collegial body of the cabinet and given it to the prime minister as the same kind of "emergency leader."[26]

The prime minister, in short, is in some respects even more powerful than the President, particularly in his ability to lead his political party and the legislature where he wishes them to go. This is by no means true, however, of all heads of government in all the parliamentary democracies, as the following discussion will show.

---

[24] This is one of the central points made by Professor R. T. McKenzie in his distinguished study of the internal power-structures of the British parties: *British Political Parties* (New York: St. Martin's Press, Inc., 1955), esp. Chs. II–III, and VI.

[25] Quoted in Herman Finer, *Theory and Practice of Modern Government* (rev. ed.; (New York: Holt, Rinehart and Winston, Inc., 1949), p. 363.

[26] See Carter, *op. cit.*, Ch. VI, for an explanation of the prime minister's increasing power.

# The Premier as Head of Government

## *Special Problems of Coalition Governments*

The British prime minister's power is firmly rooted in his leadership of a disciplined and cohesive political party that holds a majority of the seats in the House of Commons. So long as he commands its loyalty, he need not worry about how the opposition votes (he knows it will usually vote against his program). His main political concern is that the voters approve his Government's actions and renew its mandate at the next general election.

In some multiple-party democracies, e.g., Denmark, Ireland, Japan, Norway, and Sweden, one party usually comes so close to winning a majority of the parliamentary seats that it can form and sustain a one-party Government much like the British. These Governments are not significantly less stable than Britain's, and their premiers occupy positions similar to that of the British prime minister's.[27]

However, in other multiple-party democracies, e.g., Belgium, Israel, Italy, and the Netherlands, one party rarely comes close to winning a majority of the seats, and so their Governments are necessarily coalitions of several parties. The premier of such a coalition cannot rely solely on his own party's backing, for he needs the votes of the other coalition members to stay in office. Hence his first (though not his only) concern must be what his coalition partners, not the voters, think of his actions and proposals.

How does this affect his power to lead? The answer depends mainly on the nature of the other parties. If the legislature's seats are divided among a lot of little parties instead of a few big ones, he will have that many more party leaders to find ministerial offices for and keep happy. If there are deep ideological divisions among the principal parties and little willingness to compromise, he will have to construct his program very carefully. And if their leaders dislike each other personally, he will have to handle them with special tact. So being premier of such a Government is not the most desirable executive position in the world.

## *The French Premier before 1958*[28]

### Selection

The French premier under the Third (1870–1940) and Fourth (1946–1958) Republics was generally considered the prototype of the weak execu-

---

[27] Cf. Dankwart A. Rustow in Sigmund Neumann, ed., *Modern Political Parties* (Chicago: University of Chicago Press, 1956), pp. 169–193.
[28] The leading studies of the Fourth Republic include François Goguel, *France under the Fourth Republic* (Ithaca, N.Y.: Cornell University Press, 1952); and Philip Williams, *Politics in Post-war France* (New York: David McKay Company, Inc., 1954).

The Premier Often Has Difficulty Forming and Maintaining His Government: Aldo Moro, Leader of the Italian Christian Democratic Party, Shortly after He Was Asked to Form a New Government in 1964. (Wide World Photos, Inc.)

tive in a multiple-party system based on deep ideological cleavages. He was first asked by the President of the Republic (then an "elected monarch" in the sense described above) to form a Government. If he decided to give it a try, he went before the National Assembly and outlined and defended his proposed program and list of ministers. If a majority of the Assembly approved, he was confirmed in office and proceeded to fill the posts in his ministry and cabinet, appointed by the President on his advice.

The ministry was formally collectively responsible to the National Assembly, just as the British ministry was and is collectively responsible to the House of Commons. In practice, however, the two nations differed considerably. "Collective responsibility" in Great Britain means that the entire ministry stands or falls together. Thus, a vote of censure of an individual minister means that the entire ministry must resign and be replaced by an entirely new set of ministers, and an individual minister must either publicly support the ministry's policies or resign his post. The men who wrote the French Constitution of 1946 wished to establish the same kind of collective responsibility, but they could not overcome the nature of French politics of the time. When a French Government fell, all its members resigned as the Constitution required—but a substantial number of them regularly turned up again in the new Governments! The French called this process *replâtrage*—"replastering" the new Government with materials carried over from the old. According to figures compiled by Professor Finer, no newly formed French Government in the entire Fourth Republic was composed entirely of persons who had held no posts in the outgoing Government, and more often than not, well more than half of the new ministers were carry-overs from the old Government.[29] Not only did this mean that "collective responsibility" was relatively meaningless in France, but, as noted in Chapter 15, it also meant that the rapid and frequent changes in French ministries and premiers (see Figure 36) did not involve equally rapid and frequent changes in ministerial personnel or in public policy. Consequently, there was somewhat greater continuity and stability in the French executive than appears from a casual glance at Figure 36.

### Power

The Constitution of the Fourth Republic tried to strengthen the premier's position by giving him a number of impressive new powers: only he could call for a vote of confidence, countersign acts of the President of the Republic, take responsibility for the execution of the laws, make appointments to most civil and military offices, introduce the ministry's bills in the Assembly, transfer or expel individual ministers, and so on. He was even given the power to order the President of the Republic to dissolve the Assembly if in the course of an eighteen-month period the Assembly had passed two votes of no confidence. In December, 1955, M. Edgar Faure used this provision to get a dissolution—the first in France since 1877! The resulting election, however, returned an Assembly as divided and intransigent as its predecessor, and thus the new dissolution provision failed to accomplish the anticipated benefits.

Most premiers were picked and approved by the Assembly because they were relatively obscure and inoffensive deputies and, therefore, less likely to be "dictatorial" than the top party leaders. As soon as a premier began to talk and act as though he intended to exert vigorous executive leadership, his days in office were numbered. This was the fate of M. Mendès-France, M. Faure, M. Pleven, and every other premier who attempted to lead rather than content himself with presiding and negotiating.

The whole system finally collapsed in 1958. The colonial administrators and army officers in Algeria feared that the Paris Government intended to turn the province over to the native insurgents, and so they refused to obey orders. A number of army units prepared to invade France to overthrow the Government, and civil war appeared imminent. At the peak of the crisis the National Assembly called on General Charles de Gaulle to return from his self-imposed retirement and become premier. When he consented, they gave him full power to deal with the immediate crisis and to have a new

---

[29] Finer, *Governments of Greater European Powers*, p. 424.

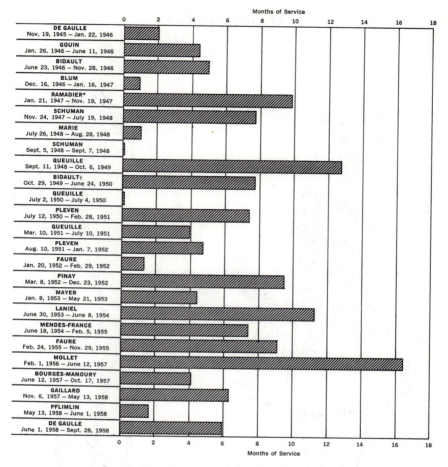

*Figure 36.* Premiers of the Fourth Republic.

Constitution drafted. He did both, and in September, 1958, the new Constitution, establishing the Fifth Republic, went into effect.

### The President and Premier under the Fifth Republic[30]

The Constitution of the Fifth Republic gives France a form of government that does not fit easily into either the traditional "presidential" or "parliamentary" categories, although it is nearer the latter than the former.

---

[30] Cf. Dorothy Pickles, *The Fifth Republic* (New York: Frederick A. Praeger, Inc., 1962); and Philip Williams and Martin Harrison, *De Gaulle's Republic* (London: David McKay Company, Inc., 1960).

# Majority Of One

*Figure 37.* *Le Grand Charles* Makes the Fifth Republic a Special Form of Government. (From *Straight Herblock,* Simon & Schuster, 1964.)

The President of the Republic is the key figure. He is directly elected by the voters for a seven-year term. He appoints the premier, nominally with a view to the distribution of party strength in the National Assembly, but actually as his personal choice. Thus de Gaulle chose as his first premier Michel Debré, a member of the Assembly and second-in-command of the new Gaullist party, the UNR. But in 1962 they disagreed about calling a national election, and Debré resigned—not, be it noted, because the National Assembly voted against him but because *le grand Charles* decided to dismiss him. De Gaulle replaced him with Georges Pompidou, a businessman and long-time loyal supporter who had never been elected to any public office. This made it clear that the premier does not hold his position because he is the number-two leader of the UNR, which has the most seats in the National Assembly; he is premier because the President wants him. He is, in short, the national commander's chief of staff.

The President has several other kingly powers. He can dissolve the National Assembly at his own discretion, whether the premier requests it or not. The famous Article 16 authorizes him in a time of threat to the nation's institutions or independence to suspend the operation of the regular governmental structure and take whatever measures he sees fit. And he can submit constitutional amendments directly to popular referenda without prior authorization by the National Assembly—as, for example, the referendum of 1962, which approved his amendment providing for direct popular election of the President.

No one can say with certainty how the Fifth Republic will operate when its creator, hero, and commander leaves the scene. But it is significant that France, which for so many years provided the classic illustration of the weak executive, has joined—and prospered under—the movement to stronger executive power evident in most modern democracies in the past century.

## The Changing Role of the Executive: A Summary

The traditional conception of the proper role and powers of the various formal governmental agencies holds that the executive should be primarily a law enforcer and an administration supervisor, not a policy maker. Yet, in the United States, Great Britain, and France the political executive has become the principal policy-making agency—and in the process, as we shall see in Chapter 19, has lost some of his ability to control effectively the administrative agencies formally subordinate to him. This basic change in the role of the executive, moreover, has by no means been confined to these nations; it has taken place to some degree in almost every other modern democracy, with the possible exceptions of Switzerland and Uruguay.

The evidence suggests that wherever this trend has occurred it has resulted from a number of factors. During the past century most democratic nations have accepted the "welfare-state" conception of the proper role of government; and the great proportion of the regulations and services undertaken have been exercised mainly by executive agencies. Big government, in other words, means a strong executive. Moreover, the increasing importance of international relations and foreign policy has added to the executive's power and importance. The time is past when any major nation can, in the fashion of the United States before 1898, sit behind its oceans or mountains or rivers and pursue a policy of "isolation" or "noninvolvement in foreign affairs." The hydrogen bomb and the intercontinental ballistic missile have made foreign policy and international relations a matter of life and death for every nation. This in itself is enough to make the executive, whose hand has always held the tiller in such matters, his nation's captain. Finally, in most modern democracies the very process of democratization itself through the broadening of the franchise has increasingly made the executive the central figure in elections—and, therefore, in the policy-making process.

Some commentators argue that these developments have made most modern democracies into something closely approaching "plebiscitary dictatorships"—systems in which the people elect an executive, turn over the whole power of government to him, and when his term of office expires express general approval or disapproval of the kind of dictator he has been. The evidence we have surveyed in the foregoing pages indicates that this picture of the omnipotent executive is a considerable exaggeration; for even the most powerful democratic executive must operate within limits laid down and enforced by legislatures, courts, party systems, and public opinion.

The most accurate statement of the executive's present role seems to be this: the political executive has replaced the legislature as the central policy-making agency in most modern democracies, and this fact has indeed given rise to a host of new problems in the organization and operation of their governments. In no democracy, however, has the executive yet become a dictator, "plebiscitary" or otherwise.

# 19

## The Administrative
## Process

**B**Y way of approaching the topic of the present chapter, consider the following hypothetical situation.

The leading issue in the 1972 American presidential election is foreign policy. The "outs" devote most of their campaign to denouncing the errors and pointing out the dangers of the policy followed by the "ins," and promise drastic changes if elected. After a hard-fought campaign, the "out" candidate is elected by a landslide.

On Inauguration Day, the incumbent Secretary of State, the Under Secretary, and all the assistant secretaries resign and are replaced by appointees of the new President. No one, not even the hottest partisan of the outgoing party, argues that the incumbents should be retained. Everyone takes it for granted that the new President has the right to replace these top officials with appointees of his own party and beliefs.

The new President, however, is not satisfied. In the campaign he had promised a "top-to-bottom house-cleaning of the whole State Department," and he believes in keeping his promises. So he issues an order dismissing *every* employee of the Department, from the Director of the Office of Intelligence Research and the Chief of the Telecommunications Division down to the last stenographer and messenger boy, and announces that all positions will be filled with faithful members of *his* party.

Immediately a great shout of protest goes up all over the nation. Newspapers of all political complexions denounce "this crass return to the spoils system." The American Political Science Association protests "this destruction of the morale, professional security, and technical competence of the civil service." Thousands of persons who had voted for the new President wire him that they had no intention of giving him a mandate to pack the government service with his political henchmen.

Hypothetical though this situation may be, few of us would doubt that any such effort by a new President to force a complete turnover in governmental personnel would produce just such a popular uproar.

For our purposes in this chapter, the interesting questions suggested by this imaginary episode are these: Why the difference? Why do we permit a new President to fire some government employees but not others? Where do we draw the line, and why?

The answers stem mainly from our acceptance of the propositions that "executive" and "political" officials differ significantly from "administrative" and "nonpolitical" officials, and that the status and tenure of the latter is and should be quite different from those of the former.

The task of the present chapter is to describe the nature, status, functions, and role of "administrative" agencies and officials. We shall begin by explaining why and in what respects such officials are generally considered to differ significantly from "executives."

## The Distinction between "Executives" and "Administrators"

### In Terms of Functions: "Policy Making" and "Policy Enforcement"

In the formative period of the American Constitution most Americans adhered to the traditional conception of the governing process as consisting of three distinct kinds of activity: lawmaking, law enforcement, and law adjudication. They also believed that power over the second of these activities should be assigned exclusively to the executive, and that the executive should confine himself largely to the enforcement of policies made by the legislature.

In Chapter 18 we observed that since the nineteenth century the executives of most democratic nations have acquired ever-increasing influence over policy making. Toward the end of the century a number of political scientists, notably Woodrow Wilson and Frank J. Goodnow, recognized that the traditional description of the executive as an enforcer rather than an initiator of policy no longer fitted the facts. Yet they wished to retain some kind of distinction between policy-making and policy-enforcing officials, and they also wished to reconcile the ideal of a permanent, professionalized civil service with the ideal of democracy. Consequently, they proposed a distinction between "political" (i.e., policy-making) officials, including the President and other executives, and "administrative" (i.e., policy-enforcing) officials. We shall return to their formula in a moment.

## In Terms of Selection and Tenure: Rotation and Permanence

Although some present-day political scientists continue to distinguish between "executives" and "administrators" in the manner just described, most of them believe that since many officials legally called "administrators" play a major role in policy making, this basis of distinction is meaningless. Few of them, however, argue that *all* public officials should be replaced whenever a majority of the voters transfer their favor from one political party to another. Most of them continue to believe, with Wilson and Goodnow, in a permanent, professionalized civil service acting under the direction and control of "political" executives and legislators.

Consequently most contemporary political scientists distinguish between "executives" and "administrators" mainly in terms of selection and tenure, as follows. "Executives," whether elected or appointed, have the top positions among and ultimate control over the policy-making agencies outside the legislature; thus, most of them are and should be active leaders of a political party, and their tenure in office rightfully depends directly upon whether their party currently commands a majority of the popular votes. All "administrators," on the other hand, are and should be appointed, and their job is to make policy recommendations to the executive and to supervise, subject to the executive's control, the body of government employees known as "the civil service." Hence, they are and/or should be selected according to their professional merit and technical competence rather than because of their partisan affiliations; and their tenure in office is and/or should be independent of changing party fortunes.[1] "Administrators" in this sense are our main concerns in the present chapter.

# The Formal Status of Governmental Administration

### Size

From the standpoint of the number of persons employed, the administrative agencies constitute by far the largest element of any modern government. In 1964, for example, the government of the United States employed a total of 2,500,492 civilians. Of these, 5810 were employed by

[1] For similar definitions of "administrators," see John A. Vieg in Fritz Morstein Marx, ed., *Elements of Public Administration* (2d ed.; Englewood Cliffs, N.J.: Prentice-Hall, Inc., 1959), p. 7; Leonard D. White, *Introduction to the Study of Public Administration* (4th ed.; New York: The Macmillan Company, 1955), pp. 1–2; and James C. Charlesworth, *Governmental Administration* (New York: Harper & Row, Publishers, 1951), p. 3.

the judicial branch, 25,041 by the legislative branch, and the remaining 2,469,641 by various executive and administrative agencies. The latter figure represented only 4.3 percent of all civilians gainfully employed in the nation, but when the state and local administrative employees are added the proportion becomes 17 percent. In the other democracies it is a bit higher: Professor Finer has estimated that in Great Britain and the European democracies something like one in every five of the gainfully employed works for a government administrative agency.[2]

## The Structure of Administrative Agencies

### Principal Types

The most common type of administrative agency in the modern democracies is the "executive department" or "ministry." Such an agency is formally headed by a member of the cabinet or ministry (see Chapter 18) and is established to formulate and administer government policy in such major areas as foreign affairs, fiscal affairs, agriculture, commerce, and labor. Each department has a number of subordinate agencies, variously called "bureaus" or "divisions" or "*directions*," and many maintain a number of field offices to conduct the department's business in particular parts of the nation subject to the direction of the department's headquarters in the nation's capital.

In some democracies (e.g., France) all administrative activities are formally conducted by these departmental agencies. Some democracies, however, also employ some "service-wide management agencies." Both the United States and Great Britain, for example, maintain civil service commissions charged with overseeing the examining, hiring, discharging, promoting, and other working conditions for the employees of most of the departments and other agencies placed under the "merit system" (see below).

Some democracies have also established a number of "government corporations," made them more or less independent of the executive departments, and charged them with duties and activities resembling those of privately owned business corporations. In the United States, for example, the Tennessee Valley Authority constructs dams and power plants and sells electric power to various state and local governments and private utilities. The Panama Railroad Company operates the Panama Canal. The Federal Deposit Insurance Corporation insures the deposits of banks and savings and loan associations, and the National Capital Housing Authority reclaims slums and builds and rents low-cost housing in the District of Columbia.

---

[2] Herman Finer, *Theory and Practice of Modern Government* (rev. ed.; New York: Holt, Rinehart and Winston, Inc., 1949), Table 22 on p. 710.

In Great Britain the British Broadcasting Corporation (BBC) sells licenses for radio receivers, prints a magazine, and with the proceeds prepares and broadcasts programs (see Chapter 11). Each of the nationalized industries, such as coal, electricity, gas, and the Bank of England, is operated by a government corporation organized much like the BBC.

A few democracies, notably the United States, have established a fourth type of administrative agency known as "independent regulatory commissions." These include such bodies as the Interstate Commerce Commission, the Federal Communications Commission, and the Civil Aeronautics Board, each of which is charged with regulating a particular area of private business and all of which are formally responsible neither to the executive departments nor to the President.

### Formal External Interrelations

The latter two types of administrative agencies are "independent" in the sense that their heads are not generally required to report or justify their decisions to the chief executive officer or any other agency. Their members, however, are appointed by the chief executive, and he can exercise at least periodic control over their activities by granting or refusing reappointment. He also has the formal power, under certain circumstances, to set aside their orders. This is true of the civil service commissions in the United States and Great Britain. Everywhere, however, the heads of the executive departments appointed by the chief executive are formally responsible to him and he may dismiss them at any time. In a great many democracies by no means all administrative agencies are formally arranged in what many students of public administration believe to be the ideal fashion: in a neat and consistent hierarchical structure of authority.

### Formal Internal Organization: Hierarchy, "Staff," and "Line"

A generation ago most students of public administration believed in certain "principles of organization"—certain correct ways of "interrelating the subdivisions of work by allotting them to men who are placed in a structure of authority, so that the work may be co-ordinated by orders of superiors to subordinates, reaching from the top to the bottom of the entire enterprise."[3] Most present-day political scientists are dubious about the universal scientific validity or practical applicability of these "principles," but many of them continue to believe that most administrative agencies should be organized in accordance with the principles of "hierarchy" and "separation of 'staff' and 'line' functions."

---

[3] Luther Gulick, "Notes on the Theory of Organization," in Luther Gulick and L. Urwick, eds., *Papers on the Science of Administration* (New York: Institute of Public Administration, 1937), p. 6.

The principle of hierarchy, or, as some call it, "scalar organization," prescribes that the personnel of any administrative agency should be formally interrelated in a pyramidal fashion, with a clear "chain of command" reaching from top to bottom and a "line of responsibility" going from bottom to top. In this fashion each employee knows just who are his superiors, equals, and inferiors, and therefore knows to whom he may give orders and from whom he must receive them. Often mentioned as models are the organization of any modern army and the priest-bishop-archbishop-pope hierarchy of the Roman Catholic Church.

The principle of separation of "staff" and "line" functions is founded on the proposition that every agency performs two basic types of function. The Department of State, for example, negotiates treaties, exchanges official communications with foreign nations, and issues passports, and all such activities are called its "line" functions. The department, if it is to be run efficiently, must also perform a number of "staff" or "housekeeping" functions, such as hiring and firing, determining promotions and pay increases, and budgeting. These two types of activities, many writers on public administration believe, should be performed by separate sets of agencies, each reporting to the agency's head but each independent of the other.

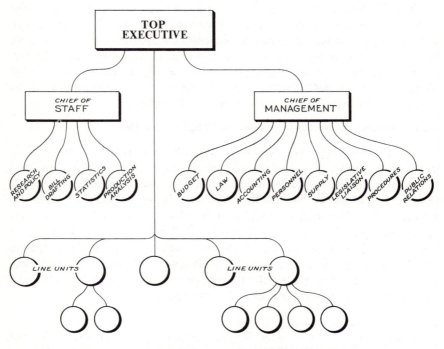

Figure 38. A Model Administrative Organization.

Thus an agency organized in full accordance with both of these principles could be represented graphically as in Figure 38.

Few actual administrative agencies, however, are as neatly and consistently organized as the model in Figure 38 in accordance with the principles of hierarchy and separation of "staff" and "line" functions. Most students of public administration recognize that the practical problems of actual agencies usually necessitate deviations from these principles.

A number of scholars, moreover, agree with the statement of two recent commentators:

> It can hardly escape the sharp-eyed observer that administrative bodies—and indeed all organizations, whether legislatures, political parties, labor unions, business enterprises, universities, churches, armies, or professional associations—respond in fact to a variety of informal patterns of influence among their membership. These are more or less at variance with the acknowledged structure of formal authority on which the organizations rests.[4]

Thus an agency's formal organization is, at most, a rough guide to and a general limitation on its "informal" or "actual" organization—and it is the latter which gets things done. As this has become more clearly perceived, a growing number of political scientists have chosen to study administrative agencies as a special aspect of the broader subject of behavior in human organizations. They focus not on legal powers and responsibilities but on the networks of interpersonal communications and influence out of which administrative decisions emerge and administrative functions are performed.[5]

### Formal Administrative Functions

From the point of view of subject matter, the functions formally assigned to administrative agencies are nearly coterminous with the functions of government itself; for every one of the governmental functions listed in Chapter 3 is performed mainly through the activities of one or a number of administrative agencies. From the point of view of the types of activities it carries on, however, we may note that every administrative agency performs one or two, but rarely all, of the following principal activities.

---

[4] From "Informal Organization" by Harvey C. Mansfield and Fritz Morstein Marx, in Marx, op. cit., p. 274. See also Herbert A. Simon, Donald W. Smithburg, and Victor A. Thompson, Public Administration (New York: Alfred A. Knopf, Inc., 1950), pp. 87–90.

[5] The leading studies include James G. March and Herbert A. Simon, Organizations (New York: John Wiley & Sons, Inc., 1958); Herbert A. Simon, Administrative Behavior (2d ed.; New York: The Macmillan Company, 1957); and Philip Selznick, Leadership in Administration (New York: Harper & Row, Publishers, 1957).

PROVIDING SERVICES.    Some agencies mainly provide services for all who wish them. The Agricultural Research Service of the Department of Agriculture, for example, conducts an elaborate program of research in such matters as pest control, farm and land management, and breeding and raising of livestock, and makes the results available at minimum cost to farmers who wish to improve their operations. The British National Health Service provides government-subsidized medical care and hospitalization for all who wish to use them. In Chapter 3 we have listed a great many other activities of the "service" type.

REGULATING.    Some agencies mainly regulate the operations of private persons and organizations to keep them from engaging in certain forbidden practices. The outstanding example of such activity, of course, is the enforcement of criminal laws by police agencies, but there are many others. The American Federal Trade Commission, for example, issues "cease-and-desist" orders to private businesses engaging in such practices as misrepresenting or misbranding their products. The American Securities and Exchange Commission regulates the trading procedures of security exchanges and determines what stocks may and may not be listed for sale. In Chapter 3 we have also listed a great many other such "regulating" activities.

LICENSING.    In most democratic nations a private person or corporation can legally conduct certain kinds of business only after obtaining from some administrative agency a license to do so. In one sense, then, licensing involves the performance of a service; but in another, it involves a considerable measure of regulation. This is illustrated by our description in Chapter 11 of how agencies like the American Federal Communications Commission and the Canadian Broadcasting Corporation use their power to grant and renew licenses for radio and television stations to control certain aspects of broadcasters' activities. Similar regulatory power is involved in any agency's power to grant or withhold licenses.

ADJUDICATING DISPUTES.    The job of settling disputes by applying the law to particular cases (see Chapter 20) is assigned exclusively to the courts of law by the traditional conception of the proper allocation of governmental powers and functions. Yet in many democratic nations in recent decades a number of administrative agencies have undertaken "quasi-judicial" functions—called "quasi" only because they are performed by administrators instead of judges. When, for example, a worker or an employer complains to the National Labor Relations Board that his employer or union is engaging in an "unfair labor practice" in violation of the 1935 (Wagner) and 1947 (Taft-Hartley) labor-management relations acts, the NLRB is empowered to hold hearings, render a decision, and dismiss the complaint or order the challenged practice stopped. In Great Britain complaints by workers about the orders of their superiors in, say, the nationalized coal industry are brought before the National Coal Board, which then decides who is in the right. This ever-increasing type of administrative activity has drawn more and more attention to the problem of the power of regular courts to review and reverse administrative decisions, and we shall have more to say about this matter later in this chapter.

INTERNAL MANAGEMENT. An eminent student of public administration, Luther Gulick, has coined a well-known catchword, POSDCORB, as a mnemonic device for recalling the internal-management functions that an administrative agency must perform if it is to carry on its external operations with maximum efficiency and economy. As he explained them, the letters in this word refer to the following functions: *P* is for planning, *O* for organization, *S* for staffing, *D* for directing, *CO* for coordinating, *R* for reporting, and B for budgeting.[6] They are mainly "staff" functions and, Gulick makes clear, the performance of any or all of these functions, by "staff" and "line" alike, involves the exercise of discretion by administrators.

## The Status and Selection of Administrative Personnel

### Political Activity

Most modern democracies have attempted to "keep politics out of administration"—that is, to remove civil servants in their professional capacities from the influence and control of political parties so that they may serve with equal faithfulness the leaders of *any* political party who may for the moment control the legislative and executive policy-making agencies. The most commonly employed means for achieving this end is to divorce the civil servants' tenure from changes in party fortunes. A number of democracies have added another: restricting the civil servants' participation in partisan political activities. In the United States, for example, members of the national "classified" civil service (see below) and state and local employees working in programs financed in whole or in part by the national government are forbidden by law from taking any active part in partisan political activities. They may vote, privately voice their opinions, and even attend party rallies as spectators. But they may not solicit party funds, make partisan public speeches, hold party office, or work for a party in any other way. In Great Britain a number of rules promulgated by the Treasury and the various departments generally prohibit "policy-making" civil servants from engaging in partisan activity, such as canvassing, making partisan public speeches, or "standing" as a candidate, that might conflict

---

[6] Gulick, *op. cit.*, p. 13.

*"Perhaps we didn't make it clear, Miss Jones, that your job with the F.B.I. is purely clerical."*

**Figure 39.** The Merit System Requires Special Qualifications for Particular Administrative Jobs. (Drawing by Alan Dunn, © 1942 The New Yorker Magazine, Inc.)

with their roles as impartial servants of the whole nation and all parties; but in recent years civil servants with "routine" posts have been permitted increasing freedom of partisan activity. France is one of the few modern democracies that places no general restrictions upon such activities, but even in France the ministers and top administrators can and often do by administrative regulation prevent their employees from actively supporting extreme anti-Government parties.[7]

### Unions and Strikes

The classic weapons of industrial workers are those of forming unions .and conducting strikes. Most modern democracies permit their civil serv-

---

[7] For more detailed discussions, see James B. Christoph, "Political Rights and Administrative Impartiality in the British Civil Service," *American Political Science Review*, LI (March, 1957), 67–87; Brian .Chapman, *The Profession of Government* (London: George Allen & Unwin, Ltd., 1959); and F. Ridley and J. Blondel, *Public Administration in France* (New York: Barnes & Noble, Inc., 1965).

ants to form unions but drastically limit or deny altogether their right to strike. For example, employees such as policemen, firemen, and postal workers are generally forbidden strikes on the ground that the continuous operation of their services is necessary to avoid national calamity. Some have developed ingenious ways of getting around this prohibition: British postal employees in the early 1960's, for example, sought higher wages by a "work-to-rule" campaign, in which they rigidly enforced every last postal regulation, with the result that mail delivery was delayed so much that their discontents were very effectively brought to their superiors' attention. Employees of nationalized railways and coal mines, on the other hand, generally have the right to strike, although every effort is made to avoid such strikes by prior arbitration. The net effect of these rules in most democracies is that the civil servants' right to organize unions is almost as well protected as that of nongovernmental workers, but their right to strike is greatly restricted.

### Selection: Patronage and Spoils versus the Merit System

At one period in its history every modern democratic nation selected its civil servants according to some standard other than technical competence. In Great Britain before the nineteenth century, for example, most governmental posts were filled by "patronage"—a system whereby members of the nobility and members of Parliament literally owned certain positions, and, as "patrons," filled them with friends, retainers, or relatives, many of whom were too incompetent to get and hold any other kind of job. In France before the Revolution of 1789, all but the few highest offices in the kingdom were regarded as a species of private property, to be sold, passed on by inheritance, or given away by their owners to whomever they pleased. In the United States before the late nineteenth century most civil service posts were filled by the "spoils system," whereby the winners in a political contest dismissed from office as many adherents of the opposition party as they pleased and replaced them with their own supporters and contributors.

Prussia (and later Germany) was the first modern nation to select its civil servants by "the merit system." This system in its ideal form uses technical competence—the civil servant's ability to perform the functions of his post with maximum efficiency—as the sole standard for selecting civil service personnel and usually measures the competence of applicants by competitive examinations of their knowledge and intelligence. Prussia instituted such a system for selecting its civil servants as early as the middle of the eighteenth century.

Beginning in the late eighteenth century "civil service reform" movements arose in most of the democratic nations calling for abolishing patronage and spoils and replacing them with merit systems on the Prus-

PERCENT

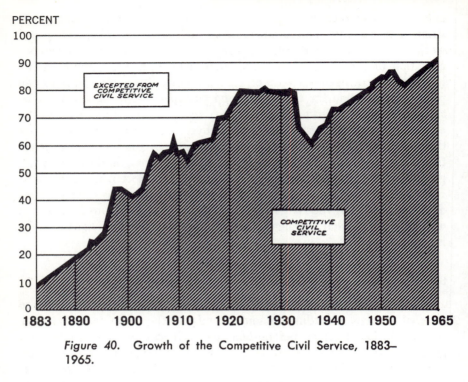

*Figure 40.* Growth of the Competitive Civil Service, 1883–
1965.

sian model. The movement succeeded earliest in France, where the Revolutionary leaders and later Napoleon I installed a professionalized civil service. In Great Britain the reform began in the 1830's when the administrators of British India set up a merit system for selecting members of the Indian Civil Service. It was extended to the whole British civil service after the publication and adoption in 1853 of the Trevelyan-Northcote Commission's Report on the Organization of the Permanent Civil Service. In the United States general national reform began in 1883 with the passage of the Pendleton Act, which established the Civil Service Commission (see above) and provided for the progressive "classification" of members of the various administrative agencies.

In most democracies at the present time all or nearly all civil service employees are selected by some kind of examination, and their tenure is largely or entirely independent of their party affiliations. The United States national civil service has been somewhat slower in this regard than most, but, as Figure 40 shows, it has come a long way since 1883.

Figure 40 shows that, as of 1965, over 90 percent of all American national civil service employees were under the merit system, and in most other democratic nations the proportion is even higher. Thus, most or all civil servants in most of the democracies are "permanent" in the sense that they are not directly subject to the approval or disapproval of the voters through the ordinary electoral processes.

How, then, can this fact be reconciled with the ideals of democracy, which, as we saw in Chapter 5, prescribe that *all* public officials do what the people want them to do and refrain from doing that which is unpopular, and rely mainly upon the popular election of such officials to guarantee this kind of performance? This is perhaps the most-discussed problem of public administration in the democracies. Let us now see what it involves.

## Politics, Administration, and Administrative Policy Making

### *The Rise and Decline of the "Politics-Administration" Dichotomy*

Many nineteenth-century American reformers, as we noted above, valued the ideal of governmental efficiency and believed that installing a Prussian type of permanent and professionalized civil service would realize it in the United States. Most of them, however, also valued the ideal of democracy and had no wish to see the entire governmental structure "Prussianized." They were reluctant to choose between these two ideals and so, for many of them, the most urgent question of the day was, How, if at all, can a permanent civil service be reconciled with the ideals and institutions of democracy?

Toward the end of the century some political scientists advanced a doctrine according to which these two ideals could be reconciled and both realized, and for several decades afterward most American students of government regarded this doctrine as having settled once and for all the problem of the proper place of professional administrators in a democratic government. Let us now examine its content, consequences, and current reputation.

#### Its Origins and Content

Most students of public administration credit the first statement of the doctrine to an article published in 1887 by a young professor of politics at Princeton named Woodrow Wilson. Briefly summarized, Wilson's argument ran as follows. The old classification of governmental powers and functions into the legislative-executive-judicial triad does not fit the facts. All governments perform only *two* basic functions: "politics," which is the making of general policies and laws; and "administration," which is the execution of these policies and laws by applying them to particular individuals and situations. Since administration is so different from politics, Wilson concluded, it must be kept nonpolitical; for, in his words, "administrative questions are not political questions. Although politics sets the tasks for administration it should not be suffered to manipulate its offices. The field of administration is a field of business."[8]

Wilson's politics-administration dichotomy was taken up by another eminent political scientist, Frank J. Goodnow, and elaborated into a broad doctrine of the proper place of administrators in a democracy, which he advanced in his book *Politics and Administration* (1900). Goodnow's position may be briefly summarized. All governmental activities are either politics ("operations necessary to the expression of [the state's] will") or administration ("operations necessary to the execution of that will"). Goodnow—unlike many of his self-proclaimed followers—believed that these two functions could not be completely separated or exclusively assigned to entirely separate governmental agencies, but recommended that so far as possible certain agencies be mainly "political" and others mainly "administrative." He concluded that in a democracy the mainly "administrative" agencies must necessarily be subordinated to, controlled by, and serve the mainly "political" agencies; for, as he put it, "popular government requires that . . . the executing authority . . . shall be subordinate to the expressing authority, since the latter in the nature of things can be made much more representative of the people than can the executing authority."[9]

## Consequences

During the following four decades the Wilson-Goodnow formula was almost universally accepted by American political scientists and deeply affected their thinking about the proper role of administrators in democratic government. As Dwight Waldo sums it up:

> Most subsequent students of administration, even when they have not read it and even when they arrive at quite opposite conclusions with respect to the application of "politics" and "administration," have regarded *Politics and Administration* much as the eighteenth-century literati regarded Newton's *Principia*.[10]

Among its specific effects may be mentioned the following.

First, for most scholars and reformers it provided an eminently satisfactory theoretical justification for the presence of a permanent, profes-

---

[8] Woodrow Wilson, "The Study of Administration," *Political Science Quarterly*, II (June, 1887), 197–222.

[9] Frank J. Goodnow, *Politics and Administration* (New York: The Macmillan Company, 1900), p. 24.

[10] Dwight Waldo, *The Administrative State; a Study of the Political Theory of Public Administration* (New York: The Ronald Press Company, 1948), p. 106.

sionalized civil service in a democracy. If administrators only carry out policies given to them by political agencies, they reasoned, there is no need to make them responsible to the voters.

Second, it provided the theoretical foundation for the new "science of public administration," which first emerged in the United States in the decade after the publication of Goodnow's book. This new branch of political science concentrated upon such problems as how to organize administrative agencies and recruit and train administrators so that the administrative function can be carried out with maximum efficiency and economy—problems similar to those dealt with by the new and rising "scientific-management" movement in private industry headed by Frederick W. Taylor, the first of the modern "efficiency experts." Nor did the new specialists in public administration feel that by concentrating on the values of efficiency and economy they were slighting the values of democracy. The latter, after all, are the concern of "politics," not "administration"—and since the two functions are distinct, students of public administration can and should focus their attention on how to improve administration and leave to others the problems of maximizing democracy.

Third, it provided a clear and satisfying set of criteria for organizing governments: let all policy-making officials be elected or appointed by elected officials, and let all administrators be selected by the merit system and hold office so long as they retain their technical competence—an idea illustrated by the hypothetical situation with which we began the present chapter. The city-manager form of municipal government, as we shall see in Chapter 21, is an effort to organize local governments in full accordance with this principle.

### Present Eclipse

Since the late 1930's an ever-growing number of political scientists, led by such students of public administration as Luther Gulick, Robert A. Dahl, Charles S. Hyneman, and Carl J. Friedrich, have rejected both the "politics-administration" dichotomy and the revised doctrine of "separation of powers" stemming from it. They reject the dichotomy because they believe it to be an inaccurate description of the governing process. The exercise of discretion, they contend, is the essence of policy determination; and every public employee, whether he is called "political" or "administrative," exercises some discretion. If "politics" means policy making and not merely partisanship, they conclude, it cannot be "taken out of administration" so long as administrators exercise discretion; and there is no way of preventing this even if it were desirable to do so.

These scholars have come to this conclusion mainly because of their observation that administrative agencies, no matter how professionalized and formally "nonpolitical," have a great deal to say about what policy *is*, and are by no means confined merely to carrying out policies laid down by legislatures and executives. These scholars are convinced, moreover, that the policy-making powers of administrators are not the result of any special hunger for power or contempt for democracy on the part of administrators, but are inevitable attributes of modern government. Let us briefly summarize the evidence on which they base these conclusions.

## Policy Making by Administrators

### Administrative Influence on Legislative and Executive Policies

In almost any human decision-making organization the expert—the man who knows the history of the organization's problems and has at his fingertips detailed technical information about the possibilities and practicality of the various proposed solutions—has an enormous advantage over the layman, who at best has only a general, partial, and probably shaky technical knowledge. The more complex and difficult the problems, moreover, the greater the expert's advantage. Since the problems of modern government are perhaps the most difficult faced by any human organization, the expert in government has a very great advantage indeed.

For a variety of reasons, an administrator has a much better chance than a legislator or an executive to become an expert in the subject matter dealt with by his particular agency. For one thing, he is a specialist in *one* area of subject matter, whether it be conservation, issuing passports, regulating railroad rates, or whatever. The legislator or the executive, on the other hand, necessarily deals with all these matters and many more besides. Unlike the administrator, therefore, the "political" official cannot afford to specialize. For another thing, the legislator or the executive is often an active leader of a political party and therefore must spend a considerable portion of his time attending party meetings, campaigning, and "politicking" in many other ways. The administrator, however, is forbidden to engage in such activities and, therefore, can spend his full time and energy on the policy questions coming before his agency. Finally, most legislators and executives are considerably less "permanent" than merit-system civil servants and do not have nearly so long a period in office in which to acquire the detailed technical knowledge and "feel" that makes for expertise.

In all modern democracies, accordingly, the impermanent, part-time, and unspecialized political officials often ask the advice of the permanent, full-time, and specialized administrative experts about the relative merits of this or that policy—and far more often than not take their advice. Administrators' own policy preferences inevitably enter into and affect their advice; for, as the British scholar Harold J. Laski wrote:

> You cannot ask an able man to concern himself with questions like education, public health, factory legislation, safety in mines, without

two consequences following. To ask him to discover facts is to ask him to indicate conclusions; and the very fact that he reports conclusions necessarily indicates a theory of action.[11]

When such men are asked for advice they can hardly avoid at least making their views known; and when, as so often is the case, "political" officials have no strong views of their own, civil servants' preferences are likely to become policy.

On some occasions, of course, the "political" official has strong views of his own that run sharply counter to the ideas of the civil servants formally subordinate to him. The Goodnow doctrine requires the administrator in such a situation to give up his own preferences cheerfully and loyally implement those of his superior. But it by no means always works this way, as the following two episodes illustrate.

One of the "planks" on which the Labour party campaigned in the British general election of 1945 was that of reversing the Conservative Government's anti-Zionist policy by permitting greater Jewish immigration into Palestine and assisting in the early formation of a Jewish state there. After they won the election and took office, Foreign Secretary Ernest Bevin discovered that the experts in the Foreign Office were unanimously against helping Zionism and maintained that only a pro-Arab policy could protect British interests in the Middle East. Their expert technical knowledge and forensic skill overcame Bevin's objections and "sold" him on continuing the previous anti-Zionist policy—which shortly became the official policy of the Labour Government.[12]

In 1950, President Harry S Truman, backed by a resolution of the United Nations General Assembly (see Chapter 23), ordered General Douglas MacArthur to take command of the American and other UN forces to repel the invasion of South Korea by the Communist North Koreans. MacArthur not only drove the invaders back but occupied most of North Korea. This brought the Chinese Communists into the war, and MacArthur had to retreat. Truman and the United Nations were committed to a policy of limiting the war to Korea and seeking a negotiated peace on the basis of the restoration of the preinvasion boundaries and guaranteed independence for South Korea. But MacArthur did not agree. He issued a number of public statements calling for direct attacks on the Chinese Communists on their home grounds as a necessary step in reoccupying the entire peninsula. "There is no substitute for victory," he declared. In April, 1951, Truman relieved him of his command on grounds of insub-

---

[11] Harold J. Laski, *Parliamentary Government in England* (London: George Allen & Unwin, Ltd., 1938), pp. 260–261.
[12] Cf. Arthur Koestler, *Promise and Fulfilment: Palestine, 1917–1949* (New York: The Macmillan Company, 1949), Chs. X–XI.

ordination; but, on returning home, MacArthur continued to rally political support for his position with considerable damage to Truman's popularity.[13]

These episodes suggest that administrators sometimes do battle for their policy preferences even when they run counter to those of the political officials. They also suggest that in such battles the administrators are far from helpless.

### Interpretation of Legislative and Executive Directives: "Administrative Legislation"

Every legislative statute and executive directive is necessarily general in expression, in the sense that its language must apply to many concrete situations and yet cannot possibly describe each of them in detail. Yet no concrete situation is exactly like any other—or exactly and in every detail identical with the wording of the statute or directive. Consequently, no administrative agency can avoid developing its own body of rules for determining what specific instances do and do not fall within the terms of the statute or directive they are administering. This kind of subordinate and derivative administrative rule making is generally known as "administrative legislation." Most students of government are convinced that making such rules necessarily involves administrators in policy making to some degree and that the broader and more general are the directives handed to the administrators, the more important "administrative legislation" becomes in determining the policy that is actually applied.

Pressure groups have long known this political fact of life. The most successful and powerful of them, accordingly, have never regarded their job as done when the legislature has passed a bill or the executive has issued a directive they desire. They have shifted their attention to the administrative agencies concerned to make sure that the latter carry out the statute or directive as the pressure groups wish it carried out. For example, the "patriotic" groups supporting restrictive immigration laws (see Chapter 7) have kept a close watch on the Immigration and Naturalization Service to make sure that no "undesirable aliens" slip through the legal nets; and the National Cooperative Milk Producers' Federation once made sure that the Bureau of Internal Revenue diligently collected the special tax on oleomargarine (see Chapter 16). Recent studies of pressure politics in the United States, indeed, show that administrative agencies are becoming targets of increasing importance for pressure groups.[14]

---

[13] The episode is discussed at length in Richard E. Neustadt, *Presidential Power* (New York: John Wiley & Sons, Inc., 1960).

[14] Cf. Donald C. Blaisdell, *American Democracy Under Pressure* (New York: The Ronald Press Company, 1957), Chs. 11, 14; and David B. Truman, *The Governmental Process* (New York: Alfred A. Knopf, Inc., 1951), Ch. XIV.

In summary, whatever may be their formal status and powers, administrative agencies make policy in every modern democracy and their activity in this regard is increasing rather than decreasing. While most democratic nations have emphasized, and to a large degree have succeeded in, "getting politics out of administration" in the sense of largely or entirely eliminating direct partisan control over the selection of administrative personnel, they have given far less attention to the significant fact that "administration has gotten into politics" in the sense of policy making.

This fact has not only made the Wilson-Goodnow "politics-administration" formula an outworn credo but it has created a grave problem for those nations who wish their governments to be democratic as well as efficient. We shall conclude the present chapter by describing the problem and reviewing some of the efforts currently made to solve it.

## "Administocracy" in a Democracy: Problem and Attempted Solutions

### The Problem

#### "Bureaucracy" and "Administocracy"

Although students of modern government frequently use the term "bureaucracy," there is no general agreement upon its meaning. Some use it merely as a synonym for "the civil service." Others use it in a highly pejorative sense to denote any administrative organization, whether a private corporation or a church or a government, that has become so concerned with its regulations and red tape that it has lost sight of its original purposes and now regards its own survival and aggrandizement as an end in itself. Still others use it to refer to any administrative organization so large that its members cannot deal with each other face to face.[15]

To refer to the problem that concerns us here we shall avoid the word "bureaucracy" and borrow the term "administocracy" (meaning an aristocracy of administrators) coined by Guy S. Claire.[16] The problem of "administocracy" may be stated as follows. Citizens of most democracies, including our own, wish their governments to be efficient. They are convinced, moreover, that a permanent and professionalized civil service whose

---

[15] For various meanings of "bureaucracy," see the selections in Albert Lepawsky, ed., *Administration* (New York: Alfred A. Knopf, Inc., 1949), Ch. 7.

[16] Cf. Guy S. Claire, *Administocracy* (New York: The Macmillan Company, 1934). More recent discussions of the problem include Charles S. Hyneman, *Bureaucracy in a Democracy* (New York: Harper & Row, Publishers, 1950); and William W. Boyer, *Bureaucracy on Trial; Policy Making by Governmental Agencies* (Indianapolis: The Bobbs-Merrill Company, Inc., 1964).

members are selected according to their technical competence and hold their posts so long as they retain this competence is best calculated to produce efficiency. They have no wish to return to the bad old days of the patronage and "spoils" systems. Yet, most of them also wish their governments to be democratic—that is, committed to realizing the ideal of popular control of government and dedicated to doing what the people want and not what some elite thinks the people ought to have. In short, most of us want both efficiency *and* democracy, and we do not wish to choose one ideal at the expense of slighting or ignoring the other.

Are these two ideals compatible? *Can* we pursue them both? These questions have long concerned political theorists. For several generations, as we noted above, most persons believed that the "politics-administration" formula of Wilson and Goodnow solved the problem. Yet most present-day political scientists believe that the Wilson-Goodnow solution, based as it is upon a misconception of what administrators actually do, is no solution at all.

Present-day political science, then, has rejected the Wilson-Goodnow solution. What, if anything, has replaced it?

### Conceptions of "Responsibility"

Most contemporary political scientists believe that the solution to the problem of "administocracy" lies, not in any misguided and futile attempt to prevent administrators from making policy, but in making sure that administrators are *responsible* in their policy-making activities. When we examine the relevant literature closely, however, we discover that its authors use the key word "responsibility" in two distinct senses; and their proposals for making administrators "responsible" reflect their differing emphases on these two meanings of the word.

"RESPONSIBILITY" AS ADHERENCE TO A PROFESSIONAL CODE.  A number of political scientists, most notably Carl J. Friedrich, have argued that the "political" responsibility of administrators established by making them accountable to elected officials can never be enforced perfectly and completely. Thus, they argue, we must place at least equal reliance on developing "functional" or "objective" responsibility—that is, we should select and train our administrators in such a way that they will operate according to certain professional standards and adhere to a professional code of ethics. Ideally, says Friedrich, administrators should be "responsible" in the same sense and for similar reasons as judges. In his words:

> Judicial decisions are relatively responsible because judges have to account for their action in terms of a somewhat rationalized and previously established set of rules. Any deviation from these rules on the part of a judge will be subjected to extensive scrutiny by his colleagues and what is known as the "legal profession." Similarly, administrative

officials seeking to apply scientific "standards" have to account for their action in terms of a somewhat rationalized and previously established set of hypotheses. Any deviation from these hypotheses will be subjected to thorough scrutiny by their colleagues in what is known as the "fellowship of science."[17]

"RESPONSIBILITY" AS ACCOUNTABILITY TO ELECTED OFFICIALS. Other political scientists, notably Herman Finer and Charles S. Hyneman, have argued that while administrative "responsibility" in Friedrich's sense is a fine thing, a democratic government must make its administrators responsible mainly by making them accountable to and controlled by elected public officials. Only thus, they contend, can we establish the popular control of administrative policy making that democratic government—which, they agree, is not necessarily synonymous with "good" government—demands. As Professor Hyneman puts it:

> Government has enormous power over us, and most of the acts of government are put into effect by the men and women who constitute the bureaucracy. It is in the power of these men and women to do us great injury, as it is in their power to advance our well-being. It is essential that they do what we want done, the way we want it done. Our concept of democratic government requires that these men and women be subject to direction and control that compel them to conform to the wishes of the people as a whole whether they wish to do so or not.[18]

In short, both the Friedrich and the Hyneman-Finer "schools" believe that some kind of external direction and control of administrative policy making is necessary to a solution of the problem of "administocracy," although they do not agree about how important this particular kind of control is. We shall conclude our discussion by briefly describing some of the principal methods of control currently employed by the democratic nations.

### Making Administrators "Representative"

Some political scientists have suggested that one of the best ways of preventing "administocracy" is to make the administrative agencies themselves represent the population rather than rely entirely upon elected representatives to keep an unrepresentative bureaucracy in line. They approve

---

[17] Carl J. Friedrich, "Responsible Government Service under the American Constitution," in *Problems of the American Public Service* (New York: McGraw-Hill Book Company, Inc., 1935), pp. 36–37. See also Phillip Monypenny, "A Code of Ethics as a Means of Controlling Administrative Conduct," *Public Administration Review*, XIII (Summer, 1953), 184–187.

[18] Hyneman, *op. cit.*, p. 38. See also Herman Finer, "Administrative Responsibility in a Democratic Government," *Public Administration Review*, I (Summer, 1941), 335–350.

and advocate the extension of various methods that administrative agencies now use to make themselves representative.

Some agencies conduct public opinion surveys in order to learn how the public feels about their policies. Many maintain advisory committees composed of spokesmen for various segments of the population. Most issue periodic reports to the public of what they are doing and why. Many take action only after consulting with the organized groups representing the major interests most likely to be strongly affected by the action. And most important of all, some agencies consider the ethnic and class affiliations of their job applicants in order to make sure that their personnel are as nearly as possible a cross section of the population.

Thus, these scholars conclude, elected legislatures and executives cannot accurately claim to be the *only* representative bodies in modern government. Some administrative agencies, despite the fact that their members are not elected, are quite as representative if not more so. If we encourage all agencies to develop themselves along these lines, these scholars contend, we will greatly reduce the danger of "administocracy."[19]

### Control by Elected Officials

#### In the United States

Political control of administrative agencies in the United States is exercised by Congress and the President, both jointly and separately. Congress and the President jointly direct and control the administrative agencies in the following ways. They pass and approve legislation creating the administrative agencies, defining their objectives and powers, and establishing standards for their performance. They raise and appropriate the money the administrative agencies spend, they propose and ratify appointments to the top administrative posts, and they establish the procedures by which lesser appointments are made. They review, criticize, and check the actions of administrators.

In addition to his joint operations with Congress, the President, as chief executive, formally controls most civil servants. He appoints the heads and chief subordinates of most executive agencies, and they are responsible to him. They, in turn, control the employees in their agencies. Thus it would seem that, like any commander in chief, the President can send orders down the administrative hierarchy, count on their being obeyed, and require reports from his subordinates that will keep him in touch with what is going on. So it would seem, but the appearance is far from the reality. Not only are the number of civil servants and the number and variety of

---

[19] Cf. Avery Leiserson, "Interest Groups in Administration," in Marx, *op. cit.*, pp. 314–338; and Simon, Smithburg, and Thompson, *op. cit.*, Chs. 19, 25.

their activities far too vast for any one man to keep an eye on, but the better executive employees are more likely to develop strong feelings about what policies ought to be followed—feelings that do not always coincide with the President's. As patriotic Americans they can do no less than work for what they believe to be in the best interests of the nation, and losing a presidential order in the bureaucratic maze is not difficult. As Jonathan Daniels, a former presidential aide, wrote of cabinet officers:

> Half of a President's suggestions, which theoretically carry the weight of orders, can be safely forgotten by a Cabinet member. And if the President asks about a suggestion a second time, he can be told that it is being investigated. If he asks a third time, a wise Cabinet officer will give him at least part of what he suggests. But only occasionally, except about the most important matters, do Presidents ever get around to asking three times.[20]

The most perceptive modern student of the presidency, Richard Neustadt, concludes that the President's power over his subordinates is not so much a power to command as a power to persuade—an opportunity "to induce them to believe that what he wants of them is what their own appraisal of their own responsibilities requires them to do in their own interest, not his."[21] So presidential control of administrators is not enough to keep them strictly obedient to the will of elected policy makers.

Congress, on the other hand, emphasizes reviewing and checking the activities of administrators. Most appropriations run for only a year or two, and when agency requests for new funds come before Congress the various subcommittees of the appropriations committee in each house use the occasion—in which administrators, understandably, are in a very tractable mood—to review the agencies' past behavior and future plans, and offer whatever criticisms the committee members think appropriate. Investigating committees, as we observed in Chapter 17, are another useful technique for making administrators toe the line. Congress frequently grants powers to administrative agencies for limited periods of time and uses the occasion of renewing the grants to review not only the policy but also the way it has been carried out.

These are but a few samples of the many means elected officials in the United States use to direct and control administrative agencies. If Congress and the President use them vigorously and intelligently with a clear understanding of what they are about and why, "administocracy" can be kept well within acceptable bounds. Professor Hyneman argues, however, that the control of administration in the United States is made difficult by

---

[20] Jonathan Daniels, *Frontier on the Potomac* (New York: The Macmillan Company, 1946), pp. 31–32.
[21] Neustadt, *op. cit.*, p. 46.

the fact that Congress and the President are formally independent of each other, that they are elected by different constituencies for different terms of office, and that more often than not, they have conflicting views about what policies administrators should pursue and by what means. Many other students of this question are skeptical of the utility of Hyneman's proposed solution of a joint executive-legislative central council to formulate policy and direct and control administration;[22] But most of them agree with his judgment that unless and until it is solved the over-all control of administrative agencies by elected officials in the United States will continue to be less effective than is desirable.

### In the Parliamentary Democracies

At first glance, the control of administrators by elected officials in the parliamentary democracies appears to be much better organized and more effective than it is in the United States, since in most of them, as we learned in Chapter 18, the legislature and executive usually speak with one voice. In such nations the administrators in each executive department are directly responsible to and formally controlled by the minister, the minister is responsible to the cabinet, and the cabinet and the legislature are always in formal agreement about both policy "ends" and administrative "means."

When we look a little closer, however, we learn that things are not quite this simple or satisfactory. For one thing, as we noted above, many of these nations have established a number of "government corporations," such as the British Broadcasting Corporation, that are not subject to direct ministerial control. For another, the members of the legislature in many of these nations apparently feel that even in the executive departments ministerial control by itself is not sufficient to prevent "administocracy." Consequently many parliamentary democracies have created institutions like the British practice of "questions" and the French practice of "interpellations," which operate as follows.

On each of the first four days of every legislative week any member of the House of Commons may, after giving the Government one or two days' notice, ask a question of any member of the ministry. The questions, both oral and written, may simply request information; or they may ask the minister to explain and justify some action taken by his department. Furthermore, the questioner and other M.P.'s may ask "supplementary" questions arising out of the minister's oral answer to the initial question. Questions are asked not only by the opposition to embarrass the Government, but also by the "back-benchers" of the majority party. Thus "question time" is not merely an arena for Government-*versus*-opposition conflict,

---

[22] Hyneman, *op. cit.*, ch. 25.

but often becomes a legislature-*versus*-administrator contest. Asking questions, indeed, is the principal method by which rank-and-file M.P.'s can review and criticize the actions of the civil service, and one of the few areas in which they can participate in the governing process free of the shackles of party discipline and cabinet control. An average of 70 to 100 oral questions are asked each day and a total of about 13,000 each year. Some observers believe that they have proved to be at least as effective as ministerial control for keeping civil servants in line.[23]

Under the Third and Fourth Republics, members of the French National Assembly also asked questions in a procedure similar to that of the House of Commons, although they were used mainly to elicit information. Far more formidable was the practice of "interpellations"—requests by deputies to ministers for the latter to explain and justify the actions of their departments. After a minister replied to a particular interpellation, a general debate was held, ending in a motion either censuring or approving the minister's reply and the action of his department. These practices constituted a powerful weapon for legislative control of administrators.

Under the Fifth Republic, however, they have been severely limited. Question time is now restricted to one day a week, and the greater power of the executive (see Chapter 18) makes it extremely unlikely that a minister or the whole cabinet will be turned out because of unsatisfactory answers to legislators' questions.

### Control by the Courts

In addition to providing these methods of ensuring that administrative agencies make and enforce policies in accordance with popular desires, all democratic nations also provide various kinds of judicial restraints to keep administrative agencies from encroaching upon the rights of indivduals as set forth in statutes, constitutions, and "common law" (see Chapter 20). If a private citizen feels that an administrative agency has maliciously used its power to harm him or his property, or stepped outside its jurisdiction in giving him an order, or exceeded its regulatory powers, or unfairly denied him a license, or the like, he can go to some kind of court and seek redress. The remedy may take the form of a suit for damages, a writ of mandamus (that is, an order by a court to a public official ordering him to do his duty as the law requires), a writ of injunction (that is, a court order prohibiting an administrative official from performing a specific action), or several other forms.

---

[23] The definitive study is D. N. Chester and Nina Bowring, *Questions in Parliament* (London: Oxford University Press, 1962).

A number of democracies, such as the United States and Great Britain, locate all such judicial review of and remedies for illegal administrative action in their ordinary courts, while others, such as France, Italy, and Sweden, have established special sets of "administrative courts" to adjudicate such disputes. We shall describe both kinds of courts in greater detail in Chapter 20. Whether exercised by regular or special courts, however, the main purpose of judicial control of administration in most nations is not to prevent "administocracy" as we have been using the term, but rather to protect the personal and property rights of individuals against administrative encroachment.

### Control by the Ombudsman

For many private citizens suing an administrative agency in the courts is not attractive or even feasible: it is time-consuming, unpleasant, and costly—and there is no guarantee the citizen will win. Hence, judicial control, which leaves the initiative up to the aggrieved person, is more of a weapon of last resort than a widely used device for keeping administrators in line.

Recognizing this difficulty, the government of Sweden as long ago as 1809 established the special office of *ombudsman* (meaning "parliamentary commissioner") to act as the private citizens' watchdog over and advocate against the administrative agencies. He is appointed by the *Riksdag* (parliament) to investigate and publicize any instance in which an administrator uses his powers wrongly or fails to act where he should. Any citizen may register a complaint with him. He investigates each complaint, and, depending on what he finds, either publicly exonerates or publicly criticizes the administrators involved. In most instances public criticism by the *ombudsman* is enough to make the erring administrator mend his ways in a hurry; but if he is adamant, the *ombudsman* is authorized to direct the public prosecutor to take the matter to court.

In this way most of the initiative and bother and all of the cost are born by the *ombudsman* rather than by the private citizen, and many observers believe the institution to be one of the most effective devices in modern democracies for keeping administrators acting as they should. As such it has attracted increasing attention from political scientists and civic reformers around the world. A number of smaller nations—Denmark, Norway, Finland, West Germany, New Zealand, and the Philippines are among them—have adopted some version of the Swedish system, and a few others, notably Great Britain, are considering it.[24]

---

[24] The practices and problems of ombudsmen in various nations are analyzed in the *University of Pennsylvania Law Review*, CIX (June, 1961), 1057–1126.

# Conclusion

Their great size and power have elevated administrative agencies to a position of great significance in all modern democracies, and their professionalization has given rise to the problem of "administocracy." Some modern Cassandras on both sides of the Atlantic, indeed, have cried that all is lost and that "administocracy" and "the new despotism" are already upon us.[25] The evidence presented in the foregoing pages, however, strongly suggests that such lamentations are, to say the least, premature. To say that administrators have a great deal of influence in the making of public policy is not to say that they have taken over the whole process and thereby become absolute and unchecked despots. The legislative and executive controls over administrators we have just surveyed can fix very definite and firm limits upon what administrators can and cannot do. So long as those who exercise them continue to do so in the confidence that they are doing what their constituents want them to do, administrators will continue to be not the masters but the valuable servants of democracy that they have been heretofore.

---

[25] Cf. Lord Hewart of Bury, *The New Despotism* (New York: Cosmopolitan Book Corp., 1929); James M. Beck, *Our Wonderland of Bureaucracy* (New York: The Macmillan Company, 1932); and Ludwig von Mises, *Bureaucracy* (New Haven, Conn.: Yale University Press, 1944).

# 20

## Law and the Judicial
## Process

"THE law," wrote the eighteenth-century playwright Charles Macklin, "is a sort of hocus-pocus science, that smiles in your face while it picks your pocket, and the glorious uncertainty of it is more use to the professors than the justice of it." But his contemporary Dr. Samuel Johnson declared, "The law is the last result of human wisdom acting upon human experience for the benefit of the public."

Some of us may sometimes be tempted to agree with Macklin—especially when, say, we have just gotten a ticket for overparking or paid a lawyer's bill. But most of us generally believe, like Dr. Johnson, that law is one of the great achievements of human civilization and that men's chances of living together happily and fruitfully in society depend largely on their ability to live according to law. The famed hope of the Massachusetts Constitution that it might establish "a government of laws, and not of men" surely expresses a desire deep in most of us that our lives and fortunes be governed, not by the passing whims of a dictator or a ruling class or even a popular majority, but by fundamental and changeless principles of right reason. The actual laws which rule us for the moment may not measure up to this dream, to be sure, but in most of us the dream is strong.

Perhaps that is why the picture most of us have of "the judge" is something close to reverential, even though no actual judge may quite live up to it. For there he sits on the bench, does our ideal judge, listening courteously and impartially to the two litigants before him, seeing to it that each side receives its full rights under the law, and making his decision, not because he thinks it will please this political party or that pressure group, but because he knows it is *right* according to the law.

There is little doubt, then, that law, and the judges and courts that interpret and apply it, occupy a place of high prestige in our attitudes toward government. To what extent do actual judges and courts live up to their ideal models? Perhaps we can suggest some answers in the present chapter, in which we shall describe the structure and role of law and the courts as they presently operate in the democracies, and contrast them with their counterparts in Communist Russia.

## The Nature of Law

### *The Meaning of "Law"*

Jurists—persons who specialize in studying the content and application of law—have long disagreed about the proper meaning of "law," and in their writings many different conceptions are put forth.[1] Three of these are particularly significant for our purposes.

### The "Natural-Law" Conception

Perhaps the basic issue on which jurists disagree is whether the essence of law—that is, the trait that distinguishes it from other rules affecting human conduct, such as those described in Chapter 2—lies in its *content* or in the *procedures* by which it is made and enforced. Some argue that "The Law" is a body of prescriptions for human behavior ordained by God or Nature, that the specific rules made and enforced by human agencies should be made to approximate these eternal principles of right and wrong, and that men have no moral obligation to obey governmental rules which contravene these eternal principles—which some jurists have called "the Higher Law" and others "the Law of Nature." Jurists who take this position are often called the "natural-law" school, and their basic views are by no means heard only in academic ivory towers. When, for example, conscientious objectors refuse to obey governmental commands to join armies and kill their nations' enemies, they regard themselves, not as acting lawlessly, but rather as obeying the "higher law" that says "thou shalt not kill." When civil-rights demonstrators lie in the streets in violation of ordinances prohibiting the obstruction of traffic, they feel they are obeying the "higher law" that says "all men of all races shall be treated equally."

### The "Positive" or "Analytical" Conception

Other jurists, sometimes called the "positive law" or "analytical" school, argue that since men have no sure way of identifying or defining universal

---

[1] Useful summaries of the different definitions are presented in George Whitecross Paton, *A Textbook of Jurisprudence* (2d ed.; Oxford: Clarendon Press, 1948), Ch. III.

principles of right and wrong, the only meaningful definition of "law" is in terms of the particular human agencies that make and enforce its rules. The nineteenth-century English jurist John Austin, for example, defined law as the command of a political superior to inferiors backed up by sanctions against those who disobey the commands. The twentieth-century American Supreme Court Justice Oliver Wendell Holmes, Jr., for another example, wrote that "the prophecies of what the courts will do in fact, and nothing more protentious, are what I mean by law."[2]

### The "Descriptive" Conception

These two schools of jurisprudence, then, have different purposes in defining "law." Natural-law jurists define law mainly for the purpose of distinguishing it from *wrong* principles of human conduct, whereas analytical jurists define law mainly for the purpose of distinguishing it from rules emanating from nongovernmental sources. Several languages, significantly enough, have different words to denote these two conceptions of law: in Latin, for example, *ius* means the eternal principles of right conduct, and *lex* means the rules enforced by the state; in French their counterparts are *droit* and *loi;* in German, *Recht* and *Gesetz;* in Italian, *diritto* and *legge;* and in Spanish, *derecho* and *ley.*[3]

In English, however, we have only the single word "law." And since our purpose in this chapter is to describe the role of courts and judges in the governing process, and to explain what most men in most nations ordinarily mean when they make such statements as "that's against the law" or "that law should be changed," we shall employ what may be called a "descriptive" definition of "law."

As we use the term in this book, accordingly, law in any nation is *the body of rules emanating from governmental agencies and applied by the courts.* Thus we distinguish it from such other kinds of behavior-directing rules as moral precepts and customs (see pages 31–34). The reader should note that, according to this definition, no particular governmental agency is regarded as having a monopoly on making laws; and the rules promulgated by any such agency achieve the full status of "law" only if the courts apply them. In Chapters 17–19 we have considered the lawmaking activities of legislators, executives, and administrators; in the present chapter we shall describe both the lawmaking activities of judges and the procedures by which they "apply" laws made by themselves and other governmental agencies.

---

[2] Oliver Wendell Holmes, Jr., *Collected Legal Papers* (New York: Harcourt, Brace & World, Inc., 1921), p. 173.

[3] Cf. Roscoe Pound, *Outlines of Lectures on Jurisprudence* (Cambridge, Mass.: Harvard University Press, 1943), p. 60.

## Some Classifications of Law

Since several different kinds of governmental agencies in any modern nation make "laws" according to our definition, and since the courts of any nation apply several different kinds of legal rules, we shall conclude our brief survey of the nature of law by describing some of the most common classifications of its rules.

### According to Source

One familiar basis for classifying laws is according to the agencies which make them. The main types of law under this system of classification are the following.

CONSTITUTIONAL LAW.   Every nation, as we learned in Chapter 6, has a constitution—a body of fundamental rules, written and unwritten, according to which its government operates. We also learned that while part of the rules consist of unwritten customs, most of them are, strictly speaking, "constitutional law" in the form of a basic written Constitution, a number of organic laws, and certain rules of interpretation laid down by the courts. Constitutional law, moreover, is everywhere regarded as the most basic of all types of law in the sense that, if any of the other types of law contravene a constitutional rule, the constitutional rule supersedes and cancels out the former. Maintaining constitutional supremacy is the special prerogative of the courts in some nations; in others the job is done by the legislature. But in every democracy constitutional law is considered the most fundamental of all types of law. The various processes by which constitutional law is made and changed and its supremacy maintained are described in Chapter 6.

STATUTORY LAW.   Statutory law consists of all the rules commanding or prohibiting some form of human behavior *enacted by the legislature*. In most nations they are collected and published in a "code" or "statutes-in-force."

ADMINISTRATIVE LAW.   In Chapter 19 we learned that in all modern democracies many executive and administrative agencies are authorized by the Constitution or the legislature to make, within certain specified limits, a number of rules and regulations. The total body of such rules is generally called "administrative law," and in most democracies it has grown to considerable size.

COMMON LAW.   In twelfth-century England a number of royal judges began traveling around the country settling various local disputes according to their understanding of the prevailing "customs of the realm." During the next centuries these judges and their successors generally followed the principle of *stare decisis* (let the decision stand), according to which judges are obligated to "follow precedent"—that is, when a judge considers a case to which a rule made in an earlier case applies, he must apply the old rule rather than make up a new one. As a consequence of their general adherence to *stare decisis* these English judges built up over the centuries an elaborate body of legal rules that came to be known as "the common law," to distinguish it from the rules laid down in acts of Parliament.[4] The common law, of course, was applied by the courts in the English colonies in various parts of the world; and when some of the latter—e.g., the United States, Canada, New Zealand, and Australia—became independent, sovereign nations their courts continued to apply English common law, although in all these nations the English principles have been revised to some degree. If any common-law rule contravenes a constitutional rule or a statutory rule, the latter take precedence. But in the nations named common law continues to govern a number of matters on which the Constitutions and statutes are silent.

EQUITY LAW.   During the time common law was developing in medieval England an increasing number of British subjects demanded relief from the injustices they claimed its rules created. So the kings turned over all such complaints to their chief legal officer, the chancellor, who in turn appointed some assistants known as "masters in chancery" to deal with them. Eventually these officials came to constitute a regular court, called the Court of Chancery. The rules outside the common law developed by this court have come to be known as "equity law," and they, too, were exported to the English colonies and then revised after those colonies won their independence. Equity law, like common law, is superseded by constitutional and statutory law in case of conflict but still governs certain matters on which the latter are silent.

ROMAN LAW AND "THE CIVIL LAW."   Every modern nation has constitutional law, statutory law, and administrative law; but common law and equity law operate mainly in the legal systems of the English-speaking nations. The nations of Western Europe and Latin America, the American state of Louisiana, and the Canadian province of Quebec supplement their constitutional, statutory, and administrative law with a system of jurisprudence commonly called "the civil law." This is a body of rules and procedures differing somewhat from nation to nation but generally similar and in all instances based upon the *ius civile* of ancient Rome, which was rediscovered and used by European judges beginning in the early Middle

---

[4] The story is told in detail in T. F. T. Plucknett, *A Concise History of the Common Law* (2d ed.; Rochester, N.Y.: The Lawyers Co-operative Publishing Co., 1936).

Ages. Its best-known and most influential codification was that made under the orders of Napoleon I in 1804, which came to be known as the *Code Napoléon* or *code civil*. The modern "civil law" differs from common law and equity not only in a number of specific rules and procedures but also in its general tone and method of growth: where common law and equity are largely judge-made and rather pragmatic in tone, the civil law to a considerable degree consists of rules expounded by writers of books on jurisprudence and has a far more rationalistic and deductive tone than its Anglo-American opposite number.[5]

Various other kinds of law (e.g., admiralty and maritime law and international law) are applied by the courts of modern nations; but the types described above are the principal elements of modern democratic legal systems.

## According to Subject Matter

One other classification of laws is significant for our purposes—that which distinguishes between "criminal" and "civil" law.

CRIMINAL LAW.   Criminal law, of course, deals with "crimes"; and a "crime" is generally considered to be a wrong committed against the whole community—"any act done in violation of those duties which an individual owes to the community, and for the breach of which the law has provided that the offender shall make satisfaction to the public."[6] Crimes are usually classified as either "felonies" (the more serious) and "misdemeanors" (the less serious) and are punishable by death, imprisonment, fine, removal from office, or disqualification from holding office.

CIVIL LAW.   Civil law deals with wrongs committed against private individuals but not considered to involve damage to the whole community. For example, if A orally spreads malicious stories about B in the hope of ruining B's reputation, he is considered to have "slandered" B but not to have hurt the whole community; so B's remedy is to sue A for damages. But if A shoots and kills B, he is considered to have damaged the basic safety and security of the whole community, and the government will prosecute him for murder; and if he is found guilty, he will be imprisoned or executed.

These, then, are the principal types of law in the modern democracies. How are the courts which apply them structured?

---

[5] A useful comparative study is W. W. Buckland and A. D. McNair, *Roman Law and Common Law* (Cambridge: Clarendon Press, 1936).

[6] *Black's Law Dictionary* (4th ed.; St. Paul, Minn.: West Publishing Company, 1951), p. 445.

# The Structure of Court Systems in the
# Democracies

## The Emergence of the Specialized Judicial Function

### The Process of Law Enforcement

Each particular instance of the various general types of law described above is a general rule made by a governmental agency either commanding or prohibiting a certain kind of human behavior. Every government from time immemorial has established certain official agencies to "enforce" the law—that is, to detect instances in which "persons" (including both flesh-and-blood individuals and corporations considered to be "legal persons") have violated these general rules, and to punish the violators. Every agency performing this function must conduct a number of basic operations, which we shall explain by the following hypothetical example.

A nation has a law against "murder," defined in the statute as one person's taking of another's life by deliberate intent and "with malice aforethought." One of its citizens, A, is found dead, and some of the people in the neighborhood tell the government they think B killed A. So the first thing the government must do is to *ascertain the facts:* Is A really dead? Did he die from a gunshot wound? Did B fire the shot that killed A? Did B fire the shot with deliberate intent and malice aforethought? And so on. Second, the government must *interpret and apply the law:* it must look at the wording of the law and decide whether what B did is an instance of the behavior prohibited by the law—whether, within the meaning of the law, it constitutes "murder." Third, if the answer to all these questions is "Yes," then the government must *penalize the law violator:* it must decide how grave a penalty is warranted by the law and the facts, pass sentence on B accordingly, and make sure the sentence is carried out.

However they may be performed, these are the three basic operations involved in law enforcement.

### The Rise of Specialized "Courts"

During most of human history, as we noted in Chapter 17, societies did not make any theoretical distinction between "lawmaking" and "law enforcement" nor did they establish governmental agencies clearly specializing in one kind of operation over the other. Kings and their ministers and "courts" (which simply meant a king's whole retinue) made *and* enforced laws. In the late Middle Ages, however, the idea began to take hold that justice is best served by having one kind of agency—which came to be called "the executive"—specialize in watching over the behavior of the king's subjects and prosecuting those it believes have violated the law, and having another kind of agency specialize in trying the persons so accused to see whether or not the executive's accusations against them are justified. The latter agencies retained the ancient title of "courts," and by the eighteenth century in most nations they were clearly distinguished in both theory and organization from "executive" agencies and had largely taken over the final fact-determining and law-interpreting-and-applying functions described above.[7]

Thus, every modern democratic nation maintains a series of specialized "courts" in this sense. Later we shall consider some theories about the role they should perform in the total process of government and describe some of the roles they actually do perform in the modern democracies. First, however, we shall describe the principal types of courts, their formal interrelations, the selection and tenure of their judges, and their formal relations with the other agencies of government.

### Principal Types of Courts

#### Regular and Administrative

We noted in Chapter 19 that in many democracies (e.g., the United States, Great Britain, the British dominions, the Scandinavian nations, and Switzerland) all legal controversies arising from the actions of administrative agencies are handled by the "regular" courts—that is, the same courts that try other kinds of civil and criminal cases. A number of continental European democracies (e.g., Italy, West Germany, and Belgium), however, have followed the lead of France in establishing a special set of "administrative courts" to give their citizens judicial remedies against arbitrary and illegal administrative decisions. The first element of the French system, for example, consists of twenty-four *Tribunaux Administratifs* (administrative courts) located in various regions to act as trial courts in cases arising out of charges and claims against local administrative agencies. The second element is the *Conseil d' État* (Council of State), which is made up of top career civil servants appointed by various ministers. The council advises the cabinet and ministry on matters of administrative policy, and its *Section du Contentieux* (litigation section) of about eighty members acts as a court of appeal for decisions made by the lower administrative courts.[8]

---

[7] Cf. Herman Finer, *Theory and Practice of Modern Government* (rev. ed.; New York: Holt, Rinehart and Winston, Inc., 1949), pp. 111–112.

[8] A useful survey of the court systems of Britain, France, and the United States is Henry J. Abraham, *The Judicial Process* (New York: Oxford University Press, 1962). A more detailed study of the French system is Arthur T. von Mehren, *The Civil Law System* (Boston: Little, Brown & Company, 1957).

## Civil and Criminal

In most democratic nations the same regular courts handle both civil and criminal cases, but some nations have established distinct sets of courts for each type of jurisdiction. In Great Britain, for example, civil cases are dealt with by a hierarchy of courts made up of the 400-odd county courts and, above them, the Supreme Court of Judicature. The latter is divided into the High Court of Justice (which tries serious civil cases in one or another of its three divisions: Queen's Bench; Chancery; and Divorce, Probate, and Admiralty) and the Court of Appeal (which hears appeals from both the county courts and the High Court). Criminal cases in Britain are dealt with by a hierarchy of courts consisting of the magistrates' courts, the Quarter Sessions courts, the Assize Courts (each presided over by a single judge from the Queen's Bench), and a Court of Criminal Appeal. The House of Lords (but, as we saw in Chapter 17, actually only about ten to fifteen of its members, including the Lord Chancellor, the nine Lords of Appeal in Ordinary, and other members who have held high judicial office) acts as the final court of appeal in *both* civil and criminal cases.[9] In West Germany each regular court at each level—local, district, appeal, and supreme—maintains one or more civil sections and one or more criminal sections. The two types of sections use somewhat different procedures, although they are not so clearly separated from each other as in Britain. In most modern democracies, we repeat, both civil and criminal cases are handled by the same set of courts.

## National and Local

In the federal democracies, as we shall see in Chapter 21, there are two sets of cosovereign governments, national and local, each with its own legislative, executive, and administrative agencies. It would seem that there should also be two complete parallel sets of courts, one national and one local; but only in the United States is this the situation. Here there is a full set of national courts, consisting mainly of the federal district courts, federal courts of appeal, and the United States Supreme Court; and in each of the states there are a number of trial courts and a supreme court, many of them also having "preliminary courts" and "intermediate courts of appeal" (see below). The Australian Constitution permits the establishment of a full set of national courts, but so far only a national High (supreme) Court and a few special courts have been set up, and most litigation is handled by the courts of the various states, which are authorized to apply national as well as state law. In Switzerland the only major

---

[9] The rather complicated structure of the British court system is lucidly described in Richard N. Jackson, *The Machinery of Justice in England* (London: Macmillan & Co., Ltd., 1960).

national court is the Federal Tribunal, and, as in Australia, most litigation is handled by the cantonal (state) courts. Canada has a more complete set of national courts than either Australia or Switzerland, but even in Canada most litigation, even on matters of dominion law, is conducted in the provincial courts.[10] It is important to note, however, that in each of the federal democracies appeals can be made from the local courts to the national court or courts on questions involving interpretation of the national Constitution or national laws; and on all such questions the national supreme courts, and not any of the local supreme courts, have the final word. We shall return to this matter in Chapter 21.

In the unitary democracies all courts are national in the sense that their judges are appointed by national authorities, although many have local courts in the sense of courts with only local jurisdictions. In Great Britain, for example, even the local justices of the peace and magistrates of the county courts are appointed by the crown on the advice of the Lord Chancellor. In France all judges are appointed by the President of the Republic on the advice of the Minister of Justice. In Italy the members of the Supreme Court of Cassation and the intermediate Appeals Courts are appointed by central authorities, and the judges of the Appeals Courts in turn appoint the judges of the lower courts in their particular regions. Similar national appointment and control of all judges is the rule in the other unitary democracies, and so they have no local courts in the sense of locally controlled courts, such as the state courts in the United States.

## Hierarchies of Appeal in National Court Systems

### Hierarchy and the Appellate Process

Every modern democratic court system features provisions whereby the decisions of some courts can be appealed—usually only on points of the proper interpretation of the law and not on findings of fact—from some courts to others. In every nation the courts are arranged in a "hierarchy of appeal," whereby the chain of appeal is structured in a pyramidal fashion from bottom to top. This is an obvious necessity for any court system; for if it were possible for the loser of any case to appeal the decision to any court of his choice in a circular and unending fashion, then the process of appeal could go on indefinitely, no final decision could ever be made, and the litigants would get poorer and poorer while the lawyers got richer and richer.

As it is, however, every democratic court system provides a process of appeal from "inferior" to "superior" courts up to but not beyond a

---

[10] K. C. Wheare, *Federal Government* (4th ed.; New York: Oxford University Press, 1964), pp. 65–68.

"supreme" court; and when that court has rendered a decision, no further judicial appeal is possible except one to the supreme court asking it to reverse its own decision.

### The General Structure of Court Hierarchies

Although the details of court names and jurisdictions vary considerably from nation to nation, most democratic court structures have four main levels.

PRELIMINARY COURTS.    In many democracies the lowest courts on the judicial ladder are what may generally be called "preliminary courts"— including such agencies as justices of the peace (in Great Britain, Switzerland, and France), *conciliatores* and *praetors* (Italy), *Amtsgerichte* (West Germany), and so on. These bodies usually have the power to try only petty civil cases and misdemeanors and must refer all major cases to the next level of courts.

GENERAL TRIAL COURTS.    Every democracy has as the first major rung of its judicial ladder a number of courts authorized to try most major civil and criminal cases. In the American national system they are called "federal district courts"; in Great Britain they are called "county courts" for civil cases and "assize courts" for criminal cases; in France, "civil tribunals"; in Switzerland, "district courts"; in West Germany, *Landsgerichte*; and so on.

INTERMEDIATE COURTS OF APPEAL.    Most democracies provide a series of intermediate courts mainly to hear appeals from the trial courts and rarely or never acting as trial courts themselves. In the American system there are ten regional federal courts of appeal and one for the District of Columbia; in Great Britain there is one national Court of Appeal for civil cases and one national Court of Criminal Appeal for criminal cases; in France there are twenty-seven regional courts of appeal; in West Germany there are several *Oberlandesgerichte*; in Switzerland there is a Court of Civil Justice in each canton; and so on.

SUPREME COURTS.    Every democracy has a national supreme court. In each nation this court acts as the final court of appeal, and in some they also act as trial courts in a few special types of cases. These bodies include the Supreme Court of the United States, the British House of Lords, and French and Italian Courts of Cassation, the German *Bundesgerichtshof*, the Swiss Federal Tribunal, and so on.

A few democracies (e.g., Italy, in its *Corte constituzionale*) have established special national tribunals in addition to their regular supreme courts for the purpose of passing upon the constitutionality of legislative and executive acts in the process known as "judicial review" (see Chapter 6). Most of the democracies using judicial review, however, vest the final reviewing power in their regular supreme courts.

## The Selection and Tenure of Judges

### Appointment and Removal

With a few exceptions, which we shall note in a moment, most modern democratic nations select all their judges, from the lowest justice of the peace to the presiding judge of the supreme court, by appointment. The appointing officials vary somewhat from nation to nation, but in many nations all judges are appointed by the chief executive or by the minister of justice or his equivalent; and in a few nations the judges of some of the lower courts are appointed by the judges of the higher courts. Generally speaking, all appointed judges hold office during "good behavior," which means that they can be removed only by a special act of the legislature, called, for example, an "Address of Parliament" in Great Britain and "impeachment" in the United States. This removal power is rarely exercised, however, and so most judges in most democratic nations hold their offices for life.

### Election and Recall

In Switzerland some of the cantons elect some or all of their judges by popular election for limited terms of office, and the twenty-six members of the Federal Tribunal, the Swiss national supreme court, are elected by the Federal Assembly for six-year terms. The major exception to the general rule that judges are appointed for life, however, is to be found in the American states.

As of 1965, in twenty-one states all judges were elected; in ten states most judges were elected and a few minor ones appointed; in seven states the higher judges were appointed and the lower elected; in seven states the higher judges were initially appointed but later had to win re-election by popular votes; and in only five states were all judges appointed for "good behavior."[11] Thus the great majority of state judges in the United States are elected rather than appointed.

In eight states, moreover, judges are subject to "the recall." Under this procedure, if a designated number of voters sign a petition asking for the recall of a certain judge, a special election is held to determine whether he should remain in office. If a majority of the voters vote to "recall" him, he immediately leaves office, and his post is filled either by appointment or by a special election.

---

[11] *The Book of the States, 1964–1965* (Chicago: Council of State Governments, 1964), Table 2 on p. 126.

Thus, in the American states there is far more direct popular control over the selection and tenure of judges than in any democratic nation except possibly Switzerland; for, we should remember, all federal judges in the United States are appointed by the President with the approval of a majority of the Senate.

DOES IT MAKE ANY DIFFERENCE?   A number of political scientists, jurists, and lawyers in the United States argue that the popular election of judges is a serious weakness in the judicial systems of the states that employ it. For many years they have pressed for replacement of present elective systems with some version of appointment and permanent tenure. They argue that a judge who has to worry about re-election must remain more a politician than a judge and so cannot develop the calm and detached judicial temperament every good judge must have. They also argue that popular election makes for frequent turnover among judges, and few of them stay in office long enough to acquire the judicial experience a man needs to be a good judge.[12]

How valid are these arguments? No one can say with certainty; for the fact is that careful, systematic, empirical studies of the relative effects of election and appointment of judges upon the judicial process are just beginning to be made. No careful study has been made of the relative "caliber" of the judges, however defined and measured, in the two types of systems. For some time to come this question is likely to be debated on the basis of hunches and general impressions rather than on systematic empirical knowledge; and there is no indication that many of the states presently using the elective system are likely to drop it.

## Formal Relations with the Legislature and Executive

### The Ideal of an Independent Judiciary

Many men and nations who do not subscribe to the doctrine of separation of powers in its entirety (see Chapter 17) nevertheless strongly support the ideal of an independent judiciary. This ideal calls for organizing the judiciary in accordance with two main precepts. First, its advocates believe that justice will not be served if the prosecutor and the judge are one and the same person or agency. In such a situation, they contend, the court loses all semblance of impartiality and becomes merely an arm of the prosecution and a "star-chamber" travesty on justice (the "star-chamber" label stems from a secret body established by the English Tudor monarchs in the sixteenth century to administer summary "justice" to their political opponents). This can be avoided only by making the courts independent

---

[12] Cf. Laurance M. Hyde, "Judges: Their Selection and Tenure," *Journal of the American Judicature Society*, XXX (February, 1947), 152–159.

of the executive. Second, these jurists argue, if the judicial process is to be well performed, it must operate in an atmosphere of calmness, deliberation, and, above all, freedom from pressures by parties and pressure groups with axes to grind. Hence the courts should also be free of the legislature. Many political theorists believe that an independent judiciary in both senses is the *sine qua non* of any governmental system intended to preserve human rights and freedoms.

## The Separation of Judges from Prosecutors

The first aspect of the ideal of an independent judiciary, the formal separation of judges from prosecutors, is most clearly and firmly established in the English-speaking democracies. At both the national and the state levels in the United States, for example, the prosecuting function is vested in an executive agency headed by an attorney general who supervises the work of a number of local United States attorneys (for the national government) and states' attorneys or district attorneys (for the state governments). In Great Britain the prosecuting function is vested mainly in the Director of Public Prosecutions, who, under the direction of the attorney general, prepares the cases against persons accused of crime and engages lawyers to prosecute the cases in court.

The continental European democracies, on the other hand, treat judges and prosecutors as different sections of the same public service. In France, for example, there is a single profession—*la magistrature*—which includes three kinds of offices: the "sitting judges," who preside over the courts much in the manner of Anglo-American judges; the *parquets*, a kind of public prosecutor's office attached to each court; and the administrative staff of the Ministry of Justice. All are regarded as civil servants under the same ministry, and any member of the *magistrature* may serve in any of these three offices. It is not uncommon, indeed, for a particular *magistrat* to move from work on the bench in one court to work in the *parquet* of another, and from there to a position in the ministry, and perhaps back again to a high judicial post. Thus, in any regular French court both the judge and the prosecutor are officers of the Ministry of Justice, and the two functions are much less clearly separated than in the English-speaking democracies. Most continental European democracies have systems similar to the French.

## The Insulation of Judges from Political Pressure

The second aspect of the ideal of an independent judiciary, the insulation of judges from political pressures, is generally established by securing the tenure of judges from partisan interference. The Constitution of the United States, for example, provides that all federal judges shall hold office "during good behavior" (i.e., until removed by impeachment), and that their salaries shall not be diminished during their term of office; and it vests the judicial power in them and in them only. Judges can be removed from office only by "impeachment" by a majority of the House of Representatives, and conviction by a two-thirds majority of the Senate. In Great Britain and the dominions, similarly, a judge may be removed from office only by "an Address" (requiring a majority vote in both houses) of Parliament.

In France and most continental European democracies before World War II, tenure, salary, and promotion of judges depended mainly upon the determinations of the various ministries of justice. Since 1945, however, a number of these nations have followed the lead of France in establishing a special body to ensure that the status of judges shall be somewhat better protected than by the ordinary procedures of the ministries. Thus, France has established a special judicial supervisory body, the *Conseil Supérieur de la Magistrature*, chosen partly by the National Assembly and partly by the judicial profession itself, to supervise the corps of judges separately from that of the *parquets* and civil servants. The ministry, however, retains the power of countersignature of the council's recommendations for appointment and promotion of judges.

On the basis of these facts, then, it seems that the English-speaking democracies come nearer to realizing the ideal of the independent judiciary than do the continental European democracies, but the latter appear to be moving in that direction.

However formally independent they may be, the actual freedom of judges from "politics" is a different matter, as we shall see below.


## The Role of Judges in the Process of Government

### *The "Mechanical" Conception*[13]

The United States Supreme Court's decisions in the school-segregation cases in the 1950's and the school prayers and legislative apportionment cases of the 1960's have unleashed a series of attacks on, and inspired a number of defenses of, the American judiciary, the like of which have not been heard in this country since President Roosevelt proposed to "pack" the Court in 1937. The Court's critics charge, among other things, that it is a bunch of politicians rather than a body of learned jurists, that it has been "brainwashed" with left-wing ideas, and, worst of all, that it has "legislated"—that is, written its own ideas of policy into the Constitution rather

---

[13] This point of view is well summarized and analyzed in Fred V. Cahill, Jr., *Judicial Legislation* (New York: The Ronald Press Company, 1952), Ch. 1.

than interpreting the latter "as it really is." Some of these critics propose impeaching the incumbent judges, others want Congress to withdraw much of the Court's appellate jurisdiction, others advocate enlarging the Court and appointing enough new judges to outvote the "radicals," and still others have proposed establishing a "Court of the Union," consisting of the chief justices of all the state supreme courts, and giving it the power to overrule decisions of the national Supreme Court. The Court's defenders reply that any such attack upon "the integrity and independence of the judiciary" will violate cherished American traditions and make us "a government of men, and not of laws."

For our purposes the most interesting aspect of this debate is the fact that so much of it is conducted in terms of *both* sides' adherence to the "mechanical" conception of the judicial function, which may be summarized as follows.

### Judges as Technicians

Under the traditional conception of the proper distribution of governmental powers, as we noted earlier in this chapter, the function of the courts is to interpret and apply the general rules formulated by lawmaking bodies in particular instances. According to this conception, judges do not *make* law; they *discover* it.

This view of the judicial function stems mainly from the views expressed in perhaps the most widely read and most influential of all books read by lawyers in the English-speaking nations for two centuries: the eighteenth-century English jurist Sir William Blackstone's *Commentaries on the Laws of England*. To Blackstone (and, apparently, to many of his readers) judges are "the living oracles . . . who are bound by an oath according to the law of the land"; and even when they reverse earlier rulings on points of law, he wrote, "it is declared not that such a sentence was *bad law*, but that it was *not law*."[14]

This Blackstonian picture of judges as skilled technicians "declaring" rather than making law is well summed up in the following statement by the nineteenth-century American jurist James C. Carter:

> That judges *declare*, and do not *make*, the law is not a fiction or a pretense, but a profound truth. If courts really made the law, they would have and feel the freedom of legislators. They could and would make it in accordance with their own views of justice and expediency. . . . I need not say that the case is precisely contrary . . . they must decide it consistently with established rules. . . . Any judge who

---

[14] *Commentaries on the Laws of England*, ed. by Thomas M. Cooley (Chicago: Callaghan and Cockcroft, 1871), I, 69.

assumed to possess that measure of *arbitrary* power which a legislator really enjoys would clearly subject himself to impeachment.[15]

## The Independent, Nonpolitical Judiciary[16]

According to the traditional conception, then, judges "declare" law that others have made and do not make it themselves. Finding out what the law *is* is thus a task for legal technicians, not politicians. Since it is a technical job demanding a high order of legal skill and training and a "judicial temperament," this conception further holds, the courts should be organized in such a way as to ensure that this difficult technical job will be performed in the best possible manner, and that the courts will be able to consider each case strictly on its legal merits without being influenced by any political considerations. To this end the judiciary, for one thing, should be made quite independent of both the legislature and the executive, both of which are necessarily political agencies. For another, the judiciary should be insulated from the selfish and noisy importunings of political parties and pressure groups. For still another, judges should be selected for their legal skill and judicial temperament, and not for their political preferences. Finally, judges should refrain from any public statement of their policy preferences and should be careful to use only the technical language of the law in writing their decisions.

Judges, in short, should themselves remain completely aloof from politics, and politics must not be permitted to begrime their deliberations. The strength of this general idea is indicated by the fact that until 1941 in the United States, state and national judges were allowed to punish for "contempt of court" any person who sought to influence a judge while a case was in process—and even then the Supreme Court decision that overruled this procedure was made by a bare majority.[17] And in Great Britain a newspaper can be fined heavily for even discussing a case in any but the vaguest terms while it is *sub judice* (under judicial consideration).

## Description or Ideal?

Many persons who hold the mechanical conception of the judicial process believe that many judges *do* behave in this fashion, although they usually disagree as to just *which* judges are acting in the proper manner. In 1937, for example, conservatives generally believed that the United States Supreme Court was acting quite properly in throwing out New Deal legislation, while the liberals accused the judges of writing their own social

---

[15] James C. Carter, "The Province of the Written and Unwritten Law" (1890), quoted in Cahill, *op. cit.*, p. 17, n. 26.

[16] This aspect of the traditional conception is perceptively described in Jack W. Peltason, *Federal Courts in the Political Process* (New York: Random House, Inc., 1955), Ch. 3.

[17] *Bridges v. California*, 314 U.S. 252 (1941).

and economic views into the Constitution. Since 1954 the tables have turned. Now the liberals praise the Court for protecting our constitutional liberties, while the conservatives attack its members for trying to foist their left-wing political philosophy on the nation.

The point is that in 1937 as well as today a great many of *both* the Court's critics and defenders adhere to the traditional "mechanical" conception, in the sense that they regard it as the correct standard to apply to actual judges—correct not only because it is morally right, but also because it is an attainable ideal if we can only get and/or keep the right kind of judges on the bench. In this sense, then, the traditional conception has had a powerful influence upon men's thinking about the role of judges in the governmental process.

### Judges as Policy-makers: "Judicial Legislation"

#### Regarded as an Avoidable Deviation

The present controversy over whether the Supreme Court is "legislating" its social and economic views or merely "declaring" the Constitution is not unique to our time. Such controversies have flared up over and over again ever since the birth of the Republic. The Jeffersonians, for example, bitterly accused John Marshall's Supreme Court and the rest of the Federalist-packed judiciary of trying to write Federalist party policies into the Constitution. Andrew Jackson and his Chief Justice, Roger B. Taney, were attacked by the Whigs on similar grounds, and the Taney Court's decision in the Dred Scott Case in 1857 was condemned perhaps more violently than any other in history. The conservative judges of the late nineteenth and early twentieth centuries were widely charged with trying to write their laissez-faire preferences into the Constitution; we have already described the controversies over the Court in 1937 and since 1954.

Thus, complaints about "judicial legislation" are endemic in the United States, and the scattered evidence available suggests that similar, though perhaps less noisy, complaints are perennial in every nation with a well-established tradition of an independent judiciary. When we examine the political views of those who attack and those who defend the courts on this score, we find a significant fact: generally speaking and with very few exceptions, persons who approve the political effects of a particular line of decisions defend the courts and say that the latter are only "enforcing the Constitution," while those who dislike those effects claim that the courts are engaging, improperly, in "judicial legislation." This fact has inclined one observer of the American judicial process to conclude that "viewed *sub specie aeternitatis*, the basic principle of American constitutional interpretation, and of American politics, is 'whose ox is gored?' "[18]

---

[18] John P. Roche, "Plessy v. Ferguson: Requiescat in Pace?" *University of Pennsylvania Law Review*, CIII (October, 1954), 53.

The point is, however, that most of those who have charged the Court with engaging in "judicial legislation" have regarded the latter as an *avoidable* deviation from the Court's true function of "declaring the law," and believe that if only we get the right kind of judges—that is, men who are skilled technicians and who accept and will adhere to the proper technical-mechanical function of "declaring the law"—the Court can be restored to its proper role in the governmental process.

### Regarded as Inherent in the Judicial Process

By no means all observers of the judicial process regard "judicial legislation" as avoidable by getting the "right kind of judges." A growing number of jurists, judges, and political scientists contend that "judicial legislation" is an inherent and inescapable consequence of the very nature of the judicial process itself. Many of them start from a premise stated by the eighteenth-century jurist and Anglican bishop, Benjamin Hoadly:

> Whoever hath an *absolute authority to interpret* any written or spoken laws, it is *he* who is truly the *Law-Giver* to all interests and purposes, and not the person who first spoke or wrote them. . . .[19]

Taking their cue from Bishop Hoadly, these writers reason that all Constitutions, statutes, executive and administrative ordinances, and other laws are necessarily to some degree general in nature and, therefore, necessarily somewhat vague. Hence, they have to be interpreted in specific cases. In most instances there is no one interpretation agreed upon by all men of good will and high technical legal training and skill. Lawyers and judges disagree to some extent among themselves about what the law means in any particular situation. The precedents of previous court decisions do not settle the question; for at least some precedents can be found for every possible interpretation—indeed, it is the duty of the lawyers for both sides to bring before the judge lists of precedents, each list calling for an opposite interpretation from the other. Thus, every judge is always faced with a number of different—but, judged by any human standard, equally reasonable—interpretations.

Each interpretation necessarily favors the interests of some groups and damages the interests of other groups. The judge cannot help choosing one of the several alternative interpretations and therefore cannot avoid promoting the interests of some groups and hurting the interests of others. Thus, when we look behind the legal jargon, we cannot avoid seeing that the process by which the judge chooses one interpretation over the others and makes his decision accordingly is political in nature; for whatever decision he makes necessarily satisfies some values and frustrates others.

This is true, these writers argue, not only for judges and courts that have

---

[19] Quoted in Cahill, *op. cit.*, p. 99.

the power of judicial review (see Chapters 6 and 20), but for *every* court, since every court has the power to "interpret" if not to "override" a law. And it will continue to be true until men perfect a machine like a cash register on which they can punch keys labeled "the facts," pull down a lever called "the law," and read "the decision" that pops out as a result.

To illustrate this characterization of the policy-making functions of the judiciary, let us see what role the United States Supreme Court has played in the conflict over racial segregation.

### "Equal Protection of the Laws" and Racial Segregation: A Case Study

The Fourteenth Amendment to the Constitution of the United States declares that "no State shall . . . deny to any person within its jurisdiction the equal protection of the laws." Beginning late in the nineteenth century the southern and border states enacted a series of "Jim Crow" laws prohibiting Negroes from attending the same schools, riding in the same cars in trains, using the same public swimming pools or golf courses, and eating in the same restaurants as whites. A number of persons, whom we may call the "antisegregation interest," felt that these laws violated the constitutional clause quoted above; while most southern whites, whom we may call the "segregation interest," had no doubt that such laws were perfectly consonant with this clause. Certainly the wording of the clause is vague enough that reasonable men can easily disagree about whether it prohibits or permits segregation laws.

Judges Make Policy Too: The Supreme Court That Decided *Brown v. Board of Education* (1954): (left to right, seated) Felix Frankfurter, Hugo Black, Earl Warren, Stanley Reed, William O. Douglas; (standing) Tom Clark, Robert Jackson, Harold H. Burton, Sherman Minton. (Wide World Photos, Inc.)

In the case of *Plessy v. Ferguson* (1896), the Supreme Court, in deciding the question of whether a state law requiring racial segregation on trains was constitutional, declared that under the "equal protection" clause segregation *in itself* was not unconstitutional so long as the accommodations provided for each race were substantially equal to those provided for the other. This ruling came to be known as the "separate-but-equal formula."

From then until the late 1930's the Court, following the Plessy doctrine, upheld all state racial-segregation laws and, indeed, was easily satisfied with what constituted "equality" of accommodations. In the 1930's, however, the Court began to take a different line. It began to insist, for example, that states which would not admit Negroes to their state universities must provide *really* equal facilities for them. In the case of *Sweatt v. Painter* (1950) they insisted that Texas either admit a Negro to the University of Texas Law School or establish one for Negroes that was its equivalent in every respect—a multimillion dollar project; and, in effect, they said that *no* segregated Negro law school could be equal to the established University school.

Finally, in the famous case of *Brown v. Board of Education* (1954) the Court overruled the Plessy Case and held that no matter what relative accommodations are provided for the two races, *segregation in itself* is a denial of "equal protection" to Negroes, and, therefore, all state laws requiring racial segregation in public schools are violations of the Fourteenth Amendment.

Many conservatives and most southern whites, as we have seen, bitterly attacked the Court for this decision; and much of the present controversy about the role of the Court stems from it. The Court's critics charge it with "making policy." So it did. But they also imply that this is something highly unusual and very wrong for a court to do; and, as we have learned above, this is far from the truth. What the critics forget, or at least do not wish to discuss, is that the phrase "equal protection of the laws" is so vague that no one interpretation is clearly indicated to all men of good will and legal expertise. The point is that the 1896 Court which declared the "separate-but-equal" formula was *also* making policy; and in throwing out that formula the 1954 Court was not making policy *de novo* but was reversing a policy made earlier.

If the present critics of the Court were given *carte blanche* to amend the Constitution and to alter the Court's personnel to their heart's desire, they could very likely force it to make the kind of policy they prefer; but there is no conceivable way, short of abolishing them entirely, of preventing courts and judges from making *some* kind of policy.[20] Policy making, in short, is inherent in the nature of the judicial process itself.

---

[20] For other illustrations of the inescapability of judicial legislation, see Victor G. Rosenblum, *Law as a Political Instrument* (New York: Random House, Inc., 1955).

## Judges in the Political Process

### The Approach of the "Legal Realists"

The statements made in the foregoing section are made and/or approved by an increasing number of contemporary political scientists, although some of the latter still regard the traditional "mechanical" view of the judicial process as a desirable and attainable ideal of what judges should do, if not an accurate description of what judges actually do. In many of the law schools and among many contemporary jurists, however, they are regarded as heresy and falsehood, for the legal profession has ever been the great stronghold of the "mechanical" conception.

Yet the lawyers, judges, and jurists have produced their own heretics. Perhaps the best known of the latter are a group of writers on legal theory, mainly such Americans as Jerome Frank, Thurman Arnold, Fred Rodell, and Edward S. Robinson, who have come to be known as the "legal realists."[21] Taking their lead from the legal philosophies of men like Oliver Wendell Holmes, Jr., and John Dewey, these writers have discarded the "mechanical" conception of the judicial function as both an inaccurate description and an impossible ideal. They recognize that judges do and must make policy, and some of them have sought to analyze and predict the decisions of particular judges on the basis of their sociological backgrounds, social and economic values, political preferences, and internal thought processes. "Legal realists" have unquestionably had a considerable impact upon contemporary American jurisprudence and some effect upon jurisprudence in other nations.

### The Political-Process Approach

In recent years a number of political scientists, whose point of view has been well stated by Jack W. Peltason in his short monograph *Federal Courts in the Political Process* (1955), have gone well beyond the "legal realists" by beginning to explore the possibilities of regarding the judicial process as simply one aspect of the total politico-governmental process, and of investigating it by many of the same techniques political scientists use to examine the legislative, executive, and administrative processes. This approach to the judicial process is too new to have produced many systematic and empirically verified explanations of how that process works; but Peltason has suggested a number of hypotheses that are worth at least a brief review here.[22]

---

[21] The main ideas of the "legal realists" are summarized in Cahill, *op. cit.*, Chs. 5–7.

[22] Cf. Peltason, *op. cit.*, Chs. 4–6. For similar hypotheses and some verification, see Glendon Schubert, ed., *Judicial Decision-Making* (New York: The Free Press of Glencoe, 1963); and Glendon Schubert, *Constitutional Politics* (New York: Holt, Rinehart and Winston, Inc., 1960).

Peltason suggests that the courts are as much involved in political con-flict, as we are using the term in this book, as any other type of govern-mental agency; for every case that comes before a court, he points out, involves a conflict of interest between the particular litigants, and many cases involve the interests of groups far broader than just the litigants themselves. In deciding each case—by ordering this man to go to jail or that corporation to release its control over other firms or the other school board to admit Negroes on an unsegregated basis—the courts lay down "authoritative value-allocations" in precisely the same sense that other governmental agencies do (see Chapter 2). Value-allocations made by the courts differ from those made by legislatures, executives, and administrators only in form, not in substance.

Peltason further suggests that for all the lip service they may pay to "judicial independence," the interests most powerfully affected by the courts' decisions have never refrained from trying to influence their out-come. Perhaps the main difference between political conflict centered upon the courts and that centered upon the other governmental agencies is that the former must be conducted within an atmosphere created by the gen-eral acceptance and respectability of the "mechanical" conception of the judicial process. Thus, let a man or a group of men say quite frankly, "We intend to put pressure on Congress, the President, and the administrative agencies to get our policies adopted," and no one will think any the worse of them for it. But let a man or a group of men say with equal frankness, "We intend to put pressure on the judges so that their decisions will be made in our favor," and many potential allies will become enemies because of their disapproval of such "crass efforts to tamper with judicial inde-pendence and The Law." Thus, while a great many political interest groups, as we shall see, *do* try to influence the outcome of judicial decisions, rarely do they *talk* as though that is what they are doing. They talk, rather, in terms of "defending the integrity of the judiciary" or "defending The Law against the depredations of political judges" or "making sure  that men with sound views of the Constitution get on the bench" or the like.

This kind of talk does not alter the *fact* of political conflict in the judicial process, but it does mean that such conflict is conducted in a rather special kind of atmosphere.

### Political Conflict in the Judicial Process

Peltason suggests that political conflict in the judicial process takes place in three main areas.

#### Over the Selection of Judges

When selecting federal judges in the United States, most Presidents and senators have *talked* as though they were selecting only technicians of jurisprudence but have *acted* as though they were selecting policy makers whose views they wished to accord with their own. "Since 1885 over 90 percent of all federal judges have been filled by members—in most cases active members—of the same party as the President who chose them and most have been supporters of the senator who nominated them."[23] The American Bar Association has asked for a greater voice in the selection of judges (after all, they ask, who can determine the technical competence of a judge better than lawyers?), but the many other interests involved have been reluctant to turn over so much power to what is, in many instances, a rival interest.[24] On the other side of the fence, a number of judges have clung to their posts long after age and failing health indicated their retirement. Why? Because they so opposed the political views of the incumbent President and Senate majority that they did not wish the latter to name their successors. As Chief Justice William Howard Taft said (in 1929!), "As long as things continue as they are, and I am able to answer in my place, I must stay on the Court in order to prevent the Bolsheviki from getting control. . . ."[25]

## Over the Making of Decisions

Interest groups try to influence the selection of judicial personnel wherever they can, but the relative stability of the bench means that for the most part they have to work with and through the judges as they are. Now an interest group may, only at great peril (see above), try to influence a judge in the same manner it might try to influence a congressman or an administrator. Thus, most groups exert direct influence only through such accepted channels as litigation, employing expensive and able lawyers, presenting the best possible "briefs," and so on. It is interesting to note in this regard that in recent decades it has become increasingly common for interest groups not directly parties to a particular case that affects their interests to submit *amicus curiae* (friend of the court) briefs and offer other legal help to litigants who represent the legal principles they want to see the courts establish or uphold. Many such were submitted for both sides, for example, in the school segregation cases of 1954 mentioned above. The ablest lawyers and the best-drawn briefs by no means always ensure victory, of course—but they help.

## Over the Implementation of Decisions

In Chapter 19 we noted that just because a law has been enacted by the legislature and approved by the executive does not necessarily mean that

---

[23] Peltason, *op. cit.*, p. 31. See also David J. Danelski, *A Supreme Court Justice Is Appointed* (New York: Random House, Inc., 1964).

[24] Cf. Joel B. Grossman, *Lawyers & Judges* (New York: John Wiley & Sons, Inc., 1965).

[25] Quoted in C. Herman Pritchett, *The Roosevelt Court* (New York: The Macmillan Company, 1948), p. 18.

it will be applied by the administrative agencies exactly, or in some instances even approximately, as its authors intended. The administrative process, in other words, can be as significant a determinant of the policies government actually follows as the legislative or executive processes.

The same thing can be said of the judicial process. Just because the Supreme Court or any other judicial body has declared what the law is on a particular point does not necessarily mean that every other court and/or governmental agency will act accordingly. For one thing, the court's decision is technically binding only upon the specific litigants in the particular case; and if interest groups similar to those represented by the losing litigants choose to ignore the decision, they can often get away with it. In 1947, for example, the Supreme Court declared that the Board of Education of Champaign County, Illinois, violated the constitutional separation of church and state in its "released-time" program, by allowing religious teachers to hold classes in the public schools, and requiring pupils either to attend the classes or to remain in a study hall. After the decision the Champaign school board discontinued its program, but in many thousands of other school districts throughout the land similar "released-time" programs were continued as though nothing had happened.[26] An even more dramatic illustration occurred in 1955 when the Supreme Court ordered the desegregation of all public schools "with all deliberate speed"; yet, today the schools in a number of southern states remain almost as segregated as they were before the 1955 order.

For another thing, the formal "hierarchical" structure of court systems described above is no guarantee that the lower courts will invariably interpret the law exactly as the higher courts wish. As Peltason points out:

> The subordinate judge's task of applying the Supreme Court's mandates is no more mechanical than is the Supreme Court's task of applying the Constitution's mandates. The high court decisions which are supposed to guide and control the subordinates are frequently just as ambiguous as is the Constitution or statute which is supposed to guide the Supreme Court, and they admit of many interpretations. Hence, just as it is said that the Constitution is what the judges say it is, so it can be said that a Supreme Court decision is what the subordinate judges who apply it say it is.[27]

Finally, groups whose interests are damaged by an adverse court decision do not need to accept their defeat as final, and rarely do. They can, for example, try to amend the Constitution so as to prevent such rulings in the future (this was the purpose of the Eleventh and Sixteenth Amendments), or to persuade the court to reverse itself (as it did, for example, in the Brown case), or to induce the lower courts to nullify it, or to "pack"

---

[26] Peltason, *op. cit.*, p. 56.
[27] *Ibid.*, p. 14. For examples of "reversals" by lower courts, see *ibid.*, pp. 60–62.

or "threaten to pack" the court. Judicial decisions, in short, do not necessarily settle once and for all the political conflicts they deal with any more than do legislative acts or executive or administrative actions. However, because of the high prestige and officially "nonpolitical" atmosphere of the judicial process, a favorable court decision is an important victory for any interest group.

### The Courts and the Democratic Political Process: A Summary

Some readers who grant that the foregoing presents a more accurate picture than does the traditional conception of what the courts in the democracies actually do may nevertheless find it depressing. Perhaps they prefer to believe that somewhere in the politico-governmental process issues are settled not because of conflict between opposing selfish groups but because some real statesmen lift themselves entirely beyond such conflict and settle the issues in accordance with eternal principles of right and wrong. Perhaps they believe, or at least hope, that they will find just such statesmen in the courts.

The author sees no reason to be depressed by this picture of the political process. After all, we have pictured democracy in this book as a process in which political conflict takes place among groups that are freely organized and at liberty to express their views; in which it is conducted by discussion and peaceful agitation, and in a spirit of respect for the other man's right to live and "pursue happiness," i.e., to try to achieve his goals; and in which value-allocations are made as the result of governmental decisions intended both to hold the society together and to promote some abstract notion of "perfect justice." If there is any validity in this view of democracy, then there is no reason to be either surprised or depressed by learning that judges and courts as well as legislatures, executives, and administrators are a part of one pervasive democratic decision-making process.

In any case, we may be sure that most democrats would greatly prefer the kind of judicial process we have described to that which operates in Communist Russia and the nations which govern themselves as Russia does.

## Law and the Courts in the Soviet Union

### The Communist Conception of Law

Some democratic political theorists, as we have noted several times in this book, believe that a democratic government and all its instrumentalities, including law, should act solely as a neutral and impartial arbiter of conflicts among its nation's interest groups. Other theorists believe that democratic governments are not only arbiters of political conflict but also to some extent participants in it; but, they feel, so long as the governmental agencies have no monopoly on the media of communications and the other tools of political power, their participation in political conflict does not violate any essential principle of democracy.

Communist political theorists view the political process in an entirely different light. As we learned in Chapters 5 and 10, Communists see all politics and, indeed, all human activity as the result and reflection of the basic struggle to the death between the bourgeoisie and the proletariat. Hence they regard any government and all its agencies as simply an instrument of the dominant class for maintaining its supremacy over the subject class; to them all the democratic theories of law outlined above are so much claptrap, either cynical or deluded, masking the naked reality of capitalist exploitation of the disfranchised workers.

Communist society, its adherents believe, recognizes the essential nature of law as a weapon in class warfare and not only turns it to the advantage of the proletariat but makes no hypocritical effort to conceal its true purpose. Thus, Article 590 of the Soviet Penal Code declares, "Law is a system of social relationships which serves the interests of the ruling classes and hence is supported by their organized power, the state."[28] Andrei Vyshinsky, once Procurator General of the Soviet Union and its quondam leading legal theorist, added:

> In the Soviet state, law is entirely and completely directed against exploitation and exploiters. Soviet law is the law of the socialist state of workers and peasants. It is invoked to meet the problems of the struggle with foes of socialism and the cause of building a socialist society.[29]

To the Communists, in short, law is the instrument of "socialist policy" —meaning the program of the Russian Communist party—and in no sense a restraint on or a counterbalance to it.

### The Purposes of the Soviet Courts

In their routine, day-to-day work the Soviet Courts perform many activities similar to those of the courts in the democracies. They hear and decide divorce cases, suits for damages between individuals, trials of persons accused of murder, rape, and similar crimes. But their underlying purposes, two of which we shall describe below, make their role quite different from that performed by courts in the democratic nations.

---

[28] Quoted in Kenneth Redden, ed., *An Introductory Survey of the Place of Law in Our Civilization* (Charlottesville, Va.: The Michie Company, 1946), p. 14.

[29] Andrei Y. Vyshinsky, *The Law of the Soviet State*, translated by Hugh W. Babb (New York: The Macmillan Company, 1948), p. 50.

# "... The Defendants, Beria, Dekanozov, Meshik..."

*Figure 41.* "The Purpose of Communist Justice Is to Destroy Communism's Enemies." (From *Herblock's Here and Now,* Simon & Schuster, 1955.)

## To Destroy Communism's Enemies

One of the leading American students of Soviet law, Harold J. Berman, points out that communist jurisprudence is obsessed with criminal law, which occupies a much greater proportion of Russian legal literature and codes than it does in their Western counterparts.[30] The Russians have

---

[30] Harold J. Berman, *Justice in Russia* (Cambridge, Mass.: Harvard University Press, 1950), p. 270.

added to the usual list of crimes a number of "economic crimes," such as habitual tardiness to and absence from work, negligence or willful mis-management by state factory and farm managers, "speculation, i.e., pur-chase and sale of commodities or other goods for profit," and the like. Economic crimes, moreover, are often regarded as more serious than the usual crimes.

Perhaps the most striking manifestation of this purpose of Soviet law is the wide range of crimes for which the penalty is death. In addition to the usual list of crimes—premeditated murder, rape, treason, espionage, sabotage, and subversion—the death penalty has been prescribed since 1962 for acts which disrupt the operations of prisons and "correctional labor camps," the counterfeiting of money or state securities, violations of cur-rency regulations, the theft of public property on a large scale, the accept-ance or giving of bribes, and "banditism."[31]

### To Educate the Masses

In Chapter 10 we learned that one major objective of Communist policy is to "educate the masses"—which means, of course, to make the masses sufficiently enthusiastic about the Communist party's policies that these policies can be pursued with a minimum of costly physical coercion. We have already described the "agitprop" apparatus established by the party for this purpose, and Berman tells us that the Soviet courts also play a significant role in the "educating" process. These bodies, he says, are sup-posed to act as "teachers and parents" for the masses. When hearing and deciding cases involving points in which the party feels the masses in the area need instruction, the courts' sessions are arranged so as to permit maxi-mum popular attendance, and the masses are "encouraged" to attend.[32] Certainly all Communist regimes have made considerable use of "purge trials," modeled on the Russian trials of 1936–1938, complete with public "confessions" of guilt and cooperation with the capitalist enemy by the accused. Communist leaders apparently believe that such trials are most useful in "educating" the masses in the immorality and folly of opposing the party.

### The Structure of the Court System and the Office of Procurator

The essentials of the Russian court system's formal structure are shown in Figure 42.

Two aspects of the system represented in Figure 42 are of especial interest for our purposes.

---

[31] W. W. Kulski, *The Soviet Regime: Communism in Practice* (Syracuse, N.Y.: Syracuse University Press, 1963), pp. 167–168.

[32] Berman, *op. cit.*, Chs. 9–10.

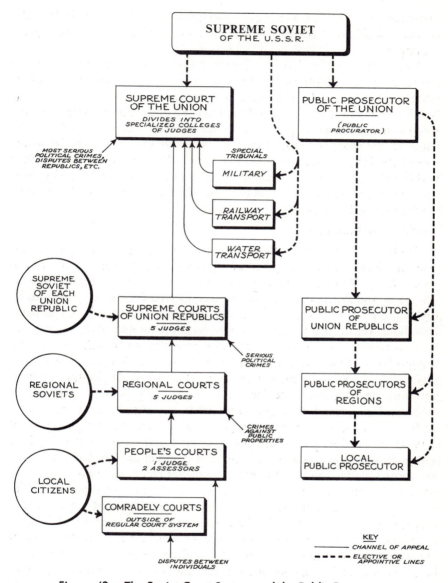

*Figure 42.* The Soviet Court System and the Public Prosecutor.

## The Selection of Judges and Assessors

The Soviet Constitution specifies that all judges shall be elected; but "election" has been interpreted to mean direct selection by the voters only in the case of the judges for the People's Courts. The judges of all the other courts are named for five-year terms by the legislative assemblies of their respective levels, up to and including the Supreme Court of the USSR, the members of which are nominally selected by the Supreme Soviet (the national legislative assembly), but actually, of course, by the party Presidium.

The judges of the People's Courts, however, are elected for five-year terms by the local voters—but from the same kind of one-candidate-per-office slate prepared by the party that confronts the voters in all other Russian elections (see Chapter 13). Each People's Court consists of one judge and two "assessors." The latter are "elected" every five years by the voters in the usual communist manner. They are supposed to be lay assistants to the judge somewhat in the manner of Western juries; but complete party dominance over the selection of all officials—assessors, elected judges, and appointed judges alike—makes any further analogy with Western institutions highly misleading.

### The Office of Procurator

Quite as important to the Soviet judicial system as the judges and assessors is the office of procurator (sometimes translated as "public prosecutor"). The institution, a revised version of an old tsarist office, is headed by the Procurator General, who is selected for a seven-year term by the Supreme Soviet and works under the close instruction of the party Presidium. He in turn selects a series of local procurators and assigns them to each court at the local, regional, and republic levels. They are strictly responsible to him and not to any local authority. Within his area each procurator is charged with seeing to it "that no single decision of local authority deviates from the law" (i.e., from party policy). Thus, he is authorized to protest to higher authorities any illegal action by a local authority; to "ferret out every single crime for punishment" by political deviants and ordinary criminals; to make sure that every arrest is legal; to appear in court to prosecute the indicted criminal and to make sure that the court upholds the law; to protest to higher courts all lower court decisions and sentences rendered in violation of the law; to supervise fulfillment of the court's sentence and even to intervene and supervise the proceedings in civil cases.[33] In short, he is one of the central party's more prominent local watchdogs not only over the behavior of individual persons but over the activities of the courts themselves. In every court proceeding he is unquestionably the dominant figure; for Soviet law and theory assign to him even more than to the courts the responsibility for making sure that Communist law and policies are carried out in the legal area. Some scholars liken the office to that of United States attorney or state's attorney, but the procurator's powers are far more extensive and he is a figure far more to be dreaded by ordinary citizens than the Western officials.

---

[33] Merle Fainsod, *How Russia Is Ruled* (rev. ed.; Cambridge, Mass.: Harvard University Press, 1963), pp. 411–413.

# Justice under Communism and Democracy:
## A Summary

Most Western observers agree that the Soviet system of justice works quite well by Western standards if and when no "political questions" (that is, questions the party regards as involving its ideals and policies) are involved; and the treatment of ordinary crimes, family disputes, and the like by Soviet courts appears not to differ widely from its counterpart in the Western democracies.

When "political questions" are involved in a legal controversy in the Soviet Union, however, justice and the will of the party are—as they are intended to be according to communist doctrine—one and the same. Law and the courts in Communist Russia, in other words, are like every other governmental agency: both in communist theory and in Russian practice they act as instruments for the party to impose its will upon the masses with a minimum of resistance by the latter and a minimum expenditure of effort by the party.

The differences between the democratic and communist conceptions and organizations of law and the judicial process, then, are one more instance—albeit one of the more striking ones—of the profound differences between the democratic and the communist processes of government.

# 21

## Local Government
## and Federalism

Under the modern state system, as we learned in Chapter 2, the earth's peoples are divided among some 126 social-political-legal entities called "nations." These are the world's principal governing units, for each claims the exclusive right to make and enforce rules governing the behavior of the people within its territory, and none formally recognizes any superior rule-making authority.

That is why we have devoted most of this book to describing government and politics in nations. Yet national communities and national governments are by no means all there is. Every nation contains a number of subnational communities, each with a population, customs, attitudes, accent, dialect, or even language, and needs that to some extent differ from those of other local communities and of the nation as a whole.

Americans, for example, are well aware of the many significant differences between New Englanders, Southerners, Midwesterners, and Westerners. Far too many of us are inclined to think of "the British (no sense of humor) and "the French" (loose morals) as homogeneous national types. But when we travel abroad or read British and French literature, we soon realize that the differences between the Highland Scots and the men of Devon and Cornwall are as great as those between Vermonters and Mississippians, and those between the Normans and the Provençals are as great as those between New Yorkers and New Mexicans.

We also learned in Chapter 2 that for most men nationalism is the highest loyalty; but this does not mean it is their *only* loyalty. Endemic in every modern-nation is conflict among its local communities for industry, population, and largesse (in the form of veterans' hospitals, military bases, defense contracts, and the like) from the national government—and conflict between the local communities and the nation over the degree to which the former can manage their own affairs without direction from the latter. Not infrequently such loyalties are strong enough to produce powerful "states' rights" or even secession movements. The revolt of the eleven Confederate States of America from 1860 to 1865 produced the greatest bloodshed of any civil war in modern times, but many modern nations have to contend with comparable, if less powerful, movements: for example, the Quebec separatist movement in Canada, the bitter conflict between the Flemings and the Walloons in Belgium, and the many tribal and provincial secessionist movements in the former Belgian Congo since it became an independent nation in 1960.

Local communities, then, are significant elements of every modern nation. Most of them have their own local governments which are authorized, in varying ways and within various limits, to make and enforce rules for persons within their particular subnational jurisdictions. Our task in the present chapter is to see what place these governments have claimed in democratic theory and to describe their principal patterns of organization and problems in modern democratic nations.

## Local Government in Democratic Theory

### Local Communities in the National Community

Some theorists of democracy, notably Jean-Jacques Rousseau and Thomas Jefferson in the eighteenth century and Baker Brownell in the twentieth, have argued that democracy's health depends to a considerable degree upon preserving the special identities of these local communities, and that maintaining strong local self-government as a means to that end should be a prime goal of governmental organization in any nation that wishes to be truly democratic. Arthur E. Morgan, onetime chairman of the Tennessee Valley Authority, spoke for all these theorists when he wrote:

> For the preservation and transmission of the fundamentals of civilization, vigorous, wholesome [local] community life is imperative. Unless many people live and work in the intimate relationships of community life, there can never emerge a truly unified nation, or a community of mankind. If I do not love my neighbor whom I know, how can I love the human race, which is but an abstraction? If I have not learned to work with a few people, how can I be effective with many?[1]

---

[1] Arthur E. Morgan, *The Small Community: Foundation of Democratic Life* (New York: Harper & Row, Publishers, 1942), p. 19. See also Baker Brownell, *The Human Community* (New York: Harper & Row, Publishers, 1950).

## The Contributions of Local Government

Although some democratic theorists regard the local community as somewhat less crucial than do the writers just mentioned, almost all of them believe that properly organized local self-government can make contributions of great value to the health of democracy. Five contributions are most frequently mentioned.

First, while there is only one national government in each nation, there are many local governments, each of which has jurisdiction over far fewer persons than the national government. Hence, many more persons can directly and continuously participate in local government than in national government, and direct participation by a maximum number of citizens in their governments makes for a healthy democracy and is a strong barrier against tyranny. Thomas Jefferson put it thus:

> Where every man is a sharer in the direction of . . . and feels that he is a participator in, the government of affairs, not merely at an election one day in the year, but every day; where there shall be not a man in the State who will not be a member of some one of its councils, great or small, he will let the heart be torn out of his body sooner than his power be wrested from him by a Caesar or a Bonaparte.[2]

Second, in the words of the English political scientist Harold J. Laski, "all problems are not central problems, and . . . problems not central in their incidence require decision at the place, and by the persons, where and by whom the incidence is most deeply felt."[3] In other words, the zoning problems of Urbana, Illinois, mainly concern and are best understood by the residents of Urbana, and not the residents of Chicago or New York or Washington. Hence, only the residents of Urbana should have the power to make Urbana's zoning ordinances.

Third, participation in local government either as a public official or as a voter is excellent training for voting in national elections and holding national public office and thereby provides an ever-fresh source of good citizens and leaders for the nation.

Fourth, local government is an invaluable sociopolitical laboratory for trying and testing on a small scale various new proposals for government organization and social and economic policies. Local failures can be borne with far less social cost than can failures of the national government, and local successes can and often do serve as models the national government may follow with a minimum of risk.

---

[2] Letter to Joseph C. Cabell, February 2, 1816, in Andrew A. Lipscomb, ed., *The Writings of Thomas Jefferson* (Washington, D.C.: The Thomas Jefferson Memorial Association, 1903), XIV, 422.

[3] Harold J. Laski, *A Grammar of Politics* (New Haven, Conn.: Yale University Press, 1925), p. 411.

Finally, a dead uniformity in all standards, policies, and organization imposed on all local areas by a national government is bound to stamp out the variety and local color that contribute so richly to the life of any nation; and strong local self-government is the most effective barrier against any such drab conformism.

### The Distribution of Functions

Few if any democratic theorists have argued that *all* governmental functions should be performed exclusively by either the national government or the local governments. At the most general (and, therefore, perhaps not very useful) level of discussion, they all agree upon what might be called the "to-each-its-own" standard: that is, let the national government deal with all problems that are mainly national in character, and let each local government deal with all problems that mainly concern its local community alone. As Jefferson put it:

> . . . the way to have good and safe government, is not to trust it to one, but to divide it among the many, distributing to every one exactly the functions he is competent to. Let the national government be entrusted with the defense of the nation, and its foreign and federal relations; the State governments with the civil rights, laws, police, and administration of what concerns the State generallly; the counties with the local concerns of the counties; and each ward direct the interests within itself.[4]

So general a standard unfortunately does not help us very much in concrete situations in which we have to decide which government should deal with this or that specific problem. For example, both Northerners and southern whites in the United States believe that the national government should handle only national matters and the states should control all purely state matters. But in the current controversy over the racial-discrimination laws of the southern states (see Chapter 9) the Southerners argue that each state's race relations are the rightful concern of that state alone and no business of the rest of the nation, while Northerners reply that since Negroes are citizens of the United States as well as of the states wherein they reside their rights are the proper concern of the whole nation. The fact that both sides are sincere in their adherence to the "to-each-its-own" standard and in their different applications of it has not made the settlement of this bitter dispute any easier.

In short, nearly every citizen of every democracy believes that both the national government and local governments have their proper place in the total scheme of things. Yet in every such nation, not just in the United

---

[4] Jefferson, *op. cit.*, p. 421.

States, there is a constant tug of war between the national and local governments over which should have the power to perform this or that public functon.

In the following account of the structure and powers of local governments in modern nations we shall describe the current state of this perennial and universal national-local contest.

## Local Governments in Unitary Situations[5]

In Chapter 4 we defined a unitary government as one in which the central government is legally supreme over all local governments within its borders. Most modern nations have unitary governments, and in each of them all local governments are legally created by the national government and made subject to whatever degree of control and supervision the national authorities think best. Even in the few nations with federal governments, as we shall see below, each of the "cosovereign" subnational governments (the states in the United States and Australia, the provinces in Canada, the *Länder* in West Germany, and the cantons in Switzerland, and so on) is unitary with respect to the local governments within its boundaries. In the present section we are concerned with the local governments operating in these unitary situations, and in the following section we shall consider local governments in federal situations.

There are, needless to say, seemingly infinite variations in detail in the legal status, governmental structure, and types and powers exercised by officials in the hundreds of thousands of local governments operating in unitary situations the world over. Nevertheless, there are enough similarities among them to warrant at least a few general descriptive statements.

### Units and Governmental Organization

#### In the American States

Most American states encompass a greater variety of units of local government and forms of local governmental organization than do any of the unitary establishments in the other democratic nations. The Census Bureau estimated in 1962 that in the fifty states there were slightly over 3000 counties, almost 18,000 cities and villages, another 17,000 towns and townships, 35,000 school districts, and about 18,000 "special districts," such as park districts, sanitary districts, drainage districts, and the like.

---

[5] A much-needed but yet unwritten book is "The Theory and Practice of Modern *Local* Government." Two modest but useful starts in this direction are G. Montagu Harris, *Comparative Local Government* (London: Hutchinson & Co., Ltd., 1948); and William A. Robson, ed., *Great Cities of the World: Their Government, Politics, and Planning* (New York: The Macmillan Company, 1954).

THE COUNTY. Every American state is entirely or largely subdivided into a number of areas known as "counties" (in Louisiana the equivalent units are called "parishes"). They vary in geographic area all the way from 20,131 square miles (San Bernardino County, California) to 24 square miles (Arlington County, Virginia), and in population from 6,038,771 (Los Angeles County, California) to 227 (Loving County, Texas). In most states the county is mainly a unit for governing rural areas, although it usually also has certain powers over and renders certain services to urban areas as well. The governmental organization of counties varies considerably from state to state, and, for that matter, from county to county within some states. In general, however, their governments are composed of two main elements.

First, there is some kind of popularly elected council, usually known as the "board of county commissioners" or the "county board of supervisors." This board generally exercises whatever regulatory powers—usually few and minor—the county may have, levies county taxes, and administers such services assigned to it by the state as laying out election precincts and appointing election officials, controlling the county courthouse, jail, hospital, "poor farm," and the like. The board acts mainly as an agency for administering and supervising certain functions assigned to it by the state rather than as a legislative body.

Second, there are a number of county officers, some elected, some appointed by the county board, and some appointed by state authorities. These include the sheriff, coroner, county clerk, recorder of deeds, county superintendent of schools, and so on. A century ago, when most Americans lived in rural areas, counties were perhaps the most significant of all units of local government; but, as we shall see below, they now take a back seat to cities in most respects.[6]

TOWNS AND TOWNSHIPS. Twenty-one American states subdivide part or all of their counties into "towns" or "townships" for purposes of rural local government, but the two types of units should not be confused with each other. In the six New England states (Connecticut, Maine, Massachusetts, New Hampshire, Rhode Island, and Vermont) the "towns," most of which include both rural and urban areas, are the leading units of local government, and, except in those areas controlled by incorporated municipalities (see below), they exercise most of the functions performed by the counties in other states. Their most noteworthy feature, of course, is their famed "town-meeting" form of government, which is so widely regarded as a

---

[6] Cf. Lane W. Lancaster, *Government in Rural America* (2d ed.; Princeton, N.J.: D. Van Nostrand Company, Inc., 1952); and Clyde F. Snider, *Local Government in Rural America* (New York: Appleton-Century-Crofts, Inc., 1957).

model of democracy. Under this form the town's citizens meet once a year, make appropriations, fix tax rates, and enact town ordinances. They also select a "board of selectmen" of three to five members to administer the town's affairs, according to the instructions and within the limits prescribed by the town meeting, until "meeting day" of the following year. In recent years, however, a number of New England towns have grown too populous for this kind of government and have replaced it with the "representative town meeting." Under the latter form the town is divided into precincts, and each elects a number of delegates who assemble as the official "town meeting" but are more like an annual representative convention.

In the other fifteen states, most of them in the Midwest and the Middle Atlantic regions, the "township" is far less prominent than the New England "town" and is used principally as an agency for administering a few minor state-assigned services, such as rural poor relief and rural roads.

OTHER LOCAL DISTRICTS.    All the states also establish certain "special purpose" districts to administer, usually through an elected board, such special local services as parks, drainage, and sanitation. By far the most significant, of course, are the school districts, which are the principal units of local educational administration in twenty-four of the states, and in such states act as the basic areas in which funds are raised and schools administered. The supervising officials in each district are usually an elected school board and, in a few instances, also a superintendent of schools, who is usually appointed by the board to act as the school system's chief administrative officer. The local school boards always operate within the limits laid down by acts of the state legislature and often also under regulations made by a state superintendent of public instruction; but in most of these twenty-four states the local school boards exercise a considerable degree of local autonomy. Local control of education, organized in this or other fashions, is one of the most widely approved and strongest aspects of all local self-government in the United States.

THE MUNICIPALITY.    A "municipality" is a *legal* entity—a "municipal corporation" established to govern an "urban area." The latter, in turn, is a *sociological* entity—a relatively well-defined area in which a number of persons live relatively close together rather than in more widely scattered places, as in a "rural" area. The legal boundaries of a municipality rarely correspond exactly to the sociological boundaries of its urban area. Thus, when we talk about "the city of New York," it is important to distinguish between the sociological entity located on both sides of the Hudson River and the legal entity located only on the east side of the river. We are here concerned only with the legal entities established by charter from a state to perform certain public services for their assigned areas. These areas and their governments are most commonly called "cities," but since they also include areas and governments called "towns" and "villages," we shall use the term "municipality" to cover them all.

Municipalities are generally considered to be the most significant units of local government in the American states. The 1960 census reported that 70 percent of all Americans live under such governments, and 60 percent live in incorporated municipalities of over 10,000 population. There is every reason to believe that the 1970 census will show an even higher degree of urbanization, and so most studies of local government in the American states rightly devote more time to municipalities than to any of the other units mentioned above.[7]

The American states vary considerably in the degree of freedom they leave to their municipalities to choose their own forms of government. A few states still use the old "special-act charter" method, whereby each municipality receives its "charter" (i.e., its authorized powers and form of government, contained not in any single document like a state or national Constitution, but consisting of all the state laws and judicial decisions that apply to its powers and form of government) by a special act of the state legislature. Many more use some version of the "general-act charter" method, one form of which is a single charter enacted by the state legislature which serves as the form of government for all municipalities. Another form is that of "classification," whereby the legislature classifies cities according to population and creates one charter and form of government for all cities in each designated range of population. In those states which use still another variation, the "optional-charter" method, the legislature enacts a series of charters, each having a somewhat different form of government, and authorizes each city to choose among them. The greatest degree of freedom is provided by the "home-rule charter" method which authorizes each municipality (either by Constitutional prescription or by legislative grant) to frame, adopt, and amend its own charter and to exercise all powers of local self-government, subject only to the general limitations laid down by the Constitution and general laws of the state. As of 1965, twenty-six states provided Constitutional home rule, and eight more provided it by legislative grant. Cities under home rule certainly have great freedom to choose their own forms of government; but, as we shall see below, they have much less freedom to decide what services they will provide and how.

American municipalities are governed by one or another of three basic forms of government: mayor-council, commission, and council-manager. Before we describe their structures, we might well heed Charles Adrian's warning that

---

[7] Cf. Charles M. Kneier, *City Government in the United States* (3d ed.; New York: Harper & Row, Publishers, 1957), pp. 3–4.

. . . there are probably no two cities in the United States that have *exactly* the same structure of government. . . . Nearly every charter commission or state legislature, in considering structure, finds it politically expedient to add its own improvisation on the given theme. . . . The variations are quite endless, and the structural descriptions that follow must be thought of as models which city charters tend to imitate.[8]

*The Mayor-Council Form.* This form has two variations, the "weak-mayor" and the "strong-mayor" forms. The "model" weak mayor–council form is graphically represented in Figure 43.

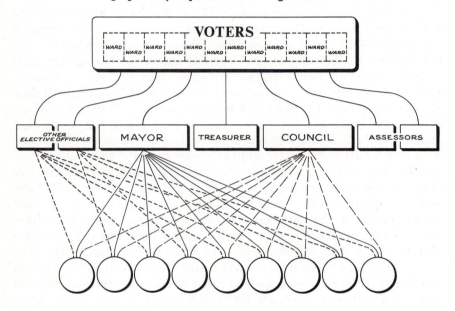

*Figure 43.*  The Weak Mayor–Council Form of Municipal Government.

The weak mayor-council structure is still the most common of all forms of municipal government in the United States, although in recent years it has been replaced in a number of municipalities by the strong-mayor and the council-manager forms. The mayor in this form is not called "weak" because he lacks powers to direct policy, for he usually presides over the council, has a veto over its actions, and often is its main political leader. He is called "weak" because he is not the "chief executive" in the

---

[8] Charles R. Adrian, *Governing Urban America* (New York: McGraw-Hill Book Company, Inc., 1955), p. 173.

sense of having the sole formal power to appoint, remove, and supervise the municipality's administrative officers and employees. As Figure 43 shows, some of these are elected by the voters, and the council shares with the mayor the power to appoint the others. Most political scientists believe this to be the worst form of municipal government, mainly because it fails to provide for administrative leadership and centralized control and responsibility, adds to the burdens of the local voters by giving them so many elective offices to fill, and violates many other "principles of public administration" (see Chapter 19). Nevertheless, it continues to be the most widely used of all forms of municipal government, particularly in small towns, although cities as large as Minneapolis, Atlanta, and Providence use it.

Many political scientists prefer the strong mayor–council variation of this form, which resembles the structure of the American national government in that the mayor, like the President, is the only elected executive official, appoints and dismisses department heads, and shares policy-making functions with the council. This form is particularly successful in large cities and is currently used by such cities as New York, Philadelphia, Detroit, Cleveland, and St. Louis.

*The Commission Form.* The structure of the "model" commission form of municipal government is shown in Figure 44.

The principal characteristics of this form, as Figure 44 shows, are its abandonment of the principle of "separation of powers" and its location of both the policy-making and administration-supervising functions in the council. It is somewhat similar to the form, described below, used by all British local governments. Many political scientists believe it to be a substantial improvement over the weak mayor–council form, because it provides a "short ballot" and establishes much greater concentration of control over and responsibility for administration. They also feel, however, that its failure to provide for a *chief* policy leader and a *chief* administrator, and its dependence upon amateurs rather than professionals to supervise administration are serious weaknesses. The number of cities using it has declined sharply since about 1917, but it is still employed by such major cities as Memphis, Portland (Oregon), and Birmingham.

*The Council-Manager Form.* The structure of the "model" council-manager form of municipal government is shown in Figure 45.

Many political scientists believe that for most municipalities the council-manager form is by far the best, and it is proposed in the "model city charter" of the National Municipal League. Its principal virtues, they believe, include the following. It provides for the "short ballot," since only the members of the council are elected. It clearly locates the policy-making and policy-administering functions in separate agencies (see Chapter 19). It not only centralizes in one man the control of and responsibility for

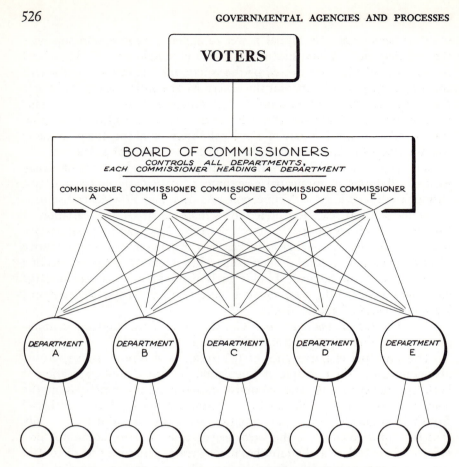

*Figure 44.* The Commission Form of Municipal Government.

supervising administration, but also enables that man to be a full-time, trained, career professional rather than a part-time amateur. Finally, since the manager is hired by the council and holds his job at its pleasure, he cannot become, as some critics charge, a "dictator."

As Professor Adrian points out, however, the council-manager plan has its weaknesses: there is a shortage of well-trained and top-quality professional managers; there is no institutional provision for policy leadership in the council; and the manager often participates actively in politics, dominates the council because of his greater expertise, and thus violates certain principles of democracy. Certainly it is no panacea for the ills of all municipalities everywhere.[9] One measure of the council-manager form's popularity in the five decades since it was first proposed is the fact that it has been

---

[9] Cf. *ibid.*, pp. 201–204.

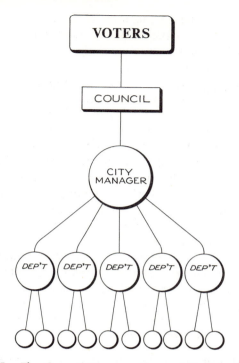

*Figure 45.* The Council-Manager Form of Municipal Government.

adopted by a steadily increasing number of municipalities, has been abandoned by very few, and is now used in nearly 50 percent of American cities with populations of over 25,000, and in over 45 percent of those with populations of between 10,000 and 25,000. The largest cities presently using it are Cincinnati, Kansas City (Missouri), Dallas, and San Antonio.

### In Great Britain

**THE STANDARD FORM OF GOVERNMENT.** After our consideration of the patchwork-quilt profusion and variety of local-government units in the American states, the structure in Great Britain seems a model of simplicity and order. For instance, there are six main types of local governing units, which we shall describe in a moment; but each of them employs the same form of government. The basic governing body in all units is an elected council. In the counties, county boroughs, and municipal boroughs the elected councillors also elect a number of "aldermen," either from among their own members or from persons outside the council, by a process known as "co-optation." The aldermen also sit on the council but have longer terms than the directly elected councillors. The whole council selects a person either from among its members or from outside as its presiding officer, called a "mayor" in the boroughs and a "chairman" in the other units. He acts as the council's presiding officer and the unit's main ceremonial figure but has no such powers as the "strong mayor" in the United States. The operation of the council is rather similar to that of the commission form of municipal government and the county board of supervisors in the United States. The whole council acts as the unit's legislature, and the council's committees acts as its administrative supervisors. For each service the unit performs the council establishes a committee, composed of both councillors and aldermen and with its members distributed among the political parties according to their strength on the whole council. Each committee then supervises the work of the professional administrator heading up the department over which it has charge. The chairmen of the various committees often act together as a sort of "cabinet" to guide both policy making and administration.

Finally, each unit has a number of permanent administrative officers. These include the town or county clerk, who is the chief administrative officer and also acts as "returning officer" in elections for Parliament (see Chapter 13); the treasurer, who presides over the collection of "rates" (local taxes) and the disbursement of local funds; the health officer; a sanitary inspector; a surveyor; and so on.

THE MAIN UNITS OF LOCAL GOVERNMENT.    The various units of British local government, then, have almost identical forms of government. The main differences among them relate to the areas over which they have jurisdiction and their relations with other units. The main units and their formal interrelations are shown in Figure 46.

Let us briefly describe each of the units shown in Figure 46.

*The Administrative County.*    The 61 modern administrative counties are the successors of the 52 ancient "shires" (e.g., Cornwall, Hampshire, Warwickshire, and Shropshire) which for many centuries were the principal units of British local government. Some of the modern units correspond to some of the ancient areas and some do not. As Figure 46 shows, the jurisdiction of each modern administrative county extends to all parts of its area except those governed by county boroughs, and its council exercises certain supervisory powers over the municipal boroughs and urban and rural districts within its boundaries.

*The County Borough.*    Each of the 83 county boroughs is a "municipality" in the American sense with the powers of an administrative county and independent of the county in which it is located. They vary in population from 1,118,500 (Birmingham) to 28,000 (Canterbury).

*The Municipal Borough.*    Each of the 317 "noncounty" or "municipal" boroughs governs an urban area and has a general power to make

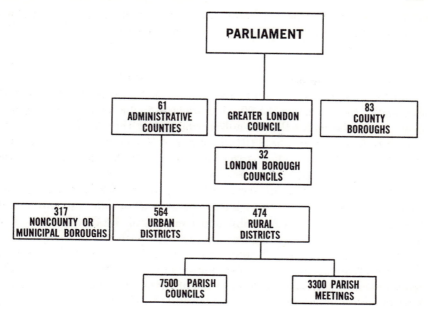

*Figure 46.* The Units of Local Government in England and Wales.

orders and bylaws for its area, subject to the supervision of the county council.

*The Urban District.* Each of the 564 urban districts is authorized to administer mainly public health, lesser roads, and housing in the urban areas of its county; unlike the municipal boroughs, these units have only the powers given them by specific grants.

*The Rural District.* Each of the 474 rural districts is in exactly the same position as the urban districts except that it operates in a rural area. Each rural district, moreover, contains one or more "parishes." The rather minimal powers of the latter are exercised either by a "parish meeting," an assembly of all the parish's voters, or by a representative parish council. The parishes act mainly as subdivisions for doing whatever their rural district councils permit or require them to do.

THE SPECIAL CASE OF LONDON.    Like the capitals of many other nations, London has its own special governmental structure. Under the major reorganization which went into effect in 1965, "Greater London"—an area including parts of 6 historic counties and a population of over 8 million—is divided into 32 London boroughs. Each of these is responsible for most functions of local gvernment in its area, but certain functions for the whole area are performed by the Greater London Council, whose members are elected from the constituent boroughs. Legally speaking, then, "London" is not a municipality but the largest and most powerful of all the administrative counties.

### In France[10]

There are two principal units of French local government. The first and territorially the larger are the 90 *départements,* including such well-known areas as the *Gironde,* the *Alpes-Maritimes,* and the *Pas-de-Calais.* The second and smaller are the 38,014 communes. There are also subdivisions of the *départements,* called *arrondissements,* but they are of too little significance to be dealt with here.

Each *département* has an elected *conseil général* (general council) whose members serve for six-year terms and some of whom are also prominent deputies in the National Assembly and members of the Government. The general council holds two regular sessions each year and as many special sessions as the prefect (see below) calls. It selects its own presiding officer and acts as an agency for performing certain functions assigned to the *département* by the national government, as a local legislature making departmental ordinances on matters permitted by the national government, and as an administrative body supervising some of the activities of the communes within its boundaries. The chief executive officer of the *département* is the *préfet* (prefect) who is *not* locally elected but is appointed by the national government. He makes up the departmental budget (although the general council can revise the budget as it wishes), supervises the departmental administrative officers and employees, takes official responsibility for maintaining order and morality in the area, exercises "tutelary" powers (see below) over the communes, and in general serves as the national government's main official agent in the *département.* The office of prefect has no counterpart in British or American local government, but a number of European democracies have created similar positions.

Each commune has an elected *conseil municipal* (municipal council) whose members also serve for six years. The council holds at least four regular sessions a year and exercises powers and functions that vary considerably from one commune to the next, since the larger communes are generally given more powers by the national government than the smaller ones. Some of the communes' functions are obligatory duties imposed on them by the national government, working mainly through the Ministry of the Interior, while others are functions permitted but not required by the national authorities. The commune's chief executive is the *maire*

---

[10] The most complete description in English is Brian Chapman, *Introduction to French Local Government* (London: George Allen & Unwin, Ltd., 1953).

(mayor). He is selected by the municipal council in the manner of all British and some American mayors, but, unlike them, he is both a local official and an agent of the central government. In his capacity as a local official he presides over the council, supervises the execution of its policies, and makes up the municipal budget; and for the proper exercise of his local duties he is responsible to the municipal council. In his capacity as an agent of the national government he is personally responsible for the public order and morality of his commune, and makes reports to and keeps registers for the national authorities; for the proper performance of his duties for the national government he is responsible to the prefect of the *département* in which his commune is located.

Paris, like London, has its own special governmental structure. The main governing body is the *Département* of the Seine, headed by two prefects: the prefect of the Seine and the prefect of police, both appointed by the Ministry of the Interior. The former is the "mayor of Paris" and an officer of the national government. Within the *département* there are twenty *arrondissements* analogous to the boroughs within Greater London, and a ninety-member municipal council of the "City of Paris" elected from these *arrondissements*. These, plus sixty other members selected in various ways, constitute the *conseil général* of the *Département* of the Seine, which is in effect the "city council" of Paris.

### In the Other Democracies

As we might expect, the structure and forms of local government within the unitary British dominions and within the unitary states or provinces of the federal dominions follow British practices more or less closely. Most European democracies, on the other hand, follow the French pattern. Speaking in the broadest terms, accordingly, we can say that in most unitary situations there are at least two main "levels" of local government; each unit at each level has some kind of elected council; each unit also has some kind of chief executive, but the powers of the latter vary all the way from the purely ceremonial and council-presiding functions of all British mayors and chairmen and the administration-supervising powers of some American mayors, many European *maires*, *Bürgermeister*, *alcaldes*, and *syndics*, to the strong policy and administrative leadership of the American "strong mayors." Each unit also has a number of administrative officers, such as town and county clerks and prefects, who are elected in some places and locally or centrally appointed in others.

The units and forms of the modern democracies' local governments vary too greatly to permit any generalizations beyond those just stated. In their functions, subjection to central control, and problems, however, their similarities are more pronounced, as we shall see.

## Functions

Although there are many variations in this regard from nation to nation and from locality to locality within particular nations, the functions most commonly performed by local governments include the following main types:

"protective" functions, such as police, fire, and public health;
"regulatory" functions, such as zoning, licensing of local businesses, parking regulations, and so on;
"assistance" functions, such as aid to the needy and sick;
"service" functions, such as providing free public education, building and maintaining roads, and providing such recreational facilities as libraries, parks, and swimming pools; and
"proprietary" functions, such as operating municipally owned electric and gas utilities, waterworks, and transportation systems.

## Degrees of Central Control

By definition, the legal powers of any local government in a unitary situation are granted by the central government, which can exercise just about any degree and form of supervision and control it prefers. There is, however, great variation in the degree of control which the central governments in various unitary situations choose to exercise. Great Britain and the British dominions, for example, generally treasure their long-standing traditions of vigorous local self-government, and so their central governments allow the local governments a considerable degree of freedom, although various national ministries—particularly the Ministry of Housing and Local Government in Great Britain—can and do supervise many local activities. This kind of local freedom is also characteristic of the Scandinavian nations, especially Denmark, and of Switzerland, Belgium, and the Netherlands.

France and most other European democracies, on the other hand, prefer a higher degree of central control and exercise what is formally known as central "tutelage" of local governments. In France, for example, the prefect can suspend from office the mayor of any commune within his *département* for a period of one month, and the Minister of the Interior can suspend any mayor for three months or, in unusually serious cases, dismiss him altogether. The prefect can also dismiss a municipal councillor from office for neglecting his duties or abusing his office for personal ends. All local budgets must be presented in a certain way and can be altered or set aside by the prefect and the ministry. Yet these central "tutelary" powers, which look rather extreme to Anglo-American eyes, are rarely used in practice, and despite the high degree of formal central control local self-government is well established in France and the other European democracies.

There is a great variation among the American states in the degree of freedom the central governments permit their local governments. Legally, of course, every local governing body is a "creature of the state" in the sense that the state creates it and gives it its legal powers. Thus, a city or county or township may legally do only what the state authorities permit it to do, and any action in excess of these powers is *ultra vires* and will be stopped by the state's administrative authorities or courts. In deciding borderline cases of local powers, moreover, most state courts follow the famous "Dillon's Rule," stated by Judge Dillon in these words:

> It is a general and undisputed proposition of law that a *municipal corporation possesses and can exercise the following powers, and no others:* First, those granted in *express words;* second, those *necessarily or fairly implied* in or *incident* to the powers expressly granted; third, those essential to the accomplishment of the declared objects and purposes of the corporation—not simply convenient, but indispensable. Any fair, reasonable, substantial doubt concerning the existence of power is resolved by the courts against the corporation, and the power is denied.[11]

Important as judicial control of local governments in the American states remains, control by state administrative officers is increasingly the main method by which local governments are kept in line. These state officials use such noncoercive procedures as requiring reports, furnishing advice and information, and providing technical aid; and such coercive procedures as withholding permits, issuing direct orders, and withholding state grants of money to local governments. All in all, local governments in the American states are rather closely controlled by the state authorities, especially in such matters as the kind and amount of taxes they can levy, the amount of indebtedness they can incur, the various types of functions they can perform, and the procedures they must use in performing them.[12] Certainly Americans cannot boast that local self-government is stronger in the United States than in any other democracy.

### Problems

Judging by articles in scholarly journals, political debates, and newspaper editorials in various parts of the world, all the modern democracies are concerned with a number of essentially similar problems relating to the status, organization, and operations of local governments. The most widely discussed of these problems are the following.

---

[11] John F. Dillon, *Commentaries on the Law of Municipal Corporations* (5th ed.; Boston: Little, Brown & Company, 1911), I, sec. 237.

[12] Cf. Kneier, *op. cit.*, Chs. 4, 7; and Adrian, *op. cit.*, Ch. 12.

## Central Control and Local Freedom

Every nation, as we noted earlier in this chapter, is a collection of local communities within a national community; and every democratic nation is to some extent committed to the desirability of local self-government. Yet, in every unitary situation (and, as we shall see in a moment, in every federal situation as well) there is a perpetual controversy over the amount of freedom from central control that should be given to local governments. Sometimes this question becomes a prominent issue in national elections. In the British general election of 1950, for example, the Conservatives charged that the Labour Government unduly interfered with the freedom of local government, and many observers believed that this charge cost the Labour party a substantial number of votes. The adherence of just about every citizen in every democracy to the "to-each-its-own" standard mentioned at the beginning of this chapter does not appear to have settled this controversy anywhere, and no nation has yet found a perfect solution to it —if, indeed, any such solution can ever be found.

## Relations among the Various Local Governments

In most democracies there has been what many observers believe to be an unjustified proliferation and overlapping of local governing units that has increased the cost and obscured the responsibility of local government in general. The most frequently discussed aspect of this problem is that of financial, service, and jurisdictional relations among the governing units within metropolitan areas. Most of the world's great cities are surrounded by suburbs whose inhabitants work in the "core cities" but are not governed by them and do not pay taxes to them. Particularly in the United States many "core cities" have to provide services to these commuting suburbanite workers without receiving commensurate tax funds from or regulatory powers over them. Political scientists in many nations have proposed the consolidation of these overlapping local authorities as the best solution to the problem, but in most democracies, as in the United States, the citizens and public officials concerned have shown relatively little disposition to accept these recommendations.

## Local Finance

In just about every modern democracy the increasing level of national taxation, the increasing costs of local services, and the many restrictions laid upon the level and types of taxation permitted local governments have combined to make many local units increasingly desperate for sources of revenue adequate to support the services they are called upon to provide. Most central authorities, however, appear to be more reluctant to give local governments freedom in the fiscal area than in any other, and so this problem too seems likely to plague local governments in many democracies for some time to come.

## Public Apathy

In Chapter 13 we noted that the voting turnouts in national elections average from 60 to 90 percent. In most democracies, however, it is rare for more than half of the eligible voters to go to the polls in local elections, and turnouts of 25 and 30 percent are quite common. The dangers of this situation from the standpoint of the democratic theories of local government expressed earlier in this chapter are too obvious to require comment. Some political scientists have proposed such remedies for the apathy of local voters as the short ballot (reducing the number of elective offices and the frequency of elections), while others have suggested that so long as the local governments remain far inferior in power and prestige to the national governments, voters will continue to be apathetic about local elections.

All of these problems arise in unitary situations, in which the local governments legally have only those powers extended to them by the central authorities but in which there is also a general belief that the central authorities should permit as much freedom to local governments as is consistent with national unity and welfare. How does the status of local governments differ when they stand in a federal relation with the national government? Let us see.

## Local Government in Federal Situations

### Federalism: Conceptions, Examples, and Problems[13]

In Chapter 4 we defined a federal government as one in which power is divided between the national government and certain local governments, each of which is supreme in its own sphere—by contrast with unitary governments, in which the national government is supreme over all local governments. Note that we did not say the power must be divided equally, only that it be divided to some degree. As political scientist William Riker correctly points out, the theoretically possible divisions range from the minimum (the national government can make decisions in only one narrowly restricted category of action without obtaining approval of the local governments) to the maximum (the national government can make deci-

---

[13] The leading comparative studies include William H. Riker, *Federalism: Origin, Operation, Significance* (Boston: Little, Brown & Company, 1964); K. C. Wheare, *Federal Government* (4th ed.; New York: Oxford University Press, 1964); and Arthur W. MacMahon, ed., *Federalism: Mature and Emergent* (New York: Columbia University Press, 1955).

sions without approval of the local governments in all but one narrowly restricted category of action).[14]

So the general definition of federalism is relatively simple and generally agreed upon. But there is surprising disagreement among political scientists about what actual governments are truly federal. For instance, Table 2 in Chapter 4 lists no fewer than twenty-one nations whose written Constitutions formally establish some degree of local autonomy. All students of federalism agree that in some of these nations the legal federal structure is simply a façade masking effective monopoly of power by the central governments. But Wheare, for one, feels that only four nations are genuinely federal.[15] Riker disagrees. *Federal* government, he points out, is not the same thing as *democratic* government; and nations like the Soviet Union and Mexico demonstrate that it is possible to combine one-party dictatorships with scrupulous maintenance of the forms of federalism. So he lists eighteen nations deserving of the label.[16]

It is not an easy problem. The Soviet Constitution, for example, follows all the standard forms of dividing authority between the All-Union (national) government and the constituent Union Republics (e.g., the Ukraine and Byelorussia) and even permits the latter to secede. Yet, the formal machinery of government, central and local alike, is controlled by the iron hand of the Communist party, which is itself a highly centralized body directed from Moscow. The party leaders have chosen to allow considerable linguistic and cultural autonomy in the Republics, but all other matters are highly centralized. Any secessionist movement is treated by the local Communists, and therefore the local governments, as treasonable counter-revolutionary activity and severely punished. And it seems clear that the national party leaders could at any time order their local followers to end even the local cultural and linguistic autonomy. So is the USSR a federal government? Riker says yes; Wheare and others say no.[17]

Another vexing instance is India. The 1950 Constitution allocates a number of powers to the states as well as to the national government, and there is in fact a considerable degree of local autonomy. But the Constitution also authorizes the national Parliament, by a two-thirds vote, to make laws in the area of state powers which will supersede any conflicting state laws. And, most centralist of all, the Constitution authorizes the President, in times of emergency, to suspend the Constitution and take over the administration of any state or states. This was actually done in 1959: the Communists in 1957 formed the Government in the state of Kerala, but

[14] Riker, *op. cit.*, pp. 5–6.
[15] Wheare, *op. cit.*, Ch. II.
[16] Riker, *op. cit.*, pp. 13–14.
[17] Cf. Wheare, *op. cit.*, pp. 24–25; and Vernon V. Aspaturian, "The Theory and Practice of Soviet Federalism," *Journal of Politics*, XII (February, 1950), 20–51.

riots and disorder grew, and in 1959 the national Government proclaimed "President's rule," removed the Communist Government, and ran things itself until the elections of 1960, in which the Kerala voters returned a non-Communist Government to power. So one authority calls India "a federal government in normal times, but a unitary government in times of emergency"; and another, "a unitary state with subsidiary federal principles."[18]

The problem is complicated even more by the fact that in such formally unitary nations as Great Britain the national government legally holds all the power but in fact permits its local governments a considerable area of freedom—more, indeed, than their counterparts enjoy in many of the formally federal nations. So perhaps we had best let others pick at this Gordian knot and confine our discussion to five nations in which, most political scientists agree, Constitutional rules *and* actual practice give certain local governments powers they can exercise as a matter of right without the national government's consent: Australia, Canada, West Germany, Switzerland, and the United States.

### Why Federalism?

In each of the nations just listed the federated local governments (called "states" in the United States and Australia, "cantons" in Switzerland, "provinces" in Canada, and *Länder* in Germany) existed as independent, sovereign governments prior to their federation. Why, then, did they join in national governments at all? And, having done so, why did they establish federal rather than unitary governments? The answer to the first of these questions, Wheare says, lies in the combination of factors present in all five situations:

> . . . in the modern federations some factors seem always to have been present. A sense of military insecurity and of the consequent need for common defence; a desire to be independent of foreign powers, and a realization that only through union could independence be secured; a hope of economic advantage from union; some political association of the communities concerned prior to their federal union . . . ; and similarity of political institutions. . . .[19]

The answer to the second question lies in the fact that in each of these five situations the prior independence of the federating units gave them a habit of self-government and a tradition of local patriotism which they were unwilling to give up altogether; their mutual economic rivalries and traditional jealousies also precluded unitarism. In Canada and the United

---

[18] Norman D. Palmer, *The Indian Political System* (Boston: Houghton Mifflin Company, 1961), pp. 94–98, 208.

[19] Wheare, *op. cit.*, p. 37. See also Riker, *op. cit.*, pp. 12–16.

States, moreover, these particularist feelings were reinforced by differing social institutions which the federating governments were unwilling to place at the mercy of an all-powerful national government—the split between the French culture of Quebec and the British culture of the rest of Canada, and between the North and the South in the United States.

These were the main factors producing federalism in each of the five situations we are considering, but some political commentators, then and now, have also hailed federalism as a strong barrier against too great governmental power in general. In Chapters 8 and 17 we noted that some writers have argued that unlimited governmental power is the mortal enemy of man's liberties of conscience, expression, and property, and that they have proposed such devices as bills of rights and separation of powers to limit such power. Some of them have also suggested that dividing power among two sets of governments in a nation will help to keep any one government from becoming powerful enough to crush men's rights. The eminent nineteenth-century British writer Lord Acton summed up this argument in these words:

> Of all checks on democracy, federation has been the most efficacious and the most congenial. . . . The federal system limits and restrains the sovereign power by dividing it and by assigning to Government only certain defined rights. It is the only method of curbing not only the majority but the power of whole people.[20]

However wide the appeal of such an argument, it is clear that in all the five situations we are considering here federalism was established mainly because the federating governments felt a need for the military, economic, and political advantages of a stronger union than "confederation" (see Chapter 4), and yet were unwilling to surrender completely their identities and power of independent action to a unitary national government. Federalism seemed to each of them an acceptable compromise between the equally undesirable extremes of confederation and unitarism.

### The Structure of Federal Governments

#### The Constitutional Division of Powers

Each of the five federal governments we are considering has a written Constitution which allocates power to the national and local governments. In all of the nations except Canada the Constitution "enumerates" (i.e., lists in more or less specific terms) the powers of the national government and locates those left over (called the "reserved" or "residual" powers)

---

[20] Quoted in Herman Finer, *Theory and Practice of Modern Government* (rev. ed.; New York: Holt, Rinehart and Winston, Inc., 1949), p. 189.

in the local governments. Only Canada "enumerates" the powers of the provinces and gives the "residual" powers to the dominion.

Some powers are granted exclusively to the national governments, others exclusively to the local governments, and still others are "concurrent"— that is, they can be exercised by both the national and local governments so long as national and local laws in these matters do not conflict with each other. All five Constitutions have a provision for "national supremacy," according to which national law supersedes local law in cases where the national and local governments have passed conflicting laws in their areas of concurrent jurisdiction. The Constitution of the United States, for example, declares:

> This Constitution, and the Laws of the United States which shall be made in Pursuance thereof; and all Treaties made, or which shall be made, under the Authority of the United States, shall be the supreme Law of the Land; and the Judges in every State shall be bound thereby, any Thing in the Constitution or Laws of any State to the Contrary notwithstanding.[21]

Note that this paragraph does not state that any national law supersedes any state law, but only any national law or treaty made "in pursuance" of the Constitution—that is, within its Constitutionally assigned area of exclusive and concurrent powers. Some such rule is stated in each of the other federal Constitutions.

Among the most significant powers assigned to the national government, either exclusively or concurrently, in all five federal Constitutions are controlling relations with foreign nations; raising, supporting, and operating armed forces; declaring war and making peace; collecting taxes and import and export duties; regulating the movement of persons and goods into, out of, and within the nation; and regulating economic matters crossing local boundaries.

Among the most significant powers generally assigned largely or exclusively to the local governments are education, public health, criminal law, marriage and divorce, licensing of businesses, and regulation and administration of elections.[22]

### Representation of Local Governments in the National Legislature

Each of the five federal Constitutions makes some provision for directly representing the local governments as such in the upper house of the national legislature. The United States, Switzerland, and Australia allow each local government regardless of its size an equal number of votes in

---

[21] Art. VI, par. 2.
[22] Cf. Wheare, *op. cit.*, Chs. VI–X; and H. R. G. Greaves, *Federal Union in Practice* (London: George Allen & Unwin, Ltd., 1940), pp. 110–119.

the upper house, while Canada and West Germany give the larger local governments more votes than the smaller. The United States, Switzerland (in most but not all cantons), and Australia are said to have "senate-type" upper houses because their members are directly elected by the voters in each of the local units. West Germany and Canada, on the other hand, are said to have "council-type" upper houses, for their members are appointed— in West Germany by the governments of the various *Länder*, and in Canada by the governor-general on the advice of the dominion prime minister. There is some reason to believe that a "council-type" upper house strengthens the hand of the local governments more than the "senate-type."[23]

### Amending Processes

Since the Constitution establishes the legal division of powers, in an ideal or model federal government neither the national nor the local governments should be able, by itself and over the objection of the other, to amend the Constitution so as to alter the division of powers. The amending procedures of the United States, Switzerland, and Australia approach this ideal more or less closely. The American Constitution has been amended only by joint actions by both sets of governments, in which the national Congress has proposed amendments by two-thirds votes of both houses, and they have been ratified by three quarters of the states acting either through their legislatures (twenty-three times) or through special ratifying conventions (once). The other amending procedure, whereby Congress calls a constitutional convention at the request of the legislatures of two thirds of the states, and whatever amendments it proposes are then ratified by three quarters of the states, has never been used. In Australia and Switzerland the national legislature proposes an amendment (in Switzerland it may also be proposed by a petition of 50,000 voters), and it must be ratified in a national popular referendum by a "double majority"—that is, both by a majority of all the voters voting over the whole nation *and* by a majority of the voters in each of a majority of the states or cantons.

Canada and West Germany, however, permit a kind of unilateral amendment by the national government. In West Germany amendments become effective if approved by a two-thirds vote of both houses of the national legislature. Yet the Constitution prohibits any amendment affecting the status and powers of the *Länder*, and in any case the fact that the members of the *Bundesrat* (the upper house) are appointed by and are

---

[23] Cf. Robert R. Bowie, "The Federal Legislature," in Robert R. Bowie and Carl J. Friedrich, eds., *Studies in Federalism* (Boston: Little, Brown & Company, 1954), pp. 8–10.

responsible to the *Länder* governments gives the latter a substantial veto power over constitutional amendments.

Canada is furthest from the ideal of bilateral amendment. The British North America Act, which is the Canadian Constitution, is an act of the *British* Parliament and, for the most part, cannot be formally amended by any Canadian agency. The British Parliament, however, has always amended the act only by request of Canadian authorities and never on its own initiative. In most of the fourteen occasions on which it has amended the act since 1867, the British government has consulted the national authorities only and has not tried to determine the wishes of the provincial governments. The British government has made it clear that any time the Canadian governments can agree upon a method of amending the act, it will gladly turn the amending process entirely over to Canadians. As yet, however, Canada has been unable to agree upon the relative roles of the dominion and provincial governments in such amendments.[24]

### "Umpiring" National-Local Disputes

We learned in Chapter 20 that all laws are inescapably vague to some degree and therefore subject to differing interpretations by men of equal good will and legal expertise. This certainly applies with full force to the clauses in federal Constitutions dividing powers between the national and local governments; and in all five nations there has been, and no doubt will continue to be, a great deal of controversy over questions of whether one government or the other has the constitutional power to engage in this or that activity.

Every federal nation, accordingly, has had to establish an "umpire" to decide all such disputes. In each of the five nations this "umpiring" function has been given to a national court: the Supreme Court of the United States, the Federal Tribunal of Switzerland, the Supreme Court of Canada (but only as recently as 1949, previous to which the function was performed by a British agency, the Judicial Committee of the Privy Council), the Federal Constitutional Court of West Germany, and the High Court of Australia. All five courts are empowered to overrule acts of local governments they find in contravention of the national Constitution, and four of the five are also authorized to overrule acts of the national government they find *ultra vires*. Only in Switzerland is the Federal Tribunal required by the Constitution to uphold all acts of the *national* legislature and permitted to set aside only cantonal acts.

How neutral and impartial have these national "umpires" been? One observer has answered: "As neutral and impartial as you could expect any

---

[24] Cf. Edward McWhinney, "Amendment of the Constitution," *ibid.*, p. 793.

umpire to be who is also a member of one of the two competing teams!"
While this quip may be something of an exaggeration, most political
scientists agree that the settlement of national-local disputes in all five
federal nations by *national* judicial agencies has had a great deal to do with
how federalism has worked out in practice.

## Federalism in Practice

### Increasing National Power

Most students of federalism agree that in each of the five nations we
are considering there has been a considerable expansion of the national
government's power from what it was originally intended to be. In Switzerland this expansion has come about mainly by formal amendments to the
Constitution, while in the other nations it has come mainly through judicial
interpretations favoring the national government. In all five nations the
growth of national power has been a response to such developments as the
increasing concern of the nations with wars and foreign affairs, the nation-
alizing of their economies and their economic problems as dramatized by
great nation-wide depressions, the acceptance of the "welfare state" and
the insistence upon national minimum standards of social welfare, and the
increasing importance of national patriotism over local patriotisms produced in part by the technological improvement in communications and
transportation.[25]

### The Concern for "States' Rights"

By no means everyone in any of these nations has been entirely satisfied
with the growth of national power, and in each there has always been and
continues to be a substantial and vocal opinion that "states' rights" must
be preserved against national encroachment.

Some of this opinion, of course, can be accounted for as the perennial
cry of the political party out of power in the national government as a
handy stick with which to belabor the party in power; in the United States
the Republicans, who from 1856 to 1933 were traditionally the strong
centralist party, have become the "states' rights" party during their long
period out of power since 1933. Some of it can also be explained as a
convenient forensic gambit for those who believe in *laissez faire* and wish
*no* government to act in this or that particular matter, and believe that the
national government is a greater threat than local governments.

Yet, when the "states' righters" of these two varieties are all accounted
for, there unquestionably remains in each of these nations a body of persons who fear that the increasing power of the national government will

---

[25] Cf. Wheare, *op. cit.*, Ch. XII.

damage or destroy the values of local self-government. In both Australia and Canada, accordingly, several Royal Commissions have been appointed to investigate the proper spheres of activity for the national and local governments. In the United States in recent years several prominent political scientists have written on this question,[26] and in 1953 Congress authorized and President Eisenhower appointed a Commission on Intergovernmental Relations to determine which functions are proper for the nation and which for the states.

The reports of these commissions and the conclusions of these writers bear a striking similarity to the discussion, noted above, of the problems of local governments in unitary situations. On the one hand, they deplore the loss of power of the local governments and warn of the dangers of overcentralization; but, on the other hand, they are not prepared to make any blanket reduction of national power, on the ground that such a move might fatally handicap the nation in dealing with the grave international and domestic problems it faces. The best answer they have come up with —which perhaps is the best answer there is—is a "to-each-government-its-own-appropriate-functions" general solution that differs little, if at all, from Jefferson's statement quoted earlier in this chapter. The American commission's report repeated this perennial standard in these words:

> Leave to private initiative all the functions that citizens can perform privately; use the level of government closest to the community for all public functions it can handle; utilize cooperative intergovernmental arrangements where appropriate to attain economic performance and popular approval; reserve National action for residual participation where State and local governments are not fully adequate, and for the continuing responsibilities that only the National Government can undertake.[27]

Few Americans would quarrel with any of these admirable propositions— but, unhappily, many Americans, like the commission itself, find them a great deal easier to state in general terms than to apply in concrete situations of national-state conflict.

The problem of intergovernmental relations in federal situations, in short, is very much like that in unitary situations. So long as men continue to have loyalties to their local communities as well as to their national communities, neither problem is likely to be solved perfectly or permanently.

---

[26] Cf. Leonard D. White, *The States and the Nation* (Baton Rouge: Louisiana State University Press, 1953); and William Anderson, *The Nation and the States, Rivals or Partners?* (Minneapolis: University of Minnesota Press, 1955).

[27] *Report of the Commission on Governmental Relations* (Washington, D.C.: Government Printing Office, 1955), p. 6.

# part five

## International Relations

# 22

## International Politics

AFTER World War I the German novelist Erich Maria Remarque wrote a scene in *All Quiet on the Western Front* that must strike a responsive chord in anyone who has ever crouched in a slit trench or peered out of a bomber at bursting flak or huddled in a bomb shelter during a raid—or who thinks that one day he may have to do so. In this scene a group of German soldiers are in a rest area behind the lines, and the following conversation ensues after one of them, Tjaden, has asked what causes wars. His comrade, Albert Kropp, replies:

"Mostly by one country badly offending another,". . .

Then Tjaden pretends to be obtuse. "A country? I don't follow. A mountain in Germany cannot offend a mountain in France. Or a river, or a wood, or a field of wheat."

"Are you really as stupid as that, or are you just pulling my leg?" growls Kropp. "I don't mean that at all. One people offends the other—"

"Then I haven't any business here at all," replies Tjaden. "I don't feel myself offended."

"Well, let me tell you," says Albert sourly, "it doesn't apply to tramps like you."

"Then I can be going home right away," retorts Tjaden, and we all laugh.

"Ach, man! he means the people as a whole, the State—" exclaims Müller.

"State, State—" Tjaden snaps his fingers contemptuously. "Gendarmes, police, taxes, that's your State;—if that's what you are talking about, no thank you."

"That's right," says Kat, "you've said something for once, Tjaden. State and home-country, there's a big difference."

"But they go together," insists Kropp, "without the State there wouldn't be any home-country."

"True, but just you consider, almost all of us are simple folk. And in France, too, the majority of men are labourers, workmen, or poor clerks. Now just why would a French blacksmith or a French shoemaker want to attack us? No, it is merely the rulers. I had never seen a Frenchman before I came here, and it will be just the same with the majority of Frenchmen as regards us. They weren't asked about it any more than we were."

And one of the soldiers proposes a solution that would surely be endorsed by a great many G.I.'s, Tommies, and *poilus*:

Kropp on the other hand is a thinker. He proposes that a declaration of war should be a kind of popular festival with entrance-tickets and bands, like a bull fight. Then in the arena the ministers and generals of the two countries, dressed in bathing-drawers and armed with clubs, can have it out among themselves. Whoever survives, his country wins. That would be much simpler and more just than this arrangement, where the wrong people do the fighting.[1]

The questions these fictional soldiers—and so many real soldiers and their sweethearts, parents, and friends—have asked are among the most difficult and most urgent facing anyone concerned with the impact of politics on modern life: What causes wars? How, if at all, can they be prevented?

In this and the following chapter we cannot hope to answer either of these questions fully and satisfactorily. We can, however, identify and explain some of the more prominent factors which political scientists believe must be taken into account in mankind's search for answers.

## The Nature of International Politics[2]

International war is part of the pathology of international politics just as civil war and domestic violence are part of the pathology of "domestic" politics—that is, politics within nations. Up to this point in our inquiry we have considered mainly the latter and some of the factors that affect

---

[1] Erich Maria Remarque, *All Quiet on the Western Front*, translated by A. W. Wheen (Boston: Little, Brown & Co., 1929), pp. 206–09, 40. Reprinted by permission of Little, Brown & Company, and of Putnam & Co., Ltd.

[2] Among the more thoughtful and suggestive, though somewhat differing, discussions of this basic question are: Inis L. Claude, Jr., *Power and International Relations* (New York: Random House, 1963); Morton A. Kaplan, *System and Process in International Politics* (New York: Science Editions, John Wiley & Sons, Inc., 1964); and C. W. Manning, *The Nature of International Society* (New York: John Wiley & Sons, Inc., 1962).

a nation's ability to conduct and resolve its internal political conflict with a minimum of domestic violence. What we have learned about domestic politics can greatly assist us in our effort to understand international politics, particularly if we begin by recognizing the principal similarities and differences between the two kinds of politics.

## Similarities with Domestic Politics

International politics is like domestic politics in the following main respects. First, like domestic politics it consists of conflict among human groups whose values—the things their members collectively desire and the common ends they wish to achieve—to some extent differ from and are incompatible with each other. Hence if some groups' values are satisfied, the values of other groups go unsatisfied; and it is impossible to satisfy equally the values of *all* groups.

Second, each group to some extent and in some manner *acts* to satisfy its values as fully as possible; and this inevitably brings it into conflict with some other group or groups holding contrary values.

In international as in domestic politics, in short, *conflict* among human groups is not an unfortunate but avoidable aberration from the political norm; it is the very essence of politics and human life itself—and international no less than domestic politics is a perpetual struggle over "who gets what, when, and how."

In both international and domestic politics, moreover, the competing groups sometimes use violence to achieve their ends (see Chapter 16). The horrors of international war sometimes make us forget that, until the 1960's at least, more people have been killed in civil wars within nations than in international wars.[3] Dramatic evidence of this for Americans is the fact that more Americans were killed in our Civil War than in all our international wars put together! Yet in the mid-1960's domestic political conflict poses far less threat than international of escalating into full-scale thermonuclear war and the literal extermination of large parts of the human race. Such domestic conflicts as those between the white supremacists and the racial egalitarians in the United States or the Flemings and Walloons in Belgium, bitter and sometimes violent though they be, are not likely to be settled by one side's dropping a hydrogen bomb on the other. But no man can predict with confidence that the disagreements between the United States and the Soviet Union or Red China will not be settled in precisely this manner. The differences between international and domestic politics, therefore, are at least as significant as their similarities.

---

[3] Cf. Lewis F. Richardson, *Statistics of Deadly Quarrels* (Pittsburgh: The Boxwood Press, 1960), pp. 32–50.

### *Differences from Domestic Politics*

International politics differs from domestic politics mainly in that its conflicts take place among different kinds of groups and are conducted within a different legal, social, and political framework.

**"BABY PLAY WITH NICE BALL?"**

*Figure 47.* Is Man's Political Maturity Equal to His Technological Achievement? (Copyright Low—London Evening Standard.)

### Nations as Contestants

The main contestants in international politics are "nations" or "nation-states,"[4] which differ from the subnational political interest groups we have considered heretofore mainly in that overlapping membership is far less frequent among nations than among subnational groups. Within any nation, as we noted in Chapter 1, each person is a member, formally or otherwise, of many different groups; he is at one and the same time, for example, a white person of Irish extraction, a Roman Catholic, a Democrat, a graduate of Fordham, and an officer of the AFL–CIO. Between nations, however, the situation is quite different. Although a few persons, as we noted in Chapter 7, have "dual citizenship" and a few others are

---

[4] Some writers distinguish between a "nation" as a group of persons sharing feelings of nationalism (see below) and a "nation-state" as a nation possessing a legally sovereign government. We, however, shall use the terms interchangeably.

"stateless," most of the world's estimated 3,218,000,000 inhabitants are legally citizens of one nation only, and very few indeed think of themselves as equally Americans and Russians or as Frenchmen and Germans—or, for that matter, as both citizens of their nation and "citizens of the world."

## The Cumulative Nature of International Conflict

In Chapters 1 and 10 we observed that conflict in domestic politics tends to be "noncumulative." In most instances, that is to say, the replacement of one issue by another in the center of the political stage is accompanied by a reshuffling of the contending individuals: some "pros" and "cons" on issue A remain associated on issue B, but some switch sides, some become "don't cares"; and some "don't cares" on issue A become partisans on issue B. Hence, the interpersonal hatreds generated by one issue are not fully reinforced by every other issue; rather, they are, to some extent, redirected and moderated by the succession of new issues.

The situation in international politics is quite different. Whereas in domestic politics a veteran may say, "I will stand with the American Legion on the bonus issue but support its opponents on the textbook-censorship issue," an American is far less likely to say, "I will support the United States in the war against the Nazis, but not against North Vietnam." Even so harsh a critic of American anticommunist foreign policy as Henry A. Wallace was in 1950 announced after the outbreak of the Korean conflict that, "I hold no brief for the past actions of either the United States or Russia, but, when my country is at war and the United Nations sanctions that war, I am on the side of my country and the United Nations."[5]

Stephen Decatur's famous toast, "My Country: may she ever be right; but, right or wrong, my Country!" was less a debatable moral slogan than an accurate description of what most men decide when they are forced to choose between loyalty to their nation and loyalty to some supernational ideal. While the lineups of friends, enemies, and neutrals among nations change from time to time and issue to issue, the persons making up the nations seldom transfer their allegiance from one to another as the issues change. As a result the personal composition of the "sides" in international political conflict changes far less from issue to issue than in domestic politics, and international conflict is thus far more "cumulative" than domestic.

## The Absence of an Authoritative Allocator of Values

In domestic politics, as we have seen, political interest groups try to achieve their ends solely or mainly by inducing the government to make

---

[5] The New York *Times*, July 16, 1950, p. 1.

and enforce policies the group favors. Every government, in other words, makes "authoritative allocations of values," and domestic politics is a contest among the nation's groups to determine the content of those allocations.

There is, however, no world government with the power to make and enforce policies binding upon all nations—no global "authoritative allocator of values." Hence, any nation seeks to achieve its goals by inducing other nations, both allies and enemies, to act as it wishes. Its power, as we shall see below, is measured by its success in getting other nations to act in this manner, and not by its success in influencing the determinations of a nonexistent world government.

International politics, in short, is like domestic politics in that the essence of both is the conflict among human groups to determine which groups' values shall be more satisfied and which groups' less satisfied. It differs from domestic politics mainly in that its contesting groups are nations with little or no overlapping membership, its conflict is "cumulative," and there is no global authoritative allocator of values. All these differences arise from the fact that international politics is conducted within the context of what political scientists call "the state system."

## The State System

The "state system," as we learned in Chapter 2, refers to the present division of the world's population among a number of "independent, sovereign nation-states." This organization of world politics emerged at the end of the Middle Ages as the result of three main developments. The first was the splintering of the ideological universalism of medieval Christendom into many different Christian denominations brought about by the Protestant Reformation, which ended the spiritual dominance of the Roman Catholic Church over the Western world. The second was the parallel disintegration of the political universalism of the Holy Roman Empire into a series of independent, sovereign nations. The third was the displacement within most of these new political units of the decentralized and contractual medieval structure of feudalism with the highly centralized and powerful national monarchies, such as those of France under Henri IV and England under Henry VIII.[6]

Since the state system provides the basic framework within which international politics is conducted in our time, we should have at least a general

---

[6] For a more detailed historical account of how the state system arose, see Carlton J. H. Hayes, *The Historical Evolution of Modern Nationalism* (New York: The Macmillan Company, 1931); and Hans Kohn, *Nationalism: Its Meaning and History* (New York: The Macmillan Company, 1955).

understanding of its legal, political, and psychological structure. Particularly important for our purposes are its characteristics of nationalism, sovereignty, and anarchy, which we shall now examine in some detail.

### The Psychological Base: Nationalism

The state system rests upon the psychological base of nationalism, and all its other characteristics—and, indeed, the whole nature of modern world politics—stems from the fact that the basic loyalty of most modern men is to their nations rather than to their churches or races or economic classes or any other group. As Professor Van Dyke rightly says:

> If men thought of themselves primarily as farmers or factory workers or businessmen or clergymen, and identified themselves primarily with their counterparts all over the world, nations could not exist. To constitute a nation, they must think of themselves primarily as Americans, Frenchmen, Germans, and regard the bonds that tie them to the country as more important than any bonds that they may have with people in other countries.[7]

In Chapter 2 we listed some of the factors—common territory, language, government—that help to generate and reinforce feelings of nationalism in particular groups of people. Yet, we should remember that nationalism itself is something that exists in men's minds. The French philosopher Renan put it this way: "What constitutes a nation is not speaking the same tongue or belonging to the same ethnic group, but having accomplished great things in the past and having the wish to accomplish them in the future."[8]

Having a common territory and/or language may help make a people feel this way. Yet Englishmen and Americans speak (approximately) the same language and are friends and allies rather than conationals, while the Swiss speak no less than four languages and yet are one of the tightest-knit nationalities in the world. For many centuries the Jews were scattered all over the earth, yet "Zionism"—the Jewish nationalism—remained a strong enough force to eventually erect a Jewish nation in Israel. Hence, we should think of nationalism as a psychological attitude (expressed by such various slogans as "God bless America," "Rule Britannia," "Vive la France," and "Deutschland über Alles") shared by a large group of persons who often, but by no means always, also share some of the "objective" features of nationalism noted in Chapter 2. As such it is the psychological base of the state system.

---

[7] Vernon Van Dyke, *International Politics* (New York: Appleton-Century-Crofts, Inc., 1957), p. 44.

[8] Quoted in Frederick H. Hartmann, *The Relations of Nations* (New York: The Macmillan Company, 1957), p. 28.

Is nationalism weakening in our time? Is the psychological base for a new system of world politics emerging? The answer to both questions appears to be "No." Perhaps the most powerful political movement in the world since 1945 has been the drive of colonial peoples everywhere to throw off their legal subjection to Western masters and win national independence. The result, as we noted in Chapter 2, has been the greatest effusion of new nations in history: of the 126 nations generally recognized in 1965, no fewer than 52 (41 percent) achieved formal independence after 1945! To be sure, many nations, new and old, have joined such international organizations as the United Nations and various regional associations; but we shall see in Chapter 23 that most have done so to advance their particular national interests, not to submerge them in a more general interest. The many fissures in once-monolithic world communism (see Chapter 3) have come mainly from the insistence of Communist leaders in various nations on practicing communism in the ways best for *their* nations, and not in the way best for, and dictated by, the Soviet Union or Red China. And the United States has found it impossible to convince its friends and allies that the version of anticommunism best for America's national interest is the policy exactly right in all respects for their (as they see it) somewhat different national interests.

So nationalism and the state system which grows from it appear to be at least as strong in our time as in any since they first emerged at the end of the Middle Ages.

### The Legal Expression: Sovereignty

The main legal expression of nationalism in the modern state system is the concept of sovereignty. The Charter of the United Nations declares that the first principle on which the organization is based is "the principle of the sovereign equality of all its Members" (Art. 2, sec. 1), which is also the basic legal principle of the state system. A nation's sovereignty may be defined as its legal power to make and enforce whatever laws for its internal affairs it sees fit and to be subjected in its external affairs only to those limitations to which it has voluntarily agreed.

Hans J. Morgenthau explains the meaning of national sovereignty by presenting the following three "synonyms" for it. (1) *Independence*. Each sovereign nation's authority over its own area is exclusive, and no nation has a legal right to interfere in the affairs of any other nation. The only limitations legally binding upon a nation are those it imposes upon itself. (2) *Equality*. If a sovereign state has supreme authority over its own territory, all sovereign states must be equal in this regard, for logically there cannot be degrees of supremacy. Hence, in the legislative aspect of international law (see Chapter 23) each nation's vote counts for as much as, but no more than, every other nation's vote. (3) *Unanimity*. As a logical consequence of the foregoing principles, any rule of international law must be unanimously agreed to by all the nations to which it applies; otherwise some nations could make law for others, in which case the latter could not be called truly sovereign.[9]

A warning: *National sovereignty is a legal concept only*, not a description of the actual relations among nations. If, for example, the Republic of Panama wanted to permit Soviet Russian troops to establish bases just outside the Panama Canal Zone, we may be sure that, one way or another, the United States would prevent it—although *legally* Panama is just as sovereign in its right to conclude agreements with other nations as is the United States. Sovereignty is a formally stated standard of how nations always *should* treat one another, not a scientific description of how they always *do* treat one another. Of course, sovereignty is just like any other legal concept in this regard; for, as we noted in Chapter 20, legal "shoulds" and actual "do's" never coincide exactly even within nations; and in Chapter 23 we shall observe how great is the disparity between the two in international law.

A second warning: Even in strictly legal terms "the sovereign equality of nations" does not mean that every nation must have exactly the same legal rights and privileges as every other nation; many nations have incurred legal burdens not imposed on others, as, for example, the reparations the losing nations agree to pay to the victors following a war. Nor, again in strictly legal terms, does the principle mean that any nation can legally divest itself of any and all of its legal obligations any time it wishes, for no nation can do this legally. The principle does mean that no basic *change* can be made in the legal rights, privileges, and obligations of a nation without its consent. In what sense and to what degree the rules of international law are "binding" upon the nations which agree to them are matters we shall take up in Chapter 23.

### The Political Result: Anarchy

Some political theorists, such as Thomas Hodgskin, Josiah Warren, Michael Bakunin, and Prince Peter Kropotkin, have argued that the ideal political organization of human society is anarchy—a situation in which there exists no government or other agency with the legal right or the physical power to force men to do what they do not wish to do, and in which men participate in joint and cooperative activities only by the free and independent consent of each, never by orders from a popular majority or a ruling class or a monarch. We noted in Chapter 2 that no human com-

---

[9] Hans J. Morgenthau, *Politics among Nations* (3d ed.; New York: Alfred A. Knopf, Inc., 1962), Ch. 19.

munity has ever formally and officially adopted anarchy as its organizing principle, although governments have from time to time broken down and lost their power to make and enforce laws—but usually for only brief periods of time.

Yet the state system, both in legal principle and in political practice, comes very close to constituting a genuinely anarchical world society. The legal principle of sovereignty, as we have just seen, provides that no international law which a nation has not at some time accepted is legally binding upon that nation. Such joint and cooperative activities as the nations may engage in they undertake because each of the participating governments decides for one reason or another to do so. There is no world legislature to make laws legally binding upon all nations, no world executive and police force to make sure they are obeyed, and no world judiciary to adjudicate violations of the law and sentence the violators. There is, to be sure, a sort of pseudo legislature in the UN General Assembly, a pseudo executive in the UN Security Council, and a pseudo supreme court in the International Court of Justice. But, as we shall see in Chapter 23, none of these institutions have any real power above and beyond what individual nations have given them—and which individual nations can withhold or withdraw whenever they desire, and successfully so if the nations are powerful enough.

The state system, in short, means that international politics is conducted within a framework of both legal and political anarchy; and this is the basic determinant of the general nature of international political conflict.

## Some General Characteristics of International Conflict

To most Americans the only serious international conflict in our time is the Cold War between ourselves and our allies and the Russians and their allies. Yet, as we are sometimes pained to learn, this is not the way things look to all other modern nations. To Egypt and some other Arab nations, for example, the most serious international issue is their Cold War with Israel. To India and some other Asian and African nations the most serious issue is the conflict between "colonialism" and "national independence and self-determination."

These, of course, are only some of the more prominent international conflicts of our time. Each of them has its own particular constellation of issues, contestants, and techniques, and is to some extent different from all other international conflicts past and present. Yet, most political scientists are convinced that to some degree all past and present international conflicts under the state system are alike and that understanding what is common in all such conflicts will greatly help us to understand what is involved in the particular conflicts with which we are most vitally concerned at the moment.

In this section, accordingly, we shall summarize what political scientists generally believe to be the enduring characteristics of all international conflict under the state system.

## Some Goals of Foreign Policy[10]

Every nation's foreign policy is the product of its policy makers' answers to these questions: What should be our national goals? If some of these are incompatible with others, what are the nation's most important goals—what are its "vital interests"? What kinds of actions are we capable of? Which are best calculated to achieve the goals we hold most dear?

The foreign policies of nations, then, begin with their national goals; and while these goals vary considerably from nation to nation, the types of goals most generally sought by all nations can be classified under five headings.

### 1. Security

Probably the prime goal of every nation and the one to which, if need be, all other goals will be sacrificed is security. It has two main aspects: first, the preservation of the nation's legal status as an independent, sovereign nation and its practical ability to rule its own affairs; and second, the creation of an atmosphere in which the nation can live relatively free of fear for its survival and independence. There is no such thing as absolute security or complete freedom from fear for any nation, of course, and so each strives for that degree of security its governors feel is reasonably attainable. Even this minimum degree of security is by no means the only goal the nation has and may often be in conflict with some of its others.

### 2. Prosperity

Every nation wishes to maintain and/or improve its citizens' standard of living. In foreign policy this goal affects a wide variety of matters, such as tariffs and trade agreements, currency exchange rates, giving or receiving economic aid and technical assistance, and so on.

### 3. Territorial Expansion

Relatively few diplomats think it politic to state openly that their nations want more territory; but just about every nation at one time or

---

[10] Cf. A. F. K. Organski, *World Politics* (New York: Alfred A. Knopf, Inc., 1961), Chs. 3–4; and Ernst B. Haas and Allen S. Whiting, *Dynamics of International Relations* (New York: McGraw-Hill Book Company, Inc, 1956), Ch. 4.

another has pursued such a goal. They have followed expansionist—or, as they are sometimes called, "imperialist"—policies for one or more reasons: more *lebensraum* for overcrowded home populations; economic advantages expected from controlling new mineral and other resources and opening up new "captive markets"; and the sheer expansive feeling of "manifest destiny" to rule ever-wider territories, such as that which characterized American western expansion in the nineteenth century.

## 4. Defending and Spreading Ideology

In recent years a number of political scientists have engaged in what some have called a "great debate" over the proper role of political and moral ideals in the formation of foreign policy.[11] Some have argued that the real goal of any nation's foreign policy is that of defending and promoting its "national interest," conceived mainly as the most advantageous "power position" (see below) for preserving and improving the nation's military, territorial, and economic security. All talk about "political ideals" and "moral values," these commentators argue, is at best a way of articulating and promoting the nation's underlying *real* interests; but if the policy makers forget the true nature and purpose of such talk and begin to take it seriously at its own face value, their naïveté will only get the nation into serious trouble. The opposing argument is that the main purpose of at least a democratic nation's foreign policy is and/or should be to promote such moral values as freedom, democracy, and equality for all men everywhere; otherwise, they say, foreign policy and international politics become merely a global chess game, hideous because it is played with human lives and meaningless because it has no higher purpose than keeping itself going.

In the present writer's opinion this debate centers upon a false issue, that of ideology *versus* other national interests, as though the two were incompatible and one or the other must be sacrificed. There is every reason to believe that both ideology *and* other national interests are in fact goals of every nation's foreign policy. We have already noted some of the other goals. Let us look at ideology for a moment.

All of us wish to preserve the independence and security of the United States and to see the "national interest" in this sense defended and promoted. But let us ask ourselves *why* preserving the United States is so important as to justify risking even thermonuclear war. Part of our answer

---

[11] Cf. the "realists": Hans J. Morgenthau, *In Defense of the National Interest* (New York: Alfred A. Knopf, Inc., 1951); and George F. Kennan, *Realities of American Foreign Policy* (Princeton, N.J.: Princeton University Press, 1954). And the "idealists": Thomas I. Cook and Malcolm Moos, *Power Through Purpose: The Realism of Idealism as a Basis for Foreign Policy* (Baltimore: The Johns Hopkins Press, 1955); and Frank Tannenbaum, *The American Tradition in Foreign Policy* (Norman: University of Oklahoma Press, 1955).

will surely be our desire to "secure the blessings of liberty to our selves and our posterity"—or, as we are more likely to put it these days, "to preserve the American way of life." That way of life includes not only a high standard of physical comfort but also a number of ideals: a certain kind of economy, religious freedom, form of government, and so on.

So it is with other peoples in other nations. After 1933, a number of Germans left Germany because they could not bear to live under the regime of Adolf Hitler. Most of them later fought with the Allies in the war against Germany. To many Germans, therefore, the Germany of Hitler was not worth preserving. How many of us would feel the same about the United States if it came to be ruled by a native Hitler or Stalin?

Such attitudes on the part of the people—who, let us never forget, make up "the nation"—help to account for some, though by no means all, of the foreign policies actually pursued by nations. In 1939, for example, a strong case could have been made that its political and economic interests in the Western Hemisphere made Great Britain a far more formidable rival than Germany for the United States. Yet we lined up with Great Britain against Germany. Why? Surely one powerful reason was that Britain, like ourselves, was a democracy and, therefore, was defending values we also held dear, while aggressively fascist Germany was attacking those ideals.

The argument made here is not that a democracy does or should support all democracies and oppose all dictatorships. After all, from 1941 to 1945 we gladly accepted Soviet Russian help against the Germans, and we now accept fascist Spain as an ally against the Russians. The point is that defending and spreading its ideology is *one* of the goals of every nation; and like every other goal, as we shall see below, it is sometimes in conflict with other goals and must compete with them for priority in the making of foreign policy. To overlook or slight the observable significance of ideology as a factor in foreign policy and international politics is therefore highly "unrealistic."

## 5. Peace

Judging by what they say, all nations and all peoples the world over cherish peace, regard war as the greatest of all evils, and condemn those who cause wars as the greatest of all villains. Thus, the Charter of the United Nations states that the organization's first purpose is "to maintain international peace and security," requires its members to "settle their international disputes by peaceful means," and opens membership to "all other peace-loving states." Both sides in the Cold War strive constantly to paint themselves as the true lovers and defenders of peace and their antagonists as "warmongers."

Individuals feel the same. Take a poll among your friends on the question, "Do you want us to go to war with Russia?" The nearly unanimous

"No's" you will get in reply would certainly be matched by a similar poll taken in the Soviet Union.

Just about every person and every nation, then, wants peace—and, we should add, sincerely wants it. Yet hardly a person or a nation in the world does not feel that thermonuclear World War III is a very real possibility. Thus, we are faced with this great apparent paradox: everyone wants peace, and no one wants war; yet, as the Bible says, there have always been "wars and rumors of wars." How can this be?

Perhaps the following catechism will provide the answer: Peace is the absence of war, and it takes two to make a fight. If the United States *really* wants peace, let it announce to all the world that under no conditions whatever will it fight another war and that it is dumping all its weapons, nuclear and otherwise, into the ocean. This policy is absolutely guaranteed to bring peace, and if you as an individual *really* want peace, you should start urging it on the President and Congress.

But, you say, that is ridiculous; if we disarmed ourselves, the Communists would simply move in and take over. True—but do you want peace or don't you? Yes, you reply, *but not at any price*; for you agree, as most persons do, with General Zapata's famous maxim: "It is better to die on your feet than to live on your knees."

The solution to our paradox is this: men and nations genuinely desire peace, but it is only one of the things they desire; and sometimes it comes into sharp conflict with some other things they also want, such as preserving their nation's independence and way of life. When this is the situation men and nations must choose which things they want most and be prepared to sacrifice the things they want least. Such choices are the very essence of foreign policy formulation.

### *Making Foreign Policy*[12]

#### Choosing Goals, Techniques, and Capabilities

Making any nation's foreign policy involves making at least thre kinds of choices.

1. *Choosing Goals.* Logically prior to other decisions is the choice of goals—deciding what should be the nation's general objectives in international politics and its specific objectives in particular situations. As we

---

[12] Useful discussions include Richard C. Snyder, H. W. Bruck, and Burton Sapin, eds., *Foreign Policy Decision Making: An Approach to the Study of International Politics* (New York: The Free Press of Glencoe, 1962); Roy C. Macridis, *Foreign Policy in World Politics* (2d ed.; Englewood Cliffs, N.J.: Prentice-Hall, Inc., 1962); Gabriel A. Almond, *The American People and Foreign Policy* (New York: Frederick A. Praeger, Inc., 1961); and Bernard C. Cohen, *The Political Process and Foreign Policy: The Making of the Japanese Peace Settlement* (Princeton, N.J.: Princeton University Press, 1957).

noted above, this choice often involves sacrificing or risking some goals in order to pursue other and more cherished ones.

2. *Choosing Techniques.* Once the goals and their order of priority are set, the next step is to select and put into operation the techniques thought most likely to achieve the chosen goals. We shall describe the most widely used techniques below.

3. *Assessing Capabilities.* Both of the first two types of choices must necessarily be influenced by the policy makers' judgment of what the nation can and cannot do relative to the capabilities of the other nations directly involved. For example, Haiti is a small and not very powerful nation; even if its dictator, Dr. Duvalier, dreamed of dominating the whole Western Hemisphere, he would be well advised not to pursue such a goal or to launch a military attack on the United States to achieve it. Like any other nation, Haiti can successfully pursue only those goals and employ only those techniques within its powers and capabilities; if it ventures beyond them, it will likely end up in a position worse than its original one. Later in this chapter we shall examine some of the factors that affect a nation's capabilities or "power."

Some political scientists have sought to understand national strategies and their effects on one another by applying "the theory of games" to international politics. This is an elaborate mathematical theory about the probable success or failure of various strategies by individual "players" in model conflict situations involving $n$ players in "zero-sum games" (i.e., those in which the losers' losses equal the winners' gains) or "non-zero-sum games" (i.e., those in which the total losses and gains do not equal each other). This mode of analysis was developed by John von Neumann, a mathematician, and first applied to economic behavior.[13] In recent years Morton Kaplan has led political scientists in applying it to international conflict; and William Riker in applying it to political conflict in general.[14] Their analyses are far too complex for a summary here, but both create mathematical models of rational choices of strategies and formation of coalitions and countercoalitions which can (somewhat like our models of democracy and dictatorship in Chapter 5) serve to measure and help explain the deviations of actual strategies from the models.

We should not, however, picture the making of any nation's foreign policy as a process in which a group of steel-nerved and sage diplomats coolly survey an infinite range of possibilities and choose those which are unmistakably calculated to promote the national interest. As many foreign-office officials who have actually engaged in making foreign policy have

---

[13] John von Neumann and Oskar Morgenstern, *The Theory of Games and Economic Behavior* (Princeton, N.J.: Princeton University Press, 1944).

[14] Kaplan, *op. cit.*; and William H. Riker, *The Theory of Political Coalitions* (New Haven, Conn.: Yale University Press, 1962).

testified, it operates like any other policy-making process: the people who make it are fallible human beings subject to a variety of external pressures from pressure groups, political parties, and public opinion—just as are the makers of any other kind of policy in a democracy. In a democracy foreign policy can never be made in complete isolation from the demands of domestic policy. The makers of foreign policy are also subject to many internal doubts and hesitations, for they are caught up in actual situations in which the possibilities do not look nearly so infinite as they may appear to their critics in college seminars and the opposition party. They have to make the best choices they can within the limits of their individual abilities and the concrete situations in which they find themselves. The eminent British diplomat and historian Sir Harold Nicolson, who knows firsthand the intricacies of foreign policy formulation, gives us something of the "feel" in this illuminating passage:

> Nobody who has not watched "policy" expressing itself in day-to-day action can realize how seldom is the course of events determined by deliberately planned purpose, or how often what in retrospect appears to have been a fully conscious intention was at the time governed and directed by that most potent of all factors—"the chain of circumstance." Few indeed are the occasions on which any statesman sees his objective clearly before him and marches towards it with undeviating stride; numerous indeed are the occasions when a decision or an event, which at the time seemed wholly unimportant, leads almost fortuitously to another decision which is no less incidental, until, little link by link, the chain of circumstances is forged.[15]

### Agencies and Officers[16]

In almost every modern nation the governmental agencies most directly and exclusively concerned with the making and conduct of foreign policy are headed by the political chief executive or head of government, although in none of the democracies does he have an unrestrained monopoly over such policy (see Chapter 18). The principal agency working under him is an executive department specializing in foreign affairs, called variously the Department of State (United States), the Foreign Office (Great Britain), the Foreign Ministry (France), the *Minindel* (Soviet Russia), and so on. The head of this department—the Secretary of State or Foreign Minister—is generally regarded as the number-two man in the executive group and often succeeds to the top position.

---

[15] Sir Harold Nicolson, *The Congress of Vienna* (New York: Harcourt, Brace & World, Inc., 1946), pp. 19–20.

[16] A useful general description is Philip W. Buck and Martin B. Travis, Jr., eds., *Control of Foreign Relations in Modern Nations* (New York: W. W. Norton & Company, 1957). For American practice, see James L. McCamy, *Conduct of the New Diplomacy* (New York: Harper & Row, Publishers, 1964).

**TEAMWORK**

*Figure 48.* American Foreign Policy Is Made by Several Agencies, Each with Its Own Ideas. (© June 24, 1960, by Mauldin. Reproduced by courtesy of Chicago Sun-Times.)

The officers and top employees under his direction are generally known as "the foreign service," which, in most nations, was one of the first administrative agencies to be put under the merit system (see Chapter 19). Foreign service officers perform one or the other of two general types of activities, "consular" and "diplomatic." The consular activities are the older but today the less important. Consuls in various foreign cities concentrate mainly on reporting the state of the economy in their locations and promoting the sale of the home country's goods there, although they also perform some services for the home country's citizens traveling abroad.

Diplomatic officials, whether stationed in the foreign affairs office at home or in the nation's various legations abroad (most nations have a policy of periodically rotating their foreign service officers from home duty to foreign duty and vice versa), perform four main types of functions. (1) *Communications and Negotiation.* This includes the transmission and reception of all official communications with foreign nations, and the negotiation of international treaties and agreements. (2) *Intelligence.* This includes studying what is going on in foreign nations now and what is likely to go on in the future that affects their foreign policies, and reporting the results to the home office. In many nations the military services also conduct intelligence operations, and in the United States we have a third major agency doing the job, the Central Intelligence Agency. (3) *Policy Recommendations.* The ultimate decisions in foreign policy belong to the foreign secretary, the chief executive, and the legislature, but subordinate officers and some employees of the foreign affairs department are expected to make policy recommendations in their particular specialized areas of concern. For reasons we discussed in Chapter 19, these recommendations more often than not become policy. (4) *Services.* These include issuing passports and visas (see Chapter 7), assisting citizens who have encountered legal trouble in foreign nations, and so on.

## Some Techniques of Foreign Policy

### Diplomacy and "Recognition"

"Diplomacy," as the term is generally used, refers to the conduct of international relations by negotiations among official envoys collectively called "diplomats." The basic formal relationship between any two nations is established by the exchange of official diplomatic "missions"—composed of a top envoy known as an "ambassador" or "minister" or "chargé d'affaires," and a number of subordinate aides, secretaries, attachés, and so on. In deciding whether or not to receive officially some particular foreign nation's diplomatic mission, each nation determines whether or not it formally "recognizes" those persons who sent the emissaries as the foreign nation's rulers. A nation or a set of rulers whose envoys are not recognized by any other nation is in a great deal of trouble, for it cannot conclude any kind of formal international treaty or agreement, provide any kind of legal protection for its citizens traveling abroad, or engage in any of the legal relationships that are a basic part of existence as an independent, sovereign nation.

Hence, the decision of whether or not to recognize a particular foreign nation can become a major question in any nation's foreign policy. The basic question involved is whether to recognize all governments which are, in fact, in full control of their particular nations, or whether to recognize only those governments which pass certain minimum standards of moral and political respectability. Some nations have attempted to answer these questions by extending "de jure" recognition to governments they approve, and "de facto" recognition to governments they disapprove but recognize as being in control of their nations. The United States, however, has on occasion refused to give any kind of formal recognition to certain governments even though the latter were in full control—the most notable instances being our refusal to recognize the Communist government of Russia from 1917 to 1933 and our refusal to recognize the Communist government of China since 1949.

Perhaps the most extreme way a nation may show its displeasure with a foreign nation short of going to war is to "sever diplomatic relations" by withdrawing its diplomatic mission and ordering the other nation's mission to leave.

From the beginning of the state system until roughly the outbreak of World War I in 1914, professional diplomats in foreign missions played a highly significant role in the formation and conduct of foreign policy. Their official titles of "ambassadors and ministers plenipotentiary" were accurate descriptions of their powers, for the difficulty and loss of time involved in communicating with officials back home necessarily gave the diplomats a very wide range of discretion in negotiating and concluding agreements with their assigned nations. Since World War I, however, professional diplomats have lost many of their powers of independent negotiation and agreement, and have become mainly cultivators of good will with and reporters of developments in their assigned nations. Most important negotiations are conducted by the foreign secretaries or even by the heads of government themselves, as in such negotiations "at the summit" as those at Teheran, Yalta, and Potsdam during World War II and at Geneva and Vienna since them. "Diplomacy by conference," in fact, has become one of the principal methods of conducting international relations.

Whoever may conduct it, diplomacy as a technique of foreign policy can be used for a number of different purposes, each of which may be illustrated with episodes from American-Russian diplomatic relations since 1945. For one thing, it can be used to seek genuine agreements, as, for example, when the Americans and British in 1963 negotiated an agreement with the Russians ending the testing of nuclear weapons in the atmosphere. For another, it can be used as a propaganda device to embarrass the nation's opponents. An example is the Soviet Union's many dramatic—and impossible—proposals for "disarmament" and "banning nuclear weapons" made since 1945, all intended not to secure genuine and workable disarmament but simply to assume the mantle of "peace-lover" for itself and pin the odious label of "warmonger" on the Western allies. Finally, diplomacy can be used to stall for time while waiting for an improvement in the military situation. An example are the long-drawn-out "peace talks" between the Chinese Communists and United Nations representatives in Korea in 1952 and 1953, in which the Chinese for over a year kept throwing up one forensic roadblock after another while continuing intermittent military offensives. Only when the Communists became convinced their military situation would not markedly improve did they begin to negotiate a truce seriously; after that, a truce was concluded in a mere two months.

For these reasons, then, diplomacy is a technique of foreign policy as well as a general term describing the formal conduct of all international relations under the state system.

### Propaganda and Subversion[17]

Any nation's efforts to achieve its goals through diplomacy are, by definition, direct and external attempts to induce the public officials of other nations to act in the desired manner. Propaganda and subversion, on the other hand, include various attempts to bring about certain internal developments in the target nations that will indirectly force their public officials to adopt the desired policies.

"Propaganda" in this context means the use of various forms of mass communications to create a climate of opinion among the target nation's general public that will induce the latter to urge their officials to act as the propagandizing nation wishes. Most major powers to some degree use propaganda for these purposes. The United States, for example, maintains the United States Information Agency to organize broadcasts, libraries, film showings, and other devices in friendly or neutral foreign nations to present the American case in the most favorable light. Through the Voice of America it beams radio broadcasts at the other side of the Iron Curtain. Through Radio Cairo, for another example, Egypt beams radio broadcasts all over the Middle East and North Africa denouncing Israel and the Western powers, and calling for all Arabs to drive out the "foreign imperialists." Russia made great use of the "Stockholm Peace Petition" to paint itself as the great defender of peace against the warmongering Western nations and used posters, films, and radio broadcasts to spread the accusation that the inhuman and bestial Americans had used germ warfare in Korea. The technological improvement of mass communications and the increasing importance of public opinion have made propaganda of this sort far more widely used than it was before World War I.

The communist and fascist nations have also made great use of sub-

---

[17] Cf. Haas and Whiting, *op. cit.*, Ch. 9.

version—that is, using sympathetic citizens of the target nations and their own undercover agents to engage in espionage, sabotage, and infiltration of other nations' governments in order to weaken their capacity to resist Russian or Nazi foreign policy. In Chapter 9 we described the techniques of Communist subversion in some detail and outlined the difficult problems they have created for the democracies. Distasteful though they may seem by contrast with the older techniques of diplomacy, it is clear that propaganda and subversion will for some time to come continue to be prominent methods for achieving foreign policy goals.

### Trade Policies and Foreign Aid

All nations have long used such trade policies as tariffs, import quotas and licenses, export controls, regulation of rates and conditions of international currency exchange, and even barter to control their economic relations. Many of them have also entered into agreements with other nations, such as the American reciprocal trade agreements and the European Economic Community, to moderate these controls reciprocally. Until recently the sole or main purpose of such trade policies was to promote the economic prosperity of the nation pursuing them, but since World War I an increasing number of nations have used them for political purposes as well: to promote the economic health of friendly nations and/or to damage that of unfriendly nations. In many nations, indeed, the economic and political purposes of trade policies are often in conflict with each other. For example, for many years the United States, in response to pressure by American beef producers, prohibited the importation of all Argentine beef, on the official ground that such beef carried hoof-and-mouth disease. Not only did this lose the Argentinians a lucrative market for their beef, but it galled their pride considerably and thereby contributed heavily to the anti-American feeling prevalent in Argentina up to World War II. During the war and since then the State Department has been able to secure permission for the importation of a limited amount of Argentine beef, and while this has been vigorously opposed by the American Meat Institute, it has helped to improve relations between the two nations.

"Foreign aid," however, is largely a post-1945 development. The United States launched it in 1947 with the creation of the famous Marshall Plan to assist the economic recovery of the European nations, and it has subsequently become a major foreign policy weapon not only for the United States but for Soviet Russia as well. Foreign aid is generally intended to accomplish two main goals: to strengthen the economies and maintain the political support of friendly nations, and to strengthen the economies and increase the good will and support of neutral nations. These goals are sought by providing outright grants of money and/or food, machinery, and other goods; by providing "technical assistance," mainly in the form of

Foreign Aid Does Not Guarantee Friendship: Panama University Students Calling for "Yankees" to Get Out of the Country. (Wide World Photos, Inc.)

technical experts and information sent abroad to show underdeveloped nations how to increase their own productivity; and by providing military weapons, matériel, and/or military advisers. From 1946 to 1962 the United States gave a total of 66 billion dollars in economic aid and another 31 billion in military aid. From 1954 to 1962 the Soviet Union gave a total of 3 billion to noncommunist nations and another 6 billion to other communist nations.[18] There is no general agreement upon how effective foreign aid has been as a device for winning friends in the neutral nations; but, judging by its survival and extension in both American and Russian policies since 1947, foreign aid is widely regarded as an effective method of maintaining the strength of friendly nations at a level where they can be of real help to the aiding nation; on the latter ground if not the former it seems likely to remain a major weapon of foreign policy—at least for relatively rich nations—for some time to come.

### War[19]

War has long been regarded by most men as perhaps the worst disease in the whole grim pathology of human affairs—and for good reason. Even before the discovery of nuclear fission, wars exacted a price in human death and suffering too enormous for the imagination to grasp. It is estimated, for example, that in World War I an unbelievable total of 37 million human beings died either on the battlefield or as a direct result of the famine and disease brought on by the war; in World War II another

---

[18] Fred Greene, *Dynamics of International Relations* (New York: Holt, Rinehart and Winston, Inc., 1964), pp. 475–477.

[19] The most comprehensive study in English of past wars is Quincy Wright, *A Study of War* (Chicago: University of Chicago Press, 1942), 2 vols. A stimulating—and frightening—study of possible future wars is Herman Kahn, *On Thermonuclear War* (Princeton, N.J.: Princeton University Press, 1961).

22 million perished in similar fashion. Wars have also damaged the quality of the human race: not only have they taken as soldiers the finest elements of the nations' populations, but the moral, social, and economic deterioration that infects both winners and losers alike after most wars leaves the world considerably poorer. Paying for past, present, and future wars is by far the greatest single economic burden borne by any large modern nation. All these things were true of war before men had discovered nuclear fission; what the costs of war are likely to be now that thermonuclear weapons are ready to be used we can only guess.

Yet, scarcely any generation in the history of any modern nation has lived out its time in peace, and many generations in many nations have fought as many as two or three major wars. Terrible though they may be, then, wars are a recurring and general phenomenon of international society. One of the most baffling and increasingly urgent questions before the student of human affairs is: How can something which is so terrible happen so regularly?

Some philosophers and theologians believe war to be a divine punishment laid upon mankind for its sins, and so it may be. Social scientists, however, must proceed from the assumption that war is not something imposed on man by forces entirely outside himself but is rather an activity he voluntarily engages in for purposes of his own. Political scientists in particular regard war much as did the great Prussian student of war Clausewitz when he declared, "War is a political instrument, a continuation of political relations, a carrying out of the same by other means."

To the political scientist, in other words, war is one of the techniques nations use to achieve their ends. For most nations it is the weapon-of-last-resort because of its tremendous cost and because it involves risking the nation's very existence. For these reasons it is used only when one of the nation's most cherished goals—preserving its independence and/or protecting its basic ideology—appears to be in mortal danger and all other means of achieving it seem to have failed. Only such a goal in such circumstances can justify the costs and risks of war.

Yet we cannot talk only of the costs and risks of war and say nothing about what wars have achieved for nations in the past; the fact is that many nations have won highly valued goals by war where they might not have done so by lesser means. The United States and Israel, for example, established their very national existence by fighting and winning wars. Great Britain and the United States may not have "made the world safe for democracy" by fighting World War II, but at least they preserved their own ways of life and made the world very unsafe for Hitler's "thousand-year Reich." Many of the world's great religions—e.g., Christianity and Islam—have, to a considerable degree, been spread among the heathen and defended against infidels and heretics by the sword. In short, we are not justified in calling *all* wars futile and barren of any accomplishment. One of the most eminent recent scholars of war sums it up thus:

> War, then, has been the instrument by which most of the great facts of political national history have been established and maintained. . . . The map of the world today has been largely determined upon the battlefield. The maintenance of civilization itself has been, and still continues to be, underwritten by the insurance of an army and navy ready to strike at any time where danger threatens.[20]

The great questions that face nations in this atomic age are these: Is war still a thinkable instrument of national policy, or has it become such technologically that it will destroy everything and achieve nothing for any nation? Can it be totally avoided or limited? We shall return to these questions in Chapter 23.

## Power: The Indispensable Means for National Ends

### The Meaning of "Power"[21]

#### As a Relationship

"Power" is one of the concepts most widely used in the discussion and analysis not only of international politics but of domestic politics as well. It is therefore not surprising that there is no general agreement upon its precise meaning or role in human affairs.

We shall use the term "power" in international relations to refer to the relationships of subordination and superordination that exist among nations which are pursuing conflicting goals. For example, everyone would say that the United States is more powerful than the Republic of Panama. Why? Not merely because the United States is richer, larger, and has more modern weapons—for these things in themselves have no political significance until they are brought to bear in some kind of international political conflict. We call the United States more powerful than Panama because

---

[20] James T. Shotwell, *War as an Instrument of National Policy* (New York: Harcourt, Brace & World, Inc., 1929), p. 15.

[21] Leading analyses of the general concept of "power" include Harold D. Lasswell, *Power and Personality* (New York: W. W. Norton & Company, Inc., 1948); Harold D. Laswell and Abraham Kaplan, *Power and Society* (New Haven, Conn.: Yale University Press, 1950); and Robert A. Dahl, *Modern Political Analysis* (Englewood Cliffs, N.J.: Prentice-Hall, Inc., 1963), Ch. 5.

we observe that in just about every instance in which a goal or policy of Panama has come into direct and clear conflict with a policy or goal of the United States, Panama's desires have been less satisfied than those of the United States. Now the superiority of American over Panamanian power may *result* from Panama's fear of being militarily conquered by the United States or from the economic sanctions they know we can apply or from the greater cleverness of our diplomats over theirs or from any of hundreds of other factors. But the power of the United States in this situation, as we shall use the term, *consists* of the fact that it regularly gets its way whenever its desires clash with Panama's. The utility of this conception of national power, in the author's opinion, is that it does not exclude, by definition, any of the factors—some of which we shall examine below— that produce particular power relationships.

### As a Means

Some writers suggest that maximizing its power—i.e., maneuvering itself into a position in which all its relations with other nations are like those of the United States with Panama—becomes an end in itself for at least some nations. Yet "power," as we are using the term, can be detected only in the conflict of specific nations over specific conflicting goals, and so it seems more useful to think of power as an indispensable means for the achievement of any goal by any nation. Thus, nation A may seek to spread communism throughout the world, B to preserve its democratic system against A's aggressions, C to annex islands belonging to D, E to extermi- nate F, and F to preserve its national existence against E—but each nation must seek sufficient power to achieve its ends against its enemies, and attempt whatever social, economic, military, or governmental changes (see below) will help it to achieve the necessary power. "Seeking power," in short, is not a particular kind of policy a nation may follow; it is an essen- tial ingredient for following successfully any policy, except perhaps one of total surrender and self-abnegation.

In short, "power" may be, as a former State Department official wrote, "the capacity to achieve intended results."[22] Any nation's capacity can be measured only in specific conflicts with specific foreign nations and only after the results have actually been achieved. Thus, if we are to try to guess before the fact what a nation's power in a given situation may be, we have to see where it and its opponents and allies stand in respect to a number of factors which in the past have been correlated with success in power conflicts.

---

[22] Charles B. Marshall, "The Nature of Foreign Policy," *Department of State Bul- letin*, March 17, 1952, p. 418.

## Factors Correlated with National Power[23]

Political analysts have found many different kinds of factors to be correlated with national power, and we shall briefly summarize the main types below. The reader should bear in mind, however, that no one of these factors by itself is enough to make a nation powerful in all circumstances, and that no nation has ever had a highly favorable position in all of the factors. While we cannot say which single factor is the most important index of power, we can say that the most powerful nations are those which score the highest—*relative always to their opponents*—in the largest number of factors.

The principal types of factors are as follows.

### 1. Physical Factors

Political analysts have found that several physical characteristics are correlated with national power. A favorable *geographic location*, such as that possessed by the United States in its separation from its main rivals by great oceans or even that possessed by Great Britain in its separation from Europe by the English Channel, makes a nation so favored difficult to invade, and gives it several advantages over nations, e.g., France or Poland, with no such natural barriers against invasion. Another significant factor is the possession of *natural resources*, including such necessary elements as food, fuel, minerals, and other industrial raw materials. For example, the fact that Great Britain has never produced enough food to feed its own citizens or any oil at all has forced it to import these basic materials from abroad and has made it more vulnerable than nations self-sufficient in both. On the other hand, the fact that both the Soviet Union and the United States have had plentiful supplies of both—and also easy access to large supplies of uranium and other sources of fissionable materials—has contributed heavily to their post-1945 positions as the world's two great "superpowers."

### 2. Demographic Factors

The sheer *size* of a nation's population, while never enough in itself to make a nation powerful, is, nevertheless, an important factor in power. Russia and the United States, generally considered to be the two most powerful nations in the world at present, rank third and fourth, respectively, in total populations; and, significantly, China and India, the largest

---

[23] Cf. Harold and Margaret Sprout, eds.. *Foundations of National Power* (Princeton, N.J.: D. Van Nostrand Company, Inc., 1951); Klaus Knorr, *The War Potential of Nations* (Princeton, N.J.: Princeton University Press, 1956); Morgenthau, *Politics among Nations*, Chs. 3, 8–10; and Van Dyke, *op. cit.*, Ch. 10.

and second-largest, respectively, are becoming increasingly powerful in international politics. A powerful nation, it seems, needs a plentiful supply of manpower to fill its armies and operate its industrial plant. The *distribution* of a nation's population among various age groups is also a significant demographic factor, for the "working-fighting" part of a population consists mainly of persons between the ages of 16 and 65, for persons over 65 are mainly pensioners and burdens on the productive groups. Thus the younger the population the more valuable from the standpoint of power.

### 3. Psychological Factors

A well-located, rich, and populous nation may still be ineffective in its international conflicts if it is seriously deficient in one or a number of various psychological factors. The *kind and degree of social tensions and consensus* may sometimes be decisive. In France in the 1930's, for example, the internal struggle among various economic classes and ideologies became so venomous that psychologically France became, in effect, several nations instead of one and was increasingly helpless both diplomatically and militarily against the German onslaught. In Great Britain during the same period, on the other hand, social and political conflict never got so bitter that the contestants forgot they were all Britons; perhaps more than any other factor this helped them make of 1940, not the tragic era of national collapse it was for France, but "their finest hour." Even more basic, though harder to assess, is national character—whatever common popular attitudes and behavior patterns make the terms "American," "British, "French," "Russian," "German," and so on, more than merely legal designations of citizenship. The "character" of a nation's people is admittedly the most elusive of all the factors mentioned here, but most students of international politics are convinced that such a thing exists and that differing national characters significantly affect the distribution of power among nations.

### 4. Organizational Factors

Several times in preceding chapters we have observed that effective organization is highly desirable, if not indispensable, for success in domestic politics; for organization is the principal method by which any human group's latent resources and strength are brought to bear upon the points of decision in the political process. So it is in international politics. For example, no matter how large a nation's population or how rich its natural resources, it is not likely to translate those advantages into political power unless they are organized into *an effective economic and productive system* convertible into military power by *an advanced technology*. By the same token, a nation must have *an effective governmental system* if it is to mobilize its geographic, economic, and other resources in such a way as to

National Power Requires Ever More Demanding Technology:
Loaded, Cocked, and Aimed at a Strategic Target Sits One of
the United States' 54 Titan II Missiles, Sheltered Deep inside
an Underground Silo Hardened to Protect It from Nuclear
Attack. (Wide World Photos, Inc.)

advance its ends in international politics. Most scholars believe that
China's long-time failure to become a major power despite its huge population and plentiful natural resources was due largely to its highly ineffective
economic system and governmental structure; and these scholars are

watching—many of them with apprehension—to see whether Mao Tse-tung will succeed, where Chiang Kai-shek, Sun Yat-sen, and the Mandarins failed, in making China into a full-fledged and powerful nation. Since the ability to wage war with maximum skill and success adds greatly to any nation's ability to get its way in war—and having a reputation as a nation skilled in war is almost equally helpful in time of peace—*an effective military establishment* considerably enhances a nation's power in both time of peace and time of war. Finally, the *skill of its diplomats* will determine how effectively a nation can bring all its other advantages in the factors listed above to bear upon its conflicts with other nations.

### The Assessment of Power

We have noted that one of the questions the makers of foreign policy must answer is, What are the nation's capabilities in the situation at hand relative to those of the other nations involved? In other words, what is the present and potential power of the nation itself, its allies, and its antagonists? These questions are so crucial in making foreign policy that a considerable part of the intelligence activities of any foreign office or military service is devoted to investigating and attempting to measure the ever-shifting power relations among the various nations, friends and foes alike, with which the nation is concerned.

The task is far too difficult to be handled perfectly by any set of analytical tools presently available to any nation's intelligence specialists. To do the job perfectly the analyst would have to know, for one thing, not only what all the factors of power are but how they relate to each other. For another, he would have to know exactly where each foreign nation and his own stand at the moment in each and every significant factor. For still another, he would have to be able to project present trends into the future. Men's present skills in these matters permit at best only "educated guesses" and often only the most general, rough, and shaky ones. The analyst can adopt Morgenthau's advice to avoid such errors as thinking of power as absolute and permanent instead of relative and changing, or trying to explain all power in terms of a single factor, such as geographical position or military might;[24] but at most this will only make his guesses more "educated," and certainly will not enable him to describe power relations and make predictions and policies on the basis of his descriptions with any scientific or mathematical certainty.

Foreign policy makers, in short, cannot avoid continually comparing their nation's power relations with others and designing their policies to fit their assessments; but the wise ones among them are likely to keep their fingers permanently crossed while going about their jobs.

---

[24] Morgenthau, *Politics among Nations*, Ch. 10.

## Politics among Nations: A Summary

International politics, like domestic politics, is basically a struggle among human groups to realize different and conflicting group values. International politics, however, differs significantly from domestic politics in several respects. First, its contestants are nations, whose memberships legally and psychologically overlap far less than do those of the contesting groups in domestic politics. Second, international political conflict is far more "cumulative" than domestic. And third, nations seek their ends mainly by trying to affect the actions of other nations rather than, as in domestic politics, by trying to affect the actions of an over-all government.

International politics since the late Middle Ages has been conducted within the framework of the "state system." The latter rests on the psychological foundation of nationalism, whereby most men's primary loyalty is given to their nation rather than to any other social or political group; its legal watchword is "the sovereign equality of nations"; and it adds up to international anarchy: political conflict conducted in the absence of a common government.

For each nation within the "state system," peace is a goal, but only one among a number of goals, with some of which it is always in conflict. By the same token, war is one of several techniques a nation may choose to pursue its ends—a technique so costly and risky, to be sure, that all nations regard it as a weapon of last resort, yet a technique that most nations on occasion have felt impelled to use to preserve some deeply cherished values or pursue some highly valued goals.

In our time, however, military technology is advancing at so frightening a pace that many men in many nations are reassessing the utility of war as an instrument of national policy and as a method of conducting international conflict. When the United States and the Soviet Union developed thermonuclear bombs in the early 1950's, they gave man weapons of hitherto unimagined destructiveness. And when they sent their Sputniks and Explorers whirling into outer space in the winter of 1957–1958, they served notice that man now has a means for delivering thermonuclear bombs to their targets against which there is no known defense.

Is it not possible, therefore, that these technological developments have made war so insupportably costly and so unbearably risky that it is unthinkable as a technique of foreign policy? Yet, may it not also be true that most men and most nations do not see it this way, and that nothing has emerged in world politics to prevent World War III from being all too real and imminent a possibility?

To these grave and perplexed questions we shall turn in Chapter 23.

# 23

## The Quest for Peace
## in the Thermonuclear Age

**I**F and when it comes, what will World War III be like? Figure 49, which shows the damage range of a thermonuclear bomb detonated over the center of Washington, D.C., suggests part of the answer (see page 578).

According to data from official tests, on which Figure 49 is based, *one* 20-megaton thermonuclear bomb[1] is more powerful than *all* the bombs dropped on Germany and Japan in World War II. One 10-megaton bomb obliterates everything within a radius of 5 miles around the blast point and leaves only a poisonously radioactive crater over 500 feet deep. The blast sets off a suffocating firestorm for a radius of 25 miles or more. More than 200 different radioactive species are created and attached to particles of debris which are swept into the air and form the familiar mushroom cloud. These deadly particles float back to earth at varying speeds, depending on their weight, and, if spread uniformly, produce lethal levels of radioactivity over about 5000 square miles.[2]

But that is only what one bomb can do. What about, say, the 150 that might be delivered in an all-out attack? In 1959 the Special Subcommittee on Radiation of the Joint Congressional Committee on Atomic Energy tried to answer this question. Its members heard testimony from military, scientific, and medical experts about the probable effects of a 1500-megaton attack on the United States. They concluded that 25 million would die the

---

[1] One "megaton" equals the destructive force of 1 million tons of TNT.

[2] The authoritative public account is Samuel Glasstone, ed., *The Effects of Nuclear Weapons* (rev. ed.; Washington, D.C.: The United States Atomic Energy Commission, 1962).

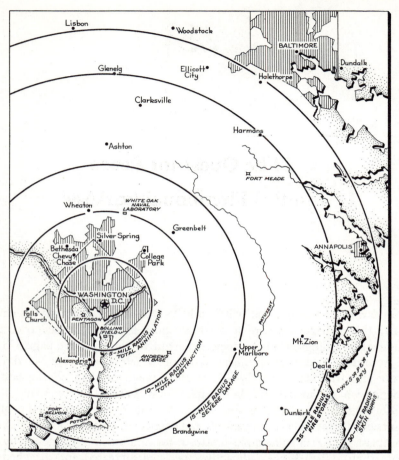

*Figure 49.*   **The Damage Range of a Thermonuclear Bomb.**

first day, another 25 million would be fatally injured, and still another 20 million would be injured but not fatally. And a 20,000-megaton attack using "dirty" bombs (those with a high fission yield) would, within sixty days, kill by fallout every American who had survived the original blasts and firestorms.[3]

At present the United States and the Soviet Union each have a stock of bombs that totals far over 20,000 megatons; indeed, the experts often use the term "overkill" to denote nuclear capability beyond what is necessary to exterminate an enemy nation's entire population. If thermonuclear bombs are delivered as the warheads of ICBM's (intercontinental ballistic

---

[3] Harrison Brown and James Real, *Community of Fear* (Santa Barbara, Calif.: Center for the Study of Democratic Institutions, 1960), pp. 14–20.

**Fireball and Fallout. (AP Wire Photo.)**

missiles) launched from deep and indestructible concrete "silos," there is no known way of preventing them from reaching their targets. No nation can hope to defend itself against thermonuclear attack; it can only retaliate by sending its own ICBM's against the aggressor—and hope that the fear of such retaliation and reciprocal annihilation will deter any potential aggressor from launching an attack. That is why a nation's nuclear arsenal and delivery system is often referred to as its "deterrent."

For these reasons, then, no one doubts that in the ICBM with a thermonuclear warhead man has at last found "the absolute weapon" with which he can literally exterminate himself and most other living things on the whole planet. Everyone recognizes that technologically the thermonuclear age is fully capable of becoming the twilight of man if he decides to fight World War III, and to fight it with thermonuclear weapons. Thus, the grim fact of our time is that the quest for peace has become a quest for the means of sheer physical survival for all men in all nations.

It is further complicated by the "nth country problem." Although at the present writing the United States and the Soviet Union are by far the biggest nuclear powers, three other nations—Great Britain, France, and Red China—also have thermonuclear weapons and some means of delivering them. Other nations are developing nuclear capabilities, and some observers have estimated that the "nuclear club" may have as many as fifteen members by the 1970's and thirty by the 1990's. So if the possession of nuclear weapons by the United States and the Soviet Union makes one a bit nervous, how about their possession by, say, Egypt and Israel, or West Germany and East Germany, or India and Pakistan? For World War III may be touched off, not by the original nuclear powers, but by the nth country to possess The Bomb.

What, then, are our chances of surviving? Some observers believe that they depend upon our ability to keep World War III from being fought with thermonuclear weapons and to confine nations to the use of old-fashioned weapons, which, however destructive, do not have the capacity to wipe out the whole race; and these writers believe the possibilities are good that nations by mutual consent will refrain from using the thermonuclear weapons. Most commentators, however, agree with the late Sir Winston Churchill that "it would be folly to suppose . . . if war should come, these weapons would [not] be used."[4] Other analysts argue that our best chance lies in keeping all future wars limited in area as well as in the number of nations involved, as were such post-1945 wars as those in Korea, Indochina, and the Middle East. Still others contend that since limiting wars is at best a chancy affair in which we have to fail only once to lose the whole game, man's only real chance for survival is to find a way of preventing *all* international wars, limited or general.

Whatever may be the direction in which they think we should look, however, all present-day students of international affairs believe that the thermonuclear age has transformed the ancient quest for peace from a search for a utopia of contentment and tranquility into a hunt for the minimum conditions of human survival. This hunt, moreover, must take place not only in the age of nuclear fission that makes it urgent but also

---

[4] Quoted in Vernon Van Dyke, *International Politics* (New York: Appleton-Century-Crofts, Inc., 1957), p. 332. *Ibid.*, pp. 323–335, Professor Van Dyke presents a thoughtful assessment of the probable costs of a thermonuclear World War III and the possibilities of lessening or avoiding the costs.

in an age of political fission by the state system that has always prevented —and may still prevent—men from finding a way to eliminate war.

In other words, war, as we noted in Chapter 22, has always been both costly and risky for any nation, and few men or nations have ever engaged in war for its own sake. Yet, under the state system just about every nation has fought wars on those occasions when its leaders and people came to believe that not fighting would bring even greater disasters than the horrors of war. We have no *a priori* reason to suppose that the enormously greater costs of thermonuclear war have basically altered this historic way of looking at international violence.

To illustrate the point just made, ask yourself this question. Suppose the United States were reduced to only two choices in its foreign policy: fighting thermonuclear World War III or permitting the Communists to take complete control of our nation. Which would you choose? You are probably correct in saying that we would never have to choose between only these two grim alternatives. *But suppose we did?* Which would you choose? Do you agree with the slogan "Better Red than Dead"? Do you believe that nothing could be worse than thermonuclear war? Or do you believe with General Zapata that "it is better to die on your feet than to live on your knees?" When you have considered the terrible costs involved in either alternative and have made your choice, you will understand something of what is involved in the quest for peace in a world not only of thermonuclear weapons but also of sovereign, independent nations with conflicting values, ways of life, and ambitions.

If peace is to come in our time, in short, it will probably come either because men and nations will have come to desire no national goal strongly enough to resort to war to achieve it, or because they will have come to feel that they can achieve any national goal by means other than war. Thus, the quest for peace in our age is a search for some kind of world political structure that will incline both men and nations to adopt either or both attitudes about war as a means for gaining their ends.

In the present chapter, accordingly, we shall examine the nature and record of some of the more prominent approaches men and nations have considered and/or tried for conducting international political conflict without war.

## Approaches to Peace within the State System

The state system, as we learned in Chapter 22, is deeply rooted in the universal hold of nationalism, that is, in the fact that most men give their basic loyalty to their nation rather than to their church or race or economic class or any of the other groups to which they belong. Hence, while men have always sought ways of resolving international conflict without resorting to war, most of them have had no desire—and even more have despaired of the possibility—to do so by eliminating such basic features of the state system as the legal right of each nation to govern its own internal and external affairs. Thus, our first general category of approaches to peace is those which employ, not any negation of the basic principles of the state system, but the voluntary actions of its sovereign independent nations.

Each of these approaches, moreover, rests upon a set of ideas about what causes wars and is intended to alleviate or remove those particular irritants from international relations.[5] We shall, accordingly, describe the rationale as well as the record of each of these approaches to peace.

### Balance of Power

#### As a Description and as an Approach to Peace

The term "balance of power" is used in several different senses by students of international affairs. In one purely descriptive sense it simply means the distribution of power among nations at any given moment and carries no necessary connotation of equality of shares. As a method for maintaining peace, however, "balance of power" means a sufficiently even distribution of power among antagonistic nations that no one of them feels strong enough to threaten or is strong enough to destroy the independence of the others; and following a "balance-of-power" policy means striving for such a distribution of power. The balance-of-power approach to peace assumes that war comes when a particular nation feels sufficiently stronger than its antagonists to believe that it can threaten or attack them with full assurance of success. Thus, it proposes to keep the peace by preventing any nation from being or feeling that much stronger than any of its rivals.[6]

#### Balancing Methods

Many nations have sought both to protect their national interests and also to avoid war by pursuing balance-of-power policies calculated to keep opposing nations or combinations of nations from becoming too strong. Among the traditional methods they have employed to this end have been *domestic measures*, such as building up their armaments and strengthening

---

[5] The theories of the causes of war underlying the various approaches to peace are perceptively identified and analyzed in Inis L. Claude, Jr., *Swords into Plowshares* (3d ed.; New York: Random House, Inc., 1964). The account in the text generally follows Professor Claude's analysis.

[6] For the various meanings of "balance of power," see Hans J. Morgenthau, *Politics among Nations* (3d ed.; New York: Alfred A. Knopf, Inc., 1962), Ch. II.

**THIS IS THE HOUSE THAT DIPLOMACY BUILT**
APRIL 7, 1935

*Figure 50.* Balance-of-Power Policies Make a Shaky Foundation for Peace. (Fitzpatrick in the St. Louis *Post-Dispatch*.)

their military organizations; *alliances,* including both acquiring allies for themselves and splitting off their opponents' allies in the ancient strategy of "divide and conquer"; *compensations,* including dividing up non-self-governing colonial areas among the great powers so that the latter will be diverted from aggression toward the other great powers; and *war,* used as a last-resort method for preventing the opposing nation or nations from becoming too powerful. The illustration usually given of a classical balance-of-power policy is that followed by Great Britain from the sixteenth century to the present in throwing her weight against the most powerful single nation in Europe—first Spain, then the Netherlands, then France, then Germany, and now Russia.

## Evaluation

Most political scientists believe that whatever balance-of-power policies may have done for the interests of individual nations, they have signally failed to keep the peace. Their failure in this regard results, for one thing, from the impossibility, noted in Chapter 22, of measuring accurately what the distribution of power *is* at any given moment, which means that no nation can ever be sure when power is "balanced" and when it is not. Another reason for the failure of such policies is the fact that most nations are convinced that prudence requires them to leave a margin for error in their calculations; and so they build up their amaments and their alliances to a level higher than what they guess to be the necessary minimum. Their antagonists, however, feel the same need for a margin of safety, and so they in turn build their armaments up to a level beyond that of the first group of nations. And so on and on, in a process familiarly known as an "arms race."

The whole idea of "balance of power," in short, rests upon a highly oversimplified and mechanistic conception of international relations, and assumes a calculability of national power and motives that does not exist. It has never succeeded in keeping the peace in the past, and it seems likely that its modern version, called by some commentators "the balance of terror," will not do so either, despite the possibility that the availability of thermonuclear weapons may make nations more hesitant to resort to war than in the past. For always before, some nation or group of nations has sooner or later come to feel that the only way to "restore the balance" is to go to war before it is too late. There is no reason to suppose that the present balance of power will work out any better.[7]

## *Collective Security*

### Meaning and Rationale

Those who seek peace through balance-of-power methods, as we have seen, assume that no nation will launch a military attack upon any other nation unless it is confident it has the preponderance of power necessary for victory. Thus, peace can be maintained, they reason, by keeping any nation from acquiring enough extra power to feel this kind of confidence.

"Collective security" is a major extension and redirection of this point of view. Briefly stated, it seeks to preserve peace through an agreement among a large number of nations that each will treat a military attack upon any of the others as an attack upon itself, and that all will fully participate in a defensive war against aggression on any of them. Collective security seeks to achieve peace by making it clear *in advance* to any would-

---

[7] Cf. *ibid.*, Ch. 14; and Van Dyke, *op. cit.*, Ch. 11.

be aggressor that the contemplated aggression will be met with overwhelming force and therefore cannot possibly succeed. It has been one of the most widely approved of all approaches to peace within the state system and, as we shall see below, is now one of the basic elements in the United Nations approach to peace.

Inis Claude points out that collective security is often confused with defensive military alliances such as the North Atlantic Treaty Organization (NATO) and the Southeast Asia Treaty Organization (SEATO). These, however, differ from true collective-security agreements mainly in that they are not intended to be universal in their membership, while such universality is at least a major goal of all genuine collective-security agreements. The NATO and SEATO alliances are new-style defensive military alliances set in what is basically a balance-of-power framework; the nearest approach to genuine collective-security systems made in the twentieth century have been certain articles in the Covenant of the League of Nations and the Charter of the United Nations.[8] We shall discuss these provisions later.

### Preconditions

The theory of collective security does not propose any alteration in the formal structure of the state system in the sense of establishing a global government with the legal and physical power to *make* nations come to each other's defense whether they want to or not. Rather, it depends upon their willingness, even eagerness, to do so voluntarily. It does, however, require a number of drastic changes in the attitudes of nations and the makers of their foreign policies. For if collective security is to work as intended, most people in most nations must, for one thing, fully accept the idea of "the indivisibility of peace"—the notion that they are deeply involved in the security and welfare of all nations, not just their own. For another, the people and policy makers of each nation must put the general requirements and obligations of collective security before their own special national interests. Finally, each nation must voluntarily surrender to some kind of international body a considerable portion of its power to make its own foreign policy.

To illustrate the differences between balance-of-power and collective-security arrangements for meeting aggression, let us consider the case of American policy toward Korea. When the North Koreans attacked the South Koreans in 1950, the United Nations under American leadership declared the North Koreans the aggressors and called for all member nations to come to South Korea's defense. The United States, which had already started to fight the North Koreans, complied with the resolution by sending large numbers of troops into Korea, although many other UN

---

[8] Claude, *op. cit.*, pp. 234–252.

members did not (see below). In this situation, then, the United States acted just as a nation should in a collective-security system.

*But* suppose the South Koreans had suddenly turned the tables, and attacked the North Koreans. Suppose, further, that the UN had branded *South* Korea the aggressor and called upon all member nations to go to the communists' defense. What would we have done? What *should* we have done? On the one hand, most of us feel that any aggression *by* communists is dangerous to American security, while any aggression *against* communists is helpful to American interests. Yet, under a collective-security agreement we would have been bound to help the communists just as diligently as we helped the anticommunists from 1950 to 1952; and if we were to honor our commitments American troops would be back in the hills of Korea, but aiming their rifles south this time. If such a situation actually arose, it is not likely that the United States would join in any collective-security defense *of* communism any more than Russia in 1950 joined in a collective-security defense *against* communism.

In these words Hans Morgenthau neatly sums up the difference between the national attitudes required by genuine collective security and those that actually prevail under the state system:

> Collective security as an ideal is directed against all aggression in the abstract; foreign policy can only operate against a particular concrete aggressor. The only question collective security is allowed to ask is: "Who has committed aggression?" Foreign policy cannot help asking: "What interest do I have in opposing this particular aggressor, and what power do I have with which to oppose him?"[9]

Until such time as the United States can be counted upon to rush to the defense of communists against anticommunist aggression, no global collective-security system in the strict sense can exist, for the good and sufficient reason that what Professor Claude calls the "subjective requirements" for it do not presently exist. We shall return to this problem in our discussion of the United Nations.

### Disarmament[10]

#### Rationale

Since the end of the Napoleonic Wars in 1815 every major nation has on occasion publicly declared itself in favor of some kind of "disarmament" —that is, some kind of agreement among nations to reduce mutually and

---

[9] Morgenthau, *op. cit.*, p. 415.
[10] Recent analyses include Bernhard G. Bechhoefer, *Postwar Negotiations for Arms Control* (Washington, D.C.: The Brookings Institution, 1961); and John W. Spanier and Joseph L. Nogee, *The Politics of Disarmament* (New York: Frederick A. Praeger, Inc., 1962).

simultaneously the general quantity of all their armed forces and weapons and/or limit or eliminate particular weapons. Nations advance such proposals for a variety of reasons, including their desire to reduce the heavy economic burdens of large military establishments, their longing to reduce the destructiveness of war if it should come, their wish to improve their power positions, and even their hope of achieving a propaganda victory over their antagonists by donning the mantle of "peace lover." The motive for disarmament proposals with which we are here concerned, however, is the desire to prevent war.

The theory of disarmament as an approach to peace is based upon the assumption that if there is no restriction on the level of armaments of the major powers, they will inevitably engage in arms races; and, since men simply cannot be trusted not to use huge military establishments if they have them, sooner or later arms races bring on wars. According to Professor Claude's vivid summary of this theory, "men are not gods, and when they gather the power of the gods in their hands they come to behave like beasts."[11] Hence, one way of approaching peace, not necessarily intended to exclude other ways but often to complement them, is to get all nations to agree to limit either the total quantity of their weapons or to forswear the use of certain weapons (e.g., poison gas, bacterial bombs, atomic bombs) or both.

## Record

Since 1815 a number of attempts have been made both at general disarmament and at localized disarmament. There have been a few instances of success in the latter, the best known being the Rush-Bagot Agreement of 1817 between the United States and Canada, which limits naval forces on the Great Lakes, and, by informal extension, has come to mean the demilitarization of the entire Canadian-American border.

The most notable examples of efforts at general disarmament have been the Holy Alliance of the immediate post-Waterloo period, the Hague Peace Conferences of 1899 and 1907, the Washington Naval Conference of 1922, the World Disarmament Conference of 1932, and the various efforts made in the disarmament commissions of the League of Nations and the United Nations. Generally speaking, such general efforts have failed to accomplish anything remotely approaching their stated objectives, for reasons we shall review in a moment.

## The Problem of Atomic Disarmament and Control

We suggested earlier in this chapter that the development of thermonuclear weapons has cast the age-old quest for peace into a brand-new

---

[11] Claude, *op. cit.*, p. 262.

atmosphere of very great urgency; much the same can be said for the problem of disarmament, which since 1945 has centered mainly upon the problem of the reduction or abolition of atomic weapons and the control of nuclear-fission materials and facilities. A brief review of the course of these negotiations should illuminate not only the special difficulties in atomic disarmament but the continuing difficulties of any effort at general disarmament made under the state system.

In 1946 the United States—which at that time, remember, had a world monopoly on nuclear weapons—laid before the Atomic Energy Commission of the United Nations its "Acheson-Lilienthal-Baruch Plan," which proposed that an international Atomic Development Authority be created as a body affiliated with but independent of the UN. This agency, the plan further proposed, should be given a world-wide monopoly over the ownership and operation of all mines and plants producing fissionable materials and over all research and testing of atomic weapons. It should also be empowered to license nations to use nuclear materials for peaceful purposes, and to make uninhibited inspections of all nations' scientific and industrial establishments to detect illicit supplies of fissionable materials and misuse of licenses for their peaceful employment. When such an authority was established and working to our satisfaction, the proposal concluded, the United States would surrender to the authority our national stockpiles of atomic bombs and fissionable materials.

The Soviet Union, however, found the proposal unacceptable. It insisted that the establishment of any international control of atomic energy be preceded by the legal prohibition of all nuclear weapons and by the United States destruction of its stocks of such weapons; and it also insisted that the proposed international authority should have no power to own, operate, or license atomic facilities, and that even in the authority's rather vague inspecting functions it should operate in clear subordination to the Security Council and its big-power veto (see below).

The General Assembly in 1948 approved a somewhat revised version of the American plan, but the Russians were so hostile to it that no serious attempt has been made to implement it. Since 1948 there have been many haggling sessions in the Disarmament Commission and the Atomic Energy Commission, and many dramatic speeches before the General Assembly—but little effective agreement.

One small ray of hope appeared in 1963 when the United States and the Soviet Union signed a treaty to end the testing of nuclear weapons in the atmosphere, outer space, and under water, in which they were joined by over 100 other nations. But the treaty provided for no system of inspection (it was thought unnecessary because the development of highly sensitive detection devices made it almost impossible to conduct such tests without the other signatories' knowledge); and the two newest members of the "nuclear club," France and Red China, refused to sign. So while the 1963 treaty was a step forward, it moved the world only a few inches along the long and rocky road to complete nuclear disarmament.

Why have these attempts at nuclear disarmament and control failed? Most students of international politics make this reply: For basically the same reasons that most general efforts at disarmament under the state system have failed. First, there are many technical difficulties even with traditional weapons—determining the proper ratios of strength to be stabilized at lower levels of armament and implementing whatever agreements can be achieved on this matter. Most atomic scientists believe that it is now so easy for any nation to hide lethal amounts of fissionable materials from any kind of inspection that no system of atomic disarmament can depend upon inspection for its enforcement.[12] Second, even if the technical difficulties could be solved, nations are unwilling to give up their weapons —especially such powerful ones—so long as they feel that by doing so they might be making themselves vulnerable to attack by other, less scrupulous nations. In other words, atomic disarmament has failed just as so many earlier attempts at general disarmament failed, basically because nations —particularly powerful nations—simply are not willing to trust their ways of life, ideologies, and national independence to the official good will and public promises of certain other nations. If the Russians were to accept the American proposal, they would have to accept the Americans' word that there would be no cheating, and they would have to trust the Atomic Development Authority not to damage Soviet interests. If the United States were to accept the Russian proposal, we would have to accept the Russians' word that they would not cheat, and that they would not use their veto on the Security Council to make the whole control system a mockery.

Most political scientists would agree with Professor Claude that the failure of attempts at atomic disarmament and control simply underscore what men have learned from comparable failures in the past: "no means have been discovered for evading the requirement that states participating in an arms regulation system be imbued with mutual trust."[13]

### Peaceful Settlement of Disputes

#### Rationale

The peaceful-settlement approach to peace rests upon the assumption that wars are mainly a technique for settling international disputes. Nations continually dispute with each other, and these disputes are sooner or later

---

[12] Cf. Eugene Rabinowitch, "Living with H-Bombs," *Bulletin of the Atomic Scientists*, January, 1955, p. 6.

[13] Claude, *op. cit.*, p. 315.

settled one way or another. Nations usually fight wars when there seems to be no other way to settle a dispute and when national tempers get hot in the negotiating process. Warfare often results from the failure of the disputants to understand all the facts in the case and from the inability of either side to endure the blow to its national pride involved in "making concessions." Since international disputes themselves cannot be eliminated, we should provide a series of peaceful techniques for settling them—techniques that will permit hot tempers to cool off, acquaint the disputing parties with all the facts, and introduce a neutral third party as a judge or arbitrator or conciliator to make decisions not involving loss of "face" for the disputants.

### Techniques

In accordance with this kind of reasoning a number of peaceful-settlement techniques have been established. One type is that of *direct negotiation,* in which the disputants try to iron out their disagreements by mutual give-and-take, and in which they often accept the "good offices" of some third nation as a mediator and conciliator—as, for example, when President Theodore Roosevelt in 1905 mediated the peace conference in Portsmouth, New Hampshire, that ended the Russo-Japanese War.

More discussed but less used than direct negotiation is the technique of *arbitration.* Although there are many variations in detail from system to system as specified in various treaties and agreements, arbitration generally involves an agreement—either made in a general treaty or *ad .hoc* for a specific dispute of the moment—between two disputing nations to establish an arbitration tribunal. Each nation usually appoints two members of the tribunal, only one of whom may be a citizen of the selecting nation; and the four arbitrators thus chosen pick a fifth. The five-man tribunal hears the arguments of both sides and makes a decision, which both sides have previously agreed to accept. A substantial number of nations have concluded bilateral (i.e., between two nations) and multilateral (i.e., among three or more nations) arbitration agreements in which they have consented to submit all disputes between or among them to such arbitration. Many of these agreements were made in the early twentieth century, when many men in many nations believed that arbitration was the best preventive of war (as Wordsworth said of early French revolutionary days, "bliss in that dawn it was to be alive, but to be young was very heaven"). The machinery, however, has been used relatively little, for reasons we shall note in a moment.

A third general technique of peaceful settlement is *adjudication*—taking disputes to the International Court of Justice for judicial settlement. We shall examine the nature and handicaps of this method in our discussion of international law below.

### Record

Arbitration machinery, as we noted above, has been used relatively little. Most of the disputes it has dealt with have been of a mainly non-political character—that is, not involving what the arbitrating nations regarded as their vital interests or power. Just about every nation has refused to submit to arbitration or adjudication anything it regards as a major political dispute. For example, Indian leaders from Gandhi and Nehru to Shastri have certainly been among the world's most prolific sources of praise for peaceful settlement and international rectitude as well as tart critics of other nations' failure to meet their own high standards. Yet, even they have consistently refused to submit the India-Pakistan dispute over the ownership of Kashmir to any kind of international arbitration or adjudication. As Nehru said, "great political questions . . . are not handed over in this way to arbitrators from foreign countries or any country."[14]

That is why peaceful settlement, arbitration, and adjudication have such a good record of compliance by the nations who have lost arbitration decisions—and why such a record is highly misleading. For, as we have seen, no nation will submit a dispute to this kind of machinery at all unless it has previously decided that it is prepared to accept and abide by an adverse ruling of the deciding tribunal. On the record, no nation will accept a ruling it feels adversely affects its vital interests and power position; and so no nation will submit to "peaceful settlement" any dispute which it feels involves these matters in any major way. Yet, it is precisely such disputes which cause wars, and so peaceful settlement by itself has never prevented wars in the past and is clearly incapable of doing so in the future.

### International Law[15]

#### As an Approach to Peace

The peculiar nature and problems of international law are suggested by the fact that jurists and political scientists disagree as to whether it really is "law." Since this debate turns upon the question of whether "real law" must emanate from an authoritative legislative source and be enforced by authoritative executive and applied by authoritative judicial agencies,

---

[14] Quoted in Morgenthau, *op. cit.*, p. 431.

[15] A leading summary and exegesis of the formal rules is J. L. Brierly, *The Law of Nations* (6th ed.; Oxford: Clarendon Press, 1963). Stimulating discussions of the nature of international law as compared with other forms of law include Charles de Visscher, *Theory and Reality in Public International Law* (Princeton, N.J.: Princeton University Press, 1957); and Morton A. Kaplan and Nicholas de B. Katzenbach, *The Political Foundations of International Law* (New York: John Wiley & Sons, Inc., 1961).

we need not linger over it. Certainly international law is not "law" in exactly the same sense as domestic law (see Chapter 20), and yet it certainly plays a significant role in international relations. Leaving aside the question of whether it is truly "law," international law may be defined as the body of rules and principles of action which civilized states usually accept as binding in their relations with one another.

Before World War I, war was entirely legal under these rules, and so international law was an approach to peace only in the sense that it provided a body of rules and principles for the settlement of international disputes and therefore helped to avoid or limit war. Since 1918, however, war —at least war waged for purposes other than "self-defense"—has become illegal according to these rules: the Covenant of the League of Nations severely restricted the circumstances in which member nations could go to war; nearly all the nations in the world ratified the Kellogg-Briand Pact of 1928, which declared that all the parties "condemn recourse to war for the solution of international controversies, and renounce it as an instrument of national policy"; and the United Nations Charter requires that all its members "shall settle their international disputes by peaceful means" and "refrain . . . from the threat or use of force against the territorial integrity or political independence of any other state" (Art. 2). Thus, international law now seeks to prevent war by making it illegal as well as by providing the rules and procedures for settling the disputes that lead to war. How effective these legal rules are and why we shall discuss in a moment.

### Scope and Content

Vernon Van Dyke offers a convenient classification of the rules of international law into four main categories.[16]

*The Law of Peace.* This category includes such rules as those affecting the legal birth of sovereign states and their recognition by other states; the definition of national boundaries; the extent of nations' legal jurisdiction over their territories; the status of alien persons and property; and so on.

*The Law of War.* This includes rules regulating the declaration and termination of war; the conduct of hostilities; the treatment of enemy civilians and their property, prisoners of war, and spies; the exclusion of certain weapons (e.g., poison gas); and so on.

*The Law of Neutrality.* This includes the definition and protection of the rights and obligations of neutrals and belligerents in their relationships with each other.

*The Laws concerning Resort to War.* As we noted above, inter-

---

[16] Van Dyke, *op. cit.*, pp. 293–296.

national law now prohibits resort to war except for purposes of "self-defense."

### Structure

The differences between domestic law and international law, all of which affect the latter's utility as an approach to peace, are mostly clearly shown by examining the legislative, judicial, and executive structure of international law.

LEGISLATION. The rules of international law arise from two principal sources. Some arise from "customs," which are ways of handling certain types of situations regularly obeyed by nations out of a sense of obligation over a long period of time. Other rules arise from "treaties"—formal international agreements among two or more nations. It is important to note that *no* rule of international law is even formally binding upon any nation that has not voluntarily accepted it: no custom is binding unless the nation acquiesces in it (although most jurists argue that such acquiescence can be implied as well as expressed); and no treaty is binding unless the nation formally ratifies it. So no new rule of international law can be forced upon a nation by some outside agency—for that would be a violation of its sovereignty (see Chapter 22).[17] Thus, the legislative process in international law is extremely decentralized when compared with domestic legislative processes (see Chapter 17).

Once a nation has accepted a custom or ratified a treaty, how binding are the rules *legally?* Two equally valid but quite contradictory legal maxims apply: *pacta sunt servanda* (agreements are to be observed), meaning that a nation cannot legally free itself at will from treaty obligations; and *rebus sic stantibus* (at this point of affairs), meaning that treaties legally cease to be obligatory as soon as the state of facts and conditions upon which they were founded has substantially changed. Who, then, shall say which treaty obligations are binding upon a nation and which are not? Who, in other words, is authorized to interpret international law? The answer is that each nation interprets the law for itself; or, if it wishes, it may submit questions of disputed interpretation to an international judicial body.

ADJUDICATION. Although some nations, as we noted above, may sometimes submit legal questions to arbitration in a sort of quasi-judicial procedure, the only body which can be said to be a permanent international

---

[17] Note, however, that the United Nations Charter provides that "the Organization shall ensure that states which are not Members of the United Nations act in accordance with these Principles so far as may be necessary for the maintenance of internaional peace and security" (Art. 2, Sec. 6). Some jurists have argued that this is an effort to "legislate" for nonmember nations without the latters' consent.

court is the International Court of Justice (ICJ). This body, which sits at The Hague, a city in the Netherlands, is made up of fifteen judges, each from a different nation and each selected for a nine-year term by concurrent action of the United Nations Security Council and General Assembly.

The ICJ, however, is a pale image of a "world supreme court." For all practical purposes it has no compulsory jurisdiction—that is, there is no legal way by which it can compel a nation to plead a case before it. The Statute of the Court declares in Article 36 that the Court's jurisdiction comprises "all cases which the parties refer it." The often-mentioned "optional clause" of the Statute, to be sure, permits the parties to make unilateral declarations "that they recognize as compulsory *ipso facto* and without special agreement, in relation to any other state accepting the same obligation, the jurisdiction of the Court" in certain kinds of cases.[18] Yet, almost half of the nations involved (including the USSR) have not made such declarations; and many of those which have (including the United States and Great Britain) have made their declarations with such accompanying hedges and reservations that they are legally quite free to refuse to take any kind of dispute to the Court if they wish. The Court cannot legally compel any nation to appear before it, nor can any nation legally "arraign" another in court against its desires. Needless to say, the lack of any effective compulsory jurisdiction sharply differentiates the ICJ from any domestic court.

The judicial function in international law, accordingly, is as decentralized as its legislative function. Each nation has the legal power to interpret the rules of international law it considers binding upon itself, and there is no clear and authoritative legal procedure by which any nation's interpretation can be overridden without its consent by another nation or by an international judicial body.

EXECUTION.   The executive process in international law is also highly decentralized. For the most part the rules are executed by the voluntary compliance of the nations themselves. Before World War I the only way a nation could legally be compelled to obey international law was by the application of such sanctions as severance of diplomatic relations, boycotts and embargoes, blockades, and even military intervention. The collective-security provisions of the League of Nations Covenant and the United Nations Charter permit the use of collective sanctions for the enforcement of international law, but, as we have seen, they have been little used for this purpose. For the most part, accordingly, the enforcement

---

[18] The Statute is reproduced in the *Yearbook of the United Nations*, published annually by the United Nations.

of international law depends upon the willingness of the nations to abide by it, not upon compulsion by some international "police force."

### Record

There is a widespread popular impression that international law is a kind of feeble political joke and that nations ignore it all the time as a matter of course. This, however, is far from the truth; for, as Professor Brierly points out,

> [International] law is normally observed because . . . the demands that it makes on states are generally not exacting, and on the whole states find it convenient to observe it; but this fact receives little notice because the interest of most people in international law is not in the ordinary routine of international legal business, but in the occasions, rare but generally sensational, on which it is flagrantly broken. Such breaches generally occur either when some great political issue has arisen between states, or in that part of the system which professes to regulate the conduct of war.[19]

In other words, the rules of international law applying to technical and nonpolitical matters are faithfully observed by nations for the excellent reason that they all find it in their self-interest to do so; and such rules make up the great bulk of international law. This service to mankind, as Professor Brierly well advises, should not be overlooked or undervalued.

By the same token, however, the few areas in which international law is largely impotent are precisely the areas in which the conflicts generally lead to war. Thus, international law in the present state of world politics makes many valuable contributions, but it is of little utility as a barrier against war. The value and limitations of its general role are well summed up by Judge Anzilotti, a former member of the International Court of Justice, as follows:

> The interests protected by international law are not those which are of major weight in the life of states. It is sufficient to think of the great political and economic rivalries to which no juridical formula applies, in order to realize the truth of this statement. International law develops its true function in a sphere considerably circumscribed and modest, not in that in which there move the great conflicts of interests which induce states to stake their very existence in order to make them prevail.[20]

---

[19] Brierly, *op. cit.*, pp. 71–72.
[20] Quoted in H. Lauterpacht, *The Function of Law in the International Community* (New York: Oxford University Press, Inc., 1933), p. 169.

## Approaches to Peace through the
## United Nations

The United Nations, like its predecessor, the League of Nations,[21] is not intended to achieve world peace by abolishing the state system; indeed, its Charter specifically states that "the Organization is based on the principle of the sovereign equality of all its Members" (Art. 2), which, as we learned in Chapter 22, is the basic legal principle of the state system. The United Nations is not, as we are using the term in this book, a "world government" in any sense.

What is it, then? Perhaps the most accurate answer is that the United Nations is an effort to do two things: first, to draw together in one world organization the various approaches to peace within the state system, outlined in the preceding section of this chapter, in an effort to operate them with maximum effectiveness; and second, to encourage and administer international cooperation in a number of largely nonpolitical matters. Thus, the United Nations is not committed to any one approach to peace but attempts to forward all approaches that do not involve any basic alterations of the state system. Professor Claude has accurately summed up its eclectic nature and purposes in these words:

> However dogmatic and monistic certain thinkers may be in explaining the cause of war and the means to peace, the founding fathers of the United Nations have clearly been prepared to try every device which shows promise of contributing to the conditions of peace, and to reject exclusive reliance upon any single device. Our present institutional structure is analogous to a shotgun rather than a rifle, inasmuch as it reflects distrust of the accuracy of anyone's aim at a solution and preference for releasing a shower of shots in the general direction of the problem; we do not know which approach to peace is valid, so we try them all, hoping that not all the shots will be wasted.[22]

The United Nations, in short, is an "international organization," and not a "world government." In our present discussion we shall not attempt to describe all the many and varied organs and activities of the UN, but shall concentrate mainly on the nature and results of those Charter provisions and organs most directly concerned with the maintenance of peace and security.

---

[21] Limitations of space preclude any discussion of the League of Nations, an organization whose structure, problems, and history contain many significant similarities to and contrasts with the United Nations. The reader who wishes to explore these matters may well consult F. P. Walters, *A History of the League of Nations* (2 vols.; New York: Oxford University Press, Inc., 1952); and Sir Alfred E. Zimmern, *The League of Nations and the Rule of Law* (New York: The Macmillan Company, 1939).

[22] Claude, *op. cit.*, p. 199.

### Establishment

The term "United Nations" was first applied to a loose association of the nations fighting against Germany and Japan in World War II, all of which on or after January 1, 1942, signed the "Declaration of the United Nations" in favor of certain general war aims and against concluding a separate peace with the Axis powers. Preliminary plans for a permanent peacetime organization of such powers were drawn up at the two Dumbarton Oaks Conferences of August and September, 1944. The Charter of the United Nations was written at the United Nations Conference on International Organization at San Francisco in April through June, 1945. The UN went into business in January, 1946, when the first General Assembly and Security Council met in London. Since 1950 the organization has had its permanent headquarters in New York City.

### Structure

#### Membership

The United Nations consists of the fifty-one nations who signed the original Charter, and the nations which have subsequently applied for admission and have been admitted by votes of the General Assembly after being recommended by the Security Council. As of May, 1965, the United Nations had 114 members, including almost all the nations of the world and a few (e.g., the Ukraine and Byelorussia) which are not full-fledged nations. Only one nation (Indonesia) has withdrawn.

#### Organs

According to the Charter (Art. 7) the UN has six principal organs: the General Assembly, Security Council, Secretariat, Economic and Social Council, International Court of Justice, and Trusteeship Council. We shall here consider only the first three.

THE GENERAL ASSEMBLY. The General Assembly is the only organ of the UN composed of all its members, and it holds annual sessions. Each nation has one vote in its deliberations, although each can send a delegation of up to five members. The body exercises powers and functions that may be categorized as "deliberative" (discussing any and all matters within the scope of the Charter); "supervisory" (controlling and regulating other organs by receiving annual reports from them and establishing certain administrative procedures for them to follow); "financial" (making up the UN's budget and apportioning its expenses among the members); "elective" (admitting new members, and choosing members for the other organs); and "constituent" (proposing amendments to the Charter). Several of these powers, as we shall see, are exercised coordinately with the

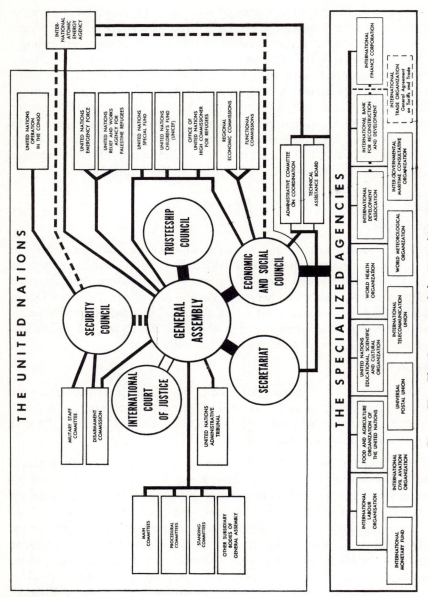

*Figure 51.* The Structure of the United Nations.

Security Council. As we shall note in a moment, the "Uniting for Peace" Resolution of 1950 has given the General Assembly an even more prominent role in the UN's affairs than it was originally intended to have. On "important questions" (defined in Article 18) its decisions are made by two thirds of the members present and voting, and on all other matters by simple majorities.

THE SECURITY COUNCIL. The Security Council consists of eleven UN members, divided into two classes: the five permanent members (Nationalist China, France, Soviet Russia, Great Britain, and the United States); and six nonpermanent members, which are elected for two-year terms by the General Assembly. The terms of the elected members are staggered so that three new members are elected each year, and no nonpermanent member may serve two consecutive terms. The Security Council, as we shall see below, was intended to bear the main responsibility for and control over the UN's machinery for maintaining peace and security, but it has lost much of its pre-eminence in this regard to the General Assembly.

The most noteworthy feature of the Security Council is its voting procedure, which provides for the famous great-power "veto." Article 27 of the Charter stipulates: "1. Each member of the Security Council shall have one vote. 2. Decisions of the Security Council on procedural matters shall be made by an affirmative vote of seven members. 3. Decisions of the Security Council on all other matters shall be made by an affirmative vote of seven members *including the concurring votes of the permanent members. . . .*" (italics added). In other words, the Security Council, which is supposed to be the UN's main acting body, cannot act unless the five great powers unanimously agree that it should act. This "veto" provision and its frequent use by the Soviet Union (which alone has registered over one hundred vetoes since 1946) are often blamed for the failure of the UN to live up to its promise; but the fact is that the United States, while it has actually never used the veto, opposes its elimination quite as much as the Russians do. The great-power veto represents, reflects, and to some extent influences the present state of international politics; but it certainly did not create them nor is it single-handedly preventing the UN from becoming a world government. We shall return to this point later.

THE SECRETARIAT AND SECRETARY-GENERAL. The UN Secretariat is the organization's "civil service" and performs a number of secretarial, research, and other administrative chores for its various agencies. It is headed by the Secretary-General, who is appointed by the General Assembly on the recommendation of the Security Council. In addition to acting as the UN's chief administrative officer, the Secretary-General plays a highly significant political role. Article 99 of the Charter authorizes him to "bring to the attention of the Security Council any matter which in his opinion may threaten international peace and security." All occupants of the office to date—Trygve Lie from 1946 to 1954, Dag Hammarsjköld from 1954 to 1961, and U Thant since 1961—have made full use of this power, and so the office of Secretary-General has come to be one of the most powerful agencies in the whole UN structure, exercising a notable influence upon its decisions.

These, then, are the principal UN organs dealing most directly with the maintenance of international peace and security. Let us now examine the Charter's provisions for handling these matters, and see how they have worked out in practice.

### Maintaining International Peace and Security

The United Nations Charter, as we noted above, incorporates many approaches to peace. In the General Assembly and Security Council it provides forums in which international issues can be discussed, "world public opinion" can be formed and registered, and negotiations can be conducted among disputing nations. The Economic and Social Council and its affiliated specialized agencies provide opportunities for many kinds of cooperation on nonpolitical and technical matters so that a "world community" (see below) may come into being. The Trusteeship Council and system not only provide a method for the enlightened administration

When the Great Powers Agree, the UN Works Well: Delegates of the USSR, the United Kingdom and the United States Raise Hands in favor of Resolution on Cyprus at UN Security Council in March 1964. The Council Asked UN Secretary General U Thant to Set Up an International Peace Force to Prevent Strife on Cyprus. (Wide World Photos, Inc.)

of non-self-governing territories by its members but also seeks to remove quarrels over colonies as a cause of war.[23] The UN also provides agencies for the mediation and conciliation of disputes, for the adjudication of legal controversies (in the International Court of Justice), and for the reduction and regulation of armaments (see above).

The approach to peace to which the Charter gives the central position, however, is that of collective security (see the general discussion above). The relevant provisions are stated mainly in Chapter VII, Articles 39 to 51, and may be briefly summarized. The Security Council is charged with determining "the existence of any threat to the peace, breach of the peace, or act of aggression" and with deciding what measures shall be taken when such situations are deemed to exist (Art. 39). It may decide to use measures not involving the use of armed force, and may call upon the members to apply any and all such measures. "These may include complete or partial interruption of economic relations and of rail, sea, air, postal, telegraphic, radio, and other means of communication, and the severance of diplomatic relations" (Art. 41). If the Security Council decides that these measures are inadequate, it may use other measures "to maintain or restore international peace and security. Such action may include demonstrations, blockades, and other operations by air, sea, or land forces of Members of the United Nations" (Art. 42). And the members are obligated to respond to the Security Council's requests that they take such action (Arts. 48–50).

These Charter provisions are clearly intended to create a strong collective-security system centered upon the Security Council as the decision-making body. How have they worked out in practice?

### The Changing UN

Since the United Nations began operations in 1946 the basic fact of international politics has been the Cold War between the United States and its allies and Soviet Russia and its allies. Hence, the fundamental prerequisite for the successful operation of the UN's collective-security system, namely, unanimity among the great powers in the Security Council, has rarely been present. Thus, in those instances of aggression or breaches of the peace in which Russia and the United States favored different combatants, the Security Council has been unable to act at all because the Russians have used or threatened to use the veto. This was the situation in such clashes between communists and anticommunists as the Greek civil war of the late 1940's, the war in Indochina and the Hungarian revolt in the 1950's, and the war between North and South Vietnam in the 1960's.

The one notable exception to this generalization, of course, was the

---

[23] Cf. James N. Murray, *The United Nations Trusteeship System* (Urbana: University of Illinois Press, 1957).

*Figure 52.*  The Truman-Led UN Internvention in Korea in 1950
May Have Saved the Organization from Collapse. (Copyright
Low—London Evening Standard.)

Korean crisis of 1950. In June of that year the Communist North Koreans
attacked the noncommunist South Koreans in as clear a case of aggression
as we are ever likely to see. By a strange twist of fate the Russians, at that
moment, were boycotting the UN in protest against its failure to admit
Red China, and so the American-proposed resolution in the Security Council to invoke Article 42 against the North Koreans was passed. The Russians
returned too late to veto it. The response of the member nations to the
Security Council's call, however, was somewhat less than unanimous and
enthusiastic cooperation. Of the sixty member nations, only sixteen sent
armed forces of any kind, and only the United States, Great Britain, and
Canada sent more than token forces. Most nations sat on the sidelines,
some of them (e.g., the Latin American nations) cheering the UN "team"
on, others (e.g., India) wringing their hands over the whole unfortunate
affair, and still others (the Communist bloc) denouncing the UN's action
as illegal, imperialistic, warmongering, and so on. The Korean episode,
accordingly, represented neither a complete collapse nor a great success
for the UN's collective-security system. Certainly, it was made possible at

all only because Russia was boycotting the UN when the Communist aggression took place. Otherwise, the Security Council would have been prevented from taking action just as it has been in the other instances of communist aggression since 1946.

## 1. Decline of the Security Council and Ascendancy of the General Assembly

The first great change in the UN has been the steady decline in the significance of the Security Council and a concomitant increase in the significance of the General Assembly. The principal formal evidence of this change is the "uniting for peace" resolution passed by the General Assembly in 1950 under the following circumstances.

Shortly after the Security Council adopted its resolutions calling for UN intervention against the North Koreans, the Russians returned to the organization in an effort to make up lost ground. They argued that while abstention from voting in the Security Council is not tantamount to a veto, absence is—and that, therefore, the UN intervention in Korea was "unconstitutional." They were unable to get the other nations to accept this view, but they were able to prevent the Council from taking further action.

The United States therefore determined to halt the Russian tactics which paralyzed UN action against communist aggression. In November, 1950, the General Assembly, under the leadership of the United States, adopted the "uniting for peace" resolution which states that in instances in which there appears to be a threat to the peace or an act of aggression and in which the Security Council, because of a veto by one of the permanent members, fails to recommend action under Articles 41 and 42, the General Assembly shall immediately consider the matter. If it deems necessary, the General Assembly shall recommend that the member nations use whatever measures, including the use of armed forces, seem appropriate to maintain or restore international peace and security.[24]

The changing relative positions of the Security Council and the General Assembly dramatized by this resolution are also indicated by these facts: since 1950 the Security Council has met far less frequently than before, while the General Assembly's annual sessions have gotten longer and longer; and since 1950 the Security Council has considered fewer and fewer political issues, while the General Assembly has considered substantially more.[25] The result is that the vetoless General Assembly has unquestionably become the main *political* as well as deliberative and supervisory organ of the UN.

---

[24] The text is given as Appendix 21 in Amry Vandenbosch and Willard N. Hogan, *The United Nations* (New York: McGraw-Hill Book Company, Inc., 1952), pp. 359–375.

[25] Claude, *op. cit.*, pp. 159–164.

## 2. Increased Power of the Afro-Asian Nations

The founders of the UN, as we have seen, intended its political activities to be dominated by the permanent members of the Security Council. The post-1950 shift of decision making from the Security Council to the General Assembly has produced a shift of power from the "Big Five" to the other member nations, particularly to the developing nations of Africa and Asia. Table 15 shows how this shift has come about.

### Table 15.   Changing Membership of the United Nations

DATE OF ADMISSION

| Blocs of Member Nations | Before 1950 | Percent | Since 1950 | Percent | Total, 1965 | Percent of Total |
|---|---|---|---|---|---|---|
| Afro-Asian | 17 | 28 | 41 | 77 | 58 | 51 |
| Communist bloc | 7 | 12 | 4 | 8 | 11 | 10 |
| Western Europe | 10 | 16 | 5 | 9 | 15 | 13 |
| British Commonwealth | 5 | 8 | 3 | 6 | 8 | 7 |
| Latin America | 20 | 33 | 0 | 0 | 20 | 17 |
| Other | 2 | 3 | 0 | 0 | 2 | 2 |
| | 61 | 100 | 53 | 100 | 114 | 100 |

SOURCE: *Yearbook of the United Nations, 1963* (New York: published by the Columbia University Press in cooperation with the United Nations, 1965), Appendix I, pp. 681–682.

Table 15 shows that before 1950 the Afro-Asian nations were the second biggest group in the General Assembly, but still had only 28 percent of the votes. Since the "uniting for peace" resolution was adopted, however, over three quarters of the UN's new members have been new nations in Africa and Asia. As a result, they now control an absolute majority of the General Assembly's votes and far outnumber all other blocs.

But has this made any difference? Several studies of voting in the General Assembly show that it has.[26] On issues of "colonialism" (e.g., resolutions condemning Portuguese suppression of Angolan independence) and "racism" (e.g., resolutions condemning *apartheid* in South Africa) the Afro-Asian nations vote together as a solid bloc. But on Cold War issues (e.g., the admission of Red China) they divide among themselves with some (Egypt, Ghana, Guinea) usually supporting Russia and others

---

[26] Cf. Hayward R. Alker, Jr., and Bruce M. Russett, *World Politics in the General Assembly* (New Haven, Conn.: Yale University Press, 1965); and Thomas Hovet, Jr., *Bloc Politics in the United Nations* (Cambridge, Mass.: Harvard University Press, 1960).

(Japan, Thailand, the Philippines) usually supporting the United States. But the point is that whereas before 1957 the United States customarily won majorities for its positions on Cold War issues with relative ease, since then it has had an increasingly difficult time lining up enough Afro-Asian nations to win. For better or worse, the latter, and not the original "Big Five," have come to dominate the General Assembly and therefore the United Nations.

### Evaluation[27]

Any evaluation of the United Nations record in dealing with the political problems of preventing war should be based upon a recognition of the fact noted at the beginning of this section: the UN is not an effort to abandon the state system and strike out in an entirely new direction. This was made painfully clear in its growing financial crisis of the mid-1960's. The UN is financed by contributions apportioned among its members according to a formula determined by the General Assembly. It assigns the largest share to the United States (32.02 percent), the second largest to the Soviet Union (14.97 percent), and the fourth largest to France (5.94 percent).[28] Article 19 of the Charter provides that any member nation more than two years in arrears in its contributions shall have no vote in the General Assembly.

After 1956 the UN incurred heavy expenses from its peace-keeping operations in the Middle East and the Congo, and the General Assembly attempted to finance them by levying special assessments on all the members. But the Communist bloc, led by the USSR, refused to pay, arguing that these operations were in violation of the Charter. In 1962 the International Court of Justice ruled that the operations were lawful and that all members were obligated to pay. However, the Communist bloc continued to refuse. France joined them, arguing that only Security Council decisions were binding on all members and that it was for members who agreed with General Assembly recommendations—not their opponents—to find means of financing them. At this point the United States demanded that Article 19 be invoked and all nonpayers be deprived of their votes—but it did not press its position, recognizing that a showdown would mean the secession of the Communist nations and France and the probable ruin of the UN. In the 1964 session of the General Assembly, accordingly, no

---

[27] Of the many evaluations of the UN's record, the most laudatory is Clark M. Eichelberger, *UN: the First Twenty Years* (New York: Harper & Row, Publishers, 1965); the most denunciatory is Chesly Manly, *The UN Record* (Chicago: Henry Regnery Company, 1955); and the most balanced is Ernest A. Gross, *The United Nations: Structure for Peace* (New York: Harper & Row, Publishers, 1962).

[28] *Yearbook of the United Nations, 1963* (New York: published by the Columbia University Press in cooperation with the United Nations, 1965), pp. 551–552.

formal votes were taken at all[29] and the members adjourned early in the hope that some compromise could be worked out. In 1965 the United States finally abandoned its insistence that Article 19 be enforced, on the ground that only thus could the UN be held together. This resolution of the problem made even clearer than before the organization's basic character as a league of independent sovereign nations rather than a world government.

The UN, then, is an effort to provide a world-wide centralization and organization of the various approaches to peace *within* the state system. It cannot escape the limitations inherent in each of these approaches, but it can and in many instances has permitted these approaches to be pursued more effectively than they could be in complete organizational isolation from one another.

So long as nations and their citizens continue to prefer national independence and self-determination to subjecting themselves to a supernational government, the UN cannot become significantly "stronger" than it now is, whether by eliminating the veto from the Security Council or by any other institutional tinkering. So long as powerful nations like the United States, Russia, and France continue to clash over such basic issues as the preservation and extension of democracy or communism, the United Nations cannot be expected to bring world peace.

Yet, despite these handicaps, the UN has already made a far better record than the League of Nations did. In 1950 it authorized military action which stopped communist aggression in Korea. In 1956 it sent a truce team to patrol the frontiers between Israel and its Arab enemies, and for over a decade prevented major violations of the truce. In 1960 it sent another military force to the former Belgian Congo to prevent secession from and maintain order in the newly independent nation—and, with Dag Hammarsjköld's death in the line of duty, gained its first genuine martyr. In 1964 it sent yet another military force to Cyprus to prevent the civil war between the Greek and Turkish Cypriots from becoming an international war between Greece and Turkey. Any of these local crises could have escalated into a major war involving the great powers, but the UN's intervention prevented it. These are no small achievements.

The UN is not intended to, nor can it, alter any basic trait of the state system. If the state system is the basic cause of international violence, the UN is powerless to prevent it. But if even within the state system there is some real hope of preventing World War III, then the UN has made a major contribution to keeping that hope alive.

---

[29] When an issue had to be decided, the President of the General Assembly, Alex Quaison-Sackley of Ghana, invited the members to give him their "opinions" privately, after which he "announced the consensus" of the Assembly.

# Approaches to Peace through World Government

### The "World-Government" Movement

World government has long been a dream of certain philosophers and poets, who have seen it as signalizing man's rising above his base, quarrelsome, chauvinistic tendencies to become a member of a truly human race. The best-known expression of this dream is Tennyson's prophetic poem *Locksley Hall* (1842) in which he foresaw the day when

> ... the war drum throbbed no longer
> and the battle flags were furled
> In the Parliament of Man, the Federation
> of the world.

Since World War II, however, world government has graduated from the status of poet's dream to that of reform movement. Mainly in Western Europe and the English-speaking nations a number of writers, including Clarence K. Streit, Cord Meyer, Emery Reeves, Norman Cousins, and Stringfellow Barr, have advocated world government, not as the fulfillment of man's highest nature, but as the minimum condition for his physical survival.[30] A number of movements have been established to hasten the achievement of this goal, and, while they differ somewhat in the details of their proposals, they are sufficiently similar that we shall consider them together as one "world-government" movement.

### The Case for World Government

Ignoring the relatively few and minor differences among them, the "world governmentalists" (or "world federalists" as they are also often called) generally base their case upon the following propositions.

Thermonuclear World War III will exterminate most human beings and annihilate civilization. This limitless disaster is almost upon us, and the clock of human destiny stands at one minute to midnight. Thus, there is no time for dallying with palliatives; we must immediately start the basic cure for the ills of international society or we perish.

The basic disease that has caused past wars and will, if left untouched,

---

[30] Cf. Clarence K. Streit, *Freedom against Itself* (New York: Harper & Row, Publishers, 1954); Cord Meyer, *Peace or Anarchy* (Boston: Little, Brown & Company, 1947); Emery Reeves, *The Anatomy of Peace* (New York: Pocket Books, Inc., 1946); Stringfellow Barr, *Citizens of the World* (New York: Doubleday & Company, Inc., 1953); and Norman Cousins, *In Place of Folly* (New York: Harper & Row, Publishers, 1961).

bring World War III is the international anarchy of the state system itself. War is the inevitable result of anarchy, and the only possible alternative to either is world government. None of the efforts at peace within the state system, including the United Nations, can prevent war because they do not get at the basic cause of wars.

If we are to survive, therefore, we have no choice but to establish a world federal government, modeled more or less closely upon the American and/or the Swiss system, that will locate all powers over international political affairs in the hands of a truly supernational world government while leaving to each nation control over its own purely domestic affairs. This can perhaps best be done by revising the United Nations Charter so as to make the UN into such a supernational government; but however it is done, it must be done soon or mankind will die.

How can we bring this about? Since the *peoples* of the various nations are far more ready for world government than are their shortsighted, timid, and confused statesmen, we must launch a world-wide propaganda (or "educational") campaign to stimulate and activate latent popular enthusiasm for this plan. When the people are aroused, the statesmen will soon be converted.

These, then, are the reasons why we must have world government and the methods by which we can get it.

### Criticisms of the World-Government Position

The world-government movement has won support from a number of intellectuals and even from a few public officials—all of them, needless to say, on this side of the Iron Curtain. Most political scientists who specialize in international affairs, however, have not been converted. Generally speaking, they object to the doctrine just outlined on grounds of desirability or practicality or both.

#### Is It Desirable?

Some political scientists, notably Professor Claude, have raised questions as to whether, entirely aside from its practicality, a world federal government would prevent war as its advocates promise. Professor Claude points out that government *within* nations has never been a magic cure for violence and civil war, and that federal governments in particular have witnessed a great deal of internecine strife—an outstanding example being the American Civil War. It may well be, he adds, that in the kind of violent and fragmented world in which we live only the most ruthless kind of world dictatorship could possibly prevent war. Should we, he asks, pay so great a price even for world peace?[31]

---

[31] Claude, *op. cit.*, pp. 380–391.

### Is It Possible?

Most political scientists, however, go along with the "world governmentalists" on the desirability of world government as a war-preventive. But, unlike its advocates, they believe that world government simply is not possible in the present state of international society.

In essence, their criticism is this. Wherever they have been successfully established and have kept domestic peace, governments have been made possible by the prior existence of a *community*. That is, the people who established them and accepted their rule did so because they consciously shared a number of common values, loyalties, and attitudes the preservation of which seemed to them to require the services of government. As we learned in Chapter 2, where no such consensus or feeling of community exists or where it is less important to the community's major groups than their own special interests, government cannot prevent domestic violence or even maintain its own existence.

The evidence, most political scientists are convinced, overwhelmingly indicates that no such world community exists at the present time. Contrary to the assumptions of "world governmentalists," the peoples of most nations are *more* nationalistic and parochial than their leaders—foreign offices and diplomats are far more often criticized as too "internationalistic" than as too "nationalistic"; and so long as national loyalties continue to run deep within the minds of most men, no world community can exist and no world government can be established or sustained.

Thus, even granting the argument that only world government can prevent World War III, most political scientists agree with Professor Claude's judgment that political science "grimly reminds man that he must do what he can; world federalism more sanguinely asserts that man can do what he must"; and that "the dilemma of the world federalist is that there is no necessary correlation between human need and human capacity."[32]

## Has Mankind a Future?

At the present state of political science, as we shall see in Chapter 24, there are many questions political scientists cannot answer with any degree of scientific probability beyond that of the educated guess. The query posed in the above subtitle is certainly an example of such a question.

Political scientists usually regret their inability to make reliable predictions on such matters; but perhaps this is an instance in which they should be glad; for if the answer to this question is "No," most of us would just

---

[32] *Ibid.*, pp. 374, 379. See also Van Dyke, *op. cit.*, Ch. 21; and Morgenthau, *op. cit.*, Ch. 29.

as soon not know it until we have to. In any case the political scientist—like anyone else—can only answer this question with "Maybe."

Political scientists can and do predict with considerable confidence, however, at least the short-term status of many of the variables that are involved in this question. Thus most students of international affairs agree that the immediate future will include at least the following elements. The essential features of the state system will remain unchanged for some time to come, although the atomistic nationalism and independent action characteristic of world politics before 1914 will increasingly be replaced by regional associations of nations with common interests and similiar ideologies, such as NATO, the European Economic Community, and the communist movement. The United Nations will continue to have its greatest successes in its nonpolitical and technical activities, such as combatting illiteracy and disease, and its greatest failures in such of its political efforts to prevent aggression and maintain peace as collective security, disarmament, and peaceful settlement of East-West tensions and disputes. Thermonuclear weapons will continue to be made, stockpiled, and held in readiness by an increasing number of nations and not by the United States and Soviet Russia alone; the means of delivering them over intercontinental distances with no possibility of successful defense will be technically perfected more and more.

In short, we must accept the fact that for an indefinite number of years ahead we are going to live in a world in which the possibility of thermonuclear war is ever-present, and in which smaller, less devastating wars will take place from time to time and pose the danger of becoming general and unlimited wars. Neither physical security nor psychic ease can be expected by any alert and intelligent person for some time to come; and we can all expect to live for many decades in what some writers have called—with only too grim accuracy—"the age of anxiety."

That much the political scientist can foretell. Has mankind a future? That—perhaps fortunately—he, like anyone else, cannot tell. As thermonuclear-age humor has it, "An optimist is one who believes the future is uncertain."

# part six

## The Current State of
## Political Science

# 24

## Inside Political Science

THE first edition of this book was written in the mid-1950's, and it then seemed appropriate to begin the concluding chapter as follows:

In the course of the hearings in the school-segregation cases before a federal district court in 1953, the attorney for the National Association for the Advancement of Colored People (NAACP), Thurgood Marshall, brought to the stand a number of "expert witnesses"—psychologists, sociologists, professors of education, and the like—to testify on the effects of segregation on Negro children. When he called an associate professor of political science, however, the defendants' counsel objected, on the ground that a political scientist is not qualified to answer the kinds of questions being asked. The following colloquy took place between the judge and Mr. Marshall:

JUDGE PARKER: Are you going to offer any more witnesses along this line?
MR. MARSHALL: No, sir. The other witnesses are REAL scientists.
JUDGE PARKER: Well, I'll take it for what it's worth. Go ahead.[1]

In a conference at Northwestern University in 1954 on the current state of political science, another political scientist confessed that "the day when children will say 'political scientist' when asked what they want to be when they grow up is remote indeed."[2]

In the decade following these rather disparaging comments, the public

---

[1] Transcript of Record in *Briggs v. Board of Trustees* (the South Carolina segregation case), October Term, 1953, p. 103, emphasis in the original.
[2] Willmoore Kendall, "Social Determinants of American Political Science," Address at Northwestern University, April 27, 1954, mimeo.

image and the self-image of political science has changed considerably. The membership of the American Political Science Association has risen from 6000 in 1955 to over 12,000 in 1965. In 1964 the National Science Foundation, established by Congress in 1950 to support basic research and education in the sciences, formally included political science in the social sciences eligible for its financial benefits.[3] The APSA's 1961 Directory listed such distinguished nonacademic members as Ralph Bunche, Paul Douglas, Barry Goldwater, Dean Rusk, Hubert H. Humphrey, Harry S. Truman, and John F. Kennedy. Newspaper columnists, television commentators, and party politicians now regularly refer to members of the profession as "political scientists" rather than (as so often before) "political economists" or "historians." And no less an authority than Richard M. Nixon ascribed the Democrats' success in 1964 in part to their ability to mobilize the support of so many political scientists; for, Nixon said, political scientists are "tremendously potent people" in political affairs.[4]

The purpose of this final chapter is to take the reader out of the classroom on a brief backstage tour of contemporary political science's main professional concerns, methods, and disputes. But first a word about why the author believes such a chapter is in order.

This book is intended to be an "introduction to political science" mainly in the sense of summarizing and explaining some of the principal conclusions political scientists have reached about the nature of politics and government in the modern world, and twenty-three of its twenty-four chapters are devoted to such material. In the author's opinion, however, the reader of an introductory survey of any area of human inquiry should acquire an additional level of information: he should learn something about the scholarly discipline itself. He should get some idea of the kinds of questions the discipline asks about the universe and how it goes about answering them, and thus gain some basis for deciding what kind and level of expertise its practitioners possess. Such understanding will help him appreciate what the discipline can and cannot do and what use, if any, he and his society can make of it in dealing with their problems.

The purpose of this chapter, then, is to provide the reader with at least a preliminary and general version of such information about political science. We may begin by noting that political science, particularly in the United States since the end of World War II, has undergone a period of intense self-examination and soul searching—perhaps the most intense of several such periods it has experienced since it emerged as a separate

---

[3] The others are cultural and physical anthropology, archaeology, demography, economics, geography, linguistics, psychology, sociology, and the history and philosophy of science.

[4] The New York *Times*, November 11, 1964, p. 26.

discipline in the late nineteenth century.[5] The learned journals have printed many articles, many books have been written, and many professional conferences have been held and committees formed—all for the purpose of re-examining the scope and methods of political science, all describing and trying to account for the discipline's deficiencies, and most offering proposals for its improvement.

One consequence of this ferment has been to make it clear that political scientists are widely and sometimes sharply divided among themselves on a number of questions about the proper organization of their discipline. In our effort in this chapter to portray the current state of political science, we shall take note of some of the areas of agreement among them and also describe some of the principal issues on which they are disagreed and the major points of view expressed on each issue.

## The Scope of Political Science

The categories most generally used to describe the nature of contemporary political science are those of its "scope" (that is, the kinds of subject matter with which it deals and the kinds of questions it asks about them); and its "methods" (that is, the techniques political scientists use to answer the questions they raise). As we shall see, there is some disagreement among political scientists about the proper scope of the discipline and a great deal of controversy about what methods it should use. Let us first consider questions of the discipline's scope.

### The Emergence of Political Science as a Distinct Discipline[6]

Men have pondered and written about the actual and ideal roles of politics and government in human society at least since the time of Socrates in the fifth century B.C.; and the writings of such giants as Plato, Aristotle, St. Thomas, Machiavelli, Hobbes, Locke, and Rousseau are still studied by students of political science in courses labeled "political theory" or "the history of political ideas." "Political science" in the modern sense,

---

[5] The three main previous official stock-takings (in 1914, 1923, and 1930) are described with bibliographical notes in *Goals for Political Science*, the Report of the Committee for the Advancement of Teaching, American Political Science Association (New York: William Sloane Associates, 1951), pp. 6–14.

[6] The histories of man's philosophizing about politics are too numerous to be mentioned here. An illuminating account of empirical analyses of politics in ancient times is William Anderson, *Man's Quest for Political Knowledge; The Study and Teaching of Politics in Ancient Times* (Minneapolis: University of Minnesota Press, 1964). For the development of political science in America, see Anna Haddow, *Political Science in American Colleges and Universities, 1636–1900* (New York: Appleton-Century-Crofts, Inc., 1939).

however, did not emerge as a distinct discipline and academic subject until the late nineteenth century, and then mainly in American colleges and universities. As we shall see later, it still has not achieved distinct academic status in the universities of many nations. In the United States it won its academic independence from other disciplines and acquired its present title mainly as a result of two developments.

### The Separation of Politics from Other Subject Matters

Socrates, Plato, Aristotle, and the other masters of political literature before the nineteenth century were not concerned—as many present-day political scientists are—with identifying the purely "political" or "governmental" in human affairs for the purpose of concentrating their studies on such matters. They were concerned not only with man-in-society but also with man-in-the-universe, and so they wrote about what we have come to call ethics, history, economics, religion, psychology, education, and so on, as well as about politics and government. They never raised the question of whether it might be profitable to distinguish these various aspects of man-in-the-universe from each other and, by division of labor, establish a discipline specializing in each. So while these writers were, in a sense, "political scientists" and "political philosophers," each of them was also, in modern terminology, a "historian," "economist," "psychologist," "ethical philosopher," and so on.

By the eighteenth century politics and government, like law and "political economy," were taught in English, American, and European universities and colleges—if at all—as branches of "moral philosophy"; for the principles of right public conduct were considered to be merely an aspect of right conduct in general, and the whole purpose of higher education was to instruct pupils in the principles of right conduct. The one exception was Uppsala University in Sweden, which in the early seventeenth century established a chair of "statecraft and eloquence" apparently for the purpose of giving instruction in politics and government as a subject separate from others. The Uppsala example, however, was not followed—even in Sweden—until well into the nineteenth century.[7]

In the late eighteenth and early nineteenth centuries a number of areas of study began to win independent academic status from moral philosophy. Among the first to be differentiated were the studies of law and "political economy." Neither, however, contributed much to the development of the specialized study of politics and government. The newly independent law schools were concerned only with questions of what the law was (see Chapter 20) and dealt little or not at all with the institutions and processes

---

[7] Cf. William A. Robson, *The University Teaching of Social Sciences: Political Science* (Leiden: published for UNESCO by A. W. Sijthoff, 1954), p. 22.

that made the law. "Political economy" became the ancestor of economics far more than of political science, for the term denoted the wealth-acquiring processes of a whole society, as opposed to "domestic economy," the well-acquiring processes of the individual family and household. So it, too, was little concerned with the policy-making and enforcement processes of government. Insofar as the latter were considered at all, they were dealt with as an aspect of history.

The study of history began to achieve academic independence in the early 1800's and by the middle of the century was well established as a separate discipline. During this same period, however, the growing intensity of the constitutional crisis in the United States that ultimately led to the Civil War produced a large volume of studies of the Constitution which were neither pure "law" nor pure "history," but rather analyses of the proper form and role of Constitutions and governments in human affairs. This development led an increasing number of writers and teachers to think of the study of politics and government as something quite distinct from either the study of history or the study of law.

In 1856 a significant episode took place. Francis Lieber, a German-born scholar who had made his career in the United States and who had published in 1838 his *Manual of Political Ethics* (a work regarded by some scholars as the first systematic treatise in political science published in this country), was elected to the Chair of History and Political Economy at Columbia College. Lieber asked the college's trustees to change the name of his chair to History and Political Science, and they agreed to do so.[8] This change signalized the emergence of the study of politics and government as something separate from the study of history.

Lieber's innovation came to full flower after the Civil War, when political science finally emerged in the United States as a distinct academic subject and scholarly discipline. By the early 1880's a number of American institutions offered courses in "government" as distinct from history or political economy, and in the late 1880's and early 1890's a number of universities and colleges created separate "government" and "political science" departments. In 1886 the *Political Science Quarterly* was established by Columbia as the first specialized political science journal. During the same period a number of political science treatises in the modern sense of the term were published, the most notable being Theodore Dwight Woolsey's *Political Science* (1878), Woodrow Wilson's *Congressional Government* (1885) and *The State* (1889), John W. Burgess's *Political Science and Comparative Constitutional Law* (1890), and one major work by an Englishman, James Bryce's *The American Commonwealth* (1888).

Finally, in 1903 the American Political Science Association was founded

---

[8] Haddow, *op. cit.*, pp. 138–140.

with Frank J. Goodnow (see Chapter 19) as its first president, and in 1906 the association began publishing the *American Political Science Review*. Political science in the United States had become well established as a distinct discipline and has remained so ever since.

### The Growth of the Idea of "Social Science"[9]

The "natural" or "physical" sciences of astronomy, chemistry, physics, and so on, first emerged in their modern versions in the sixteenth century, and from then on achieved an ever-growing and impressive body of empirically verified laws describing the behavior of various facets of the physical universe. By the nineteenth century these disciplines had won great prestige in the eyes of many philosophers and laymen, and had developed a well-understood "scientific method" (see below) for dealing with their subject matters. By the middle of that century a number of students of human affairs had come to accept the doctrine, most notably advanced by the French philosopher Auguste Comte in his work *Cours de philosophie positive* (1830–1842), that human society in all its aspects can and should be studied in exactly the same spirit and by substantially the same methods as those used by the natural scientists in their studies of physical phenomena. Thus, the idea of "social science" in the modern sense of the term was born and took a grip on the imaginations and aspirations of many students of human affairs that has since increased rather than diminished.[9]

It is not surprising, therefore, that many of the same nineteenth-century scholars who, as we have just seen, believed that politics and government should be studied apart from ethics, history, law, and "political economy," also came to believe in Comte's "positivist" philosophy that these matters can and should be studied scientifically. Many who pressed for the independence of political and governmental studies took up the term "political science" to describe both the scope and method of the discipline they hoped to establish.

### The Current Status of the "Political Science" Label

By no means every student of political and governmental affairs, then or now, has accepted both developments implicit in the label "political science." Some scholars, for example, have preferred to speak of the "political sciences," the plural form representing their conviction that *all* the aspects of society which relate to government, such as law, economics, sociology, history, and so on, should be studied together, and that politics and government alone constitute too narrow a focus for profitable study. This, as we shall see below, is the predominant view in the academic structures of most European universities.

---

[9] The story is well told in Maurice Duverger, *An Introduction to the Social Sciences*, translated by Malcolm Anderson (New York: Frederick A. Praeger, Inc., 1964), Ch. 1.

Other scholars grant that politics and government are a proper subject for special study, but deny that they can or should be studied "scientifically" in the Comtian or "positivist" sense of the term. Hence they refuse to accept the term "political *science*" as a proper designation for the discipline, and in a number of American colleges and universities the departments teaching the matters we have considered in this book are officially called departments of "government" or "politics" or "public affairs."

Later in this chapter we shall outline the major issues involved and the positions taken on the question of whether the subject matter of "political science" can be studied "scientifically." For our present purposes, however, we should recognize that in the United States "political science" is by far the most commonly used term for the kinds of studies we have dealt with in this book. Far more American academic departments dealing with such matters are officially designated "political science" than anything else; the name of the professional association to which most of their members belong is the American Political Science Association; and "political scientist" is the term most commonly used to describe teachers and scholars of these subjects.

"Political science," in short, may not be a precise designation for the scholarly enterprises we consider in this chapter. But it certainly is so widely accepted that everyone who engages in them knows what kinds of activity it refers to (although there is disagreement, as we shall see, about what kinds of activity it *should* denote); moreover, any other label is likely to muddy the waters of identification and discussion more than "political science" does.

### Political Science around the World[10]

Political science, as we have defined it, has had by far its greatest development in the United States. A survey conducted in 1962 by the staff of the APSA's national office in Washington, D.C., reported that a total of 786 degree-granting colleges and universities offered courses under the title "political science," "government," or "politics." Four hundred and sixty-six had separate departments, 162 had joint history and political science departments, 129 gave the courses in general departments of social studies, and 29 joined political science with some other discipline, such as economics or sociology.[11] Professor William Robson estimates that there are more political scientists in the United States than in all other nations combined. Most of this chapter, accordingly, deals with the current state of

---

[10] The most comprehensive surveys are Robson, *op. cit.*; and *Contemporary Political Science* (Paris: UNESCO Publication No. 426, 1950).

[11] "Political Science as a Discipline," *American Political Science Review*, LVI (June, 1962), 417–42.

American political science; however, the status of political science elsewhere in the world merits comment.

The academic and professional status of political science varies considerably from nation to nation outside the United States. It is perhaps
most firmly established in Sweden, where, following the early lead of
Uppsala University (see above), the nation's other three universities have
also established the study of politics and government as a separate academic division; it is also an examination subject in the governmental
institutes which train civil servants. It is probably least firmly established in
the Asian nations, although in India and Japan political science is a major
independent area of study in most universities.

The other nations appear to fall somewhere between these two extremes. In Great Britain, for example, politics and government are taught
to some extent in all universities and university colleges, but the subject
has achieved independent status and prominence mainly at the University
of London, with its famous London School of Economics and Political
Science; Oxford University, where it plays a prominent role in the honors
curriculum known, in the mysterious British fashion, as "Modern Greats"
and where distinguished research is conducted under the aegis of Nuffield
College; the University of Manchester; and a few of the new universities,
such as the University of Essex. Cambridge University has a Chair of Political Science, presently held by the distinguished political scientist Sir Denis
Brogan; but even so the subject can be taken by a student only as a minor
option in an honors degree in history or economics. So it is in other
British universities.

In France the plural term "political sciences" (*les sciences politiques*)
remains almost as popular as it was in 1872, when the *École Libre des
Sciences Politiques* was founded. This well-known school, established by
private initiative but later made an institute of the University of Paris,
gives instruction in all matters considered to bear upon the making of public policy: political ideologies, economic history and theory, political and
social geography, and so on. Thus it offers broader coverage than do political science departments in the United States. Similar institutes have been
set up at six of France's sixteen other universities, but for the most part
politics and government are studied in France as part of the curriculum in
law and treated in a heavily legalistic and formalistic manner; the other
"political sciences" are scattered between the faculties of letters and
science.

The rest of the European nations generally follow the French patterns.
A few have established special institutes similar to the *École Libre*, the
outstanding example being the *Deutsche Hochschule für Politik* in Berlin,
but they have no independent academic departments called "political

science," and even the "political sciences" are dispersed among the various divisions of their universities.

There is reason to believe, however, that "political science" in the American sense of the term is achieving increasing recognition in Europe. For example, when a number of scholars of political and governmental matters met in Paris in 1948 under the auspices of the United Nations Educational, Scientific and Cultural Organization (UNESCO) to form an international professional association, they specifically rejected the continental designation of "political sciences" and the British designation of "political studies," and officially named the new organization the International Political Science Association. To be sure, many of the new association's European and Asian members (well over half of its members are Americans) hold professorships of law or psychology or sociology in their home institutions. But the very existence of the association is encouraging the development abroad of "political science" in the American sense, although it will be many years before it achieves in any other nation the degree of academic independence and prominence it has gained in the United States.

### The Traditional Focus of Political Science

Since 1945, as we noted above, many American political scientists have been engaged in re-examining and re-evaluating both the scope and the methods of their discipline. In the sizable body of literature that has emerged from this soul searching one can discern both a considerable area of agreement about what political scientists have regarded as the discipline's proper scope and a great many disagreements about what *should* be its scope.[12] In what follows we shall note the areas of agreement and disagreement.

#### "Legal Governments" and Their "Politics"

Those who have surveyed the literature and classroom instruction of political science in the United States generally agree that political scientists have had at least one thing in common: their primary focus upon the structure and operations of the world's "legal governments" (as opposed to

---

[12] These self-appraisals are too numerous to be listed, let alone summarized, in such a general survey as this. Four of the most comprehensive are David Easton, *The Political System: An Inquiry into the State of Political Science* (New York: Alfred A. Knopf, Inc., 1953); Charles S. Hyneman, *The Study of Politics: The Present State of American Political Science* (Urbana: University of Illinois Press, 1959); Vernon Van Dyke, *Political Science: A Philosophical Analysis* (Stanford, Calif.: Stanford University Press, 1960); and Harold D. Lasswell, *The Future of Political Science* (New York: Atherton Press, 1963).

the "private governments" of unofficial groups, such as churches, trade unions, and so on), and upon the "politics" associated with them.[13] Both of these terms, moreover, have been given working definitions substantially similar to those presented in Chapters 1 and 2 of this book.

In their investigations of politics and government, political scientists have asked at least five basic types of questions about the making and enforcing of governmental policy: (1) What are the policies of this or that government (that is, what is their content)? (2) Are they good or bad (that is, do they help or hinder in the effort to achieve the good society)? (3) How are these policies made and enforced (that is, what is the actual nature of the particular society's political and governmental institutions and processes)? (4) Is that a good or a bad way to make policies (that is, do those institutions and processes get the results the society wants, and do they damage other values the society holds)? (5) How are policy-making and enforcement institutions constructed and maintained, and/or how should they be constructed and maintained?

Not all political scientists, of course, have been equally interested in all five questions. Some, for example, have concentrated on describing the policy-making and enforcement processes and institutions, and have professed little or no *professional* concern with value-judgments. Others have been mainly concerned with evaluating and reforming processes, but have refrained from stating their preferences for the content of policies. Still others have regarded themselves mainly as policy advisers to the nation and have seen their main professional task as one of steering public officials and/or the general public toward "good" policies and away from "bad" ones.

Taken altogether, therefore, political science has dealt with both policy content and policy process, and has considered each of them both descriptively and evaluatively.

### The "Fields" of Political Science

The subject matter of every academic discipline is subdivided by its practitioners into a number of constituent "fields" for purposes of division of labor in teaching and investigation. Political science is no exception, and we shall take note of two such sets of subdivisions.

The 1948 Paris conference at which the International Political Science Association was founded (see above) agreed that the subject should be divided into the following four fields, each with its subordinate divisions.[14]

---

[13] The most thorough post-1945 survey of what American political scientists have been doing is Hyneman, *op. cit.* Most of the factual statements in this section are based on Hyneman's report.

[14] *Contemporary Political Science*, p. 4.

I. Political theory
   1. Political theory
   2. History of political ideas
II. Political institutions
   1. The constitution
   2. National government
   3. Regional and local government
   4. Public administration
   5. Economic and social functions of government
   6. Comparative political institutions
III. Parties, groups, and public opinion
   1. Political parties
   2. Groups and associations
   3. Participation of the citizen in the government and the administration
   4. Public opinion
IV. International relations
   1. International politics
   2. International organization and administration
   3. International law

At the 1965 annual convention of the American Political Science Association in Washington, D.C., the program was organized to reflect the prevailing fields of instruction in the larger American academic departments of political science. Thus, its panels and discussions were classified under nine headings: American national government and politics; American state and local government and politics; political theory; public administration; public law; comparative government and politics, Western areas; comparative government and politics, developing nations; comparative government and politics, Communist nations; and international relations and foreign policy.

### The Current Debate over Scope

Most political scientists, as we have stated, would agree with our description of the traditional scope of political science. Some believe it to be fully adequate for further progress and see no reason to search for another definition. Others, however, are convinced that one of the reasons for what they regard as political science's failure to produce very significant or useful results is the result of the present definition of its scope.

Thus, some writers argue that chopping up the actual unity of human social life into "the economic," "the political," and so on, prevents us from gaining a full and rounded understanding of how society operates. They contend that we should abandon all efforts to define a proper scope for a narrow *political* science (or economic science or social psychology or cultural anthropology) and start developing a broad and unified *social* science.

Other political scientists, however, take the opposite position. They believe that there is great utility in a proper division of labor in the social sciences so long as it is made in terms of certain nuclei of main concerns for each discipline rather than in terms of constant border warfare among them over who is improperly invading whose field. It is impossible for anyone to study everything at once, they argue, and so division of labor is just as profitable in the study of human affairs as it is in the production of material wealth or in any other complicated human endeavor. One of the troubles with political science, they contend, is that the content it has presumed to adopt is far too broad, while the data it uses to investigate that content are far too narrow. The way out of this *cul-de-sac*, they believe, is for political science to focus upon a certain kind of human *relationship* rather than on a particular institution, such as "government" or "the state." Some of them, notably George Catlin and Harold Lasswell, suggest "power" (see Chapter 22) or "influence" as the most fruitful relationship on which to focus.[15] Others agree with David Easton that "the authoritative allocation of values for a society" is the best orienting concept.[16]

In such a general survey as this we can only pause to note the existence of this debate and identify some of the major positions taken in it. If and when one of these views comes to dominate the thinking of most political scientists, the nature of the discipline will unquestionably undergo a major change. All we can say at present, however, is that none of them has yet gained any such general acceptance, and until one does, the main concern of most political scientists will continue to be what it has been: the study of whatever aspects of legal governments and their politics they choose to explore.

## The Methods of Political Science

Although, as we have seen, there is some disagreement among contemporary political scientists about the discipline's proper scope, there is considerably more disagreement among them over various issues of "methodology." This term is generally used to refer to what political scientists do with their subject matter; that is, the kinds of questions they consider worth answering and answerable, the techniques they use to get answers, the standards by which they distinguish good answers from bad, and the like.

---

[15] Cf. George E. G. Catlin, A *Study of the Principles of Politics* (London: George Allen & Unwin, Ltd., 1930), and *Systematic Politics: Elementa Politica et Sociologica* (Toronto: University of Toronto Press, 1962). See also Harold D. Lasswell and Abraham Kaplan, *Power and Society* (New Haven, Conn.: Yale University Press, 1950).

[16] Cf. Easton, *op. cit.*, Chs. 4–5. See also Easton's A *Systems Analysis of Political Life* (New York: John Wiley & Sons, Inc., 1965).

In the limited space of the present chapter we cannot describe in any detail even a few of the many different "epistemological"[17] positions held and methods used by contemporary political scientists. It is enough for our purposes to note that they include a great variety of different operations, such as, for example, logical analyses of others' writings, statistical analyses of election returns, interviews with public officials, reproducing newspaper accounts of political events, sample surveys, and many, many more. This whole book, indeed, is something of a catalogue of these methods, for the professional literature it cites and the many different kinds of evidence on which its generalizations are based constitute a kind of cross-section sample of current political science methods.

Rather than attempt to describe any of the specific methods political scientists use, we shall take note of the most prominent issue in the postwar debate over methodology.

### The Dispute over Behavioralism

#### The Meaning of "Behavioralism"

Much of the post-1945 dispute over the proper concerns and methods of political science has centered on something variously called "political behavior," "behavioralism," or "behaviorism." Most political scientists regard themselves as to some extent "probehavioral" or "antibehavioral,"[18] but there has been no clear agreement, either between the two camps or within them, as to just what the conflict is about. At first the term "political behavior" was often used to designate the activities we have called "voting behavior" (see Chapter 14). In the mid-1960's, however, this usage has been generally dropped, and most of the disputants agree with Robert Dahl that what is at issue is a particular *approach* to the study of all political and governmental phenomena.[19] Hence the preferred usage now is the

---

[17] "Epistemology" is the branch of philosophy that deals with the scope, methods, and validity of human knowledge. It is concerned with such questions as these: What sorts of knowledge have we? How valid are they? How can we test their validity? How can we acquire knowledge? How can we determine which ways of acquiring knowledge are best? And so on.

[18] In 1963 Professors Albert Somit and Joseph Tanenhaus analyzed the views of a random sample of 431 political scientists about various professional issues. They found that the dispute over behavioralism separates the profession substantially more than any other issue: *American Political Science: A Profile of a Discipline* (New York: Atherton Press, 1964), pp. 21–24.

[19] The conflict is accurately described and calmly analyzed from a probehavioral position in Professor Dahl's "The Behavioral Approach to Political Science: Epitaph for a Monument to a Successful Protest," *American Political Science Review*, LV (December, 1961), 763–772. See also Evron M. Kirkpatrick's comprehensive survey of the relevant literature, "The Impact of the Behavioral Approach on Traditional Political Science," in Austin Ranney, ed., *Essays on the Behavioral Study of Politics* (Urbana: University of Illinois Press, 1962), pp. 1–29.

adjectival form, as in "the behavioral study of politics," and its advocates are most often called "behavioralists."

But what is the behavioral approach? Some have confused it with the "behavioristic" doctrines of such psychologists as J. B. Watson. Others have defined it as the substitution of the individual human being for the political institution as the basic unit for political analysis. Still others consider it to be a protest against the formalism and weak evidential base of prewar political science.[20]

However, despite this confusion the dispute over behavioralism has been mainly concerned with the general issue of the proper meaning and role of science in political science. In dealing with this issue the disputants have argued mostly about the following two questions.

### What Is "Science"?

The word "science," like the word "democracy," has acquired such strongly favorable emotional connotations for so many people in our time that it is used to denote all sorts of disparate things. We often hear people speak, for example, not only of the "sciences" of chemistry and physics, but also of the "sciences" of wrestling and cooking, of "scientific" bidding in bridge, and of "Christian Science" as a form of religion.

Most political scientists, however, use the term "science" to denote a particular method of inquiry—one which is distinguished from other methods of inquiry by its insistence upon the following objectives, techniques, and standards.[21]

OBJECTIVES.   The main objective of science is to discover, state, and verify the fundamental "laws" that govern the universe. A scientific law, of course, differs from a governmental law in that the former is *descriptive* (that is, it states the regular and recurring patterns of behavior observed in this or that body of natural phenomena, and thus states how things *do* behave), while the latter is *prescriptive* (that is, it states a rule of behavior that human beings *should* obey but in fact may or may not obey).

Scientists, of course, would not try to discover scientific laws if they thought that no such laws exist and that there are no discoverable uniformities and regularities in nature. They operate on the basic assumption, as one philosopher puts it, that

---

[20] The various meanings are analyzed in David Easton, "The Current Meaning of 'Behavioralism' in Political Science," in James C. Charlesworth, ed., *The Limits of Behavioralism in Political Science* (Philadelphia: The Amercan Academy of Political and Social Science, 1962), pp. 1–25.

[21] The following discussion in the text is drawn largely from the conception of science presented in Morris R. Cohen, *Reason and Nature* (New York: Harcourt, Brace & World, 1931), pp. 83–114. The problems involved in applying scientific method to the study of social and political problems are well considered in Abraham Kaplan, *The Conduct of Inquiry: Methodology for Behavioral Science* (San Francisco: Chandler Publishing Company, 1964).

the universe is a cosmos, not a chaos. The scientist has faith that . . . events in the world can be comprehended if he can learn some law or set of laws that "govern" them, and he believes that his methods can lead to the discovery of these laws.[22]

**SCIENTIFIC METHOD.**   Modern science has developed a well-defined and generally accepted method for discovering descriptive general laws. The principal operations in that method may be described as follows, although they are by no means always conducted in the same chronological order given here.

1. *Selecting Problems.*   Scientific inquiry begins when a scientist becomes dissatisfied with the existing state of knowledge on a particular matter. He may be dissatisfied with the way some aspect of the universe —such as bad weather or disease—affects human life, and may conclude that the ill cannot be cured until we know what causes it. He may be dissatisfied with the adequacy of some accepted explanation of a particular phenomenon—such as the phlogiston theory of combustion or the supply-and-demand theory of price formation—and resolve to seek a better one. In any case, scientific inquiry begins because a scientist is bothered by some problem and wishes to solve it.[23]

2. *Formulating Hypotheses.*   The scientist next formulates working hypotheses—that is, tentative statements about the forces governing the particular phenomena which his problem leads him to study.

3. *Gathering Data and Testing Hypotheses.*   On the basis of his hypotheses he makes certain predictions about the future course of events— that is, he reasons that if his guess at the forces governing the phenomena in question is correct, then under conditions A and B events X and Y must happen. He then gathers data about what events actually have taken place under conditions A and B, and on the basis of his observations decides whether his hypotheses provide a valid, invalid, or partially valid explanation of the forces in question.

4. *Using the Results.*   Students of scientific method often distinguish between "pure science" and "applied science" or "engineering" in the following manner. The "pure scientist" is concerned only with the state of knowledge and understanding, and so he uses the results of his studies only to support, refute, or modify existing scientific theories. The "applied scientist" or "engineer," on the other hand, is concerned with using scientific laws to manipulate natural and/or social forces to achieve some "practical" goal beyond that of understanding alone. So he uses the

---

[22] Lewis White Beck, *Philosophic Inquiry* (Englewood Cliffs, N.J.: Prentice-Hall, Inc., 1952), p. 118.

[23] For an analysis of the successive stages of scientific inquiry and the techniques appropriate to each stage, see F. S. C. Northrop, *The Logic of the Sciences and the Humanities* (New York: The Macmillan Company, 1947), Chs. I–IV.

results of scientific inquiry to construct or modify physical devices or social institutions for the betterment of human life: he builds an atomic bomb or an electrical power plant, he creates a new form of municipal government, he develops a new vaccine or antitoxin, and so on.

THE STANDARDS OF SCIENCE.    Scientists evaluate their own research and the research of others by three main standards.

*Accuracy and Measurement.*    Every investigator seeks to describe the aspect of the universe he is investigating in a way that will most accurately represent its nature and manner of operation. Accuracy is a standard not only of the physical sciences but also of all forms of human investigation. The physical sciences believe that the most accurate form of description is *measurement:* reducing all phenomena to units of similar nature that can be expressed and compared in terms of numbers. Thus, for example, they prefer to describe the temperature of a liquid as "83° C." rather than as "hot," the weight of a man as "230 pounds, 10 ounces" rather than as "heavy," and the height of a mountain as "15,352 feet, 7 inches above sea level" rather than as "high."

*Universality.*    Scientists seek generalizations that, in the manner of the law of gravitation or the law of the conservation of energy, apply to particular phenomena wherever they may be found, and not merely as they appear in some places.

*System.*    The ultimate goal of science is *systematic* theory—that is, a body of logically consistent and connected statements explaining all aspects of the universe.

### How Scientific Should Political Scientists Try to Be?

The preceding description of science is, of course, a "model"—an ideal that may be pursued and a standard by which actual research may be measured and evaluated. It is, moreover, a highly rigorous and demanding model to which the actual work of chemists, physicists, biologists, and botanists by no means always measures up.

Political scientists are widely split over the questions of how closely political science can approach this model, and whether it should even try to approach it. Most behavioralists argue that political science can become much more scientific than it now is, and that it should settle for nothing less than becoming as scientific as is possible. Most antibehavioralists dispute this. Some argue that there are no regularities in human behavior comparable to the presumed uniformities in nature. They contend that the existence of free will in human beings makes them basically unlike stars, atoms, and animals. Human behavior, accordingly, is always determined by whim, caprice, and reasoned judgment, not by compulsions beyond the individual's control. It is even insulting and immoral, some of them argue, to think of man as subject to such compulsions.

Others argue that if such regularities exist in human behavior, they are not significant for understanding relationships among men; or if they exist and are significant, they cannot be identified by means of "scientific techniques"—"what counts can't be counted," as some of them are fond of saying.[24]

The author agrees with Professor Charles Hyneman's judgment that

> there is no way of learning which side is right on this issue except by making the search for regularities and either finding some which gain general acceptance or, failing to find them, there is general agreement that further research is futile.[25]

Some political scientists, however, do not agree with even so modest a conclusion as this. They contend that even the *attempt* to find such regularities is not only futile but dangerous and morally wrong: it is doomed to failure and is therefore a waste of time; but, even more, they argue, "scientism" and "gnosticism" assume that *no* knowledge is beyond man and that *no* questions are too sacred for men to ask. This, they say, means that man puts himself in the place of God, which turns men's eyes from the eternal principles of right and wrong, and opens the door for evil to triumph in human affairs.[26]

This conflict over the proper role of science is closely related to the second major issue in current discussions of political-science methodology.

### The Problem of Values

#### The Influence of Values in Political Science

Not long ago a number of political scientists debated the desirability of erecting a "value-free" political science—that is, a purely descriptive science of what *is*, with the views of its practitioners about what *should* be totally excluded.[27]

This debate has now largely faded out, however, mainly because most political scientists recognize that, aside from whether or not it would be desirable, such a "value-free" political science is simply not possible. Every political scientist, despite what some of his students may think, is a human

---

[24] The most comprehensive attack on the behavioral position is Herbert J. Storing, ed., *Essays on the Scientific Study of Politics* (New York: Holt, Rinehart and Winston, Inc., 1962). For a sharp criticism of the volume see the critique by John H. Schaar and Sheldon S. Wolin in the *American Political Science Review*, LVII (March, 1963), 125–150. For replies by the authors, see *ibid.*, pp. 151–160.

[25] Mimeographed report, used with its author's permission.

[26] The most learned and impressive exposition of this point of view is Eric Voegelin, *The New Science of Politics* (Chicago: University of Chicago Press, 1952).

[27] Cf. the debate between William F. Whyte, "A Challenge to Political Scientists," *American Political Science Review*, XXXVII (August, 1943), 692–697; and John H. Hallowell, "Politics and Ethics," *American Political Science Review*, XXXVIII (August, 1944), 639–655.

being, and every human being, as we learned in Chapter 1, has a set of values, a body of beliefs about what is good, true, and beautiful—whether he is conscious of all of them or not. No political scientist can completely divorce his professional investigating and teaching activities from his values. This begins to become apparent when we ask, Why does anyone bother to undertake any kind of research? Different researchers no doubt have different reasons for doing so. Some may feel that research is "good for its own sake"—that is, it will interest, absorb, and otherwise entertain them; others may believe that they will make money and acquire prestige thereby; others may wish to benefit mankind; still others may wish to keep their wives from upbraiding them for laziness; and many may have a combination of these and other reasons. The point is that any researcher—including one who attempts the "value-free" variety—undertakes research because he thinks it is a *good* thing to do. If he did not think so, he would not undertake it; and he cannot determine what is and what is not a good thing to do except according to his values.

Any political scientist, moreover, wishes to investigate and teach significant matters rather than frivolous or silly or insignificant ones. His decisions about which matters are significant enough to warrant investigation and class discussion are inescapably determined by his values. For example, a professor of politics at the University of Moscow is not likely to study whether two-party systems or multiple-party systems better express the popular will. Being a devout Communist, he does not believe that the popular will in nations corrupt enough to tolerate noncommunist parties should be expressed at all. He is more likely to deal with such questions as how noncommunist governments exploit the proletariat in the interests of the capitalists, how societies may more speedily progress from capitalism to communism, the role of the Communist party in hastening things along, and so on. A professor of political science at the University of Illinois, on the other hand, is not likely to study the most effective methods of running slave-labor camps, for the whole idea of such camps is abhorrent to him.

Most political scientists in the nonauthoritarian nations are committed to the belief that democracy is the best kind of political system. Most of them, accordingly, devote their research and teaching to such matters as the mechanisms of popular control of government, the process of adjusting competing group interests, the nature and extent of popular participation in politics—in short, matters such as those we have discussed in the preceding chapters of this book.[28]

---

[28] For a perceptive discussion of how a political scientist's values affect the kinds of questions he asks and how he goes about getting answers, see Easton, *The Political System*, Ch. 9.

## How Should Values Be Treated?

Granted, then, that there is no way of totally excluding values from the study of politics and government (or anything else) even if it were desirable to do so, the question remains as to how values should be treated in political science. Professor Hyneman detects in the current professional literature the following three main treatments of values. First, the identification of what men value and the description of the value-sytems of particular societies. Second, "value-analysis": the determination of compatibilities and incompatibilities in the values held by particular men and societies, and the determination of what values support and reinforce one another or impair and hinder realization of one another. And third, the statement of the author's or the teacher's personal preferences, in which particular values are extolled or deplored, and all good men are urged to line up for or against them.[29]

Some political scientists contend that all three are proper ways to treat values, and that the best works are those which move forward along all three lines. Others, particularly those most committed to the scientific study of politics, feel that, at most, only the first is a proper enterprise for political scientists. A few argue that the third is not only a proper way to treat values but the main reason for the very existence of political science and the primary task of every political scientist who takes seriously his responsibilities to God and/or the community.

Perhaps the most widely held position, however, is that which holds the first and second to be operations proper and useful for political scientists to perform, but regards the third as quite improper. The political scientist, these writers contend, has no professional expertise in determining which social and personal goals are good and which are bad, and, therefore, no right to tell the community *in his capacity as a professional political scientist* what the good life consists of and urge it to pursue this goal and abandon that one.

## Keeping Value Preferences and Descriptive Statements Distinct

Most political scientists believe that at least some kinds of value questions are proper for professional consideration. Many of them add, however, that political science will be served best if its practitioners strive always to keep their value preferences and their descriptive statements as distinct as they possibly can. Their reasons for this conviction can be briefly summarized.

Whatever may be the views of a particular political scientist about the

---

[29] Hyneman, *The Study of Politics*, pp. 181–189.

relative professional importance of describing the politico-governmental system before him, or of urging his fellow men to preserve it or alter it, he can work toward either end most effectively if he can accurately describe and thoroughly understand that system as it is.

Now the validity of any descriptive statement he may make about these matters depends upon its correspondence to the way the system is, and not upon its correspondence to the way the political scientist would like it to be.[30] For example, to say that political bosses are bad and should be deprived of power is very different from saying that they have no power; and to say that World War III will destroy the world and should be prevented is very different from predicting that it will be prevented.

The more a political scientist permits his "should" feelings to occupy the center of his attention, moreover, the more likely he is to distort his perceptions of how things actually are. To illustrate this point we may note that in the heyday of the "progressive era" in the United States from about 1890 to about 1920, American political scientists wrote a great deal about political bosses and machines. Most of these writers were deeply repelled by both institutions, and their dislikes apparently dominated their thinking about the situation. Most of their writings emphasized how bad bosses are and contained lengthy exhortations to their readers to throw the rascals out and so forward the cause of good government. So convinced were these writers that nothing good can be said about the bosses that they could explain the latters' continuing survival in the face of the many reform movements of the time only in terms of apathy, laziness, and lack of public spirit on the part of the voters. Indeed, they talked about politics as though it were simply a contest between good men (the reformers) and bad men (the bosses)—a contest which the latter won with disheartening frequency.

This body of literature did not, however, provide an adequate explanation of *why* the bad men usually won, or, for that matter, why the good men occasionally won. Its authors took little account, for example, of the hypothesis that no man is entirely good or bad but rather a mixture of both, the proportions of which change from time to time. Their preoccupation with the badness of the bosses, in other words, estopped them from exploring even so elementary a question as whether the bosses might not be performing services which the majority of the voters regarded as necessary and which no other social or political institutions were providing—in short, whether some hypothesis other than the low moral character of the voters might not more adequately explain the phenomenon of bossism.

The moral of this story, many political scientists believe, is this: while recognizing that he cannot entirely divorce his research and teaching from his values, the student of politics must, nevertheless, try his best not to

---

[30] This position is well put by Kaplan, *op. cit.*, Ch. X.

confuse his notions of how things should be with his conceptions of how things actually are. His ability to avoid this kind of confusion is likely to play an important role in his attempts to understand how politics and government operate. Such an understanding is vital to the effective performance of whatever may be his conception of the proper functions and ultimate goals of political science.

## Political Science and the Governing of Men

Every political scientist should walk humbly with his profession, and most do. Ambitious as are the objectives of the physical sciences, the ultimate goals of political science are even more so, for they are nothing less than acquiring an understanding of government and politics that will enable men to use those agencies to realize whatever vision of the good life they may have. Since a man's reach should indeed exceed his grasp, then, however else we may criticize political science, we cannot condemn it for pursuing petty and insignificant goals.

When political scientists measure the knowledge they have against the knowledge they want—or compare their achievements with those of the natural sciences or even some of the other social sciences—they should, and most do, feel very humble indeed. Yet, even in its present state of development political science is far from being a complete failure; for surely human society is far better off for having the kind of information and understanding—which, after all, has been developed mainly by political scientists—that we have summarized in this book than it would be without it.[31]

Political science may well never become as exact or as useful a discipline as chemistry or physics or even medicine or meteorology. But surely its efforts to become *more* exact and *more* useful cannot help benefiting mankind. For, as the late, great American historian and political scientist Charles A. Beard wisely said:

> No one can deny that the idea is fascinating—the idea of subduing the phenomena of politics to the laws of causation, of penetrating to the mystery of its transformations, of symbolizing the trajectory of its future; in a word, of grasping destiny by the forelock and bringing it prostrate to earth. The very idea is worthy of the immortal gods. . . . If nothing ever comes of it, its very existence will fertilize thought and enrich imagination.[32]

---

[31] For a judicious estimate of the failures and successes of political science and a convincing conclusion that it has had a number of impressive scholarly successes and has made valuable contributions to human welfare, see Dwight Waldo, *Perspectives on Administration* (University: University of Alabama Press, 1956), Ch. I.

[32] Quoted in Easton, *The Political System*, p. vii.

# Selected Bibliography

This book has not attempted so impossible a task as trying to tell the reader everything he may ever want to know about the governing of men. It is an *introduction* to political science, and one of its main hopes is that the reader's intellectual appetites will be whetted rather than satisfied or killed. What follows is a list of some of the leading works dealing with each of the areas we have discussed to which the reader eager for more may turn. It is not, needless to say, an exhaustive list of all the works ever written on these subjects. It is intended, rather, to be a sampling of the rich literature on politics and government, and to provide at least a starting point for the further exploration of the governing of men. Limitations of space have necessitated excluding all but a few items from the voluminous and valuable periodical literature available.

## Section One: General Themes and Principal Variations

### The General Nature of Politics and Government

*PLATO, *The Republic* and *The Laws*. Many editions. These and Aristotle's works are the first systematic studies of the ideal and the actual in politics and government, and continue to be of far more than historical interest for the modern student.

ALMOND, GABRIEL A., and COLEMAN, JAMES S., eds., *The Politics of Developing Areas*. Princeton, N.J.: Princeton University Press, 1957. Influential study of comparative political institutions especially notable for theoretical scheme in first and last chapters.

BENTLEY, ARTHUR F., *The Process of Government*. Chicago: University of Chicago Press, 1908; reprinted by the Principia Press of Evanston, Illinois. The classic statement of the group structure of politics, and one of the most influential works of twentieth-century political science.

TRUMAN, DAVID B., *The Governmental Process*. New York: Alfred A. Knopf, Inc., 1951. An updating of Bentley's thesis, with particular attention to the operations of American pressure groups.

*DAHL, ROBERT A., *Modern Political Analysis*. Englewood Cliffs, N.J.: Prentice-Hall, Inc., 1963. A short but rich introduction to the study of politics by a distinguished political scientist.

*DEWEY, JOHN, *The Public and Its Problems*. New York: Holt, Rinehart and

---

\* Books marked with an asterisk are available in paperback editions.

[ 634 ]

Winston, Inc., 1927. Difficult but influential analysis of the nature of politics and government.

Downs, Anthony, *An Economic Theory of Democracy*. New York: Harper & Row, Publishers, 1957. An original and provocative model of decision making in a democracy drawn from economic theories of perfect competition.

Easton, David, *A Systems Analysis of Political Life*. New York: John Wiley & Sons, Inc., 1965. A major effort to conceptualize politics and government in terms of systems theory.

Emerson, Rupert, *From Empire to Nation*. Cambridge, Mass. Harvard University Press, 1960. A useful analysis of the emergence and problems of the developing nations.

Finer, Herman, *Theory and Practice of Modern Government*. Rev. ed. New York: Holt, Rinehart and Winston, Inc., 1949. Comprehensive survey of political problems and governmental institutions in various modern nations, both democracies and dictatorships.

*Lasswell, Harold D., *Politics, Who Gets What, When, How*. New York: McGraw-Hill Book Company, Inc., 1936. Theory of politics emphasizing value conflicts.

*————, and Kaplan, Abraham, *Power and Society*. New Haven, Conn.: Yale University Press, 1950. Abstract and difficult but important and influential theory of politics based on "power" as key concept.

MacIver, Robert M., *The Web of Government*. New York: The Macmillan Company, 1947. A distinguished sociologist considers government in its social setting.

Merriam, Charles E., *Public and Private Government*. New Haven, Conn.: Yale University Press, 1944. Analysis of similarities and differences between government and private organizations.

*Millikan, Max F., and Blackmer, Donald L. M., *The Emerging Nations*. Boston: Little, Brown & Company, 1961. Useful general survey of political problems and institutions in the developing nations.

*von der Mehden, Fred R., *Politics of the Developing Nations*. Englewood Cliffs, N.J.: Prentice-Hall, Inc., 1964. Short but useful comparative study of politics and government in developing nations.

*Wallas, Graham, *Human Nature in Politics*. Boston: Houghton Mifflin Company, 1908. Pioneer application of modern psychology to analysis of politics.

Weber, Max, *The Theory of Social and Economic Organization*, translated by A. M. Henderson and Talcott Parsons. New York: Oxford University Press, 1947. Useful collection of much of work on society and politics by one of the most influential modern writers.

## Political Novels

One of the best ways of getting a "feel" for politics by vicarious participation in it is by reading novels focusing on political conflict. The following is a short list of novels dealing with politics in various settings.

*Burdick, Eugene L., *The Ninth Wave*. Boston: Houghton Mifflin Company, 1956.

CAMUS, ALBERT. *The Plague,* translated by Stuart Gilbert. New York: Alfred
     A. Knopf, Inc., 1948.
*DOSTOYEVSKY, FYODOR, *The Possessed,* translated by Constance Garnett. New
     York: Modern Library, Inc., 1936.
FIENBURGH, WILFRED, *No Love for Johnnie.* London: Hutchinson & Co.,
     Ltd., 1959.
FORSTER, E. M., *A Passage to India.* New York: Modern Library, Inc., 1940.
*KOESTLER, ARTHUR, *Darkness at Noon,* translated by Daphne Hardy. New
     York: Modern Library, Inc., 1941.
*O'CONNOR, EDWIN, *The Last Hurrah.* Boston: Little, Brown & Company,
     1955.
*ORWELL, GEORGE, *1984.* New York: New American Library of World Litera-
     ture, Inc., 1951.
*PATON, ALAN, *Cry, the Beloved Country.* New York: Charles Scribner's Sons,
     1948.
*SILONE, IGNAZIO, *Bread and Wine,* translated by Gwenda David and Eric
     Mosbacher. New York: Harper & Row, Publishers, 1937.
*SNOW, C. P., *The Masters.* New York: The Macmillan Company, 1951.
SPRING, HOWARD, *Fame Is the Spur.* New York: The Viking Press, Inc., 1949.
*TROLLOPE, ANTHONY, *Barchester Towers.* New York: Modern Library, Inc.,
     1950.
————, *Phineas Finn.* New York: Oxford University Press, Inc., 1949.
————, *The Prime Minister.* New York: Oxford University Press, Inc., 1951.
*WARREN, ROBERT PENN, *All the King's Men.* New York: Bantam Books, Inc.,
     1950.

## Functions of Modern Governments

BUCKLEY, WILLIAM F., JR., *Up From Liberalism.* New York: Ivan Obolensky,
     Inc., 1959. Popular exposition of conservative *laissez faire.*
*DAHL, ROBERT A., AND LINDBLOM, CHARLES E., *Politics, Economics and
     Welfare.* New York: Harper & Row, Publishers, 1953. Explores interre-
     lated patterns of political and economic power, and role of government
     in modern economies.
FAINSOD, MERLE, *How Russia Is Ruled.* Rev. ed. Cambridge, Mass.: Harvard
     University Press, 1962. Most authoritative account in English of govern-
     ment and politics in the USSR.
*FINER, HERMAN, *The Road to Reaction.* Boston: Little, Brown & Company,
     1945. Defense of the welfare state and attack on Hayek and *laissez faire.*
GIRVETZ, HARRY K., *From Wealth to Welfare.* Stanford, Calif.: Stanford
     University Press, 1950. History of the rise of the welfare state.
*GRIFFITH, WILLIAM E., *The Sino-Soviet Rift.* Cambridge, Mass.: The M.I.T.
     Press, 1964. Account of the great schism in the communist movement.
HALL, P., *The Social Services of Modern England.* London: Routledge &
     Kegan Paul, Ltd., 1959. Description of English socialism.
*HAYEK, FRIEDRICH A., *The Road to Serfdom.* Chicago: University of Chicago
     Press, 1944. Defense of *laissez faire* and attack on welfare state.
KENDALL, WILLMOORE, *The Conservative Affirmation.* Chicago: Henry Reg-

nery Company, 1963. Exposition of conservative philosophy with only minor stress on *laissez faire*.

MEYER, FRANK S., *In Defense of Freedom: A Conservative Credo*. Chicago: Henry Regnery Company, 1962. Exposition of conservatism with heavy emphasis on *laissez faire*.

POLANYI, KARL, *The Great Transformation*. New York: Holt, Rinehart and Winston, Inc., 1944. Account of rise and decline of *laissez faire*.

ROBSON, WILLIAM A., *Nationalized Industry and Public Ownership*. London: George Allen & Unwin, Ltd., 1960. Analysis of English socialism in practice.

*SCHUMPETER, JOSEPH, *Capitalism, Socialism, and Democracy*. 3d ed. New York: Harper & Row, Publishers, 1950. Influential analytical discussion of different theories of role of government in economic affairs.

ZAGORIA, DONALD, S., *The Sino-Soviet Conflict, 1956–61*. New York: Atheneum Publishers, 1964. Account of origins and consequences of split in world communism.

## Forms of Government

ARENDT, HANNAH, *The Origins of Totalitarianism*. New York: Harcourt, Brace & World, Inc., 1954. Imaginative analysis of psychological and philosophical sources of nondemocratic governments.

*BARBU, ZEVEDEI, *Democracy and Dictatorship: Their Psychology and Patterns of Life*. New York: Grove Press, Inc., 1956. Psychosocial analysis of forms of government.

*BRZEZINSKI, ZBIGNIEW AND HUNTINGTON, SAMUEL P., *Political Power: USA/ USSR*. New York: The Viking Press, 1965. A stimulating discussion of how the American and Soviet governments and political processes work, with comparisons and contrasts noted at every point.

*FRIEDRICH, CARL J., AND BRZEZINSKI, ZBIGNIEW, 2d. ed. *Totalitarian Dictatorship and Autocracy*. Cambridge, Mass.: Harvard University Press, 1965. Analysis of fascist and communist dictatorships.

MACRIDIS, ROY, AND BROWN, BERNARD, *The de Gaulle Republic: Quest for Unity*. Homewood, Ill.: The Dorsey Press, Inc., 1960. Analysis of the French Fifth Republic.

MAYO, H. B., *Democracy and Marxism*. New York: Oxford University Press, 1955. Comparative analysis of communist dictatorships and democracies.

NEUMANN, SIGMUND, *Permanent Revolution*. New York: Harper & Row, Publishers, 1942. Influential analysis of fascist dictatorships.

PICKLES, DOROTHY, *The Fifth Republic*. New York: Frederick A. Praeger, Inc., 1962. Analysis of the Fifth Republic.

WILLIAMS, PHILIP, AND HARRISON, MARTIN, *De Gaulle's Republic*. London: Longmans, Green & Co., Ltd., 1960. Analysis of the Fifth Republic.

## Models of Democracy and Dictatorship

*DAHL, ROBERT A., *A Preface to Democratic Theory*. Chicago: University of Chicago Press, 1956. Develops a model of democracy and analyzes alternative models.

HATTERSLEY, A. N., *A Short History of Democracy*. London: Cambridge University Press, 1930. Describes development of democratic ideas and institutions from time of Periclean Athens.

KENDALL, WILLMOORE, *John Locke and the Doctrine of Majority Rule*. Urbana: University of Illinois Press, 1941. Explanation of origins and content of "absolute majority-rule" position.

LINDSAY, A. D., *The Essentials of Democracy*. 2d ed. London: Oxford University Press, 1942. Emphasizes role of discussion and consensus.

*———, *The Modern Democratic State*. New York: Oxford University Press, 1947. Description of some of modern democracy's leading institutions and problems.

*MAYO, H. B., *Introduction to Democratic Theory*. New York: Oxford University Press, 1960. Takes a moderate position between limited and absolute majority-rule positions.

MIMS, EDWARD, JR., *The Majority of the People*. New York: Modern Age Books, Inc., 1941. Exposition of "absolute majority-rule" position.

PENNOCK, J. ROLAND, *Liberal Democracy: Its Merits and Prospects*. New York: Holt, Rinehart and Winston, Inc., 1950. Emphasizes civil rights and restraints on majority rule as essentials of democracy.

RANNEY, AUSTIN, AND KENDALL, WILLMOORE, *Democracy and the American Party System*. New York: Harcourt, Brace & World, Inc., 1956. Chapters 1 through 3 present conception of democracy employed in this book.

*SARTORI, GIOVANNI. *Democratic Theory*. New York: Frederick A. Praeger, Inc., 1965. Perhaps the most exhaustive discussion of the various meanings of "democracy."

SIMON, YVES R., *Philosophy of Democratic Government*. Chicago: University of Chicago Press, 1939. Emphasis on philosophical beliefs necessary to sustain belief in democratic government.

STAPLETON, LAURENCE, *The Design of Democracy*. New York: Oxford University Press, 1949. Emphasizes social preconditions for democracy.

*THORSON, THOMAS LANDON, *The Logic of Democracy*. New York: Holt, Rinehart and Winston, Inc., 1962. Stimulating philosophical analysis of problems in definition and implementation of democracy.

### Section Two: The Constitutional Position of the Individual

#### The Nature of Constitutions

BAGEHOT, WALTER, *The English Constitution*. London: Oxford University Press, 1936. First published in 1867. Classic study of the "real" and "literary" constitutions of England.

JENNINGS, SIR IVOR, *The British Constitution*. 3d ed. London: Cambridge University Press, 1950. Leading modern study of written and unwritten aspects of the British constitution.

McBAIN, HOWARD L., *The Living Constitution*. First published in 1927. An illuminating pioneer analysis of the relations among the written and unwritten parts of the American constitutional system.

PEASLEE, AMOS J., ED., *Constitutions of Nations.* 2d ed., 3 vols. The Hague: Martinus Nijhoff, 1956. Compilation of written Constitutions of modern nations with tables summarizing incidence of various forms of government and governmental institutions.

STRONG, C. F., *Modern Political Constitutions.* London: Sidgwick & Jackson, Ltd., 1950. General survey.

WHEARE, K. C., *Modern Constitutions.* New York: Oxford University Press, 1951. Useful brief discussion of the nature and role of and variations in the constitutions of modern nations.

## The Doctrine of Constitutionalism

FRIEDRICH, CARL J., *Constitutional Government and Democracy.* Rev. ed. Boston: Ginn & Company, 1950. Description of theory and practice of constitutionalism in modern Europe and America.

*McILWAIN, CHARLES H., *Constitutionalism, Ancient and Modern.* Ithaca, N.Y.: Cornell University Press, 1940. Standard history of meaning and development of constitutionalism.

WORMUTH, FRANCIS D., *The Origins of Modern Constitutionalism.* New York: Harper & Row, Publishers, 1949. More recent treatment of the same subject.

## Citizenship

GETTYS, LUELLA, *The Law of Citizenship in the United States.* Chicago: University of Chicago Press, 1934. Outdated in some respects, but still the most comprehensive study available.

ROELOFS, H. MARK, *The Tension of Citizenship.* New York: Holt, Rinehart and Winston, Inc., 1957. Analysis of meaning and obligations of citizenship.

UNITED NATIONS, DEPARTMENT OF SOCIAL AFFAIRS, *A Study of Statelessness.* New York: United Nations Publication, 1949. Authoritative summary.

UNITED NATIONS LEGISLATIVE SERVICE, *Laws concerning Nationality.* New York: United Nations Publication, 1954. Authoritative summary.

## Immigration

BERNARD, WILLIAM S., ZELENY, CAROLYN, AND MILLER, HENRY, EDS., *American Immigration Policy.* New York: Harper & Row, Publishers, 1950. Most complete description, and also includes summaries of policies followed by other nations.

HANDLIN, OSCAR, *The Uprooted.* Boston: Little, Brown & Company, 1951. Study of problems and role of immigrants in American life.

KONVITZ, MILTON R., *Civil Rights in Immigration.* Ithaca, N.Y.: Cornell University Press, 1953. Critical analysis of American immigration and naturalization policy.

SCHECHTMAN, JOSEPH B., *The Refugee in the World.* New York: A. S. Barnes and Company, 1963. Most complete survey of the post-1945 refugee problem.

## Theories of Civil Liberties

*BECKER, CARL L., *The Declaration of Independence*. New York: Alfred A. Knopf, Inc., 1951. First published in 1922. Historical study of the natural-law theories underlying this famous document.

*———, *Freedom and Responsibility in the American Way of Life*. New York: Alfred A. Knopf, Inc., 1945. History and analysis of American concepts of civil liberties.

CARR, ROBERT K., *Federal Protection of Civil Rights*. Ithaca, N.Y.: Cornell University Press, 1947. Emphasizes role of government as a protector of rights.

CHAFEE, ZECHARIAH, JR., *Free Speech in the United States*. Cambridge, Mass.: Harvard University Press, 1941. Influential defense of idea of free speech.

GELLHORN, WALTER, *American Rights*. New York: The Macmillan Company, 1960. Survey of the law of civil rights.

HOCKING, WILLIAM E., *Freedom of the Press: A Framework of Principle*. Chicago: University of Chicago Press, 1947. A distinguished philosopher's theory of civil liberties.

HOLCOMBE, ARTHUR H., *Human Rights in the Modern World*. New York: New York University Press, 1947. Survey of the legal and actual status of civil liberties in various modern nations.

HOOK, SIDNEY, *Heresy, Yes—Conspiracy, No!* New York: The John Day Company, Inc., 1953. Analysis of the limits of free speech in the face of communist subversion.

HYNEMAN, CHARLES S., "Free Speech: At What Price?" *American Political Science Review*, LVI (December, 1962), 847–852. Presidential address to the American Political Science Association emphasizing necessity of limiting free speech to preserve other values.

MEIKLEJOHN, ALEXANDER, *Free Speech and Its Relation to Self-Government*. New York: Harper & Row, Publishers, 1948. Best modern exposition of "absolute" free-speech doctrine.

*MILL, JOHN STUART, *On Liberty* (1859). Many editions. Classic defense of free speech.

MILTON, JOHN, *Areopagitica* (1644). Many editions. One of the earliest and still influential arguments for free speech.

*STREET, HARRY, FREEDOM, *The Individual, and The Law*. Harmondsworth, Middlesex, England: Penguin Books, Ltd., 1963. Most comprehensive survey of civil rights in Britain.

## Civil Liberties and Church-State Relations

BOLES, DONALD E., *The Bible, Religion, and the Public Schools*. Ames: Iowa State University Press, 1961. Analysis of arguments pro and con complete separation.

FELLMAN, DAVID, *Religion in American Law*. Boston: Boston University Press, 1965. Most comprehensive recent survey of judicial decisions on church-state relations.

STOKES, ANSON P., *Church and State in the United States*. Rev. ed. New York: Harper & Row, Publishers, 1964. Useful survey complementing Fellman.

## Civil Liberties and Communist Subversion

BROWN, RALPH S., JR., *Loyalty and Security*. New Haven, Conn.: Yale University Press, 1958. Analysis of national loyalty-security program.

CHASE, HAROLD W., *Security and Liberty: The Problem of Native Communists, 1947–1955*. New York: Doubleday & Company, Inc., 1955. More comprehensive analysis of American handling of communist subversion.

O'BRIAN, JOHN LORD, *National Security and Individual Freedom*. Cambridge, Mass.: Harvard University Press, 1955. Critical evaluation of loyalty-security program.

ROURKE, FRANCIS E., *Secrecy and Publicity: Dilemmas of Democracy*. Baltimore: The Johns Hopkins Press, 1961. Analysis of problems involved in maintaining government security.

STOUFFER, SAMUEL A., *Communism, Conformity, and Civil Liberties*. New York: Doubleday & Company, Inc., 1955. A sample-survey study of American attitudes on these matters.

## Civil Liberties and Racial Discrimination

ABRAMS, CHARLES, *Forbidden Neighbors: A Study of Prejudice in Housing*. New York: Harper & Row, Publishers, 1955. Problems of discrimination in housing in the United States.

CARTER, GWENDOLEN, M., *The Politics of Inequality*. 2d ed. New York: Frederick A. Praeger, Inc., 1959. Analysis of *apartheid* in South Africa.

HANDLIN, OSCAR, *Fire-Bell in the Night: The Crisis in Civil Rights*. Boston: Little, Brown & Company, 1964. Description of crises leading to passage of American Civil Rights Act of 1964.

MARQUAND, LEOPOLD, *The Peoples and Policies of South Africa*. 3d ed. New York: Oxford University Press, 1962. More on *apartheid*.

McENTIRE, DAVIS, *Residence and Race*. Berkeley: University of California Press, 1960. Housing discrimination in the United States.

NEWBY, I. A., *Jim Crow's Defense: Anti-Negro Thought in America, 1900–1930*. Baton Rouge: Louisiana State University Press, 1965. Useful description of white-supremacy views underlying racial segregation laws.

PELTASON, JACK W., *Fifty-Eight Lonely Men*. New York: Harcourt, Brace & World, Inc., 1961. Study of desegregation of schools in the South focused on role of federal district court judges.

ROSE, ARNOLD, M., ED., "The Negro Protest," *Annals of the American Academy of Political and Social Science*, Vol. CCCLVII (January, 1965). Good collection of articles on Negro civil rights movement.

ROUX, EDWARD, *Time Longer Than Rope*. 2d ed. Madison: University of Wisconsin Press, 1964. One of best discussions of *apartheid*.

RUCHAMES, LOUIS, *Race, Jobs, and Politics: The Story of F.E.P.C.* New York: Columbia University Press, 1953. Problems of governmental regulation of discrimination in employment before the 1964 Civil Rights Act.

Nature and Determinants of Public Opinion

ALBIG, WILLIAM, *Modern Public Opinion*. New York: McGraw-Hill Book Company, Inc., 1956. Sociologist's analysis of public opinion.

*ALMOND, GABRIEL A., AND VERBA, SIDNEY, *The Civic Culture*. Boston: Little, Brown & Company, 1965. Comparative sample-survey study of political attitudes in the United States, Great Britain, West Germany, Italy, and Mexico.

*CANTRIL, HADLEY, *The Psychology of Social Movements*. New York: John Wiley & Sons, Inc., 1941. Social Psychologist's analysis of public opinion.

CENTERS, RICHARD, *The Psychology of Social Classes*. Princeton, N.J.: Princeton University Press, 1949. Social psychologist's analysis of influence of class on political attitudes.

DAVIES, JAMES C., *Human Nature in Politics*. New York: John Wiley & Sons, Inc., 1963. Focuses on individual's psychological structure as it bears upon his political behavior.

FESTINGER, LEON, *A Theory of Cognitive Dissonance*. New York: Harper & Row, Publishers, 1957. Leading exposition of theory that people's reality perceptions are affected by what they want to perceive.

HENNESSY, BERNARD C., *Public Opinion*. Belmont, Calif.: Wadsworth Publishing Company, Inc., 1965. A useful introduction to the subject incorporating much recent research.

HOMANS, GEORGE C., *The Human Group*. New York: Harcourt, Brace & World, Inc., 1950. Summary of conclusions reached by various studies of primary-group leadership and opinion formation.

HYMAN, HERBERT H., *Political Socialization*. New York: The Free Press of Glencoe, 1959. Summary of conclusions reached by various studies of how persons acquire their political attitudes from childhood on.

INKELES, ALEX, *Public Opinion in Soviet Russia*. Cambridge, Mass.: Harvard University Press, 1950. Illuminating description of meaning and manipulation of public opinion in the USSR.

KEY, V. O., JR., *Public Opinion and American Democracy*. New York: Alfred A. Knopf, Inc., 1961. Distinguished political scientist's analysis of public opinion.

LANE, ROBERT E., *Political Ideology*. New York: The Free Press of Glencoe, 1962. In-depth analysis of political attitudes of a few selected respondents.

*————, AND SEARS, DAVID O., *Public Opinion*. Englewood Cliffs, N.J.: Prentice-Hall, Inc., 1964. Useful short introduction to the subject.

Mass Communications and Public Opinion

BERELSON, BERNARD, AND JANOWITZ, MORRIS, EDS., *Reader in Public Opinion and Communication*. New York: The Free Press of Glencoe, 1950. Selected readings.

COHEN, BERNARD C., *The Press and Foreign Policy*. Princeton, N.J.: Princeton University Press, 1963. Analysis of role of press in shaping opinions affecting foreign policy.

DEUTSCH, KARL W., *The Nerves of Government: Models of Political Com-

*munication and Control.* New York: The Free Press of Glencoe, 1963. Difficult but stimulating general theory about government as a series of interconnected communications processes.

KATZ, ELIHU, AND LAZARSFELD, PAUL F., *Personal Influence.* New York: The Free Press of Glencoe, 1955. Leading exposition of the "opinion leader" phenomenon.

KLAPPER, JOSEPH T., *The Effects of Mass Communications.* New York: The Free Press of Glencoe, 1960. Leading study of impact of mass media on opinion formation.

SCHRAMM, WILBUR, ED., *The Process and Effects of Mass Communications.* Urbana: University of Illinois Press, 1954. Selected readings.

SIEPMANN, CHARLES A., *Radio, Television, and Society.* New York: Oxford University Press, 1950. Special emphasis on role in opinion formation.

THOMSON, CHARLES A. H., *Television and Presidential Politics.* Washington, D.C.: The Brookings Institution, 1956. Evaluation of impact on political campaigns.

### Public Opinion Polls

*BACKSTROM, CHARLES H., AND HURSH, GERALD D., Survey Research. Evanston, Ill.: Northwestern University Press, 1963. Useful elementary how-to-do-it manual.

GALLUP, GEORGE, *A Guide to Public Opinion Polls.* 2d ed. Princeton, N.J.: Princeton University Press, 1948. Description and defense of polls by the leading commercial practitioner.

REMMERS, H. H., *Introduction to Opinion and Attitude Measurement.* New York: Harper & Row, Publishers, 1954. Detailed description of sample-survey problems and techniques.

ROBINSON, CLAUDE E., *Straw Votes: A Study in Political Prediction.* New York: Columbia University Press, 1932. Description of the sample surveys' predecessors.

ROGERS, LINDSAY, *The Pollsters.* New York: Alfred A. Knopf, Inc., 1949. Attack on the polls' validity and utility.

*STEPHAN, FREDERICK F., AND MCCARTHY, PHILIP J., *Sampling Opinions: An Analysis of Survey Procedure.* New York: John Wiley & Sons, Inc., 1958. Detailed description of sample-survey problems and techniques.

### Representation

BURKE, EDMUND, "Address to the Electors of Bristol," in *Works,* Vol. II. Boston: Little, Brown & Company, 1871. Classic exposition of the "independence" theory of representative-constituent relations.

CLARKE, MAUDE V., *Medieval Representation and Consent.* London: Longmans, Green & Co., Ltd., 1936. Description of predemocratic theories and institutions.

COLE, G. D. H., *Guild Socialism Re-stated.* Philadelphia: J. B. Lippincott Company, 1920. Leading exposition of functional-representation position.

DE GRAZIA, ALFRED, *Public and Republic.* New York: Alfred A. Knopf, Inc., 1951. Summary and analysis of various theories of representation.

EDELMAN, MURRAY, *The Symbolic Uses of Politics*. Urbana: University of Illinois Press, 1964. Stimulating analysis of role of symbols in political conflict and representation.

FIELD, G. LOWELL, *The Syndical and Corporative Institutions of Italian Fascism*. New York: Columbia University Press, 1938. Description of fascist version of functional representation.

FORD, HENRY JONES, *Representative Government*. New York: Holt, Rinehart and Winston, Inc., 1924. Historical description of development of democratic representation.

HOGAN, JAMES, *Election and Representation*. Cork, Ireland: Cork University Press, 1945. Summary and analysis of various theories of representation.

*MILL, JOHN STUART, *Considerations on Representative Government* (1861). Many editions. Classic statement of democratic theory of representation.

NOVA, FRITZ, *Functional Representation*. Dubuque, Iowa: William C. Brown Company, 1950. Recent exposition of functional-representation view.

O'SULLIVAN, DONAL, *The Irish Free State and Its Senate*. London: Faber & Faber, Ltd., 1940. Description of a democratic attempt to incorporate functional representation in a legislative body.

PITKIN, HANNA, *The Concept of Representation*. Berkeley: University of California Press, 1966. The most comprehensive and illuminating analysis of the leading theories of representation.

ROUSSEAU, JEAN-JACQUES, *Considerations on the Government of Poland* (1778). Several editions. Classic exposition of the "mandate" theory of representative-constituent relations.

### Direct Legislation

BONJOUR, FELIX, *Real Democracy in Action*. Philadelphia: J. B. Lippincott Company, 1920. Description and praise of Swiss direct-legislation system.

GOSNELL, HAROLD F., AND SCHMIDT, MARGARET J., "Popular Law-Making in the United States, 1924–1936," in *Proceedings of the New York State Constitutional Convention, 1938*, Vol. VII. Summary of American experience with direct legislation.

MUNRO, WILLIAM B., ED., *The Initiative, Referendum, and Recall*. New York: Appleton-Century-Crofts, Inc., 1912. Leading American exposition of direct legislation.

### Suffrage

ABRAHAM, HENRY J., *Compulsory Voting*. Washington, D.C.: Public Affairs Press, 1955. Description and evaluation.

GOSNELL, HAROLD F., *Democracy, the Threshold of Freedom*. New York: The Ronald Press Company, 1948. Features analysis of theories of the right to vote.

PORTER, KIRK H., *A History of Suffrage in the United States*. Chicago: University of Chicago Press, 1918. Standard history of events leading up to the Nineteenth Amendment.

*Report of the President's Commission on Registration and Voting Participa-

*tion*. Washington, D.C.: Government Printing Office, 1963. Summary of registration and voting procedures in the United States, and recommendations for making voting easier.

## Nominations and Candidate Selection

DALLINGER, FREDERICK W., *Nominations for Elective Office in the United States*. New York: David McKay Company, Inc., 1897. Standard history of methods used before advent of direct primary.

*DAVID, PAUL T., GOLDMAN, RALPH M., AND BAIN, RICHARD C., *The Politics of National Party Conventions*. Washington, D.C.: The Brookings Institution, 1960. Comprehensive description and analysis of nominations of presidential candidates. An abridged paperback edition is also available.

HARRIS, JOSEPH P., *A Model Direct Primary System*. New York: National Municipal League, 1951. Defense of the direct-primary system and suggestions for improving it.

MERRIAM, CHARLES E., AND OVERACKER, LOUISE, *Primary Elections*. Rev. ed. Chicago: University of Chicago Press, 1928. Standard history and description of American direct primary system.

MEYER, ERNST C., *Nominating Systems*. Madison, Wis.: Published by the author, 1902. Historical survey covering various nations.

RANNEY, AUSTIN, *Pathways to Parliament*. Madison: University of Wisconsin Press, 1965. Detailed study of selection of British parliamentary candidates since 1945.

*WHITE, THEODORE, H., *The Making of the President, 1960*. New York: Atheneum Publishers, 1961. Presents an outstanding account of John F. Kennedy's successful drive for the Democratic nomination.

## Elections

BUTLER, DAVID E., *The Electoral System in Britain since 1918*. 2d ed. Oxford: Clarendon Press, 1963. Useful analysis of development of legal machinery and its effects on party fortunes.

———, *Elections Abroad*. London: Macmillan & Co., Ltd., 1959. Detailed studies of elections in France, Ireland, Poland, and South Africa, 1957–1958.

CAMPBELL, PETER, *French Electoral Systems and Elections, 1789–1957*. New York: Frederick A. Praeger, Inc., 1958. Useful historical analysis of changing French systems and their effects on distribution of power.

HARRIS, JOSEPH P., *Election Administration in the United States*. Washington, D.C.: The Brookings Institution, 1934. Outdated in several respects, but still the most comprehensive survey.

LAKEMAN, ENID, AND LAMBERT, JAMES D., *Voting in Democracies*. London: Faber & Faber, Ltd., 1955. Most comprehensive comparative study written from a pro-PR point of view.

*LEONARD, RICHARD L., *Guide to the General Election*. London: Pan Books, Ltd., 1964. Useful introduction to the conduct of British general elections.

MACKENZIE, W. J. M., *Free Elections*. New York: Holt, Rinehart and Winston, Inc., 1958. A short and well-written introduction to the problems and institutions of elections in democratic nations.

PARKER, F. R., *The Powers, Duties, and Liabilities of an Election Agent.* London: Charles Knight & Co., Ltd., 1950. Most comprehensive description of this unique British institution.

SCHOFIELD, A. N., *Parliamentary Elections.* 2d ed. London: Shaw & Sons, Ltd., 1955. Authoritative detailed exposition of British election laws.

SMITH, T. E., *Elections in Developing Countries.* New York: St. Martin's Press, 1960. General survey of procedures and problems of elections in developing nations.

WIATR, JERZY J., "Elections and Voting Behavior in Poland," in Austin Ranney, ed., *Essays on the Behavioral Study of Politics.* Urbana: University of Illinois Press, 1962, pp. 235–251. Ingenious argument about role of elections as opinion-indicators in communist nations.

### Proportional Representation

HERMENS, FERDINAND A., *Democracy or Anarchy?* Notre Dame, Ind.: The Review of Politics, 1941. Leading attack on PR.

HOAG, CLARENCE G., AND HALLETT, GEORGE H., *Proportional Representation.* New York: The Macmillan Company, 1926. For many years the standard exposition of the case for PR.

ROSS, J. F. S., *Elections and Electors.* London: Eyre & Spottiswoode, Ltd., 1955. Attack on single-member plurality systems and advocacy of single-transferable-vote system of PR.

### Voting Behavior

ALFORD, ROBERT R., *Party and Society.* Chicago: Rand McNally & Company, 1963. Comparative survey of voting patterns in the United States, Great Britain, Canada, and Australia based on polling data.

ALLARDT, ERIK, AND LITTUNEN, YRJÖ, EDS., *Cleavages, Ideologies, and Party Systems.* Turku, Finland: Transactions of the Westermarck Society, Vol. X, 1964. Essays on voting behavior in the United States, Scandinavia, and Europe.

BEAN, LOUIS H., *How to Predict Elections.* New York: Alfred A. Knopf, Inc., 1948. Aggregate data study of trends in presidential elections.

BENNEY, MARK, GRAY, A. P., AND PEAR, R. H., *How People Vote.* London: Routledge & Kegan Paul, Ltd., 1956. Sample-survey study of English voters in Greenwich constituency.

BERELSON, BERNARD, LAZARSFELD, PAUL F., AND McPHEE, WILLIAM N., *Voting.* Chicago: University of Chicago Press, 1954. Sample-survey study of the 1948 presidential election in Elmira, New York. Summary of findings by other studies of determinants of voting behavior.

*BLONDEL, JEAN, *Voters, Parties, and Leaders.* Harmondsworth, Middlesex, England: Penguin Books, Ltd., 1963. Perceptive survey of British voting patterns.

*BONE, HUGH A., AND RANNEY, AUSTIN, *Politics and Voters.* New York:

McGraw-Hill Book Company, Inc., 1963. Introductory survey of voting patterns in the United States.

BURDICK, EUGENE, AND BRODBECK, ARTHUR J., EDS., *American Voting Behavior*. New York: The Free Press of Glencoe, 1959. Collection of essays on various aspects of American voting behavior.

*CAMPBELL, ANGUS, CONVERSE, PHILIP E., MILLER, WARREN E., AND STOKES, DONALD E., *The American Voter*. New York: John Wiley & Sons, Inc., 1960. Generally regarded as the leading work on American voting behavior, based on sample-survey studies of the 1952 and 1956 presidential elections. Abridged paperback edition also available.

EWING, CORTEZ A. M., *Congressional Elections, 1896–1944*. Norman: University of Oklahoma Press, 1947. Aggregate data study.

GOSNELL, HAROLD F., *Why Europe Votes*. Chicago: University of Chicago Press, 1930. Pioneer study of voting behavior in Europe using aggregate data.

KEY, V. O., JR., *American State Politics: An Introduction*. New York: Alfred A. Knopf, Inc., 1956. Analysis of election patterns at state level, using aggregate data.

KITZINGER, UWE W., *German Electoral Politics: A Study of the 1957 Campaign*. Oxford: Clarendon Press, 1960. Study of recent German voting patterns.

LANE, ROBERT E., *Political Life*. New York: The Free Press of Glencoe, 1959. General survey of factors making for high and low participation in politics.

LIPSET, SEYMOUR MARTIN, *Political Man*. New York: Doubleday & Company, Inc., 1960. Broad comparative survey of preference and participation patterns in many countries.

LUBELL, SAMUEL, *The Future of American Politics*. New York: Harper & Row, Publishers, 1952. Widely read journalistic analysis of voting trends in the United States.

MERRIAM, CHARLES E., AND GOSNELL, HAROLD F., *Non-Voting*. Chicago: University of Chicago Press, 1924. Pioneer study of one aspect of voting behavior.

TINGSTEN, HERBERT, *Political Behavior*. London: P. S. King & Staples, Ltd., 1937. Pioneer aggregate data study by a Swedish political scientist of voting patterns in various nations.

## Democratic Political Parties

*BURNS, JAMES MACGREGOR, *The Deadlock of Democracy*. Englewood Cliffs, N.J.: Prentice-Hall, Inc., 1963. Plea for greater centralization and discipline in American parties.

COMMITTEE ON POLITICAL PARTIES OF THE AMERICAN POLITICAL SCIENCE ASSOCIATION, *Toward a More Responsible Two-Party System*. New York: Holt, Rinehart and Winston, Inc., 1950. Criticisms of American parties from responsible-parties model, and proposals for reform.

*DUVERGER, MAURICE, *Political Parties*. New York: John Wiley & Sons, Inc., 1954. Influential work by French political scientist outlining a general theory of political parties applying to many nations.

ELDERSVELD, SAMUEL J., *Political Parties*: A *Behavioral Analysis*. Chicago: Rand McNally & Company, 1964. Development of general empirical theory about local party organization based on intensive study of Detroit area.

GUTTSMAN, W. L., *The British Political Elite*. London: MacGibbon & Kee, 1963. Sociological analysis of British party leadership.

HARRISON, MARTIN, *Trade Unions and the Labour Party since 1945*. London: George Allen & Unwin, Ltd., 1960. Authoritative account of special role of unions in the Labour party's structure and policies.

*HEARD, ALEXANDER, *The Costs of Democracy*. Chapel Hill: The University of North Carolina Press, 1960. The authoritative work on American party finance.

HERRING, PENDLETON, *The Politics of Democracy*. New York: Holt, Rinehart and Winston, Inc., 1940. Classic defense of decentralized American party system.

KEY, V. O., JR., *Politics, Parties, & Pressure Groups*. 5th ed. New York: Thomas Y. Crowell Company, 1964. The most comprehensive and influential general description of the American party system.

LEISERSON, AVERY, *Parties and Politics: An Institutional and Behavioral Approach*. New York: Alfred A. Knopf, Inc., 1958. General survey of political parties with special attention to the American system.

*MCKENZIE, ROBERT T., *British Political Parties*. 2d ed. London: Mercury Books, 1963. Principal study of the British party system, with special attention to distribution of power within each.

*MICHAELS, ROBERT, *Political Parties*. New York: The Free Press of Glencoe, 1949. First published in 1915. Development of the influential "iron law of oligarchy" based on study of European socialist parties in the early twentieth century.

NEUMANN, SIGMUND, ED., *Modern Political Parties*. Chicago: University of Chicago Press, 1956. Useful descriptions of various party systems throughout the world.

*OSTROGORSKI, M. I., *Democracy and the Organization of Political Parties*. 2 vols. New York: The Macmillan Company, 1902. Classic study of the history and organization of British and American parties up to 1900, and attack on "permanent parties." Also available in abridged paperback edition.

*RANNEY, AUSTIN, *The Doctrine of Responsible Party Government*. Urbana: University of Illinois Press, 1954. Description of origins of responsible-parties position, and criticism of present expositions.

RANNEY, AUSTIN, AND KENDALL, WILLMOORE, *Democracy and the American Party System*. New York: Harcourt, Brace & World, Inc., 1956. General survey of American parties with special attention to their viability as agencies of democratic government.

SCHATTSCHNEIDER, E. E., *Party Government*. New York: Holt, Rinehart and Winston, Inc., 1942. Influential exposition of responsible-parties model and criticism of American parties.

*———, *The Semi-Sovereign People*. New York: Holt, Rinehart and Winston, Inc., 1960. A further explication of this point of view.

*Sorauf, Frank J., *Political Parties in the American System*. Boston: Little, Brown & Company, 1964. A brief but provocative analysis of American parties with reference to democratic theory.

Valen, Henry, and Katz, Daniel, *Political Parties in Norway*. London: Tavistock Publications, 1964. A general survey of the Norwegian system with an exploration-in-depth of voters, party leaders, and party organization in the Stavanger area.

Weiner, Myron, *Party Politics in India*. Princeton, N.J.: Princeton University Press, 1957. Skillful account of India's fascinating and significant party system.

Williams, Philip, *Politics in Post-War France*. 2d ed. New York: David McKay Company, Inc., 1958. The best account of parties in the Fourth Republic.

## Semi- and Nondemocratic Parties

Armstrong, John A., *The Politics of Totalitarianism*. New York, Random House, Inc., 1961. History and contemporary operation of the Communist party of the Soviet Union.

Carter, Gwendolen, M., ed., *African One-Party States*. Ithaca, N.Y.: Cornell University Press, 1962. Essays on one-party systems in some of Africa's new nations.

Crossman, R. H. S., ed., *The God that Failed*. New York: Harper & Row, Publishers, 1950. Essays by various ex-Communists explaining why they joined the party and why they left it.

Einaudi, Mario, Domenach, Jean-Marie, and Garosci, Aldo, *Communism in Western Europe*. Ithaca, N.Y.: Cornell University Press, 1951. Description of Communist parties in European democracies.

*Hodgkin, Thomas, *African Political Parties*. Harmondsworth, Middlesex, England: Penguin Books, Ltd., 1961. General analysis of African party regimes.

Kautsky, John H., *Moscow and the Communist Party of India*. New York: John Wiley & Sons, Inc., 1956. Emphasis on methods of direction from Moscow.

Rossi, Angelo, *A Communist Party in Action*. New Haven, Conn.: Yale University Press, 1949. Description of French Communist party up to 1944 by a former member.

*Scott, Robert E., *Mexican Government in Transition*. Urbana: University of Illinois Press, 1959. Illuminating description of Mexico's one-party-dominant system.

## Pressure Groups in General

Blaisdell, Donald C., *American Democracy under Pressure*. New York: The Ronald Press Company, 1957. General description of objectives and tactics of American pressure groups.

BONDURANT, JOAN V., *Conquest of Violence: The Gandhian Philosophy of Conflict*. Princeton, N.J.: Princeton University Press, 1958. Description of development of philosophy and tactics of nonviolent resistance which have become increasingly important in pressure-group politics.

*EHRMANN, HENRY W., ED., *Interest Groups on Four Continents*. Pittsburgh: University of Pittsburgh Press, 1958. Essays on pressure-group objectives and tactics in a number of nations.

FINER, SAMUEL E., *Anonymous Empire*. London: Pall Mall Press, 1958. Pressure-group objectives and tactics in Britain.

LATHAM, EARL, *The Group Basis of Politics*. Ithaca, N.Y.: Cornell University Press, 1952. General discussion of pressure politics illustrated by a case study.

MEYNAUD, JEAN, *Les Groupes de Pression en France*. Paris: Armand Colin, 1959. Objectives and tactics of pressure groups in France.

MILBRATH, LESTER W., *The Washington Lobbyists*. Chicago: Rand McNally Company, 1963. Detailed study of pressure tactics.

POTTER, ALLEN, *Organized Groups in British National Politics*. London: Faber & Faber, Ltd., 1961. Same for Britain.

ZEIGLER, HARMON, *Interest Groups in American Society*. Englewood Cliffs, N.J.: Prentice-Hall, Inc., 1964. Same for the United States, but with emphasis on general theory.

## Special Pressure Groups

BAKER, ROSCOE, *The American Legion and American Foreign Policy*. New York: Bookman Associates, 1954.

BAUER, RAYMOND A., POOL, ITHIEL DE SOLA, AND DEXTER, LEWIS ANTHONY, *American Business and Public Policy: The Politics of Foreign Trade*. New York: Atherton Press, 1963.

BELL, DANIEL, ED., *The Radical Right*. New York: Doubleday & Company, Inc., 1963.

BUNZEL, JOHN H., *The American Small Businessman*. New York: Alfred A. Knopf, Inc., 1962.

DERBER, MILTON, AND YOUNG, EDWIN, EDS., *Labor and the New Deal*. Madison: University of Wisconsin Press, 1957.

EBERSOLE, LUKE E., *Church Lobbying in the Nation's Capital*. New York: The Macmillan Company, 1951.

ECKSTEIN, HARRY, *Pressure Group Politics: The Case of the British Medical Association*. London: George Allen & Unwin, Ltd., 1960.

EHRMANN, HENRY W., *Organized Business in France*. Princeton, N.J.: Princeton University Press, 1957.

GARCEAU, OLIVER, *The Political Life of the American Medical Association*. Cambridge, Mass.: Harvard University Press, 1941.

GARFINKEL, HERBERT, *When Negroes March*. New York: The Free Press of Glencoe, 1959.

GROSSMAN, JOEL B., *Lawyers and Judges: The American Bar Association and the Politics of Judicial Selection*. New York: John Wiley & Sons, Inc., 1965.

MAASS, ARTHUR, *Muddy Waters*. Cambridge, Mass.: Harvard University Press, 1951. Study of the Army Corps of Engineers.

ODEGARD, PETER H., *Pressure Politics: The Story of the Anti-Saloon League*. New York: Columbia University Press, 1928.

WILSON, H. H., *Pressure Group: The Campaign for Commercial Television in England*. New Brunswick, N.J.: Rutgers University Press, 1961.

WILSON, JAMES Q., *Negro Politics*. New York: The Free Press of Glencoe, 1960.

ZEIGLER, HARMON, *The Politics of Small Business*. Washington, D.C.: Public Affairs Press, 1961.

### Section Four: Governmental Agencies and Processes

#### The Legislative Process

*BAILEY, STEPHEN K., *Congress Makes a Law*. New York: Columbia University Press, 1950. Congressional procedures illuminated by a case study.

BARBER, JAMES DAVID, *The Lawmakers*. New Haven, Conn.: Yale University Press, 1965. Study of freshman legislators' attitudes in Connecticut.

CAMPION, GILBERT, ET AL., *Parliament: A Survey*. London: George Allen & Unwin, Ltd., 1955. Detailed description of procedures.

*CLAPP, CHARLES L., *The Congressman: His Work As He Sees It*. Washington, D.C.: The Brookings Institution, 1963. Perceptions of members of U.S. House of Representatives.

FINER, S. E., BERRINGTON, H. B., AND BARTHOLOMEW, D., *Backbench Opinion in the House of Commons, 1955–1959*. London: Pergamon Press, 1961. Ingenious study of individual attitudes masked by party discipline.

GALLOWAY, GEORGE B., *The Legislative Process in Congress*. New York: Thomas Y. Crowell Company, 1953. Description of legal and party agencies.

GROSS, BERTRAM M., *The Legislative Struggle*. New York: McGraw-Hill Book Company, 1953. Procedures and power viewed from Bentleyan group-conflict framework.

INTER-PARLIAMENTARY UNION, *Parliaments*. New York: Frederick A. Praeger, Inc., 1961. Useful summary of formal procedures and most of world's legislatures.

JENNINGS, SIR IVOR, *Parliament*. London: Cambridge University Press, 1939. Long the leading study of the British legislature.

KEEFE, WILLIAM J., AND OGUL, MORRIS S., *The American Legislative Process: Congress and the States*. Englewood Cliffs, N.J.: Prentice-Hall, Inc., 1964. Comprehensive survey of American legislative processes at both the national and state levels.

*MATTHEWS, DONALD R., *U.S. Senators and Their World*. Chapel Hill: University of North Carolina Press, 1960. Useful study of role perceptions of members of upper U.S. house.

*MORRISON, HERBERT, *Government and Parliament: A Survey from Inside*. London: Oxford University Press, 1954. Analysis by a former Labour minister.

RICHARDS, PETER G., *Honourable Members*. London: Faber & Faber, Ltd., 1959. Description of position of British back-benchers.

STEINER, GILBERT Y., *The Congressional Conference Committee*. Urbana: University of Illinois Press, 1951. Analysis of procedures and relative power of the two houses.

WAHLKE, JOHN C., EULAU, HEINZ, BUCHANAN, WILLIAM, AND FERGUSON, LE ROY C., *The Legislative System*. New York: John Wiley & Sons, Inc., 1962. Massive and influential study of legislators in four states based on extensive interviewing.

*WHEARE, K. C., *Legislatures*. London: Oxford University Press, 1963. Introductory survey of principal features of legislatures in democratic nations.

WHITE, WILLIAM S., *Citadel: The Story of the U.S. Senate*. New York: Harper & Row, Publishers, 1957. Description of Senate's group life, and praise of it as an institution.

YOUNG, ROLAND A., *The American Congress*. New York: Harper & Row, Publishers, 1958. Effort to explain why Congress acts as it does.

————, *The British Parliament*. London: Faber & Faber, Ltd., 1962. Comparable study of British Parliament.

## The Executive Process

BINKLEY, WILFRED E., *The President and Congress*. New York: Alfred A. Knopf, Inc., 1947. Study of presidential-congressional relations in legislation.

CARTER, BYRUM E., *The Office of Prime Minister*. Princeton, N.J.: Princeton University Press, 1956. A recent study of the office.

*CORWIN, EDWARD S., *The President: Office and Powers*. 3d ed. New York: New York University Press, 1948. Comprehensive and authoritative legal analysis of the office.

DONOVAN, ROBERT J., *Eisenhower: The Inside Story*. New York: Harper & Row, Publishers, 1956. Revealing description based on private records and cabinet minutes.

JENNINGS, SIR IVOR, *Cabinet Government*. London: Cambridge University Press, 1947. Leading British study.

*NEUSTADT, RICHARD E., *Presidential Power*. New York: John Wiley & Sons, Inc., 1960. Perceptive and influential study of President's relations with his subordinates illustrated by three case studies.

RANSONE, COLEMAN B., JR., *The Office of Governor in the United States*. University: University of Alabama Press, 1956. Useful for comparisons with presidency.

*ROSSITER, CLINTON, *The American Presidency*. New York: Harcourt, Brace & World, Inc., 1956. Sprightly popular discussion.

## The Administrative Process

APPLEBY, PAUL H., *Policy and Administration*. University: University of Alabama Press, 1949. Theoretical discussion of problems by an observer with experience in administration and academic political science.

CHAPMAN, BRIAN, *The Profession of Government*. London: George Allen &

Unwin, Ltd., 1959. Comparative analysis of status and tenure of civil servants.

CHESTER, D. N., AND BOWRING, NINA, *Questions in Parliament*. London: Oxford University Press, 1962. Authoritative study of a significant institution.

GOODNOW, FRANK J., *Politics and Administration*. New York: The Macmillan Company, 1900. Classic statement of the "politics-administration" formula.

GULICK, LUTHER, AND URWICK, L., EDS., *Papers on the Science of Administration*. New York: Institute of Public Administration, 1937. Essays on the "principles" of administration.

HYNEMAN, CHARLES S., *Bureaucracy in a Democracy*. New York: Harper & Row, Publishers, 1950. Discussion of problem and methods of democratic control of administrators.

MACKENZIE, W. J. M., AND GROVE, J. W., *Central Administration in Great Britain*. London: Longmans, Green & Co., Ltd., 1957. The most comprehensive description of the British civil service

MARCH, JAMES G., AND SIMON, HERBERT A., *Organizations*. New York: John Wiley & Sons, Inc., 1958. General theory of organizational behavior with special attention to government administrative agencies.

RIDLEY, F., AND BLONDEL, JEAN, *Public Administration in France*. New York: Barnes & Noble, Inc., 1965. Leading study in English.

ROBSON, WILLIAM A., ED., *The Civil Service in Britain and France*. London: Hogarth Press., Ltd., 1956. Collection of essays useful for comparisons.

SELZNICK, PHILIP, *Leadership in Administration*. New York: Harper & Row, Publishers, 1957. Study of administration by a political sociologist.

SIMON, HERBERT A., *Administrative Behavior*. 2d ed. New York: The Macmillan Company, 1957. Influential study of administrative decision making from a nontraditional viewpoint.

———, SMITHBURG, DONALD W., AND THOMPSON, VICTOR A., *Public Administration*. New York: Alfred A. Knopf, Inc., 1950. The first major behavioral analysis of public administration.

WHITE, LEONARD D., *Introduction to the Study of Public Administration*. 4th ed. New York: The Macmillan Company, 1955. Most influential of the traditional textbook descriptions of the American system.

## Law and Court Structures

*ABRAHAM, HENRY J., *The Judicial Process*. New York: Oxford University Press, 1962. Clear and informative description of court structures and procedures in the United States, France, and Great Britain.

ALLEN, CARLETON KEMP, *Law in the Making*. 6th ed. London: Oxford University Press, 1958. Analysis of development of principal legal systems.

BECK, F., AND GOODIN, E., *Russian Purges and the Extraction of Confession*. New York: The Viking Press, Inc., 1951. Description of the "educative" functions of communist justice.

BERMAN, HAROLD J., *Justice in Russia*. Cambridge, Mass.: Harvard University Press, 1950. Analysis of Communist system of justice.

JACKSON, RICHARD N., *The Machinery of Justice in England*. London: Mac-

millan & Co., Ltd., 1960. Survey of court organization and administration
of justice in England.

*Jacob, Herbert, *Justice in America*. Boston: Little, Brown & Company, 1965.
Survey of court structures and legal systems in the United States.

Kelsen, Hans, *The Communist Theory of Law*. New York: Frederick A.
Praeger, Inc., 1955. Emphasis on theories of Marx and Engels.

Sieghart, Marguerite A., *Government by Decree: A Comparative History
of the Ordinance in English and French Law*. New York: Frederick A.
Praeger, Inc., 1950. Study of administrative law in the two nations.

von Mehren, Arthur T., *The Civil Law System*. Boston: Little, Brown &
Company, 1957. Comparative study of French and German legal systems.

Vyshinsky, Andrei Y., *The Law of the Soviet State*. New York: The Macmillan Company, 1948. Exposition of Communist conception of law and
justice.

## The Judicial Process

Cahill, Fred V., Jr., *Judicial Legislation*. New York: The Ronald Press
Company, 1952. Description of judges' policy-making role, and analysis
of "mechanical" and "legal realist" schools of jurisprudence.

Cardozo, Benjamin N., *The Nature of the Judicial Process*. New Haven,
Conn.: Yale University Press, 1921. Early anticipation of "legal realism"
by distinguished American judge and jurist.

Corwin, Edward S., *Court over Constitution*. 2d ed. New York: Peter Smith,
1950. Description and evaluation of judicial review.

*Danelski, David J., *A Supreme Court Justice Is Appointed*. New York: Random House, Inc., 1964. Study of the politics of judicial appointments.

Frank, Jerome, *Law and the Modern Mind*. New York: Brentano's, 1930.
Leading exposition of "legal realism."

Haines, Charles Grove, *The American Doctrine of Judicial Supremacy*. 2d
ed., 2 vols. Berkeley: University of California Press, 1932. Analysis and
evaluation of American system of judicial review.

*Peltason, Jack W., *Federal Courts in the Political Process*. New York:
Doubleday & Company, Inc., 1955. Influential exposition of conception
of judicial process as part of political process.

*Rosenblum, Victor G., *Law As a Political Instrument*. New York: Doubleday & Company, Inc., 1955. Case studies showing policy-making role of
judges.

Schubert, Glendon, *Constitutional Politics*. New York: Holt, Rinehart and
Winston, Inc., 1960. Most comprehensive behavioral analysis of judicial
process.

————, ed., *Judicial Decision-Making*. New York: The Free Press of Glencoe,
1963. Collection of essays in behavioral analysis of judicial process.

## Local Government

Adrian, Charles R., *Governing Urban America*. New York: McGraw-Hill
Book Company, Inc., 1955. General description.

Brownell, Baker, *The Human Community*. New York: Harper & Row,

Publishers, 1950. Theory of local government as a key institution in a healthy democracy.

CHAPMAN, BRIAN, *Introduction to French Local Government*. London: George Allen & Unwin, Ltd., 1953. Major study in English.

CHESTER, D. N., *Central and Local Government, Financial and Administrative Relations*. London: Macmillan & Co., Ltd., 1951. Survey of "intergovernmental relations" in Great Britain.

CLARKE, JOHN J., *The Local Government of the United Kingdom*. 15th ed. London: Sir Isaac Pitman & Sons, Ltd., 1956. Most comprehensive description.

HARRIS, G. MONTAGU, *Comparative Local Government*. London: Hutchinson's Universal Library, 1948. Description of structure and problems of local government in various nations.

JACOB, HERBERT, AND VINES, KENNETH N., eds., *Politics in the American States*. Boston: Little, Brown and Company, 1965. Comparative analysis of various aspects of state government.

*KAUFMAN, HERBERT, *Politics and Policies in State and Local Governments*. Englewood Cliffs, N.J.: Prentice-Hall, Inc., 1963. Imaginative and well-written introductory survey.

KNEIER, CHARLES M., *City Government in the United States*. 3d ed. New York: Harper & Row, Publishers, 1957. General description.

LOCKARD, DUANE, *The Politics of State and Local Government*. New York: The Macmillan Company, 1963. General description with emphasis on politics.

MORGAN, ARTHUR E., *The Small Community: Foundation of Democratic Life*. New York: Harper & Row, Publishers, 1942. Importance of local self-government for democracy.

ROBSON, WILLIAM A., ED., *Great Cities of the World: Their Government, Politics, and Planning*. New York: The Macmillan Company, 1954. Description of various metropolitan governments in various nations.

SNIDER, CLYDE F., *American State and Local Government*. 2d ed. New York: Appleton-Century-Crofts, Inc., 1965. Most complete structural survey.

Federalism

ANDERSON, WILLIAM, *The Nation and the States: Rivals or Partners?* Minneapolis: University of Minnesota Press, 1955. Argument by a distinguished political scientist that the two levels need not be in competition.

FRIEDRICH, CARL J., AND BOWIE, ROBERT R., EDS., *Studies in Federalism*. Boston: Little, Brown & Company, 1954. Essays on various aspects of federalism.

MACMAHON, ARTHUR W., ED., *Federalism: Mature and Emergent*. New York: Doubleday & Company, Inc., 1955. Essays on practice and problems of federalism in old and new nations.

*Report of the Commission on Governmental Relations*. Washington, D.C.: Government Printing Office, 1955. Report on the proper distribution of functions between the national and state governments.

*RIKER, WILLIAM H., *Federalism: Origin, Operation, Significance*. Boston:

Little, Brown & Company, 1964. A fresh look at the nature and consequences of federalism.

*WHEARE, K. C., *Federal Government*. 4th ed. London: Oxford University Press, 1964. More formal description and analysis by leading British scholar.

## Section Five: International Relations

### International Politics

CLAUDE, INIS L., JR., *Power and International Relations*. New York: Random House, Inc., 1963. Analysis of basic structure of international politics as it affects chances for maintaining peace.

DEUTSCH, KARL W., *Nationalism and Social Communication*. New York: John Wiley & Sons, Inc., 1953. Analysis of effects of nationalism on attitudes and communication.

HAAS, ERNST B., AND WHITING, ALLEN S., *Dynamics of International Relations*. New York: McGraw-Hill Book Company, Inc., 1956. Emphasizes social-psychological categories for explaining international politics.

HAYES, CARLTON J. H., *The Historical Evolution of Modern Nationalism*. New York: The Macmillan Company, 1931. Origins of the state system.

*KAPLAN, MORTON A., *System and Process in International Relations*. New York: John Wiley & Sons, Inc., 1964. Highly abstract theorizing about international relations, using theory of games as an explanatory tool.

KOHN, HANS, *Nationalism: Its Meaning and History*. New York: The Macmillan Company, 1955. Analysis of the psychological basis of the state system.

MANNING, C. W., *The Nature of International Society*. New York: John Wiley & Sons, Inc., 1962. General survey from behavioral point of view.

MORGENTHAU, HANS J., *Politics Among Nations*. 3d ed. New York: Alfred A. Knopf, Inc., 1962. Description and explanation in terms of "power" as basic orienting concept.

ORGANSKI, A. F. K., *World Politics*. New York: Alfred A. Knopf, Inc., 1961. General survey based on power concept.

VAN DYKE, VERNON, *International Politics*. New York: Appleton-Century-Crofts, Inc., 1957. General description.

### Principles and Processes of Foreign Policy

*ALMOND, GABRIEL A., *The American People and Foreign Policy*. New York: Harcourt, Brace & World, Inc., 1950. Description of pressures on making of foreign policy in the United States.

BELOFF, MAX, *Foreign Policy and the Democratic Process*. Baltimore: The Johns Hopkins Press, 1955. Discussion of problems of making foreign policy in a democracy.

BUCK, PHILLIP W., AND TRAVIS, MARTIN B., JR., *Control of Foreign Relations in Modern Nations*. New York: W. W. Norton & Company, Inc., 1957. Description of governmental machinery for making and administering foreign policy in various nations.

COHEN, BERNARD C., *The Political Process and Foreign Policy: The Making of the Japanese Peace Settlement.* Princeton, N.J.: Princeton University Press, 1957. A carefully analyzed case study illuminating the general process.

COOK, THOMAS I., AND MOOS, MALCOLM, *Power Through Purpose: The Realism of Idealism as a Basis for Foreign Policy.* Baltimore: The Johns Hopkins Press, 1955. Exposition of the "idealist" view.

*DAHL, ROBERT A., *Congress and Foreign Policy.* New York: Harcourt, Brace & World, Inc., 1950. Roles of Congress, the President, and civil servants in making foreign policy.

HILSMAN, ROGER, *Strategic Intelligence and National Decisions.* New York: The Free Press of Glencoe, 1956. Role of intelligence operations in making foreign policy.

KENNAN, GEORGE F., *Realities of American Foreign Policy.* Princeton, N.J.: Princeton University Press, 1954. Exposition of the "realist" view.

KNORR, KLAUS, *The War Potential of Nations.* Princeton, N.J.: Princeton University Press, 1956. Analysis of elements and evaluation of national power.

MACRIDIS, ROY C., *Foreign Policy in World Politics.* 2d ed. Englewood Cliffs, N.J.: Prentice-Hall, Inc., 1962. Process of making foreign policy in various nations.

MARSHALL, CHARLES B., *The Limits of Foreign Policy.* New York: Holt, Rinehart and Winston, Inc., 1954. Analysis of problems of making foreign policy.

McCAMY, JAMES L., *Conduct of the New Diplomacy.* New York: Harper & Row, Publishers, 1964. Description of administration of foreign policy.

MORGENTHAU, HANS J., *In Defense of the National Interest.* New York: Alfred A. Knopf, Inc., 1951. Exposition of the "realist" view.

RIKER, WILLIAM H., *The Theory of Political Coalitions.* New Haven, Conn.: Yale University Press, 1962. Application of game theory to political conflict.

SNYDER, RICHARD C., BRUCK, H. W., AND SAPIN, BURTON, EDS., *Foreign Policy Decision Making: An Approach to the Study of International Politics.* New York: The Free Press of Glencoe, 1962. Essays on process and problems of making foreign policy.

SPROUT, HAROLD, AND SPROUT, MARGARET, EDS., *Foundations of National Power.* Princeton, N.J.: D. Van Nostrand Company, Inc., 1951. Essays on elements and evaluation of national power.

WESTERFIELD, H. B., *Foreign Policy and Party Politics.* New Haven, Conn.: Yale University Press, 1956. Analysis of problems of maintaining a "bipartisan" foreign policy after World War II.

WOLFERS, ARNOLD, AND MARTIN, LAWRENCE W., *The Anglo-American Tradition in Foreign Policy.* New Haven, Conn.: Yale University Press, 1956. Historical-comparative analysis.

## The Costs and Causes of War

*BROWN, HARRISON, AND REAL, JAMES, *Community of Fear.* Santa Barbara,

Calif.: Center for the Study of Democratic Institutions, 1960. Popular short discussion of probable effects of thermonuclear war.

CANTRIL, HADLEY, ED., *Tensions That Cause Wars*. Urbana: University of Illinois Press, 1951. Essays emphasizing social-psychological causes of war.

GLASSTONE, SAMUEL, ED., *The Effects of Nuclear Weapons*. Rev. ed. Washington, D.C.: The United States Atomic Energy Commission, 1962. Authoritative description of effects of thermonuclear weapons.

KAHN, HERMAN, *On Thermonuclear War*. Princeton, N.J.: Princeton University Press, 1961. "Thinking about the unthinkable."

NEF, JOHN U., *War and Human Progress*. Cambridge, Mass.: Harvard University Press, 1950. Analysis of effects of past wars on human welfare.

ROBBINS, LIONEL, *The Economic Causes of War*. London: Jonathan Cape, Ltd., 1939. As indicated by the title.

SHOTWELL, JAMES T., *War as an Instrument of National Policy*. New York: Harcourt, Brace & World, Inc., 1929. Political analysis of causes of war.

WRIGHT, QUINCY, *A Study of War*. 2 vols. Chicago: University of Chicago Press, 1942. Most comprehensive study.

## Approaches to Peace

ALKER, HAYWARD R., AND RUSSETT, BRUCE M., *World Politics in the General Assembly*. New Haven, Conn.: Yale University Press, 1965. Voting patterns in the UN.

BARR, STRINGFELLOW, *Citizens of the World*. New York: Doubleday & Company, Inc., 1953. Exposition of the world-government view.

BECHHOEFER, BERNHARD, *Postwar Negotiations for Arms Control*. Washington, D.C.: The Brookings Institution, 1961. Discussion of problems of disarmament.

BRIERLY, J. L., *The Law of Nations*. 6th ed. Oxford: Clarendon Press, 1963. Contains both summaries of rules and description of general nature and role of international law.

CARR, E. H., *The Conditions of Peace*. New York: The Macmillan Company, 1944. General discussion.

CLAUDE, INIS L., JR., *Swords into Plowshares*. 3d ed. New York: Random House, Inc., 1964. Analysis of theories and results of various approaches to peace within the state system.

*COUSINS, NORMAN, *In Place of Folly*. New York: Harper & Row, Publishers, 1961. Exposition of world-government position.

*DEUTSCH, KARL W., *Political Community at the International Level: Problems of Definition and Measurement*. New York: Doubleday & Company, Inc., 1954. Analysis of methodological problems involved in assessing the preconditions for world government.

DE VISSCHER, CHARLES, *Theory and Reality in Public International Law*. Princeton, N.J.: Princeton University Press, 1957. Analysis of role of international law.

EICHELBERGER, CLARK M., *UN: The First Twenty Years*. New York: Harper & Row, Publishers, 1965. Most favorable appraisal of UN's record.

Gross, Ernest A., *The United Nations: Structure for Peace*. New York: Harper & Row, Publishers, 1962. Judicious appraisal.

Hovet, Thomas, Jr., *Bloc Politics in the United Nations*. Cambridge, Mass.: Harvard University Press, 1960. Voting patterns in the UN General Assembly.

Kaplan, Morton A., and Katzenbach, Nicholas de B., *The Political Foundations of International Law*. New York: John Wiley & Sons, Inc., 1961. Analyzes origins and limitations.

Mangone, Gerard J., *The Idea and Practice of World Government*. New York: Columbia University Press, 1951. General analysis of the idea of world government.

————, *A Short History of International Organization*. New York: McGraw-Hill Book Company, Inc., 1954. Useful introduction to this approach to peace.

Manly, Chesly, *The UN Record*. Chicago: Henry Regnery Company, 1955. Denunciation of UN as a subversive force.

Spanier, John W., and Nogee, Joseph L., *The Politics of Disarmament*. New York: Frederick A. Praeger, Inc., 1962. Analysis of postwar problems in disarmament.

Streit, Clarence K., *Freedom against Itself*. New York: Harper & Row, Publishers, 1954. Exposition of world-federalist position.

Walters, F. P., *A History of the League of Nations*. 2 vols. New York: Oxford University Press, 1952. Most comprehensive description.

Zimmern, Sir Alfred E., *The League of Nations and the Rule of Law*. New York: The Macmillan Company, 1939. Sympathetic evaluation.

### Section Six: The Current State of Political Science

#### The Emergence and Present Status of Political Science

Anderson, William, *Man's Quest for Political Knowledge: The Study and Teaching of Politics in Ancient Times*. Minneapolis: University of Minnesota Press, 1964. Survey of empirical analyses of politics from ancient Greeks to Middle Ages.

*Contemporary Political Science*. Paris: UNESCO Publication No. 426, 1950. Essays describing status of political science in various nations in immediate post-war period; now out of date in many respects.

Duverger, Maurice, *An Introduction to the Social Sciences*. New York: Frederick A. Praeger, Inc., 1964. Contains useful history of emergence of political science as a distinct discipline.

Haddow, Anna, *Political Science in American Colleges and Universities, 1636–1900*. New York: Appleton-Century-Crofts, Inc., 1939. As indicated by the title.

Robson, William A., *The University Teaching of Social Sciences: Political Science*. Leiden: Published for UNESCO by A. W. Sijthoff, 1954. Useful short survey of academic status of political science in various nations.

Somit, Albert, and Tanenhaus, Joseph, *American Political Science: A Pro-*

*file of a Discipline*. New York: Atherton Press, 1964. A careful and illuminating sample-survey study of political scientists' attitudes about the discipline.

## The Scope and Methods of Political Science

*ALKER, HAYWARD R., JR., Mathematics & Politics*. New York: The Macmillan Company, 1965. Introductory survey of uses of mathematical methods in analysis of political behavior.

BECK, LEWIS WHITE, *Philosophic Inquiry*. Englewood Cliffs, N.J.: Prentice-Hall, Inc., 1952. Analysis of the presuppositions and techniques of various forms of human inquiry.

CATLIN, GEORGE E. G., *The Science and Method of Politics*. New York: Alfred A. Knopf, Inc., 1927. Pioneer systematic analysis of politics emphasizing power as orienting concept.

————, *Systematic Politics: Elementa Politica et Sociologica*. Toronto: University of Toronto Press, 1962. Recent reflections on the same subjects.

*CHARLESWORTH, JAMES C., ED., The Limits of Behavioralism in Political Science*. Philadelphia: American Academy of Political and Social Science, 1962. Essays by both pro- and antibehavioralists.

COHEN, MORRIS R., *Reason and Nature*. New York: Harcourt, Brace & World, Inc., 1931. Influential discussion of scientific method in physical and social sciences.

CRICK, BERNARD, *The American Science of Politics*. Berkeley: University of California Press, 1959. Attack upon the behavioralist approach.

EASTON, DAVID, *The Political System*. New York: Alfred A. Knopf, Inc., 1953. Survey of contemporary political science emphasizing need for and lack of broad systematic theory.

————, *A Framework for Political Analysis*. Englewood Cliffs, N.J.: Prentice-Hall, Inc., 1965. General scheme for understanding politics, based on systems theory.

*EULAU, HEINZ, The Behavioral Persuasion*. New York: Random House, Inc., 1963. Urbane introduction to the behavioral point of view.

HYNEMAN, CHARLES S., *The Study of Politics*. Urbana: University of Illinois Press, 1959. Most comprehensive description of the activities of American political scientists.

KAPLAN, ABRAHAM, *The Conduct of Inquiry*. San Francisco: The Chandler Publishing Company, 1964. Leading recent survey of behavioral framework for study of social affairs.

LASSWELL, HAROLD D., *The Future of Political Science*. New York: Atherton Press, 1963. Survey of present state and future possibilities for political science by one of its most distinguished practitioners.

NORTHROP, F. S. C., *The Logic of the Sciences and the Humanities*. New York: The Macmillan Company, 1947. Analysis of the presuppositions and techniques of various forms of human inquiry.

RANNEY, AUSTIN, ED., *Essays in the Behavioral Study of Politics*. Urbana: University of Illinois Press, 1962. Essays on the achievements and problems of behavioral analysis in various areas of political science.

SCHAAR, JOHN H., AND WOLIN, SHELDON S., "Essays on the Scientific Study of Politics: A Critique," *American Political Science Review*, LVII (March, 1963), 125–150. A sharp attack on the Storing volume. The latter authors' rejoinders appear in the same issue.

STORING, HERBERT J., ED., *Essays on the Scientific Study of Politics*. New York: Holt, Rinehart and Winston, Inc., 1962. Most concentrated attack upon the behavioral point of view.

VAN DYKE, VERNON, *Political Science: A Philosophical Analysis*. Stanford, Calif.: Stanford University Press, 1960. Appraisal of political science methodology from moderate behavioral point of view.

VOEGELIN, ERIC, *The New Science of Politics*. Chicago: University of Chicago Press, 1952. Attack on positivism, "scientism," and moral relativism in current political science.

YOUNG, ROLAND, ED., *Approaches to the Study of Politics*. Evanston, Ill.: Northwestern University Press, 1958. Essays on various aspects of the study of politics, mostly from a behavioral point of view.

# Index

Abraham, Henry J., 288n, 491n
Access, 374
Acton, Lord, 538
Adams, John, 435
Adenauer, Konrad, 319
"Administocracy," problem and attempted solution, 475–481
Administration, public, administrative law, 487; formal functions, 463–465; "principles" of, 462–463, 470; problem of external control and responsibility, 476–482; separation of "staff" and "line," 462–463; theory of separation from "politics," 469–472, 475; types of agencies, 460–463; see also Civil service
Administrative courts, 481–482, 491
Administrators, advantages over elected officials, 472–473; conception of "responsibility" of, 476–477; control by courts, 481–482; control by elected officials, 478–480; control by ombudsman, 482; distinguished from "executives," 458–459; partisan activities permitted, 465–466; policy making by, 472–475; as "representatives," 477–478; as targets of pressure groups, 474
Adrian, Charles R., 524n, 527
Afro-Asian nations, 604–605
Agitators, Russian, 226–228, 307
Agitprop, Russian, 227, 247, 512
Agricultural pressure groups, 369–370
Albania, 61, 66, 99, 111, 117n
Albig, William, 233, 234n, 238n, 240n
Alford, Dale, 423n
Alford, Robert R., 222n, 320n
Algeria, 30, 66, 134
Alker, Hayward R., Jr., 604n
Aliens, 134–140
Allardt, Erik, 320n, 346n
Allegiance, 127
Alliances, international, 583
Almond, Gabriel A., 28n, 30n, 211, 212n, 344n, 362n, 367n, 560n
Amendments, constitutional, 119–120, 122, 400, 540–541
American Association of University Professors, 370, 380
American Bar Association, 370, 507
American Civil Liberties Union, 372
American Farm Bureau Federation (AFBF), 369, 373, 381
American Federation of Labor-Congress of

Industrial Organization (AFL-CIO), 368, 369, 373, 376, 380, 381, 383, 402, 417
American Heritage Foundation, 286
American Institute of Architects, 370, 373, 381
American Institute of Public Opinion, 248, 249, 250
American Legion, 371, 380
American Medical Association, 11, 332, 374, 381
American Petroleum Institute, 368
American Political Science Association, 289, 370, 457, 614, 617, 619, 623
American Veterans Committee, 371, 380
Amicus curiae, 507
Anarchy, in domestic politics, 21, 34, 153, 161; in international politics, 38, 555–556
Anderson, Charles W., 72
Anderson, Clinton, 415
Anderson, William, 543n, 615n
Anti-Saloon League, 372
Apartheid, in South Africa, 17, 198–201
Apoliticals, 311
Appellate courts, 493–494
Apportionment, legislative, 266–268
Aquinas, St. Thomas, 615
Arendt, Hannah, 99n
Argentina, conflict with the United States, 567; constitution, 63, 66, 74; immigration, 146–147; nationality laws, 129, 133
Aristocracy, 64, 90
Aristotle, 3, 615, 616
Armstrong, John A., 52n
Arnold, Thurman, 505
Aron, Raymond, 186n
Arrondissements, 531
Aspaturian, Vernon, 308n, 536n
Association of American Railroads, 368, 375
Atomic Energy Commission, 588
Attlee, Clement, 183
Austin, John, 486
Australia, compulsory voting, 287; constitution, 66, 120; court system, 488; electoral system, 273, 275, 287, 295; federalism, 63; immigration, 134, 140, 141, 145–146; organization of Senate, 260, 272; political parties, 353
"Australian ballot," 295

Austria, 66, 273, 403, 429
Authority, 22–23, 35–36
Autocracy, 64, 65, 90; *see also* Dictatorship

Backstrom, Charles H., 251n
Bain, Richard C., 345n
Bakunin, Michael, 555
Balance of power, *see* Peace; Power
Ballots, 295, 299
Barber, James David, 420n
Barker, Ernest, 257, 307n
Barr, Stringfellow, 607
Bartholomew, D., 418n
Beard, Charles A., 633
Bechhoefer, Bernhard G., 586n
Beck, James M., 483n
Beck, Lewis White, 627n
Becker, Carl, 85, 149n
Beer, Samuel H., 385
Behavior, drives affecting human, 214;
   political, 625–626; voting, *see* Voting
   behavior
Behavioralism, 625–629
Belgium, compulsory voting, 287; constitu-
   tion, 63, 66, 120; court system, 491;
   elections, 273, 287
Belief systems, 77–78
Beloff, Max, 397n
Ben Bella, Ahmed, 362
Bennett, John W., 222n
Benney, Mark, 319n
Bentley, Arthur F., 373n
Berelson, Bernard R., 215, 243n, 245n,
   246
Berman, Daniel M., 410n
Berman, Harold J., 511, 512
Bernstein, Marver H., 302n
Berrington, H. B., 418n
Betancourt, Romulo, 209, 318
Bevan, Aneurin, 355
Bevin, Ernest, 473
Bicameralism, 403–405
Bills, legislative, main steps in passing,
   407–410; types of, 407
Bills of rights, *see* Civil rights; Constitutions
Blackmer, Donald L. M., 30n
Blackstone, William, 499
Blair, George S., 300n
Blaisdell, Donald C., 367n, 373n, 474n
"Block vote" system, 297
Blondel, Jean, 74n, 317n, 345n, 466n
Bondurant, Joan V., 378n
Bone, Hugh A., 310n
Bonjour, Felix, 280n
Borough government, British, 528
Bowring, Nina, 481n
Boyer, William W., 475n
Brady, Alexander, 197n
Brandt, Willy, 50
Brazil, constitution, 61, 66, 117, 159; elec-
   tions and nominations, 273, 286, 293;
   immigration, 146–147
Brezhnev, Leonid, 52, 225
Bribery, 387
Brierly, J. L., 138n, 591n, 595

Britain, *see* United Kingdom
British Broadcasting Corporation, 239,
   461, 480
Brodbeck, Arthur J., 210n
Brogan, D. W., 53n, 76n
"Broker parties," 341–345
*Brown v. Board of Education of Topeka*,
   123, 193, 195, 504, 508
Brown, Bernard E., 176n
Brown, Harrison, 578n
Brown, J. A., Jr., 226n
Brownell, Baker, 517
Brownlow, Louis, 440n
Bruck, H. W., 560n
Bryce, James, 107, 617
Brzezinski, Zbigniew, 99n, 100n, 356n
Buchanan, William, 420
Buck, Philip, 418n, 462n
Buckland, W. W., 489n
Buckley, William F., 54n
Bulgaria, 61, 66, 117
Bunche, Ralph, 614
Burdick, Eugene, 210n
Bureau of Internal Revenue, 474
Bureaucracy, *see* Administration; Adminis-
   trators; Civil Service
Burgess, John W., 393, 617
Burke, Edmund, 47, 107, 264, 270
Burns, James M., 168n, 180n, 182n, 254
Business pressure groups, 53, 367–368
Butler, D. E., 266n
Butler, R. A., 431
Byrd, Harry F., 115n, 417

Cabinet, American, 438; British, 447–448
Caesar, Julius, 99
Cahill, Fred V., Jr., 498n, 500n, 502n
Caligula (Gaius Caesar), 100
Calvin, John, 174
Campaigns, effect on voters, 247; importance of, 334; purposes and techniques,
   376; in USSR, 307
Campbell, Angus, 211n, 212n, 216n, 312n,
   313n, 314n, 316n, 317n, 318n, 323n,
   326n, 328, 329
Canada, bilingual nature, 27; constitution,
   63, 66, 115–116, 118, 123; court system,
   488, 541; elections and nominations,
   271, 273, 275, 276, 292; federalism, 63,
   272, 537, 538, 540; immigration policy,
   134, 141, 145–146; organization of
   Senate, 261, 272; radio and television
   in, 239–240
Candidate orientation, 318–319
Carter, Byrum E., 446n, 449n
Carter, Gwendolyn M., 197n, 201, 362n
Carter, James C., 499
Case, Francis, 388
Catlin, George, 624
Caucus, legislative, 416; nominating, 291
"Cease-and-desist" order, 464
Cecil, Robert, 449
Centers, Richard, 222n
Centralization, in political parties, 345–
   347

Ceylon, 66, 273, 275
Chapman, Brian, 466n, 530n
Chapman, D. E., 287
Chapple, Eliot D., 32n
Charlesworth, James C., 459n, 626n
Chase, Harold W., 180n
Checks and balances, 397; see also Separation of powers
Chester, D. N., 481n
Chiang Kai-shek, 575
Chiefs of state, defined, 276; functions, 430–432; principal types, 428–429; selection, 62–63
Chile, 30, 66, 273, 293
China, Communist, boundary dispute, 25; coercive measures, 21, 40; foreign policy, 566; government of, 37, 61, 67, 99; population, 75n
Christian Democratic parties (Catholic), 343, 344, 345, 350–351n
Christoph, James B., 466n
Churches, separation from state, 174–177; tax exemption to, 175
Churchill, Winston, 4, 319, 580
Citizenship, acquisition, 128–131; dual, 132–133; meaning, 126–128; termination, 131–132
City government, see Borough government; Municipal government
City-states, 127–129
Civil law, the, 488–489
Civil rights, American judicial tests for limits of, 168–169; conflicts among groups, 169–170; definition, 150; government as defender of, 165–166; government as enemy of, 160–163; incidence of, in modern constitutions (table), 160; nongovernmental threats to, 163–165; nonviolence, 378–380; philosophical foundations of, 150–157; political conflict over, 170–171; types of, 157–159
Civil Rights Act of 1964, 36, 166, 195–197, 443
Civil service, American and British loyalty and security programs in, 181, 182–184; control by courts, 481–482; control by elected officials, 478–480; merit system, patronage and spoils in, 468–469; place of, in modern democracy, 458–459; politics and, 465–466; "representative" nature, 477–478; strikes and unions, 466–467
Civil Service Commission, 468
Civil War, American, 517, 549, 608
Claire, Guy S., 475
Clapp, Charles L., 420n
Classes, social, 217–218
Claude, Inis L., Jr., 548n, 582n, 585, 586, 587, 589, 596, 603n, 608, 609
"Clear and present danger" test, 168
Cloture, legislative, 413–415
Code civil, 489
Coercion, 39–40
Cohen, Bernard C., 560n

Cohen, Morris R., 626n
Cohesion, in political parties, 348–349, 416–417; in pressure groups, 381–383
Cold war, 556, 559
Cole, G. D. H., 261
Coleman, James S., 28n, 30n, 344n, 362n, 367n
Collective security, general, 584–586; in the UN, 600–601
Collegial executives, 430
Cominform, 360
Comintern, 360
Committee on Political Education (COPE), 377, 383
Committees, legislative, 408, 410–413; see also Legislatures
Common law, 129, 487–488
Commons, House of, see Legislatures; United Kingdom
Communes, French, 530
Communication, definition and general role, 233; elements of, 233–235; face-to-face media, 242–243, 245; influence on public opinion, 243–247; mass media, 235–242; world distribution of facilities (figures), 238
Communism, aggression of, 5–6; American methods of handling subversion, 179–182; British methods of handling subversion, 182–184; Chinese, 40, 50, 52, 178, 473; concept of "class," 222; concept of "democracy," 85–86; conception of public opinion, 226–231; economy under, 76; French method of handling subversion, 185–187; ideology, 224; justice, 512, 515; method of handling, in South Africa, 200; objective and methods, 37, 177–179; relation to socialism, 50; role of criticism, 224–226; role of parties in, 358–360; Russian, 50, 52, 178, 306–307, 358, 359; similarities with fascism, 360, 361
Communist Control Act (1954), 181
Communist parties, American, 178, 179; British, 182; Chinese, 333; French, 178, 360; general, 50, 178, 339, 357; Russian, 50, 177, 306–307, 358–359, 510
Community, membership in, 89–90; as prerequisite to a government, 609
Compromise, in politics, 38–39
Compulsory voting, 286–288
Comte, Auguste, 618
Conceptualization, politics and, 216
Confederation, 64, 538
Confédération Française des Travailleurs (CFTC), 368, 369
Confédération Génerale du Travail (CGT), 185, 368, 369, 377
Confédération Génerale des Viniculteurs, 368
Confédération Nationale du Patronat Français, 368
"Confidence," parliamentary, 400
Conflict, consensus and, 209–210; domestic, 7–11, 31–32, 46; international, 551

Conformity, pressures for, in social groups, 242
Congress, *see* Legislatures; United States
Congress of Racial Equality (CORE), 191, 366, 372
*Conseil d'Etat,* 491
*Conseil Supérieur de la Magistrature,* 498
Consensus, 77, 209–210
Conservative party, British, 53, 73, 337–338, 345
Conservatism, 351–352
Constituencies, legislative, 272–275, 297–298
Constituents' relations with representatives, 268–271, 422–423
"Constitutional rights," 171
Constitutionalism, definition, 108; distinguished from democracy, 97; origins, 112, 161–162; present status, 162
Constitutions, amendments to, 119–120, 122; changing, 121–124; checks and balances in, 397; concepts of, 106–108; contents of, 116–120; definition, 107–108; "flexible" and "rigid," 119–120; interpretation of, 502; judicial review of, 110; origin of, 120–121; power of legislatures over, 400; relation to ordinary law, 108–110; veto provisions, 79; written and unwritten, 107, 111
Consuls, 563–564
Conventions, nominating, 291–292
Converse, Philip E., 211n, 212n, 216n, 259n, 312n, 313n, 314n, 315n, 316n, 326n
Cook, Thomas I., 558n
Cooley, Thomas M., 499n
Coon, Carleton S., 32n
"Corporate state," 262
Corporations, government, 461
*Cortes,* 396
Corwin, Edward S., 439n, 443n
Costa Rica, 67, 273, 275
Cotter, Cornelius P., 340n
Council of Five Hundred, 395
County government, American, 521
*Coup d'etat,* 378
Courts, civil and criminal, 492; conflict with President, 445; emergence as specialized agencies, 490–491; formal relations with executive and legislature, 496–498; hierarchies of appeal, 493–494; in international law, 594; involved in the political process, 9–10; national and local, 492–493; regular and administrative, 481–482, 491; role in Communist subversion, 181–182; role in democratic process, 509; role in protecting civil rights, 162–163, 168–169; role in religious education, 176–177; in USSR, 509–519
Cousins, Norman, 607
Cree, Nathan, 297n
Criminal law, 489, 511
Cromwell, Oliver, 121
Crossley, Archibald, 249

Cuba, 67, 117, 439
Culture, as an element of nationalism, 27
Cumulative vote system, 300
*Curia Regis,* 395
Currency regulations, for international travelers, 137
Cushman, Robert E., 180n
Customs, constitutional, 113–116, 124; social, 33
Customs regulations, 137
Cyprus, 67, 606
Czechoslovakia, 61, 66, 111, 117n

Dahl, Robert A., 88n, 208n, 471, 570n, 625
Danelski, David J., 507n
Daniels, Jonathan, 479
David, Paul T., 345n
Davies, James C., 214n
Dawn, C. Ernest, 72
Dawson, Robert M., 276n
Debate, legislative, 402, 408, 413–415
Decentralization, 345–346
Declaration of Independence, 149, 152
Declaration of the Rights of Man and of the Citizen, 152
Deener, David, 110n
Democracy, author's conception of, 88–97; classical Greek concept, 96; Communist conception of, 85–86, 229, 231; Communist and non-Communist conceptions contrasted, 229–231; contemporary confusion over meaning of, 79; contemporary controversy over meaning of, 84–85; definition, 85; distinguished from constitutionalism, 97; non-Communist conception, 60–61, 86–88, 229–231; parliamentary type, 65, 398, 408, 430; place of civil service, 458, 475–482; place of political parties, 331; presidential, 65, 398, 400, 430; role of courts, 509; role of pressure groups, 386–389; role of public opinion, 206–213; structure of court system, 490–498; system of selecting representatives (table), 273–274; theory of local government, 517–519; theory of suffrage, 283
"Democratic centralism," 359
Democratic party, 236, 312, 317, 327, 336, 340, 365, 369
Denaturalization, 132
Denmark, constitution, 43, 63, 67, 120; elections and nominations, 273, 293; government monopoly of broadcasting, 239; unicameral legislature, 405
*Départements,* 530
Departments, governmental, *see* Administration
Deutsch, Karl W., 25n, 233n
*Deutsche Hochschule für Politik,* 620
De Valera, Eamon, 262
Developing nations, 362
Dewey, John, 505
Dewey, Thomas E., 215
Dexter, Lewis A., 250n

*Dharna,* 380
Dialectical materialism, 357
Dictatorship, 60–63, 77, compared to totalitarianism, 99–100; essentials of, 98–100; functional representation in legislature, 262–263; historical meaning of, 98; modern conception of, 98–99; one-party system of, 356–357; *see also* China; Communism; Fascism; Hitler, Mussolini; Stalin; USSR
Diefenbaker, John, 319
Dillon's Rule, 533
Diplomats, changing role and power, 563–564; legal status, 139–140; role of President as, 439
Direct legislation, 278–281; *see also* Initiative; Referendum
Direct primary, American, organization, 290–291; political effects, 336
Disarmament, 565, 586–589
Discipline, in political parties, 347–348, 416–417
Displaced persons, 134, 144
Displaced Persons Act of 1948, 144
Dissolution, legislative, 294, 448, 452
Dixiecrats, 115n
Dominican Republic, 67, 111
Donovan, Robert J., 442n
Douglas, Paul, 614
Dred Scott Case, 501
Drury, Allen, 422n
Duclos, Jacques, 187
"Due process of law," 171
Dupeux, Georges, 259n, 313n, 315n
Duvalier, François, 98, 99, 561
Duverger, Maurice, 304n, 331n, 341n, 346, 356n, 618n

Easton, David, 394n, 621n, 624, 626n, 630n, 633n
Ecclesia, 395
*École Libre des Sciences Politiques,* 620
Economic systems as influences in governmental forms, 75–76
Edelman, Murray, 237n, 259n
Eden, Anthony, 431
Education, Civil Rights Act and, 196; contrasted with propaganda, 234–235; local control of, in the United States, 221; racial segregation in South Africa, 199; racial segregation in the United States, 192–194; religious, 176
Ehrmann, Henry W., 367n
Eichelberger, Clark M., 605n
Eisenhower, Dwight D., 259, 315, 318, 323, 329, 383, 442
Elections, campaigns for, 334, 376; fraud in, 296; representativeness of, 296–297; secret ballot, 295; timing and frequency, 293–295; in USSR, 304–308
Electoral College, American, 114–115, 436; *see also* President of United States, selection of
Electoral systems, majority, 297–298; proportional, 300–303; relation to party system, 304; semiproportional, 298–300

Emergency Powers Act (1920), 183
Emerson, Rupert, 30n
Emerson, Thomas I., 158n
Emigration, sources of (figure), 142
Employment, Civil Rights Act and, 196; racial discrimination in, 195
Engels, Friedrich, 50
Epistemology, 625
Epstein, Leon D., 336n, 348n
"Equal protection of the laws," interpretation of, 123, 503–504
Equality, political, 87, 90–91; racial, *see* Racial discrimination
Equity law, 488
Ethiopia, 30, 63, 67, 129, 362
Ethnic pressure groups, 372
Eulau, Heinz, 420
European Defense Community (EDC), 377
Executives, changing role of, 454–456; chief of state and head of government roles, 276–277, 428–434; collegial, 430; increasing power and importance, 282, 427; method of selection, 276, 401; plural, in Switzerland and Uruguay, 274; premier type, 450–453; presidential type, 410, 443, 435–445; prime minister type, 446–449; relations with administrators, 458–459, 472–473, 478–480; relations with courts, 496–498; relations with legislatures, 426
Expatriation, 131–132
Experts, 18–19, 472

Fabian Society, 372
Fainsod, Merle, 226n, 308n, 358n, 514n
Farrand, Max, 269n
Fascism, 50, 133, 361; *see also* Hitler; Germany; Italy; Mussolini
Federal Bureau of Investigation, 179, 180
Federal Communications Commission, 123, 237, 461
Federal Regulation of Lobbying Act (1946), 387
Federalism, as cause for ticket splitting, 322; constitutional amending procedures, 119–120, 540–541; definition and incidence, 63, 535–536; distribution of powers, 118; increasing centralization in federal nations, 542; pseudo-federalism in USSR, 536; reasons for adoption, 537–538; representation of local governments in national legislatures, 272, 539–540; umpiring national-local disputes, 541–542
*Federalist* papers, 396, 397
Fellman, David, 175n
Fenno, Richard F., 438n
Ferguson, LeRoy C., 420
Festinger, Leon, 215n
Feudalism, 129
Field, G. Lowell, 262n
Filibuster, legislative, 413–415

Finer, Herman, 108n, 152n, 280n, 303n, 396n, 399n, 408n, 433, 449n, 451, 460, 477, 491n, 538n
Finer, Samuel E., 367n, 418n
Finland, 67, 117, 129, 273, 293, 415n
Force, 24; see also Coercion; Sanctions; Violence; War
Ford, Henry Jones, 394
Foreign aid, 567–568
Foreign policy, 5–6, agencies and officers, 562–564; diplomacy in, 564–566; formulating process, 560–562; goals, 557–560; international travel and, 137; "realism" versus "idealism" in, 558
Forms of government, in modern nations (table), 66–72; process and utility of classifying, 61–62, 83; social influences on, 73–78
Force Ouvrière, 368, 369
France, civil service, 461, 466, 467; communism in, 185–187; constitution, 63, 67, 121, 386; court system, 491, 493, 494, 498; elections and nominations, 273, 275, 292; internal ideological and social divisions, 185–186; legislative control of administrators, 481; local government, 530–531; 532; nationality laws, 129; political parties, 339, 340; pressure groups, 368–369; role of president, 454; selection and position of executive, 450–454; strikes, 377; structure of legislature, 273, 275, 403, 411
Franchise, see Suffrage
Franco, Francisco, 98
Frank, Jerome, 505
Fraud, in elections, 296
Free enterprise, 54; see also Laissez-faire
Free market, as social science model, 80–81
Freedom, conflict with security, 150, 166–169
Freedom of speech, 171
Frei, Eduardo, 318
Friedrich, Carl J., 99n, 100n, 161n, 213, 356n, 471, 476
Führerprinzip, 619
Functions, governmental, debate over, 45–49; list of, in the United States, 43–45

Gaitskell, Hugh, 50, 339
Gallup, George, 248, 249, 255
"Gallup poll," see American Institute of Public Opinion
Gandhi, Mohandas, 363, 378, 379, 380, 591
Garceau, Oliver, 374n
Gaudet, Hazel, 245n
Gaulle, Charles de, 4, 259, 452
Gellhorn, Walter, 158n
Genghis Khan, 100
Geopolitics, 217
Germany, East, 68
Germany, Nazi, 40
Germany, Weimar, 121, 280

Germany, West, abandonment of direct legislation, 280; constitution, 63, 67, 110, 386, 540; court system, 491, 492, 494, 541; judicial review, 110; organization of Bundesrat, 261; selection of representatives, 273, 275
Gerrymandering, 268
Ghana, 30, 67
Girod, Roger, 347n
Girvetz, Harry K., 53n
Gladstone, William, 105
Glasstone, Samuel, 577n
Glickman, Harry, 182n
Godfrey, E. Drexel, Jr., 187
Goebbels, Josef, 84
Goguel, François, 186n, 450n
Goldman, Ralph M., 345n
Goldwater, Barry, 9, 54, 95, 194, 208, 209, 216, 289, 318, 323, 377, 614
Golombiewski, Robert T., 218n
Gompers, Samuel, 368
Goodnow, Frank J., 458, 459, 470, 471, 473, 475, 476, 618
Gosnell, Harold F., 280n, 310
Gouldner, Alvin W., 384n
Gove, Samuel K., 280n
Government, and civil rights, 160–163, 165–166; coalition, 450; debate over proper functions of, 45–49; definition, 21; different from other social organizations, 22–24; forms of, 60–72; functions performed by, 42–45; general role in modern life, 55–58; interaction with public opinion, 256; local, see Local government; official and unofficial aspects, 393–395; organization of, by political parties, 334–335; reasons for existence, 34–38; role of coercion, 39–40; role of compromise, 38–39; role of models, 81–82; social influence on, 73–78; spectrum classification, 65, 82–83; views of proper divisions of power, 395–399; world, 607–609
"Government, the," in parliamentary democracies, 408, 412, 413
"Gravity of evil" test, 169, 181
Gray, A. P., 319n
Grazia, Alfred de, 258n
Great Britain, see United Kingdom
Greaves, H. R. G., 539n
Greece, 68, 273, 275
Greene, Fred, 568n
"Gresham's law," 48
Griffith, William E., 52n
Gross, Ernest A., 605n
Grossman, Joel B., 507n
Groups, categoric, relation to primary groups, 219–222; types of, 11–12, 217, 366; voting behavior of (table), 16, 310–311
Groups, in French parties, 349
Groups, interest, defined, 11, 366; direct representation of, 277–278; formation of, 11–14; overlapping membership of, 13, 15, 37

Groups, political, defined, 12; imperfect mobilization of, 15–17; related to individual, 213–214; types, 366

Groups, primary, effect on opinion of, 218–219; influence on voting behavior, 219; pressures for conformity within, 242; relation to categoric groups, 219–222

Groups, social, influence on opinion formation, 219–222; overlapping membership, 15; role of, in politics, 8–9; types, 11–12, 217

"Guillotine" cloture, 415

Gulick, Luther, 462n, 465, 471

Gunther, John, 200n

Gurin, Gerald, 318n, 328, 329

Guttsman, W. L., 74n, 345n

Gyorgy, Andrew, 360n

Haas, Ernest B., 557n

Haber, David, 158n

Haddow, Anna, 615n, 617n

Hagan, Charles B., 281n

Haiti, 68, 561

Hallett, George H., 300n

Hallowell, John H., 49, 261n, 629n

Hammarsjköld, Dag, 600, 606

Handlin, Oscar, 190n

Harris, G. Montagu, 520n

Harris, Joseph P., 296n

Harris, Louis, 250

Harris, Robert J., 192n

Harrison, Martin, 369n, 453n

Hartmann, Frederick H., 553n

Hayes, Carlton J. H., 552n

Hays, Brooks, 423n

Heads of government, 276–277, 433–445, 450–454

Hennessy, Bernard C., 340n

Hermens, F. A., 303n

Herodotus, 64

Herring, Pendleton, 294n, 389, 444n

Hewart, Lord of Bury, 483n

Hierarchy, 23, 462–463, 493–494

Hitler, Adolf, 84, 98, 99, 259, 265, 361, 559, 569

Hoadly, Benjamin, 502

Hoag, Clarence G., 300n

Hobbes, Thomas, 615

Hodges, A. G., 440n

Hodgskin, Thomas, 331n, 555

Hoffa, Jimmy, 402

Hogan, Willard N., 603n

Holmes, Oliver Wendell, Jr., 156, 486, 505

Homans, George C., 218n

Home, Lord, 431

Home rule, municipal, 523; see also Local government, American

Housing, racial segregation in United States, 194

Hovet, Thomas, Jr., 604n

Hughes, Christopher, 430n

Huitt, Ralph K., 420

Humphrey, Hubert H., 614

Hungary, 61, 68, 111, 117n, 129, 134, 230–231

Hursh, Gerald D., 251n

Hyde, Lawrence M., 496n

Hydrogen bombs, 576, 577–580

Hyman, Herbert H., 223n, 437, 438n

Hyneman, Charles S., 471, 475n, 477, 479, 480, 621n, 622n, 629, 631

Iceland, 68, 273, 429

Identification, party, 312

Ideology, in political parties, 341–345, 349–350

Immigration, definition, 138; destination, (figure), 142; ethnic composition (figure), 145; reception by various nations (figure), 141; regulation, American, 140–145

Immigration and Naturalization Service, 132, 474

Impeachment, 401, 498

"Implied powers," doctrine of, 124

Incitement to Disaffection Act (1934), 183

Incitement to Mutiny Act (1797), 183

Income taxes, 47

Independence among voters, 316

India, boundary disputes, 25; constitution, 68, 118, 159, 536; nationality laws, 129; party system, 363; selection of representatives, 273, 275

Indians, American, legal status of, 128

Individuals, determinants of opinions of, 213–216; primacy of, 155

Indonesia, 68

Information, as basis of public opinion, 211–212

Initiative, legislative, 93, 279

Inkeles, Alex, 224n, 225n, 231n

Institutions, 21, 55

Intercontinental ballistic missiles (ICBM), 578–580

Interests, "national" and "special," 17–19, 31, 37

Internal Security Act (1950), 180, 182

International Court of Justice, 590, 594, 601, 605

International Political Science Association, 621, 622

International Refugee Organization (IRO), 134

Interstate Commerce Commission, 123, 461

Intimidation, 387

Ireland (Eire), constitution, 27, 68, 119, 120, 429; functional representation in the Senate, 262; selection of representatives, 273; single transferable-vote system, 303

Irion, Frederick C., 242n

Israel, constitution, 27, 30, 68; elections and nominations, 248, 293, 301–302; immigration, 134, 141, 147; legislature, 416n; proportional representation, 301–302

Issues, effect on voting behavior, 316–318
Italy, constitution, 68; court system, 491, 494; nationality laws, 129; proportional representation, 304; selection of representatives, 262, 273

Jackson, Andrew, 436
Jackson, Richard N., 492n
Jamaica, 69, 273
Japan, constitution, 63, 69; elections and nominations, 273, 292; judicial review, 110; nationality laws, 131; proportional representation, 304
Jefferson, Thomas, 4, 149, 286, 396, 517, 518, 519, 543
Jennings, Ivor, 406n, 446n
Jewell, Malcolm, E., 349n
"Jim Crow" laws, 9, 192n, 195, 503
Johnson, Andrew, 401
Johnson, Lyndon B., 9, 95, 208, 209, 216, 340, 347, 435
Johnson, Samuel, 58, 484
Joliot-Curie, Frederic, 186
Judges, appointment, election and removal, 495–496, 506–507; as constitution makers, 112–113; ideal of independence of, 496–497; involvement in political process, 497–498, 505–509; as legal technicians, 499–501; popular reverence toward, 484–485; relations with executive and legislature, 496–498; in USSR, 513-514; viewed as policy makers, 501–504
"Judicial legislation," 501–504
Judicial review, 110, 112–113, 495
Judiciary, see Courts
Judiciary Act of 1789, 112
Jurists, 485
Jus sanguinis, 128–129, 133
Jus soli, 129–130, 132
Justice, democratic and communist conceptions, 509, 514–515

Kahn, Herman, 568n
"Kangaroo" cloture, 415
Kaplan, Abraham, 5n, 80n, 570n, 624n, 626n
Kaplan, Morton A., 548n, 561, 591n
Katz, Elihu, 243n
Katzenbach, Nicholas de B., 591n
Kautsky, John H., 30n
Keefe, William J., 406n, 410n, 417n
Kefauver, Estes, 115n, 402
Kellogg-Briand Pact, 592
Kendall, Willmoore, 15n, 54n, 60n, 88n, 209n, 291n, 309n, 332n, 346n, 349n, 444n, 613n
Kennan, George F., 558n
Kennedy, John F., 115, 194, 195, 250, 318, 439, 614
Key, V. O., Jr., 205n, 207, 212, 213n, 243n, 256n, 291n, 296n, 332n, 371, 373n
Khrushchev, Nikita, 52
King, Martin Luther, Jr., 191, 378, 379, 380

Kinship, 126
Kirkpatrick, Evron M., 625n
Kitzinger, Uwe W., 322n
Klapper, Joseph T., 243n, 245n
Kneier, Charles M., 523n, 533n
Knesset, 416n
Koenig, Louis W., 443n
Koestler, Arthur, 473n
Kohn, Hans, 25n, 552n
Komsomols, 228, 359
Korea, North, 69, 473
Korea, South, 69, 117, 473
Korean War, 432, 439, 473, 551, 585–586, 602
Kosygin, Alexei, 52, 225
Kropotkin, Peter, 555
Ku Klux Klan, 190
Kuchel, Thomas H., 417
Kulski, W. W., 304n, 512n

Labor party, Norwegian, 350
Labor pressure groups, 368–369
Labor unions, see Trade unions
Labour party, British, 50, 52, 73, 182, 339, 345, 348, 369, 473
Lagting, 403n
Laissez-faire, 48–49, 52, 53–54
Lakeman, Enid, 297n
Lambert, James D., 297n
Lancaster, Lane W., 521n
Lane, Robert E., 207n, 214n, 311n
Language, as an element of nationalism, 27
LaPalombara, Joseph G., 281n
Laski, Harold J., 472–473, 518
Laswell, Harold D., 5n, 570n, 621n, 624
Latham, Earl, 373n
Laue, James H., 191n
Lauterpacht, H., 595n
Law, domestic, civil contrasted with criminal, 489; classification of, 487–489; common, 487–488; Communist conception of, 509–510; conceptions of, 485–486; constitutional and ordinary, 108–109, 487; definition, 33–34, 486; distinguished from "statutes," 399–400; enforcement of, 490; equity, 488; "natural," 152, 485; organic, 112, 487
Law, international, achievements and failures, 595; content and structure, 592–594; status of aliens in, 138; status of citizenship in, 127; status of diplomats in, 139–140; status of war in, 591–592
Lazarsfeld, Paul F., 215, 243n
Leadership, general nature and functions, 383–384; in political parties, 344–345, 346
League of Nations, 585, 592, 594, 596n
League of Women Voters, 372
Lebanon, 69, 273
Lee, A. M., 234n
Lee, E. B., 234n
Left-right ideological spectrum, 350
Legion of Decency, 371
Legislation, direct, 278–281; in international law, 593; judicial, 501–504

Legislatures, bases of representation in upper houses, 262; bicameralism versus unicameralism, 403–405; bill passing procedure, 407–410; cloture, debate and filibuster, 402–403, 413–415; control of administrators, 479; factors influencing votes in, 268–271; functions, 399–403; party organization, 335; power and structure of committees, 408, 409, 410–413; presiding officer, 405–406; relation with courts, 496–498; roles of members, 418–423; selection, 271–276; size (table), 275; structure and organization, 403–417
Leiserson, Avery, 277n, 331n, 478n
Lenin, Nikolai, 50, 224, 225
Leonard, R. L., 276n
Lepawsky, Albert, 475n
Lewis, Edward G., 278n
Lewis, John D., 84n
*L'Humanité*, 178, 235
Libel, 163, 387
Liberal party, Canadian, 344
Liberal party, South African, 200
Liberalism, 345, 351
Liberia, 65, 69, 117
Libya, 63, 69, 134, 362, 429
Licensing, 464
Lie, Trygve, 600
Lieber, Francis, 617
Lilburne, John, 269
Lincoln, Abraham, 4, 282, 438, 439, 440
"Line" agencies, 462–463
Lipscomb, Andrew A., 518n
Lipset, Seymour Martin, 212n, 320n, 325
Lipson, Leslie, 304n, 436n
Literature, as an element of nationalism, 27
Littunen, Yrjö, 320n, 346n
Lobbying, 278, 374–375, 388
Local government, common functions of, 532; contributions of, 518; in democratic theory, 517–519; division of functions with central government, 519–520, 532–533; in federal situation, 272; in France, 530–531, 532; in Great Britain, 527–530, 532; problems of, 533–535
Locke, John, 48, 151–152, 161, 162, 175, 286, 396, 615
"Logrolling," 375
London, governmental structure, 529–530
Long, Huey, 355
Louis XIV, King, 63, 100
Lowell, A. Lawrence, 394
Loyalty, 127, 181, 516
Loyalty-Security Program, 181
Lubell, Samuel, 355n
Luethy, Herbert, 186n
Luther, Martin, 174
Luthuli, Albert, 201

MacArthur, Douglas, 473–474
McCamy, James L., 234n, 562n
McCarran-Walter Act of 1952, 144
McCarthy, Joseph R., 184, 355, 402, 411

McClellan, John, 388, 402
McClosky, Herbert, 93n
McDonald, Neil A., 332n
McEntire, Davis, 194n
Machiavelli, Niccolo, 615
McIlwain, Charles H., 107n, 161n
MacIver, R. M., 32n
McKenzie, Robert T., 339n, 449n
MacKenzie, W. J. M., 283n, 286n, 297n
MacKinder, Halford J., 217n
Macklin, Charles, 484
MacMahon, Arthur W., 535n
Macmillan, Harold, 431
McNair, A. D., 489n
McPhee, William N., 215
Macridis, Roy C., 185n, 308n, 340n, 413n, 560n
McWhinney, Edward, 541n
Madison, James, 397, 439
Majority rule, defined, 92; "limited," 87, 93; as a principle of democracy, 92–93; "unlimited," 87, 93–95
Mallory, Walter H., 72
Mandate, representation by, 269
Manly, Chesly, 605n
Manning, C. W., 548n
Mansfield, Harvey C., 463n
Mao Tse-tung, 50, 99, 575
March, James G., 463n
Marquard, Leopold, 197n
Marshall, Charles B., 571n
Marshall, John, 110, 501
Marshall, Thurgood, 193, 613
Marshall Plan, 377, 567
Marx, Fritz Morstein, 459n, 463n, 478n
Marx, Karl, 50, 76, 222, 357
Mass media, description, 235–242; effectiveness compared with that of face-to-face media, 345; world distribution of facilities (figure), 238
Matthews, Donald R., 420n
Maxson, Charles H., 126n
Mayo, Henry B., 88n
"Medicare," 443
Mehden, Fred R. von der, 28n, 72, 84n, 362n
Mehren, Arthur T. von, 491n
Meisel, John, 347n
Membership, in communities, 89–90; in political parties, 312–315, 335–338; in pressure groups, 382–383; in social groups, 15, 16, 22, 32
Mendés-France, Pierre, 368, 452
Merit system, 461, 467–469; *see also* Administrators; Civil service
Merriam, Charles E., 310
Mexico, 30, 63, 70, 363
Meyer, Cord, 607
Meyer, Frank S., 54n, 224n
Meynaud, Jean, 367n
Micaud, Charles A., 185n
Michels, Robert, 337
Migration, international, 140
Milbrath, Lester W., 374n, 388n
Mill, John Stuart, 295

Miller, Warren E., 211n, 212n, 216n, 258n, 312n, 313n, 314n, 316n, 318n, 323n, 326n, 328, 329, 422n, 423
Millikan, Max F., 30n
Milton, John, 156, 175
Ministry, British, 447–448; French, 451–452
Minority rule, 94–95
Mises, Ludwig von, 483
"Missionary parties," 341–345
Models, definition, 81; description, 81; nature and role in social sciences, 80–84; normative, 81
Monarchs, constitutional, 60–63, 276, 428–429, 431
Monypenny, Phillip, 477n
Montesquieu, Charles de, 396
Moos, Malcolm, 558n
Morality, as a regulator of human behavior, 32–33
Morgan, Arthur E., 517
Morgenstern, Oskar, 561n
Morgenthau, Hans J., 554, 555n, 558n, 575, 582n, 586, 609n
Morrison, Herbert, 446n
Motion pictures, in the democracies, 241; in USSR, 229
Motivation, patterns of, related to political participation and preference (tables), 328, 329
Mouvement Républican Populaire, 340, 369
Multiple party systems, 350–353
Munger, Frank J., 336n
Municipal government, American, charters, 523; commission form, 525, (figure), 526; council-manager form, 525–527, (figure), 527; importance, 522–523; mayor-council form (figure), 524; see also Local government
Munro, William B., 279n
Murphy, Frank, 166
Murray, James N., 601n
Mussolini, Benito, 84, 259, 262, 361

Napoleon I, 129, 489
National Association for the Advancement of Colored People (NAACP), 9, 11, 35, 36, 37, 85, 191, 193, 366, 372, 613
National Association of Manufacturers (NAM), 367, 373, 376
National Opinion Research Center, 248
National-origins quota system, 144
National Science Foundation, 371, 614
National Socialist German Workers ("Nazi") party, German, 361
National Urban League, 191
Nationalism, definition and elements, 26–28; increasing strength of, 554; role, 553–554; symbols and ceremonies, 430–431
Nations, characteristics of, 25–28; compared with "nation state," 550n
Nations, as contestants in international politics, 550–551; "developing," 28–31;

forms of government classified (table), 66–72; problems of internal unity, 31–32; recognition of in international law, 564–565
Natural-law philosophy, 152, 485
Naturalization, 130–131
Negroes, discrimination against, 188–195; drive for equal rights, 9, 11, 35–36, 164–165, 191–192; suffrage, 284; voting behavior of (figure), 189
Negroes, South African, discrimination against, 197–201
Nehru, Jawaharlal, 363, 591
Neofascism, 352
Netherlands, 63, 70, 120, 272, 274, 287
Neumann, John von, 561
Neumann, Sigmund, 331n, 346n, 364n, 450n
Neustadt, Richard E., 437n, 445n, 474n, 479
New Zealand, constitution, 70, 109, 119; courts, 488; elections and nominations, 292; political parties, 344, 353; selection of representatives, 274; 275; unicameral legislature, 403
Newspapers, in the democracies, 235–237; in USSR, 228–229, 235
Nicolson, Harold, 562
Nigeria, 70, 274, 275
Nixon, Raymond B., 237n
Nixon, Richard M., 115n, 318, 614
Nkrumah, Kwame, 333, 362
Nogee, Joseph L., 586n
Nominations, American legal procedures, 290–293; legal procedures in other democracies, 292–293; legal procedures in USSR, 305–306; parties' power over, 346; party processes, 288–289; significance, 333
"Nonviolent civil disobedience," 378–380
Nonvoting, 286–287, 310, 311
North Atlantic Treaty Organization (NATO), 339, 377, 585, 610
Northrup, F. S. C., 62n, 627n
Norway, 63, 70, 274, 314, 317, 403n
Nova, Fritz, 261n
Nugent, Thomas, 397n

Ochs, Robert D., 146n
Odegard, Peter, 372n
Odelsting, 403n
Official Secrets Act (1911), 183
Ogul, Morris S., 406n, 410n, 417n
Oligarchy, 64, 65, 87, 90
Ombudsman, 482
One-party systems, 356–363
Opinion leaders, 311
Opposition, leader of the British, 347–348
Opposition, political, 14–15
Organization, general nature and role, 12; of political parties, 338–340; of pressure groups, 373–374
Organization activists, 311
Organizations, nongovernmental, compared and contrasted with government, 22–24

Organski, A. F. K., 557n
Orwell, George, 99
O'Sullivan, Donal, 262n

Page, Charles H., 32n
Paine, Thomas, 74, 106, 107, 108
Palmer, Norman D., 537n
*Panachage*, 302
Panama, 70, 274, 555, 570–571
Parliament, *see* Legislatures; United Kingdom
Parliamentary democracies, 65, 276, 480–481
Parsons, Talcott, 210
Participation, political, 328, 333–334
Partisanship, 328
Party identification, definition, 312; distribution, 314–315; impact of, 315–316
Party-list systems, 301
Party systems, Communist one-party, 358–360; defined, 349; Fascist one-party, 361; modified one-party in developing nations, 362–363; multiple, 311, 350–353; one-party in developing nations, 362; relation to electoral system, 304; totalitarian, 356–357; two-party, 301, 311, 353–355
Passports, 136
Paterson, William, 269
Paton, George Whitecross, 485n
Patronage, 443–444, 467
Peace, world, balance-of-power approach, 582–584; collective-security approach, 584–586; disarmament approach, 586–589; as a goal of foreign policy, 559–560; international-law approach, 591–595; peaceful-settlement approach, 589–591; UN approach, 596–606; world-government approach, 607–609
Pear, R. H., 319n
Peaslee, Amos J., 63n, 72, 110n, 158n, 160
Peltason, Jack W., 168n, 170n, 180n, 182n, 254, 500n, 505, 506, 508n
Pendleton Act, 468
Pennock, J. Roland, 111n
People's Courts, Russian, 514
People's party (the "Populists"), 368
Perception, politics and, 215–216
*Personalismo*, 259
Peru, 70, 109
Petitions, nominating, 292
Philippine Republic, constitution, 65, 70, 117; elections, 274, 275
Physiocrats, the, 48
Pickles, Dorothy, 453n
Pitkin, Hanna Fenichel, 257n, 258n, 300n
Pius XI, Pope, 261
Plato, 64, 615, 616
Pleven, René, 452
Plucknett, T. F. T., 488n
Pluralism, 389
Poland, 27, 61, 70, 99, 117n
Polanyi, Karl, 53n
Policy, 5

Political economy, 616–617
Political parties, American, changes in affiliation, 224; decentralization of control, 345–346; development, 313; identification with, 312; membership, 312–315; presidential leadership, 440–442, 444; regional influence, 321; varying cohesion, 349, 417; *see also* Democratic party; Republican party; Socialist Labor party
Political parties, British, centralization, 347; cohesion, 349, 417; *see also* Conservative party; Labour party
Political parties, democratic, activities of, 333–335; centralization, 345–347; compared with pressure groups, 366; contrasted with totalitarian parties, 333; definition, 332; discipline in, 347–348; educational and social activities, 335; extragovernmental and intragovernmental agencies, 338–339; legislative organization, 415–417; means and nature of discipline, 347–348; membership, 335–338; organization, 338–340; pressure groups' operation inside, 376; types of party systems, 349–356; varying degrees of cohesion, 348–349, 416–417; varying role of ideology in, 340–344; varying social composition of leadership and support, 344–345
Political parties, European, ideologies, 317
Political parties, French, 313, 346, 352
Political science, contemporary scope of, 394–395; current debate over proper scope, 623–624; debate over methodology, 609–610; emergence as a distinct discipline, 615–619; "fields" of, 622–623; goals of, 633; methods of, 624–632; problem of values in, 629–633; self-examination in, 614–615; status of, in various nations, 619–620; traditional subject matter, 21, 621–623
Political socialization, 223–224
Politicians, theory of voting behavior, 309
Politics, domestic, civil service and, 465–466; in clashes over civil rights, 170–172, 173–174; conception of, 4–6; definition, 5; in the judicial process, 505–509; popular attitudes toward, 4–5; pressure-group tactics as only one aspect of, 366; principal aspects, 6; role of "access," 374; role of conflict, 7–11; role of groups, 9–11; role of "national interest," 17–19; role of opposition, 14–15; role of organization, 12; role of values, 8–9; role of violence, 378; Wilson-Goodnow theory of separation from "administration," 470–471, 473–475
Politics, international, anarchy and war in, 38; compared with domestic, 549–552; goals of foreign policy, 557–560; nature and role of power, 570–575; "theory of games" applied to, 561
Polls, *see* Public opinion polls

Pope, Alexander, 59
Popular consultation, 91–92
Popular sovereignty, 89–90
Population, 25, 57n, 75, 572–573
Portugal, 70, 110, 263
"Positive law," 485–486
Positivism, 153
Potter, Allen, 367n
Poujade, Pierre, 186
Pound, Roscoe, 486n
Power, national, assessment of, 575; balance of, 582–584; constitutional distribution of, 118; definition, 570–571; factors correlated with, 572–575
Pragmatism, 153
*Pravda*, 228
Prefects, 530
Preferential ballot, 298
Premier, French, in coalition government, 450; duration in office (figure), 453; powers and handicaps, 452–453; selection, 434, 450–452
President of France, 454
President of the United States, compared with prime minister and premier, 444–445; control of administrators by, 478–479; expansion of power, 435–436; as legislator, 442; limitations to power, 445; as party leader, 347, 440–442, 444; relations with Congress, 426, 443; roles of, 436–444; selection of, 61, 114–115, 276, 289, 327
Presidential democracies, 65, 118, 276, 294
Presidium, Russian, 359
Pressure groups, in British politics, 376, 385; compared with political parties, 332; definition, 12; factors affecting success, 380–386; impact on policy formation, 388–389; influence on administrators, 474; legal status, 386–388; list of American, 13–14; principal types, 367–372; role in democratic government, 386–389; weapons, 373–380
Primaries, *see* Direct primary
Prime minister, British, contrasted with premier and president, 444–445; general role, 446–449; increasing power, 449; status, 434; weapons of party leadership, 347–348
Primogeniture, 428
Pritchett, C. Herman, 507n
Privy Council, 123
Procurator, Russian, 512–514
Progressive-Conservative party, Canadian, 344
Prohibition party, 372
Propaganda, Communist use of, 226–229; contrasted with "education," 234–235; in foreign policy, 566–567; limitations on effectiveness, 244–247; by pressure groups, 278, 375
Proportional representation, criticism, 303–304; organization, 301–303; rationale, 300–301

Prosecutors, separation from judges, 497
Public opinion, alleged distortion by two-party systems, 301; characteristics of, 209–213; contrast of democratic and communist conceptions, 229–231; definition, 207; in the democracies, 206–213; as a democratic process and symbol, 205–207; determinants of, 213–224; direction of, 207–209; distribution, J-shaped curve (figure), 210; distribution, U-shaped curve (figure), 208; influence of biological needs, 214; influence of motion pictures, 229, 241; influence of newspapers, 228–229, 235–237; influence of primary groups, 218–19; influence of psychological needs, 214–215; influence of radio, 229; influence of social groups, 217–224; intensity of, 207–209; interaction with government, 256; latent, 213; problems and techniques of measurement, 247–248; representation and, 278; role of communication, 243–247; role of opinion leaders, 243; socialization and, 223–224; in USSR, 224, 229
Public opinion polls, accuracy, 252–255; advisory role in government, 256; influence, 255–256; nature and present status, 248–250; procedures, 251–252; record in predicting presidential elections (table), 254
"Purge trials," 512
Pye, Lucian, 30n

*Quadrigesimo Anno*, 261
Quadros, Janio, 318
"Question time," 480

Rabinowitch, Eugene, 589n
Racial discrimination, Civil Rights Act and, 195–197; definition, 188; in education, 192–194; in employment, 195; in housing, 194; Negro action against, 191–192; political conflict over, in the United States, 35–37, 188–197, 197–201; in public and service accommodations, 195; in voting, 192
Radio, in the democracies, 237–240; in USSR, 229
Ransone, Coleman, Jr., 436n
Rappard, William E., 280n
*Rapporteurs*, 411
Real, James, 578n
Reale, Egidio, 136n
Recognition, in international law, 439, 564–565
Redden, Kenneth, 34n, 510n
Reeves, Emery, 607
Referendum, 93, 279
Reform pressure groups, 372–373
Reformation, Protestant, 174
Refugee Relief Act of 1953, 145
Refugees, 134, 147
"Regime," concept of, 73–75
Registration, 285

Religion, effect on voting behavior, 322; public opinion and, 220; separation of church and state, 174–177
Religious pressure groups, 371
Remarque, Erich Maria, 547–548
Remmers, H. H., 250n
*Replâtrage*, 451
Representation, bases for selecting representatives, 271–276; Communist and Fascist conceptions, 262–265; contrasted with direct legislation, 278–279; defined, 258; democratic theories, 263–265, 269–271; direct, 265; elections as devices for, 297–304; functional, 261–262, 386; instrumental function, 258; of interests, 260–263; by mandate, 269; medieval, 260; of persons, 263–265; problem of apportionment, 266–268; symbolic function, 258–259; virtual, 264–265
Representatives, acting on mandate, 269; administrators as, 477–478; independent action by, 269–271; relations with constituents, 268–271, 422–423; system of selection (table), 273–274
Representatives, House of, *see* Legislatures; United States
Republican party, American, 289, 317, 327, 336, 365
Republics, 61, 62, 63
Responsibility, of administrators, 476–477
"Restrictive covenants," 194
Returned Soldiers' League, 371
Revolutions, 133, 230–231
Richards, Peter G., 270n, 418n
Richardson, Lewis F., 549n
"Riders," 443
Ridley, F., 466n
"Right," 350n
Rights, *see* Civil rights; Constitutionalism; Democracy; Liberalism
Riker, William, 535, 536, 561
Robert's Rules of Order, 407, 415
Robertson, Nathan, 54n
Robinson, Claude E., 249n
Robinson, Edward S., 505
Robson, William A., 520n, 616n, 619
Roche, John P., 501n
Rockefeller, Nelson, 289
Rodell, Fred, 505
Roelofs, H. Mark, 126n
Rogers, Lindsay, 255, 256n
Roman law, 488–489
Roosevelt, Franklin D., 4, 124, 346, 347, 439, 498
Roosevelt, Theodore, 124, 590
Roper, Elmo B., 249
Rosa, Ruth Amende, 85n
Rose, Arnold M., 190n, 191n
Rose, Richard, 313n
Rosenblum, Victor G., 504n
Rossiter, Clinton, 435n, 436n, 445n
Rousseau, Jean-Jacques, 269, 278, 286, 396, 517, 615
Roux, Edward, 197n

Ruggiero, Guido de, 351n
Rules, constitutional, 108–109, 113; legislative, 407; social, 20, 22–23, 32–34
Rural district councils, British, 529
Rush-Bagot Agreement of 1817, 587
Rusk, Dean, 614
Russett, Bruce M., 604n
Rustow, Dankwart A., 346n, 450n

Sackley, Alex Quaison, 606n
Salazar, Oliveira, 263
*Samokritika*, 225–226
Sampling, theory of, 251
San Marino, 25n, 71, 274
Sanctions, 20, 23–24
Sapin, Burton, 560n
Saudi Arabia, 30, 63, 70, 111, 118, 362, 398, 429
Schaar, John H., 629n
Schattschneider, E. E., 12n, 304n, 331n, 333, 348n, 364, 389n
Schechtman, Joseph B., 134n
Schmidt, Margaret J., 280n
Schofield, A. N., 292n
Schramm, Wilbur, 237n
Schubert, Glendon A., 17n, 505n
Schumpeter, Joseph A., 88n
Schurz, William Lytle, 146n
Science, meaning and objectives, 626–627; standards of, 628
Scientific method, debate over role of, in study of politics, 628–629; nature, 627–629; rise of, 618; use of models in, 80–81
Scott, Robert E., 363n
Scranton, William, 289
Sears, David O., 207n
Secession, 517
Secret ballot, 295
Security, in American civil service, 181; in British civil service, 183–184; conflict with freedom, 166–169; in French civil service, 185; as a goal of foreign policy, 557
Segregation, racial, court action in, 503–504; school, 192–194; in South Africa, 198–201; *see also* Racial discrimination
Selassie, Haile, 98
Seligman, Lester G., 384n
Selznick, Philip, 463n
Senate, American, *see* Legislatures; United States
Separation of church and state, 174–177
Separation of powers, 118, 322, 395–399
Sexes, voting behavior, 326
Shastri, Lal Bahadur, 591
Shotwell, James T., 570n
Sihanouk, Norodom, 362
Simon, Herbert A., 463n
Single-member-district system, 297–298
Single-nontransferable-vote system, 298–300
Single-transferable-vote system, 303
Slander, 387
Smith, Adam, 48, 49, 54

Smith, David G., 111n
Smith Act of 1940, 180, 182
Smithburg, Donald W., 463n
Smuts, Jan Christian, 200
Snider, Clyde F., 280n, 521n
Snyder, Richard C., 560n
Social democratic parties, European, 50, 350
Social structure, 76
Socialism, definition, 49; in European parties, 350; relation to communism, 50
Socialist Labor party, American, 342, 343
Socialist parties, European, 50, 341, 343, 369
Socialist party, American, 50
Socialist Workers party, American, 343
Society, conflict in, 31–32; influence on forms of government, 73–78; role of government in, 55–58
Society for the Preservation of the White Race, 372
Socrates, 616
Soltau, Roger H., 150
Somit, Albert, 625n
Sorauf, Frank J., 332n
Sorel, Georges, 377
South Vietnam, 61, 72, 74
Southeast Asia Treaty Organization (SEATO), 585
Southern Christian Leadership Conference, 191, 372
Sovereignty, in international law, 25, 26, 354; popular, as a principle of democracy, 89
Spanier, John W., 586n
Speakers, legislative, 116, 406
Spectrum classification of governments, 65, 82–83, (chart), 83
"Spoils" system, 467–468
"Staff" agencies, 462–463
Stalin, Josef, 50, 52, 99, 361
"Star-chamber" court, 162
State system, approaches to peace with, 581–595; definition, 24–25, 552; features, 553–556
Statelessness, 133–134
"States rights," 517, 542–543
Statesmen, popular conception of, 4–5
Statutes, distinguished from laws, 399–400
Steiner, Gilbert Y., 410n
Stevenson, Adlai E., 115n, 329, 383
Stodgill, Ralph M., 384n
Stoicism, 155
Stokes, Donald E., 211n, 212n, 216n, 258n, 312n, 313n, 314n, 316n, 326n, 422n, 423
Storing, Herbert J., 629n
Storting, 403n
Straetz, Ralph A., 336n
"Straw votes," 249
Street, Harry, 182n, 184n
Streit, Clarence K., 607
Strikes, 377–378, 466–467
Student Nonviolent Co-ordinating Committee (SNCC), 191–192

Subversion, Communist, 177–188; as a technique of foreign policy, 566–567
Suffrage, attempts to exclude Negroes from, in South Africa, 199; attempts to exclude Negroes from, in the United States, 192; in democratic theory, 283; historical democratization, 283, 284; requirements, 284–286
Sun Yat-sen, 575
Survey Research Center, 208, 211, 212, 216, 249, 310, 312, 313, 323, 325, 326, 327
Swearer, Howard, 52n
Sweden, constitution, 21, 43, 63, 71, 120, 415n; control of administrators, 482; government monopoly of broadcasting, 238; proportional representation, 302; selection of legislators, 274
Switzerland, citizenship, 131; constitution, 43, 63, 71, 109, 120; court system, 494, 495, 541; direct legislation, 280; election of judges, 277; federalism, 63; function of executive, 430; nationality laws, 130; organization of Senate, 260, 272; plural executive, 274; selection of representatives, 274, 403
Syria, 71, 110, 129
Systematic theory, 628

Taft, William Howard, 507
Taft-Hartley Act, 215, 367
Tanenhaus, Joseph, 625n
Taney, Roger B., 501
Tannenbaum, Frank, 558n
Tariffs, 137, 567
Tax, income, 47
Taylor, Frederick, W., 471
Teamsters' Union, 402
Television, 237–240
Tennessee Valley Authority, 46, 517
Tensions, social, 77
Territory, as an element of nationalism, 25, 26, 75
Thailand, 71
Thermonuclear weapons, 577–580
Thompson, Victor A., 463n
Thoreau, Henry David, 378n
Thorson, Thomas Landon, 88n, 93n
Thurmond, J. Strom, 115n
Ticket-splitting, 322
Timasheff, N. S., 85n, 86n
Tocqueville, Alexis de, 105
Tomlinson, F. R., 201
Totalitarianism, characteristics of, 100, 150; compared to dictatorship, 99–100; see also Communism; Dictatorship; Fascism
Town meetings, 521–522
Towns and townships, 521–522
Trade unions, 368, 466–467
Trades Union Congress, 368
Travis, Martin B., Jr., 562n
Treason, 127
Tribunaux Administratifs, 491; see also Administration; Courts

Trinidad, 71, 274
Truman, David B., 11, 373n, 374n, 385n, 389n, 474n
Truman, Harry S, 115n, 215, 432, 439, 445, 473–474, 614
Tumin, Melvin W., 222n
Two-party systems, 353–355

Unicameralism, 403–405
*Union pour la Nouvelle République*, 340
Union of South Africa, conflict over *apartheid*, 17, 198–201; constitution, 71; proportional representation, 303; selection of representatives, 286, 303
Union of Soviet Socialist Republics (USSR), agitation and propaganda operations, 40; Communist party of, 50; constitution, 60–61, 63, 71, 111, 117; elections and nominations, 304–308; foreign policy, 566, 572; nationality laws, 129; as nuclear power, 580; one-party system, 358–359; pseudo-federalism, 63; public opinion, 224–229; radio and motion pictures, 229; role of law and courts, 509–515; *samokritika*, 225, 226; status of diplomats, 139
Unitary states, 63, 118, 520–535
United Kingdom of Great Britain and Northern Ireland, church, 174, 175; citizenship, 130, 133; civil service, 461, 465–466, 467; constitution, 43, 60–61, 63, 72, 106, 109, 111, 120, 538, 541; direct representation of interest groups, 277; elections and nominations, 266, 274, 275, 276, 285–286, 292, 294, 295; foreign policy, 559, 572, 573, 583; handling of Communist subversion, 182–184; immigration, 134, 146; interrelations between social structure and government, 73–74; law, courts and judges, 487–488, 492, 494, 495; legislative control of administrators, 481; local government, 525, 527–530, 532; monarchy, 428–429; organization, cohesion and role of political parties, 344, 346–347, 349, 353–354; organization and power of House of Commons, 73, 372, 407–408; pressure groups, 368, 370, 371, 372, 376; "question time," 480; radio and television, 239; role of legislators, 419, 422–423; structure and power of House of Lords, 60, 372, 401–402, 403; structure and power of legislative committees, 408, 411, 412; structure and role of ministry, cabinet and prime minister, 424–426, 446–449
United Nations, changing membership (table), 604; changing roles of General Assembly and Security Council, 603; charter, 554, 559, 585, 592, 593n, 594, 596, 599, 600, 605; collective security arrangements, 600–601; disarmament attempts, 588; evaluation, 605–606; financial problems, 605; handling refugees, 134; human rights and, 157; increasing power of Afro-Asian nations, 604–605; Korean War and, 602; origin, 597; purposes, 596; record, 601–602; structure, 597–600, (chart), 598; veto in Security Council, 599
United States of America, civil service, 459–460; "collective responsibility," 451; conflict over racial discrimination, 35–37, 39, 188–197, 197–201; Constitution, 60–61, 63, 72, 107, 110, 111, 112, 113, 117, 175, 372, 539; direct representation of interest groups, 277–278; distribution of party identification (table), 314; election and organization of House of Representatives, 297; elections, 294; federalism, 63, 537, 539; foreign policy, 558, 560, 565; functions performed by governments of, 42–45; handling of Communist subversion, 179–182; immigration, 134, 140, 141, 142–145; local government, 520–527; nationality laws, 129, 133; as nuclear power, 580; policy toward Korea, 585; political parties, 353, 355; population, 75n; role of members of legislature, 420–423; role of pressure groups, 384–385; selection and organization of House of Representatives, 266–268, 274, 275, 276; selection and organization of Senate, 260, 274, 403–404, 415; selection and role of President, 289, 400, 426, 435–445; status of administrators, 478–480; status of diplomats, 139; structure and role of law, courts and judges, 110, 113, 123, 168–169, 181–182, 277, 488, 492, 494, 541
"Uniting for peace" resolution, 599, 603
Universal Declaration of Human Rights, 157
Uruguay, 72, 274, 430
Urwick, L., 462n
Utilitarianism, 153

Valen, Henry, 312n, 314, 317n
Values, problem of, in political science, 629–633; role in international politics, 549, 552; role in politics, 8–9; sources of, 154–155
Van Dyke, Vernon, 553, 580n, 584n, 592, 609n, 621n
Vandenbosch, Amry, 603n
Variables, definition, 62n; social, 75–78
Venezuela, 63, 72, 209, 274
Verba Sidney, 211, 212n, 218n
Verney, Douglas V., 53n
Verwoerd, Hendrik, 200
Veterans of Foreign Wars, 371
Veterans pressure groups, 371
Veto, constitutional provisions for, 79; by minorities, 94; by President, 443; in the UN Security Council, 599
Vieg, John A., 459n
Vietnam, North, 72

Vietnam, South, 61, 72, 74
Violence, 378, 387; *see also* Coercion; Sanctions; War
Visas, 136
Visscher, Charles de, 591
Voegelin, Eric, 629n
Voice of America, 566
Volstead Act, 372
Voter, definition, 311; independent, 316
Voting, compulsory, 287–288
Voting behavior, candidate orientation and, 318–319; Civil Rights Act and, 196; dependent variables, 311; dimensions, 310–311; effect of issues on, 316–318; intervening variables, 311–312; patterns of, 319–326; politicians' theory of, 309; psychological motivating factors, 327–330; racial discrimination in, 192; regional differences, 320–321; religion and, 322; as result of "pressures," 327–329; social influences on, 320, 325–326; turnouts in general elections (table), 287; turnouts in municipal elections, 535
Voting Rights Act of 1965, 443
Vyshinsky, Andrei, 510

Wahlke, John C., 420
Waldo, Dwight, 470, 633n
Wallace, George, 9
Wallace, Henry, 551
Walters, F. P., 596n
War, civil, 549; costs of, 568–569, 581; international, 549; new destructiveness of, 580–581; "preventive," 9; as a technique of foreign policy, 568–570
"War on poverty," 443
Ward, Robert E., 185n, 308n, 340n, 413n
Warren, Earl, 193
Warren, Josiah, 555
Washington, George, 435
Watson, J. B., 626
Weiner, Myron, 363n
Welfare state, 52–53, 455
West, S. George, 263n
Westin, Alan F., 190n
Wheare, K. C., 64n, 112n, 119, 120,

121n, 403n, 406n, 493n, 535n, 536, 537n, 539n, 542n
"Whip," 416, 447
White, Leonard D., 459n, 543n
White, William S., 420
White Citizens' Councils, 9, 85, 190, 372
"White supremacy," 36, 39, 190
Whiting, Allen S., 557n
Whyte, William F., 629n
Wiatr, Jerzy J., 308n
Wiener, Norbert, 233n
Wilkins, Roy, 9
Williams, Philip, 450n, 453n
Williamson, René de Visme, 265n
Wilson, H. H., 182n
Wilson, Harold, 319
Wilson, James O., 336n
Wilson, Woodrow, 393, 412, 439, 458, 459, 469–470, 475, 476, 617
Wolin, Sheldon S., 629n
Woman suffrage, 284
Woman's National Sabbath Alliance, 371
Woodward, C. Vann, 192n
Woolsey, Theodore Dwight, 394, 617
World government movement, arguments for, 607–608; criticism of, 608–609; origin, 607
World War I, 565, 566, 568
World War II, 565, 568, 569
World War III, 560, 580, 581, 606, 607, 609, 632
Wormuth, Francis D., 108n, 161n
Wright, Quincy, 568n

Yanaga, Chitoshi, 320n
Young, Arthur, 107n
Young, M. Crawford, 72
Young, Roland, 418n
Yugoslavia, 50, 61, 63, 72, 99, 133

Zagoria, Donald S., 52n
Zapata, Emiliano, 560, 581
Zeigler, Harmon, 367n, 373n
Zeller, Belle, 388n
Zimmern, Alfred E., 596n
Zionism, 473, 553